ETHICAL THEORIES

A Book of Readings

ETHICAL THEORIES

A Book of Readings

SECOND EDITION WITH REVISIONS

A. I. MELDEN, Ph.D., Editor

Professor of Philosophy
University of California
Irvine, California

Prentice-Hall, Inc., Englewood Cliffs, New Jersey

CURRENT PRINTING (LAST DIGIT):

22 21

C

Library of Congress Catalog Card Number: 67:12379
Printed in the United States of America.

PRENTICE-HALL INTERNATIONAL, INC., *London*
PRENTICE-HALL OF AUSTRALIA, PTY. LTD., *Sydney*
PRENTICE-HALL OF CANADA, LTD., *Toronto*
PRENTICE-HALL OF INDIA (PRIVATE) LTD., *New Delhi*
PRENTICE-HALL OF JAPAN, INC., *Tokyo*

Preface

My assumption in preparing this volume of readings has been that the most effective way in which an understanding of ethics or moral philosophy can be promoted is through a reading of the original source materials—essays written by outstanding and representative thinkers.

In choosing the materials for this volume, I have been guided by several considerations: (a) the extreme importance of presenting fairly complete essays, with as few deletions of material as possible, in order to avoid presenting fragmentary selections that are intelligible only in the light of the omitted context; (b) the desirability of limiting the selections to those that are most relevant to contemporary ethical theory; and (c) the importance of including materials from the recent as well as the remote past. Although selections have been arranged chronologically, there are important omissions. The most unfortunate of these is Spinoza. Only material from the *Ethics* will do, but the discussions of ethics in that work are inextricably woven together with discussions of the theory of knowledge, psychology, and metaphysics. In the First Edition of this book, similar considerations prompted the omission of the examples of Christian ethics from the writings of Augustine and Aquinas; only fragmentary samples of the ethical theories of these thinkers could have been included, and my objective was to supply actual texts that could be understood and studied on their own account. The difficult problem of choosing readings was complicated throughout by the necessary limitation of space. How well the aforementioned considerations of this volume have been met by the selections chosen is a matter on which there will be differences of opinion. Inevitably, compromises have been necessary.

The Second Edition provided fairly complete selections from the writings of the great moral philosophers of the past. Additions were made to the selections from Aristotle, Butler, Hume, Mill, and Sidgwick. To help meet the need for writings from the medieval period, selections from Augustine were also included. This material was added—despite the fact that the ethical doctrines of Augustine are closely interwoven with his other philosophical and theological views—first, because the complete omission of writings from the medieval period would be serious, and second, because certain of the problems raised by Augustine, notably that of the freedom of the will, are important on their own account. Bradley's essay "My Station and Its Duties" was substituted for his essay "Why Should I Be Moral?" The latter offers considerable difficulties to the student not familiar with Bradley's metaphysics, whereas the former presents a striking doctrine that needs to be considered.

One further change in the previous edition deserves explanation. To attempt to include materials from contemporary writings would not be in keeping with the objective of providing selections from the great moral philosophers of the past and would add enormously to the length of the volume. Accordingly, the selections now conclude with Prichard's famous essay of 1912.

The present revision embodies several more substantial changes. Some of the material from Saint Augustine included in the earlier editions has now been deleted: namely, that portion pertaining to the freedom of the will. Mill's essay on utilitarianism is presented in its entirety with the addition of Chapter V on justice. Selections from the *Summa Theologica* are also included here; they present Aquinas' doctrine of the natural law foundation of morals. Finally, the present edition includes selections drawn from various writings of Nietzsche. These, in the editor's opinion, afford the reader a relatively well-organized statement of some of Nietzsche's most interesting views on the nature of morality.

I am deeply grateful to all those who have so generously spent time and effort in submitting criticisms and suggestions. For their help in providing a new translation of the Nietzsche writings specifically designed for the present volume, my gratitude goes to Professors Fred Hagen and Ursula Mahlendorf. Special thanks are also due Professor John Ladd, not only for helpful criticisms of the translation but also for detailed suggestions, which are embodied in a number of changes represented in this revision.

A. I. M.

Table of Contents

ETHICAL THEORIES

A Book of Readings

On the Nature and Problems of Ethics

1. MORALS AND MORAL RULES

The term "ethics" is derived from the Greek word "ethos," which originally meant customs, habitual conduct, usages, and, later, character. The term "morals" is derived from the Latin "mores," which signifies customs or habits. But customs and practices, particularly those of one's own group, evoke approval, hence "ethics" and "morals" have reference, in one of their important uses, to the things, whether customs or conduct, motives or character, of which we approve as good, desirable, right, obligatory, worthy, and so forth. In this sense, the terms are honorific, and are to be contrasted with the terms "unethical" and "immoral." In a wider sense, however, the terms refer to conduct, character, motives, and so on, toward which such approval *or* disapproval (the latter being expressed by such terms as "bad," "undesirable," "wrong," "evil," "unworthy") is relevant. In this sense the terms "ethical" and "moral" are to be contrasted with "non-ethical" and "non-moral" respectively. But when we speak of the ethics and morals of a person, we usually refer to a set of rules or principles—expressed either in the indicative or in the imperative mood—which are taken to specify the kinds of conduct that he regards as desirable. We speak of the ethics or morals of this or that person even where we disapprove; and we contrast a person having an ethics—i.e., a code of conduct—with one who has none at all, who is unprincipled, who follows or respects no set of rules that mark, in his opinion at least, desirable conduct.

We are all familiar with such rules of conduct. Each society, religion, professional group, or distinguishable community has its principles, its standards of conduct. As persons who are concerned with being reasonable in our conduct, we rely ordinarily upon a body of principles for guidance in conduct. "Tell the truth." "Physicians ought to save human life whenever possible." "Teachers ought to encourage and develop intellectual curiosity and inquiry." Not to be guided by such rules or principles is to be unpredictable in one's behavior, to be devoid of character

1

upon which others may count, to be unreliable and an object of wary attention, uncertainty, and suspicion. But, to be guided by such principles, however much our conduct may elicit the respect and approval of others, is not to preclude all moral perplexity and resolve all moral doubt. For instance, the truth ought to be told and physicians are obligated to save human life, but should the physician be truthful to his critically ill patient when the patient's knowledge of his condition will make his recovery unlikely or impossible? To honor one principle of conduct is to violate the other; it appears impossible to avoid rejecting one or the other. Further, we cannot depend wholly upon such principles for guidance, simply because it is impossible to lay down a set of rules complete enough to anticipate all possible occasions for moral decision. To be useful, moral principles must be general; but, being general, their utility is inescapably limited. The future, however much it may resemble the past, provides its own novelties. A set of moral principles covering all possible moral eventualities is just as impossible as a set of laws so complete that no further legislation is necessary.

2. MORALISTS AND MORAL PHILOSOPHERS

Not all moral problems, then, can be resolved by appealing to our common moral rules. Traditionally, the morally perplexed have referred their problems to moralists—to persons who, for one reason or another, are believed to be of special competence in arriving at morally valid answers. The moralist may assume a variety of social guises, ecclesiastical or secular; he may be a "lonely hearts" editor, a man of reputed wisdom or experience, a pastor, or a physician. Whatever his social status, he performs an important function. That the moralist's advice is not always followed is indicative of a human failing of which we can cite parallel instances in other fields of experience, e.g., the patient who consults his physician and ignores his prescriptions, or the patient who "shops around" until he meets a physician who gives him a congenial or a relatively pleasant diagnosis.

It would be a mistake, however, to identify the moralist with the moral philosopher. Unlike the physician, whose diagnoses are assumed to be based upon a knowledge of the medical sciences, the moralist need have no competence in the corresponding *theory* of morals. To be sure, he may be a Plato, an Epictetus, or a Kant whose moral counsel and practical concern to promote the good are supported by a more or less systematic body of theory; but he may also be a poet or prophet whose moral counsel is the fruit of long experience, and of that practical moral sensibility to which we give the name "wisdom." Rare is the moral philosopher who does not offer moral counsel, but not at all rare is the moral counselor or the moralist for whom moral philosophy is an unexplored, unknown territory.

What, then, is moral philosophy, the theory of morals or ethics, or—to follow one current usage—ethics? It is, to begin with, a field of inquiry, the subject of a theoretical discipline. Interest in it may and normally does spring from our practical concern with good conduct, the desire to live well and reasonably. Nevertheless, the theoretical interest in the subject matter of ethics, whatever the conditions of its origin may be, must not be confused with the practical interest of moral beings. The theoretical interest is concerned with knowing; the practical interest is concerned with doing. Let us bear in mind the importance of the formation of habits in the development of moral character and conduct, and thus avoid the mistake of supposing that a knowledge of moral theory is sufficient for the improvement of our moral practice. Further, it would be dangerous, in advance of a systematic study of the subject, to argue that moral philosophy will improve our soundness in moral judgment. Some moral philosophers, to be sure, have made this claim. Plato, Epicurus, and Epictetus, among others, have argued that a knowledge of the basic principles of morality will enable us to correct ordinary misconceptions concerning what is good or bad, right or wrong. On the other hand, the contrary opinion has also been expressed. Aristotle commented that good judgment in ethical theory is possible only for those who by virtue of their training and resulting character know, to begin with, what is good and what is bad.[1] If it takes a good man to know what is good, and if it takes a man who knows what is good to be a moral philosopher, then to argue that moral philosophy will improve moral judgment is to put the cart before the horse. More recently, Prichard has argued that moral philosophy rests upon a mistake if it supposes that it can, by virtue of its analyses, supplant moral doubts with moral knowledge.[2] Clearly the only intelligent way of deciding between these opposed views is to engage in the study of moral philosophy itself.

Granted that moral philosophy is a field of inquiry, into what does it inquire? In reply to such a question, it would be ill-advised to attempt a definition. The definition of any subject matter, if accurate, is likely to be couched in terms that are fully intelligible only to those who have achieved a large measure of competence in the field of inquiry. What is required is not the definition of a term but the general account of a subject

---

[1] *Nicomachean Ethics*, 1095 a. See p. 90 below.

[2] *Does Moral Philosophy Rest on a Mistake?* See p. 480 below.

matter, and for this purpose nothing less than an introduction to the inquiry itself is needed.

Let us return, for purposes of illustration, to the moral problem faced by the physician who, it would seem, must reject either the moral principle concerning truth or the moral principle that requires that he save the life of his patient. Both rules, presumably, prescribe good conduct, but good conduct in this instance cannot satisfy both rules. How shall we resolve the dilemma?

We would probably agree that the physician ought to tell his patient an encouraging untruth. Moralists and moral philosophers (with the sole possible exception of Kant [3]) would argue for saving the patient's life. Surely a physician who sacrificed his patient's life through an unconditional devotion to the truth would be exposed to charges of malpractice, and liable to considerable penalties, civil and professional. The lie, we would say, is a "white lie." But if we ask "Why is it 'white,' not 'black'?," if we ask the moralist for a reason for his moral judgment, a variety of answers, all familiar to common sense, may be forthcoming. He may, as an ecclesiastic, refer us to the expressed will of God as revealed in sacred writings or as delivered by ecclesiastical authority. He may, as a professed humanitarian, cite the welfare of humanity which the recommended action promotes. He may refer to the authority of conscience, to simple and not further explicable moral insight, to the authority or the approval of society, to the conditions of evolutionary development or progress, the promotion of the good, the general happiness, the functions and responsibilities of physicians, the happiness of the patient, the self-interest of the agent, and so on. In any case, he will be advancing a reason, and the recommended action will, on that ground, be termed "reasonable."

But, although this may be the end of the moralist's interest in the matter—for the moralist is concerned simply to secure right or good conduct by determining what, in his opinion, is right or good—it marks the beginning of moral philosophy. It may be unquestionable that the physician ought to tell the untruth. But it is not unquestionable that any one of the reasons mentioned above is adequate. True beliefs can be, and often are, supported by bad reasons, and what we would like to know is what distinguishes a good from a bad reason. In logic, we are concerned to make clear what it means to say that an argument is reasonable, and we become clear about this only when we examine in detail the nature and criteria of

[3] See his essay "On a Supposed Right To Lie From Altruistic Motives," which reveals Kant in his most rigorous mood. It may be found in the volume of Immanuel Kant's essays entitled *Critique of Practical Reason and Other Writings in Moral Philosophy*, translated and edited by Lewis White Beck, The University of Chicago Press, 1949.

valid and probable inference. In ethical theory, similarly, we are concerned to know what it means to say that conduct and attitudes are reasonable, and this we can do only by making clear what the nature and criteria of valid moral judgments are. What *is* a good moral reason? The history of moral philosophy can be summed up as the history of the attempt of philosophers to clarify the conditions and criteria of moral reasonableness, of that reasonableness in conduct and attitudes that distinguishes the moral person, in the best sense of that term, from the nonmoral or immoral person.

Let us consider briefly one of the suggested answers to the moral problem we posed earlier. The devout might seize upon the will of God as an answer to our question. Traditionally, religion has functioned as the vehicle for moral instruction, criticism, and progress. Indeed, the claim is perennially advanced by the protagonists of each established religion that a morality that professes independence from religion, from the will of God as revealed in its canonical writings or pronouncements, is founded only on illusion and arrogance. Unfortunately for such claims, the problem raised by Socrates in the dialogue *Euthyphro* in connection with the nature of holiness is applicable here, and the kind of objection raised there is fatal to the claim that religion and its theology do provide a satisfactory solution to the problems of moral philosophy. Socrates asked: Is a thing holy because it is loved by the gods or is it loved by the gods because it is holy? And so we may ask, concerning the nature of right or good, whether things are right or good because God wills them or whether God wills them because they are right or good. The question must not be dismissed as a sophistical verbalism. If "good" means conforming with God's will, then "God's will is good" reduces to the trivial statement that He wills what He wills. But "A wills what he wills" is true whether A's will is good or bad. The statement, then, that God's will is good is not trivial, and hence we cannot identify what we mean by "right" or "good" with what we mean by "the will of God." And if this is the case, then we should still want to ask, "What does it mean to say that anything is right, good?" It may well be that if we knew what God's will is, we could know *what* things are *indeed* right or wrong. We would then have a satisfactory moral criterion, and in that case we would be assured, as moralists, that our moral judgments are correct. But we would be no closer to the solution of the problem for moral philosophy, of providing an account and analysis of what it is that our criterion is a criterion of. Suppose that someone offered, as a criterion of valid inference, the known congruence of inference with that of an infallible, divine reasoner. Would that provide any clarification of what is meant by "valid inference"? Would the reference to the deity assist us in understanding the principles of logic? Clearly not. If theology is irrelevant to logic, then, by the same token, it is irrelevant to ethical theory or moral philosophy.

3. THE SCIENTISTIC CHALLENGE

It may be asked, however, "What is meant by an analysis of the fundamental notions employed in moral discourse such as right and wrong, good and bad?" Surely, it may be suggested, morality, like any other phenomenon having to do with human behavior and attitudes, is the proper object of inquiry of the various sciences of man: sociology, psychology, anthropology, and so forth. Sometimes this claim is advanced by those who pride themselves on their devotion to scientific method, on their tough-mindedness. It is advanced by those who find an object lesson in the manifest inability of moral philosophers to reach agreement after more than two thousand years of reflection and dispute. "Let's be realistic," these people say. If there is any doubt about the meaning of critical ethical terms, look them up in the dictionary, and see for yourself that right and wrong, good and bad, have reference to norms or standards that moral rules describe, and if there is any question concerning the nature of these norms or standards, examine the function they perform, the ends they serve, in their actual use. The trouble with philosophy, they say, is that it is confused about the questions it asks, and where the questions are clarified the answers can be gained only by going to science.

4. PROBLEMS INHERENT IN THE APPEAL TO SCIENCE

We have seen already, however, that our moral rules do not and cannot preclude all moral perplexity. These rules, on occasion at least, conflict. Hence the identification of morality with the actual set of moral rules we have won't do, for we still want to know, and the question is surely reasonable, "What in such cases ought we to do? Which course of action is right, which wrong?" And there are, as we also indicated, the inevitably novel situations that arise for which pre-existing moral rules are inadequate. However, apart from all such troubling cases, even if we found no instances of conflicting moral principles and lacked none for any eventuality that might arise, what reason is there for abiding by them? Those who have turned to psychology, sociology, and anthropology for an understanding of morality must meet the same challenge in a different form. Nothing is more impressive than the relativity of moral codes and rules.

What is right for one community is wrong for another. Time and place seem to make all the difference between right and wrong. The moral rules of one society prohibit polygamy; those of another permit or even praise it. Morals and ethics, to consider their dictionary meaning, have reference to approved conduct and character, but the approvals of one group are matched by the disapprovals of another. There is scarcely one norm or standard of good conduct that, in another time and place, does not serve to mark bad conduct. So far at least the empirical sciences of man do report. But what reason is there for accepting any given standard or norm in any given society? It won't do to reply that the only reason that can be given is that it is the standard or norm. Standards vary from one time and place to another. Is it possible for all to be right? If all are right, is it simply because they are the standards of their respective communities? In that case, "x is right" would mean simply that x conforms to the norm or standard, and the question "Is this standard right?," which surely is meaningful, would degenerate into the absurd question "Is this standard a standard?" On what basis, then, can we maintain that all the varieties of norms or standards are correct? If, however, only *our* norms are correct, how can we support this contention? The fact that we are concerned with one particular set of standards rather than with another is an accident of our birth; it is not any reason at all for our moral obligation to respect and abide by them.

A moral reason for acceptance is required. We need to be able to show that the moral rules we honor serve a moral end. No doubt, a scientific account of the phenomenon of morality would explore the causes and effects, the costs and consequences of the psychology and practice of morality. Such information would be eminently useful in providing techniques for social control, moral education, and data for intelligent moral judgment. But scientific explanation is one thing, moral justification and evaluation seem to be something else. The one is concerned with actual fact—with the way in which human beings do in fact behave in the broad sense of that term. The other is concerned with what would be worth while and desirable, with how man ought to behave. Moral philosophy, in its attempt to articulate what a moral ideal is, what the nature and conditions of valid moral judgment are, seems to be a normative, not a descriptive, inquiry into human conduct and attitudes. And if the demand is made for an account of the relation between norms and practice, fact and ideal, what is and what ought to be—if it is demanded that we give an account of the relevance of empirical fact to moral evaluation—surely that is a matter for philosophical analysis, for the kind of analysis that falls within the province of moral philosophy.

5. THE CHALLENGE OF THE MORAL SKEPTIC

The challenge, expressed earlier, to provide a moral justification of the moral rules or principles of one's society must then be met. In Plato's day, as in our own, the recognition of the relativity of moral codes suggested a skepticism concerning morals. Such a skepticism is often abetted by skepticism about religion; where religion provides the main or sole support of morality, the skepticism that challenges religion soon finds morality for an object of attack. Whatever the causes may have been in Plato's own time, however, a vivid picture of a moral skeptic is presented in the characterization of Thrasymachus in Book I of Plato's *Republic*. Thrasymachus identifies morality with the *de facto* moral rules, justice with the rules of justice. He argues for the factual thesis, that these rules are designed for the selfish interest of the strong, namely, the rulers. And he concludes with the moral skepticism expressed by the well-known statement that might is right. The rules of justice are simply the cunning contrivances of the self-interested strong to which the weak and stupid, perforce, submit. Hence the thesis emerges during the course of the argument in Book I of the *Republic* that injustice is more profitable than justice, that only the foolish will be just when, as is sometimes the case, self-interest can be furthered by injustice.

We need not dwell at this point upon Thrasymachus' affirmation of the doctrine of psychological egoism. This doctrine, which can be summed up in the statement that men are by nature selfish, has played a curious role in the history of moral philosophy. For Thrasymachus, it aids and abets his moral skepticism; for Hobbes, on the other hand, it serves to recommend to one's intelligence the reasonableness of accepting the whole system of moral conventions. But whatever our conclusions concerning the truth of the doctrine of man's selfishness may be, the allegedly conventional character of morals presents a serious challenge. To be sure, skepticism has not been associated, in the main, with the doctrine that bases morality on the will of God, whereas skepticism has emerged from the doctrine that founds morality on the will of man. But this difference rests solely upon the recognition that men, unlike God, can be deceived and that their punishment, unlike that of God, can be avoided. Even this difference, however, tends on occasion to disappear. For some religious institutions, as Adeimantus observed in Book II of the *Republic*, have provided ways of allowing their members to purchase the good will of God or the gods by means of sacrifices and other offerings.

A careful reading of the remarkable speech by Glaucon, which opens the discussion in Book II of Plato's *Republic*, will reward those who are concerned with tracing the manner in which philosophy attempted to meet this skeptical attack. Glaucon distinguishes, to begin with, between three types of goods: (a) those that are good *intrinsically*, that is, those that are valued for their own sakes and apart from all consequences; (b) those that are good only *instrumentally*, that is, are to be endured or suffered only for the sake of things other than themselves which they bring to pass; and (c) those things (e.g., knowledge, health) that are good both instrumentally and intrinsically. According to the social contract theory, which Glaucon describes as the intellectually fashionable opinion of his time (and which Hobbes later adopted for different ends), men are by nature selfish, desiring their intrinsic goods even at the expense of others. In the natural condition of man, insecurity, fear, and suffering are rampant—men are too weak to resist the so-called injustices committed by others. Hence self-interest forces men to enter into a social compact which brings law into being, and, with it, social sanctions and the distinctions between just and unjust, right and wrong. Justice is valued, therefore, not as an intrinsic good but as a purely instrumental good, something to be endured as a lesser evil than that greater evil that would otherwise spring, as from Pandora's box, from man's selfish nature.

At least two distinct problems are raised by Glaucon which set the stage for the discussions that follow in the *Republic*, and which, as we shall see, have played an important role in a good deal of subsequent moral philosophy. (1) Justice is commonly valued not for its rewards, but for its own sake. The child who is punished for stealing will miss the moral point that stealing is wrong if the only lesson he derives from the punishment is that it is painful to be caught. Hence the problem is posed by Glaucon of how we can show, by means of an analysis of justice and its related ethical concepts, that there are moral reasons for approving the kinds of actions and character that just or moral men favor. This, in part at least, is the meaning of Glaucon's demand that Socrates show justice to be intrinsically good: that he provide an analysis that will demonstrate what the relevant *moral* reasons are for praising the kinds of things called "just" independently of the rewards they usually bring. (2) The just or moral life is commonly praised for its own sake as the happy life. Crime and immorality, we often say, do not pay. Notwithstanding Thrasymachus and other immoralists, justice profits a man far more than injustice. So goes the common belief, one persuasive device of moral instruction, and a familiar theme in literature. If this is so, let us pose a test case, an extreme case. It is for this reason that Glaucon relates the story of the Ring of Gyges. Gyges, by using a magic ring that gave him the advantage of becoming invisible at will, became king after a series of brutal crimes.

Society would not only condemn a Gyges who profited in external goods from the injustices he was enabled to commit with impunity, it would also contend that, in a larger sense, he could not profit from, or "get away with," his injustices. Hence the demand is made by Glaucon: Show that a Gyges, who is not subject to the ordinary weaknesses of men, and hence is able not only to avoid the usual penalties for wrong-doing but also to enjoy a reputation for decency, is far worse off than the man who remains steadfastly just even in the face of all the punishments that society inflicts upon him, in the mistaken belief that he is unjust or immoral. The demand, then, that Socrates show that justice is an intrinsic good is, in part at least, the demand that he show that it is no mere instrumental good in the specific sense that it is something to be endured or suffered in order to forestall a greater evil—that, unlike a distasteful medicine taken in order to remove a greater unpleasantness, it is something *good for the agent*, in the sense that it makes for his well-being or profit. Justice, in short, must be shown to be more profitable than injustice under any and all circumstances.

6. MORAL SKEPTICISM AND MORAL PHILOSOPHY

It is no passing accident that these two distinct issues are not distinguished in the *Republic*. Indeed, they are not distinguished clearly by any of the great Greek moral philosophers. Aristotle, to be sure, does consider the effect of tragedy upon the happiness of a virtuous Priam, but his solution—namely, that such a person is merely deprived of blessedness and that he nevertheless avoids a wretchedness which those without virtue would suffer in similar external circumstances—leaves many a modern reader dissatisfied.[4] For the Epicureans, the good life is a life with a minimum of pains and a maximum of pleasure or cheerfulness. For the Stoic, the virtuous man alone will be cheerful by the cultivation of his reason and his resulting indifference to all the externals that are of no value at all and only a source of anxiety, disappointment, and misery to the unwise. For all, the moral life, which the Greek took to be the life of virtue, is the life of well-being, happiness. Hence it is that the term "eudaemonistic" (from the Greek word meaning well-being or happiness) describes their ethics. The fundamental question for Greek moral philosophy is not "What ought I to do?," but rather "How should I live in order to achieve happiness, well-being, the enjoyment of the good?" In this respect, Greek philosophy is characteristically teleological, that is, it takes the concept of good as basic, and values virtue for the good it secures; but

---

[4] *Nicomachean Ethics*, Book I, Chapter X.

unlike modern teleological ethics which values the virtues merely because these are viewed as means toward a resulting good whether in the agent or in anyone else, Greek eudaemonism characteristically values the virtues because of the happiness that they provide in the soul of the agent. Thus the proponent of a modern teleological ethics will understand the question "What ought I to do?" as the question "What action maximizes the good?," which, he will recognize, is quite a different question from the characteristically Greek question "How should I live in order to achieve happiness?" And Greek ethical theories are even more removed from those views, which, like that of Kant, take the concept of duty as fundamental. The confidence of Plato, Aristotle, the Epicureans, and the Stoics that a virtuous life is a happy one stands in sharp contrast to Kant's striking and stern appeal to duty for duty's sake regardless of the loss of well-being or happiness to the agent or to anyone else.

The problem, then, of the relation between self-interest and right action forms one of the major themes in the history of ethics or moral philosophy. Hobbes premises his moral theory upon the doctrine of man's selfishness; for him, of course, duty and self-interest coincide. Bishop Butler, whose refutation of psychological egoism (the doctrine of the selfishness of man) is as decisive as anything we are likely to encounter in philosophy, argues, nevertheless, for the perfect congruence of virtue and reasoned self-interest. Even Kant and Sidgwick, with a perhaps sounder appreciation of the tragedies that befall good men in this imperfect world, looked to the prospects of immortality as one way of ensuring a happiness which, as they recognized, good men deserve but often miss.

There is, however, a more fundamental question that the reader must face if he is to profit in understanding from his reading. It may be the case that, as a matter of fact, the virtuous life is always the happy life, that duty and self-interest always coincide. On this issue, the Socratics and Stoics, to mention but a few, have been charged with an unrealistic optimism. But assume for the sake of discussion that this coincidence is, in fact, invariable. Is it the case that the justification of the acceptance of our common moral rules, of the development and possession of virtue, or of right action, can be given in terms of self-interest? In one well-known passage, Butler remarks as follows: "Let it be allowed, though virtue or moral rectitude does indeed consist in affection to and pursuit of what is right and good, as such; yet, that when we sit down in a cool hour, we can neither justify to ourselves this or any other pursuit, till we are convinced that it will be for our happiness, or at least not contrary to it."[5] This passage has perplexed scholars. To some, it has seemed to be the

---

[5] *Sermon XI*, p. 240 below.

assertion of an egoism which Butler, to all appearances, had taken great pains to refute. But whatever the correct interpretation may be of Butler's intent, it does pose the problem of specifying the kind of reason that is relevant to our moral judgments. Self-interest can and often does provide an inducement; for one not already inclined to do so, it may serve to induce one to act as a good man would act if we impress upon the agent that his self-interest will be promoted. But is this a moral reason? Consider the question "Why should I be kind to my neighbor?" Is this question the same as "What self-interest would be served by my being kind to my neighbor?" It is immaterial to reply that my self-interest is in fact always promoted by my kindness. That may be true as a matter of fact. But we can conceive of a world ordered by an evil demon in which kindness always pleases the recipient but not the donor; and, within limits, we would still want to say that in such a world men ought to be kind. Hence the moral reason for being kind cannot be identified with the private advantage that may as a matter of fact accrue from being kind. In short, however self-interest may serve as an inducement to the agent for performing an act of a given kind, it in itself provides no moral reason for doing so. Moral purpose and private interest are distinguishable. If this is so, any attempt to show that justice is an intrinsic good in the specific sense that it profits one, so that even a morally indifferent Gyges may be persuaded to become just, raises a number of doubts.

Can self-interest provide a reason for being moral? Hobbes' view that reason leads men, in self-protection, to enter into the social compact in consequence of which alone the distinction between right and wrong, justice and injustice, emerges is particularly open to attack because of his underlying psychological egoism. Morality imposes upon men the obligation, among others, of forgetting one's self in the interests of others. But, as Kant has rightly urged, obligation obtains only in those cases in which, in some sense, we are free to act and will in the prescribed manner. Hence, if Hobbes' doctrine of psychological egoism is true, it is false that we ought to forget our own interest and desire the happiness of others. But quite apart from this special difficulty, what reason is there for one, who, because of the special circumstance of his private powers, cunning, and so forth, needs no further protection from the mischief that others may visit upon him, for continuing to abide by the social compact? Hobbes' answer is that any such deviation from the terms of the social compact "is somewhat like to that, which in the disputations of scholars is called *absurdity*. For as it is there called an absurdity to contradict what one maintained in the beginning; so in the world, it is called injustice, and injury, voluntarily to undo that which from the beginning he had voluntarily done." [6] Hobbes' answer, unfortunately, involves a confusion be-

6 *Leviathan* Chap XIV See p. 200 below.

tween logical consistency and constancy in belief and attitude. Inconstancy in belief or attitude involves no logical inconsistency; it occurs whenever we change our minds. Why not then change one's mind? By hypothesis, self-interest will not be served, and yet we ought to abstain from injuring others, from performing the kinds of acts specifically prohibited by the terms of the covenant. Hence the reason for abstaining from such acts cannot be self-interest; it must be a moral reason.

A similar consideration is pertinent to one suggested interpretation of Butler's statement quoted above. It has been suggested that all that Butler meant to do was to show that self-interest, when reasonably and fully considered, does not conflict with the moral deliverances of conscience.[7] Hence one could appeal to the rational egoist on the basis of his self-interest alone. The reader may wonder, indeed, whether such self-interest is not premised upon the assumption that the rational egoist is rational in at least this sense that he is, as Butler argues, endowed with a human nature in which conscience exercises its authority, and thus penalizes the egoist for his moral derelictions by the familiar pangs and disquiets. Is not the premise of the contention that immorality, injustice, will not really profit a man, that the man to begin with is moral or just, in some degree at least, and hence that he cannot, to that degree, live comfortably with himself and act immorally?

Moral discourse, it would seem, is addressed to moral men, who can recognize, understand, and be moved by moral reasons. On this point even such widely divergent moral philosophers as Hume and Prichard are in basic agreement. Hume agrees on the ground that, in the absence of the sentiment of sympathy, the contemplation of the happiness or sufferings of another leaves one indifferent, provides no occasion for the moral approvals or disapprovals that define virtue and vice, good and bad, and leaves one utterly unmoved by the persuasive devices of moral discourse. Hence Hume recommends that the moral skeptic had best be let alone, that "the only way, therefore, of converting an antagonist of this kind, is to leave him to himself" in the hopes that his own moral nature will prevail and at last bring him over to the side of common sense and reason.[8] And Prichard would agree on the ground that in the absence of moral insight or intelligence, the contemplation of any act or situation would preclude all possibility of an intuition of right or wrong, good or bad, which alone can serve as a moral reason for the particular moral judgments we reach. The lesson, then, is an old one, but too often it is

[7] Cf. C. D. Broad's *Five Types of Ethical Theory*, Chap. III, Harcourt, Brace and Co., 1930.

[8] *Enquiry Concerning the Principles of Morals*, p. 248 below.

forgotten. If, as Aristotle remarked, it takes a good man to know what is good, it also takes a good man to recognize what is a moral reason. It is for this reason that critical students have been dissatisfied with the outcome of Plato's venture in the *Republic*—to persuade one who, like our legendary Gyges, is not just or moral, to become just or moral. The student senses that the appeal to self-interest won't do, that there is no self-contradiction in the conception of a Nietzschean superman, morally indifferent Gyges, or conscienceless intelligence who is smugly content with the pleasures he is able to muster for himself even at the expense of untold harm to others. Hence he is led to reject Plato's analysis of the virtues, Butler's account of conscience, and the moral philosophy of each philosopher who has attempted, on the grounds of self-interest, to meet the challenge of the moral skeptic, when the real root of the trouble is that no such answer should have been attempted in the first place. But the question "Why Should I Be Moral?," in this context, is senseless. "Should" calls for a reason, but the only one that is pertinent is one that the skeptic won't recognize and the moral man doesn't require for the purpose of being moral, since he is moral to begin with. To suppose that moral skepticism can be countered by providing reasons sufficient to persuade one who is not moral to become moral, may well be as absurd as to suppose that a skepticism about the whole business of logic can be met by providing logical arguments that will persuade the skeptic. One must be logical in order to recognize the force of a logical argument, and one must be moral in order to be moved by a moral reason or argument. Our best procedure in both cases is to leave the skeptic and get on with the business of analysis.

7. THEMES AND VARIATIONS IN MORAL PHILOSOPHY

When, however, the reader addresses himself to the task of understanding how philosophers have attempted to analyze what is meant by a valid moral reason, his first reaction is likely to be one of bewilderment. He will encounter widely different approaches and, consequently, radically different types of answers in the writings of moral philosophers. But the reader must be reminded that a first reading is likely to miss the extent of the agreements that lie concealed beneath the differences in idiom, that the problem is complex and the difficulties are many, and that a hasty conclusion is most likely to be superficial and inadequate. And even when philosophers have been mistaken, the study of their methods and results is likely to be far more illuminating than many a success of the unseasoned novice. Indeed, closer examination of the literature will reveal that a comparatively small number of themes run through the philosophy of morals, that each thinker has selected some one or more of these themes for variation and development.

Consider, for example, the development and modification by Plato and Aristotle of one of the theses in the early so-called Socratic dialogues, namely, that virtue is knowledge, and vice ignorance, a thesis that is expressed even within the rubric of a hedonistic or pleasure theory of the good in the dialogue *Protagoras*. For both Plato and Aristotle, man is a political or social being and the Good, to which all moral justification must appeal in the last analysis, is something that can be realized only in man's social or political relations. Hence the necessity for Plato of delineating the features of the ideal republic and for Aristotle of considering the *Ethics* as a preface to the *Politics*. Yet if we look closely at both accounts of the Good, we cannot miss the extent to which knowledge is at least a necessary condition of its realization.

For Plato the Supreme Good is achieved with the realization of the state of justice in the individual soul, and, as Aristotle explicitly adds, with its actual exercise or functioning. It won't do to rest content with the description of justice as a harmony of soul; a harmony is an arrangement of parts that meets our moral or aesthetic preferences, hence we need to know what kind of arrangement this harmony is. Plato's answer is as follows: The kind of harmony that constitutes justice is the harmony that is obtained when wisdom, courage, and temperance are present in the soul. Of these three, wisdom is the fundamental virtue. Without it, courage and temperance (and therefore justice) are impossible. Thus temperance without wisdom is a vulgar prudence based upon nothing more substantial than habit and custom, and uncertain in the face of temptation. Without wisdom, it is no more like the temperance of the ideally just than the counterfeit wisdom of common sense with its rules of thumb gathered from experience is like that wisdom achieved through a thorough grounding in the exact sciences culminating in the highest knowledge—the intuitive vision of an indescribable and unanalyzable Form of the Good. Plato's view poses a number of problems to the critical student: How can the several virtues of the philosopher-king be distinguished? How are they related to the ordinary virtues and to common-sense moral rules? How far has Plato been guilty of changing the subject, by attempting to meet Glaucon's demand for an analysis of moral concepts as they are ordinarily understood in terms of an analysis of moral concepts as they are quite differently and ideally construed? In any case, however, the earlier Socratic thesis has been developed into one in which the highest virtue is that excellence which occurs when and only when there is knowledge of the Form of the Good.

When we turn to Aristotle, we are, at first, impressed with a radically different attitude toward morals. There is no single Good for all earthly things. Like Plato, Aristotle understands good to be the excellence with which a thing performs its proper function; but, unlike Plato, Aristotle denies that there is a common goodness, or Form of the Good, for all things. Hence Aristotle is much more favorable to the virtues of ordinary non-philosophical men, to *their* good or happiness, which he defines, in general, as an active life of virtue. It is for this reason that we find in Aristotle's writings a detailed account of the moral virtues as these appear within the social framework of Greek society of his time, and a resulting well-rounded picture of a virtuous Greek gentleman. However, when we look more closely at Aristotle's account of the virtues, we must not over-look the important function of reason in moral decision and in the attain-ment of the highest Good or Happiness. For even the life in accordance with the moral virtues is the life guided by reason, by the application of rational principle in moral decision—if nothing else, by the application of the rule of the golden mean. And if we are dissatisfied by Plato's intuitionism (to use a modern term), that is, by his appeal to an intuition or experience of an unanalyzable objective or absolute Goodness, we shall not be comforted by Aristotle's account. Unfortunately, the rule of the golden mean does not tell us *what* the good for man is but, roughly, *where* it is. The account of Happiness, the good for man, hinges upon the key word "proper" in the so-called proper function or activity peculiar to man. Since what is peculiar to man is his reason, the Supreme Good turns out, in the last analysis, to be the life of reason. Such a life man can attain only intermittently, in contemplation, and although the object of this contemplation, according to Aristotle, is not the Form of the Good, it is, nonetheless, that supreme Form who is God. Hence even if Aristotle is more charitable than Plato to a lesser grade of happiness, it remains true for Aristotle that happiness in any form requires the use of reason, and, in its highest form, the activity of reason in contemplating the eternal and divine.

The theme that the moral life is the rational life, that right moral decision involves the use of reason or intelligence, is one of the recurrent themes in the writings of moral philosophy. The Stoics, for example, harked back to the Socratic dictum that virtue is knowledge. The Sum-mum Bonum, indeed the only good, is virtue, namely, the life according to nature. It is this that gives moral point to right action. Nature, how-ever, must be known if we are to live according to it; and what it is known to be, by the exceptional Stoic sage, is rational, excellent, good. And if the Stoic's thesis is of little help, if for no other reason than because of its obvious circularity (the good = virtue, virtue = knowledge, knowledge = the knowledge of the good), his persistent thesis is that the good life is the rational life. Similarly, Hobbes argued for justice by an appeal to the natural light of reason, even identifying injustice—the violation of the terms of the social compact—with logical absurdity or contradiction. Even Butler's appeal to conscience can be described as an appeal to a kind of rational faculty. Conscience, being naturally supreme, is no mere arbitrary authority, but a source of insight, a faculty that reveals the nature and extent of our obligations, the path of virtuous action. If Butler does not attempt to say more about the latter—to make clear what it is that conscience reveals—the answer lies mainly in the fact that his chief concern lay elsewhere: to win men of intelligence from the fashionable moral and religious skepticism to which, in large measure, a mistaken psychology had contributed. Again, Kant's appeal to the conception of a rational will for the derivation of the fundamental principles of morality, his reliance upon the principle of contradiction for the determination of valid moral rules, is surely one bold identification of the moral with the rational. Finally, we may mention the empirical use of reason that Dewey urges in our moral reasoning. The basic data for Dewey are the satisfactions of the *de facto* needs or interests of men interacting with their natural and social environments. Reason's function in morals is essential. Moral justifications are explanations, by means of the findings of all the empirical sciences that bear upon man and his behavior, of the manner in which satisfaction of desires is promoted and the frustrations of interests avoided by the consequences of our action.

It is possible, similarly, to examine in detail how moral philosophers have developed another key concept, that of human nature. For Plato and Aristotle, Butler, Hume, and Kant, to mention but a few, the appeal to human nature is central in one form or another—for Plato and Aristotle, in their account of the virtues as the excellences with which man's various and proper functions are performed; for Butler, in his account of human nature and the alleged natural supremacy or authority of conscience; for Hume, in his account of moral approval and disapproval in terms of the *de facto* operations of the sentiment of sympathy or benevolence; and for Kant, in his appeal to man's nature as a being endowed with a rational will, in his account of moral obligation.

8. PROBLEMS AND CAUTIONS

Whether the basic theme is the appeal to rationality or to the constitution and functions of human nature, the same problems are expressible in the idiom appropriate to the selected theme. If the theme is reason, what is its method, empirical or *a priori*, and what does it reveal? Is the conception of good fundamental, and the notion of right and obligation definable in terms of it? Are these independent notions? Or, is the conception of duty basic and that of good definable in terms of it? If the conception of good is fundamental, what is the nature of intrinsic, as distinguished from instrumental, good? Can it be identified with pleasure, the object of an interest, and so on, or is it indefinable or unanalyzable, as modern intuitionists like Moore declare who, in this respect, follow the example of Plato? In any case, is the theory of moral value the theory of value in general, and if not, what are the differentiating characteristics of moral values? How, finally, are we to construe the normative character of ethics? Are there normative facts, and if so how are these facts different from non-normative facts? Similarly, if the theme is the appeal to human nature, it must clearly be an appeal to human nature in so far as it is moral. Thus, in the phrase "man's proper nature or function," by which Aristotle, among others, seeks to elucidate the virtues and the good, the term "proper" is central. The nature and function of man that are "properly" his, if they are to be taken as a key to an understanding of morals, is that nature and function of man that are morally relevant. And precisely the same questions that we raised above now appear. Is it man's nature in so far as he is capable of enjoying the good? In so far as he is subject to moral obligations? If the former, what is the nature of intrinsic good that provides the moral justification of the rules of conduct, of reasonable moral decision? If the latter, what is the source of the demands to which moral men respond, the character of the moral law that commands? What is the nature and status of norms; how far, for example, is Hume enabled to provide a satisfactory account of norms in terms of his *de facto* account of the operation of the mechanism of human nature? And so our questions appear once more, rephrased in a different form.

This very flexibility of discourse poses a source of difficulty and misunderstanding for the reader. We have commented upon the similarities that often lie concealed beneath the differences of verbal expression, but it is apparent by now that the appeal to reason, to human nature, by various philosophers often conceals important differences. Key terms, therefore, like "reason," "human nature," which permit of such latitude in their meaning, application, and results, are and should be the objects of careful scrutiny by the student. Man is, by his human nature, a moral being. So it is often said. The pertinent question is: By virtue of what factor or factors in that human nature is he moral? To be moral is to be rational. So one common thesis goes. The pertinent question, here again, is: In what sense is "rationality" employed, and precisely what does this rationality discover in the way of moral facts that validate our moral judgments? The reader, therefore, will be well advised to be cautious and critical, cautious lest he be misled into mistaking verbal differences for differences in doctrine, critical lest he be misled by fashionable or persuasive idioms into supposing that there is agreement when in fact there are important differences in interpretations of key terms and hence in ethical doctrine. He must be wary at all times lest he be misled into supposing that what in fact is difficult, obscure, or confused is simple, obvious, or clear.

But however difficult and hazardous it may be, the study of moral philosophy can be and is rewarding. To be sure, if the reader's objective is to find quickly and effortlessly the answers to the problems we have raised, he will be bewildered and disappointed. The truth is not mined easily and comfortably. Nature has not contrived to satisfy our desire for ease. But the various moral philosophers have provided us with examples of their efforts, the lessons of their mistakes, and the positive achievements of their insights. From all these the reader can and should profit. And his profit will be all the greater because of the intellectual effort it requires and the advantage the study affords of introducing him to some of the great minds in moral philosophy.

Plato (428/7 – 348/7 B.C.)

A member of an aristocratic Athenian family, Plato spent his youth during the turbulent and disastrous years of the Peloponnesian War. During these times of crisis it was Socrates who stood out in sharp relief from his fellow Athenians. His aloofness from the sordid political squabbles of the day, his complete integrity, and his persistent inquiry into the things that matter most made a deep impression on the mind of the young Plato. The trial of Socrates (see the *Apology*) and his subsequent execution turned Plato away from his earlier thought of a public career; for he saw that effective and desirable social action was impossible without the wisdom Socrates persistently sought to achieve. After Socrates' death in 399 B.C., Plato left Athens and retired to Megara along with other disciples of Socrates, resolved to defend the memory of his revered master and to continue his work. Thus began the composition of the Platonic dialogues, which constitute a remarkable monument of artistic as well as philosophic achievement. When Plato was about forty years of age, he engaged in his one political venture — the attempt through Dion, brother-in-law of Dionysius, tyrant of Syracuse, to bring kingship under philosophic control and direction. The enterprise ended disastrously — one story is that Plato was sold into slavery and rescued by his friends. However, Plato never dismissed from his mind the dream of a good society, one ruled over by philosopher-kings. It forms the basic theme of the *Republic* and has continued to capture the imaginations of men down to the present day. Shortly after the adventure at Syracuse, Plato returned to Athens, where he founded the Academy. Students were taught there chiefly by means of the conversational approach that has come to be known as the Socratic method. It would be difficult to exaggerate the importance of the influence of Plato, through both his writings and the work begun by him in the Academy, upon the subsequent history of ideas down to the present day. Plato's dialogues, his only published writings, are too numerous to mention here. The most important of the dialogues for moral philosophy are, in the probable order of their composition, *Protagoras*, the *Apology, Crito, Gorgias, Meno*, the *Republic, Philebus*, and the *Laws*.

THE REPUBLIC OF PLATO [1]

PART I (BOOK I)

SOME CURRENT VIEWS OF JUSTICE

The main question to be answered in the REPUBLIC is: *What does Justice mean, and how can it be realized in* human society? *The Greek word for 'just' has as many senses as the English*

[1] Reprinted from *The Republic of Plato*, translated by F. M. Cornford, Oxford University Press, New York, 1945, with the permission of the publisher. The divisions of the text into parts and chapters together with all prefatory notes and footnotes are by the translator.

20

'right.' It can mean: observant of custom or of duty, righteous; fair, honest; legally right, lawful; what is due to or from a person, deserts, rights; what one ought to do. Thus it covers the whole field of the individual's conduct in so far as it affects others — all that they have a 'right' to expect from him or he has a right to expect from them, whatever is right as opposed to wrong. A proverbial saying declared that justice is the sum of all virtue.

The demand for a definition of Justice seems to imply that there is some conception in which all these applications of the word meet like lines converging to a common centre; or, in more concrete terms, that there is some principle whereby human life might be so organized that there would exist a just society composed of just men. The justice of the society would secure that each member of it should perform his duties and enjoy his rights. As a quality residing in each individual, justice would mean that his personal life — or as a Greek would say, his soul — was correspondingly ordered with respect to the rights and duties of each part of his nature.

A society so composed and organized would be ideal, in the sense that it would offer a standard of perfection by which all existing societies might be measured and appraised according to the degrees in which they fell short of it. Any proposed reform, moreover, might be judged by its tendency to bring us nearer to, or farther from, this goal. The REPUBLIC is the first systematic attempt ever made to describe this ideal, not as a baseless dream, but as a possible framework within which man's nature, with its unalterable claims, might find well-being and happiness. Without some such goal in view, statecraft must be either blind and aimless or directed (as it commonly is) to false and worthless ends.

If a man of sceptical and inquiring mind were to ask, in any mixed company of intelligent people, for a definition of 'right' or 'justice,' the answers produced would be likely to be superficial and to cover only some part of the field. They might also reveal fundamental differences of conviction about what Socrates calls the most important of all questions: how we ought to live. In the first Part of the REPUBLIC Socrates opens up the whole range of inquiry by eliciting some typical views of the nature of justice and criticizing them as either inadequate or false. The criticism naturally reveals some glimpses of the principles which will guide the construction that is to follow.

CHAPTER I (I. 327–331 D)

CEPHALUS: JUSTICE AS HONESTY IN WORD AND DEED

The whole imaginary conversation is narrated by Socrates to an unspecified audience. The company who will take part in it assemble at the house of Cephalus, a retired manufacturer living at the Piraeus, the harbour town about five miles from Athens. It includes, besides Plato's elder brothers, Glaucon and Adeimantus, Cephalus' sons, Polemarchus, Lysias, well known as a writer of speeches, and Euthydemus; Thrasymachus of Chalcedon, a noted teacher of rhetoric, who may have formulated the definition of justice as 'the interest of the stronger,' though hardly any evidence about his opinions exists outside the REPUBLIC; and a number of Socrates' young friends. The occasion is the festival of Bendis, a goddess whose cult had been *imported from Thrace. Cephalus embodies the wisdom of a long life honourably spent in business. He is well-to-do, but values money as a means to that peace of mind which comes of honesty and the ability to render to gods and men their due. This is what he understands by 'right' conduct or justice.*

SOCRATES. I walked down to the Piraeus yesterday with Glaucon, the son of Ariston, to make my prayers to the goddess. As this was the first celebration of her festival, I wished also to see how the ceremony would be conducted. The Thracians, I thought, made as fine a show in the procession as our own people, though they did well enough. The prayers and the spectacle were over, and we were leaving to go back to the city, when from some way off Polemarchus, the son of Cephalus, caught sight of us starting homewards and sent his slave running to ask us to wait for him. The boy caught my garment from behind and gave me the message.

I turned round and asked where his master was.

There, he answered; coming up behind. Please wait.

Very well, said Glaucon; we will.

A minute later Polemarchus joined us, with Glaucon's brother, Adeimantus, and Niceratus, the son of Nicias, and some others who must have been at the procession.

Socrates, said Polemarchus, I do believe you are starting back to town and leaving us.

You have guessed right, I answered.

Well, he said, you see what a large party we are?

I do.

Unless you are more than a match for us, then, you must stay here.

Isn't there another alternative? said I; we might convince you that you must let us go.

How will you convince us, if we refuse to listen?

We cannot, said Glaucon.

Well, we shall refuse; make up your minds to that.

Here Adeimantus interposed: Don't you even know that in the evening there is going to be a torch-race on horseback in honour of the goddess?

On horseback! I exclaimed; that is something new. How will they do it? Are the riders going to race with torches and hand them on to one another?

Just so, said Polemarchus. Besides, there will be a festival lasting all night, which will be worth seeing. We will go out after dinner and look on. We shall find plenty of young men there and we can have a talk. So please stay, and don't disappoint us.

It looks as if we had better stay, said Glaucon.

Well, said I, if you think so, we will.

Accordingly, we went home with Polemarchus; and there we found his brothers, Lysias and Euthydemus, as well as Thrasymachus of Chalcedon, Charmantides of Paeania, and Cleitophon, the son of Aristonymus. Polemarchus' father, Cephalus, was at home too. I had not seen him for some time, and it struck me that he had aged a good deal. He was sitting in a cushioned chair, wearing a garland, as he had just been conducting a sacrifice in the courtyard. There were some chairs standing round, and we sat down beside him.

As soon as he saw me, Cephalus greeted me. You don't often come down to the Piraeus to visit us, Socrates, he said. But you ought to. If I still had the strength to walk to town easily, you would not have to come here; we would come to you. But, as things are, you really ought to come here oftener. I find, I can assure you, that in proportion as bodily pleasures lose their savour, my appetite for the things of the mind grows keener and I enjoy discussing them more than ever. So you must not disappoint me. Treat us like old friends, and come here often to have a talk with these young men.

To tell the truth, Cephalus, I answered, I enjoy talking with very old people. They have gone before us on a road by which we too may have to travel, and I think we do well to learn from them what it is like, easy or difficult, rough or smooth. And now that you have reached an age when your foot, as the poets say, is on the threshold, I should like to hear what report you can give and whether you find it a painful time of life.

I will tell you by all means what it seems like to me, Socrates. Some of us old men often meet, true to the old saying that people of the same age like to be together. Most of our company are very sorry for themselves, looking back with regret to the pleasures of their young days, all the delights connected with love affairs and merrymaking. They are vexed at being deprived of what seems to them so important; life was good in those days, they think, and now they have no life at all. Some complain that their families have no respect for their years, and make that a reason for harping on all the miseries old age has brought. But to my mind, Socrates, they are laying the blame on the wrong shoulders. If the fault were in old age, so far as that goes, I and all who have ever reached my time of life would have the same experience; but in point of fact, I have met many who felt quite differently. For instance, I remember someone asking Sophocles, the poet, whether he was still capable of enjoying a woman. 'Don't talk in that way,' he answered; 'I am only too

glad to be free of all that; it is like escaping from bondage to a raging madman.' I thought that a good answer at the time, and I still think so; for certainly a great peace comes when age sets us free from passions of that sort. When they weaken and relax their hold, most certainly it means, as Sophocles said, a release from servitude to many forms of madness. All these troubles, Socrates, including the complaints about not being respected, have only one cause; and that is not old age, but a man's character. If you have a contented mind at peace with itself, age is no intolerable burden; without that, Socrates, age and youth will be equally painful.

I was charmed with these words and wanted him to go on talking; so I tried to draw him out. I fancy, Cephalus, said I, most people will not accept that account; they imagine that it is not character that makes your burden light, but your wealth. The rich, they say, have many consolations.

That is true, he replied; they do not believe me; and there is something in their suggestion, though not so much as they suppose. When a man from Seriphus [2] taunted Themistocles and told him that his fame was due not to himself but to his country, Themistocles made a good retort: 'Certainly, if I had been born a Seriphian, I should not be famous; but no more would you, if you had been born at Athens.' And so one might say to men who are not rich and feel old age burdensome: If it is true that a good man will not find it easy to bear old age and poverty combined, no more will riches ever make a bad man contented and cheerful.

And was your wealth, Cephalus,

[2] An insignificant island, among the Cyclades.

mostly inherited or have you made your own fortune?

Made my fortune, Socrates? As a man of business I stand somewhere between my grandfather and my father. My grandfather, who was my namesake, inherited about as much property as I have now and more than doubled it; whereas my father Lysanias reduced it below its present level. I shall be content if I can leave these sons of mine not less than I inherited, and perhaps a little more.

I asked, said I, because you strike me as not caring overmuch about money; and that is generally so with men who have not made their own fortune. Those who have are twice as fond of their possessions as other people. They have the same affection for the money they have earned that poets have for their poems, or fathers for their children: they not merely find it useful, as we all do, but it means much to them as being of their own creation. That makes them disagreeable company; they have not a good word for anything but riches.

That is quite true.

It is indeed, I said; but one more question: what do you take to be the greatest advantage you have got from being wealthy?

One that perhaps not many people would take my word for. I can tell you, Socrates, that, when the prospect of dying is near at hand, a man begins to feel some alarm about things that never troubled him before. He may have laughed at those stories they tell of another world and of punishments there for wrongdoing in this life; but now the soul is tormented by a doubt whether they may not be true. Maybe from the weakness of old age, or perhaps because, now that he is nearer to what lies beyond, he begins to get some glimpse of it himself—at any rate he is beset with fear and misgiving; he begins thinking over the past:

is there anyone he has wronged? If he finds that his life has been full of wrongdoing, he starts up from his sleep in terror like a child, and his life is haunted by dark forebodings; whereas, if his conscience is clear, that 'sweet Hope' that Pindar speaks of is always with him to tend his age. Indeed, Socrates, there is great charm in those lines describing the man who has led a life of righteousness:

Hope is his sweet companion, she who guides
Man's wandering purpose, warms his heart
And nurses tenderly his age.

That is admirably expressed, admirably. Now in this, as I believe, lies the chief value of wealth, not for everyone, perhaps, but for the right-thinking man. It can do much to save us from going to that other world in fear of having cheated or deceived anyone even unintentionally or of being in debt to some god for sacrifice or to some man for money. Wealth has many other uses, of course; but, taking one with another, I should regard this as the best use that can be made of it by a man of sense.

You put your case admirably, Cephalus, said I. But take this matter of doing right: can we say that it really consists in nothing more nor less than telling the truth and paying back anything we may have received? Are not these very actions sometimes right and sometimes wrong? Suppose, for example, a friend who had lent us a weapon were to go mad and then ask for it back, surely anyone would say we ought not to return it. It would not be 'right' to do so; nor yet to tell the truth without reserve to a madman.

No, it would not.

Right conduct, then, cannot be defined as telling the truth and restoring anything we have been trusted with.

Yes, it can, Polemarchus broke in, at least if we are to believe Simonides.

Well, well, said Cephalus, I will bequeath the argument to you. It is time for me to attend to the sacrifice.

Your part, then, said Polemarchus, will fall to me as your heir.

By all means, said Cephalus with a smile; and with that he left us, to see to the sacrifice.

CHAPTER II (I. 331 E-336 A)

POLEMARCHUS: JUSTICE AS HELPING
FRIENDS AND HARMING ENEMIES

Criticism now begins. No doubt it is generally right or just to tell the truth and pay one's debts; but no list of external actions such as these can tell us what is meant by justice, the name of the quality they have in common. Also what is superficially the same action, e.g. repayment of a loan, may completely change its character when we take into account the antecedents and consequences which form its wider context.

Polemarchus can only meet this objection by citing a maxim borrowed from a famous poet. In Greece, where there was no sacred book like the Bible, the poets were regarded as inspired authorities on religion and morals; but Socrates, when he questioned them, found them unable to give any rational account of their teaching (APOLOGY, 22 B). Polemarchus, too, has never thought out the implications of defining justice as 'giving every man his due.' What is it that is due, and to whom?

Socrates' first object is to bring home to Polemarchus the vagueness of his ideas by leading him on to an absurd conclusion. In approaching a very large and obscure question, the first step is to convince one who thinks he can answer it with a compact formula

that he knows much less than he imagines and cannot even understand his own formula.

Plato often, as here, compares the practice of morality to the useful (not the fine) arts or crafts: medicine, navigation, shoemaking. He even speaks of an 'art of justice.' He adopted Socrates' belief that there should be an art of living, analogous to the craftsman's knowledge and consequent ability to achieve a purposed end. A builder, building a house, knows what he is setting out to do and how to do it; he can account for all his actions as contributing to his end. This knowledge and ability constitute the craft embodied in the builder and his special excellence or 'virtue' (areté), qua builder. Similarly a man can live well only if he knows clearly what is the end of life, what things are of real value, and how they are to be attained. This knowledge is the moral virtue of man, qua man, and constitues the art of living. If a man imagines that the end of life is to gain wealth or power, which are valueless in themselves, all his actions will be misdirected. This doctrine is fundamental in the RE-PUBLIC. It leads to the central thesis that society must be ruled by men who have learnt, by long and severe training, not only the true end of human life, but the meaning of goodness in all its forms.

Then, said I, if you are to inherit this discussion, tell me, what is this saying of Simonides about right conduct which you approve?

That it is just to render every man his due. That seems to me a fair statement.

It is certainly hard to question the inspired wisdom of a poet like Simonides; but what this saying means you may know, Polemarchus, but I do not. Obviously it does not mean what we were speaking of just now — returning something we have been entrusted with to the owner even when he has gone out of his mind. And yet surely it is his due, if he asks for it back?

Yes.

But it is out of the question to give it back when he has gone mad?

True.

Simonides, then, must have meant something different from that when he said it was just to render a man his due.

Certainly he did; his idea was that, as between friends, what one owes to another is to do him good, not harm.

I see, said I; to repay money entrusted to one is not to render what is due, if the two parties are friends and the repayment proves harmful to the lender. That is what you say Simonides meant?

Yes, certainly.

And what about enemies? Are we to render whatever is their due to them?

Yes certainly, what really is due to them; which means, I suppose, what is appropriate to an enemy — some sort of injury.

It seems, then, that Simonides was using words with a hidden meaning, as poets will. He really meant to define justice as rendering to everyone what is appropriate to him; only he called that his 'due.'

Well, why not?

But look here, said I. Suppose we could question Simonides about the art of medicine — whether a physician can be described as rendering to some object what is due or appropriate to it; how do you think he would answer?

That the physician administers the appropriate diet or remedies to the body.

And the art of cookery — can that be described in the same way?

Yes; the cook gives the appropriate seasoning to his dishes.

Good. And the practice of justice?

If we are to follow those analogies, Socrates, justice would be rendering services or injuries to friends or enemies.

So Simonides means by justice doing good to friends and harm to enemies?

I think so.

And in matters of health who would be the most competent to treat friends and enemies in that way?

A physician.

And on a voyage, as regards the dangers of the sea?

A ship's captain.

In what sphere of action, then, will the just man be the most competent to do good or harm?

In war, I should imagine; when he is fighting on the side of his friends and against his enemies.

I see. But when we are well and staying on shore, the doctor and the ship's captain are of no use to us.

True.

Is it also true that the just man is useless when we are not at war?

I should not say that.

So justice has its uses in peace-time too?

Yes.

Like farming, which is useful for producing crops, or shoemaking, which is useful for providing us with shoes. Can you tell me for what purposes justice is useful or profitable in time of peace?

For matters of business, Socrates.

In a partnership, you mean?

Yes.

But if we are playing draughts, or laying bricks, or making music, will the just man be as good and helpful a partner as an expert draught-player, or a builder, or a musician?

No.

Then in what kind of partnership will he be more helpful?

Where money is involved, I suppose.

Except, perhaps, Polemarchus, when we are putting our money to some use. If we are buying or selling a horse, a judge of horses would be a better partner; or if we are dealing in ships, a shipwright or a sea-captain.

I suppose so.

Well, when will the just man be specially useful in handling our money?

When we want to deposit it for safekeeping.

When the money is to lie idle, in fact?

Yes.

So justice begins to be useful only when our money is out of use?

Perhaps so.

And in the same way, I suppose, if a pruning-knife is to be used, or a shield, or a lyre, then a vine-dresser, or a soldier, or a musician will be of service; but justice is helpful only when these things are to be kept safe. In fact justice is never of any use in using things; it becomes useful when they are useless.

That seems to follow.

If that is so, my friend, justice can hardly be a thing of much value. And here is another point. In boxing or fighting of any sort skill in dealing blows goes with skill in keeping them off; and the same doctor that can keep us from disease would also be clever at producing it by stealth; or again, a general will be good at keeping his army safe, if he can also cheat the enemy and steal his plans and disposi-tions. So a man who is expert in keep-ing things will always make an expert thief.

Apparently.

The just man, then, being good at keeping money safe, will also be good at stealing it.

That seems to be the conclusion, at any rate.

So the just man turns out to be a kind of thief. You must have learnt

that from Homer, who showed his predilection for Odysseus' grandfather Autolycus by remarking that he sur-passed all men in cheating and per-jury. Justice, according to you and Homer and Simonides, turns out to be a form of skill in cheating, provided it be to help a friend or harm an enemy. That was what you meant?

Good God, no, he protested; but I have forgotten now what I did mean. All the same, I do still believe that justice consists in helping one's friends and harming one's enemies.

[*The argument now becomes more serious. Polemarchus, though puzzled, clings to the belief that it must be right to help friends and harm ene-mies. This was a traditional maxim of Greek morality, never doubted till Socrates denied it: no one had ever said that we ought to do good, or even refrain from doing harm, to them that hate us. Socrates' denial rests on his principle, later adopted by the Stoics, that the only thing that is good in it-self is the goodness, virtue, well-being of the human soul. The only way really to injure a man is to make him a worse man. This cannot be the func-tion of justice.*]

Which do you mean by a man's friends and enemies — those whom he believes to be good honest people and the reverse, or those who really are, though they may not seem so?

Naturally, his loves and hates de-pend on what he believes.

But don't people often mistake an honest man for a rogue, or a rogue for an honest man; in which case they regard good people as enemies and bad people as friends?

No doubt.

But all the same, it will then be right for them to help the rogue and to injure the good man?

Apparently.

And yet a good man is one who is not given to doing wrong.

True.

According to your account, then, it is right to ill-treat a man who does no wrong.

No, no, Socrates; that can't be sound doctrine.

It must be the wrongdoers, then, that it is right to injure, and the honest that are to be helped.

That sounds better.

Then, Polemarchus, the conclusion will be that for a bad judge of character it will often be right to injure his friends, when they really are rogues, and to help his enemies, when they really are honest men—the exact opposite of what we took Simonides to mean.

That certainly does follow, he said. We must shift our ground. Perhaps our definition of friend and enemy was wrong.

What definition, Polemarchus?

We said a friend was one whom we believe to be an honest man.

And how are we to define him now?

As one who really is honest as well as seeming so. If he merely seems so, he will be only a seeming friend. And the same will apply to enemies.

On this showing, then, it is the good people that will be our friends, the wicked our enemies.

Yes.

You would have us, in fact, add something to our original definition of justice: it will not mean merely doing good to friends and harm to enemies, but doing good to friends who are good, and harm to enemies who are wicked.

Yes, I think that is all right.

Can it really be a just man's business to harm any human being?

Certainly; it is right for him to harm bad men who are his enemies.

But does not harming a horse or a dog mean making it a worse horse or dog, so that each will be a less perfect creature in its own special way?

Yes.

Isn't that also true of human beings —that to harm them means making them worse men by the standard of human excellence?

Yes.

And is not justice a peculiarly human excellence?

Undoubtedly.

To harm a man, then, must mean making him less just.

I suppose so.

But a musician or a riding-master cannot be exercising his special skill, if he makes his pupils unmusical or bad riders.

No.

Whereas the just man is to exercise his justice by making men unjust? Or, in more general terms, the good are to make men bad by exercising their virtue? Can that be so?

No, it cannot.

It can no more be the function of goodness to do harm than of heat to cool or of drought to produce moisture. So if the just man is good, the business of harming people, whether friends or not, must belong to his opposite, the unjust.

I think that is perfectly true, Socrates.

So it was not a wise saying that justice is giving every man his due, if that means that harm is due from the just man to his enemies, as well as help to his friends. That is not true; because we have found that it is never right to harm anyone.

I agree.

Then you and I will make common cause against anyone who attributes that doctrine to Simonides or to any of the old canonical sages, like Bias or Pittacus.

Yes, he said, I am prepared to support you.

Do you know, I think that account

of justice, as helping friends and harming enemies, must be due to some despot, so rich and powerful that he thought he could do as he liked— someone like Periander, or Perdiccas, or Xerxes, or Ismenias of Thebes.

That is extremely probable.

Very good, said I; and now that we have disposed of that definition of justice, can anyone suggest another?

CHAPTER III (I. 336 B-347 E)

THRASYMACHUS: JUSTICE AS THE INTEREST OF THE STRONGER

Socrates has opposed to the popular conception of justice one of his own deepest convictions. Polemarchus' ready acceptance of this provokes a violent protest from Thrasymachus, who represents the doctrine that might is right in an extreme form. He holds that justice or right is nothing but the name given by the men actually holding power in any state to any actions they enjoin by law upon their subjects; and that all their laws are framed to promote their own personal or class interests. 'Just' accordingly means what is for the interest of the stronger, ruling party. Right and wrong have no other meaning at all. This is not a theory of social contract: it is not suggested that the subject has ever made a bargain with the ruler, sacrificing some of his liberty to gain the benefits of a social order. The ruler imposes his 'rights' by sheer force. The perfect example of such a ruler is the despot (the Greek 'tyrant'), whose position Thrasymachus regards as supremely enviable. He is precisely the man who has the will and the power to 'do good to himself and his friends and to harm his enemies.'

The discussion begins by clearing up the ambiguities of Thrasymachus' formula. The word translated 'stronger' commonly means also 'superior' or 'better'; but 'better' has no moral sense for Thrasymachus, who does not recognize the existence of morality. The superiority of the stronger lies in the skill and determination which enable them to seize and hold power. 'Interest,' again, means the personal satisfaction and aggrandizement of the ruling individuals.

All this time Thrasymachus had been trying more than once to break in upon our conversation; but his neighbours had restrained him, wishing to hear the argument to the end. In the pause after my last words he could keep quiet no longer; but gathering himself up like a wild beast he sprang at us as if he would tear us in pieces. Polemarchus and I were frightened out of our wits, when he burst out to the whole company:

What is the matter with you two, Socrates? Why do you go on in this imbecile way, politely deferring to each other's nonsense? If you really want to know what justice means, stop asking questions and scoring off the answers you get. You know very well it is easier to ask questions than to answer them. Answer yourself, and tell us what you think justice means. I won't have you telling us it is the same as what is obligatory or useful or advantageous or profitable or expedient; I want a clear and precise statement; I won't put up with that sort of verbiage.

I was amazed by this onslaught and looked at him in terror. If I had not seen this wolf before he saw me, I really believe I should have been struck dumb; [3] but fortunately I had looked at him earlier, when he was beginning to get exasperated with our argument; so I was able to reply, though rather tremulously:

[3] A popular superstition, that if a wolf sees you first, you become dumb.

Don't be hard on us, Thrasymachus. If Polemarchus and I have gone astray in our search, you may be quite sure the mistake was not intentional. If we had been looking for a piece of gold, we should never have deliberately allowed politeness to spoil our chance of finding it; and now when we are looking for justice, a thing much more precious than gold, you cannot imagine we should defer to each other in that foolish way and not do our best to bring it to light. You must believe we are in earnest, my friend; but I am afraid the task is beyond our powers, and we might expect a man of your ability to pity us instead of being so severe.

Thrasymachus replied with a burst of sardonic laughter.

Good Lord, he said; Socrates at his old trick of shamming ignorance! I knew it; I told the others you would refuse to commit yourself and do anything sooner than answer a question.

Yes, Thrasymachus, I replied; because you are clever enough to know that if you asked someone what are the factors of the number twelve, and at the same time warned him: 'Look here, you are not to tell me that 12 is twice 6, or 3 times 4, or 6 times 2, or 4 times 3; I won't put up with any such nonsense' — you must surely see that no one would answer a question put like that. He would say: 'What do you mean, Thrasymachus? Am I forbidden to give any of these answers, even if one happens to be right? Do you want me to give a wrong one?' What would you say to that?

Humph! said he. As if that were a fair analogy!

I don't see why it is not, said I; but in any case, do you suppose our barring a certain answer would prevent the man from giving it, if he thought it was the truth?

Do you mean that you are going to give me one of those answers I barred?

I should not be surprised, if it seemed to me true, on reflection.

And what if I give you another definition of justice, better than any of those? What penalty are you prepared to pay? [4]

The penalty deserved by ignorance, which must surely be to receive instruction from the wise. So I would suggest that as a suitable punishment.

I like your notion of a penalty! he said; but you must pay the costs as well.

I will, when I have any money.

That will be all right, said Glaucon; we will all subscribe for Socrates. So let us have your definition, Thrasymachus.

Oh yes, he said; so that Socrates may play the old game of questioning and refuting some one else, instead of giving an answer himself!

But really, I protested, what can you expect from a man who does not know the answer or profess to know it, and, besides that, has been forbidden by no mean authority to put forward any notions he may have? Surely the definition should naturally come from you, who say you do know the answer and can tell it us. Please do not disappoint us. I should take it as a kindness, and I hope you will not be chary of giving Glaucon and the rest of us the advantage of your instruction.

Glaucon and the others added their entreaties to mine. Thrasymachus was evidently longing to win credit, for he was sure he had an admirable answer ready, though he made a show of insisting that I should be the one to

---

[4] In certain lawsuits the defendant, if found guilty, was allowed to propose a penalty alternative to that demanded by the prosecution. The judges then decided which should be inflicted. The 'costs' here means the fee which the sophist, unlike Socrates, expected from his pupils.

reply. In the end he gave way and exclaimed:

So this is what Socrates' wisdom comes to! He refuses to teach, and goes about learning from others without offering so much as thanks in return.

I do learn from others, Thrasymachus; that is quite true; but you are wrong to call me ungrateful. I give in return all I can — praise; for I have no money. And how ready I am to applaud any idea that seems to me sound, you will see in a moment, when you have stated your own; for I am sure that will be sound.

Listen then, Thrasymachus began. What I say is that 'just' or 'right' means nothing but what is to the interest of the stronger party. Well, where is your applause? You don't mean to give it me.

I will, as soon as I understand, I said. I don't see yet what you mean by right being the interest of the stronger party. For instance, Polydamas, the athlete, is stronger than we are, and it is to his interest to eat beef for the sake of his muscles; but surely you don't mean that the same diet would be good for weaker men and therefore be right for us?

You are trying to be funny, Socrates. It's a low trick to take my words in the sense you think will be most damaging.

No, no, I protested; but you must explain.

Don't you know, then, that a state may be ruled by a despot, or a democracy, or an aristocracy?

Of course.

And that the ruling element is always the strongest?

Yes.

Well then, in every case the laws are made by the ruling party in its own interest; a democracy makes democratic laws, a despot autocratic

ones, and so on. By making these laws they define as 'right' for their subjects whatever is for their own interest, and they call anyone who breaks them a 'wrongdoer' and punish him accordingly. That is what I mean: in all states alike 'right' has the same meaning, namely what is for the interest of the party established in power, and that is the strongest. So the sound conclusion is that what is 'right' is the same everywhere: the interest of the stronger party.

Now I see what you mean, said I; whether it is true or not, I must try to make out. When you define right in terms of interest, you are yourself giving one of those answers you forbade to me; though, to be sure, you add 'to the stronger party.'

An insignificant addition, perhaps!

Its importance is not clear yet; what is clear is that we must find out whether your definition is true. I agree myself that right is in a sense a matter of interest; but when you add 'to the stronger party,' I don't know about that. I must consider.

Go ahead, then.

I will. Tell me this. No doubt you also think it is right to obey the men in power?

I do.

Are they infallible in every type of state, or can they sometimes make a mistake?

Of course they can make a mistake.

In framing laws, then, they may do their work well or badly?

No doubt.

Well, that is to say, when the laws they make are to their own interest; badly, when they are not?

Yes.

But the subjects are to obey any law they lay down, and they will then be doing right?

Of course.

If so, by your account, it will be right to do what is not to the interest of the stronger party, as well as what is so.

What's that you are saying?

Just what you said, I believe; but let us look again. Haven't you admitted that the rulers, when they enjoin certain acts on their subjects, sometimes mistake their own best interests, and at the same time that it is right for the subjects to obey, whatever they may enjoin?

Yes, I suppose so.

Well, that amounts to admitting that it is right to do what is not to the interest of the rulers or the stronger party. They may unwittingly enjoin what is to their own disadvantage; and you say it is right for the others to do as they are told. In that case, their duty must be the opposite of what you said, because the weaker will have been ordered to do what is against the interest of the stronger. You with your intelligence must see how that follows.

Yes, Socrates, said Polemarchus, that is undeniable.

No doubt, Cleitophon broke in, if you are to be a witness on Socrates' side.

No witness is needed, replied Polemarchus; Thrasymachus himself admits that rulers sometimes ordain acts that are to their own disadvantage, and that it is the subjects' duty to do them.

That is because Thrasymachus said it was right to do what you are told by the men in power.

Yes, but he also said that what is to the interest of the stronger party is right; and, after making both these assertions, he admitted that the stronger sometimes command the weaker subjects to act against their interests. From all which it follows that what is in the stronger's interest is no more right than what is not.

No, said Cleitophon; he meant whatever the stronger *believes* to be

in his own interest. That is what the subject must do, and what Thrasymachus meant to define as right.

That was not what he said, rejoined Polemarchus.

No matter, Polemarchus, said I; if Thrasymachus says so now, let us take him in that sense. Now, Thrasymachus, tell me, was that what you intended to say — that right means what the stronger thinks is to his interest, whether it really is so or not?

Most certainly not, he replied. Do you suppose I should speak of a man as 'stronger' or 'superior' at the very moment when he is making a mistake?

I did think you said as much when you admitted that rulers are not always infallible.

That is because you are a quibbler, Socrates. Would you say a man deserves to be called a physician at the moment when he makes a mistake in treating his patient and just in respect of that mistake; or a mathematician, when he does a sum wrong and just in so far as he gets a wrong result? Of course we do commonly speak of a physician or a mathematician or a scholar having made a mistake; but really none of these, I should say, is ever mistaken, in so far as he is worthy of the name we give him. So strictly speaking — and you are all for being precise — no one who practises a craft makes mistakes. A man is mistaken when his knowledge fails him; and at that moment he is no craftsman. And what is true of craftsmanship or any sort of skill is true of the ruler: he is never mistaken so long as he is acting as a ruler; though anyone might speak of a ruler making a mistake, just as he might of a physician. You must understand that I was talking in that loose way when I answered your question just now; but the precise statement is this. The ruler, in so far as he is acting as a ruler, makes no mistakes and consequently enjoins what is best for himself; and that is what the subject is to do. So, as I said at first, 'right' means doing what is to the interest of the stronger.

Very well, Thrasymachus, said I. So you think I am quibbling?

I am sure you are.

You believe my questions were maliciously designed to damage your position?

I know it. But you will gain nothing by that. You cannot outwit me by cunning, and you are not the man to crush me in the open.

Bless your soul, I answered, I should not think of trying. But, to prevent any more misunderstanding, when you speak of that ruler or stronger party whose interest the weaker ought to serve, please make it clear whether you are using the words in the ordinary way or in that strict sense you have just defined.

I mean a ruler in the strictest possible sense. Now quibble away and be as malicious as you can. I want no mercy. But you are no match for me.

Do you think me mad enough to beard a lion or try to outwit a Thrasymachus?

You did try just now, he retorted, but it wasn't a success.

[*Thrasymachus has already shifted his ground. At first 'the stronger' meant only the men ruling by superior force; but now their superiority must include the knowledge and ability needed to govern without making mistakes. This knowledge and ability constitute an art of government, comparable to other useful arts or crafts requiring special skill. The ruler in his capacity as ruler, or the craftsman* qua *craftsman, can also be spoken of as the craft personified, since a craft exists only in the man who embodies it, and we are considering the man only as the embodiment of this special* capacity, neglecting all personal characteristics and any other capacities he may chance to have. When Socrates talks of the art or craft in this abstract way as having an interest of its own, he means the same thing as if he spoke of the interest of the craftsman* qua *craftsman. Granted that there is, as Thrasymachus suggested, an art of government exercised by a ruler who,* qua *ruler, is infallible and so in the full sense 'superior,' the question now is, what his interest should be, on the analogy of other crafts.*]

Enough of this, said I. Now tell me about the physician in that strict sense you spoke of: is it his business to earn money or to treat his patients? Remember, I mean your physician who is worthy of the name.

To treat his patients.

And what of the ship's captain in the true sense? Is he a mere seaman or the commander of the crew?

The commander.

Yes, we shall not speak of him as a seaman just because he is on board a ship. That is not the point. He is called captain because of his skill and authority over the crew.

Quite true.

And each of these people has some special interest? [5]

No doubt.

And the craft in question exists for the very purpose of discovering that interest and providing for it?

Yes.

Can it equally be said of any craft that it has an interest, other than its own greatest possible perfection?

[5] All the persons mentioned have some interest. The craftsman *qua* craftsman has an interest in doing his work as well as possible, which is the same thing as serving the interest of the subjects on whom his craft is exercised; and the subjects have their interest, which the craftsman is there to promote.

What do you mean by that?

Here is an illustration. If you ask me whether it is sufficient for the human body just to be itself, with no need of help from without, I should say, Certainly not; it has weaknesses and defects, and its condition is not all that it might be. That is precisely why the art of medicine was invented: it was designed to help the body and provide for its interests. Would not that be true?

It would.

But now take the art of medicine itself. Has that any defects or weaknesses? Does any art stand in need of some further perfection, as the eye would be imperfect without the power of vision or the ear without hearing, so that in their case an art is required that will study their interests and provide for their carrying out those functions? Has the art itself any corresponding need of some further art to remedy its defects and look after its interests; and will that further art require yet another, and so on for ever? Or will every art look after its own interests? Or, finally, is it not true that no art needs to have its weaknesses remedied or its interests studied either by another art or by itself, because no art has in itself any weakness or fault, and the only interest it is required to serve is that of its subject-matter? In itself, an art is sound and flawless, so long as it is entirely true to its own nature as an art in the strictest sense — and it is the strict sense that I want you to keep in view. Is not that true?

So it appears.

Then, said I, the art of medicine does not study its own interest, but the needs of the body, just as a groom shows his skill by caring for horses, not for the art of grooming. And so every art seeks, not its own advantage — for it has no deficiencies — but the interest of the subject on which it is exercised.

It appears so.

But surely, Thrasymachus, every art has authority and superior power over its subject.

To this he agreed, though very reluctantly.

So far as arts are concerned, then, no art ever studies or enjoins the interest of the superior or stronger party, but always that of the weaker over which it has authority.

Thrasymachus assented to this at last, though he tried to put up a fight. I then went on:

So the physician, as such, studies only the patient's interest, not his own. For as we agreed, the business of the physician, in the strict sense, is not to make money for himself, but to exercise his power over the patient's body; and the ship's captain, again, considered strictly as no mere sailor, but in command of the crew, will study and enjoin the interest of his subordinates, not his own.

He agreed reluctantly.

And so with government of any kind no ruler, in so far as he is acting as ruler, will study or enjoin what is for his own interest. All that he says and does will be said and done with a view to what is good and proper for the subject for whom he practises his art.

[Thrasymachus can hardly challenge his last argument, based as it is on his own 'precise' distinction of the ruler acting in his special capacity with knowledge and ability like the craftsman's and impeccable. Accordingly he takes refuge in an appeal to facts. The ruler, from the Homeric king onwards, had been called the shepherd of the people. Thrasymachus truly remarks that these shepherds have commonly been less concerned with the good of their flock than with shearing and butchering them for their own profit and aggrandizement. This behavior is called 'in-

*justice' because it means getting more
than one's fair share; but the entirely
selfish autocrat who practises it on a
grand scale is envied and admired;
and Thrasymachus himself regards
him as the happiest of men. Justice,
fairness, honesty, he concludes, never
pay; the life of injustice is always more
profitable.*

*Socrates leaves this more general
proposition to be challenged in the
next chapter. Here he is still concerned with the art of government.
He takes up the analogy of the shepherd and applies once more Thrasymachus' own distinction of 'capacities.' The shepherd* qua *shepherd
cares for his flock; he receives wages
in a different capacity,* qua *wage-
earner. The fact that the rulers of
mankind expect to be rewarded shows
that the proper task of governing is
commonly regarded as an irksome and
unprofitable business.]*

At this point, when everyone could
see that Thrasymachus' definition of
justice had been turned inside out,
instead of making any reply, he said:

Socrates, have you a nurse?

Why do you ask such a question as
that? I said. Wouldn't it be better to
answer mine?

Because she lets you go about snif-
fling like a child whose nose wants
wiping. She hasn't even taught you to
know a shepherd when you see one,
or his sheep either.

What makes you say that?

Why, you imagine that a herdsman
studies the interests of his flocks or
cattle, tending and fattening them up
with some other end in view than his
master's profit or his own; and so you
don't see that, in politics, the genuine
ruler regards his subjects exactly like
sheep, and thinks of nothing else,
night and day, but the good he can
get out of them for himself. You are
so far out in your notions of right and

wrong, justice and injustice, as not to
know that 'right' actually means what
is good for some one else, and to be
'just' means serving the interest of the
stronger who rules, at the cost of the
subject who obeys; whereas injustice
is just the reverse, asserting its authority over those innocents who are called
just, so that they minister solely to
their master's advantage and happiness, and not in the least degree to
their own. Innocent as you are yourself, Socrates, you must see that a just
man always has the worst of it. Take
a private business: when a partnership is wound up, you will never find
that the more honest of two partners
comes off with the larger share; and in
their relations to the state, when there
are taxes to be paid, the honest man
will pay more than the other on the
same amount of property; or if there
is money to be distributed, the dishonest will get it all. When either of
them hold some public office, even if
the just man loses in no other way, his
private affairs at any rate will suffer
from neglect, while his principles will
not allow him to help himself from
the public funds; not to mention the
offence he will give to his friends and
relations by refusing to sacrifice those
principles to do them a good turn. Injustice has all the opposite advantages.
I am speaking of the type I described
just now, the man who can get the
better of other people on a large scale:
you must fix your eye on him, if you
want to judge how much it is to one's
own interest not to be just. You can
see that best in the most consummate
form of injustice, which rewards
wrongdoing with supreme welfare and
happiness and reduces its victims, if
they won't retaliate in kind, to misery.
That form is despotism, which uses
force or fraud to plunder the goods of
others, public or private, sacred or
profane, and to do it in a wholesale
way. If you are caught committing

any one of these crimes on a small scale, you are punished and disgraced; they call it sacrilege, kidnapping, burglary, theft and brigandage. But if, besides taking their property, you turn all your countrymen into slaves, you will hear no more of those ugly names; your countrymen themselves will call you the happiest of men and bless your name, and so will everyone who hears of such a complete triumph of injustice; for when people denounce injustice, it is because they are afraid of suffering wrong, not of doing it. So true is it, Socrates, that injustice, on a grand enough scale, is superior to justice in strength and freedom and autocratic power; and 'right,' as I said at first, means simply what serves the interest of the stronger party; 'wrong' means what is for the interest and profit of oneself.

Having deluged our ears with this torrent of words, as the man at the baths might empty a bucket over one's head, Thrasymachus meant to take himself off; but the company obliged him to stay and defend his position. I was specially urgent in my entreaties.

My good Thrasymachus, said I, do you propose to fling a doctrine like that at our heads and then go away without explaining it properly or letting us point out to you whether it is true or not? Is it so small a matter in your eyes to determine the whole course of conduct which every one of us must follow to get the best out of life?

Don't I realize it is a serious matter? he retorted.

Apparently not, said I; or else you have no consideration for us, and do not care whether we shall lead better or worse lives for being ignorant of this truth you profess to know. Do take the trouble to let us into your secret; if you treat us handsomely, you may be sure it will be a good investment; there are so many of us to show

our gratitude. I will make no secret of my own conviction, which is that injustice is not more profitable than justice, even when left free to work its will unchecked. No; let your unjust man have full power to do wrong, whether by successful violence or by escaping detection; all the same he will not convince me that he will gain more than he would by being just. There may be others here who feel as I do, and set justice above injustice. It is for you to convince us that we are not well advised.

How can I? he replied. If you are not convinced by what I have just said, what more can I do for you? Do you want to be fed with my ideas out of a spoon?

God forbid! I exclaimed; not that. But I do want you to stand by your own words; or, if you shift your ground, shift it openly and stop trying to hoodwink us as you are doing now. You see, Thrasymachus, to go back to your earlier argument, in speaking of the shepherd you did not think it necessary to keep to that strict sense you laid down when you defined the genuine physician. You represent him, in his character of shepherd, as feeding up his flock, not for their own sake but for the table or the market, as if he were out to make money as a caterer or a cattle-dealer, rather than a shepherd. Surely the sole concern of the shepherd's art is to do the best for the charges put under its care; its own best interest is sufficiently provided for, so long as it does not fall short of all that shepherding should imply. On that principle it followed, I thought, that any kind of authority, in the state or in private life, must, in its character of authority, consider solely what is best for those under its care. Now what is your opinion? Do you think that the men who govern states — I mean rulers in the strict sense — have no reluctance to hold office?

I don't think so, he replied; I know it.

Well, but haven't you noticed, Thrasymachus, that in other positions of authority no one is willing to act unless he is paid wages, which he demands on the assumption that all the benefit of his action will go to his charges? Tell me: Don't we always distinguish one form of skill from another by its power to effect some particular result? Do say what you really think, so that we may get on.

Yes, that is the distinction.

And also each brings us some benefit that is peculiar to it: medicine gives health, for example; the art of navigation, safety at sea; and so on.

Yes.

And wage-earning brings us wages; that is its distinctive product. Now, speaking with that precision which you proposed, you would not say that the art of navigation is the same as the art of medicine, merely on the ground that a ship's captain regained his health on a voyage, because the sea air was good for him. No more would you identify the practice of medicine with wage-earning because a man may keep his health while earning wages, or a physician attending a case may receive a fee.

No.

And, since we agreed that the benefit obtained by each form of skill is peculiar to it, any common benefit enjoyed alike by all these practitioners must come from some further practice common to them all?

It would seem so.

Yes, we must say that if they all earn wages, they get that benefit in so far as they are engaged in wage-earning as well as in practicing their several arts.

He agreed reluctantly.

This benefit, then—the receipt of wages—does not come to a man from his special art. If we are to speak strictly, the physician, as such, produces health; the builder, a house; and then each, in his further capacity of wage-earner, gets his pay. Thus every art has its own function and benefits its proper subject. But suppose the practitioner is not paid; does he then get any benefit from his art?

Clearly not.

And is he doing no good to anyone either, when he works for nothing?

No, I suppose he does some good.

Well then, Thrasymachus, it is now clear that no form of skill or authority provides for its own benefit. As we were saying some time ago, it always studies and prescribes what is good for its subject—the interest of the weaker party, not of the stronger. And that, my friend, is why I said that no one is willing to be in a position of authority and undertake to set straight other men's troubles, without demanding to be paid; because, if he is to do his work well, he will never, in his capacity of ruler, do, or command others to do, what is best for himself, but only what is best for the subject. For that reason, if he is to consent, he must have his recompense, in the shape of money or honour, or of punishment in case of refusal.

What do you mean, Socrates? asked Glaucon. I recognize two of your three kinds of reward; but I don't understand what you mean by speaking of punishment as a recompense.

Then you don't understand the recompense required by the best type of men, or their motive for accepting authority when they do consent. You surely know that a passion for honours or for money is rightly regarded as something to be ashamed of.

Yes, I do.

For that reason, I said, good men are unwilling to rule, either for money's sake or for honour. They have no wish to be called mercenary for demanding to be paid, or thieves for making a secret profit out of their office, nor yet will honours tempt them, for they are not ambitious. So they must be forced to consent under threat of penalty; that may be why a readiness to accept power under no such constraint is thought discreditable. And the heaviest penalty for declining to rule is to be ruled by someone inferior to yourself. That is the fear, I believe, that makes decent people accept power; and when they do so, they face the prospect of authority with no idea that they are coming into the enjoyment of a comfortable berth; it is forced upon them because they can find no one better than themselves, or even as good, to be entrusted with power. If there could ever be a society of perfect men, there might well be as much competition to evade office as there is now to gain it; and it would then be clearly seen that the genuine ruler's nature is to seek only the advantage of the subject, with the consequence that any man of understanding would sooner have another to do the best for him than be at the pains to do the best for that other himself. On this point, then, I entirely disagree with Thrasymachus' doctrine that right means what is to the interest of the stronger.

CHAPTER IV (I. 347 E-354 C)

THRASYMACHUS: IS INJUSTICE MORE PROFITABLE THAN JUSTICE?

Socrates now turns from the art of government to Thrasymachus' whole view of life: that injustice, unlimited self-seeking, pursued with enough force of character and skill to ensure success, brings welfare and happiness.

This is what he ultimately means by the interest of the stronger.

Socrates and Thrasymachus have a common ground for argument in that both accept the notion of an art of living, comparable to the special crafts in which trained intelligence creates some product. The goodness, excellence, or virtue of a workman lies in his efficiency, the Greek areté, a word which, with the corresponding adjective agathos, 'good,' never lost its wide application to whatever does its work or fulfills its function well, as a good knife is one that cuts efficiently. The workman's efficiency involves trained intelligence or skill, an old sense of the word sophia, which also means wisdom. None of these words necessarily bears any moral sense; but they can be applied to the art of living. Here the product to be aimed at is assumed to be a man's own happiness and well-being. The efficiency which makes him good at attaining this end is called 'virtue'; the implied knowledge of the end and of the means to it is like the craftsman's skill and may be called 'wisdom.' But as it sounds in English almost a contradiction to say that to be unjust is to be virtuous or good and wise, the comparatively colourless phrase 'superior in character and intelligence' will be used instead.

Where Socrates and Thrasymachus differ is in their views of the nature of happiness or well-being. Thrasymachus thinks it consists in getting more than your fair share of what are commonly called the good things of life, pleasure, wealth, power. Thus virtue and wisdom mean to him efficiency and skill in achieving injustice.

However, I continued, we may return to that question later. Much more important is the position Thrasymachus is asserting now: that a life of injustice is to be preferred to a life of justice. Which side do you take,

Glaucon? Where do you think the truth lies?

I should say that the just life is the better worth having.

You heard Thrasymachus' catalogue of all the good things in store for injustice?

I did, but I am not convinced.

Shall we try to convert him, then, supposing we can find some way to prove him wrong?

By all means.

We might answer Thrasymachus' case in a set speech of our own, drawing up a corresponding list of the advantages of justice; he would then have the right to reply, and we should make our final rejoinder; but after that we should have to count up and measure the advantages on each list, and we should need a jury to decide between us. Whereas, if we go on as before, each securing the agreement of the other side, we can combine the functions of advocate and judge. We will take whichever course you prefer.

I prefer the second, said Glaucon.

Come then, Thrasymachus, said I, let us start afresh with our questions. You say that injustice pays better than justice, when both are carried to the furthest point?

I do, he replied; and I have told you why.

And how would you describe them? I suppose you would call one of them an excellence and the other a defect?

Of course.

Justice an excellence, and injustice a defect?

Now is that likely, when I am telling you that injustice pays, and justice does not?

Then what do you say?

The opposite.

That justice is a defect?

No; rather the mark of a good-natured simpleton.

Injustice, then, implies being ill-natured?

No; I should call it good policy.

Do you think the unjust are positively superior in character and intelligence, Thrasymachus?

Yes, if they are the sort that can carry injustice to perfection and make themselves masters of whole cities and nations. Perhaps you think I was talking of pickpockets. There is profit even in that trade, if you can escape detection; but it doesn't come to much as compared with the gains I was describing.

I understand you now on that point, I replied. What astonished me was that you should class injustice with superior character and intelligence and justice with the reverse.

Well, I do, he rejoined.

That is a much more stubborn position, my friend; and it is not so easy to see how to assail it. If you would admit that injustice, however well it pays, is nevertheless, as some people think, a defect and a discreditable thing, then we could argue on generally accepted principles. But now that you have gone so far as to rank it with superior character and intelligence, obviously you will say it is an admirable thing as well as a source of strength, and has all the other qualities we have attributed to justice.

You read my thoughts like a book, he replied.

However, I went on, it is no good shirking; I must go through with the argument, so long as I can be sure you are really speaking your mind. I do believe you are not playing with us now, Thrasymachus, but stating the truth as you conceive it.

Why not refute the doctrine? he said. What does it matter to you whether I believe it or not?

It does not matter, I replied.

[*Socrates attacks separately three points in Thrasymachus' position:* (1) *that the unjust is superior to the just*

*in character ('virtue') and intelligence;
(2) that injustice is a source of
strength; (3) that it brings happiness.*

*(1) The first argument (349 B-350
C) is omitted here, because only a very
loose paraphrase could liberate the
meaning from the stiff and archaic
form of the original. Thrasymachus
has upheld the superman who will try
to outdo everyone else and go to any
lengths in getting the better of his
neighbours. Socrates attacks this ideal
of unlimited self-assertion, relying
once more on the admitted analogy
between the art of living and other
arts. The musician, tuning an instrument, knows that there is for each
string a certain pitch which is absolutely right. He shows his excellence
and mastery of the art by aiming at
that 'limit' or 'measure' (as the Greeks
would call it), and he would be satisfied if he could attain it. In doing so
he would be outdoing or 'going one
better than' less skilful musicians or
the unmusical; but he would not be
showing superior skill if he tried to
outdo a musician who acknowledged
the same measure and had actually
attained it. Socrates holds that in
moral conduct also there is a measure
which is absolutely right, whether we
recognize it or not. The just man, who
does recognize it, shows a wisdom and
virtue corresponding to the skill of the
good musician. The unjust, who acknowledges no measure or limit, because there is no limit to getting more
and more for yourself at others' expense and that is his object, is, by all
analogy, exhibiting rather a lack of
intelligence and character. As a man,
and therefore a moral agent, he is no
more 'wise and good' than an instru-
mentalist who should refuse to recognize such a thing as the right pitch.
Jowett quotes: 'When workmen strive
to do better than well, They do confound their skill in covetousness' (K.
John iv. 2). Socrates concludes:*

*'It is evident, then, that it is the just
man that is wise and good (superior in
character and intelligence), the unjust
that is ignorant and bad.'*

*(2) In the following passage Socra-
tes has little difficulty in showing that
unlimited self-assertion is not a source
of strength in any association formed
for a common purpose. 'Honour
among thieves' is common sense,
which Thrasymachus cannot challenge. Socrates infers that injustice
will have the same effect within the
individual soul, dividing a man against
himself and destroying a unity of purpose. The various desires and impulses in his nature will be in conflict,
if each asserts an unlimited claim to
satisfaction. This view of justice as a
principle of internal order and unity
will become clearer when the soul
has been analysed into its principal
elements.]*

Thrasymachus' assent was dragged
out of him with a reluctance of which
my account gives no idea. He was
sweating at every pore, for the
weather was hot; and I saw then what
I had never seen before—Thrasymachus blushing. However, now that we
had agreed that justice implies superior character and intelligence, injustice
a deficiency in both respects, I went
on:

Good; let us take that as settled.
But we were also saying that injustice was a source of strength. Do you
remember, Thrasymachus?

I do remember; only your last argument does not satisfy me, and I could
say a good deal about that. But if I
did, you would tell me I was harangu-
ing you like a public meeting. So
either let me speak my mind at length,
or else, if you want to ask questions,
ask them, and I will nod or shake my
head, and say 'Hm?' as we do to encourage an old woman telling us a
story.

No, please, said I; don't give your assent against your real opinion.

Anything to please you, he rejoined, since you won't let me have my say. What more do you want?

Nothing, I replied. If that is what you mean to do, I will go on with my questions.

Go on, then.

Well, to continue where we left off. I will repeat my question: What is the nature and quality of justice as compared with injustice? It was suggested, I believe, that injustice is the stronger and more effective of the two; but now we have seen that justice implies superior character and intelligence, it will not be hard to show that it will also be superior in power to injustice, which implies ignorance and stupidity; that must be obvious to anyone. However, I would rather look deeper into this matter than take it as settled off-hand. Would you agree that a state may be unjust and may try to enslave other states or to hold a number of others in subjection unjustly?

Of course it may, he said; above all if it is the best sort of state, which carries injustice to perfection.

I understand, said I; that was your view. But I am wondering whether a state can do without justice when it is asserting its superior power over another in that way.

Not if you are right, that justice implies intelligence; but if I am right, injustice will be needed.

I am delighted with your answer, Thrasymachus; this is much better than just nodding and shaking your head.

It is all to oblige you.

Thank you. Please add to your kindness by telling me whether any set of men—a state or an army or a band of robbers or thieves—who were acting together for some unjust purpose would be likely to succeed, if they were always trying to injure one another. Wouldn't they do better, if they did not?

Yes, they would.

Because, of course, such injuries must set them quarrelling and hating each other. Only fair treatment can make men friendly and of one mind.

Be it so, he said; I don't want to differ from you.

Thank you once more, I replied. But don't you agree that, if injustice has this effect of implanting hatred wherever it exists, it must make any set of people, whether freemen or slaves, split into factions, at feud with one another and incapable of any joint action?

Yes.

And so with any two individuals: injustice will set them at variance and make them enemies to each other as well as to everyone who is just.

It will.

And will it not keep its character and have the same effect, if it exists in a single person?

Let us suppose so.

The effect being, apparently, wherever it occurs—in a state or a family or an army or anywhere else—to make united action impossible because of factions and quarrels, and moreover to set whatever it resides in at enmity with itself as well as with any opponent and with all who are just.

Yes, certainly.

Then I suppose it will produce the same natural results in an individual. He will have a divided mind and be incapable of action, for lack of singleness of purpose; and he will be at enmity with all who are just as well as with himself?

Yes.

And 'all who are just' surely includes the gods?

Let us suppose so.

The unjust man, then, will be a god-forsaken creature; the good-will of heaven will be for the just.

Enjoy your triumph, said Thrasymachus. You need not fear my contradicting you. I have no wish to give offence to the company.

[(3) *The final question is, whether justice (now admitted to be a virtue) or injustice brings happiness. The argument turns on the doctrine (adopted as fundamental in Aristotle's* ETHICS) *that man, like any other living species, has a peculiar work or function or activity, in the satisfactory exercise of which his well-being or happiness will consist; and also a peculiar excellence or virtue, namely a state of his soul from which that satisfactory activity will result. Aristotle argues* (ETH. NIC. i. 7) *that, a thing's function being the work or activity of which it alone is capable, man's function will be an activity involving the use of reason, which man alone possesses. Man's virtue is 'the state of character which makes him a good man and makes him do his work well'* (ibid. ii. 6). *It is the quality which enables him to 'live well,' for living is the soul's function; and to live well is to be happy.*

'Here again,' writes Nettleship on the following passage, 'the argument is intensely abstract. We should be inclined to break in on it and say that virtue means something very different in morality from what it means in the case of seeing or hearing, and that by happiness we mean a great many other things besides what seems to be meant here by living well. All depends, in this argument, on the strictness of the terms, upon assuming each of them to have a definite and distinct meaning. The virtues of a man and of a horse are very different, but what is the common element in them which makes us call them virtue? Can we call anything virtue which does not involve the doing well of the function, never mind what, of the agent that

possesses the virtue? Is there any other sense in which we can call a thing good or bad, except that it does or does not do well that which it was made to do? Again, happiness in its largest sense, welfare, well-being, or doing well, is a very complex thing, and one cannot readily describe in detail all that goes to make it up; but does it not necessarily imply that the human soul, man's vital activity as a whole, is in its best state, or is performing well the function it is made to perform? If by virtue and by happiness we mean what it seems we do mean, this consequence follows: when men are agreed that a certain sort of conduct constitutes virtue, if they mean anything at all, they must mean that in that conduct man finds happiness. And if a man says that what he calls virtue has nothing to do with what he calls happiness or well-being, then either in calling the one virtue he does not really mean what he says, or in calling the other happiness he does not really mean what he says This is substantially the position that Plato takes up in this section.' (LECTURES ON PLATO'S REPUBLIC, p. 42.)]

You will make my enjoyment complete, I replied, if you will answer my further questions in the same way. We have made out so far that just men are superior in character and intelligence and more effective in action. Indeed without justice men cannot act together at all; it is not strictly true to speak of such people as ever having effected any strong action in common. Had they been thoroughly unjust, they could not have kept their hands off one another; they must have had some justice in them, enough to keep them from injuring one another at the same time with their victims. This it was that enabled them to achieve what they did achieve: their injustice only partially incapacitated them for their career of wrongdoing; if perfect, it would have disabled them for any action whatsoever. I can see that all this is true, as against your original position. But there is a further question which we postponed: Is the life of justice the better and happier life? What we have said already leaves no doubt in my mind; but we ought to consider more carefully, for this is no light matter: it is the question, what is the right way to live?

Go on, then.

I will, said I. Some things have a function;[6] a horse, for instance, is useful for certain kinds of work. Would you agree to define a thing's function in general as the work for which that thing is the only instrument or the best one?

I don't understand.

Take an example. We can see only with the eyes, hear only with the ears; and seeing and hearing might be called the functions of those organs.

Yes.

Or again, you might cut vine-shoots with a carving-knife or a chisel or many other tools, but with none so well as with a pruning-knife made for the purpose; and we may call that its function.

True.

Now, I expect, you see better what I meant by suggesting that a thing's function is the work that it alone can do, or can do better than anything else.

Yes, I will accept that definition.

Good, said I; and to take the same examples, the eye and the ear, which we said have each its particular function: have they not also a specific excellence or virtue? Is not that always the case with things that have some appointed work to do?

Yes.

6 The word translated 'function' is the common word for 'work.' Hence the need for illustrations to confine it to the narrower sense of 'function,' here defined for the first time.

Now consider: is the eye likely to do its work well, if you take away its peculiar virtue and substitute the corresponding defect?

Of course not, if you mean substituting blindness for the power of sight.

I mean whatever its virtue may be; I have not come to that yet. I am only asking, whether it is true of things with a function — eyes or ears or anything else — that there is always some specific virtue which enables them to work well; and if they are deprived of that virtue, they work badly.

I think that is true.

Then the next point is this. Has the soul a function that can be performed by nothing else? Take for example such actions as deliberating or taking charge and exercising control: is not the soul the only thing of which you can say that these are its proper and peculiar work?

That is so.

And again, living — is not that above all the function of the soul?

No doubt.

And we also speak of the soul as having a certain specific excellence or virtue?

Yes.

Then, Thrasymachus, if the soul is robbed of its peculiar virtue, it cannot possibly do its work well. It must exercise its power of controlling and taking charge well or ill according as it is itself in a good or a bad state.

That follows.

And did we not agree that the virtue of the soul is justice, and injustice its defect?

We did.

So it follows that a just soul, or in other words a just man, will live well; the unjust will not.

Apparently, according to your argument.

But living well involves well-being and happiness.

Naturally.

Then only the just man is happy; injustice will involve unhappiness.

Be it so.

But you cannot say it pays better to be unhappy.

Of course not.

Injustice then, my dear Thrasymachus, can never pay better than justice.

Well, he replied, this is a feast-day, and you may take all this as your share of the entertainment.

For which I have to thank you, Thrasymachus; you have been so gentle with me since you recovered your temper. It is my own fault if the entertainment has not been satisfactory. I have been behaving like a greedy guest, snatching a taste of every new dish that comes round before he has properly enjoyed the last. We began by looking for a definition of justice; but before we had found one, I dropped that question and hurried on to ask whether or not it involved superior character and intelligence; and then, as soon as another idea cropped up, that injustice pays better, I could not refrain from pursuing that.

So now the whole conversation has left me completely in the dark; for so long as I do not know what justice is, I am hardly likely to know whether or not it is a virtue, or whether it makes a man happy or unhappy.

PART II (Books II-IV, 445 b)

Justice in the State and
in the Individual

chapter v (ii. 357 a-367 e)
the problem stated

The question, what Justice or Right ultimately mean, being still unanswered, the conversation so far amounts to a preliminary survey of the ground to be covered in the rest of the Republic. *Plato does not pretend that an immoralist like Thrasymachus could be silenced by summary arguments which seem formal and unconvincing until the whole view of life that lies behind them has been disclosed.*

The case which Socrates has to meet is reopened by Glaucon and Adeimantus, young men with a generous belief that justice has a valid meaning, but puzzled by the doctrine, current in intellectual circles, that it is a mere matter of social convention, imposed from without, and is practised as an unwelcome necessity. They demand a proof that justice is not merely useful as bringing external rewards, but intrinsically good as an inward state of the soul, even though the just man be persecuted rather than rewarded. In dealing with inquirers like these, who really wish to discover the truth, Socrates drops his role of ironical critic and becomes constructive.

Glaucon opens with one of the earliest statements of the Social Contract theory. The essence of this is that all the customary rules of religion and moral conduct imposed on the individual by social sanctions have their origin in human intelligence and will and always rest on tacit consent. They are neither laws of nature nor divine enactments, but conventions which man who made them can alter, as laws are changed or repealed by legislative bodies. It is assumed that, if all these artificial restraints were removed, the natural man would be left only with purely egoistic instincts and desires, which he would indulge in all that Thrasymachus commended as injustice.

Adeimantus supplements Glaucon's case by an attack on current moral education and some forms of mystery religion, as tacitly encouraging im-

morality by valuing justice only for the rewards it brings. Since these can be gained in this life by seeming just without being so, and after death by buying the favour of heaven, the young conclude that the ideal is injustice masked by a good reputation and atoned for by bribery. Both speakers accordingly demand that external rewards shall be ruled out of account and justice proved to be worth having for its own sake. The prospect of rewards and punishments after death is reserved for the myth at the end of the dialogue.

I thought that, with these words, I was quit of the discussion; but it seems this was only a prelude. Glaucon, undaunted as ever, was not content to let Thrasymachus abandon the field.

Socrates, he broke out, you have made a show of proving that justice is better than injustice in every way. Is that enough, or do you want us to be really convinced?

Certainly I do, if it rests with me.

Then you are not going the right way about it. I want to know how you classify the things we call good. Are there not some which we should wish to have, not for their consequences, but just for their own sake, such as harmless pleasures and enjoyments that have no further result beyond the satisfaction of the moment?

Yes, I think there are good things of that description.

And also some that we value both for their own sake and for their consequences — things like knowledge and health and the use of our eyes?

Yes.

And a third class which would include physical training, medical treatment, earning one's bread as a doctor or otherwise — useful, but burdensome things, which we want only for the sake of the profit or other benefit they bring.

Yes, there is that third class. What then?

In which class do you place justice?

I should say, in the highest, as a thing which anyone who is to gain happiness must value both for itself and for its results.

Well, that is not the common opinion. Most people would say it was one of those things, tiresome and disagreeable in themselves, which we cannot avoid practising for the sake of reward or a good reputation.

I know, said I; that is why Thrasymachus has been finding fault with it all this time and praising injustice. But I seem to be slow in seeing his point.

Listen to me, then, and see if you agree with mine. There was no need, I think, for Thrasymachus to yield so readily, like a snake you had charmed into submission; and nothing so far said about justice and injustice has been established to my satisfaction. I want to be told what each of them really is, and what effect each has, in itself, on the soul that harbours it, when all rewards and consequences are left out of account. So here is my plan, if you approve. I shall revive Thrasymachus' theory. First, I will state what is commonly held about the nature of justice and its origin; secondly, I shall maintain that it is always practised with reluctance, not as good in itself, but as a thing one cannot do without; and thirdly, that this reluctance is reasonable, because the life of injustice is much the better life of the two — so people say. That is not what I think myself, Socrates; only I am bewildered by all that Thrasymachus and ever so many others have dinned into my ears; and I have never yet heard the case for justice stated as I wish to hear it. You, I believe, if anyone, can tell me what is to be said in praise of justice in and for itself; that is what I want. Accordingly, I shall set you an example by glorifying the life of injustice with all the energy that I hope you will show later in denouncing it and exalting justice in its stead. Will that plan suit you?

Nothing could be better, I replied. Of all subjects this is one on which a sensible man must always be glad to exchange ideas.

Good, said Glaucon. Listen then, and I will begin with my first point: the nature and origin of justice.

What people say is that to do wrong is, in itself, a desirable thing; on the other hand, it is not at all desirable to suffer wrong, and the harm to the sufferer outweighs the advantage to the doer. Consequently, when men have had a taste of both, those who have not the power to seize the advantage and escape the harm decide that they would be better off if they made a compact neither to do wrong nor to suffer it. Hence they began to make laws and covenants with one another; and whatever the law prescribed they called lawful and right. That is what right or justice is and how it came into existence; it stands half-way between the best thing of all — to do wrong with impunity — and the worst, which is to suffer wrong without the power to retaliate. So justice is accepted as a compromise, and valued, not as good in itself, but for lack of power to do wrong; no man worthy of the name, who had that power, would ever enter into such a compact with anyone; he would be mad if he did. That, Socrates, is the nature of justice according to this account, and such the circumstances in which it arose.

The next point is that men practise it against the grain, for lack of power to do wrong. How true that is, we shall best see if we imagine two men, one just, the other unjust, given full licence to do whatever they like, and then follow them to observe where each will be led by his desires. We shall catch the just man taking the same road as the unjust; he will be moved by self-interest, the end which it is natural to every creature to pursue as good, until forcibly turned aside by law and custom to respect the principle of equality.

Now, the easiest way to give them the complete liberty of action would be to imagine them possessed of the talisman found by Gyges, the ancestor of the famous Lydian. The story tells how he was a shepherd in the King's service. One day there was a great storm, and the ground where his flock was feeding was rent by an earthquake. Astonished at the sight, he went down into the chasm and saw, among other wonders of which the story tells, a brazen horse, hollow, with windows in its sides. Peering in, he saw a dead body, which seemed to be of more than human size. It was naked save for a gold ring, which he took from the finger and made his way out. When the shepherds met, as they did every month, to send an account to the King of the state of his flocks, Gyges came wearing the ring. As he was sitting with the others, he happened to turn the bezel of the ring inside his hand. At once he became invisible, and his companions, to his surprise, began to speak of him as if he had left them. Then, as he was fingering the ring, he turned the bezel outwards and became visible again. With that, he set about testing the ring to see if it really had this power, and always with the same result: according as he turned the bezel inside or out he vanished and reappeared. After this discovery he contrived to be one of the messengers sent to the court. There he seduced the Queen, and with her help murdered the King and seized the throne.

Now suppose there were two such magic rings, and one were given to the just man, the other to the unjust. No one, it is commonly believed, would have such iron strength of mind as to stand fast in doing right or keep his hands off other men's goods, when he could go the the marketplace and fearlessly help himself to anything he wanted, enter houses and sleep with any woman he chose, set prisoners free and kill men at his pleasure, and in a word go about among men with the powers of a god. He would behave no better than the other; both would take the same course. Surely this would be strong proof that men do right only under compulsion; no individual thinks of it as good for him personally, since he does wrong whenever he finds he has the power. Every man believes that wrongdoing pays him personally much better, and, according to this theory, that is the truth. Granted full licence to do as he liked, people would think him a miserable fool if they found him refusing to wrong his neighbours or to touch their belongings, though in public they would keep up a pretence of praising his conduct, for fear of being wronged themselves. So much for that.

Finally, if we are really to judge between the two lives, the only way is to contrast the extremes of justice and injustice. We can best do that by imagining our two men to be perfect types, and crediting both to the full with the qualities they need for their respective ways of life. To begin with the unjust man: he must be like any consummate master of a craft, a physician or a captain, who, knowing just what his art can do, never tries to do more, and can always retrieve a false step. The unjust man, if he is to reach perfection, must be equally discreet in his criminal attempts, and he must not be found out, or we shall think him a bungler; for the highest pitch of injustice is to seem just when you are not. So we must endow our

man with the full complement of injustice; we must allow him to have secured a spotless reputation for virtue while committing the blackest crimes; he must be able to retrieve any mistake, to defend himself with convincing eloquence if his misdeeds are denounced, and, when force is required, to bear down all opposition by his courage and strength and by his command of friends and money.

Now set beside this paragon the just man in his simplicity and nobleness, one who, in Aeschylus' words, 'would be, not seem, the best.' There must, indeed, be no such seeming; for if his character were apparent, his reputation would bring him honours and rewards, and then we should not know whether it was for their sake that he was just or for justice's sake alone. He must be stripped of everything but justice, and denied every advantage the other enjoyed. Doing no wrong, he must have the worst reputation for wrong-doing, to test whether his virtue is proof against all that comes of having a bad name; and under this lifelong imputation of wickedness, let him hold on his course of justice unwavering to the point of death. And so, when the two men have carried their justice and injustice to the last extreme, we may judge which is the happier.

My dear Glaucon, I exclaimed, how vigorously you scour these two characters clean for inspection, as if you were burnishing a couple of statues! [7]

I am doing my best, he answered. Well, given two such characters, it is not hard, I fancy, to describe the sort of life that each of them may expect;

[7] At Elis and Athens officials called *phaidryntai*, 'burnishers,' had the duty of cleaning cult statues (A. B. Cook, *Zeus*, iii. 967). At 612 c, where this passage is recalled, it is admitted to be an extravagant supposition, that the just and unjust should exchange reputations.

and if the description sounds rather coarse, take it as coming from those who cry up the merits of injustice rather than from me. They will tell you that our just man will be thrown into prison, scourged and racked, will have his eyes burnt out, and, after every kind of torment, be impaled. That will teach him how much better it is to seem virtuous than to be so. In fact those lines of Aeschylus I quoted are more fitly applied to the unjust man, who, they say, is a realist and does not live for appearances: 'he would be, not seem' unjust,

> reaping the harvest sown
> In those deep furrows of the thoughtful heart
> Whence wisdom springs.

With his reputation for virtue, he will hold offices of state, ally himself by marriage to any family he may choose, become a partner in any business, and, having no scruples about being dishonest, turn all these advantages to profit. If he is involved in a lawsuit, public or private, he will get the better of his opponents, grow rich on the proceeds, and be able to help his friends and harm his enemies.[8] Finally, he can make sacrifices to the gods and dedicate offerings with due magnificence, and, being in a much better position than the just man to serve the gods as well as his chosen friends, he may reasonably hope to stand higher in the favour of heaven. So much better, they say, Socrates, is the life prepared for the unjust by gods and men.

Here Glaucon ended, and I was meditating a reply, when his brother Adeimantus exclaimed:

Surely, Socrates, you cannot suppose that that is all there is to be said.

Why, isn't it? said I.

[8] To help friends and harm enemies, offered as a definition of Justice by Polemarchus, now appears as the privilege of the unjust.

The most essential part of the case has not been mentioned, he replied.

Well, I answered, there is a proverb about a brother's aid. If Glaucon has failed, it is for you to make good his shortcomings; though, so far as I am concerned, he has said quite enough to put me out of the running and leave me powerless to rescue the cause of justice.

Nonsense, said Adeimantus; there is more to be said, and you must listen to me. If we want a clear view of what I take to be Glaucon's meaning, we must study the opposite side of the case, the arguments used when justice is praised and injustice condemned. When children are told by their fathers and all their pastors and masters that it is a good thing to be just, what is commended is not justice in itself but the respectability it brings. They are to let men see how just they are, in order to gain high positions and marry well and win all the other advantages which Glaucon mentioned, since the just man owes all these to his good reputation.

In this matter of having a good name, they go farther still: they throw in the favourable opinion of heaven, and can tell us of no end of good things with which they say the gods reward piety. There is the good old Hesiod,[9] who says the gods make the just man's oak-trees 'bear acorns at the top and bees in the middle; and their sheep's fleeces are heavy with wool,' and a great many other blessings of that sort. And Homer[10] speaks in the same strain:

As when a blameless king fears the gods and upholds right judgment; then the dark earth yields wheat and barley, and the trees are laden with fruit; the young of his flocks are strong, and the sea gives abundance of fish.

[9] *Works and Days*, 232.
[10] *Odyssey*, xix. 109.

Musaeus and his son Eumolpus [11] enlarge in still more spirited terms upon the rewards from heaven they promise to the righteous. They take them to the other world and provide them with a banquet of the Blest, where they sit for all time carousing with garlands on their heads, as if virtue could not be more nobly recompensed than by an eternity of intoxication. Others, again, carry the rewards of heaven yet a stage farther: the pious man who keeps his oaths is to have children's children and to leave a posterity after him. When they have sung the praises of justice in that strain, with more to same effect, they proceed to plunge the sinners and unrighteous men into a pool of mud in the world below, and set them to fetch water in a sieve. Even in this life, too, they give them a bad name, and make out that the unjust suffer all those penalties which Glaucon described as falling upon the good man who has a bad reputation: they can think of no others. That is how justice is recommended and injustice denounced.

Besides all this, think of the way in which justice and injustice are spoken of, not only in ordinary life, but by the poets. All with one voice reiterate that self-control and justice, admirable as they may be, are difficult and irksome, whereas vice and injustice are pleasant and very easily to be had; it is mere convention to regard them as discreditable. They tell us that dishonesty generally pays better than honesty. They will cheerfully speak of a bad man as happy and load him with honours and social esteem, provided he be rich and otherwise powerful; while they despise and disregard one who has neither power nor wealth, though all the while they acknowledge that he is the better man of the two.

Most surprising of all is what they say about the gods and virtue: that heaven itself often allots misfortunes and a hard life to the good man, and gives prosperity to the wicked. Mendicant priests and soothsayers come to the rich man's door with a story of a power they possess by the gift of heaven to atone for any offence that he or his ancestors have committed with incantations and sacrifice, agreeably accompanied by feasting. If he wishes to injure an enemy, he can, at a trifling expense, do him a hurt with equal ease, whether he be an honest man or not, by means of certain invocations and spells which, as they profess, prevail upon the gods to do their bidding. In support of all these claims they call the poets to witness. Some, by way of advertising the easiness of vice, quote the words: 'Unto wickedness men attain easily and in multitudes; smooth is the way and her dwelling is very near at hand. But the gods have ordained much sweat upon the path to virtue' [12] and a long road that is rough and steep.

Others, to show that men can turn the gods from their purpose, cite Homer: 'Even the gods themselves listen to entreaty. Their hearts are turned by the entreaties of men with sacrifice and humble prayers and libation and burnt offering, whensoever anyone transgresses and does amiss.' [13] They produce a whole farrago of books in which Musaeus and Orpheus, described as descendants of the Muses and the Moon, prescribe their ritual; and they persuade entire communities, as well as individuals, that, both in this life and after death, wrongdoing may be absolved and purged away by means of sacrifices

[11] Legendary figures, to whom were attributed poems setting forth the doctrines of the mystery religion known as Orphism.

[12] Hesiod, *Works and Days*, 287.

[13] *Iliad* ix. 497.

and agreeable performances which they are pleased to call rites of initiation. These deliver us from punishment in the other world, where awful things are in store for all who neglect to sacrifice.

Now, my dear Socrates, when all this stuff is talked about the estimation in which virtue and vice are held by heaven and by mankind, what effect can we suppose it has upon the mind of a young man quick-witted enough to gather honey from all these flowers of popular wisdom and to draw his own conclusions as to the sort of person he should be and the way he should go in order to lead the best possible life? In all likelihood he would ask himself, in Pindar's words: 'Will the way of right or the by-paths of deceit lead me to the higher fortress,' where I may entrench myself for the rest of my life? For, according to what they tell me, I have nothing to gain but trouble and manifest loss from being honest, unless I also get a name for being so; whereas, if I am dishonest and provide myself with a reputation for honesty, they promise me a marvellous career. Very well, then; since 'outward seeming,' as wise men inform me, 'overpowers the truth' and decides the question of happiness, I had better go in for appearances wholeheartedly. I must ensconce myself behind an imposing façade designed to look like virtue, and trail the fox behind me, 'the cunning shifty fox' [14] — Archilochus knew the world as well as any man. You may say it is not so easy to be wicked without ever being found out. Perhaps not; but great things are never easy. Anyhow, if we are to reach happiness, everything we have been told points to this as the road to be followed. We will form secret societies to save us from exposure; besides, there are men who

[14] An allusion to a fable by Archilochus.

teach the art of winning over popular assemblies and courts of law; so that, one way or another, by persuasion or violence, we shall get the better of our neighbours without being punished. You might object that the gods are not to be deceived and are beyond the reach of violence. But suppose that there are no gods, or that they do not concern themselves with the doings of men; why should we concern ourselves to deceive them? Or, if the gods do exist and care for mankind, all we know or have ever heard about them comes from current tradition and from the poets who recount their family history, and these same authorities also assure us that they can be won over and turned from their purpose 'by sacrifice and humble prayers' and votive offerings. We must either accept both these statements or neither. If we are to accept both, we had better do wrong and use part of the proceeds to offer sacrifice. By being just we may escape the punishment of heaven, but we shall be renouncing the profits of injustice; whereas by doing wrong we shall make our profit and escape punishment into the bargain, by means of those entreaties which win over the gods when we transgress and do amiss. But then, you will say, in the other world the penalty for our misdeeds on earth will fall either upon us or upon our children's children. We can counter that objection by reckoning on the great efficacy of mystic rites and the divinities of absolution, vouched for by the most advanced societies and by the descendants of the gods who have appeared as poets and spokesmen of heavenly inspiration.

What reason, then, remains for preferring justice to the extreme of injustice, when common belief and the best authorities promise us the fulfillment of our desires in this life and the next if only we conceal our ill-doing under a veneer of decent behaviour? The upshot is, Socrates, that no man possessed of superior powers of mind or person or rank or wealth will set any value on justice; he is more likely to laugh when he hears it praised. So, even one who could prove my case false and were quite sure that justice is best, far from being indignant with the unjust, will be very ready to excuse them. He will know that, here and there, a man may refrain from wrong because it revolts some instinct he is graced with or because he has come to know the truth; no one else is virtuous of his own will; it is only lack of spirit or the infirmity of age or some other weakness that makes men condemn the iniquities they have not the strength to practise. This is easily seen: give such a man the power, and he will be the first to use it to the utmost.

What lies at the bottom of all this is nothing but the fact from which Glaucon, as well as I, started upon this long discourse. We put it to you, Socrates, with all respect, in this way. All you who profess to sing the praises of right conduct, from the ancient heroes whose legends have survived down to the men of the present day, have never denounced injustice or praised justice apart from the reputation, honours, and rewards they bring; but what effect either of them in itself has upon its possessor when it dwells in his soul unseen of gods or men, no poet or ordinary man has ever yet explained. No one has proved that a soul can harbour no worse evil than injustice, no greater good than justice. Had all of you said that from the first and tried to convince us from our youth up, we should not be keeping watch upon our neighbours to prevent them from doing wrong to us, but everyone would keep a far more effectual watch over himself, for fear lest by wronging others he should open his doors to the worst of all evils.

That, Socrates, is the view of justice and injustice which Thrasymachus and, no doubt, others would state, perhaps in even stronger words. For myself, I believe it to be a gross perversion of their true worth and effect; but, as I must frankly confess, I have put the case with all the force I could muster because I want to hear the other side from you. You must not be content with proving that justice is superior to injustice; you must make clear what good or what harm each of them does to its possessor, taking it simply in itself and, as Glaucon required, leaving out of account the reputation it bears. For unless you deprive each of its true reputation and attach to it the false one, we shall say that you are praising or denouncing nothing more than the appearances in either case, and recommending us to do wrong without being found out; and that you hold with Thrasymachus that right means what is good for someone else, being the interest of the stronger, and wrong is what really pays, serving one's own interest at the expense of the weaker. You have agreed that justice belongs to that highest class of good things which are worth having not only for their consequences, but much more for their own sakes — things like sight and hearing, knowledge, and health, whose value is genuine and intrinsic, not dependent on opinion. So I want you, in commending justice, to consider only how justice, in itself, benefits a man who has it in him, and how injustice harms him, leaving rewards and reputation out of account. I might put up with others dwelling on those outward effects as a reason for praising the one and condemning the other; but from you, who have spent your life in the study of this question, I must beg leave to demand something better.

You must not be content merely to prove that justice is superior to injustice, but explain how one is good, the other evil, in virtue of the intrinsic effect each has on its possessor, whether gods or men see it or not.

CHAPTER VI (II. 367 E-372 A)

THE RUDIMENTS OF
SOCIAL ORGANIZATION

Socrates has been challenged to define justice and its effects in the individual soul. Since the life of a political society manifests the life of the men composing it on a larger scale, he proposes to look first for the principle which makes a state just and then to see if the same principle has similar effects in a man. So he starts to build up a social structure from its necessary rudiments.

Plato is not here describing the historical development of any actual state. (In Laws iii he says that civilization has often been destroyed by natural cataclysms, and he traces its growth from a simple pastoral phase on lines quite unlike those followed here.) He takes the type of state in which he lived, the Greek city-state. The construction is based on an analysis of such a society into parts corresponding to fundamental needs of human nature. These parts are put together successively in a logical, not an historical, order.

As against the social contract theory, Plato denies that society is 'unnatural,' either as being the artificial outcome of an arbitrary compact or as thwarting the individual's natural instincts, which Thrasymachus assumed to be purely egoistic impulses to unlimited self-assertion. Men are not born self-sufficient or all alike; hence an organized society in which they are interdependent and specialize according to innate aptitudes is, according to Plato, both natural and advantageous to all the individuals.

.   .   .

I was delighted with these speeches from Glaucon and Adeimantus, whose gifts I had always admired. How right, I exclaimed, was Glaucon's lover to begin that poem of his on your exploits at the battle of Megara by describing you two as the

sons divine
Of Ariston's noble line!

Like father, like sons: there must indeed be some divine quality in your nature, if you can plead the cause of injustice so eloquently and still not be convinced yourselves that it is better than justice. That you are not really convinced I am sure from all I know of your dispositions, though your words might well have left me in doubt. But the more I trust you, the harder I find it to reply. How can I come to the rescue? I have no faith in my own powers, when I remember that you were not satisfied with the proof I thought I had given to Thrasymachus that it is better to be just. And yet I cannot stand by and hear justice reviled without lifting a finger. I am afraid to commit a sin by holding aloof while I have breath and strength to say a word in its defence. So there is nothing for it but to do the best I can.

Glaucon and the others begged me to step into the breach and carry through our inquiry into the real nature of justice and injustice, and the truth about their respective advantages. So I told them what I thought. This is a very obscure question, I said, and we shall need keen sight to see our way. Now, as we are not remarkably clever, I will make a suggestion as to how we should proceed. Imagine a rather short-sighted person told to read an inscription in small letters from some way off. He would think it a godsend if someone pointed out that the same inscription was written up elsewhere on a bigger scale, so that he could first read the larger characters and then make out whether the smaller ones were the same.

No doubt, said Adeimantus; but what analogy do you see in that to our inquiry?

I will tell you. We think of justice as a quality that may exist in a whole community as well as in an individual, and the community is the bigger of the two. Possibly, then, we may find justice there in larger proportions, easier to make out. So I suggest that we should begin by inquiring what justice means in a state. Then we can go on to look for its counterpart on a smaller scale in the individual.

That seems a good plan, he agreed.

Well then, I continued, suppose we imagine a state coming into being before our eyes. We might then be able to watch the growth of justice or of injustice within it. When that is done, we may hope it will be easier to find what we are looking for.

.   .   .

CHAPTER XIII (IV. 434 D-441 C)

THE THREE PARTS OF THE SOUL

It has been shown that justice in the state means that the three chief social functions — deliberative and governing, executive, and productive — are kept distinct and rightly performed. Since the qualities of a community are those of the component individuals, we may expect to find three corresponding elements in the individual soul. All three will be present in every soul; but the structure of society is based on the fact that they are de-veloped to different degrees in different types of character.

The existence of three elements or 'parts' of the soul is established by an analysis of the conflict of motives. A simple case is the thirsty man's appetite for drink, held in check by the rational reflection that to drink will be bad for him. That two distinct elements must be at work here follows from the general principle that the same thing cannot act or be affected in two opposite ways at the same time. By 'thirst' is meant simply the bare craving for drink; it must not be confused with a desire for some good (e.g., health or pleasure) expected as a consequence of drinking. This simple craving says, 'Drink'; Reason says, 'Do not drink': the contradiction shows that two elements are at work.

A third factor is the 'spirited' element, akin to our 'sense of honour,' manifested in indignation, which takes the side of reason against appetite, but cannot be identified with reason, since it is found in children and animals and it may be rebuked by reason.

This analysis is not intended as a complete outline of psychology; that could be reached only by following 'a longer road.' It is concerned with the factors involved in moral behaviour. Later (Chap. XXXIII) they will be represented as three forms of desire, each with its characteristic object: wisdom; honour; gain as a means to the satisfaction of bodily appetites. In Plato's myth of creation (the TIMAEUS) the three parts are lodged in the head, the chest, and the belly and organs of generation; and the reason alone is immortal and separable from the body. But in Chapter XXXVIII, it will be indicated that this mythical picture must not be taken literally as implying that the soul is like a material thing, which can be destroyed by being broken up into parts out of which it has been put together.

We must not be too positive yet, said I. If we find that this same quality when it exists in the individual can equally be identified with justice, then we can at once give our assent; there will be no more to be said; otherwise, we shall have to look further. For the moment, we had better finish the inquiry which we began with the idea that it would be easier to make out the nature of justice in the individual if we first tried to study it in something on a larger scale. That larger thing we took to be a state, and so we set about constructing the best one we could, being sure of finding justice in a state that was good. The discovery we made there must now be applied to the individual. If it is confirmed, all will be well; but if we find that justice in the individual is something different, we must go back to the state and test our new result. Perhaps if we brought the two cases into contact like flint and steel, we might strike out between them the spark of justice, and in its light confirm the conception in our own minds.

A good method. Let us follow it.

Now, I continued, if two things, one large, the other small, are called by the same name, they will be alike in that respect to which the common name applies. Accordingly, in so far as the quality of justice is concerned, there will be no difference between a just man and a just society.

No.

Well, we decided that a society was just when each of the three types of human character it contained performed its own function; and again, it was temperate and brave and wise by virtue of certain other affections and states of mind of those same types.

True.

Accordingly, my friend, if we are to be justified in attributing those same virtues to the individual, we shall expect to find that the individual soul contains the same three elements and that they are affected in the same way as are the corresponding types in society.

That follows.

Here, then, we have stumbled upon another little problem: Does the soul contain these three elements or not? Not such a very little one, I think. It may be a true saying, Socrates, that what is worth while is seldom easy.

Apparently; and let me tell you, Glaucon, it is my belief that we shall never reach the exact truth in this matter by following our present methods of discussion; the road leading to that goal is longer and more laborious.[15] However, perhaps we can find an answer that will be up to the standard we have so far maintained in our speculations.

Is not that enough? I should be satisfied for the moment.

Well, it will more than satisfy me, I replied.

Don't be disheartened, then, but go on.

Surely, I began, we must admit that the same elements and characters that appear in the state must exist in every one of us; where else could they have come from? It would be absurd to imagine that among peoples with a reputation for a high-spirited character, like the Thracians and Scythians and northerners generally, the states have not derived that character from their individual members; or that it is otherwise with the love of knowledge, which would be ascribed chiefly to our own part of the world, or with the love of money, which one would specially connect with Phoenicia and Egypt.

Certainly.

So far, then, we have a fact which is easily recognized. But here the difficulty begins. Are we using the same

[15] Socrates refers to this 'longer road' later, at 504 B.

part of ourselves in all these three experiences, or a different part in each? Do we gain knowledge with one part, feel anger with another, and with yet a third desire the pleasures of food, sex, and so on? Or is the whole soul at work in every impulse and in all these forms of behaviour? The difficulty is to answer that question satisfactorily.

I quite agree.

Let us approach the problem whether these elements are distinct or identical in this way. It is clear that the same thing cannot act in two opposite ways or be in two opposite states at the same time, with respect to the same part of itself, and in relation to the same object. So if we find such contradictory actions or states among the elements concerned, we shall know that more than one must have been involved.

Very well.

Consider this proposition of mine, then. Can the same thing, at the same time and with respect to the same part of itself, be at rest and in motion?

Certainly not.

We had better state this principle in still more precise terms, to guard against misunderstanding later on. Suppose a man is standing still, but moving his head and arms. We should not allow anyone to say that the same man was both at rest and in motion at the same time, but only that part of him was at rest, part in motion. Isn't that so?

Yes.

An ingenious objector might refine still further and argue that a peg-top, spinning with its peg fixed at the same spot, or indeed any body that revolves in the same place, is both at rest and in motion as a whole. But we should not agree, because the parts in respect of which such a body is moving and at rest are not the same. It contains an axis and a circumference; and in respect of the axis it is at rest inasmuch as the axis is not inclined in any direction, while in respect of the circumference it revolves; and if, while it is spinning, the axis does lean out of the perpendicular in all directions, then it is in no way at rest.

That is true.

No objection of that sort, then, will disconcert us or make us believe that the same thing can ever act or be acted upon in two opposite ways, or be two opposite things, at the same time, in respect of the same part of itself, and in relation to the same object.

I can answer for myself at any rate.

Well, anyhow, as we do not want to spend time in reviewing all such objections to make sure that they are unsound, let us proceed on this assumption, with the understanding that, if we ever come to think otherwise, all the consequences based upon it will fall to the ground.

Yes, that is a good plan.

Now, would you class such things as assent and dissent, striving after something and refusing it, attraction and repulsion, as pairs of opposite actions or states of mind—no matter which?

Yes, they are opposites.

And would you not class all appetites such as hunger and thirst, and again willing and wishing, with the affirmative members of those pairs I have just mentioned? For instance, you would say that the soul of a man who desires something is striving after it, or trying to draw to itself the thing it wishes to possess, or again, in so far as it is willing to have its want satisfied, it is giving its assent to its own longing, as if to an inward question.

Yes.

And, on the other hand, disinclination, unwillingness, and dislike, we should class on the negative side with acts of rejection or repulsion.

Of course.

That being so, shall we say that appetites form one class, the most conspicuous being those we call thirst and hunger?

Yes.

Thirst being desire for drink, hunger for food?

Yes.

Now, is thirst, just in so far as it is thirst, a desire in the soul for anything more than simply drink? Is it, for instance, thirst for hot drink or for cold, for much drink or for little, or in a word for drink of any particular kind? Is it not rather true that you will have a desire for cold drink only if you are feeling hot as well as thirsty, and for hot drink only if you are feeling cold; and if you want much drink or little, that will be because your thirst is a great thirst or a little one? But, just in itself, thirst or hunger is a desire for nothing more than its natural object, drink or food, pure and simple.

Yes, he agreed, each desire, just in itself, is simply for its own natural object. When the object is of such and such a particular kind, the desire will be correspondingly qualified.[16]

We must be careful here, or we might be troubled by the objection that no one desires mere food and drink, but always wholesome food and drink. We shall be told that what we desire is always something that is good; so if thirst is a desire, its object

must be, like that of any other desire, something—drink or whatever it may be—that will be good for one.[17]

Yes, there might seem to be something in that objection.

But surely, wherever you have two correlative terms, if one is qualified, the other must always be qualified too; whereas if one is unqualified, so is the other.

I don't understand.

Well, 'greater' is a relative term; and the greater is greater than the less; if it is much greater, then the less is much less; if it is greater at some moment, past or future, then the less is less at that same moment. The same principle applies to all such correlatives, like 'more' and 'fewer,' 'double' and 'half'; and again to terms like 'heavier' and 'lighter,' 'quicker' and 'slower,' and to things like hot and cold.

Yes.

Or take the various branches of knowledge: is it not the same there? The object of knowledge pure and simple is the knowable—if that is the right word—without any qualification; whereas a particular kind of knowledge has an object of a particular kind. For example, as soon as men learnt how to build houses, their craft was distinguished from others under the name of architecture, because it had a unique character, which was itself due to the character of its object; and all other branches of craft and knowledge were distinguished in the same way.

True.

This, then, if you understand me now, is what I meant by saying that,

16 The object of the following subtle argument about relative terms is to distinguish thirst as a mere blind craving for drink from a more complex desire whose object includes the pleasure or health expected to result from drinking. We thus forestall the objection that all desires have 'the good' (apparent or real) for their object and include an intellectual or rational element, so that the conflict of motives might be reduced to an intellectual debate, in the same 'part' of the soul, on the comparative values of two incompatible ends.

17 If this objection were admitted, it would follow that the desire would always be correspondingly qualified. It is necessary to insist that we do experience blind cravings which can be isolated from any judgment about the goodness of their object.

where there are two correlatives, the one is qualified if, and only if, the other is so. I am not saying that the one must have the same quality as the other—that the science of health and disease is itself healthy and diseased, or the knowledge of good and evil is itself good and evil—but only that, as soon as you have a knowledge that is restricted to a particular kind of object, namely health and disease, the knowledge itself becomes a particular kind of knowledge. Hence we no longer call it merely knowledge, which would have for its object whatever can be known, but we add the qualification and call it medical science.

I understand now and I agree.

Now, to go back to thirst: is not that one of these relative terms? It is essentially thirst for something.

Yes, for drink.

And if the drink desired is of a certain kind, the thirst will be correspondingly qualified. But thirst which is just simply thirst is not for drink of any particular sort—much or little, good or bad—but for drink pure and simple.

Quite so.

We conclude, then, that the soul of a thirsty man, just in so far as he is thirsty, has no other wish than to drink. That is the object of its craving, and towards that it is impelled.

That is clear.

Now if there is ever something which at the same time pulls it the opposite way, that something must be an element in the soul other than the one which is thirsting and driving it like a beast to drink; in accordance with our principle that the same thing cannot behave in two opposite ways at the same time and towards the same object with the same part of itself. It is like an archer drawing the bow: it is not accurate to say that his hands are at the same time both pushing and

pulling it. One hand does the pushing, the other the pulling.

Exactly.

Now, is it sometimes true that people are thirsty and yet unwilling to drink?

Yes, often.

What, then, can one say of them, if not that their soul contains something which urges them to drink and something which holds them back, and that this latter is a distinct thing and overpowers the other?

I agree.

And is it not true that the intervention of this inhibiting principle in such cases always has its origin in reflection; whereas the impulses driving and dragging the soul are engendered by external influences and abnormal conditions? [18]

Evidently.

We shall have good reason, then, to assert that they are two distinct principles. We may call that part of the soul whereby it reflects, rational; and the other, with which it feels hunger and thirst and is distracted by sexual passion and all the other desires, we will call irrational appetite, associated with pleasure in the replenishment of certain wants.

Yes, there is good ground for that view.

Let us take it, then, that we have now distinguished two elements in the soul. What of that passionate element which makes us feel angry and indignant? Is that a third, or identical in nature with one of those two?

It might perhaps be identified with appetite.

I am more inclined to put my faith in a story I once heard about Leon-

---

[18] Some of the most intense bodily desires are due to morbid conditions, e.g. thirst in fever, and even milder desires are caused by a departure from the normal state, which demands 'replenishment' (*Philebus*, 45–46).

tius, son of Aglaion. On his way up from the Piraeus outside the north wall, he noticed the bodies of some criminals lying on the ground, with the executioner standing by them. He wanted to go and look at them, but at the same time he was disgusted and tried to turn away. He struggled for some time and covered his eyes, but at last the desire was too much for him. Opening his eyes wide, he ran up to the bodies and cried, 'There you are, curse you; feast yourselves on this lovely sight!'

Yes, I have heard that story too.

The point of it surely is that anger is sometimes in conflict with appetite, as if they were two distinct principles. Do we not often find a man whose desires would force him to go against his reason, reviling himself and indignant with this part of his nature which is trying to put constraint on him? It is like a struggle between two factions, in which indignation takes the side of reason. But I believe you have never observed, in yourself or anyone else, indignation make common cause with appetite in behaviour which reason decides to be wrong.

No, I am sure I have not.

Again, take a man who feels he is in the wrong. The more generous his nature, the less can he be indignant at any suffering, such as hunger and cold, inflicted by the man he has injured. He recognizes such treatment as just, and, as I say, his spirit refuses to be roused against it.

That is true.

But now contrast one who thinks it is he that is being wronged. His spirit boils with resentment and sides with the right as he conceives it. Persevering all the more for the hunger and cold and other pains he suffers, it triumphs and will not give in until its gallant struggle has ended in success or death; or until the restraining voice of reason, like a shepherd calling off his dog, makes it relent.

An apt comparison, he said; and in fact it fits the relation of our Auxiliaries to the Rulers: they were to be like watch-dogs obeying the shepherds of the commonwealth.

Yes, you understand very well what I have in mind. But do you see how we have changed our view? A moment ago we were supposing this spirited element to be something of the nature of appetite; but now it appears that, when the soul is divided into factions, it is far more ready to be up in arms on the side of reason.

Quite true.

Is it, then, distinct from the rational element or only a particular form of it, so that the soul will contain no more than two elements, reason and appetite? Or is the soul like the state, which had three orders to hold it together, traders, Auxiliaries, and counsellors? Does the spirited element make a third, the natural auxiliary of reason, when not corrupted by bad upbringing?

It must be a third.

Yes, I said, provided it can be shown to be distinct from reason, as we saw it was from appetite.

That is easily proved. You can see that much in children: they are full of passionate feelings from their very birth; but some, I should say, never become rational, and most of them only late in life.

A very sound observation, said I, the truth of which may also be seen in animals. And besides, there is the witness of Homer in that line I quoted before: 'He smote his breast and spoke, chiding his heart.' The poet is plainly thinking of the two elements as distinct, when he makes the one which has chosen the better course after reflection rebuke the other for its unreasoning passion.

I entirely agree.

CHAPTER XIV (IV. 441c-445B)

THE VIRTUES IN THE INDIVIDUAL

The virtues in the state were the qualities of the citizen, as such, considered as playing the special part in society for which he was qualified by the predominance in his nature of the philosophic, the pugnacious, or the commercial spirit. But all three elements exist in every individual, who is thus a replica of society in miniature. In the perfect man reason will rule, with the spirited element as its auxiliary, over the bodily appetites. Self-control or temperance will be a condition of internal harmony, all the parts being content with their legitimate satisfactions. Justice finally appears, no longer only as a matter of external behaviour towards others, but as an internal order of the soul, from which right behaviour will necessarily follow. Injustice is the opposite state of internal discord and faction. To ask whether justice or injustice pays the better is now seen to be as absurd as to ask whether health is preferable to disease.

And so, after a stormy passage, we have reached the land. We are fairly agreed that the same three elements exist alike in the state and in the individual soul.

That is so.

Does it not follow at once that state and individual will be wise or brave by virtue of the same element in each and in the same way? Both will possess in the same manner any quality that makes for excellence.

That must be true.

Then it applies to justice: we shall conclude that a man is just in the same way that a state was just. And we have surely not forgotten that justice in the state meant that each of the three orders in it was doing its own proper work. So we may henceforth bear in mind that each one of us likewise will be a just person, fulfilling his proper function, only if the several parts of our nature fulfil theirs.

Certainly.

And it will be the business of reason to rule with wisdom and forethought on behalf of the entire soul; while the spirited element ought to act as its subordinate and ally. The two will be brought into accord, as we said earlier, by that combination of mental and bodily training which will tune up one string of the instrument and relax the other, nourishing the reasoning part on the study of noble literature and allaying the other's wildness by harmony and rhythm. When both have been thus nurtured and trained to know their own true functions, they must be set in command over the appetites, which form the greater part of each man's soul and are by nature insatiably covetous. They must keep watch lest this part, by battening on the pleasures that are called bodily, should grow so great and powerful that it will no longer keep to its own work, but will try to enslave the others and usurp a dominion to which it has no right, thus turning the whole of life upside down. At the same time, those two together will be the best of guardians for the entire soul and for the body against all enemies from without: the one will take counsel, while the other will do battle, following its ruler's commands and by its own bravery giving effect to the ruler's designs.

Yes, that is all true.

And so we call an individual brave in virtue of this spirited part of his nature, when, in spite of pain or pleasure, it holds fast to the injunctions of reason about what he ought or ought not to be afraid of.

True.

And wise in virtue of that small part which rules and issues these injunctions, possessing as it does the knowledge of what is good for each of the three elements and for all of them in common.

Certainly.

And, again, temperate by reason of the unanimity and concord of all three, when there is no internal conflict between the ruling element and its two subjects, but all are agreed that reason should be ruler.

Yes, that is an exact account of temperance, whether in the state or in the individual.

Finally, a man will be just by observing the principle we have so often stated.

Necessarily.

Now is there any indistinctness in our vision of justice, that might make it seem somehow different from what we found it to be in the state?

I don't think so.

Because, if we have any lingering doubt, we might make sure by comparing it with some commonplace notions. Suppose, for instance, that a sum of money were entrusted to our state or to an individual of corresponding character and training, would anyone imagine that such a person would be specially likely to embezzle it?

No.

And would he not be incapable of sacrilege and theft, or of treachery to friend or country; never false to an oath or any other compact; the last to be guilty of adultery or of neglecting parents or the due service of the gods?

Yes.

And the reason for all this is that each part of his nature is exercising its proper function, of ruling or of being ruled.

Yes, exactly.

Are you satisfied, then, that justice is the power which produces states or individuals of whom that is true, or must we look further?

There is no need; I am quite satisfied.

And so our dream has come true—I mean the inkling we had that, by some happy chance, we had lighted upon a rudimentary form of justice from the very moment when we set about founding our commonwealth. Our principle that the born shoemaker or carpenter had better stick to his trade turns out to have been an adumbration of justice; and that is why it has helped us. But in reality justice, though evidently analogous to this principle, is not a matter of external behaviour, but of the inward self and of attending to all that is, in the fullest sense, a man's proper concern. The just man does not allow the several elements in his soul to usurp one another's functions; he is indeed one who sets his house in order, by self-mastery and discipline coming to be at peace with himself, and bringing into tune those three parts, like the terms in the proportion of a musical scale, the highest and lowest notes and the mean between them, with all the intermediate intervals. Only when he has linked these parts together in well-tempered harmony and has made himself one man instead of many, will he be ready to go about whatever he may have to do, whether it be making money and satisfying bodily wants, or business transactions, or the affairs of state. In all these fields when he speaks of just and honourable conduct, he will mean the behaviour that helps to produce and to preserve this habit of mind; and by wisdom he will mean the knowledge which presides over such conduct. Any action which tends to break down this habit will be for him unjust; and the notions governing it he will call ignorance and folly.

That is perfectly true, Socrates.

Good, said I. I believe we should not be thought altogether mistaken, if we claimed to have discovered the just man and the just state, and wherein their justice consists.

Indeed we should not.

Shall we make that claim, then?

Yes, we will.

So be it, said I. Next, I suppose, we have to consider injustice.

Evidently.

This must surely be a sort of civil strife among the three elements, whereby they usurp and encroach upon one another's functions and some one part of the soul rises up in rebellion against the whole, claiming a supremacy to which it has no right because its nature fits it only to be the servant of the ruling principle. Such turmoil and aberration we shall, I think, identify with injustice, intemperance, cowardice, ignorance, and in a word with all wickedness.

Exactly.

And now that we know the nature of justice and injustice, we can be equally clear about what is meant by acting justly and again by unjust action and wrongdoing.

How do you mean?

Plainly, they are exactly analogous to those wholesome and unwholesome activities which respectively produce a healthy or unhealthy condition in the body; in the same way just and unjust conduct produce a just or unjust character. Justice is produced in the soul, like health in the body, by establishing the elements concerned in their natural relations of control and subordination, whereas injustice is like disease and means that this natural order is inverted.

Quite so.

It appears, then, that virtue is as it were the health and comeliness and well-being of the soul, as wickedness is disease, deformity, and weakness.

True.

And also that virtue and wickedness are brought about by one's way of life, honourable or disgraceful.

That follows.

So now it only remains to consider which is the more profitable course: to do right and live honourably and be just, whether or not anyone knows what manner of man you are, or to do wrong and be unjust, provided that you can escape the chastisement which might make you a better man.

But really, Socrates, it seems to me ridiculous to ask that question now that the nature of justice and injustice has been brought to light. People think that all the luxury and wealth and power in the world cannot make life worth living when the bodily constitution is going to rack and ruin; and are we to believe that, when the very principle whereby we live is deranged and corrupted, life will be worth living so long as a man can do as he will, and wills to do anything rather than to free himself from vice and wrongdoing and to win justice and virtue?

Yes, I replied, it is a ridiculous question.

PART III (Books V, 471 c-VII)

The Philosopher-King

CHAPTER XXIII (VI. 502 c-509 c)

THE GOOD AS THE HIGHEST OBJECT OF KNOWLEDGE

Granted that a Philosopher-King might possibly be produced, how is he to be trained? The rest of this Part describes the higher education in mathematics and moral philosophy which the prospective Rulers, after the elementary education of Chapter IX and two or three years of intensive physical training, will receive from the age of twenty to thirty-five (537 B). The account may also be taken as a sort of ideal programme of studies at the Academy.

Plato first defines the ultimate goal, the knowledge of the Good. For the saviour of society the one thing needful is a certain and immediate knowledge of values, the ends which all life, private or public, should realize. Both Plato (CHARMIDES, 173, EUTHYDEMUS, 288 D ff.) and Aristotle (ETHICS, I. i) picture social life as a domain in which all forms of 'art' or specialized skill have their several fields, each with its peculiar end: medicine producing health, the art of war victory, business wealth, and so on. Above them all is the Royal Art, or Art of Statesmanship ('Politics'), which sees these special ends as means to, or elements in, the ultimate end or perfection (telos) of life, human well-being or happiness, 'the Good for man.' All effort will be perverted and falsely orientated if this end is misconceived—if a statesman, e.g., believes that his nation should aim at imperial domination or unlimited wealth, or if an individual imagines that wealth or power or pleasure will suffice to make him happy. It is of this 'Human Good' that Plato first speaks, as the most important object of knowledge. He rejects the popular belief that it is pleasure. The more refined view, that it is 'knowledge' (insight, wisdom) may be attributed to the Socrates pictured in Plato's early dialogues. He held that man's happiness consists in the full realization of his characteristic virtue and function (Chap. IV), and that his virtue, as a rational being, is a clear insight into the true end of life, 'knowledge of the Good.' Such knowledge, once attained, cannot fail to determine will and action.

But in the latter part of this chapter (506 B ff.) 'the Good' receives the much wider meaning it bears in Plato's own theory of Forms ('Ideas'). In Greek 'the Good' is normally synonymous with 'Goodness itself.' This is the supreme Form or Essence manifested not only in the special kinds of moral goodness, Justice, Courage, etc., but throughout all Nature (for every living creature has its own 'good') and especially in the beautiful and harmonious order of the heavenly bodies (592 B). The knowledge of the Good, on which well-being depends, is now to include an understanding of the moral and physical order of the whole universe. As the object of a purpose attributed to a divine Reason operating in the world, this supreme Good makes the world intelligible, as a work of human craftsmanship becomes intelligible when we see the purpose it is designed to serve. As thus illuminating and accounting for the rational aspect of the universe, the Good is analogous to the Sun, which, as the source of light, is the cause of vision and of visibility, and also of all mortal existence.

Socrates refuses to define this supreme Good. The apprehension of it is rather to be thought of as a revelation which can only follow upon a long intellectual training (540 A). Neither Glaucon nor the readers of the REPUBLIC have been so prepared. Also Plato would never commit his deepest thoughts to writing (EPISTLE vii. 341 c).

One difficulty, then, has been surmounted. It remains to ask how we can make sure of having men who will preserve our constitution. What must they learn, and at what age should they take up each branch of study?

Yes, that is the next point.

I gained nothing by my cunning in putting off those thorny questions of the possession of wives and children and the appointment of Rulers. I knew that the ideal plan would give offence and be hard to carry out; none the less I have had to discuss these matters. We have now disposed of the women and children, but we must start all over again upon the training of the Rulers. You remember how their love for their country was to be proved, by the tests of pain and pleasure, to be a faith that no toil or danger, no turn of fortune could make them abandon.[19] All who failed were to be rejected; only the man who came out flawless, like gold tried in the fire, was to be made a Ruler with privileges and rewards in life and after death. So much was said, when our argument turned aside, as if hoping, with veiled face, to slip past the danger that now lies in our path.

Quite true, I remember.

Yes, I shrank from the bold words which have now been spoken; but now we have ventured to declare that our Guardians in the fullest sense must be philosophers.[20] So much being granted, you must reflect how few are likely to be available. The natural gifts we required will rarely grow together into one whole; they tend to split apart.

How do you mean?

Qualities like ready understanding, a good memory, sagacity, quickness, together with a high-spirited, generous temper, are seldom combined with willingness to live a quiet life of sober constancy. Keen wits are apt to lose all steadiness and to veer about in every direction. On the other hand,

the steady reliable characters, whose impassivity is proof against the perils of war, are equally proof against instruction. Confronted with intellectual work, they become comatose and do nothing but yawn.

That is true.

But we insist that no one must be given the highest education or hold office as Ruler, who has not both sets of qualities in due measure. This combination will be rare. So, besides testing it by hardship and danger and by the temptations of pleasure, we may now add that its strength must be tried in many forms of study, to see whether it has the courage and endurance to pursue the highest kind of knowledge, without flinching as others flinch under physical trials.

By all means; but what kinds of study do you call the highest?

You remember how we deduced the definitions of justice, temperance, courage, and wisdom by distinguishing three parts of the soul?

If I had forgotten that, I should not deserve to hear any more.

Do you also remember my warning you beforehand[21] that in order to gain the clearest possible view of these qualities we should have to go round a longer way, although we could give a more superficial account in keeping with our earlier argument. You said that would do; and so we went on in a way which seemed to me not sufficiently exact; whether you were satisfied, it is for you to say.

We all thought you gave us a fair measure of truth.

No measure that falls in the least degree short of the whole truth can be quite fair in so important a matter. What is imperfect can never serve as a measure; though people sometimes think enough has been done and there is no need to look further.

---

[19] Chap. X.

[20] The constancy of *belief* required of all Guardians in the earlier passage referred to (413) is not enough for those few who will be the Rulers obeyed by the rest. They must have the philosopher's immediate *knowledge* of the Good.

[21] At 435 D.

Yes, indolence is common enough.

But the last quality to be desired in the Guardian of a commonwealth and its laws. So he will have to take the longer way and work as hard at learning as at training his body; otherwise he will never reach the goal of the highest knowledge, which most of all concerns him.

Why, are not justice and the other virtues we have discussed the highest? Is there something still higher to be known?

There is; and of those virtues themselves we have as yet only a rough outline, where nothing short of the finished picture should content us. If we strain every nerve to reach precision and clearness in things of little moment, how absurd not to demand the highest degree of exactness in the things that matter most.

Certainly. But what do you mean by the highest kind of knowledge and with what is it concerned? You cannot hope to escape that question.

I do not; you may ask me yourself. All the same, you have been told many a time; but now either you are not thinking, or, as I rather suspect, you mean to put me to some trouble with your insistence. For you have often been told that the highest object of knowledge is the essential nature of the Good, from which everything that is good and right derives its value for us. You must have been expecting me to speak of this now, and to add that we have no sufficient knowledge of it. I need not tell you that, without that knowledge, to know everything else, however well, would be of no value to us, just as it is of no use to possess anything without getting the good of it. What advantage can there be in possessing everything except what is good, or in understanding everything else while of the good and desirable we know nothing?

None whatever.

Well then, you know too that most people identify the Good [22] with pleasure, whereas the more enlightened think it is knowledge.

Yes, of course.

And further that these latter cannot tell us what knowledge they mean, but are reduced at last to saying, 'knowledge of the Good.'

It is; first they reproach us with not knowing the Good, and then tell us that it is knowledge of the Good, as if we did after all understand the meaning of that word 'Good' when they pronounce it.

Quite true.

What of those who define the Good as pleasure? Are they any less confused in their thoughts? They are obliged to admit that there are bad pleasures; from which it follows that the same things are both good and bad.[23]

Quite so.

Evidently, then, this is a matter of much dispute. It is also evident that, although many are content to do what seems just or honourable without really being so, and to possess a mere semblance of these qualities, when it comes to good things, no one is satisfied with possessing what only seems good: here all reject the appearance and demand the reality.

Certainly.

A thing, then, that every soul pursues as the end of all her actions, dimly divining its existence, but perplexed and unable to grasp its nature with the same clearness and assurance as in dealing with other things, and so missing whatever value those other things might have—a thing of such supreme importance is not a matter about which those chosen Guardians of the whole fortunes of our commonwealth can be left in the dark.

[22] Here 'the Good' obviously means 'the Human Good' or end of human life.

[23] This admission is extracted in the *Gorgias* (499 B) from Callicles, who has maintained extreme hedonism.

Most certainly not.

At any rate, institutions or customs which are desirable and right will not, I imagine, find a very efficient guardian in one who does not know in what way they are good. I should rather guess that he will not be able to recognize fully that they are right and desirable.

No doubt.

So the order of our commonwealth will be perfectly regulated only when it is watched over by a Guardian who does possess this knowledge.

That follows. But Socrates, what is your own account of the Good? Is it knowledge, or pleasure, or something else? [24]

There you are! I exclaimed; I could see all along that you were not going to be content with what other people think.

Well, Socrates, it does not seem fair that you should be ready to repeat other people's opinions but not to state your own, when you have given so much thought to this subject.

And do you think it fair of anyone to speak as if he knew what he does not know?

No, not as if he knew, but he might give his opinion for what it is worth.

Why, have you never noticed that opinion without knowledge is always a shabby sort of thing? At the best it is blind. One who holds a true belief without intelligence is just like a blind man who happens to take the right road, isn't he? [25]

No doubt.

Well, then, do you want me to produce one of these poor blind cripples,

when others could discourse to you with illuminating eloquence?

No, really, Socrates, said Glaucon, you must not give up within sight of the goal. We should be quite content with an account of the Good like the one you gave us of justice and temperance and the other virtues.

So should I be, my dear Glaucon, much more than content! But I am afraid it is beyond my powers; with the best will in the world I should only disgrace myself and be laughed at. No, for the moment let us leave the question of the real meaning of good; to arrive at what I at any rate believe it to be would call for an effort too ambitious for an inquiry like ours. However, I will tell you, though only if you wish it, what I picture to myself as the offspring of the Good and the thing most nearly resembling it.

Well, tell us about the offspring, and you shall remain in our debt for an account of the parent.

I only wish it were within my power to offer, and within yours to receive, a settlement of the whole account. But you must be content now with the interest only;[26] and you must see to it that, in describing this offspring of the Good, I do not inadvertently cheat you with false coin.

We will keep a good eye on you. Go on.

First we must come to an understanding. Let me remind you of the distinction we drew earlier and have often drawn on other occasions,[27] between the multiplicity of things that we call good or beautiful or whatever it may be and, on the other hand,

---

[24] Here it begins to appear that the discussion is not confined to the 'Human Good' but extends to the supreme Form, 'Goodness itself.'

[25] At *Meno* 97 the man who has a correct belief at second-hand about the way from Athens to Larisa is contrasted with one who has certain knowledge of the road from having travelled by it himself.

[26] The Greek has a play on two meanings of the word *tokos*—'offspring' and 'interest' on a loan, 'a breed for barren metal.'

[27] Perhaps an allusion to the *Phaedo* (especially 78 E ff.), where the theory of Forms was first explicitly stated in similar terms. The earlier passage in the *Republic* is at 475 E ff.

Goodness itself or Beauty itself and so on. Corresponding to each of these sets of many things, we postulate a single Form or real essence, as we call it.

Yes, that is so.

Further, the many things, we say, can be seen, but are not objects of rational thought; whereas the Forms are objects of thought, but invisible.

Yes, certainly.

And we see things with our eyesight, just as we hear sounds with our ears and, to speak generally, perceive any sensible thing with our sense-faculties.

Of course.

Have you noticed, then, that the artificer who designed the senses has been exceptionally lavish of his materials in making the eyes able to see and their objects visible?

That never occurred to me.

Well, look at it in this way. Hearing and sound do not stand in need of any third thing, without which the ear will not hear nor sound be heard;[28] and I think the same is true of most, not to say all, of the other senses. Can you think of one that does require anything of the sort?

No, I cannot.

But there is this need in the case of sight and its objects. You may have the power of vision in your eyes and try to use it, and colour may be there in the objects; but sight will see nothing and the colours will remain invisible in the absence of a third thing peculiarly constituted to serve this very purpose.

By which you mean—?

Naturally I mean what you call light; and if light is a thing of value, the sense of sight and the power of being visible are linked together by a very precious bond, such as unites no other sense with its object.

No one could say that light is not a precious thing.

And of all the divinities in the skies [29] is there one whose light, above all the rest, is responsible for making our eyes see perfectly and making objects perfectly visible?

There can be no two opinions: of course you mean the Sun.

And how is light related to this deity? Neither sight nor the eye which contains it is the Sun, but of all the sense-organs it is the most sun-like; and further, the power it possesses is dispensed by the Sun, like a stream flooding the eye.[30] And again, the Sun is not vision, but it is the cause of vision and also is seen by the vision it causes.

Yes.

It was the Sun, then, that I meant when I spoke of that offspring which the Good has created in the visible world, to stand there in the same relation to vision and visible things as that which the Good itself bears in the intelligible world to intelligence and to intelligible objects.

How is that? You must explain further.

You know what happens when the colours of things are no longer irradiated by the daylight, but only by the fainter luminaries of the night: when

---

[28] Plato held that the hearing of sound is caused by blows inflicted by the air (*Timaeus* 67 B, 80 A); but the air is hardly analogous to light.

[29] Plato held that the heavenly bodies are immortal living creatures, i.e. gods.

[30] Plato's theory of vision involves three kinds of fire or light: (1) daylight, a body of pure fire diffused in the air by the Sun; (2) the visual current or 'vision,' a pure fire similar to daylight, contained in the eye-ball and capable of issuing out in a stream directed towards the object seen; (3) the colour of the external object, 'a flame streaming off from every body, having particles proportioned to those of of the visual current, so as to yield sensation' when the two streams meet and coalesce (*Timaeus,* 45 B, 67 C).

you look at them, the eyes are dim and seem almost blind, as if there were no unclouded vision in them. But when you look at things on which the Sun is shining, the same eyes see distinctly and it becomes evident that they do contain the power of vision.

Certainly.

Apply this comparison, then, to the soul. When its gaze is fixed upon an object irradiated by truth and reality, the soul gains understanding and knowledge and is manifestly in possession of intelligence. But when it looks towards that twilight world of things that come into existence and pass away, its sight is dim and it has only opinions and beliefs which shift to and fro, and now it seems like a thing that has no intelligence.

That is true.

This, then, which gives to the objects of knowledge their truth and to him who knows them his power of knowing, is the Form or essential nature of Goodness. It is the cause of knowledge and truth; and so, while you may think of it as an object of knowledge, you will do well to regard it as something beyond truth and knowledge and, precious as these both are, of still higher worth. And, just as in our analogy light and vision were to be thought of as like the Sun, but not identical with it, so here both knowledge and truth are to be regarded as like the Good, but to identify either with the Good is wrong. The Good must hold a yet higher place of honour.

You are giving it a position of extraordinary splendour, if it is the source of knowledge and truth and itself surpasses them in worth. You surely cannot mean that it is pleasure.

Heaven forbid, I exclaimed. But I want to follow up our analogy still further. You will agree that the Sun not only makes the things we see visible, but also brings them into existence and gives them growth and nourishment; yet he is not the same thing as existence.[31] And so with the objects of knowledge: these derive from the Good not only their power of being known, but their very being and reality; and Goodness is not the same thing as being, but even beyond being, surpassing it in dignity and power.

Glaucon exclaimed with some amusement at my exalting Goodness in such extravagant terms.

It is your fault, I replied; you forced me to say what I think.

PART IV (BOOKS VIII-IX)

THE DECLINE OF SOCIETY AND OF THE SOUL. COMPARISON OF THE JUST AND THE UNJUST LIVES

CHAPTER XXXII (VIII 562A-IX. 576B)

DESPOTISM AND THE DESPOTIC MAN

The Greeks called an absolute, unconstitutional ruler a 'tyrant,' but the word by no means always bore the sinister associations which are now gathering round its modern equivalent, the once honourable name of 'dictator.' A tyrant might be, like Peisistratus at Athens, a comparatively benevolent champion of the common people against the oppression of a landed aristocracy; but then, as now, Acton's saying was true: 'all power corrupts; absolute power corrupts ab-

[31] The ambiguity of *genesis* can hardly be reproduced. The Sun 'gives things their *genesis*' (generation, birth), but 'is not itself *genesis*' (becoming, the existence in time of things which begin and cease to exist, as opposed to the real being of eternal things in the intelligible world).

solutely.' Little as Plato valued what he has described as democratic liberty, no democrat could surpass him in detestation of the despotism which is the triumph of injustice and the very negation of the liberty he did believe in.

Democratic anarchy, carried to the classes: a growing number of ruined spendthrift and desperadoes; the capitalists, quietly amassing wealth; and the mass of country people, working their own small farms and uninterested in politics. The most unscrupulous 'drones' lead an attack upon property, which drives the capitalists in self-defence to form a reactionary party. The people then put forward a champion who, having tasted blood, is fated to become a human wolf, the enemy of mankind. Threatened with assassination, he successfully demands a bodyguard or private army, seizes absolute power, and makes the people his slaves. This account of the rise of despotism is adapted to Plato's psychological standpoint, rather than to the normal course of Greek history. At Athens, for example, the 'tyranny' of Peisistratus broke the power of the landed nobility and prepared the way for democracy. On the other hand democracy sometimes passed into despotism, as at Syracuse in Plato's time.

A picture follows of the miserable condition to which the despot is driven to reduce himself by murdering his opponents and possible rivals, till he is left with only scoundrels for company and loathed by the people when they realize how they have been enslaved.

In the individual soul despotism means the dominion of one among those unlawful appetites whose existence, even in decent people, is revealed in dreams. The democratic man allowed equal rights to all his desires; but this balance is easily destroyed by the growth of a master passion, which will gradually enslave every

other element in the soul. So at last the portrait of the perfectly unjust man is completed for comparison with the perfectly just philosopher-king.

Now there remains only the most admired of all constitutions and characters—despotism and the despot. How does despotism arise? That it comes out of democracy is fairly clear. Does the change take place in the same sort of way as the change from oligarchy to democracy? Oligarchy was established by men with a certain aim in life: the good they sought was wealth, and it was the insatiable appetite for money-making to the neglect of everything else that proved its undoing. Is democracy likewise ruined by greed for what it conceives to be the supreme good?

What good do you mean?

Liberty. In a democratic country you will be told that liberty is its noblest possession, which makes it the only fit place for a free spirit to live in.

True; that is often said.

Well then, as I was saying, perhaps the insatiable desire for this good to the neglect of everything else may transform a democracy and lead to a demand for despotism. A democratic state may fall under the influence of unprincipled leaders, ready to minister to its thirst for liberty with too deep draughts of this heady wine; and then, if its rulers are not complaisant enough to give it unstinted freedom, they will be arraigned as accursed oligarchs and punished. Law-abiding citizens will be insulted as nonentities who hug their chains; and all praise and honour will be bestowed, both publicly and in private, on rulers who behave like subjects and subjects who behave like rulers. In such a state the spirit of liberty is bound to go to all lengths.

Inevitably.

It will make its way into the home,

until at last the very animals catch the infection of anarchy. The parent falls into the habit of behaving like the child, and the child like the parent: the father is afraid of his sons, and they show no fear or respect for their parents, in order to assert their freedom. Citizens, resident aliens, and strangers from abroad are all on an equal footing. To descend to smaller matters, the schoolmaster timidly flatters his pupils, and the pupils make light of their masters as well as of their attendants. Generally speaking, the young copy their elders, argue with them, and will not do as they are told; while the old, anxious not to be thought disagreeable tyrants, imitate the young and condescend to enter into their jokes and amusements. The full measure of popular liberty is reached when the slaves of both sexes are quite as free as the owners who paid for them; and I had almost forgotten to mention the spirit of freedom and equality in the mutual relations of men and women.

Well, to quote Aeschylus, we may as well speak 'the word that rises to our lips.'

Certainly; so I will. No one who had not seen it would believe how much more freedom the domestic animals enjoy in a democracy than elsewhere. The very dogs behave as if the proverb 'like mistress, like maid' applied to them; and the horses and donkeys catch the habit of walking down the street with all the dignity of freemen, running into anyone they meet who does not get out of their way. The whole place is simply bursting with the spirit of liberty.

No need to tell me that. I have often suffered from it on my way out of the town.

Putting all these items together, you can see the result: the citizens become so sensitive that they resent the slightest application of control as intolerable tyranny, and in their resolve to have no master they end by disregarding even the law, written or unwritten.

Yes, I know that only too well.

Such then, I should say, is the seed, so full of fair promise, from which springs despotism.

Promising indeed. But what is the next stage?

The same disease that destroyed oligarchy breaks out again here, with all the more force because of the prevailing licence, and enslaves democracy. The truth is that, in the constitution of society, quite as much as in the weather or in plants and animals, any excess brings about an equally violent reaction. So the only outcome of too much freedom is likely to be excessive subjection, in the state or in the individual; which means that the culmination of liberty in democracy is precisely what prepares the way for the cruellest extreme of servitude under a despot. But I think you were asking rather about the nature of that disease which afflicts democracy in common with oligarchy and reduces it to slavery.

Yes, I was.

What I had in mind was that set of idle spendthrifts, among whom the bolder spirits take the lead. We compared these leaders, if you remember, to drones armed with stings, the stingless drones being their less enterprising followers. In any society where these two groups appear they create disorder, as phlegm and bile do in the body. Hence the lawgiver, as a good physician of the body politic, should take measures in advance, no less than the prudent bee-keeper who tries to forestall the appearance of drones, or, failing that, cuts them out, cells and all, as quickly as he can.

Quite true.

Then, to gain a clearer view of our problem, let us suppose the democratic commonwealth to be divided into three parts, as in fact it is. One consists of the drones we have just described. Bred by the spirit of licence, in a democracy this class is no less numerous and much more energetic than in an oligarchy, where it is despised and kept out of office and so remains weak for lack of exercise. But in a democracy it furnishes all the leaders, with a few exceptions; its keenest members make the speeches and transact the business, while the other drones settle on the benches round, humming applause to drown any opposition. Thus nearly the whole management of the commonwealth is in its hands.

Quite true.

Meanwhile, a second group is constantly emerging from the mass. Where everyone is bent upon making money, the steadiest characters tend to amass the greatest wealth. Here is a very convenient source from which the drones can draw an abundance of honey.

No doubt; they cannot squeeze any out of men of small means.

'The rich,' I believe, is what they call this class which provides provender for the drones.

Yes.

The third class will be the 'people,' comprising all the peasantry who work their own farms, with few possessions and no interest in politics. In a democracy this is the largest class and, when once assembled, its power is supreme.

Yes, but it will not often meet, unless it gets some share of the honey.

Well, it always does get its share, when the leaders are distributing to the people what they have taken from the well-to-do, always provided they can keep the lion's share for themselves.[32] The plundered rich are driven to defend themselves in debate before the Assembly and by any measures they can compass; and then, even if they have no revolutionary designs, the other party accuse them of plotting against the people and of being reactionary oligarchs. At last, when they see the people unwittingly misled by such denunciation into attempts to treat them unjustly, then, whether they wish it or not, they become reactionaries in good earnest. There is no help for it; the poison is injected by the sting of those drones we spoke of. Then follow impeachments and trials, in which each party arraigns the other.

Quite so.

And the people always put forward a single champion of their interests, whom they nurse to greatness. Here, plainly enough, is the root from which despotism invariably springs.[33]

Yes.

How does the transformation of the people's champion into a despot begin? You have heard the legend they tell of the shrine of Lycaean Zeus in Arcadia: how one who tastes a single piece of human flesh mixed in with the flesh of the sacrificial victims is fated to be changed into a wolf. In the same way the people's champion, finding himself in full control of the mob, may not scruple to shed a brother's blood; dragging him before

[32] Pericles had introduced the payment of a small fee to enable country people to come to Athens for service on juries. This was later increased to an amount compensating for the loss of a day's work. After the Peloponnesian War, citizens were paid for attending the Assembly. There were also distributions of surplus revenue, corn-doles, and payments for festivals.

[33] Aristotle (*Politics*, v. 5) observes that in the old days most despots had risen from being demagogues. Cf. Herod. iii. 82.

a tribunal with the usual unjust charges, he may foully murder him, blotting out a man's life and tasting kindred blood with unhallowed tongue and lips; he may send men to death or exile with hinted promises of debts to be cancelled and estates to be redistributed. Is it not thenceforth his inevitable fate either to be destroyed by his enemies or to seize absolute power and be transformed from a human being into a wolf?

It is.

Here, then, we have the party-leader in the civil war against property. If he is banished, and then returns from exile in despite of his enemies, he will come back a finished despot. If they cannot procure his banishment or death by denouncing him to the state, they will conspire to assassinate him. Then comes the notorious device of all who have reached this stage in the despot's career, the request for a bodyguard to keep the people's champion safe for them. The request is granted, because the people, in their alarm on his account, have no fear for themselves.

Quite true.

This is a terrifying sight for the man of property, who is charged with being not merely rich but the people's enemy. He will follow the oracle's advice to Croesus,

To flee by Hermus' pebbly shore,
Dreading the coward's shame no more.[34]

Well, he would have little chance to dread it a second time.

True; if he is caught, no doubt he will be done to death; whereas our champion himself does not, like Hector's charioteer,[35] 'measure his towering length in dust,' but on the contrary, overthrows a host of rivals and stands erect in the chariot of the state,

[34] Herodotus, i. 55.
[35] Iliad, xvi. 776.

no longer protector of the people, but its absolute master.

Yes, it must come to that.

And now shall we describe the happy condition of the man and of the country which harbours a creature of this stamp?

By all means.

In the early days he has a smile and a greeting for everyone he meets; disclaims any absolute power; makes large promises to his friends and to the public; sets about the relief of debtors and the distribution of land to the people and to his supporters; and assumes a mild and gracious air towards everybody. But as soon as he has disembarrassed himself of his exiled enemies by coming to terms with some and destroying others, he begins stirring up one war after another, in order that the people may feel their need of a leader, and also be so impoverished by taxation that they will be forced to think of nothing but winning their daily bread, instead of plotting against him. Moreover, if he suspects some of cherishing thoughts of freedom and not submitting to his rule, he will find a pretext for putting them at the enemy's mercy and so making away with them. For all these reasons a despot must be constantly provoking wars.

He must.

This course will lead to his being hated by his countrymen more and more. Also, the bolder spirits among those who have helped him to power and now hold positions of influence will begin to speak their mind to him and among themselves and to criticize his policy. If the despot is to maintain his rule, he must gradually make away with all these malcontents, until he has not a friend or an enemy left who is of any account. He will need to keep a sharp eye open for anyone who is courageous or high-minded or intelligent or rich; it is his happy fate to be at war with all such, whether he likes it or not, and to lay his plans against them until he has purged the commonwealth.[36]

A fine sort of purgation!

Yes, the exact opposite of the medical procedure, which removes the worst elements in the bodily condition and leaves the best.

There seems to be no choice, if he is to hold his power.

No; he is confined to the happy alternatives of living with people most of whom are good for nothing and who hate him into the bargain, or not living at all. And the greater the loathing these actions inspire in his countrymen, the more he will need trustworthy recruits to strengthen his bodyguard. Where will he turn to find men on whom he can rely?

They will come flocking of their own accord, if he offers enough pay.

Foreigners of all sorts, you mean — yet another swarm of drones. But why not draw upon the home supply? He could rob the citizens of their slaves, emancipate them, and enroll them in his bodyguard.

No doubt they would be the most faithful adherents he could find.

What an enviable condition for the despot, to put his trust in such friends as these, when he has made away with his earlier supporters! He will, of course, be the admiration of all this band of new-made citizens, whose company he will enjoy when every decent person shuns him with loath-

ing. It is not for nothing that the tragic drama is thought to be a storehouse of wisdom, and above all Euripides, whose profundity of thought appears in the remark that 'despots grow wise by converse with the wise,' meaning no doubt by the wise these associates we have described.

Yes, and Euripides praises absolute power as godlike, with much more to the same effect. So do the other poets.[37]

That being so, the tragedians will give a further proof of their wisdom if they will excuse us and all states whose constitution resembles ours, when we deny them admittance on the ground that they sing the praises of despotism. At the same time, I expect they will go the round of other states, where they will hire actors with fine sonorous voices to sway the inclination of the assembled crowd towards a despotic or a democratic constitution. Naturally they are honoured and well paid for these services, by despots chiefly, and in a less degree by democracies. But the higher they mount up the scale of commonwealths, the more their reputation flags, like a climber who gives in for lack of breath. However, we are wandering from our subject. Let us go back to the despot's army. How is he to maintain this fine, ever-shifting array of nondescripts?

No doubt he will spend any treasure there may be in the temples,[38] so long as it will last, as well as the property

[36] At *Gorg.* 510 B Socrates remarks that a despot cannot make friends with his betters, whom he will fear, or with his inferiors, whom he will despise, but only with men of like character, who will truckle to him. In *Ep.* vii 332 c Plato says that Dionysius I was too clever to trust anyone, and 'there is no surer sign of moral character than the lack of trustworthy friends.'

[37] The ancients often quote lines from the tragedians, as many people now quote Shakespeare, without regard to the context or the fact that a dramatist is not responsible for all the sentiments expressed by his characters.

[38] In the ancient world temples were to some extent used like banks for the safe deposit of valuables, since robbery would involve the additional guilt of sacrilege.

of his victims, thus lightening the war-taxes imposed on the people.

And when that source fails?

Clearly he will support himself, with his boon-companions, minions, and mistresses, from his parent's estate.

I understand: the despot and his comrades will be maintained by the common people which gave him birth.

Inevitably.

But how if the people resent this and say it is not right for the father to support his grown-up son — it ought to be the other way about; they did not bring him into being and set him up in order that, when he had grown great, they should be the slaves of their own slaves and support them together with their master and the rest of his rabble; he was to be the champion to set them free from the rich and the so-called upper class. Suppose they now order him and his partisans to leave the country, as a father might drive his son out of the house along with his riotous friends?

Then, to be sure, the people will learn what sort of a creature it has bred and nursed to greatness in its bosom, until now the child is too strong for the parent to drive out.

Do you mean that the despot will dare to lay violent hands on this father of his and beat him if he resists?

Yes, when once he has disarmed him.

So the despot is a parricide, with no pity for the weakness of age. Here, it seems, is absolutism openly avowed. The people, as they say, have escaped the smoke only to fall into the fire, exchanging service to free men for the tyranny of slaves. That freedom which knew no bounds must now put on the livery of the most harsh and bitter servitude, where the slave has become the master.

Yes, that is what happens.

May we say, then, that we have now sufficiently described the transition from democracy to despotism, and what despotism is like when once established?

Yes, quite sufficiently.

Last comes the man of despotic character. It remains to ask how he develops from the democratic type, what he is like, and whether his life is one of happiness or of misery.

Yes.

Here I feel the need to define, more fully than we have so far done, the number and nature of the appetites. Otherwise it will not be so easy to see our way to a conclusion.

Well, it is not too late.

Quite so. Now, about the appetites, here is the point I want to make plain. Among the unnecessary pleasures and desires,[39] some, I should say, are unlawful. Probably they are innate in everyone; but when they are disciplined by law and by the higher desires with the aid of reason, they can in some people be got rid of entirely, or at least left few and feeble, although in others they will be comparatively strong and numerous.

What kind of desires do you mean?

Those which bestir themselves in dreams, when the gentler part of the soul slumbers and the control of reason is withdrawn; then the wild beast in us, full-fed with meat or drink, becomes rampant and shakes off sleep to go in quest of what will gratify its own instincts. As you know, it will cast away all shame and prudence at such moments and stick at nothing. In phantasy it will not shrink from intercourse with a mother or anyone else, man, god, or brute, or from forbidden food or any deed of blood. In a word, it will go to any length of shamelessness and folly.

Quite true.

It is otherwise with a man sound in

[39] Distinguished at 558 D.

body and mind, who, before he goes to sleep, awakens the reason within him to feed on high thoughts and questionings in collected meditation. If he has neither starved nor surfeited his appetites, so that, lulled to rest, no delights or griefs of theirs may trouble that better part, but leave it free to reach out, in pure and independent thought, after some new knowledge of things past, present, or to come; if, likewise, he has soothed his passions so as not to fall asleep with his anger roused against any man; if, in fact, he does not take his rest until he has quieted two of the three elements in his soul and awakened the third wherein wisdom dwells, then he is in a fair way to grasp the truth of things, and the visions of his dreams will not be unlawful. However, we have been carried away from our point, which is that in every one of us, even those who seem most respectable, there exist desires, terrible in their untamed lawlessness, which reveal themselves in dreams. Do you agree?

I do.

Remember, then, our account of the democratic man, how his character was shaped by his early training under a parsimonious father, who respected only the businesslike desires, dismissing the unnecessary ones as concerned with frivolous embellishments. Then, associating with more sophisticated people who were a prey to those lawless appetites we have just described, he fell into their ways, and hatred of his father's miserliness drove him into every sort of extravagance. But, having a better disposition than his corrupters, he came to a compromise between the two conflicting ways of life, making the best of both with what he called moderation and avoiding alike the meanness of the one and the licence of the other. So the oligarchical man was transformed into the democratic type.

Yes, I hold by that description.

Now imagine him grown old in his turn, with a young son bred in his ways, who is exposed to the same influences, drawn towards the utter lawlessness which his seducers call perfect freedom, while on the other side his father and friends lend their support to the compromise. When those terrible wizards who would conjure up an absolute ruler in the young man's soul begin to doubt the power of their spells, in the last resort they contrive to engender in him a master passion, to champion the mob of idle appetites which are for dividing among themselves all available plunder — a passion that can only be compared to a great winged drone. Like a swarm buzzing round this creature, the other desires come laden with incense and perfumes, garlands and wine, feeding its growth to the full on the pleasures of a dissolute life, until they have implanted the sting of a longing that cannot be satisfied.[40] Then at last this passion, as leader of the soul, takes madness for the captain of its guard and breaks out in frenzy; if it can lay hold upon any thoughts or desires that are of good report and still capable of shame, it kills them or drives them forth, until it has purged the soul of all sobriety and called in the partisans of madness to fill the vacant place.

That is a complete picture of how the despotic character develops.

Is not this the reason why lust has long since been called a tyrant? A drunken man, too, has something of this tyrannical spirit; and so has the lunatic who dreams that he can lord it over all mankind and heaven besides. Thus, when nature or habit or both have combined the traits of drunkenness, lust, and lunacy, then

[40] The winged drone, it will be remembered, is naturally stingless (552 c). The word translated by 'passion' is *Eros*, and *Eros* was commonly pictured with wings.

you have the perfect specimen of the despotic man.

Quite true.

Such, then, being his origin and character, what will his life be like?

I give it up. You must tell me.

I will. When a master passion is enthroned in absolute dominion over every part of the soul, feasting and revelling with courtesans and all such delights will become the order of the day. And every day and night a formidable crop of fresh appetites springs up, whose numerous demands quickly consume whatever income there may be. Soon he will be borrowing and trenching on his capital; and when all resources fail, the lusty brood of appetites will crowd about him clamouring. Goaded on to frenzy by them and above all by that ruling passion to which they serve as a sort of bodyguard, he will look out for any man of property whom he can rob by fraud or violence. Money he must have, no matter how, if he is not to suffer torments.

All that is inevitable.

Now, just as a succession of new pleasures asserted themselves in his soul at the expense of the older ones, so this young man will claim the right to live at his parents' expense and help himself to their property when his own portion is spent. If they resist, he will first try to cheat them; and failing that, he will rob them by force. If the old people still hold out, will any scruple restrain him from behaving like a despot?

I should not have much hope for the parents of such a son.

And yet consider, Adeimantus: his father and mother have been bound to him by the closest ties all his life; and now that they are old and faded, would he really be ready to beat them for the sake of the charms of some new-found mistress or favourite who

has no sort of claim on him? Is he going to bring these creatures under the same roof and let them lord it over his parents?

I believe he would.

It is no very enviable lot, then, to give birth to a despotic son.

It is not.

And now suppose that his parents' resources begin to fail, while his appetites for new pleasures have mustered into a great swarm in his soul; he will begin by breaking into someone's house or robbing a traveller by night, and go on to sweep some temple clean of its treasures. Meanwhile, the old approved beliefs about right and wrong which he had as a child will be overpowered by thoughts, once held in subjection, but now emancipated to second that master passion whose bodyguard they form. In his democratic days when he was still under the control of his father and of the laws, they broke loose only in sleep; but now that this passion has set up an absolute dominion, he has become for all his waking life the man he used to be from time to time in his dreams, ready to shed blood or eat forbidden food or do any dreadful deed. The desire that lives in him as sole ruler in a waste of lawless disrule will drive him, as a tyrant would drive his country, into any desperate venture which promises to maintain it with its horde of followers, some of whom evil communication has brought in from without, while others have been released from bondage by the same evil practices within. Is that a fair account of his manner of life?

If there are a few such characters in a country where most men are law-abiding, they will go elsewhere to join some despot's bodyguard or serve as mercenaries in any war that is toward. In quiet times of peace, they stay at home and commit crimes on a small scale, as thieves, burglars, pickpockets, temple-robbers, kidnappers; or, if they have a ready tongue, they may take to selling their services as informers and false witnesses.

Such crimes will be a small matter, you mean, so long as the criminals are few in number.

Small is a relative term; and all of them put together do not, as they say, come within sight of the degradation and misery of society under a despot. When the number of such criminals and their hangers-on increases and they become aware of their strength, then it is they who, helped by the folly of the common people, create the despot out of that one among their number whose soul is itself under the most tyrannical despotism.

Yes, such a state of mind would naturally be his best qualification.

All goes smoothly if men are ready to submit. But the country may resist; and then, just as he began by calling his father and mother to order, so now he will discipline his once loved fatherland, or motherland as the Cretans call it, and see that it shall live in subjection to the newfound partisans he has called in to enslave it. So this man's desires come to their fulfilment.

Yes, that is true.

In private life, before they gain power, men of this stamp either consort with none but parasites ready to do them any service, or, if they have a favour to beg, they will not hesitate themselves to cringe and posture in simulated friendliness, which soon cools off when their end is gained. So, throughout life, the despotic character has not a friend in the world; he is sometimes master, sometimes slave, but never knows true friendship or freedom. There is no faithfulness in him; and, if we were right in our notion of justice, he is the perfect example of the unjust man.

Certainly.

CHAPTER XXXIII (IX 576B-588A)

THE JUST AND THE UNJUST LIVES
COMPARED IN RESPECT OF
HAPPINESS

By tracing the portraits of the philosopher-king and of the despot, Socrates has now set in contrast the ideally just man and the ideally unjust, in response to the original demand of Glaucon and Adeimantus (Chap. V). It remains to point out which life is the happiest. Three arguments are advanced.

(1) The man whose soul is under the despotism of a master passion is the unhappiest by three tests of well-being: freedom, wealth, and security from fear. His unlimited licence to 'do what he likes' is not genuine freedom, which consists in doing what the true, i.e. the reasonable, self wills for the good of the whole man. (In the Gorgias 446 ff. Socrates argues against Polus that the autocrat is least of all men able to do what he wills in this sense.) No man is rich whose desires can never be satisfied. The despot, moreover, as the enemy of mankind, must live haunted by fear.

(2) When the two lives are compared in respect of pleasantness, the best judge is the philosopher, who alone has experienced the peculiar pleasures of all three parts of the soul, and whose experience is supported by insight and reasoning. (It appears here, more clearly than elsewhere, that each part of the soul has its characteristic desire, and that desires are defined by differences in their objects. This fits in with the suggestion at 485 D that desire is a single fund of energy which can be turned from one object to another 'like a stream diverted into another bed.')

(3) The third proof· turns on the distinction between pure or positive

pleasure and pleasure which is illusory because exaggerated by contrast with a preceding pain of want. Thus the pleasure of eating is enhanced by the pain of hunger which it relieves; and this is said to be true of most sensual pleasures, but not (it is implied) of the pleasures enjoyed by the soul independently of the body. Intellectual satisfactions are also more real, in proportion as the mind and the truth it feeds on are more real than the body and its earthly food. The despot, being enslaved to the lowest of all desires and appetites, is at the farthest remove from the pure and real pleasures accessible to the philosophic ruler. (The distinctions between true and false, or pure and mixed, pleasures are drawn in greater detail in the PHILEBUS.)

To sum up, then: this worst type of man is he who behaves in waking life as we said men do in their dreams. The born despot who gains absolute power must come to this, and the longer he lives as a tyrant, the more this character grows upon him.

Inevitably, said Glaucon, who now took his turn to answer.

Now shall we find that the lowest depth of wickedness goes with the lowest depth of unhappiness, and that the misery of the despot is really in proportion to the extent and duration of his power, though the mass of mankind may hold many different opinions?

Yes, that much is certain.

It is true, is it not? that each type of individual — the despotic, the democratic, and so on — resembles the state with the corresponding type of constitution, and will be good and happy in a corresponding degree.

Yes, of course.

In point of excellence, then, how does a state under a despotism com-

pare with the one governed by kings, such as we first described?

They are at opposite extremes: the best and the worst.

I shall not ask which is which, for that is obvious. Is your estimate the same with respect to their degrees of happiness or misery? We must not let our eyes be dazzled by fixing them only on the despot himself and some few of his supporters; we should not decide until we have looked into every corner and inspected the life of the whole community.

That is a fair demand. Everyone must see that a state is most wretched under a despot and happiest under a true king.

And in judging between the corresponding individuals, is it not equally fair to demand the verdict of one who is not dazzled, like a child, by the outward pomp and parade of absolute power, but whose understanding can enter into a man's heart and see all that goes on within? Should we not all do well to listen to such a competent judge, if he had also lived under the same roof and witnessed the despot's behaviour, not only in the emergencies of public life, but towards intimates in his own household, where he can best be seen stripped of his theatrical garb? We might then ask for a report on the happiness or misery of the despot as compared with the rest of the world.

Yes, that would be perfectly fair.

Shall we, then, make believe that we ourselves are qualified to judge from having been in contact with despots, so that we may have someone to answer our questions? [41]

By all means.

Bearing in mind, then, the analogy

[41] Plato, it is generally agreed, here implies that he himself is qualified to judge by his experience of living at the court of Dionysius I of Syracuse on his first visit to the West in 388/7 B.C.

between state and individual, you shall tell me what you think of the condition of each in turn. To begin with the state: is it free under a despot, or enslaved?

Utterly enslaved.

And yet you see it contains some who are masters and free men.

Yes, a few; but almost the whole of it, including the most respectable part, is degraded to a miserable slavery.

If the individual, then, is analogous to the state, we shall find the same order of things in him: a soul labouring under the meanest servitude, the best elements in it being enslaved, while a small part, which is also the most frenzied and corrupt, plays the master. Would you call such a condition of the soul freedom or slavery?

Slavery, of course.

And just as a state enslaved to a tyrant cannot do what it really wishes, so neither can a soul under a similar tyranny do what it wishes as a whole. Goaded on against its will by the sting of desire, it will be filled with confusion and remorse. Like the corresponding state, it must always be poverty-stricken, unsatisfied, and haunted by fear. Nowhere else will there be so much lamentation, groaning, and anguish as in a country under a despotism, and in a soul maddened by the tyranny of passion and lust.

It cannot be otherwise.

These, I think, were the considerations that made you judge such a state to be the most unhappy of all.

Was I not right?

Certainly. But, in view of the same facts, what would you say of the despotic type of individual?

That he is by far the most miserable of men.

There I think you are wrong. You will perhaps agree that there is a still lower depth of misery, to be found in a man of this temperament who has not the good fortune to remain in a private station but is thrust by circum-stance into the position of an actual despot.

Judging by what we have said already, I should think that must be true.

Yes; but this is the most important of all questions, the choice between a good and an evil life; and we must be content with nothing short of a reasoned conviction. Am I right in thinking that some light may be gained from considering those wealthy private individuals who own a large number of slaves? In that respect they are like the despot, though his subjects are still more numerous. Now, as you know, they do not live in terror of their servants.

No; what have they to fear?

Nothing. But do you see why?

Yes; it is because the individual is protected by the whole community.

True; but imagine a man owning fifty or more slaves, miraculously caught up with his wife and children and planted, along with all his household goods and servants, in some desert place where there were no freemen to come to his rescue. Would he not be horribly afraid that his servants would make away with him and his family? He would be driven to fawn upon some of the slaves with liberal promises and give them their freedom, much against his will. So he would become a parasite, dependent on his own henchmen.

That would be his only way to escape destruction.

Moreover, the place he was transported to might be surrounded by neighbours who would not tolerate the claims of one man to lord it over others, but would retaliate fiercely on anyone they caught in such an attempt.

In that case he would be in still more desperate straits, hemmed in on all sides by enemies.

Is not that a picture of the prison to which the despot is confined? His nature is such as we have described, infested with all manner of fears and lusts. However curious he may be, he alone can never travel abroad to attend the great festivals which every freeman wants to witness, but must live like a woman ensconced in the recesses of his house, envying his countrymen who can leave their homes to see what is worth seeing in foreign lands. You spoke just now of the despotic character, ill governed in his own soul, as the most miserable of men; but these disadvantages I have mentioned add to his wretchedness when he is driven by ill luck out of his private station to become an actual despot and undertake to rule others when he is not his own master. You might as well force a paralytic to leave the sheltered life of an invalid and spend his days in fighting or in trials of physical strength.

Quite true, Socrates; that is a fair comparison.

So the despot's condition, my dear Glaucon, is supremely wretched, even harder than the life you pronounced the hardest of all. Whatever people may think, the actual tyrant is really the most abject slave, a parasite of the vilest scoundrels. Never able to satisfy his desires, he is always in need, and, to an eye that sees a soul in its entirety, he will seem the poorest of the poor. His condition is like that of the country he governs, haunted throughout life by terrors and convulsed with anguish. Add to this what we said before, that power is bound to exaggerate every fault and make him ever more envious, treacherous, unjust, friendless, impure, harbouring every vice in his bosom, and hence only less of a calamity to all about him than he is to himself.

No man of sense will dispute that.

Then the time has come for you, as the final judge in this competition, to decide who stands first in point of happiness and to arrange in order all our five types of character, the kingly, the timocratic, the oligarchic, the democratic, the despotic.

The decision is easy. In respect both of goodness and of happiness I range them in the order in which they have entered the lists.

Shall we hire a herald, then, or shall I myself proclaim that, in the judgment of the son of Ariston, the happiest man is he who is first in goodness and justice, namely the true king who is also king over himself; and the most miserable is that lowest example of injustice and vice, the born despot whose tyranny prevails in his own soul and also over his country.

Yes, you may proclaim that.

May I add that it would make no difference if the true character of both should remain unknown to heaven and to mankind?

You may.

Very well, said I; that may stand as one of our proofs. But I want to consider a second one, which can, I think, be based on our division of the soul into three parts, corresponding to the three orders in the state. Each part seems to me to have its own form of pleasure and its peculiar desire; and any one of the three may govern the soul.

How do you mean?

There was the part with which a man gains knowledge and understanding, and another whereby he shows spirit. The third was so multifarious that we could find no single appropriate name; we called it after its chief and most powerful characteristic 'appetite,' because of the intensity of all the appetites connected with eating and drinking and sex and so on. We also called it money-loving, because money is the principal means of satisfying desires of this kind. Gain is the source of its pleasures and the object of its affection; so 'money-loving' or 'gain-loving' might be the best single expression to sum up the nature of this part of the soul for the purpose of our discussion.

I agree.

The spirited element, again, we think of as wholly bent upon winning power and victory and a good name. So we might call it honour-loving or ambitious.

Very suitably.

Whereas the part whereby we gain knowledge and understanding is least of all concerned with wealth or reputation. Obviously its sole endeavor is to know the truth, and we may speak of it as loving knowledge and philosophic.

Quite so.

And the human soul is sometimes governed by this principle, sometimes by one of the other two, as the case may be. Hence we recognise three main classes of men, the philosophic, the ambitious, and the lovers of gain. So there will also be three corresponding forms of pleasure.

Certainly.

Now, if you choose to ask men of these three types, which of their lives is the pleasantest, each in turn will praise his own above the rest. The man of business will say that, as compared with profit-making, the pleasures of winning a high reputation or of learning are worthless, except in so far as they bring in money. The ambitious man will despise the pleasure derived from money as vulgar, and the pleasure of learning, if it does not bring fame, as moonshine. The philosopher, again, will think that the satisfaction of knowing the truth and always gaining fresh understanding is beyond all comparison with those other pleasures, which he will call 'necessary' in the fullest sense; for he would have no use for them, if they were not unavoidable. In this dispute about the pleasures of each class and as to which of the three lives as a whole is not merely better

and nobler but actually pleasanter or less painful, how is one to know whose judgment is the truest?

I am not prepared to say.

Well, think of it in this way. What is required for a sound judgment? Can it rest on any better foundation than experience, or insight, or reasoning?

Surely not.

Take experience, then. Which of our three men has the fullest acquaintance with all the pleasures we have mentioned? Has the lover of gain such an understanding of the truth as to know by experience the pleasure of knowledge better than the philosopher knows the pleasure of gain?

No, all the advantage lies with the philosopher, who cannot help experiencing both the other kinds of pleasure from childhood up; whereas the lover of gain is under no necessity to taste the sweetness of understanding the truth of things; rather he would not find it easy to gain that experience, however hard he should try.

In experience of both sorts of pleasure, then, the philosopher has the advantage over the lover of gain. How does he compare with the ambitious man? Is he less well acquainted with the pleasures of honour than the other is with the pleasures of wisdom?

No, honour comes to them all, if they accomplish their several purposes; the rich man is esteemed by many people, and so are the brave man and the wise. So the pleasure of being honoured is familiar to them all; but only the philosopher can know how sweet it is to contemplate the truth.

Then, so far as experience goes, he is the best judge of the three.

Yes, by far.

And the only one in whom experience is seconded by insight.[42]

---

[42] Insight or intelligence will help him to learn more from a less amount of experience.

Yes.

Further, we agreed that the decision must be reached by means of reasoning; and this is peculiarly the tool of the philosopher, not of the money-lover or of the ambitious man.

No doubt.

Now, if wealth and profit were the most satisfactory criteria, the judgments of value passed by the lover of gain would be nearest to the truth; and if honour, courage, and success were the test, the best judge would be the man who lives for honour and victory; but since the tests are experience, insight, and reasoning—?

The truest values must be those approved by the philosopher, who uses reason for the pursuit of wisdom.

Of the three kinds of pleasure, then, the sweetest will belong to that part of the soul whereby we gain understanding and knowledge, and the man in whom that part predominates will have the pleasantest life.

It must be so; in praising his own life the wise man speaks with authority.

What life or form of pleasure will this judge rank second?

Obviously, that of the warlike and ambitious temperament. It comes nearer than the business man's to his own.

And the pleasure of gain will come last, it seems.

Surely.

So now the just man has scored a second victory over the unjust. There remains the third round, for which the wrestlers at the Great Games invoke Olympian Zeus, the Preserver; [43] and

a fall in this bout should be decisive. I seem to have heard some wise man say that only the pleasures of intelligence are entirely true and pure; all the others are illusory.

That should settle the matter. But what does it mean?

I shall discover the meaning, if you will help me by answering my questions. We speak of pain as the contrary of pleasure. Is there not also a neutral state between the two, in which the mind feels neither pleasure nor pain, but is as it were at rest from both?

Yes.

Well, you must have heard people say, when they are ill, that nothing is pleasanter than to be well, though they never knew it until they were ill; and people in great pain will tell you that relief from pain is the greatest pleasure in the world. There are many such cases in which you find the sufferer saying that the height of pleasure is not positive enjoyment, but the peace which comes with the absence of pain.

Yes; I suppose at such moments the state of rest becomes pleasurable and all that can be desired.

In the same way, then, when enjoyment comes to an end, the cessation of pleasure will be painful.

I suppose so.

If so, that state of rest which, we said, lies between pleasure and pain, will be sometimes one, sometimes the other. But if it is neither of the two, how can it become both?

I do not think it can.

And besides, both pleasure and pain are processes of change [44] which take place in the mind, are they not? whereas the neutral condition ap-

---

[43] At banquets the third libation was offered to Zeus the Preserver. This passage seems to imply that competitors at the Olympic Games had a corresponding custom. Plato is fond of quoting the phrase 'the third (libation) to the Preserver,' where his arguments culminate at the third stage.

[44] Plato is thinking specially of pleasures, like that of satisfying hunger, which accompany the physical process of restoring the normal (neutral) state, which has been depleted with accompanying pain.

peared to be a state of rest between the two. So can it be right to regard the absence of pain as pleasant or the absence of enjoyment as painful?

No, it cannot.

It follows, then, that the state of rest is not really either pleasant or painful, but only appears so in these cases by contrast. There is no soundness in these appearances; by the standard of true pleasure they are a sort of imposture.

That seems to be the conclusion.

You might be tempted, in these instances, to suppose that pleasure is the same thing as relief from pain, and pain the same as the cessation of pleasure; but, as an instance to the contrary, consider pleasures which do not follow on pain. There are plenty of them; the best example is the pleasures of smell. These occur suddenly with extraordinary intensity; they are not preceded by any pain and they leave no pain behind when they cease.

Quite true.

We are not to be persuaded, then, that relief from pain is the same thing as pure pleasure, or cessation of pleasure the same as pure pain.

No.

On the other hand, the class of pleasures which do involve some sort of relief from pain may be said to include the great majority and the most intense of all the pleasures, so called, which reach the mind by way of the body; and the same description applies to the pleasures or pains of anticipation which precede them.

Yes.

Here is an analogy, to illustrate their nature. You think of the world as divided into an upper region and a lower, with a centre between them.[45] Now if a person were transported from below to the centre, he would be sure

to think he was moving 'upwards'; and when he was stationed at the centre and looking in the direction he had come from, he would imagine he was in the upper region, if he had never seen the part which is really above the centre. And supposing he were transported back again, he would think he was travelling 'downwards,' and this time he would be right. His mistake would be due to his ignorance of the real distinctions between the upper and lower regions and the centre.

Clearly.

You will not be surprised, then, if people whose ignorance of truth and reality gives them many unsound ideas, are similarly confused about pleasure and pain and the intermediate state. When the movement is towards a painful condition, they are right in believing that the pain is real; but when they are passing from a state of pain to the neutral point, they are firmly convinced that they are approaching the pleasure of complete satisfaction. In their ignorance of true pleasure, they are deceived by the contrast between pain and the absence of pain, just as one who had never seen white might be deceived by the contrast between black and grey.

Certainly; I should be much more surprised if it were not so.

Then look at it in this way. As hunger and thirst are states of bodily inanition, which can be replenished by food, so ignorance and unwisdom in the soul are an emptiness to be filled by gaining understanding. Of the two sorts of nourishment, will not the more real yield the truer satisfaction?

Clearly.

Which kind of nourishment, then, has the higher claim to pure reality—food-stuffs like bread and meat and drink, or such things as true belief, knowledge, reason, and in a word all the excellences of the mind? You may decide by asking yourself whether

---

[45] A popular view, adopted for purposes of illustration here, but corrected at *Timeaus* 62 c.

something which is closely connected with the unchanging and immortal world of truth and itself shares that nature together with the thing in which it exists, has more or less reality than something which, like the thing which contains it, belongs to a world of mortality and perpetual change.

No doubt it is much more real.

And a higher or lower degree of reality goes with a greater or less measure of knowledge and so of truth.[46]

Necessarily.

And is there not, to speak generally, less of truth and reality in the things which serve the needs of the body than in those which feed the soul?

Much less.

And, again, less in the body itself than in the soul?

Certainly.

And in proportion as the sustenance and the thing sustained by it are more real, the satisfaction itself is a more real satisfaction.

Of course.

Accordingly, if the appropriate satisfaction of natural needs constitutes pleasure, there will be more real enjoyment of true pleasure in such a case; whereas in the opposite case the satisfaction is not so genuine or secure and the pleasure is less true and trustworthy.

Inevitably.

To conclude, then: those who have no experience of wisdom and virtue and spend their whole time in feasting and self-indulgence are all their lives, as it were, fluctuating downwards from the central point and back to it again, but never rise beyond it into the true upper region, to which they have not lifted their eyes. Never really satisfied with real nourishment, the pleasure they taste is uncertain and impure. Bent over their tables, they feed like cattle with stooping heads and eyes fixed upon the ground; so they grow fat and breed, and in their greedy struggle kick and butt one another to death with horns and hoofs of steel, because they can never satisfy with unreal nourishment that part of themselves which is itself unreal and incapable of lasting satisfaction.

Your description of the way most people live is quite in the oracular style, Socrates.

Does it not follow that the pleasures of such a life are illusory phantoms of real pleasure, in which pleasure and pain are so combined that each takes its colour and apparent intensity by contrast with the other? Hence the frenzied desire they implant in the breasts of fools, who fight for them as Stesichorus says the combatants at Troy fought, in their blindness, for a phantom Helen.[47]

Yes, that is bound to be so.

Take, again, the satisfaction of the spirited element in our nature. Must not that be no less illusory, when a man seeks, at all costs, to gratify his ambition by envy, his love of victory

---

[46] The text here is corrupt and much disputed. With the slight change of $\epsilon\iota$ to $\hat{\eta}$ at 585 c 12 the MS. text can be literally rendered as follows: 'And does the substance of an always unchanging thing partake any more of reality than of knowledge? — No. — Or of truth? — No. (In other words, the substance of an always unchanging thing partakes of knowledge and so of truth *just as much as* it does of reality.) $\hat{\eta}$ δὲ (sc. οὐσία) ἀληθείας ἧττον (μετέχει) οὐ χαὶ οὐσίας (ἧττον μετέχει); And does not the substance which partakes less of truth, also partake less of reality? — Necessarily.' ('To partake of knowledge' here seems to mean 'to be knowable.')

[47] At *Phaedrus* 243 A Plato refers to the legend that the poet Stesichorus, divinely punished with blindness for defaming Helen, regained his sight only by writing a recantation declaring that she never went to Troy, but was all the while in Egypt. Euripides' *Helen* is based on this story.

by violence, and his ill-temper by outbursts of passion, without sense or reason?

It must.

What then? May we boldly assert that all the desires both of the gain-loving and of the ambitious part of our nature will win the truest pleasures of which they are capable, if they accept the guidance of knowledge and reason and pursue only those pleasures which wisdom approves? Such pleasures will be true, because truth is their guide, and will also be proper to their nature, if it is a fact that a thing always finds in what is best for it something akin to its real self.

Well, that is certainly a fact.

To conclude, then, each part of the soul will not only do its own work and be just when the whole soul, with no inward conflict, follows the guidance of the wisdom-loving part, but it also will enjoy the pleasures that are proper to it and the best and truest of which it is capable; [48] whereas if either of the other two parts gains the upper hand, besides failing to find its own proper pleasure, it will force the others to pursue a false pleasure uncongenial to their nature.

Yes.

Now would not these evil effects be most of all produced by the elements farthest removed from philosophy and reason, that is to say, from subordination to law? Such, we have seen, are the lustful and despotic appetites; whereas the orderly and kingly desires stand nearest to the controlling reason. Accordingly, the despot is at the farthest remove from the true pleasure proper to man's nature, and his life is the least pleasant, in contrast with the king's, who stands at the opposite extreme. Have you any notion how much less pleasant it is?

[48] Not that Plato does not hold that lower desires should be altogether suppressed or mortified.

There are, it seems, three kinds of pleasure, one genuine and two spurious.[49] The despot, in his flight from law and reason, goes beyond the bounds even of the spurious kinds, to surround himself with pleasures comparable to a bodyguard of slaves.[50] The measure of his inferiority can hardly be expressed, unless perhaps in this way. The despot, you remember, was at the third remove from the oligarch; for the democratic man came between. If that was right, the pleasure he enjoys will be a phantom three times less real than the oligarch's. And the oligarch himself was third in rank below the king, if we identify kingship with the rule of the best. So the number representing the distance that separates this phantom pleasure of the despot from reality will be three times three; and when that number is squared and cubed, calculation will show how great the interval becomes. Conversely, you will find that, in respect of truth and reality, the kingly life is seven hundred and twenty-nine times the pleasanter, and the despot's more painful by the same amount.[51]

I feel quite overwhelmed by your estimate of the difference between the just and unjust man, on the score of pleasure and pain.

All the same, my figure is correct and applicable to the lives of men as surely as the reckoning of days and

[49] Corresponding to the three parts of the soul and to the king, the timocrat, and the oligarch.

[50] As described at 573 D.

[51] The translation here simplifies the text, which is perhaps intentionally obscure. It is not explained why 9 is to be raised to the third power, 729. J. A. Stewart, *Myths of Plato*, 349, notes the importance attached later to this number which is the square of 27 as well as the cube of 9. Plutarch makes it the number of the Sun (*de anim. proc.* 31), which stands for Reason (*nous*) in *de fac. in orbe lunae*, 28.

nights, months, and years.[52] And if the good and just man is so far superior to the bad and unjust in point of pleasure, there is no saying by how much more his life will surpass the other's in grace, nobility, and virtue.

I entirely agree.

CHAPTER XXXIV (IX. 588 B-592 B)

JUSTICE, NOT INJUSTICE
IS PROFITABLE

Socrates now gives the final answer to Thrasymachus' contention, restated in Glaucon's opening speech at 360 E ff., that injustice pays when it goes unpunished. The question of rewards and punishments after death, expressly excluded at the outset, is still reserved for the closing myth in Chapter XL.

This chapter ends with a doubt whether the ideal state can ever be founded on earth. There is more hope that, here and there, some man may come near to realizing the ideal of justice in the economy of his own soul. Plato had before him the example of Socrates himself, the one man he knew who seemed to have found complete happiness in 'living well.'

Good, said I. And now that the argument has brought us to this point, let us recall something that was said at the outset, namely, if I remember aright, that wrongdoing is profitable when a man is completely unjust but has a reputation for justice.

[52] According to Censorinus *de die nat.* 18–19 (Diels-Kranz, *Vors.*[5] 44 A 22) the Pythagorean Philolaus reckoned 364½ days (and presumably the same number of nights) to the year, and 2 × 364½ = 729. This may explain 'days and nights.' He had also a 'great year' of 729 months. These numerical correspondences between macrocosm and microcosm, which seem to us fantastic, may not be literally meant, but they cannot have been mere nonsense to Plato.

Yes, that position was stated.

Well, we are now agreed about the real meaning and consequences of doing wrong as well as of doing right, and the time has come to point out to anyone who maintains that position what his statement implies. We may do so by likening the soul to one of those many fabulous monsters said to have existed long ago, such as the Chimaera or Scylla or Cerberus, which combined the forms of several creatures in one. Imagine, to begin with, the figure of a multifarious and many-headed beast, girt round with heads of animals, tame and wild, which it can grow out of itself and transform at will.

That would tax the skill of a sculptor; but luckily the stuff of imagination is easier to mould than wax.

Now add two other forms, a lion and a man. The many-headed beast is to be the largest by far, and the lion next to it in size. Then join them in such a way that the three somehow grow together into one. Lastly, mould the outside into the likeness of one of them, the man, so that, to eyes which cannot see inside the outward sheath, the whole may look like a single creature, a human being.

Very well. What then?

We can now reply to anyone who says that for this human creature wrongdoing pays and there is nothing to be gained by doing right. This simply means, we shall tell him, that it pays to feed up and strengthen the composite beast and all that belongs to the lion, and to starve the man till he is so enfeebled that the other two can drag him whither they will, and he cannot bring them to live together in peace, but must leave them to bite and struggle and devour one another. On the other hand, to declare that justice pays is to assert that all our words and actions should tend towards giving the man within us complete mastery over the whole human creature, and letting him take the many-headed beast under his care and tame its wildness, like the gardener who trains his cherished plants while he checks the growth of weeds. He should enlist the lion as his ally, and, caring for all alike, should foster their growth by first reconciling them to one another and to himself.

Yes, such are the implications when justice or injustice is commended.

From every point of view, then, whether of pleasure or reputation or advantage, one who praises justice speaks the truth; he who disparages it does not know what it is that he idly condemns.

I agree; he has no conception.

But his error is not wilful; so let us reason with him gently. We will ask him on what grounds conduct has come to be approved or disapproved by law and custom. Is it not according as conduct tends to subdue the brutish parts of our nature to the human—perhaps I should rather say to the divine in us—or to enslave our humanity to the savagery of the beast? Will he agree?

Yes, if he has any regard for my opinion.

On that showing, then, can it profit a man to take money unjustly, if he is thereby enslaving the best part of his nature to the vilest? No amount of money could make it worth his while to sell a son or daughter as slaves into the hands of cruel and evil men; and when it is a matter of ruthlessly subjugating all that is most godlike in himself to whatsoever is most ungodly and despicable, is not the wretch taking a bribe far more disastrous than the necklace Eriphyle took as the price of her husband's life? [53]

[53] Eriphyle was bribed with a necklace by Polynices to persuade her husband, the seer Amphiaraos, to become one of the seven champions who made war on Thebes and of whom all but one lost their lives.

Far more, said Glaucon, if I may answer on his behalf.

You will agree, too, with the reasons why certain faults have always been condemned: profligacy, because it gives too much license to the multiform monster; self-will and ill temper, when the lion and serpent [54] part of us is strengthened till its sinews are overstrung: luxury and effeminacy, because they relax those sinews till the heart grows faint; flattery and meanness, in that the heart's high spirit is subordinated to the turbulent beast, and for the sake of money to gratify the creature's insatiable greed the lion is browbeaten and schooled from youth up to become an ape. Why, again, is mechanical toil discredited as debasing? Is it not simply when the highest thing in a man's nature is naturally so weak that it cannot control the animal parts but can only learn how to pamper them?

I suppose so.

Then, if we say that people of this sort ought to be subject to the highest type of man, we intend that the subject should be governed, not, as Thrasymachus thought, to his own detriment, but on the same principle as his superior, who is himself governed by the divine element within him. It is better for everyone, we believe, to be subject to a power of godlike wisdom residing within himself, or, failing that, imposed from without, in order that all of us, being under one guidance, may be so far as possible equal and united. This, moreover, is plainly the intention of the law in lending its support to every member of the community, and also of the government of children; for we allow them to go free only when we have established in each one of them as it were a constitutional ruler, whom we have trained to take over the guardianship

[54] The serpent, perhaps a symbol of cunning, occurs here only (if the text is sound).

from the same principle in ourselves.

True.

On what ground, then, can we say that it is profitable for a man to be unjust or self-indulgent or to do any disgraceful act which will make him a worse man, though he may gain money and power? Or how can it profit the wrongdoer to escape detection and punishment? He will only grow still worse; whereas if he is found out, chastisement will tame the brute in him and lay it to rest, while the gentler part is set free; and thus the entire soul, restored to its native soundness, will gain, in the temperance and righteousness which wisdom brings, a condition more precious than the strength and beauty which health brings to the body, in proportion as the soul itself surpasses the body in worth. To this end the man of understanding will bend all his powers through life, prizing in the first place those studies only which will fashion these qualities in his soul; and, so far from abandoning the care of his bodily condition to the irrational pleasures of the brute and setting his face in that direction, he will not even make health his chief object. Health, strength, and beauty he will value only in so far as they bring soundness of mind, and you will find him keeping his bodily frame in tune always for the sake of the resulting concord in the soul.

Yes, if he is to have true music in him.

And in the matter of acquiring wealth he will order his life in harmony with the same purpose. He will not be carried away by the vulgar notion of happiness into heaping up an unbounded store which would bring him endless troubles. Rather, in adding to or spending his substance, he will, to the best of his power, be guided by watchful care that neither want nor abundance may unsettle the constitution set up in his soul. Again, in accepting power and honours he will keep the same end in view, ready to enjoy any position in public or private life which he thinks will make him a better man, and avoiding any that would break down the established order within him.

Then, if that is his chief concern, he will have no wish to take part in politics.

Indeed he will, in the politics of his own commonwealth, though not perhaps in those of his country, unless some miraculous chance should come about.

I understand, said Glaucon: you mean this commonwealth we have been founding in the realm of discourse; for I think it nowhere exists on earth.

No, I replied; but perhaps there is a pattern set up in the heavens [55] for one who desires to see it and, seeing it, to found one in himself. But whether it exists anywhere or ever will exist is no matter; for this is the only commonwealth in whose politics he can ever take part.

I suspect you are right.

[55] 'The heavens' probably means the visible order (cosmos) of the universe (sometimes called 'the heaven') and in particular of the heavenly bodies, which preserves the stars from wrong and manifests, though imperfectly, the divine order which the philosopher tries to reproduce in himself (500 B ff. Cf. the account of the Astronomer-Guardians in *Laws* xii. 965 ff.). The word has not the Christian associations of 'heaven' or of the kingdom of heaven. But this passage inspired both Stoics and Christians with the idea of the City of God.

Aristotle (384–323 B.C.)

Aristotle was born in Stagira, Thrace, the son of the court physician to Amnytas II, King of Macedonia, father of Philip the Great. At the age of 18, Aristotle came to the Academy in Athens where he remained as a student of Plato for twenty years, until the latter's death in 348-7 B.C. Following this, he traveled, doing research work and occasionally teaching. In 343-2, he became tutor to the thirteen-year-old Alexander (later Alexander the Great). The instruction lasted about three years, until Alexander became of age and was appointed regent for his father, Philip. There is little or no reason to suppose that Aristotle's relation to Alexander had any effect upon the conqueror's character or policies. It was not until 335–4 that Aristotle returned to Athens. For twelve years after his return, Aristotle devoted himself to the establishment of his school, the Lyceum, in which a remarkable program of investigation and instruction was carried forward in almost every field of inquiry. During this period Aristotle wrote voluminously. Unfortunately none of his published writings remain, but the evidence indicates that they were, following Plato, in the dialogue form. His extant writings have been regarded generally as lecture notes, probably worked up in consultation with, or edited by, his advanced students. In 323, at the death of Alexander the Great, the Athenians rebelled against the Macedonians. Because of his association with Alexander, Aristotle was under fire. A charge of impiety was brought against him, but he fled Athens lest, as he is alleged to have said, Athens sin twice against philosophy. The *Nicomachean Ethics*, from which the material below is taken, is one of three ethical treatises that remain; it is of unquestioned authenticity. The *Magna Moralia* is most probably spurious and bears the mark of much later composition during the third or the second century B.C. The *Eudemian Ethics* has often been regarded as the work of Aristotle's pupil Eudemus, but it is possible that both the *Eudemian* and the *Nicomachean Ethics* are editions, by Eudemus and Nicomachus respectively, of two distinct courses given by Aristotle. In any case, the *Nicomachean Ethics* is to be considered as the first part of a treatise of which the *Politics* is the concluding section.

THE NICOMACHEAN ETHICS [1]

BOOK I

THE GOOD FOR MAN

1. Every art and every inquiry, and similarly every action and pursuit, is thought to aim at some good; and for this reason the good has rightly been declared [2] to be that at which all things aim. But a certain difference is found among ends; some are activities, others are products apart from the activities that produce them.

[1] From Aristotle's *The Nicomachean Ethics*, translated by W. D. Ross, with the permission of The Clarendon Press, Oxford. Footnotes are by the translator.

[2] Perhaps by Eudoxus.

Where there are ends apart from the actions, it is the nature of the products to be better than the activities. Now, as there are many actions, arts, and sciences, their ends also are many; the end of the medical art is health, that of shipbuilding a vessel, that of strategy victory, that of economics wealth. But where such arts fall under a single capacity—as bridlemaking and the other arts concerned with the equipment of horses fall under the art of riding, and this and every military action under strategy, in the same way other arts fall under yet others—in all of these the ends of the master arts are to be preferred to all the subordinate ends; for it is for the sake of the former that the latter are pursued. It makes no difference whether the activities themselves are the ends of the actions, or something else apart from the activities, as in the case of the sciences just mentioned.

2. If, then, there is some end of the things we do, which we desire for its own sake (everything else being desired for the sake of this), and if we do not choose everything for the sake of something else (for at that rate the process would go on to infinity, so that our desire would be empty and vain), clearly this must be the good and the chief good. Will not the knowledge of it, then, have a great influence on life? Shall we not, like archers who have a mark to aim at, be more likely to hit upon what is right? If so, we must try, in outline at least to determine what it is, and of which of the sciences or capacities it is the object. It would seem to belong to the most authoritative art and that which is most truly the master art. And politics appears to be of this nature; for it is this that ordains which of the sciences should be studied in a state, and which each class of citizens should learn and up

to what point they should learn them; and we see even the most highly esteemed of capacities to fall under this, e.g. strategy, economics, rhetoric; now, since politics uses the rest of the sciences, and since, again, it legislates as to what we are to do and what we are to abstain from, the end of this science must include those of the others, so that this end must be the good for man. For even if the end is the same for a single man and for a state, that of the state seems at all events something greater and more complete whether to attain or to preserve; though it is worth while to attain the end merely for one man, it is finer and more godlike to attain it for a nation or for city-states. These, then, are the ends at which our inquiry aims, since it is political science, in one sense of that term.

3. Our discussion will be adequate if it has as much clearness as the subject-matter admits of, for precision is not to be sought for alike in all discussions, any more than in all the products of the crafts. Now fine and just actions, which political science investigates, admit of much variety and fluctuation of opinion, so that they may be thought to exist only by convention, and not by nature. And goods also give rise to similar fluctuation because they bring harm to many people; for before now men have been undone by reason of their wealth, and others by reason of their courage. We must be content, then, in speaking of such subjects and with such premises to indicate the truth roughly and in outline, and in speaking about things which are only for the most part true and with premises of the same kind to reach conclusions that are no better. In the same spirit, therefore, should each type of statement be *received;* for it is the mark of an educated man

to look for precision in each class of things just so far as the nature of the subject admits; it is evidently equally foolish to accept probable reasoning from a mathematician and to demand from a rhetorician scientific proofs.

Now each man judges well the things he knows, and of these he is a good judge. And so the man who has been educated in a subject is a good judge of that subject, and the man who has received an all-round education is a good judge in general. Hence a young man is not a proper hearer of lectures on political science; for he is inexperienced in the actions that occur in life, but its discussions start from these and are about these; and, further, since he tends to follow his passions, his study will be vain and unprofitable, because the end aimed at is not knowledge but action. And it makes no difference whether he is young in years or youthful in character; the defect does not depend on time, but on his living, and pursuing each successive object, as passion directs. For to such persons, as to the incontinent, knowledge brings no profit; but to those who desire and act in accordance with a rational principle knowledge about such matters will be of great benefit.

These remarks about the student, the sort of treatment to be expected, and the purpose of the inquiry, may be taken as our preface.

4. Let us resume our inquiry and state, in view of the fact that all knowledge and every pursuit aims at some good, what it is that we say political science aims at and what is the highest of all goods achievable by action. Verbally there is very general agreement; for both the general run of men and people of superior refinement say that it is happiness, and identify living well and doing well with being happy; but with regard to what happiness is they differ, and the many do not give the same account as the wise. For the former think it is some plain and obvious thing, like pleasure, wealth, or honour; they differ, however, from one another—and often even the same man identifies it with different things, with health when he is ill, with wealth when he is poor; but, conscious of their ignorance, they admire those who proclaim some great ideal that is above their comprehension. Now some [3] thought that apart from these many goods there is another which is self-subsistent and causes the goodness of all these as well. To examine all the opinions that have been held were perhaps somewhat fruitless; enough to examine those that are most prevalent or that seem to be arguable.

Let us not fail to notice, however, that there is a difference between arguments from and those to the first principles. For Plato, too, was right in raising this question and asking, as he used to do, 'are we on the way from or to the first principles?' [4] There is a difference, as there is in a race course between the course from the judges to the turning-point and the way back. For, while we must begin with what is known, things are objects of knowledge in two senses—some to us, some without qualification. Presumably, then, we must begin with things known to *us*. Hence any one who is to listen intelligently to lectures about what is noble and just and, generally, about the subjects of political science must have been brought up in good habits. For the fact is the starting-point, and if this is sufficiently plain to him, he will not at the start need the reason as well; and the man who has been well brought up has or can easily get starting-points. And as for him who neither has nor can get them, let him hear the words of Hesiod:

[3] The Platonic School.
[4] Cf. *Rep.* 511 B.

Far best is he who knows all things
  himself;
Good, he that hearkens when men counsel
  right;
But he who neither knows, nor lays to
  heart
Another's wisdom, is a useless wight.

5. Let us, however, resume our discussion from the point at which we digressed. To judge from the lives that men lead, most men, and men of the most vulgar type, seem (not without some ground) to identify the good, or happiness, with pleasure; which is the reason why they love the life of enjoyment. For there are, we may say, three prominent types of life—that just mentioned, the political, and thirdly the contemplative life. Now the mass of mankind are evidently quite slavish in their tastes, preferring a life suitable to beasts, but they get some ground for their view from the fact that many of those in high places share the tastes of Sardanapallus. A consideration of the prominent types of life shows that people of superior refinement and of active disposition identify happiness with honour; for this is, roughly speaking, the end of the political life. But it seems too superficial to be what we are looking for, since it is thought to depend on those who bestow honour rather than on him who receives it, but the good we divine to be something proper to a man and not easily taken from him. Further, men seem to pursue honour in order that they may be assured of their goodness; at least it is by men of practical wisdom that they seek to be honoured, and among those who know them, and on the ground of their virtue; clearly, then, according to them, at any rate, virtue is better. And perhaps one might even suppose this to be, rather than honour, the end of the political life. But even this appears somewhat incomplete; for possession of virtue seems actually compatible with being asleep, or with lifelong inactivity, and, further, with the greatest sufferings and misfortunes; but a man who was living so no one would call happy, unless he were maintaining a thesis at all costs. But enough of this; for the subject has been sufficiently treated even in the current discussions. Third comes the contemplative life, which we shall consider later.

The life of money-making is one undertaken under compulsion, and wealth is evidently not the good we are seeking; for it is merely useful and for the sake of something else. And so one might rather take the aforenamed objects to be ends; for they are loved for themselves. But it is evident that not even these are ends; yet many arguments have been thrown away in support of them. Let us leave this subject, then.

6. We had perhaps better consider the universal good and discuss thoroughly what is meant by it, although such an inquiry is made an uphill one by the fact that the Forms have been introduced by friends of our own. Yet it would perhaps be thought to be better, indeed to be our duty, for the sake of maintaining the truth even to destroy what touches us closely, especially as we are philosophers or lovers of wisdom; for, while both are dear, piety requires us to honour truth above our friends.

The men who introduced this doctrine did not posit Ideas of classes within which they recognized priority and posteriority (which is the reason why they did not maintain the existence of an Idea embracing all numbers); but the term 'good' is used both in the category of substance and in that of quality and in that of relation, and that which is *per se*, i. e. substance, is prior in nature to the relative (for the latter is like an offshoot and accident of being); so that there could not be a common Idea set over all these goods. Further, since 'good' has as many senses as 'being' (for it is predicated both in the category of substance, as of God and of reason, and in quality, i. e. of the virtues, and in quantity, i. e. of that which is moderate, and in relation, i. e. of the useful, and in time, i. e. of the right opportunity, and in place, i. e. of the right locality and the like), clearly it cannot be something universally present in all cases and single; for then it could not have been predicated in all the categories but in one only. Further, since of the things answering to one Idea there is one science, there would have been one science of all the goods; but as it is there are many sciences even of the things that fall under one category, e. g. of opportunity, for opportunity in war is studied by strategics and in disease by medicine, and the moderate in food is studied by medicine and in exercise by the science of gymnastics. And one might ask the question, what in the world they *mean* by 'a thing itself,' if (as is the case) in 'man himself' and in a particular man the account of man is one and the same. For in so far as they are man, they will in no respect differ; and if this is so, neither will 'good itself' and particular goods, in so far as they are good. But again it will not be good any the more for being eternal, since that which lasts long is no whiter than that which perishes in a day. The Pythagoreans seem to give a more plausible account of the good, when they place the one in the column of goods; and it is they that Speusippus seems to have followed. But let us discuss these matters elsewhere; an objection to what we have said, however, may be discerned in the fact that the Platonists have not been speaking about *all* goods, and that the goods that are pursued and loved for themselves are called good by reference to a single Form, while those which tend to produce or to preserve these somehow or to prevent their contraries are called so by reference to these, and in a secondary sense. Clearly, then, goods must be spoken of in two ways, and some must be good in themselves, the others by reason of these. Let us separate, then, things good in themselves from things useful, and consider whether the former are called good by reference to a single Idea. What sort of goods would one call good in themselves? Is it those that are pursued even when isolated from others, such as intelligence, sight, and certain pleasures and honours? Certainly, if we pursue these also for the sake of something else, yet one would place them among things good in themselves. Or is nothing other than the Idea of good good in itself? In that case the Form will be empty. But if the things we have named are also things good in themselves, the account of the good will have to appear as something identical in them all, as that of whiteness is identical in snow and in white lead. But of honour, wisdom, and pleasure, just in respect of their goodness, the accounts are distinct and diverse. The good, therefore, is not some common element answering to one Idea.

But what then do we mean by the good? It is surely not like the things that only chance to have the same name. Are goods one, then, by being derived from one good or by all contributing to one good, or are they rather one by analogy? Certainly as sight is in the body, so is reason in the soul, and so on in other cases. But perhaps these subjects had better be dismissed for the present; for perfect precision about them would be more appropriate to another branch of philosophy.[5] And similarly with regard to the Idea; even if there is some one

[5] Cf. *Met.* iv. 2.

good which is universally predicable of goods or is capable of separate and independent existence, clearly it could not be achieved or attained by man; but we are now seeking something attainable. Perhaps, however, some one might think it worth while to recognize this with a view to the goods that *are* attainable and achievable; for having this as a sort of pattern we shall know better the goods that are good for us, and if we know them shall attain them. This argument has some plausibility, but seems to clash with the procedure of the sciences; for all of these, though they aim at some good and seek to supply the deficiency of it, leave on one side the knowledge of *the* good. Yet that all the exponents of the arts should be ignorant of, and should not even seek, so great an aid is not probable. It is hard, too, to see how a weaver or a carpenter will be benefited in regard to his own craft by knowing this 'good itself,' or how the man who has viewed the Idea itself will be a better doctor or general thereby. For a doctor seems not even to study health in this way, but the health of man, or perhaps rather the health of a particular man; it is individuals that he is healing. But enough of these topics.

7. Let us again return to the good we are seeking, and ask what it can be. It seems different in different actions and arts; it is different in medicine, in strategy, and in the other arts likewise. What then is the good of each? Surely that for whose sake everything else is done. In medicine this is health, in strategy victory, in architecture a house, in any other sphere something else, and in every action and pursuit the end; for it is for the sake of this that all men do whatever else they do. Therefore, if there is an end for all that we do, this will be the good achievable by action, and

if there are more than one, these will be the goods achievable by action.

So the argument has by a different course reached the same point; but we must try to state this even more clearly. Since there are evidently more than one end, and we choose some of these (e. g. wealth, flutes, and in general instruments) for the sake of something else, clearly not all ends are final ends; but the chief good is evidently something final. Therefore, if there is only one final end, this will be what we are seeking, and if there are more than one, the most final of these will be what we are seeking. Now we call that which is in itself worthy of pursuit more final than that which is worthy of pursuit for the sake of something else, and that which is never desirable for the sake of something else more final than the things that are desirable both in themselves and for the sake of that other thing, and therefore we call final without qualification that which is always desirable in itself and never for the sake of something else.

Now such a thing happiness, above all else, is held to be; for this we choose always for itself and never for the sake of something else, but honour, pleasure, reason, and every virtue we choose indeed for themselves (for if nothing resulted from them we should still choose each of them), but we choose them also for the sake of happiness, judging that by means of them we shall be happy. Happiness, on the other hand, no one chooses for the sake of these, nor, in general, for anything other than itself.

From the point of view of self-sufficiency the same result seems to follow; for the final good is thought to be self-sufficient. Now by self-sufficient we do not mean that which is sufficient for a man by himself, for one who lives a solitary life, but also for parents, children, wife, and in general for his friends and fellow citizens, since man is born for citizenship. But some limit must be set to this; for if we extend our requirement to ancestors and descendants and friends' friends we are in for an infinite series. Let us examine this question, however, on another occasion; the self-sufficient we now define as that which when isolated makes life desirable and lacking in nothing; and such we think happiness to be; and further we think it most desirable of all things, without being counted as one good thing among others—if it were so counted it would clearly be made more desirable by the addition of even the least of goods; for that which is added becomes an excess of goods, and of goods the greater is always more desirable. Happiness, then, is something final and self-sufficient, and is the end of action.

Presumably, however, to say that happiness is the chief good seems a platitude, and a clearer account of what it is is still desired. This might perhaps be given, if we could first ascertain the function of man. For just as for a flute-player, a sculptor, or any artist, and, in general, for all things that have a function or activity, the good and the 'well' is thought to reside in the function, so would it seem to be for man, if he has a function. Have the carpenter, then, and the tanner certain functions or activities, and has man none? Is he born without a function? Or as eye, hand, foot, and in general each of the parts evidently has a function, may one lay it down that man similarly has a function apart from all these? What then can this be? Life seems to be common even to plants, but we are seeking what is peculiar to man. Let us exclude, therefore, the life of nutrition and growth. Next there would be a life of perception, but *it* also seems to be common even to the horse, the ox, and every

animal. There remains, then, an active life of the element that has a rational principle; of this, one part has such a principle in the sense of being obedient to one, the other in the sense of possessing one and exercising thought. And, as 'life of the rational element' also has two meanings, we must state that life in the sense of activity is what we mean; for this seems to be the more proper sense of the term. Now if the function of man is an activity of soul which follows or implies a rational principle, and if we say 'a so-and-so' and 'a good so-and-so' have a function which is the same in kind, e. g. a lyre-player and a good lyre-player, and so without qualification in all cases, eminence in respect of goodness being added to the name of the function (for the function of a lyre-player is to play the lyre, and that of a good lyre-player is to do so well): if this is the case, [and we state the function of man to be a certain kind of life, and this to be an activity or actions of the soul implying a rational principle, and the function of a good man to be the good and noble performance of these, and if any action is well performed when it is performed in accordance with the appropriate excellence: if this is the case,] human good turns out to be activity of soul in accordance with virtue, and if there are more than one virtue, in accordance with the best and most complete.

But we must add 'in a complete life.' For one swallow does not make a summer, nor does one day; and so too one day, or a short time, does not make a man blessed and happy.

Let this serve as an outline of the good; for we must presumably first sketch it roughly, and then later fill in the details. But it would seem that any one is capable of carrying on and articulating what has once been well outlined, and that time is a good discoverer or partner in such a work; to which facts the advances of the arts are due; for any one can add what is lacking. And we must also remember what has been said before, and not look for precision in all things alike, but in each class of things such precision as accords with the subject-matter, and so much as is appropriate to the inquiry. For a carpenter and a geometer investigate the right angle in different ways; the former does so in so far as the right angle is useful for his work, while the latter inquires what it is or what sort of thing it is; for he is a spectator of the truth. We must act in the same way, then, in all other matters as well, that our main task may not be subordinated to minor questions. Nor must we demand the cause in all matters alike; it is enough in some cases that the *fact* be well established, as in the case of the first principles; the fact is the primary thing or first principle. Now of first principles we see some by induction, some by perception, some by a certain habituation, and others too in other ways. But each set of principles we must try to investigate in the natural way, and we must take pains to state them definitely, since they have a great influence on what follows. For the beginning is thought to be more than half of the whole, and many of the questions we ask are cleared up by it.

8. We must consider it, however, in the light not only of our conclusion and our premises, but also of what is commonly said about it; for with a true view all the data harmonize, but with a false one the facts soon clash. Now goods have been divided into three classes,[6] and some are described as external, others as relating to soul or to body; we call those that relate to soul most properly and truly goods,

6 Pl. *Euthyd.* 279 AB, *Phil.* 48 E, *Laws,* 743 E.

and physical actions and activities we class as relating to soul. Therefore our account must be sound, at least according to this view, which is an old one and agreed on by philosophers. It is correct also in that we identify the end with certain actions and activities; for thus it falls among goods of the soul and not among external goods. Another belief which harmonizes with our account is that the happy man lives well and does well; for we have practically defined happiness as a sort of good life and good action. The characteristics that are looked for in happiness seem also, all of them, to belong to what we have defined happiness as being. For some identify happiness with virtue, some with practical wisdom, others with a kind of philosophic wisdom, others with these, or one of these, accompanied by pleasure or not without pleasure; while others include also external prosperity. Now some of these views have been held by many men and men of old, others by a few eminent persons; and it is not probable that either of these should be entirely mistaken, but rather that they should be right in at least some one respect or even in most respects.

With those who identify happiness with virtue or some one virtue our account is in harmony; for to virtue belongs virtuous activity. But it makes, perhaps, no small difference whether we place the chief good in possession or in use, in state of mind or in activity. For the state of mind may exist without producing any good result, as in a man who is asleep or in some other way quite inactive, but the activity cannot; for one who has the activity will of necessity be acting, and acting well. And as in the Olympic Games it is not the most beautiful and the strongest that are crowned but those who compete (for it is some of these that are victorious), so those who act win, and rightly win, the noble and good things in life.

Their life is also in itself pleasant. For pleasure is a state of *soul,* and to each man that which he is said to be a lover of is pleasant; e. g. not only is a horse pleasant to the lover of horses, and a spectacle to the lover of sights, but also in the same way just acts are pleasant to the lover of justice and in general virtuous acts to the lover of virtue. Now for most men their pleasures are in conflict with one another because these are not by nature pleasant, but the lovers of what is noble find pleasant the things that are by nature pleasant; and virtuous actions are such, so that these are pleasant for such men as well as in their own nature. Their life, therefore, has no further need of pleasure as a sort of adventitious charm, but has its pleasure in itself. For, besides what we have said, the man who does not rejoice in noble actions is not even good; since no one would call a man just who did not enjoy acting justly, nor any man liberal who did not enjoy liberal actions; and similarly in all other cases. If this is so, virtuous actions must be in themselves pleasant. But they are also *good* and *noble,* and have each of these attributes in the highest degree, since the good man judges well about these attributes; his judgement is such as we have described.[7] Happiness then is the best, noblest, and most pleasant thing in the world, and these attributes are not severed as in the inscription at Delos—

Most noble is that which is justest, and best is health;
But pleasantest is it to win what we love.

For all these properties belong to the best activities; and these, or one—the

[7] I. e., he judges that virtuous actions are good and noble in the highest degree.

best—of these, we identify with happiness.

Yet evidently, as we said, it needs the external goods as well; for it is impossible, or not easy, to do noble acts without the proper equipment. In many actions we use friends and riches and political power as instruments; and there are some things the lack of which takes the lustre from happiness, as good birth, goodly children, beauty; for the man who is very ugly in appearance or ill-born or solitary and childless is not very likely to be happy, and perhaps a man would be still less likely if he had thoroughly bad children or friends or had lost good children or friends by death. As we said, then, happiness seems to need this sort of prosperity in addition; for which reason some identify happiness with good fortune, though others identify it with virtue.

9. For this reason also the question is asked, whether happiness is to be acquired by learning or by habituation or some other sort of training, or comes in virtue of some divine providence or again by chance. Now if there is *any* gift of the gods to men, it is reasonable that happiness should be god-given, and most surely god-given of all human things inasmuch as it is the best. But this question would perhaps be more appropriate to another inquiry; happiness seems, however, even if it is not god-sent but comes as a result of virtue and some process of learning or training, to be among the most godlike things; for that which is the prize and end of virtue seems to be the best thing in the world, and something godlike and blessed.

It will also on this view be very generally shared; for all who are not maimed as regards their potentiality for virtue may win it by a certain kind of study and care. But if it is better to be happy thus than by chance, it is reasonable that the facts should be so, since everything that depends on the action of nature is by nature as good as it can be, and similarly everything that depends on art or any rational cause, and especially if it depends on the best of all causes. To entrust to chance what is greatest and most noble would be a very defective arrangement.

The answer to the question we are asking is plain also from the definition of happiness; for it has been said to be a virtuous activity of soul, of a certain kind. Of the remaining goods, some must necessarily pre-exist as conditions of happiness, and others are naturally co-operative and useful as instruments. And this will be found to agree with what we said at the outset; for we stated the end of political science to be the best end, and political science spends most of its pains on making the citizens to be of a certain character, viz. good and capable of noble acts.

It is natural, then, that we call neither ox nor horse nor any other of the animals happy, for none of them is capable of sharing in such activity. For this reason also a boy is not happy; for he is not yet capable of such acts, owing to his age; and boys who are called happy are being congratulated by reason of the hopes we have for them. For there is required, as we said, not only complete virtue but also a complete life, since many changes occur in life, and all manner of chances, and the most prosperous may fall into great misfortunes in old age, as is told of Priam in the Trojan Cycle; and one who has experienced such chances and has ended wretchedly no one calls happy.

10. Must no one at all, then, be called happy while he lives; must we, as Solon says, see the end? Even if we are to lay down this doctrine, is it also the case that a man *is* happy when he is *dead?* Or is not this quite absurd, especially for us who say that happiness is an activity? But if we do not call the dead man happy, and if Solon does not mean this, but that one can then safely *call* a man blessed as being at last beyond evils and misfortunes, this also affords matter for discussion; for both evil and good are thought to exist for a dead man, as much as for one who is alive but not aware of them; e. g. honours and dishonours and the good or bad fortunes of children and in general of descendants. And this also presents a problem; for though a man has lived happily up to old age and has had a death worthy of his life, many reverses may befall his descendants—some of them may be good and attain the life they deserve, while with others the opposite may be the case; and clearly too the degrees of relationship between them and their ancestors may vary indefinitely. It would be odd, then, if the dead man were to share in these changes and become at one time happy, at another wretched; while it would also be odd if the fortunes of the descendants did not for *some* time have *some* effect on the happiness of their ancestors.

But we must return to our first difficulty; for perhaps by a consideration of it our present problem might be solved. Now if we must see the end and only then call a man happy, not as being happy but as having been so before, surely this is a paradox, that when he is happy the attribute that belongs to him is not to be truly predicated of him because we do not wish to call living men happy, on account of the changes that may befall them, and because we have assumed happiness to be something permanent and by no means easily changed, while a single man may suffer many turns of fortune's wheel. For clearly if we were to keep pace with his fortunes, we should often call the same man happy and again wretched, making the happy man out to be a 'chameleon and insecurely based.' Or is this keeping pace with his fortunes quite wrong? Success or failure in life does not depend on these, but human life, as we said, needs these as mere additions, while virtuous activities or their opposites are what constitute happiness or the reverse.

The question we have now discussed confirms our definition. For no function of man has so much permanence as virtuous activities (these are thought to be more durable even than knowledge of the sciences), and of these themselves the most valuable are more durable because those who are happy spend their life most readily and most continuously in these; for this seems to be the reason why we do not forget them. The attribute in question,[8] then, will belong to the happy man, and he will be happy throughout his life; for always, or by preference to everything else, he will be engaged in virtuous action and contemplation, and he will bear the chances of life most nobly and altogether decorously, if he is 'truly good' and 'foursquare beyond reproach.' [9]

Now many events happen by chance, and events differing in importance; small pieces of good fortune or of its opposite clearly do not weigh down the scales of life one way or the other, but a multitude of great events if they turn out well will make life happier (for not only are they themselves such as to add beauty to life, but the way a man deals with them may be noble and good), while if they turn out ill they crush and maim happiness; for they both bring pain with them and hinder many activities. Yet even in these nobility shines through,

when a man bears with resignation many great misfortunes, not through insensibility to pain but through nobility and greatness of soul.

If activities are, as we said, what gives life its character, no happy man can become miserable; for he will never do the acts that are hateful and mean. For the man who is truly good and wise, we think, bears all the chances of life becomingly and always makes the best of circumstances, as a good general makes the best military use of the army at his command and a good shoemaker makes the best shoes out of the hides that are given him; and so with all other craftsmen. And if this is the case, the happy man can never become miserable—though he will not reach *blessedness*, if he meet with fortunes like those of Priam.

Nor, again, is he many-coloured and changeable; for neither will he be moved from his happy state easily or by any ordinary misadventures, but only by many great ones, nor, if he has had many great misadventures, will he recover his happiness in a short time, but if at all, only in a long and complete one in which he has attained many splendid successes.

Why then should we not say that he is happy who is active in accordance with complete virtue and is sufficiently equipped with external goods, not for some chance period, but throughout a complete life? Or must we add 'and who is destined to live thus and die as befits his life'? Certainly the future is obscure to us, while happiness, we claim, is an end and something in every way final. If so, we shall call happy those among living men in whom these conditions are, and are to be, fulfilled—but happy *men*. So much for these questions.

11. That the fortunes of descendants and of all a man's friends should not affect his happiness at all seems a

[8] Durability.
[9] Simonides.

very unfriendly doctrine, and one opposed to the opinions men hold; but since the events that happen are numerous and admit of all sorts of difference, and some come more near to us and others less so, it seems a long—nay, an infinite—task to discuss each in detail; a general outline will perhaps suffice. If, then, as some of a man's own misadventures have a certain weight and influence on life while others are, as it were, lighter, so too there are differences among the misadventures of our friends taken as a whole, and it makes a difference whether the various sufferings befall the living or the dead (much more even than whether lawless and terrible deeds are presupposed in a tragedy or done on the stage), this difference also must be taken into account; or rather, perhaps, the fact that doubt is felt whether the dead share in any good or evil. For it seems, from these considerations, that even if anything whether good or evil penetrates to them, it must be something weak and negligible, either in itself or for them, or if not, at least it must be such in degree and kind as not to make happy those who are not happy nor to take away their blessedness from those who are. The good or bad fortunes of friends, then, seem to have some effects on the dead, but effects of such a kind and degree as neither to make the happy unhappy nor to produce any other change of the kind.

12. These questions having been definitely answered, let us consider whether happiness is among the things that are praised or rather among the things that are prized; for clearly it is not to be placed among *potentialities.* Everything that is praised seems to be praised because it is of a certain kind and is related somehow to something else; for we praise the just or brave man and in general both the good man

and virtue itself because of the actions and functions involved, and we praise the strong man, the good runner, and so on, because he is of a certain kind and is related in a certain way to something good and important. This is clear also from the praises of the gods; for it seems absurd that the gods should be referred to our standard, but this *is* done because praise involves a reference, as we said, to something else. But if praise is for things such as we have described, clearly what applies to the best things is not praise, but something greater and better, as is indeed obvious; for what we do to the gods and the most godlike of men is to call them blessed and happy. And so too with good *things;* no one praises happiness as he does justice, but rather calls it blessed, as being something more divine and better.

Eudoxus also seems to have been right in his method of advocating the supremacy of pleasure; he thought that the fact that, though a good, it is not praised indicated it to be better than the things that are praised, and that this is what God and the good are; for by reference to these all other things are judged. *Praise* is appropriate to virtue, for as a result of virtue men tend to do noble deeds; but *encomia* are bestowed on acts, whether of the body or of the soul. But perhaps nicety in these matters is more proper to those who have made a study of encomia; to us it is clear from what has been said that happiness is among the things that are prized and perfect. It seems to be so also from the fact that it is a first principle; for it is for the sake of this that we all do all that we do, and the first principle and cause of goods is, we claim, something prized and divine.

13. Since happiness is an activity of soul in accordance with perfect virtue, we must consider the nature

of virtue; for perhaps we shall thus see better the nature of happiness. The true student of politics, too, is thought to have studied virtue above all things; for he wishes to make his fellow citizens good and obedient to the laws. As an example of this we have the lawgivers of the Cretans and the Spartans, and any others of the kind that there may have been. And if this inquiry belongs to political science, clearly the pursuit of it will be in accordance with our original plan. But clearly the virtue we must study is human virtue; for the good we were seeking was human good and the happiness human happiness. By human virtue we mean not that of the body but that of the soul; and happiness also we call an activity of soul. But if this is so, clearly the student of politics must know somehow the facts about soul, as the man who is to heal the eyes or the body as a whole must know about the eyes or the body; and all the more since politics is more prized and better than medicine; but even among doctors the best educated spend much labour on acquiring knowledge of the body. The student of politics, then, must study the soul, and must study it with these objects in view, and do so just to the extent which is sufficient for the questions we are discussing; for further precision is perhaps something more laborious than our purposes require.

Some things are said about it, adequately enough, even in the discussion outside our school, and we must use these; e. g. that one element in the soul is irrational and one has a rational principle. Whether these are separated as the parts of the body or of anything divisible are, or are distinct by definition but by nature inseparable, like convex and concave in the circumference of a circle, does not affect the present question.

Of the irrational element one division seems to be widely distributed, and vegetative in its nature, I mean that which causes nutrition and growth; for it is this kind of power of the soul that one must assign to all nurslings and to embryos, and this same power to full-grown creatures; this is more reasonable than to assign some different power to them. Now the excellence of this seems to be common to all species and not specifically human; for this part or faculty seems to function most in sleep, while goodness and badness are least manifest in sleep (whence comes the saying that the happy are no better off than the wretched for half their lives; and this happens naturally enough, since sleep is an inactivity of the soul in that respect in which it is called good or bad), unless perhaps to a small extent some of the movements actually penetrate to the soul, and in this respect the dreams of good men are better than those of ordinary people. Enough of this subject, however; let us leave the nutritive faculty alone, since it has by its nature no share in human excellence.

There seems to be also another irrational element in the soul—one which in a sense, however, shares in a rational principle. For we praise the rational principle of the continent man and of the incontinent, and the part of their soul that has such a principle, since it urges them aright and towards the best objects; but there is found in them also another element naturally opposed to the rational principle, which fights against and resists that principle. For exactly as paralysed limbs when we intend to move them to the right turn on the contrary to the left, so is it with the soul; the impulses of incontinent people move in contrary directions. But while in the body we see that which moves astray, in the soul we do not. No doubt, however, we must none the less suppose that in the soul too there is something contrary to the rational principle, resisting and opposing it. In what sense it is distinct from the other elements does not concern us. Now even this seems to have a share in a rational principle, as we said; at any rate in the continent man it obeys the rational principle—and presumably in the temperate and brave man it is still more obedient; for in him it speaks, on all matters, with the same voice as the rational principle.

Therefore the irrational element also appears to be twofold. For the vegetative element in no way shares in a rational principle, but the appetitive, and in general the desiring element in a sense shares in it, in so far as it listens to and obeys it; this is the sense in which we speak of 'taking account' of one's father or one's friends, not that in which we speak of 'accounting' for a mathematical property. That the irrational element is in some sense persuaded by a rational principle is indicated also by the giving of advice and by all reproof and exhortation. And if this element also must be said to have a rational principle, that which has a rational principle (as well as that which has not) will be twofold, one subdivision having it in the strict sense and it itself, and the other having a tendency to obey as one does one's father.

Virtue too is distinguished into kinds in accordance with this difference; for we say that some of the virtues are intellectual and others moral, philosophic wisdom and understanding and practical wisdom being intellectual, liberality and temperance moral. For in speaking about a man's character we do not say that he is wise or has understanding but that he is good-tempered or temperate; yet we praise the wise man also with respect to his state of mind; and of states of mind we call those which merit praise virtues.

BOOK II

MORAL VIRTUE

1. Virtue, then, being of two kinds, intellectual and moral, intellectual virtue in the main owes both its birth and its growth to teaching (for which reason it requires experience and time), while moral virtue comes about as a result of habit, whence also its name *ethike* is one that is formed by a slight variation from the word *ethos* (habit). From this it is also plain that none of the moral virtues arises in us by nature; for nothing that exists by nature can form a habit contrary to its nature. For instance the stone which by nature moves downwards cannot be habituated to move upwards, not even if one tries to train it by throwing it up ten thousand times; nor can fire be habituated to move downwards, nor can anything else that by nature behaves in one way be trained to behave in another. Neither by nature, then, nor contrary to nature do the virtues arise in us; rather we are adapted by nature to receive them, and are made perfect by habit.

Again, of all the things that come to us by nature we first acquire the potentiality and later exhibit the activity (this is plain in the case of the senses; for it was not by often seeing or often hearing that we got these senses, but on the contrary we had them before we used them, and did not come to have them by using them); but the virtues we get by first exercising them, as also happens in the case of the arts as well. For the things we have to learn before we can do them, we learn by doing them, e. g. men become builders by building and lyre-players by playing the lyre; so too we become just by doing just acts, temperate by doing temperate acts, brave by doing brave acts.

This is confirmed by what happens in states; for legislators make the citizens good by forming habits in them, and this is the wish of every legislator, and those who do not effect it miss their mark, and it is in this that a good constitution differs from a bad one.

Again, it is from the same causes and by the same means that every virtue is both produced and destroyed, and similarly every art; for it is from playing the lyre that both good and bad lyre-players are produced. And the corresponding statement is true of builders and of all the rest; men will be good or bad builders as a result of building well or badly. For if this were not so, there would have been no need of a teacher, but all men would have been born good or bad at their craft. This, then, is the case with the virtues also; by doing the acts that we do in our transactions with other men we become just or unjust, and by doing the acts that we do in the presence of danger, and being habituated to feel fear or confidence, we become brave or cowardly. The same is true of appetites and feelings of anger; some men become temperate and good-tempered, others self-indulgent and irascible, by behaving in one way or the other in the appropriate circumstances. Thus, in one word, states of character arise out of like activities. This is why the activities we exhibit must be of a certain kind; it is because the states of character correspond to the differences between these. It makes no small difference, then, whether we form habits of one kind or of another from our very youth; it makes a very great difference, or rather *all* the difference.

2. Since, then, the present inquiry does not aim at theoretical knowledge like the others (for we are inquiring not in order to know what virtue is, but in order to become good, since otherwise our inquiry would have been of no use), we must examine the nature of actions, namely how we ought to do them; for these determine also the nature of the states of character that are produced, as we have said. Now, that we must act according to the right rule is a common principle and must be assumed—it will be discussed later, i. e. both what the right rule is, and how it is related to the other virtues. But this must be agreed upon beforehand, that the whole account of matters of conduct must be given in outline and not precisely, as we said at the very beginning that the accounts we demand must be in accordance with the subject-matter; matters concerned with conduct and questions of what is good for us have no fixity, any more than matters of health. The general account being of this nature, the account of particular cases is yet more lacking in exactness; for they do not fall under any art or precept but the agents themselves must in each case consider what is appropriate to the occasion, as happens also in the art of medicine or of navigation.

But though our present account is of this nature we must give what help we can. First, then, let us consider this, that it is the nature of such things to be destroyed by defect and excess, as we see in the case of strength and of health (for to gain light on things imperceptible we must use the evidence of sensible things); both excessive and defective exercise destroys the strength, and similarly drink or food which is above or below a certain amount destroys the health, while that which is proportionate both produces and increases and preserves it. So too is it, then, in the case of temperance and courage and the other virtues. For the man who flies from and fears everything and does not stand his ground against anything becomes a coward, and the man who fears nothing at all but goes to meet every danger becomes rash; and similarly the man who indulges in every pleasure and abstains from none becomes self-indulgent, while the man who shuns every pleasure, as boors do, becomes in a way insensible; temperance and courage, then, are destroyed by excess and defect, and preserved by the mean.

But not only are the sources and causes of their origination and growth the same as those of their destruction, but also the sphere of their actualization will be the same; for this is also true of the things which are more evident to sense, e. g. of strength; it is produced by taking much food and undergoing much exertion, and it is the strong man that will be most able to do these things. So too is it with the virtues; by abstaining from pleasures we become temperate, and it is when we have become so that we are most able to abstain from them; and similarly too in the case of courage; for by being habituated to despise things that are terrible and to stand our ground against them we become brave, and it is when we have become so that we shall be most able to stand our ground against them.

3. We must take as a sign of states of character the pleasure or pain that ensues on acts; for the man who abstains from bodily pleasures and delights in this very fact is temperate, while the man who is annoyed at it is self-indulgent, and he who stands his ground against things that are terrible and delights in this or at least is not pained is brave, while the man who is pained is a coward. For moral excellence is concerned with pleasures and pains; it is on account of the pleasure that we do bad things, and on account of the pain that we abstain from noble ones. Hence we ought to have been brought up in a particular way from our very youth, as Plato says,[10] so as both to delight in and to be pained by the things that we ought; for this is the right education.

Again, if the virtues are concerned with actions and passions, and every passion and every action is accompanied by pleasure and pain, for this reason also virtue will be concerned with pleasures and pains. This is indicated also by the fact that punishment is inflicted by these means; for it is a kind of cure, and it is the nature of cures to be effected by contraries.

Again, as we said but lately, every state of soul has a nature relative to and concerned with the kind of things by which it tends to be made worse or better; but it is by reason of pleasures and pains that men become bad, by pursuing and avoiding these—either the pleasures and pains they ought not or when they ought not or as they ought not, or by going wrong in one of the other similar ways that may be distinguished. Hence men [11] even define the virtues as certain states of impassivity and rest; not well, however, because they speak absolutely, and do not say 'as one ought' and 'as one ought not' and 'when one ought or ought not,' and the other things that may be added. We assume, then, that this kind of excellence tends to do what is best with regard to pleasures and pains, and vice does the contrary.

The following facts also may show us that virtue and vice are concerned with these same things. There being three objects of choice and three of avoidance, the noble, the advantageous, the pleasant, and their contraries, the base, the injurious, the painful, about all of these the good man tends to go right and the bad man to go wrong, and especially about pleasure;

[10] *Laws*, 653 A ff., *Rep.* 401 E–402 A.
[11] Probably Speusippus is referred to.

for this is common to the animals, and also it accompanies all objects of choice; for even the noble and the advantageous appear pleasant.

Again, it has grown up with us all from our infancy; this is why it is difficult to rub off this passion, engrained as it is in our life. And we measure even our actions, some of us more and others less, by the rule of pleasure and pain. For this reason, then, our whole inquiry must be about these; for to feel delight and pain rightly or wrongly has no small effect on our actions.

Again, it is harder to fight with pleasure than with anger, to use Heraclitus' phrase, but both art and virtue are always concerned with what is harder; for even the good is better when it is harder. Therefore for this reason also the whole concern both of virtue and of political science is with pleasures and pains; for the man who uses these well will be good, he who uses them badly bad.

That virtue, then, is concerned with pleasures and pains, and that by the acts from which it arises it is both increased and, if they are done differently, destroyed, and that the acts from which it arose are those in which it actualizes itself—let this be taken as said.

4. The question might be asked, what we mean by saying that we must become just by doing just acts, and temperate by doing temperate acts; for if men do just and temperate acts, they are already just and temperate, exactly as, if they do what is in accordance with the laws of grammar and of music, they are grammarians and musicians.

Or is this not true even of the arts? It is possible to do something that is in accordance with the laws of grammar, either by chance or at the suggestion of another. A man will be a gramma-

rian, then, only when he has both done something grammatical and done it grammatically; and this means doing it in accordance with the grammatical knowledge in himself.

Again, the case of the arts and that of the virtues are not similar; for the products of the arts have their goodness in themselves, so that it is enough that they should have a certain character, but if the acts that are in accordance with the virtues have themselves a certain character it does not follow that they are done justly or temperately. The agent also must be in a certain condition when he does them; in the first place he must have knowledge, secondly he must choose the acts, and choose them for their own sakes, and thirdly his action must proceed from a firm and unchangeable character. These are not reckoned in as conditions of the possession of the arts, except the bare knowledge; but as a condition of the possession of the virtues knowledge has little or no weight, while the other conditions count not for a little but for everyting, i. e. the very conditions which result from often doing just and temperate acts.

Actions, then, are called just and temperate when they are such as the just or the temperate man would do; but it is not the man who does these that is just and temperate, but the man who also does them *as* just and temperate men do them. It is well said, then, that it is by doing just acts that the just man is produced, and by doing temperate acts the temperate man; without doing these no one would have even a prospect of becoming good.

But most people do not do these, but take refuge in theory and think they are being philosophers and will become good in this way, behaving somewhat like patients who listen attentively to their doctors, but do none of the things they are ordered to do. As the latter will not be made well in body by such a course of treatment, the former will not be made well in soul by such a course of philosophy.

5. Next we must consider what virtue is. Since things that are found in the soul are of three kinds—passions, faculties, states of character—virtue must be one of these. By passions I mean appetite, anger, fear, confidence, envy, joy, friendly feeling, hatred, longing, emulation, pity, and in general the feelings that are accompanied by pleasure or pain; by faculties the things in virtue of which we are said to be capable of feeling these, e. g. of becoming angry or being pained or feeling pity; by states of character the things in virtue of which we stand well or badly with reference to the passions, e. g. with reference to anger we stand badly if we feel it violently or too weakly, and well if we feel it moderately; and similarly with reference to the other passions.

Now neither the virtues nor the vices are *passions*, because we are not called good or bad on the ground of our passions, but are so called on the ground of our virtues and our vices, and because we are neither praised nor blamed for our passions (for the man who feels fear or anger is not praised, nor is the man who simply feels anger blamed, but the man who feels it in a certain way), but for our virtues and our vices we are praised or blamed.

Again, we feel anger and fear without choice, but the virtues are modes of choice or involve choice. Further, in respect of the passions we are said to be moved, but in respect of the virtues and the vices we are said not to be moved but to be disposed in a particular way.

For these reasons also they are not *faculties;* for we are neither called good nor bad, nor praised nor blamed,

for the simple capacity of feeling the passions; again, we have the faculties of nature, but we are not made good or bad by nature; we have spoken of this before.

If, then, the virtues are neither passions nor faculties, all that remains is that they should be *states of character*.

Thus we have stated what virtue is in respect of its genus.

6. We must, however, not only describe virtue as a state of character, but also say what sort of state it is. We may remark, then, that every virtue or excellence both brings into good condition the thing of which it is the excellence and makes the work of that thing be done well; e. g. the excellence of the eye makes both the eye and its work good; for it is by the excellence of the eye that we see well. Similarly the excellence of the horse makes a horse both good in itself and good at running and at carrying its rider and at awaiting the attack of the enemy. Therefore, if this is true in every case, the virtue of man also will be the state of character which makes a man good and which makes him do his own work well.

How this is to happen we have stated already, but it will be made plain also by the following consideration of the specific nature of virtue. In everything that is continuous and divisible it is possible to take more, less, or an equal amount, and that either in terms of the thing itself or relatively to us; and the equal is an intermediate between excess and defect. By the intermediate in the object I mean that which is equidistant from each of the extremes, which is one and the same for all men; by the intermediate relatively to us that which is neither too much nor too little—and this is not one, nor the same for all. For instance, if ten is many and two is few, six is the intermediate, taken in terms of the object; for it exceeds and is exceeded by an equal amount; this is intermediate according to arithmetical proportion. But the intermediate relatively to us is not to be taken so; if ten pounds are too much for a particular person to eat and two too little, it does not follow that the trainer will order six pounds; for this also is perhaps too much for the person who is to take it, or too little—too little for Milo,[12] too much for the beginner in athletic exercises. The same is true of running and wrestling. Thus a master of any art avoids excess and defect, but seeks the intermediate and chooses this—the intermediate not in the object but relatively to us.

If it is thus, then, that every art does its work well—by looking to the intermediate and judging its works by this standard (so that we often say of good works of art that it is not possible either to take away or to add anything, implying that excess and defect destroy the goodness of works of art, while the mean preserves it; and good artists, as we say, look to this in their work), and if, further, virtue is more exact and better than any art, as nature also is, then virtue must have the quality of aiming at the intermediate. I mean moral virtue; for it is this that is concerned with passions and actions, and in these there is excess, defect, and the intermediate. For instance, both fear and confidence and appetite and anger and pity and in general pleasure and pain may be felt both too much and too little, and in both cases not well; but to feel them at the right times, with reference to the right objects, towards the right people, with the right motive, and in the right way, is what is both intermediate and best, and this is characteristic of virtue. Similarly with regard to actions also there is excess, defect, and the intermediate.

[12] A famous wrestler.

Now virtue is concerned with passions and actions, in which excess is a form of failure, and so is defect, while the intermediate is praised and is a form of success; and being praised and being successful are both characteristics of virtue. Therefore virtue is a kind of mean, since, as we have seen, it aims at what is intermediate.

Again, it is possible to fail in many ways (for evil belongs to the class of the unlimited, as the Pythagoreans conjectured, and good to that of the limited), while to succeed is possible only in one way (for which reason also one is easy and the other difficult—to miss the mark easy, to hit it difficult); for these reasons also, then, excess and defect are characteristic of vice, and the mean of virtue;

> For men are good in but one way,
>   but bad in many.

FINAL

Virtue, then, is a state of character concerned with choice, lying in a mean, i. e. the mean relative to us, this being determined by a rational principle, and by that principle by which the man of practical wisdom would determine it. Now it is a mean between two vices, that which depends on excess and that which depends on defect; and again it is a mean because the vices respectively fall short of or exceed what is right in both passions and actions, while virtue both finds and chooses that which is intermediate. Hence in respect of its substance and the definition which states its essence virtue is a mean, with regard to what is best and right and extreme.

But not every action nor every passion admits of a mean; for some have names that already imply badness, e. g. spite, shamelessness, envy, and in the case of actions adultery, theft, murder; for all of these and suchlike things imply by their names that they are themselves bad, and not the exesses or deficiencies of them. It is not possible, then, ever to be right with regard to them; one must always be wrong. Nor does goodness or badness with regard to such things depend on committing adultery with the right woman, at the right time, and in the right way, but simply to do any of them is to go wrong. It would be equally absurd, then, to expect that in unjust, cowardly, and voluptuous action there should be a mean, an excess, and a deficiency; for at that rate there would be a mean of excess and of deficiency, an excess of excess, and a deficiency of deficiency. But as there is no excess and deficiency of temperance and courage because what is intermediate is in a sense an extreme, so too of the actions we have mentioned there is no mean nor any excess and deficiency, but however they are done they are wrong; for in general there is neither a mean of excess and deficiency, nor excess and deficiency of a mean.

7. We must, however, not only make this general statement, but also apply it to the individual facts. For among statements about conduct those which are general apply more widely, but those which are particular are more genuine, since conduct has to do with individual cases, and our statements must harmonize with the facts in these cases. We may take these cases from our table. With regard to feelings of fear and confidence courage is the mean; of the people who exceed, he who exceeds in fearlessness has no name (many of the states have no name), while the man who exceeds in confidence is rash, and he who exceeds in fear and falls short in confidence is a coward. With regard to pleasures and pains—not all of them, and not so much with regard to the pains--the mean is temperance, the excess self-indulgence. Persons de-

ficient with regard to the pleasures are not often found; hence such persons also have received no name. But let us call them 'insensible.'

With regard to giving and taking of money the mean is liberality, the excess and the defect prodigality and meanness. In these actions people exceed and fall short in contrary ways; the prodigal exceeds in spending and falls short in taking, while the mean man exceeds in taking and falls short in spending. (At present we are giving a mere outline or summary, and are satisfied with this; later these states will be more exactly determined.) With regard to money there are also other dispositions—a mean, magnificence (for the magnificent man differs from the liberal man; the former deals with large sums, the latter with small ones), and excess, tastelessness and vulgarity, and a deficiency, niggardliness; these differ from the states opposed to liberality, and the mode of their difference will be stated later.

With regard to honour and dishonour the mean is proper pride, the excess is known as a sort of 'empty vanity,' and the deficiency is undue humility; and as we said liberality was related to magnificence, differing from it by dealing with small sums, so there is a state similarly related to proper pride, being concerned with small honours while that is concerned with great. For it is possible to desire honour as one ought, and more than one ought, and less, and the man who exceeds in his desires is called ambitious, the man who falls short unambitious, while the intermediate person has no name. The dispositions also are nameless, except that that of the ambitious man is called ambition. Hence the people who are at the extremes lay claim to the middle place; and we ourselves sometimes call the intermediate person ambitious and sometimes unambitious, and sometimes praise the ambitious man and sometimes the unambitious. The reason of our doing this will be stated in what follows; but now let us speak of the remaining states according to the method which has been indicated.

With regard to anger also there is an excess, a deficiency, and a mean. Although they can scarcely be said to have names, yet since we call the intermediate person good-tempered let us call the mean good temper; of the persons at the extremes let the one who exceeds be called irascible, and his vice irascibility, and the man who falls short an inirascible sort of person, and the deficiency inirascibility.

There are also three other means, which have a certain likeness to one another, but differ from one another: for they are all concerned with intercourse in words and actions, but differ in that one is concerned with truth in this sphere, the other two with pleasantness; and of this one kind is exhibited in giving amusement, the other in all the circumstances of life. We must therefore speak of these two, that we may the better see that in all things the mean is praiseworthy, and the extremes neither praiseworthy nor right, but worthy of blame. Now most of these states also have no names, but we must try, as in the other cases, to invent names ourselves so that we may be clear and easy to follow. With regard to truth, then, the intermediate is a truthful sort of person and the mean may be called truthfulness, while the pretence which exaggerates is boastfulness and the person characterized by it a boaster, and that which understates is mock modesty and the person characterized by it mock-modest. With regard to pleasantness in the giving of amusement the intermediate person is ready-witted and the disposition ready wit, the excess is buffoonery and the person characterized by it a buffoon, while the man who falls

short is a sort of boor and his state is boorishness. With regard to the remaining kind of pleasantness, that which is exhibited in life in general, the man who is pleasant in the right way is friendly and the mean is friendliness, while the man who exceeds is an obsequious person if he has no end in view, a flatterer if he is aiming at his own advantage, and the man who falls short and is unpleasant in all circumstances is a quarrelsome and surly sort of person.

There are also means in the passions and concerned with the passions; since shame is not a virtue, and yet praise is extended to the modest man. For even in these matters one man is said to be intermediate, and another to exceed, as for instance the bashful man who is ashamed of everything; while he who falls short or is not ashamed of anything at all is shameless, and the intermediate person is modest. Righteous indignation is a mean between envy and spite, and these states are concerned with the pain and pleasures that are felt at the fortunes of our neighbours; the man who is characterized by righteous indignation is pained at undeserved good fortune, the envious man, going beyond him, is pained at all good fortune, and the spiteful man falls so far short of being pained that he even rejoices. But these states there will be an opportunity of describing elsewhere; with regard to justice, since it has not one simple meaning, we shall, after describing the other states, distinguish its two kinds and say how each of them is a mean; and similarly we shall treat also of the rational virtues.

8. There are three kinds of disposition, then, two of them vices, involving excess and deficiency respectively, and one a virtue, viz. the mean, and all are in a sense opposed to all; for the extreme states are contrary both to

the intermediate state and to each other, and the intermediate to the extremes; as the equal is greater relatively to the less, less relatively to the greater, so the middle states are excessive relatively to the deficiencies, deficient relatively to the excesses, both in passions and in actions. For the brave man appears rash relatively to the coward, and cowardly relatively to the rash man; and similarly the temperate man appears self-indulgent relatively to the insensible man, insensible relatively to the self-indulgent, and the liberal man prodigal relatively to the mean man, mean relatively to the prodigal. Hence also the people at the extremes push the intermediate man each over to the other, and the brave man is called rash by the coward, cowardly by the rash man, and correspondingly in the other cases.

These states being thus opposed to one another, the greatest contrariety is that of the extremes to each other, rather than to the intermediate; for these are further from each other than from the intermediate, as the great is further from the small and the small from the great than both are from the equal. Again, to the intermediate some extremes show a certain likeness, as that of rashness to courage and that of prodigality to liberality; but the extremes show the greatest unlikeness to each other; now contraries are defined as the things that are furthest from each other, so that things that are further apart are more contrary.

To the mean in some cases the deficiency, in some the excess is more opposed; e. g. it is not rashness, which is an excess, but cowardice, which is a deficiency, that is more opposed to courage, and not insensibility, which is a deficiency, but self-indulgence, which is an excess, that is more opposed to temperance. This happens from two reasons, one being drawn from the thing itself; for because one

extreme is nearer and liker to the intermediate, we oppose not this but rather its contrary to the intermediate. E. g., since rashness is thought liker and nearer to courage, and cowardice more unlike, we oppose rather the latter to courage; for things that are further from the intermediate are thought more contrary to it. This, then, is one cause, drawn from the thing itself; another is drawn from ourselves; for the things to which we ourselves more naturally tend seem more contrary to the intermediate. For instance, we ourselves tend more naturally to pleasures, and hence are more easily carried away towards self-indulgence than towards propriety. We describe as contrary to the mean, then, rather the directions in which we more often go to great lengths; and therefore self-indulgence, which is an excess, is the more contrary to temperance.

9. That moral virtue is a mean, then, and in what sense it is so, and that it is a mean between two vices, the one involving excess, the other deficiency, and that it is such because its character is to aim at what is intermediate in passions and in actions, has been sufficiently stated. Hence also it is no easy task to be good. For in everything it is no easy task to find the middle, e. g. to find the middle of a circle is not for every one but for him who knows; so, too, any one can get angry—that is easy—or give or spend money; but to do this to the right person, to the right extent, at the right time, with the right motive, and in the right way, *that* is not for every one, nor is it easy; wherefore goodness is both rare and laudable and noble.

Hence he who aims at the intermediate must first depart from what is the more contrary to it, as Calypso advises—

Hold the ship out beyond that surf and
spray.[13]

For of the extremes one is more erroneous, one less so; therefore, since to
hit the mean is hard in the extreme,
we must as a second best, as people
say, take the least of the evil; and this
will be done best in the way we describe.

But we must consider the things towards which we ourselves also are easily carried away; for some of us tend
to one thing, some to another; and this
will be recognizable from the pleasure and the pain we feel. We must
drag ourselves away to the contrary
extreme; for we shall get into the intermediate state by drawing well away
from error, as people do in straighten-
ing sticks that are bent.

Now in everything the pleasant or
pleasure is most to be guarded against;
for we do not judge it impartially. We
ought, then, to feel towards pleasure
as the elders of the people felt towards
Helen, and in all circumstances repeat
their saying; for if we dismiss pleasure
thus we are less likely to go astray.
It is by doing this, then, (to sum the
matter up) that we shall best be able
to hit the mean.

But this is no doubt difficult, and especially in individual cases; for it is
not easy to determine both how and
with whom and on what provocation
and how long one should be angry;
for we too sometimes praise those who
fall short and call them good-tempered, but sometimes we praise those
who get angry and call them manly.
The man, however, who deviates little
from goodness is not blamed, whether
he do so in the direction of the more
or of the less, but only the man who
deviates more widely; for *he* does not

[13] *Od.* xii. 219 f. (Mackail's trans.). But
it was Circe who gave the advice (xii.
108), and the actual quotation is from
Odysseus' orders to his steersman.

fail to be noticed. But up to what point
and to what extent a man must deviate
before he becomes blameworthy it is
not easy to determine by reasoning,
any more than anything else that is
perceived by the senses; such things
depend on particular facts, and the
decision rests with perception. So
much, then, is plain, that the intermediate state is in all things to be praised,
but that we must incline sometimes
towards the excess, sometimes towards
the deficiency; for so shall we most
easily hit the mean and what is right.

BOOK III

Responsible Action

1. Since virtue is concerned with
passions and actions, and on voluntary
passions and actions praise and blame
are bestowed, on those that are involuntary pardon, and sometimes also
pity, to distinguish the voluntary and
the involuntary is presumably necessary for those who are studying the
nature of virtue, and useful also for
legislators with a view to the assigning
both of honours and of punishments.

Those things, then, are thought involuntary, which take place under
compulsion or owing to ignorance; and
that is compulsory of which the moving principle is outside, being a principle in which nothing is contributed
by the person who is acting or is feeling the passion, e. g. if he were to be
carried somewhere by a wind, or by
men who had him in their power.

But with regard to the things that
are done from fear of greater evils or
for some noble object (e. g. if a tyrant
were to order one to do something
base, having one's parents and children in his power, and if one did the
action they were to be saved, but
otherwise would be put to death), it
may be debated whether such actions

are involuntary or voluntary. Something of the sort happens also with regard to the throwing of goods overboard in a storm; for in the abstract no one throws goods away voluntarily, but on condition of its securing the safety of himself and his crew any sensible man does so. Such actions, then, are mixed, but are more like voluntary actions; for they are worthy of choice at the time when they are done, and the end of an action is relative to the occasion. Both the terms, then, 'voluntary' and 'involuntary,' must be used with reference to the moment of action. Now the man acts voluntarily; for the principle that moves the instrumental parts of the body in such actions is in him, and the things of which the moving principle is in a man himself are in his power to do or not to do. Such actions, therefore, are voluntary, but in the abstract perhaps involuntary; for no one would choose any such act in itself.

For such actions men are sometimes even praised, when they endure something base or painful in return for great or noble objects gained; in the opposite case they are blamed, since to endure the greatest indignities for no noble end or for a trifling end is the mark of an inferior person. On some actions praise indeed is not bestowed, but pardon is, when one does what he ought not under pressure which overstrains human nature and which no one could withstand. But some acts, perhaps, we cannot be forced to do, but ought rather to face death after the most fearful sufferings; for the things that 'forced' Euripides' Alcmaeon to slay his mother seem absurd. It is difficult sometimes to determine what should be chosen at what cost, and what should be endured in return for what gain, and yet more difficult to abide by our decisions; for as a rule what is expected is painful, and what we are forced to do is base, whence

praise and blame are bestowed on those who have been compelled or have not.

What sort of acts, then, should be called compulsory? We answer that without qualification actions are so when the cause is in the external circumstances and the agent contributes nothing. But the things that in themselves are involuntary, but now and in return for these gains are worthy of choice, and whose moving principle is in the agent, are in themselves involuntary, but now and in return for these gains voluntary. They are more like voluntary acts; for actions are in the class of particulars, and the particular acts here are voluntary. What sort of things are to be chosen, and in return for what, it is not easy to state; for there are many differences in the particular cases.

But if some one were to say that pleasant and noble objects have a compelling power, forcing us from without, all acts would be for him compulsory; for it is for these objects that all men do everything they do. And those who act under compulsion and unwillingly act with pain, but those who do acts for their pleasantness and nobility do them with pleasure; it is absurd to make external circumstances responsible, and not oneself, as being easily caught by such attractions, and to make oneself responsible for noble acts but the pleasant objects responsible for base acts. The compulsory, then, seems to be that whose moving principle is outside, the person compelled contributing nothing.

Everything that is done by reason of ignorance is not voluntary; it is only what produces pain and repentance that is involuntary. For the man who has done something owing to ignorance, and feels not the least vexation at his action, has not acted voluntarily, since he did not know what he was doing, nor yet involuntarily, since he is not pained. Of people, then, who act by reason of ignorance he who repents is thought an involuntary agent, and the man who does not repent may, since he is different, be called a not voluntary agent; for, since he differs from the other, it is better that he should have a name of his own.

Acting by reason of ignorance seems also to be different from acting *in* ignorance; for the man who is drunk or in a rage is thought to act as a result not of ignorance but of one of the causes mentioned, yet not knowingly but in ignorance.

Now every wicked man is ignorant of what he ought to do and what he ought to abstain from, and it is by reason of error of this kind that men become unjust and in general bad; but the term 'involuntary' tends to be used not if a man is ignorant of what is to his advantage—for it is not mistaken purpose that causes involuntary action (it leads rather to wickedness), nor ignorance of the universal (for *that* men are *blamed*), but ignorance of particulars, i. e. of the circumstances of the action and the objects with which it is concerned. For it is on these that both pity and pardon depend, since the person who is ignorant of any of these acts involuntarily.

Perhaps it is just as well, therefore, to determine their nature and number. A man may be ignorant, then, of who he is, and what he is doing, what or whom he is acting on, and sometimes also what (e. g. what instrument) he is doing it with, and to what end (e. g. he may think his act will conduce to some one's safety), and how he is doing it (e. g. whether gently or violently). Now of all of these no one could be ignorant unless he were mad, and evidently also he could not be ignorant of the agent; for how could he not know himself? But of what he is doing a man might be ignorant, as for instance people say 'it slipped out of

their mouths as they were speaking,' or 'they did not know it was a secret', as Aeschylus said of the mysteries, or a man might say he 'let it go off when he merely wanted to show its working', as the man did with the catapult. Again, one might think one's son was an enemy, as Merope did, or that a pointed spear had a button on it, or that a stone was pumice-stone; or one might give a man a draught to save him, and really kill him; or one might want to touch a man, as people do in sparring, and really wound him. The ignorance may relate, then, to any of these things, i. e. of the circumstances of the action, and the man who was ignorant of any of these is thought to have acted involuntarily, and especially if he was ignorant on the most important points; and these are thought to be the circumstances of the action and its end. Further, the doing of an act that is called involuntary in virtue of ignorance of this sort must be painful and involve repentance.

Since that which is done under compulsion or by reason of ignorance is involuntary, the voluntary would seem to be that of which the moving principle is in the agent himself, he being aware of the particular circumstances of the action. Presumably acts done by reason of anger or appetite are not rightly called involuntary.[14] For in the first place, on that showing none of the other animals will act voluntarily, nor will children; and secondly, is it meant that we do not do voluntarily *any* of the acts that are due to appetite or anger, or that we do the noble acts voluntarily and the base acts involuntarily? Is not this absurd, when one and the same thing is the cause? But it would surely be odd to describe as involuntary the things one ought to desire; and we ought both to

[14] A reference to Pl. *Laws* 863 B, ff., where anger and appetite are coupled with ignorance as sources of wrong action.

be angry at certain things and to have an appetite for certain things, e. g. for health and for learning. Also what is involuntary is thought to be painful, but what is in accordance with appetite is thought to be pleasant. Again, what is the difference in respect of involuntariness between errors committed upon calculation and those committed in anger? Both are to be avoided, but the irrational passions are thought not less human than reason is, and therefore also the actions which proceed from anger or appetite are the man's actions. It would be odd, then, to treat them as involuntary.

2. Both the voluntary and the involuntary having been delimited, we must next discuss choice; for it is thought to be most closely bound up with virtue and to discriminate characters better than actions do.

Choice, then, seems to be voluntary, but not the same thing as the voluntary; the latter extends more widely. For both children and the lower animals share in voluntary action, but not in choice, and acts done on the spur of the moment we describe as voluntary, but not as chosen.

Those who say it is appetite or anger or wish or a kind of opinion do not seem to be right. For choice is not common to irrational creatures as well, but appetite and anger are. Again, the incontinent man acts with appetite, but not with choice; while the continent man on the contrary acts with choice, but not with appetite. Again, appetite is contrary to choice, but not appetite to appetite. Again, appetite relates to the pleasant and the painful, choice neither to the painful nor to the pleasant.

Still less is it anger; for acts due to anger are thought to be less than any others objects of choice.

But neither is it wish, though it seems near to it; for choice cannot relate to impossibles, and if any one said he chose them he would be thought silly; but there may be a wish even for impossibles, e. g. for immortality. And wish may relate to things that could in no way be brought about by one's own efforts, e. g. that a particular actor or athlete should win in a competition; but no one chooses such things, but only the things that he thinks could be brought about by his own efforts. Again, wish relates rather to the end, choice to the means; for instance, we wish to be healthy, but we choose the acts which will make us healthy, and we wish to be happy and say we do, but we cannot well say we choose to be so; for, in general, choice seems to relate to the things that are in our own power.

For this reason, too, it cannot be opinion; for opinion is thought to relate to all kinds of things, no less to eternal things and impossible things than to things in our own power; and it is distinguished by its falsity or truth, not by its badness or goodness, while choice is distinguished rather by these.

Now with opinion in general perhaps no one even says it is identical. But it is not identical even with any kind of opinion; for by choosing what is good or bad we are men of a certain character, which we are not by holding certain opinions. And we choose to get or avoid something good or bad, but we have opinions about what a thing is or whom it is good for or how it is good for him; we can hardly be said to opine to get or avoid anything. And choice is praised for being related to the right object rather than for being rightly related to it, opinion for being truly related to its object. And we choose what we best know to be good, but we opine what we do not quite know; and it is not the same people that are thought to make the best choices and to have the best opinions, but some are thought to have fairly good opinions, but by reason of vice to choose what they should not. If opinion precedes choice or accompanies it, that makes no difference; for it is not this that we are considering, but whether it is *identical with some* kind of opinion.

What, then, or what kind of thing is it, since it is none of the things we have mentioned? It seems to be voluntary, but not all that is voluntary to be an object of choice. Is it, then, what has been decided on by previous deliberation? At any rate choice involves a rational principle and thought. Even the name seems to suggest that it is what is chosen before other things.

3. Do we deliberate about everything, and is everything a possible subject of deliberation, or is deliberation impossible about some things? We ought presumably to call not what a fool or a madman would deliberate about, but what a sensible man would deliberate about, a subject of deliberation. Now about eternal things no one deliberates, e. g. about the material universe or the incommensurability of the diagonal and the side of a square. But no more do we deliberate about the things that involve movement but always happen in the same way, whether of necessity or by nature or from any other cause, e. g. the solstices and the risings of the stars; nor about things that happen now in one way, now in another, e. g. droughts and rains; nor about chance events, like the finding of treasure. But we do not deliberate even about all human affairs; for instance, no Spartan deliberates about the best constitution for the Scythians. For none of these things can be brought about by our own efforts.

We deliberate about things that are in our power and can be done; and these are in fact what is left. For nature, necessity, and chance are thought to be causes, and also reason and everything that depends on man. Now every class of men deliberates about the things that can be done by their own efforts. And in the case of exact and self-contained sciences there is no deliberation, e. g. about the letters of the alphabet (for we have no doubt how they should be written); but the things that are brought about by our own efforts, but not always in the same way, are the things about which we deliberate, e. g. questions of medical treatment or of money-making. And we do so more in the case of the art of navigation than in that of gymnastics, inasmuch as it has been less exactly worked out, and again about other things in the same ratio, and more also in the case of the arts than in that of the sciences; for we have more doubt about the former. Deliberation is concerned with things that happen in a certain way for the most part, but in which the event is obscure, and with things in which it is indeterminate. We call in others to aid us in deliberation on important questions, distrusting ourselves as not being equal to deciding.

We deliberate not about ends but about means. For a doctor does not deliberate whether he shall heal, nor an orator whether he shall persuade, nor a statesman whether he shall produce law and order, nor does any one else deliberate about his end. They assume the end and consider how and by what means it is to be attained; and if it seems to be produced by several means they consider by which it is most easily and best produced, while if it is achieved by one only they consider how it will be achieved by this and by what means *this* will be achieved, till they come to the first cause, which in the order of discovery is last. For the person who deliberates seems to investigate and analyse in the way described as though he were analysing a geometrical construction [15] (not all investigation appears to be deliberation—for instance mathematical investigations—but all deliberation is investigation), and what is last in the order of analysis seems to be first in the order of becoming. And if we come on an impossibility, we give up the search, e. g. if we need money and this cannot be got; but if a thing appears possible we try to do it. By 'possible' things I mean things that might be brought about by our own efforts, and these in a sense include things that can be brought about by the efforts of our friends, since the moving principle is in ourselves. The subject of investigation is sometimes the instruments, sometimes the use of them; and similarly in the other cases— sometimes the means, sometimes the mode of using it or the means of bringing it about. It seems, then, as has been said, that man is a moving principle of actions; now deliberation is about the things to be done by the agent himself, and actions are for the sake of things other than themselves. For the end cannot be a subject of deliberation, but only the means; nor indeed can the particular facts be a subject of it, as whether this is bread or has been baked as it should; for these are matters of perception. If we are to be always deliberating, we shall have to go on to infinity.

The same thing is deliberated upon

[15] Aristotle has in mind the method of discovering the solution of a geometrical problem. The problem being to construct a figure of a certain kind, we suppose it constructed and then analyse it to see if there is some figure by constructing which we can construct the required figure, and so on till we come to a figure which our existing knowledge enables us to construct.

and is chosen, except that the object of choice is already determinate, since it is that which has been decided upon as a result of deliberation that is the object of choice. For every one ceases to inquire how he is to act when he has brought the moving principle back to himself and to the ruling part of himself; for this is what chooses. This is plain also from the ancient constitutions, which Homer represented; for the kings announced their choices to the people. The object of choice being one of the things in our own power which is desired after deliberation, choice will be deliberate desire of things in our own power; for when we have decided as a result of deliberation, we desire in accordance with our deliberation.

We may take it, then, that we have described choice in outline, and stated the nature of its objects and the fact that is concerned with means.

4. That *wish* is for the end has already been stated; some think it is for the good, others for the apparent good. Now those who say that the good is the object of wish must admit in consequence that that which the man who does not choose aright wishes for is not an object of wish (for if it is to be so, it must also be good; but it was, if it so happened, bad); while those who say the apparent good is the object of wish must admit that there is no natural object of wish, but only what seems good to each man. Now different things appear good to different people, and, if it so happens, even contrary things.

If these consequences are unpleasing, are we to say that absolutely and in truth the good is the object of wish, but for each person the apparent good; that that which is in truth an object of wish is an object of wish to the good man, while any chance thing may be so to the bad man, as in the case of bodies also the things that are in truth wholesome are wholesome for bodies which are in good condition, while for those that are diseased other things are wholesome—or bitter or sweet or hot or heavy, and so on; since the good man judges each class of things rightly, and in each the truth appears to him? For each state of character has its own ideas of the noble and the pleasant, and perhaps the good man differs from others most by seeing the truth in each class of things, being as it were the norm and measure of them. In most things the error seems to be due to pleasure; for it appears a good when it is not. We therefore choose the pleasant as a good, and avoid pain as an evil.

5. The end, then, being what we wish for, the means what we deliberate about and choose, actions concerning means must be according to choice and voluntary. Now the exercise of the virtues is concerned with means. Therefore virtue also is in our own power, and so too vice. For where it is in our power to act it is also in our power not to act, and *vice versa;* so that, if to act, where this is noble, is in our power, not to act, which will be base, will also be in our power, and if not to act, where this is noble, is in our power, to act, which will be base, will also be in our power. Now if it is in our power to do noble or base acts, and likewise in our power not to do them, and this was what being good or bad meant, then it is in our power to be virtuous or vicious.

The saying that 'no one is voluntarily wicked nor involuntarily happy' seems to be partly false and partly true; for no one is involuntarily happy, but wickedness *is* voluntary. Or else we shall have to dispute what has just been said, at any rate, and deny that man is a moving principle or begetter of his actions as of children. But if

these facts are evident and we cannot refer actions to moving principles other than those in ourselves, the acts whose moving principles are in us must themselves also be in our power and voluntary.

Witness seems to be borne to this both by individuals in their private capacity and by legislators themselves; for these punish and take vengeance on those who do wicked acts (unless they have acted under compulsion or as a result of ignorance for which they are not themselves responsible), while they honour those who do noble acts, as though they meant to encourage the latter and deter the former. But no one is encouraged to do the things that are neither in our power nor voluntary; it is assumed that there is no gain in being persuaded not to be hot or in pain or hungry or the like, since we shall experience these feelings none the less. Indeed, we punish a man for his very ignorance, if he is thought responsible for the ignorance, as when penalties are doubled in the case of drunkenness; for the moving principle is in the man himself, since he had the power of not getting drunk and his getting drunk was the cause of his ignorance. And we punish those who are ignorant of anything in the laws that they ought to know and that is not difficult, and so too in the case of anything else that they are thought to be ignorant of through carelessness; we assume that it is in their power not to be ignorant, since they have the power of taking care.

But perhaps a man is the kind of man not to take care. Still they are themselves by their slack lives responsible for becoming men of that kind, and men make themselves responsible for being unjust or self-indulgent, in the one case by cheating and in the other by spending their time in drinking bouts and the like; for it is activities exercised on particular objects that make the corresponding character. This is plain from the case of people training for any contest or action; they practice the activity the whole time. Now not to know that it is from the exercise of activities on particular objects that states of character are produced is the mark of a thoroughly senseless person. Again, it is irrational to suppose that a man who acts unjustly does not wish to be unjust or a man who acts self-indulgently to be self-indulgent. But if *without* being ignorant a man does the things which will make him unjust, he will be unjust voluntarily. Yet it does not follow that if he wishes he will cease to be unjust and will be just. For neither does the man who is ill become well on those terms. We may suppose a case in which he is ill voluntarily, through living incontinently and disobeying his doctors. In that case it was *then* open to him not to be ill, but not now, when he has thrown away his chance, just as when you have let a stone go it is too late to recover it; but yet it was in your power to throw it, since the moving principle was in you. So, too, to the unjust and to the self-indulgent man it was open at the beginning not to become men of this kind, and so they are unjust and self-indulgent voluntarily; but now that they have become so it is not possible for them not to be so.

But not only are the vices of the soul voluntary, but those of the body also for some men, whom we accordingly blame; while no one blames those who are ugly by nature, we blame those who are so owing to want of exercise and care. So it is, too, with respect to weakness and infirmity; no one would reproach a man blind from birth or by disease or from a blow, but rather pity him, while every one would blame a man who was blind from drunkenness or some other form of self-indulgence. Of vices of the body, then, those in our own power are blamed, those not in our power are not. And if this be so, in the other cases also the vices that are blamed must be in our own power.

Now some one may say that all men desire the apparent good, but have no control over the appearance, but the end appears to each man in a form answering to his character. We reply that if each man is somehow responsible for his state of mind, he will also be himself somehow responsible for the appearance; but if not, no one is responsible for his own evildoing, but every one does evil acts through ignorance of the end, thinking that by these he will get what is best, and the aiming at the end is not self-chosen but one must be born with an eye, as it were, by which to judge rightly and choose what is truly good, and he is well endowed by nature who is well endowed with this. For it is what is greatest and most noble, and what we cannot get or learn from another, but must have just such as it was when given us at birth, and to be well and nobly endowed with this will be perfect and true excellence of natural endowment. If this is true, then, how will virtue be more voluntary than vice? To both men alike, the good and the bad, the end appears and is fixed by nature or however it may be, and it is by referring everything else to this that men do whatever they do.

Whether, then, it is not by nature that the end appears to each man such as it does appear, but something also depends on him, or the end is natural but because the good man adopts the means voluntarily virtue is voluntary, vice also will be none the less voluntary; for in the case of the bad man there is equally present that which depends on himself in his actions even if not in his end. If, then, as is asserted, the virtues are voluntary (for we are ourselves somehow partly responsible for our states of character, and it is by being persons of a certain kind that we assume the end to be so and so), the vices also will be voluntary; for the same is true of them.

With regard to the virtues in *general* we have stated their genus in outline, viz. that they are means and that they are states of character, and that they tend, and by their own nature, to the doing of the acts by which they are produced, and that they are in our power and voluntary, and act as the right rule prescribes. But actions and states of character are not voluntary in the same way; for we are masters of our actions from the beginning right to the end, if we know the particular facts, but though we control the beginning of our states of character the gradual progress is not obvious, any more than it is in illnesses; because it was in our power, however, to act in this way or not in this way, therefore the states are voluntary.

BOOK VI

KNOWLEDGE AND PRACTICAL WISDOM

1. Since we have previously said that one ought to choose that which is intermediate, not the excess nor the defect, and that the intermediate is determined by the dictates of the right rule, let us discuss the nature of these dictates. In all the states of character we have mentioned, as in all other matters, there is a mark to which the man who has the rule looks, and heightens or relaxes his activity accordingly, and there is a standard which determines the mean states which we say are intermediate between excess and defect, being in accordance with the right rule. But such a statement, though true, is by no means clear; for not only here but in all other pursuits which are objects of knowledge it is indeed true to say that we must not exert ourselves nor relax our efforts too much nor too little, but to an intermediate extent and as the right rule dictates; but if a man had only this knowledge he would be none the wiser—e. g. we should not know what sort of medicines to apply to our body if some one were to say 'all those which the medical art prescribes, and which agree with the practice of one who possesses the art.' Hence it is necessary with regard to the states of the soul also not only that this true statement should be made, but also that it should be determined what is the right rule and what is the standard that fixes it.

We divided the virtues of the soul and said that some are virtues of character and others of intellect. Now we have discussed in detail the moral virtues; with regard to the others let us express our view as follows, beginning with some remarks about the soul. We said before that there are two parts of the soul—that which grasps a rule or rational principle, and the irrational; let us now draw a similar distinction within the part which grasps a rational principle. And let it be assumed that there are two parts which grasp a rational principle — one by which we contemplate the kind of things whose originative causes are invariable, and one by which we contemplate variable things; for where objects differ in kind the part of the soul answering to each of the two is different in kind, since it is in virtue of a certain likeness and kinship with their objects that they have the knowledge they have. Let one of these parts be called the scientific and the other the calculative; for to deliberate and to calculate are the same thing, but no one deliberates about the invariable. Therefore the calculative is one part of the faculty which grasps a rational principle. We must, then, learn what is the best state of each of these two parts; for this is the virtue of each.

2. The virtue of a thing is relative to its proper work. Now there are three things in the soul which control action and truth—sensation, reason, desire.

Of these sensation originates no action; this is plain from the fact that the lower animals have sensation but no share in action.

What affirmation and negation are in thinking, pursuit and avoidance are in desire; so that since moral virtue is a state of character concerned with choice, and choice is deliberate desire, therefore both the reasoning must be true and the desire right, if the choice is to be good, and the latter must pursue just what the former asserts. Now this kind of intellect and of truth is practical; of the intellect which is contemplative, not practical nor productive, the good and the bad state are truth and falsity respectively (for this is the work of everything intellectual); while of the part which is practical and intellectual the good state is truth in agreement with right desire.

The origin of action—its efficient, not its final cause—is choice, and that of choice is desire and reasoning with a view to an end. This is why choice cannot exist either without reason and intellect or without a moral state; for good action and its opposite cannot exist without a combination of intellect and character. Intellect itself, however, moves nothing, but only the intellect which aims at an end and is practical; for this rules the productive intellect as well, since every one who makes makes for an end, and that which is made is not an end in the unqualified sense (but only an end in a particular relation, and the end of a particular operation)—only that which is *done* is that; for good action

is an end, and desire aims at this. Hence choice is either desiderative reason or ratiocinative desire, and such an origin of action is a man. (It is to be noted that nothing that is past is an object of choice, e. g. no one chooses to have sacked Troy; for no one *deliberates* about the past, but about what is future and capable of being otherwise, while what is past is not capable of not having taken place; hence Agathon is right in saying

> For this alone is lacking even to God,
> To make undone things that have
>   once been done.)

The work of both the intellectual parts, then, is truth. Therefore the states that are most strictly those in respect of which each of these parts will reach truth are the virtues of the two parts.

3. Let us begin, then, from the beginning, and discuss these states once more. Let it be assumed that the states by virtue of which the soul possesses truth by way of affirmation or denial are five in number, i. e. art, scientific knowledge, practical wisdom, philosophic wisdom, intuitive reason; we do not include judgement and opinion because in these we may be mistaken.

Now what *scientific knowledge* is, if we are to speak exactly and not follow mere similarities, is plain from what follows. We all suppose that what we know is not even capable of being otherwise; of things capable of being otherwise we do not know, when they have passed outside our observation, whether they exist or not. Therefore the object of scientific knowledge is of necessity. Therefore it is eternal; for things that are of necessity in the unqualified sense are all eternal; and things that are eternal are ungenerated and imperishable. Again, every science is thought to be capable of being taught, and its object of being learned. And all teaching starts from what is already known, as we maintain in the *Analytics* also; for it proceeds sometimes through induction and sometimes by syllogism. Now induction is the starting-point which knowledge even of the universal presupposes, while syllogism proceeds *from* universals. There are therefore starting-points from which syllogism proceeds, which are not reached by syllogism; it is therefore by induction that they are acquired. Scientific knowledge is, then, a state of capacity to demonstrate, and has the other limiting characteristics which we specify in the *Analytics;* for it is when a man believes in a certain way and the starting-points are known to him that he has scientific knowledge, since if they are not better known to him than the conclusion, he will have his knowledge only incidentally.

Let this, then, be taken as our account of scientific knowledge.

4. In the variable are included both things made and things done; making and acting are different (for their nature we treat even the discussions outside our school as reliable); so that the reasoned state of capacity to act is different from the reasoned state of capacity to make. Hence too they are not included one in the other; for neither is acting making nor is making acting. Now since architecture is an art and is essentially a reasoned state of capacity to make, and there is neither any art that is not such a state nor any such state that is not an art, *art* is identical with a state of capacity to make, involving a true course of reasoning. All art is concerned with coming into being, i. e. with contriving and considering how something may come into being which is capable of either being or not being, and whose

origin is in the maker and not in the thing made; for art is concerned neither with things that are, or come into being, by necessity, nor with things that do so in accordance with nature (since these have their origin in themselves). Making and acting being different, art must be a matter of making, not of acting. And in a sense chance and art are concerned with the same objects; as Agathon says, 'art loves chance and chance loves art'. Art, then, as has been said, is a state concerned with making, involving a true course of reasoning, and lack of art on the contrary is a state concerned with making, involving a false course of reasoning; both are concerned with the variable.

5. Regarding *practical wisdom* we shall get at the truth by considering who are the persons we credit with it. Now it is thought to be the mark of a man of practical wisdom to be able to deliberate well about what is good and expedient for himself, not in some particular respect, e. g. about what sorts of thing conduce to health or to strength, but about what sorts of thing conduce to the good life in general. This is shown by the fact that we credit men with practical wisdom in some particular respect when they have calculated well with a view to some good end which is one of those that are not the object of any art. It follows that in the general sense also the man who is capable of deliberating has practical wisdom. Now no one deliberates about things that are invariable, nor about things that it is impossible for him to do. Therefore, since scientific knowledge involves demonstration, but there is no demonstration of things whose first principles are variable (for all such things might actually be otherwise), and since it is impossible to deliberate about things that are of necessity, practical wisdom can-

not be scientific knowledge nor art; not science because that which can be done is capable of being otherwise, not art because action and making are different kinds of thing. The remaining alternative, then, is that it is a true and reasoned state of capacity to act with regard to the things that are good or bad for man. For while making has an end other than itself, action cannot; for good action itself is its end. It is for this reason that we think Pericles and men like him have practical wisdom, viz. because they can see what is good for themselves and what is good for men in general; we consider that those can do this who are good at managing households or states. (This is why we call temperance (*sophrosyne*) by this name; we imply that it preserves one's practical wisdom (*sodsousa ten phronesin*). Now what it preserves is a judgement of the kind we have described. For it is not any and every judgment that pleasant and painful objects destroy and pervert, e. g. the judgement that the triangle has or has not its angles equal to two right angles, but only judgements about what is to be done. For the originating causes of the things that are done consist in the end at which they are aimed; but the man who has been ruined by pleasure or pain forthwith fails to see any such originating cause—to see that for the sake of this or because of this he ought to choose and do whatever he chooses and does; for vice is destructive of the originating cause of action.)

Practical wisdom, then, must be a reasoned and true state of capacity to act with regard to human goods. But further, while there is such a thing as excellence in art, there is no such thing as excellence in practical wisdom; and in art he who errs willingly is preferable, but in practical wisdom, as in the virtues, he is the reverse. Plainly, then, practical wisdom is a virtue and not an art. There being two parts of the soul that can follow a course of reasoning, it must be the virtue of one of the two, i. e. of that part which forms opinions; for opinion is about the variable and so is practical wisdom. But yet it is not only a reasoned state; this is shown by the fact that a state of that sort may be forgotten but practical wisdom cannot.

6. Scientific knowledge is judgement about things that are universal and necessary, and the conclusions of demonstration, and all scientific knowledge, follow from first principles (for scientific knowledge involves apprehension of a rational ground). This being so, the first principle from which what is scientifically known follows cannot be an object of scientific knowledge, of art, or of practical wisdom; for that which can be scientifically known can be demonstrated, and art and practical wisdom deal with things that are variable. Nor are these first principles the objects of philosophic wisdom, for it is a mark of the philosopher to have *demonstration* about some things. If, then, the states of mind by which we have truth and are never deceived about things invariable or even variable are scientific knowledge, practical wisdom, philosophic wisdom, and intuitive reason, and it cannot be any of the three (i. e. practical wisdom, scientific knowledge, or philosophic wisdom), the remaining alternative is that it is *intuitive reason* that grasps the first principles.

7. *Wisdom* (1) in the arts we ascribe to their most finished exponents, e. g. to Phidias as a sculptor and to Polyclitus as a maker of portrait-statues, and here we mean nothing by wisdom except excellence in art; but (2) we think that some people are wise in general, not in some particular

field or in any other limited respect, as Homer says in the *Margites,*

Him did the gods make neither a digger
    nor yet a ploughman
Nor wise in anything else.

Therefore wisdom must plainly be the most finished of the forms of knowledge. It follows that the wise man must not only know what follows from the first principles, but must also possess truth about the first principles. Therefore wisdom must be intuitive reason combined with scientific knowledge—scientific knowledge of the highest objects which has received as it were its proper completion.

Of the highest objects, we say; for it would be strange to think that the art of politics, or practical wisdom, is the best knowledge, since man is not the best thing in the world. Now if what is healthy or good is different for men and for fishes, but what is white or straight is always the same, any one would say that what is wise is the same but what is practically wise is different; for it is to that which observes well the various matters concerning itself that one ascribes practical wisdom, and it is to this that one will entrust such matters. This is why we say that some even of the lower animals have practical wisdom, viz. those which are found to have a power of foresight with regard to their own life. It is evident also that philosophic wisdom and the art of politics cannot be the same; for if the state of mind concerned with a man's own interests is to be called philosophic wisdom, there will be many philosophic wisdoms; there will not be one concerned with the good of all animals (any more than there is one art of medicine for all existing things), but a different philosophic wisdom about the good of each species.

But if the argument be that man is

the best of the animals, this makes no difference; for there are other things much more divine in their nature even than man, e. g., most conspicuously, the bodies of which the heavens are framed. From what has been said it is plain, then, that philosophic wisdom is scientific knowledge, combined with intuitive reason, of the things that are highest by nature. This is why we say Anaxagoras, Thales, and men like them have philosophic but not practical wisdom, when we see them ignorant of what is to their own advantage, and why we say that they knew things that are remarkable, admirable, difficult, and divine, but useless; viz. because it is not human goods that they seek.

Practical wisdom on the other hand is concerned with things human and things about which it is possible to deliberate; for we say this is above all the work of the man of practical wisdom, to deliberate well, but no one deliberates about things invariable, nor about things which have not an end, and that a good that can be brought about by action. The man who is without qualification good at deliberating is the man who is capable of aiming in accordance with calculation at the best for man of things attainable by action. Nor is practical wisdom concerned with universals only—it must also recognize the particulars; for it is practical, and practice is concerned with particulars. This is why some who do not know, and especially those who have experience, are more practical than others who know; for if a man knew that light meats are digestible and wholesome, but did not know which sorts of meat are light, he would not produce health, but the man who knows that chicken is wholesome is more likely to produce health.

Now practical wisdom is concerned with action; therefore one should have both forms of it, or the latter in preference to the former. But of practical as of philosophic wisdom there must be a controlling kind.

8. Political wisdom and practical wisdom are the same state of mind, but their essence is not the same. Of the wisdom concerned with the city, the practical wisdom which plays a controlling part is legislative wisdom, while that which is related to this as particulars to their universal is known by the general name 'political wisdom'; this has to do with action and deliberation, for a decree is a thing to be carried out in the form of an individual act. This is why the exponents of this art are alone said to 'take part in politics'; for these alone 'do things' as manual labourers 'do things'.

Practical wisdom also is identified especially with that form of it which is concerned with a man himself—with the individual; and this is known by the general name 'practical wisdom'; of the other kinds one is called household management, another legislation, the third politics, and of the latter one part is called deliberative and the other judicial. Now knowing what is good for oneself will be one kind of knowledge, but it is very different from the other kinds; and the man who knows and concerns himself with his own interests is thought to have practical wisdom, while politicians are thought to be busybodies; hence the words of Euripides,

But how could I be wise, who might at
   ease,
Numbered among the army's multitude,
Have had an equal share? . . .
For those who aim too high and do too
   much . . . .

Those who think thus seek their own good, and consider that one ought to do so. From this opinion, then, has come the view that such men have

practical wisdom; yet perhaps one's own good cannot exist without household management, nor without a form of government. Further, how one should order one's own affairs is not clear and needs inquiry.

What has been said is confirmed by the fact that while young men become geometricians and mathematicians and wise in matters like these, it is thought that a young man of practical wisdom cannot be found. The cause is that such wisdom is concerned not only with universals but with particulars, which become familiar from experience, but a young man has no experience, for it is length of time that gives experience; indeed one might ask this question too, why a boy may become a mathematician, but not a philosopher or a physicist. Is it because the objects of mathematics exist by abstraction, while the first principles of these other subjects come from experience, and because young men have no conviction about the latter but merely use the proper language, while the essence of mathematical objects is plain enough to them?

Further, error in deliberation may be either about the universal or about the particular; we may fail to know either that all water that weighs heavy is bad, or that this particular water weighs heavy.

That practical wisdom is not scientific knowledge is evident; for it is, as has been said, concerned with the ultimate particular fact, since the thing to be done is of this nature. It is opposed, then, to intuitive reason; for intuitive reason is of the limiting premisses, for which no reason can be given, while practical wisdom is concerned with the ultimate particular, which is the object not of scientific knowledge but of perception—not the perception of qualities peculiar to one sense but a perception akin to that by which we perceive that the particular figure before us is a triangle; for in that direction as well as in that of the major premiss there will be a limit. But this is rather perception than practical wisdom, though it is another kind of perception than that of the qualities peculiar to each sense.

9. There is a difference between inquiry and deliberation; for deliberation is inquiry into a particular kind of thing. We must grasp the nature of excellence in deliberation as well—whether it is a form of scientific knowledge, or opinion, or skill in conjecture, or some other kind of thing. *Scientific knowledge* it is not; for men do not inquire about the things they know about, but good deliberation is a kind of deliberation, and he who deliberates inquires and calculates. Nor is it *skill in conjecture;* for this both involves no reasoning and is something that is quick in its operation, while men deliberate a long time, and they say that one should carry out quickly the conclusions of one's deliberations, but should deliberate slowly. Again, *readiness of mind* is different from excellence in deliberation; it is a sort of skill in conjecture. Nor again is excellence in deliberation *opinion* of any sort. But since the man who deliberates badly makes a mistake, while he who deliberates well does so correctly, excellence in deliberation is clearly a kind of correctness, but neither of knowledge nor of opinion; for there is no such thing as correctness of knowledge (since there is no such thing as error of knowledge), and correctness of opinion is truth; and at the same time everything that is an object of opinion is already determined. But again excellence in deliberation involves reasoning. The remaining alternative, then, is that it is correctness *of thinking;* for this is not yet assertion, since, while even opinion is not inquiry but has reached the stage of assertion, the man who is deliberating, whether he does so well or ill, is searching for something and calculating.

But excellence in deliberation is a certain correctness of deliberation; hence we must first inquire what deliberation is and what it is about. And, there being more than one kind of correctness, plainly excellence in deliberation is not any and every kind; for (1) the incontinent man and the bad man, if he is clever, will reach as a result of his calculation what he sets before himself, so that he will have deliberated correctly, but he will have got for himself a great evil. Now to have deliberated well is thought to be a good thing; for it is this kind of correctness of deliberation that is excellence in deliberation, viz. that which tends to attain what is good. But (2) it is possible to attain even good by a false syllogism, and to attain what one ought to do but not by the right means, the middle term being false; so that this too is not yet excellence in deliberation—this state in virtue of which one attains what one ought but not by the right means. Again (3) it is possible to attain it by long deliberation while another man attains it quickly. Therefore in the former case we have not yet got excellence in deliberation, which is rightness with regard to the expedient—rightness in respect both of the end, the manner, and the time. (4) Further it is possible to have deliberated well either in the unqualified sense or with reference to a particular end. Excellence in deliberation in the unqualified sense, then, is that which succeeds with reference to what is the end in the unqualified sense, and excellence in deliberation in a particular sense is that which succeeds relatively to a particular end. If, then, it is characteristic of men of practical wisdom to have deliberated well, excellence in deliberation will be correctness with regard to what conduces to the end of which practical wisdom is the true apprehension.

10. Understanding, also, and goodness of understanding, in virtue of which men are said to be men of understanding or of good understanding, are neither entirely the same as opinion or scientific knowledge (for at that rate all men would have been men of understanding), nor are they one of the particular sciences, such as medicine, the science of things connected with health, or geometry, the science of spatial magnitudes. For understanding is neither about things that are always and are unchangeable, nor about any and every one of the things that come into being, but about things which may become subjects of questioning and deliberation. Hence it is about the same objects as practical wisdom; but understanding and practical wisdom are not the same. For practical wisdom issues commands, since its end is what ought to be done or not to be done; but understanding only judges. (Understanding is identical with goodness of understanding, men of understanding with men of good understanding.) Now understanding is neither the having nor the acquiring of practical wisdom; but as learning is called understanding when it means the exercise of the faculty of knowledge, so 'understanding' is applicable to the exercise of the faculty of opinion for the purpose of judging of what some one else says about matters with which practical wisdom is concerned—and of judging soundly; for 'well' and 'soundly' are the same thing. And from this has come the use of the name 'understanding' in virtue of which men are said to be 'of good understanding', viz. from the application of the word to the grasping of scientific truth; for we often call such grasping understanding.

11. What is called judgment, in virtue of which men are said to 'be sympathetic judges' and to 'have judgement', is the right discrimination of the equitable. This is shown by the fact that we say the equitable man is above all others a man of sympathetic judgment, and identify equity with sympathetic judgement about certain facts. And sympathetic judgement is judgement which discriminates what is equitable and does so correctly; and correct judgement is that which judges what is true.

Now all the states we have considered converge, as might be expected, to the same point; for when we speak of judgement and understanding and practical wisdom and intuitive reason we credit the same people with possessing judgement and having reached years of reason and with having practical wisdom and understanding. For all these faculties deal with ultimates, i. e. with particulars; and being a man of understanding and of good or sympathetic judgement consists in being able to judge about the things with which practical wisdom is concerned; for the equities are common to all good men in relation to other men. Now all things which have to be done are included among particulars or ultimates; for not only must the man of practical wisdom know particular facts, but understanding and judgement are also concerned with things to be done, and these are ultimates. And intuitive reason is concerned with the ultimates in both directions; for both the first terms and the last are objects of intuitive reason and not of argument, and the intuitive reason which is presupposed by demonstrations grasps the unchangeable and first terms, while the intuitive reason involved in practical reasons grasps the last and variable fact, i. e. the minor premiss. For these variable facts are the starting-points for the apprehension of the end, since the universals are reached from the particulars; of these therefore we must have perception, and this perception is intuitive reason.

This is why these states are thought to be natural endowments—why, while no one is thought to be a philosopher by nature, people are thought to have by nature judgement, understanding, and intuitive reason. This is shown by the fact that we think our powers correspond to our time of life, and that a particular age brings with it intuitive reason and judgment; this implies that nature is the cause. [Hence intuitive reason is both beginning and end; for demonstrations are from these and about these.] Therefore we ought to attend to the undemonstrated sayings and opinions of experienced and older people or of people of practical wisdom not less than to demonstrations; for because experience has given them an eye they see aright.

We have stated, then, what practical and philosophic wisdom are, and with what each of them is concerned, and we have said that each is the virtue of a different part of the soul.

12. Difficulties might be raised as to the utility of these qualities of mind. For (1) philosophic wisdom will contemplate none of the things that will make a man happy (for it is not concerned with any coming into being), and though practical wisdom has *this* merit, for what purpose do we need it? Practical wisdom is the quality of mind concerned with things just and noble and good for man, but these are the things which it is the mark of a *good* man to do, and we are none the more able to act for *knowing* them if the virtues are states of *character*, just as we are none the better able to act for knowing the things that are healthy and sound, in the sense not of producing but of issuing from the state of health; for we are none the more able

to act for having the art of medicine or of gymnastics. But (2) if we are to say that a man should have practical wisdom not for the sake of knowing moral truths but for the sake of becoming good, practical wisdom will be of no use to those who *are* good; but again it is of no use to those who have *not* virtue; for it will make no difference whether they have practical wisdom themselves or obey others who have it, and it would be enough for us to do what we do in the case of health; though we wish to become healthy, yet we do not learn the art of medicine. (3) Besides this, it would be thought strange if practical wisdom, being inferior to philosophic wisdom, is to be put in authority over it, as seems to be implied by the fact that the art which produces anything rules and issues commands about that thing.

These, then, are the questions we must discuss; so far we have only stated the difficulties.

(1) Now first let us say that in themselves these states must be worthy of choice because they are the virtues of the two parts of the soul respectively, even if neither of them produce anything.

(2) Secondly, they do produce something, not as the art of medicine produces health, however, but as health produces health;[16] so does philosophic wisdom produce happiness; for, being a part of virtue entire, by being possessed and by actualizing itself it makes a man happy.

(3) Again, the work of man is achieved only in accordance with practical wisdom as well as with moral virtue; for virtue makes us aim at the right mark, and practical wisdom makes us take the right means. (Of the fourth part of the soul—the nutri-

16 i.e. as health, as an inner state, produces the activities which we know as constituting health.

tive[17]—there is no such virtue; for there is nothing which it is in its power to do or not to do.)

(4) With regard to our being none the more able to do because of our practical wisdom what is noble and just, let us begin a little further back, starting with the following principle. As we say that some people who do just acts are not necessarily just, i. e. those who do the acts ordained by the laws either unwillingly or owing to ignorance or for some other reason and not for the sake of the acts themselves (though, to be sure, they do what they should and all the things that the good man ought), so is it, it seems, that in order to be good one must be in a certain state when one does the several acts, i.e. one must do them as a result of choice and for the sake of the acts themselves. Now virtue makes the choice right, but the question of the things which should naturally be done to carry out our choice belongs not to virtue but to another faculty. We must devote our attention to these matters and give a clearer statement about them. There is a faculty which is called cleverness; and this is such as to be able to do the things that tend towards the mark we have set before ourselves, and to hit it. Now if the mark be noble, the cleverness is laudable, but if the mark be bad, the cleverness is mere smartness; hence we call even men of practical wisdom clever or smart. Practical wisdom is not the faculty, but it does not exist without this faculty. And this eye of the soul acquires its formed state not without the aid of virtue, as has been said and is plain; for the syllogisms which deal with acts to be done are things which involve a starting-point, viz. 'since the end, i. e. what is best, is of such and such a nature', whatever it may be (let it for the sake

17 The other three being the scientific, the calculative, and the desiderative.

of argument be what we please); and this is not evident except to the good man; for wickedness perverts us and causes us to be deceived about the starting-points of action. Therefore it is evident that it is impossible to be practically wise without being good.

13. We must therefore consider virtue also once more; for virtue too is similarly related; as practical wisdom is to cleverness—not the same, but like it—so is natural virtue to virtue in the strict sense. For all men think that each type of character belongs to its possessors in some sense by nature; for from the very moment of birth we are just or fitted for self-control or brave or have the other moral qualities; but yet we seek something else as that which is good in the strict sense—we seek for the presence of such qualities in another way. For both children and brutes have the natural dispositions to these qualities, but without reason these are evidently hurtful. Only we seem to see this much, that, while one may be led astray by them, as a strong body which moves without sight may stumble badly because of its lack of sight, still, if a man once acquires reason, that makes a difference in action; and his state, while still like what it was, will then be virtue in the strict sense. Therefore, as in the part of us which forms opinions there are two types, cleverness and practical wisdom, so too in the moral part there are two types, natural virtue and virtue in the strict sense, and of these the latter involves practical wisdom. This is why some say that all the virtues are forms of practical wisdom, and why Socrates in one respect was on the right track while in another he went astray; in thinking that all the virtues were forms of practical wisdom he was right. This is confirmed by the fact that even now all men, when they define virtue, after naming

the state of character and its objects add 'that (state) which is in accordance with the right rule'; now the right rule is that which is in accordance with practical wisdom. All men, then, seem somehow to divine that this kind of state is virtue, viz. that which is in accordance with practical wisdom. But we must go a little further. For it is not merely the state in accordance with the right rule, but the state that implies the *presence* of the right rule, that is virtue; and practical wisdom is a right rule about such matters. Socrates, then, thought the virtues were rules or rational principles (for he thought they were, all of them, forms of scientific knowledge), while we think they *involve* a rational principle.

It is clear, then, from what has been said, that it is not possible to be good in the strict sense without practical wisdom, nor practically wise without moral virtue. But in this way we may also refute the dialectical argument whereby it might be contended that the virtues exist in separation from each other; the same man, it might be said, is not best equipped by nature for all the virtues, so that he will have already acquired one when he has not yet acquired another. This is possible in respect of the natural virtues, but not in respect of those in respect of which a man is called without qualification good; for with the presence of the one quality, practical wisdom, will be given all the virtues. And it is plain that, even if it were of no practical value, we should have needed it because it is the virtue of the part of us in question; plain too that the choice will not be right without practical wisdom any more than without virtue; for the one determines the end and the other makes us do the things that lead to the end.

But again it is not *supreme* over philosophic wisdom, i. e. over the superior part of us, any more than the art of medicine is over health; for it does not use it but provides for its coming into being; it issues orders, then, for its sake, but not to it. Further, to maintain its supremacy would be like saying that the art of politics rules the gods because it issues orders about all the affairs of the state.

BOOK X

Pleasure. Happiness

A. PLEASURE

1. After these matters we ought perhaps next to discuss pleasure. For it is thought to be most intimately connected with our human nature, which is the reason why in educating the young we steer them by the rudders of pleasure and pain; it is thought, too, that to enjoy the things we ought and to hate the things we ought has the greatest bearing on virtue of character. For these things extend right through life, with a weight and power of their own in respect both to virtue and to the happy life, since men choose what is pleasant and avoid what is painful; and such things, it will be thought, we should least of all omit to discuss, especially since they admit of much dispute. For some[18] say pleasure is the good, while others,[19] on the contrary, say it is thoroughly bad—some no doubt being persuaded that the facts are so, and others thinking it has a better effect on our life to exhibit pleasure as a bad thing even if it is not; for most people (they think) incline towards it and are the slaves of their pleasures, for which reason they ought to lead them in the opposite direction, since thus they will reach

[18] The school of Eudoxus. Aristippus is perhaps also referred to.
[19] The school of Speusippus.

the middle state. But surely this is not correct. For arguments about matters concerned with feelings and actions are less reliable than facts: and so when they clash with the facts of perception they are despised, and discredit the truth as well; if a man who runs down pleasure is once seen to be aiming at it, his inclining towards it is thought to imply that it is all worthy of being aimed at; for most people are not good at drawing distinctions. True arguments seem, then, most useful, not only with a view to knowledge, but with a view to life also; for since they harmonize with the facts they are believed, and so they stimulate those who understand them to live according to them.—Enough of such questions; let us proceed to review the opinions that have been expressed about pleasure.

2. Eudoxus thought pleasure was the good because he saw all things, both rational and irrational, aiming at it, and because in all things that which is the object of choice is what is excellent, and that which is most the object of choice the greatest good; thus the fact that all things moved towards the same object indicated that this was for all things the chief good (for each thing, he argued, finds its own good, as it finds its own nourishment); and that which is good for all things and at which all aim was *the* good. His arguments were credited more because of the excellence of his character than for their own sake; he was thought to be remarkably self-controlled, and therefore it was thought that he was not saying what he did say as a friend of pleasure, but that the facts really were so. He believed that the same conclusion followed no less plainly from a study of the contrary of pleasure; pain was in itself an object of aversion to all things, and therefore its contrary must

be similarly an object of choice. And again that is most an object of choice which we choose not because or for the sake of something else, and pleasure is admittedly of this nature; for no one asks to what end he is pleased, thus implying that pleasure is in itself an object of choice. Further, he argued that pleasure when added to any good, e. g. to just or temperate action, makes it more worthy of choice, and that it is only by itself that the good can be increased.

This argument seems to show it to be one of the goods, and no more a good than any other; for every good is more worthy of choice along with another good than taken alone. And so it is by an argument of this kind that Plato[20] proves the good *not* to be pleasure; he argues that the pleasant life is more desirable with wisdom than without, and that if the mixture is better, pleasure is not the good; for the good cannot become more desirable by the addition of anything to it. Now it is clear that nothing else, any more than pleasure, can be the good if it is made more desirable by the addition of any of the things that are good in themselves. What, then, is there that satisfies this criterion, which at the same time we can participate in? It is something of this sort that we are looking for.

Those who object that that at which all things aim is not necessarily good are, we may surmise, talking nonsense. For we say that that which every one thinks really is so; and the man who attacks this belief will hardly have anything more credible to maintain instead. If it is senseless creatures that desire the things in question, there might be something in what they say; but if intelligent creatures do so as well, what sense can there be in this view? But perhaps even in inferior creatures there is some natural

[20] *Phil.* 60 B–E.

good stronger than themselves which aims at their proper good.

Nor does the argument about the contrary of pleasure seem to be correct. They say that if pain is an evil it does not follow that pleasure is a good; for evil is opposed to evil and at the same time both are opposed to the neutral state—which is correct enough but does not apply to the things in question. For if both pleasure and pain belonged to the class of evils they ought both to be objects of aversion, while if they belonged to the class of neutrals neither should be an object of aversion or they should both be equally so; but in fact people evidently avoid the one as evil and choose the other as good; that then must be the nature of the opposition between them.

3. Nor again, if pleasure is not a quality, does it follow that it is not a good; for the activities of virtue are not qualities either, nor is happiness.

They say,[21] however, that the good is determinate, while pleasure is indeterminate, because it admits of degrees. Now if it is from the feeling of pleasure that they judge thus, the same will be true of justice and the other virtues, in respect of which we plainly say that people of a certain character are so more or less, and act more or less in accordance with these virtues; for people may be more just or brave, and it is possible also to act justly or temperately more or less. But if their judgement is based on the various pleasures, surely they are not stating the real cause,[22] if in fact some pleasures are unmixed and other mixed. Again, just as health admits of degrees without being indeterminate, why should not pleasure? The same proportion is not found in all

things, nor a single proportion always in the same thing, but it may be relaxed and yet persist up to a point, and it may differ in degree. The case of pleasure also may therefore be of this kind.

Again, they assume[23] that the good is perfect while movements and comings into being are imperfect, and try to exhibit pleasure as being a movement and a coming into being. But they do not seem to be right even in saying that it is a movement. For speed and slowness are thought to be proper to every movement, and if a movement, e. g. that of the heavens, has not speed or slowness in itself, it has it in relation to something else; but of pleasure neither of these things is true. For while we may *become* pleased quickly as we may become angry quickly, we cannot *be* pleased quickly, not even in relation to some one else, while we *can* walk, or grow, or the like, quickly. While, then, we can change quickly or slowly into a state of pleasure, we cannot quickly exhibit the activity of pleasure, i.e. be pleased. Again, how can it be a coming into being? It is not thought that any chance thing can come out of any chance thing, but that a thing is dissolved into that out of which it comes into being; and pain would be the destruction of that of which pleasure is the coming into being.

They say, too,[24] that pain is the lack of that which is according to nature, and pleasure is replenishment. But these experiences are bodily. If then pleasure is replenishment with that which is according to nature, that which feels pleasure will be that in which the replenishment takes place, i. e. the body; but that is not thought to be the case; therefore the replenishment is not pleasure, though one

[21] Ib. 24 E–25 A, 31 A.

[22] Sc., of the badness of (some) pleasures.

[23] Pl. *Phil.* 53 C–54 D.

[24] Ib. 31 E–32 B, 42 C, D.

would be pleased when replenishment was taking place, just as one would be pained if one was being operated on.[25] This opinion seems to be based on the pains and pleasures connected with nutrition; on the fact that when people have been short of food and have felt pain beforehand they are pleased by the replenishment. But this does not happen with all pleasures; for the pleasures of learning and, among the sensuous pleasures, those of smell, and also many sounds and sights, and memories and hopes, do not presuppose pain. Of what then will these be the coming into being? There has not been lack of anything of which they could be the supplying anew.

In reply to those who bring forward the disgraceful pleasures one may say that these are not pleasant; if things are pleasant to people of vicious constitution, we must not suppose that they are also pleasant to others than these, just as we do not reason so about the things that are wholesome or sweet or bitter to sick people, or ascribe whiteness to the things that seem white to those suffering from a disease of the eye. Or one might answer thus—that the pleasures are desirable, but not from *these* sources, as wealth is desirable, but not as the reward of betrayal, and health, but not at the cost of eating anything and everything. Or perhaps pleasures differ in kind; for those derived from noble sources are different from those derived from base sources, and one cannot get the pleasure of the just man without being just, nor that of the musical man without being musical, and so on.

The fact, too, that a friend is different from a flatterer seems to make it plain that pleasure is not a good or

that pleasures are different in kind; for the one is thought to consort with us with a view to the good, the other with a view to our pleasure, and the one is reproached for his conduct while the other is praised on the ground that he consorts with us for different ends. And no one would choose to live with the intellect of a child throughout his life, however much he were to be pleased at the things that children are pleased at, nor to get enjoyment by doing some most disgraceful deed, though he were never to feel any pain in consequence. And there are many things we should be keen about even if they brought no pleasure, e. g. seeing, remembering, knowing, possessing the virtues. If pleasures necessarily do accompany these, that makes no odds; we should choose these even if no pleasure resulted. It seems to be clear, then, that neither is pleasure the good nor is all pleasure desirable, and that some pleasures *are* different in kind or in their sources from the others. So much for the things that are said about pleasure and pain.

4. What pleasure, is or what kind of thing it is, will become plainer if we take up the question again from the beginning. Seeing seems to be at any moment complete, for it does not lack anything which coming into being later will complete its form; and pleasure also seems to be of this nature. For it is a whole, and at no time can one find a pleasure whose form will be completed if the pleasure lasts longer. For this reason, too, it is not a movement. For every movement (e. g. that of building) takes time and is for the sake of an end, and is complete when it has made what it aims at. It is complete, therefore, only in the whole time or at that final moment. In their parts and during the time they occupy, all movements are

---

25 The point being that the being replenished no more *is* pleasure than the being operated on *is* pain. For the instance, see Plato's *Timaeus* 65 B.

incomplete, and are different in kind from the whole movement and from each other. For the fitting together of the stones is different from the fluting of the column, and these are both different from the making of the temple; and the making of the temple is complete (for it lacks nothing with a view to the end proposed), but the making of the base or of the triglyph is incomplete; for each is the making of only a part. They differ in kind, then, and it is not possible to find at any and every time a movement complete in form, but if at all, only in the whole time. So, too, in the case of walking and all other movements. For if locomotion is a movement from here to there, it, too, has differences in kind—flying, walking, leaping, and so on. And not only so, but in walking itself there are such differences; for the whence and whither are not the same in the whole racecourse and in a part of it, nor in one part and in another, nor is it the same thing to traverse this line and that; for one traverses not only a line but one which is in a place, and this one is in a different place from that. We have discussed movement with precision in another work,[26] but it seems that it is not complete at any and every time, but that the many movements are incomplete and different in kind, since the whence and whither give them their form. But of pleasure the form is complete at any and every time. Plainly, then, pleasure and movement must be different from each other, and pleasure must be one of the things that are whole and complete. This would seem to be the case, too, from the fact that it is not possible to move otherwise than in time, but it *is* possible to be pleased; for that which takes place in a moment is a whole.

From these considerations it is clear, too, that these thinkers are not right

[26] *Phys.* vi–viii.

in saying there is a movement or a coming into being *of* pleasure. For these cannot be ascribed to all things, but only to those that are divisible and not wholes; there is no coming into being of seeing nor of a point nor of a unit, nor is any of these a movement or coming into being; therefore ther¢ is no movement or coming into being of pleasure either; for it is a whole.

Since every sense is active in relation to its object, and a sense which is in good condition acts perfectly in relation to the most beautiful of its objects (for perfect activity seems to be ideally of this nature; whether we say that *it* is active, or the organ in which it resides, may be assumed to be immaterial), it follows that in the case of each sense the best activity is that of the best-conditioned organ in relation to the finest of its objects. And this activity will be the most complete and pleasant. For, while there *is* pleasure in respect of any sense, and in respect of thought and contemplation no less, the most complete is pleasantest, and that of a well-conditioned organ in relation to the worthiest of its objects is the most complete; and the pleasure completes the activity. But the pleasure does not complete it in the same way as the combination of object and sense, both good, just as health and the doctor are not in the same way the cause of a man's being healthy. (That pleasure is produced in respect to each sense is plain; for we speak of sights and sounds as pleasant. It is also plain that it arises most of all when both the sense is at its best and it is active in reference to an object which corresponds; when both object and perceiver are of the best there will always be pleasure, since the requisite agent and patient are both present.) Pleasure completes the activity not as the corresponding permanent state does, by its immanence, but as an end which supervenes as the bloom of youth does on those in the flower of their age. So long, then, as both the intelligible or sensible object and the discriminating or contemplative faculty are as they should be, the pleasure will be involved in the activity; for when both the passive and the active factor are unchanged and are related to each other in the same way, the same result naturally follows.

How, then, is it that no one is continuously pleased? Is it that we grow weary? Certainly all human things are incapable of continuous activity. Therefore pleasure also is not continuous; for it accompanies activity. Some things delight us when they are new, but later do so less, for the same reason; for at first the mind is in a state of stimulation and intensely active about them, as people are with respect to their vision when they look hard at a thing, but afterwards our activity is not of this kind, but has grown relaxed; for which reason the pleasure also is dulled.

One might think that all men desire pleasure because they all aim at life; life is an activity, and each man is active about those things and with those faculties that he loves most; e. g. the musician is active with his hearing in reference to tunes, the student with his mind in reference to theoretical questions, and so on in each case; now pleasure completes the activities, and therefore life, which they desire. It is with good reason, then, that they aim at pleasure too, since for every one it completes life, which is desirable. But whether we choose life for the sake of pleasure or pleasure for the sake of life is a question we may dismiss for the present. For they seem to be bound up together and not to admit of separation, since without activity pleasure does not arise, and every activity is completed by the attendant pleasure.

5. For this reason pleasures seem,

too, to differ in kind. For things different in kind are, we think, completed by different things (we see this to be true both of natural objects and of things produced by art, e. g. animals, trees, a painting, a sculpture, a house, an implement); and, similarly, we think that activities differing in kind are completed by things differing in kind. Now the activities of thought differ from those of the senses, and both differ among themselves, in kind; so, therefore, do the pleasures that complete them.

This may be seen, too, from the fact that each of the pleasures is bound up with the activity it completes. For an activity is intensified by its proper pleasure, since each class of things is better judged of and brought to precision by those who engage in the activity with pleasure; e. g. it is those who enjoy geometrical thinking that become geometers and grasp the various propositions better, and, similarly, those who are fond of music or of building, and so on, make progress in their proper function by enjoying it; so the pleasures intensify the activities, and what intensifies a thing is proper to it, but things different in kind have properties different in kind.

This will be even more apparent from the fact that activities are hindered by pleasures arising from other sources. For people who are fond of playing the flute are incapable of attending to arguments if they overhear some one playing the flute, since they enjoy flute-playing more than the activity in hand; so the pleasure connected with flute-playing destroys the activity concerned with argument. This happens, similarly, in all other cases, when one is active about two things at once; the more pleasant activity drives out the other, and if it is much more pleasant does so all the more, so that one even ceases from the other. This is why when we enjoy anything very much we do not throw ourselves into anything else, and do one thing only when we are not much pleased by another; e. g. in the theatre the people who eat sweets do so most when the actors are poor. Now since activities are made precise and more enduring and better by their proper pleasure, and injured by alien pleasures, evidently the two kinds of pleasure are far apart. For alien pleasures do pretty much what proper pains do, since activities are destroyed by their proper pains; e. g. if a man finds writing or doing sums unpleasant and painful, he does not write, or does not do sums, because the activity is painful. So an activity suffers contrary effects from its proper pleasures and pains, i.e. from those that supervene on it in virtue of its own nature. And alien pleasures have been stated to do much the same as pain; they destroy the activity, only not to the same degree.

Now since activities differ in respect of goodness and badness, and some are worthy to be chosen, others to be avoided, and others neutral, so, too, are the pleasures; for to each activity there is a proper pleasure. The pleasure proper to a worthy activity is good and that proper to an unworthy activity bad; just as the appetites for noble objects are laudable, those for base objects culpable. But the pleasures involved in activities are more proper to them than the desires; for the latter are separated both in time and in nature, while the former are close to the activities, and so hard to distinguish from them that it admits of dispute whether the activity is not the same as the pleasure. (Still, pleasure does not seem to *be* thought or perception—that would be strange; but because they are not found apart they appear to some people the same.) As activities are different, then, so are the corresponding pleasures. Now sight is superior to touch in purity, and hearing and smell to taste; the pleasures, there-fore, are similarly superior, and those of thought superior to these, and with-in each of the two kinds some are superior to others.

Each animal is thought to have a proper pleasure, as it has a proper function; viz. that which corresponds to its activity. If we survey them species by species, too, this will be evident; horse, dog, and man have different pleasures, as Heraclitus says 'asses would prefer sweepings to gold'; for food is pleasanter than gold to asses. So the pleasures of creatures different in kind differ in kind, and it is plausible to suppose that those of a single species do not differ. But they vary to no small extent, in the case of men at least; the same things delight some people and pain others, and are painful and odious to some, and pleasant to and liked by others. This happens, too, in the case of sweet things; the same things do not seem sweet to a man in a fever and a healthy man—nor hot to a weak man and one in good condition. The same happens in other cases. But in all such matters that which appears to the good man is thought to be really so. If this is correct, as it seems to be, and virtue and the good man as such are the measure of each thing, those also will be pleasures which appear so to him, and those things pleasant which he enjoys. If the things he finds tiresome seem pleasant to some one, that is nothing surprising; for men may be ruined and spoilt in many ways; but the things are not pleasant, but only pleasant to these people and to people in this condition. Those which are admittedly disgraceful plainly should not be said to be pleasures, except to a perverted taste; but of those that are thought to be good what kind of pleasure or what pleasure should be said to be that proper to man? Is it not plain from the corresponding activities? The pleasures follow these. Whether, then, the perfect and supremely happy man has one or more activities, the pleasures that perfect these will be said in the strict sense to be pleasures proper to man, and the rest will be so in a secondary and fractional way, as are the activities.

B. HAPPINESS

6. Now that we have spoken of the virtues, the forms of friendship, and the varieties of pleasure, what remains is to discuss in outline the nature of happiness, since this is what we state the end of human nature to be. Our discussion will be the more concise if we first sum up what we have said already. We said, then, that it is not a disposition; for if it were it might belong to some one who was asleep throughout his life, living the life of a plant, or, again, to some one who was suffering the greatest misfortunes. If these implications are unacceptable, and we must rather class happiness as an activity, as we have said before, and if some activities are necessary, and desirable for the sake of something else, while others are so in themselves, evidently happiness must be placed among those desirable in themselves, not among those desirable for the sake of something else; for happiness does not lack anything, but is self-sufficient. Now those activities are desirable in themselves from which nothing is sought beyond the activity. And of this nature virtuous actions are thought to be; for to do noble and good deeds is a thing desirable for its own sake.

Pleasant amusements also are thought to be of this nature; we choose them not for the sake of other things; for we are injured rather than benefited by them, since we are led to neglect our bodies and our property. But most of the people who are deemed happy take refuge in such pastimes, which is the reason why those who are ready-witted at them are highly esteemed at the courts of tyrants; they make themselves pleasant companions in the tyrants' favourite pursuits, and that is the sort of man they want. Now these things are thought to be of the nature of happiness because people in despotic positions spend their leisure in them, but perhaps such people prove nothing; for virtue and reason, from which good activities flow, do not depend on despotic position; nor, if these people, who have never tasted pure and generous pleasure, take refuge in the bodily pleasures, should these for that reason be thought more desirable; for boys, too, think the things that are valued among themselves are the best. It is to be expected, then, that, as different things seem valuable to boys and to men, so they should to bad men and to good. Now, as we have often maintained, those things are both valuable and pleasant which are such to the good man; and to each man the activity in accordance with his own disposition is most desirable, and, therefore, to the good man that which is in accordance with virtue. Happiness, therefore, does not lie in amusement; it would, indeed, be strange if the end were amusement, and one were to take trouble and suffer hardship all one's life in order to amuse oneself. For, in a word, everything that we choose we choose for the sake of something else—except happiness, which is an end. Now to exert oneself and work for the sake of amusement seems silly and utterly childish. But to amuse oneself in order that one may exert oneself, as Anacharsis puts it, seems right; for amusement is a sort of relaxation, and we need relaxation because we cannot work continuously. Relaxation, then, is not an end; for it is taken for the sake of activity.

The happy life is thought to be virtuous; now a virtuous life requires exertion, and does not consist in amusement. And we say that serious things are better than laughable things and those connected with amusement, and that the activity of the better of any two things—whether it be two elements of our being or two men—is the more serious; but the activity of the better is *ipso facto* superior and more of the nature of happiness. And any chance person—even a slave—can enjoy the bodily pleasures no less than the best man; but no one assigns to a slave a share in happiness—unless he assigns to him also a share in human life. For happiness does not lie in such occupations, but, as we have said before, in virtuous activities.

7. If happiness is activity in accordance with virtue, it is reasonable that *it* should be in accordance with the highest virtue; and this will be that of the best thing in us. Whether it be reason or something else that is this element which is thought to be our natural ruler and guide and to take thought of things noble and divine, whether it be itself also divine or only the most divine element in us, the activity of this in accordance with its proper virtue will be perfect happiness. That this activity is contemplative we have already said.

Now this would seem to be in agreement with what we said before and with the truth. For, firstly, this activity is the best (since not only is reason the best thing in us, but the objects of reason are the best of knowable objects); and, secondly, it is the most continuous, since we can contemplate truth more continuously than we can *do* anything. And we think happiness has pleasure mingled with it, but the activity of philosophic wisdom is admittedly the pleasantest of virtuous activities; at all events the pursuit of

it is thought to offer pleasures marvellous for their purity and their enduringness, and it is to be expected that those who know will pass their time more pleasantly than those who inquire. And the self-sufficiency that is spoken of must belong most to the contemplative activity. For while a philosopher, as well as a just man or one possessing any other virtue, needs the necessaries of life, when they are sufficiently equipped with things of that sort the just man needs people towards whom and with whom he shall act justly, and the temperate man, the brave man, and each of the others is in the same case, but the philosopher, even when by himself, can contemplate truth, and the better the wiser he is; he can perhaps do so better if he has fellow-workers, but still he is the most self-sufficient. And this activity alone would seem to be loved for its own sake; for nothing arises from it apart from the contemplating, while from practical activities we gain more or less apart from the action. And happiness is thought to depend on leisure; for we are busy that we may have leisure, and make war that we may live in peace. Now the activity of the practical virtues is exhibited in political or military affairs, but the actions concerned with these seem to be unleisurely. War-like actions are completely so (for no one chooses to be at war, or provokes war, for the sake of being at war; any one would seem absolutely murderous if he were to make enemies of his friends in order to bring about battle and slaughter); but the action of the statesman is also unleisurely, and—apart from the political action itself—aims at despotic power and honours, or at all events happiness, for him and his fellow citizens—a happiness different from political action, and evidently sought as being different. So if among virtuous actions political and military actions are distinguished by nobility and greatness, and these are unleisurely and aim at an end and are not desirable for their own sake, but the activity of reason, which is contemplative, seems both to be superior in serious worth and to aim at no end beyond itself, and to have its pleasure proper to itself (and this augments the activity), and the self-sufficiency, leisureliness, unweariedness (so far as this is possible for man), and all the other attributes ascribed to the supremely happy man are evidently those connected with this activity, it follows that this will be the complete happiness of man, if it be allowed a complete term of life (for none of the attributes of happiness is *incom*plete).

But such a life would be too high for man; for it is not in so far as he is man that he will live so, but in so far as something divine is present in him; and by so much as this is superior to our composite nature is its activity superior to that which is the exercise of the other kind of virtue. If reason is divine, then, in comparison with man, the life according to it is divine in comparison with human life. But we must not follow those who advise us, being men, to think of human things, and, being mortal, of mortal things, but must, so far as we can, make ourselves immortal, and strain every nerve to live in accordance with the best thing in us; for even if it be small in bulk, much more does it in power and worth surpass everything. This would seem, too, to be each man himself, since it is the authoritative and better part of him. It would be strange, then, if he were to choose not the life of his self but that of something else. And what we said before will apply now; that which is proper to each thing is by nature best and most pleasant for each thing; for man, therefore, the life according to

reason is best and pleasantest, since reason more than anything else *is* man. This life therefore is also the happiest.

8. But in a secondary degree the life in accordance with the other kind of virtue is happy; for the activities in accordance with this befit our human estate. Just and brave acts, and other virtuous acts, we do in relation to each other, observing our respective duties with regard to contracts and services and all manner of actions and with regard to passions; and all of these seem to be typically human. Some of them seem even to arise from the body, and virtue of character to be in many ways bound up with the passions. Practical wisdom, too, is linked to virtue of character, and this to practical wisdom, since the principles of practical wisdom are in accordance with the moral virtues and rightness in morals is in accordance with practical wisdom. Being connected with the passions also, the moral virtues must belong to our composite nature; and the virtues of our composite nature are human; so, therefore, are the life and the happiness which correspond to these. The excellence of the reason is a thing apart; we must be content to say this much about it, for to describe it precisely is a task greater than our purpose requires. It would seem, however, also to need external equipment but little, or less than moral virtue does. Grant that both need the necessaries, and do so equally, even if the statesman's work is the more concerned with the body and things of that sort; for there will be little difference there; but in what they need for the exercise of their activities there will be much difference. The liberal man will need money for the doing of his liberal deeds, and the just man too will need it for the returning of services (for wishes are hard to discern, and even people who are not just pre-

tend to wish to act justly); and the brave man will need power if he is to accomplish any of the acts that correspond to his virtue, and the temperate man will need opportunity; for how else is either he or any of the others to be recognized? It is debated, too, whether the will or the deed is more essential to virtue, which is assumed to involve both; it is surely clear that its perfection involves both; but for deeds many things are needed, and more, the greater and nobler the deeds are. But the man who is contemplating the truth needs no such thing, at least with a view to the exercise of his activity; indeed they are, one may say, even hindrances, at all events to his contemplation; but in so far as he is a man and lives with a number of people, he chooses to do virtuous acts; he will therefore need such aids to living a human life.

But that perfect happiness is a contemplative activity will appear from the following consideration as well. We assume the gods to be above all other beings blessed and happy; but what sort of actions must we assign to them? Acts of justice? Will not the gods seem absurd if they make contracts and return deposits, and so on? Acts of a brave man, then, confronting dangers and running risks because it is noble to do so? Or liberal acts? To whom will they give? It will be strange if they are really to have money or anything of the kind. And what would their temperate acts be? Is not such praise tasteless, since they have no bad appetites? If we were to run through them all, the circumstances of action would be found trivial and unworthy of gods. Still, every one supposes that they *live* and therefore that they are active; we cannot suppose them to sleep like Endymion. Now if you take away from a living being action, and still more production, what is left but contemplation?

Therefore the activity of God, which surpasses all others in blessedness, must be contemplative; and of human activities, therefore, that which is most akin to this must be most of the nature of happiness.

This is indicated, too, by the fact that the other animals have no share in happiness, being completely deprived of such activity. For while the whole life of the gods is blessed, and that of men too in so far as some likeness of such activity belongs to them, none of the other animals is happy, since they in no way share in contemplation. Happiness extends, then, just so far as contemplation does, and those to whom contemplation more fully belongs are more truly happy, not as a mere concomitant but in virtue of the contemplation; for this is in itself precious. Happiness, therefore, must be some form of contemplation.

But, being a man, one will also need external prosperity; for our nature is not self-sufficient for the purpose of contemplation, but our body also must be healthy and must have food and other attention. Still, we must not think that the man who is to be happy will need many things or great things, merely because he cannot be supremely happy without external goods; for self-sufficiency and action do not involve excess, and we can do noble acts without ruling earth and sea; for even with moderate advantages one can act virtuously (this is manifest enough; for private persons are thought to do worthy acts no less than despots—indeed even more); and it is enough that we should have so much as that; for the life of the man who is active in accordance with virtue will be happy. Solon, too, was perhaps sketching well the happy man when he described him as moderately furnished with externals but as having done (as Solon thought) the noblest acts, and lived temperately; for one can with but moderate possessions do what one ought. Anaxagoras also seems to have supposed the happy man not to be rich nor a despot, when he said that he would not be surprised if the happy man were to seem to most people a strange person; for they judge by externals, since these are all they perceive. The opinions of the wise seem, then, to harmonize with our arguments. But while even such things carry some conviction, the truth in practical matters is discerned from the facts of life; for these are the decisive factor. We must therefore survey what we have already said, bringing it to the test of the facts of life, and if it harmonizes with the facts we must accept it, but if it clashes with them we must suppose it to be mere theory. Now he who exercises his reason and cultivates it seems to be both in the best state of mind and most dear to the gods. For if the gods have any care for human affairs, as they are thought to have, it would be reasonable both that they should delight in that which was best and most akin to them (i. e. reason) and that they should reward those who love and honour this most, as caring for the things that are dear to them and acting both rightly and nobly. And that all these attributes belong most of all to the philosopher is manifest. He, therefore, is the dearest to the gods. And he who is that will presumably be also the happiest; so that in this way too the philosopher will more than any other be happy.

9. If these matters and the virtues, and also friendship and pleasure, have been dealt with sufficiently in outline, are we to suppose that our programme has reached its end? Surely, as the saying goes, where there are things to be done the end is not to survey and recognize the various things, but rather to do them; with regard to virtue, then, it is not enough to know, but we must try to have and use it, or try any other way there may be of becoming good. Now if arguments were in themselves enough to make men good, they would justly, as Theognis says, have won very great rewards, and such rewards should have been provided; but as things are, while they seem to have power to encourage and stimulate the generous-minded among our youth, and to make a character which is gently born, and a true lover of what is noble, ready to be possessed by virtue, they are not able to encourage the many to nobility and goodness. For these do not by nature obey the sense of shame, but only fear, and do not abstain from bad acts because of their baseness but through fear of punishment; living by passion they pursue their own pleasures and the means to them, and avoid the opposite pains, and have not even a conception of what is noble and truly pleasant, since they have never tasted it. What argument would remould such people? It is hard, if not impossible, to remove by argument the traits that have long since been incorporated in the character; and perhaps we must be content if, when all the influences by which we are thought to become good are present, we get some tincture of virtue.

Now some think that we are made good by nature, others by habituation, others by teaching. Nature's part evidently does not depend on us, but as a result of some divine causes is present in those who are truly fortunate; while argument and teaching, we may suspect, are not powerful with all men, but the soul of the student must first have been cultivated by means of habits for noble joy and noble hatred, like earth which is to nourish the seed. For he who lives as passion directs will not hear argument that dissuades him, nor understand it if he does; and how can we persuade one in such a state to change his ways? And in general passion seems to yield not to argument but to force. The character, then, must somehow be there already with a kinship to virtue, loving what is noble and hating what is base.

But it is difficult to get from youth up a right training for virtue if one has not been brought up under right laws; for to live temperately and hardily is not pleasant to most people, especially when they are young. For this reason their nurture and occupations should be fixed by law; for they will not be painful when they have become customary. But it is surely not enough that when they are young they should get the right nature and attention; since they must, even when they are grown up, practise and be habituated to them, we shall need laws for this as well, and generally speaking to cover the whole of life; for most people obey necessity rather than argument, and punishments rather than the sense of what is noble.

This is why some think [27] that legislators ought to stimulate men to virtue and urge them forward by the motive of the noble, on the assumption that those who have been well advanced by the formation of habits will attend to such influences; and that punishments and penalties should be imposed on those who disobey and are of inferior nature, while the incurably bad should be completely banished.[28] A good man (they think), since he lives with his mind fixed on what is noble, will submit to argument, while a bad man, whose desire is for pleasure, is corrected by pain like a beast of burden. This is, too, why they say the pains inflicted should be those that are most opposed to the pleasures such men love.

[27] Pl. *Laws* 722 D ff.
[28] Pl. *Prot.* 325 A.

However that may be, if (as we have said) the man who is to be good must be well trained and habituated, and go on to spend his time in worthy occupations and neither willingly nor unwillingly do bad actions, and if this can be brought about if men live in accordance with a sort of reason and right order, provided this has force— if this be so, the paternal command indeed has not the required force or compulsive power (nor in general has the command of one man, unless he be a king or something similar), but the law *has* compulsive power, while it is at the same time a rule proceeding from a sort of practical wisdom and reason. And while people hate *men* who oppose their impulses, even if they oppose them rightly, the law in its ordaining of what is good is not burdensome.

In the Spartan state alone, or almost alone, the legislator seems to have paid attention to questions of nurture and occupations; in most states such matters have been neglected, and each man lives as he pleases, Cyclops-fashion 'to his own wife and children dealing law.' [29] Now it is best that there should be a public and proper care for such matters; but if they are neglected by the community it would seem right for each man to help his children and friends towards virtue, and that they should have the power, or at least the will, to do this.

It would seem from what has been said that he can do this better if he makes himself capable of legislating. For public control is plainly effected by laws, and good control by good laws; whether written or unwritten would seem to make no difference, nor whether they are laws providing for the education of individuals or of groups—any more than it does in the case of music or gymnastics and other such pursuits. For as in cities laws and

[29] *Od.* ix. 114 f.

prevailing types of character have force, so in households do the injunctions and the habits of the father, and these have even more because of the tie of blood and the benefits he confers; for the children start with a natural affection and disposition to obey. Further, private education has an advantage over public, as private medical treatment has; for while in general rest and abstinence from food are good for a man in a fever, for a particular man they may not be; and a boxer presumably does not prescribe the same style of fighting to all his pupils. It would seem, then, that the detail is worked out with more precision if the control is private; for each person is more likely to get what suits his case.

But the details can be best looked after, one by one, by a doctor or gymnastic instructor or any one else who has the general knowledge of what is good for every one or for people of a certain kind (for the sciences both are said to be, and are, concerned with what is universal); not but what some particular detail may perhaps be well looked after by an unscientific person, if he has studied accurately in the light of experience what happens in each case, just as some people seem to be their own best doctors, though they could give no help to any one else. None the less, it will perhaps be agreed that if a man does wish to become master of an art or science he must go to the universal, and come to know it as well as possible; for, as we have said, it is with this that the sciences are concerned.

And surely he who wants to make men, whether many or few, better by his care must try to become capable of legislating, if it is through laws that we can become good. For to get any one whatever—any one who is put before us—into the right condition is not for the first chance comer; if any one can do it, it is the man who knows, just as in medicine and all other matters which give scope for care and prudence.

Must we not, then, next examine whence or how one can learn how to legislate? Is it, as in all other cases, from statesmen? Certainly it was thought to be a part of statesmanship. Or is a difference apparent between statesmanship and the other sciences and arts? In the others the same people are found offering to teach the arts and practising them, e. g. doctors or painters; but while the sophists profess to teach politics, it is practised not by any of them but by the politicians, who would seem to do so by dint of a certain skill and experience rather than of thought; for they are not found either writing or speaking about such matters (though it were a nobler occupation perhaps than composing speeches for the law-courts and the assembly), nor again are they found to have made statesmen of their own sons or any other of their friends. But it was to be expected that they should if they could; for there is nothing better than such a skill that they could have left to their cities, or could prefer to have for themselves, or, therefore, for those dearest to them. Still, experience seems to contribute not a little; else they could not have become politicians by familiarity with politics; and so it seems that those who aim at knowing about the art of politics need experience as well.

But those of the sophists who profess the art seem to be very far from teaching it. For, to put the matter generally, they do not even know what kind of thing it is nor what kinds of things it is about; otherwise they would not have classed it as identical with rhetoric or even inferior to it, nor have thought it easy to legislate by collecting the laws that are thought well of; they say it is possible to select the best laws, as though even the selection did not demand intelligence and as though right judgement were not the greatest thing, as in matters of music. For while people experienced in any department judge rightly the works produced in it, and understand by what means or how they are achieved, and what harmonizes with what, the inexperienced must be content if they do not fail to see whether the work has been well or ill made—as in the case of painting. Now laws are as it were the 'works' of the political art; how then can one learn from them to be a legislator, or judge which are best? Even medical men do not seem to be made by a study of textbooks. Yet people try, at any rate, to state not only the treatments, but also how particular classes of people can be cured and should be treated—distinguishing the various habits of body; but while this seems useful to experienced people, to the inexperienced it is valueless. Surely, then, while collection of laws, and of constitutions also, may be serviceable to those who can study them and judge what is good or bad and what enactments suit what circumstances, those who go through such collections without a practised faculty will not have right judgement (unless it be as a spontaneous gift of nature), though they may perhaps become more intelligent in such matters.

Now our predecessors have left the subject of legislation to us unexamined; it is perhaps best, therefore, that we should ourselves study it, and in general study the question of the constitution, in order to complete to the best of our ability our philosophy of human nature. First, then, if anything has been said well in detail by earlier thinkers, let us try to review it; then in the light of the constitutions we have collected let us study what sorts of influence preserve and destroy states, and what sorts preserve or destroy the particular kinds of constitution, and to what causes it is due that some are well and others ill administered. When these have been studied we shall perhaps be more likely to see with a comprehensive view, which constitution is best, and how each must be ordered, and what laws and customs it must use, if it is to be at its best.[30] Let us make a beginning of our discussion.

[30] This paragraph is a programme for the *Politics*, agreeing to a large extent with the existing contents of that work.

Epicurus (342/1 — 270 B.C.)

Epicurus, the son of an Athenian citizen, was born on the island of Samos. Although he claimed to be self-taught, he is said to have been instructed in the systems of Democritus and Plato. His professed scorn for and clear ignorance of the finer intellectual achievements of his time do point, however, to an inadequate education. About 306 B.C. Epicurus founded his famous Garden of Epicurus in Athens. This school or cult continued to flourish; within fifty years after its founder's death, Epicureanism was transferred to Rome, where it gained numerous converts, including Lucretius, whose *De Rerum Natura*, a magnificent poem, contains the most complete extant exposition of Epicurean doctrine. The immediate success of this doctrine, which combined a Democritean atomism with hedonism, was due no doubt to the remarkably warm and winning personality of Epicurus. But its lasting success was due in large measure to the hope of salvation it offered—the peace of mind it promised those beset by superstitious fear and troubled by the cares and uncertainties of a declining society. Epicurus received almost religious veneration. The members of the Garden lived a peaceful and abstemious life of retreat in a way directly opposed to the life that the term "epicurean," in its common use, now connotes. Following Epicurus' death, which terminated a painful illness borne calmly and courageously, his blessed memory was celebrated by his followers in their monthly common meals, for which he had provided in his will. Although Epicurus wrote extensively, his only literary remains are several letters and a number of fragments.

EPICURUS TO MENOECEUS [1]

Let no one when young delay to study philosophy, nor when he is old grow weary of his study. For no one can come too early or too late to secure the health of his soul. And the man who says that the age for philosophy has either not yet come or has gone by is like the man who says that the age for happiness is not yet come to him, or has passed away. Wherefore both when young and old a man must study philosophy, that as he grows old he may be young in blessings through the grateful recollection of what has been, and that in youth he may be old as well, since he will know no fear of what is to come. We must then meditate on the things that make our happiness, seeing that when that is with us we have all, but when it is absent we do all to win it.

The things which I used unceasingly

[1] With the permission of The Clarendon Press, Oxford. Translated by C. Bailey.

to commend to you, these do and practise, considering them to be the first
principles of the good life. First of
all believe that god is a being immortal
and blessed, even as the common idea
of a god is engraved on men's minds,
and do not assign to him anything
alien to his immortality or ill-suited
to his blessedness: but believe about
him everything that can uphold his
blessedness and immortality. For gods
there are, since the knowledge of
them is by clear vision. But they
are not such as the many believe them
to be: for indeed they do not consistently represent them as they believe
them to be. And the impious man is
not he who denies the gods of the
many, but he who attaches to the gods
the beliefs of the many. For the statements of the many about the gods are
not conceptions derived from sensation, but false suppositions, according
to which the greatest misfortunes befall the wicked and the greatest blessings the good by the gift of the gods.
For men being accustomed always
to their own virtues welcome those
like themselves, but regard all that is
not of their nature as alien.

Become accustomed to the belief
that death is nothing to us. For all
good and evil consists in sensation, but
death is deprivation of sensation. And
therefore a right understanding that
death is nothing to us makes the mortality of life enjoyable, not because it
adds to it an infinite span of time, but
because it takes away the craving for
immortality. For there is nothing terrible in life for the man who has truly
comprehended that there is nothing
terrible in not living. So that the man
speaks but idly who says that he fears
death not because it will be painful
when it comes, but because it is painful in anticipation. For that which
gives no trouble when it comes, is but
an empty pain in anticipation. So
death, the most terrifying of ills, is

nothing to us, since so long as we
exist death is not with us; but when
death comes, then we do not exist. It
does not then concern either the living
or the dead, since for the former it is
not, and the latter are no more.

But the many at one moment shun
death as the greatest of evils, at another yearn for it as a respite from the
evils in life. But the wise man neither
seeks to escape life nor fears the cessation of life, for neither does life offend
him nor does the absence of life seem
to be any evil. And just as with food
he does not seek simply the larger
share and nothing else, but rather
the most pleasant, so he seeks to enjoy
not the longest period of time, but the
most pleasant.

And he who counsels the young man
to live well, but the old man to make
a good end, is foolish, not merely because of the desirability of life, but
also because it is the same training
which teaches to live well and to die
well. Yet much worse still is the man
who says it is good not to be born, but

'once born make haste to pass the
    gates of Death.'
        (Theognis, 427)

For if he says this from conviction why
does he not pass away out of life? For
it is open to him to do so, if he had
firmly made up his mind to this. But
if he speaks in jest, his words are idle
among men who cannot receive them.

We must then bear in mind that the
future is neither ours, nor yet wholly
not ours, so that we may not altogether expect it as sure to come, nor
abandon hope of it, as if it will certainly not come.

We must consider that of desires
some are natural, others vain, and of
the natural some are necessary and
others merely natural; and of the necessary some are necessary for happiness, others for the repose of the body,
and others for very life. The right

understanding of these facts enables us to refer all choice and avoidance to the health of the body and the soul's freedom from disturbance, since this is the aim of the life of blessedness. For it is to obtain this end that we always act, namely, to avoid pain and fear. And when this is once secured for us, all the tempest of the soul is dispersed, since the living creature has not to wander as though in search of something that is missing, and to look for some other thing by which he can fulfil the good of the soul and the good of the body. For it is then that we have need of pleasure, when we feel pain owing to the absence of pleasure; but when we do not feel pain, we no longer need pleasure. And for this cause we call pleasure the beginning and end of the blessed life. For we recognize pleasure as the first good innate in us, and from pleasure we begin every act of choice and avoidance, and to pleasure we return again, using the feeling as the standard by which we judge every good.

And since pleasure is the first good and natural to us, for this very reason we do not choose every pleasure, but sometimes we pass over many pleasures, when greater discomfort accrues to us as the result of them: and similarly we think many pains better than pleasures, since a greater pleasure comes to us when we have endured pains for a long time. Every pleasure then because of its natural kinship to us is good, yet not every pleasure is to be chosen: even as every pain also is an evil, yet not all are always of a nature to be avoided. Yet by a scale of comparison and by the consideration of advantages and disadvantages we must form our judgement on all these matters. For the good on certain occasions we treat as bad, and conversely the bad as good.

And again independence of desire we think a great good—not that we

may at all times enjoy but a few things, but that, if we do not possess many, we may enjoy the few in the genuine persuasion that those have the sweetest pleasure in luxury who least need it, and that all that is natural is easy to be obtained, but that which is superfluous is hard. And so plain savours bring us a pleasure equal to a luxurious diet, when all the pain due to want is removed; and bread and water produce the highest pleasure, when one who needs them puts them to his lips. To grow accustomed therefore to simple and not luxurious diet gives us health to the full, and makes a man alert for the needful employments of life, and when after long intervals we approach luxuries, disposes us better towards them, and fits us to be fearless of fortune.

When, therefore, we maintain that pleasure is the end, we do not mean the pleasures of profligates and those that consist in sensuality, as is supposed by some who are either ignorant or disagree with us or do not understand, but freedom from pain in the body and from trouble in the mind. For it is not continuous drinkings and revellings, nor the satisfaction of lusts, nor the enjoyment of fish and other luxuries of the wealthy table, which produce a pleasant life, but sober reasoning, searching out the motives for all choice and avoidance, and banishing mere opinions, to which are due the greatest disturbance of the spirit.

Of all this the beginning and the greatest good is prudence. Wherefore prudence is a more precious thing even than philosophy: for from prudence are sprung all the other virtues, and it teaches us that it is not possible to live pleasantly without living prudently and honourably and justly, nor, again, to live a life of prudence, honour, and justice without living pleasantly. For the virtues are by nature bound up with the pleasant life, and the pleasant life is inseparable from them. For indeed who, think you, is a better man than he who holds reverent opinions concerning the gods, and is at all times free from fear of death, and has reasoned out the end ordained by nature? He understands that the limit of good things is easy to fulfil and easy to attain, whereas the course of ills is either short in time or slight in pain: he laughs at destiny, whom some have introduced as the mistress of all things. He thinks that with us lies the chief power in determining events, some of which happen by necessity and some by chance, and some are within our control; for while necessity cannot be called to account, he sees that chance is inconstant, but that which is in our control is subject to no master, and to it are naturally attached praise and blame. For, indeed, it were better to follow the myths about the gods than to become a slave to the destiny of the natural philosophers; for the former suggests a hope of placating the gods by worship, whereas the latter involves a necessity which knows no placation. As to chance, he does not regard it as a god as most men do (for in god's acts there is no disorder), nor as an uncertain cause of all things: for he does not believe that good and evil are given by chance to man for the framing of a blessed life, but that opportunities for great good and great evil are afforded by it. He therefore thinks it better to be unfortunate in reasonable action than to prosper in unreason. For it is better in a man's actions that what is well chosen should fail, rather than that what is ill chosen should be successful owing to chance.

Meditate therefore on these things and things akin to them night and day by yourself, and with a companion like to yourself, and never shall you be disturbed waking or asleep, but you shall live like a god among men. For a man who lives among immortal blessings is not like to a mortal being.

PRINCIPAL DOCTRINES [2]

I. The blessed and immortal nature knows no trouble itself nor causes trouble to any other, so that it is never constrained by anger or favour. For all such things exist only in the weak.

II. Death is nothing to us: for that which is dissolved is without sensation; and that which lacks sensation is nothing to us.

III. The limit of quantity in pleasures is the removal of all that is painful. Wherever pleasure is present, as long as it is there, there is neither pain of body nor of mind, nor of both at once.

IV. Pain does not last continuously in the flesh, but the acutest pain is there for a very short time, and even that which just exceeds the pleasure in the flesh does not continue for many days at once. But chronic illnesses permit a predominance of pleasure over pain in the flesh.

V. It is not possible to live pleasantly without living prudently and honourably and justly, nor again to live a life of prudence, honour, and justice without living pleasantly. And the man who does not possess the pleasant life, is not living prudently and honourably and justly, and the man who does not possess the virtuous life, cannot possibly live pleasantly.

VI. To secure protection from men anything is a natural good, by which you may be able to attain this end.

VII. Some men wished to become famous and conspicuous, thinking that they would thus win for themselves safety from other men. Wherefore if

2 With the permission of The Clarendon Press, Oxford. Translated by C. Bailey.

the life of such men is safe, they have obtained the good which nature craves; but if it is not safe, they do not possess that for which they strove at first by the instinct of nature.

VIII. No pleasure is a bad thing in itself; but the means which produce some pleasures bring with them disturbances many times greater than the pleasures.

IX. If every pleasure could be intensified so that it lasted and influenced the whole organism or the most essential parts of our nature, pleasures would never differ from one another.

X. If the things that produce the pleasures of profligates could dispel the fears of the mind about the phenomena of the sky and death and its pains, and also teach the limits of desires and of pains, we should never have cause to blame them: for they would be filling themselves full with pleasures from every source and never have pain of body or mind, which is the evil of life.

XI. If we were not troubled by our suspicions of the phenomena of the sky and about death, fearing that it concerns us, and also by our failure to grasp the limits of pains and desires, we should have no need of natural science.

XII. A man cannot dispel his fear about the most important matters if he does not know what is the nature of the universe but suspects the truth of some mythical story. So that without natural science it is not possible to attain our pleasures unalloyed.

XIII. There is no profit in securing protection in relation to men, if things above and things beneath the earth and indeed all in the boundless universe remain matters of suspicion.

XIV. The most unalloyed source of protection from men, which is secured to some extent by a certain force of expulsion, is in fact the immunity which results from a quiet life and the retirement from the world.

XV. The wealth demanded by nature is both limited and easily procured; that demanded by idle imaginings stretches on to infinity.

XVI. In but few things chance hinders a wise man, but the greatest and most important matters reason has ordained and throughout the whole period of life does and will ordain.

XVII. The just man is most free from trouble, the unjust most full of trouble.

XVIII. The pleasure in the flesh is not increased, when once the pain due to want is removed, but is only varied: and the limit as regards pleasure in the mind is begotten by the reasoned understanding of these very pleasures and of the emotions akin to them, which used to cause the greatest fear to the mind.

XIX. Infinite time contains no greater pleasure than limited time, if one measures by reason the limits of pleasure.

XX. The flesh perceives the limits of pleasure as unlimited and unlimited time is required to supply it. But the mind, having attained a reasoned understanding of the ultimate good of the flesh and its limits and having dissipated the fears concerning the time to come, supplies us with the complete life, and we have no further need of infinite time: but neither does the mind shun pleasure, nor, when circumstances begin to bring about the departure from life, does it approach its end as though it fell short in any way of the best life.

XXI. He who has learned the limits of life knows that that which removes the pain due to want and makes the whole of life complete is easy to obtain; so that there is no need of actions which involve competition.

XXII. We must consider both the real purpose and all the evidence of direct perception, to which we always refer the conclusions of opinion; otherwise, all will be full of doubt and confusion.

XXIII. If you fight against all sensations, you will have no standard by which to judge even those of them which you say are false.

XXIV. If you reject any single sensation and fail to distinguish between the conclusion of opinion as to the appearance awaiting confirmation and that which is actually given by the sensation or feeling, or each intuitive apprehension of the mind, you will confound all other sensations as well with the same groundless opinion, so that you will reject every standard of judgement. And if among the mental images created by your opinion you affirm both that which awaits confirmation and that which does not, you will not escape error, since you will have preserved the whole cause of doubt in every judgement between what is right and what is wrong.

XXV. If on each occasion instead of referring your actions to the end of nature, you turn to some other nearer standard when you are making a choice or an avoidance, your actions will not be consistent with your principles.

XXVI. Of desires, all that do not lead to a sense of pain, if they are not satisfied, are not necessary, but involve a craving which is easily dispelled, when the object is hard to procure or they seem likely to produce harm.

XXVII. Of all the things which wisdom acquires to produce the blessedness of the complete life, far the greatest is the possession of friendship.

XXVIII. The same conviction which has given us confidence that there is nothing terrible that lasts for ever or even for long, has also seen the protection of friendship most fully completed in the limited evils of this life.

XXIX. Among desires some are natural and necessary, some natural but not necessary, and others neither natural nor necessary, but due to idle imagination.

XXX. Wherever in the case of desires which are physical, but do not lead to a sense of pain, if they are not fulfilled, the effort is intense, such pleasures are due to idle imagination, and it is not owing to their own nature that they fail to be dispelled, but owing to the empty imaginings of the man.

XXXI. The justice which arises from nature is a pledge of mutual advantage to restrain men from harming one another and save them from being harmed.

XXXII. For all living things which have not been able to make compacts not to harm one another or be harmed, nothing ever is either just or unjust; and likewise too for all tribes of men which have been unable or unwilling to make compacts not to harm or be harmed.

XXXIII. Justice never is anything in itself, but in the dealings of men with one another in any place whatever and at any time it is a kind of compact not to harm or be harmed.

XXXIV. Injustice is not an evil in itself, but only in consequence of the fear which attaches to the apprehension of being unable to escape those appointed to punish such actions.

XXXV. It is not possible for one who acts in secret contravention of the terms of the compact not to harm or be harmed, to be confident that he will escape detection, even if at present he escapes a thousand times. For up to the time of death it cannot be certain that he will indeed escape.

XXXVI. In its general aspect justice is the same for all, for it is a kind of mutual advantage in the dealings of men with one another: but with reference to the individual peculiarities of a country or any other circumstances the same thing does not turn out to be just for all.

XXXVII. Among actions which are sanctioned as just by law, that which is proved on examination to be of advantage in the requirements of men's dealings with one another, has the guarantee of justice, whether it is the same for all or not. But if a man makes a law and it does not turn out to lead to advantage in men's dealings with each other, then it no longer has the essential nature of justice. And even if the advantage in the matter of justice shifts from one side to the other, but for a while accords with the general concept, it is none the less just for that period in the eyes of those who do not confound themselves with empty sounds but look to the actual facts.

XXXVIII. Where, provided the circumstances have not been altered, actions which were considered just, have been shown not to accord with the general concept in actual practice, then they are not just. But where, when circumstances have changed, the same actions which were sanctioned as just no longer lead to advantage, there they were just at the time when they were of advantage for the dealings of fellow-citizens with one another; but subsequently they are no longer just, when no longer of advantage.

XXXIX. The man who has best ordered the element of disquiet arising from external circumstances has made those things that he could akin to himself and the rest at least no alien: but with all to which he could not do even this, he has refrained from mixing, and has expelled from his life all which it was of advantage to treat thus.

XL. As many as possess the power to procure complete immunity from their neighbours, these also live most pleasantly with one another, since they have the most certain pledge of security, and after they have enjoyed the fullest intimacy, they do not lament the previous departure of a dead friend, as though he were to be pitied.

Epictetus (?—first part of second century A.D.)

Little is known of the life of Epictetus. He is said to have been a Greek, a native of Hieropolis in Phrygia. It is recorded that early in life he became a slave in Rome, one account being that his parents sold him into slavery as a child. His known lameness is said to have been due to the punishment or torture he received from a cruel master, but this is conjectural. It seems true, however, that his evident intelligence caused his master to send him to attend the lectures of a Stoic philosopher, a circumstance that is consistent at least with the fact that some of the wealthier Romans could reckon among their many slaves culti-vated poets, rhetoricians, and philosophers. In some way, Epictetus secured his freedom and began his teaching of philosophy in Rome. This was terminated in A.D. 89 with the expulsion of the philosophers from Rome by order of the Emperor Domitian. Epictetus thereupon retired to Nicopolis where he taught until his death. All of the so-called writings of Epictetus were written under his name by a devoted pupil, Arrian, who took down his master's discourses. Of these writings the *Discourses* and the *Encheiridion,* or *Manual,* alone remain. They rank with the *Meditations* of Marcus Aurelius as the most influential of the Stoic writings. All three documents are high on the list of those that have provided men in trouble with the consolations of philosophy.

THE ENCHEIRIDION, OR MANUAL [1]

I.

Of things some are in our power, and others are not. In our power are opin-ion, movement toward a thing, desire, aversion (turning from a thing); and in a word, whatever are our own acts: not in our power are the body, prop-erty, reputation, offices (magisterial power), and in a word, whatever are not our own acts. And the things in our power are by nature free, not sub-ject to restraint nor hindrance: but the things not in our power are weak, slav-ish, subject to restraint, in the power of others. Remember then that if you think the things which are by nature slavish to be free, and the things which are in the power of others to be your own, you will be hindered, you will lament, you will be disturbed, you will blame both gods and men: but if you think that only which is your own to be your own, and if you think that

[1] Translated by G. Long. London, 1877.

150

what is another's, as it really is, belongs to another, no man will ever compel you, no man will hinder you, you will never blame any man, you will accuse no man, you will do nothing involuntarily (against your will), no man will harm you, you will have no enemy, for you will not suffer any harm.

If then you desire (aim at) such great things, remember that you must not (attempt to) lay hold of them with a small effort; but you must leave alone some things entirely, and postpone others for the present. But if you wish for these things also (such great things), and power (office) and wealth, perhaps you will not gain even these very things (power and wealth) because you aim also at those former things (such great things): certainly you will fail in those things through which alone happiness and freedom are secured. Straightway then practice saying to every harsh appearance, You are an appearance, and in no manner what you appear to be. Then examine it by the rules which you possess, and by this first and chiefly, whether it relates to the things which are in our power or to the things which are not in our power: and if it relates to anything which is not in our power, be ready to say, that it does not concern you.

II.

Remember that desire contains in it the profession (hope) of obtaining that which you desire; and the profession (hope) in aversion (turning from a thing) is that you will not fall into that which you attempt to avoid: and he who fails in his desire is unfortunate; and he who falls into that which he would avoid, is unhappy. If then you attempt to avoid only the things contrary to nature which are within your power, you will not be involved in any of the things which you would avoid. But if you attempt to avoid disease or death or poverty, you will be unhappy. Take away then aversion from all things which are not in our power, and transfer it to the things contrary to nature which are in our power. But destroy desire completely for the present. For if you desire anything which is not in our power, you must be unfortunate: but of the things in our power, and which it would be good to desire, nothing yet is before you. But employ only the power of moving toward an object and retiring from it; and these powers indeed only slightly and with exceptions and with remission.

III.

In everything which pleases the soul, or supplies a want, or is loved, remember to add this to the (description, notion); what is the nature of each thing, beginning from the smallest? If you love an earthen vessel, say it is an earthen vessel which you love; for when it has been broken, you will not be disturbed. If you are kissing your child or wife, say that it is a human being whom you are kissing, for when the wife or child dies, you will not be disturbed.

IV.

When you are going to take in hand any act, remind yourself what kind of an act it is. If you are going to bathe, place before yourself what happens in the bath: some splashing the water, others pushing against one another, others abusing one another, and some stealing: and thus with more safety you will undertake the matter, if you say to yourself, I now intend to bathe, and to maintain my will in a manner comfortable to nature. And so you will do in every act: for thus if any hindrance to bathing shall happen, let this thought be ready; it was not this only that I intended, but I intended also to maintain my will in a way comfortable to nature; but I shall not maintain it so, if I am vexed at what happens.

V.

Men are disturbed not by the things which happen, but by the opinions about the things: for example, death is nothing terrible, for if it were, it would have seemed so to Socrates; for the opinion about death, that it is terrible, is the terrible thing. When then we are impeded or disturbed or grieved, let us never blame others, but ourselves, that is, our opinions. It is the act of an ill-instructed man to blame others for his own bad condition; it is the act of one who has begun to be instructed, to lay the blame on himself; and of one whose instruction is completed, neither to blame another, nor himself.

VI.

Be not elated at any advantage (excellence), which belongs to another. If a horse when he is elated should say, I am beautiful, one might endure it. But when you are elated, and say, I have a beautiful horse, you must know that you are elated at having a good horse. What then is your own? The use of appearances. Consequently when in the use of appearances you are conformable to nature, then be elated, for then you will be elated at something good which is your own.

VII.

As on a voyage when the vessel has reached a port, if you go out to get water, it is an amusement by the way to pick up a shell-fish or some bulb, but your thoughts ought to be di-

rected to the ship, and you ought to be constantly watching if the captain should call, and then you must throw away all those things, that you may not be bound and pitched into the ship like sheep: so in life also, if there be given to you instead of a little bulb and a shell a wife and child, there will be nothing to prevent (you from taking them). But if the captain should call, run to the ship, and leave all those things without regard to them. But if you are old, do not even go far from the ship, lest when you are called you make default.

VIII.

Seek not that the things which happen should happen as you wish; but wish the things which happen to be as they are, and you will have a tranquil flow of life.

IX.

Disease is an impediment to the body, but not to the will, unless the will itself chooses. Lameness is an impediment to the leg, but not to the will. And add this reflection on the occasion of everything that happens; for you will find it an impediment to something else, but not to yourself.

X.

On the occasion of every accident (event) that befalls you, remember to turn to yourself and inquire what power you have for turning it to use. If you see a fair man or a fair woman, you will find that the power to resist is temperance (continence). If labor (pain) be presented to you, you will find that it is endurance. If it be abusive words, you will find it to be patience. And if you have been thus formed to the (proper) habit, the appearances will not carry you along with them.

XI.

Never say about anything, I have lost it, but say I have restored it. Is your child dead? It has been restored. Is your wife dead? She has been restored. Has your estate been taken from you? Has not then this also been restored? But he who has taken it from me is a bad man. But what is it to you, by whose hands the giver demanded it back? So long as he may allow you, take care of it as a thing which belongs to another, as travelers do with their inn.

XII.

If you intend to improve, throw away such thoughts as these: if I neglect my affairs, I shall not have the means of living: unless I chastise my slave, he will be bad. For it is better to die of hunger and so be released from grief and fear than to live in abundance with perturbation; and it is better for your slave to be bad than for you to be unhappy. Begin then from little things. Is the oil spilled? Is a little wine stolen? Say on the occasion, at such price is sold freedom from perturbation; at such price is sold tranquillity, but nothing is got for nothing. And when you call your slave, consider that it is possible that he does not hear; and if he does hear, that he will do nothing which you wish. But matters are not so well with him, but altogether well with you, that it should be in his power for you to be not disturbed.

XIII.

If you would improve, submit to be considered without sense and foolish with respect to externals. Wish to be considered to know nothing: and if you shall seem to some to be a person of importance, distrust yourself. For you should know that it is not easy both to keep your will in a condition conformable to nature and (to secure) external things; but if a man is careful about the one, it is an absolute necessity that he will neglect the other.

XIV.

If you would have your children and your wife and your friends to live forever, you are silly; for you would have the things which are not in your power to be in your power, and the things which belong to others to be yours. So if you would have your slave to be free from faults, you are a fool; for you would have badness not to be badness, but something else. But if you wish not to fail in your desires, you are able to do that. Practice then this which you are able to do. He is the master of every man who has the power over the things, which another person wishes or does not wish, the power to confer them on him or to take them away. Whoever then wishes to be free, let him neither wish for anything nor avoid anything which depends on others: if he does not observe this rule, he must be a slave.

XV.

Remember that in life you ought to behave as at a banquet. Suppose that something is carried round and is opposite to you. Stretch out your hand and take a portion with decency. Suppose that it passes by you. Do not detain it. Suppose that it is not yet come to you. Do not send your desire forward to it, but wait till it is opposite to you. Do so with respect to children, so with respect to a wife, so with respect to magisterial offices, so with respect to wealth, and you will be some time a worthy partner of the banquets of the gods. But if you take none of the things which are set before you, and even despise them, then you will be not only a fellow-banqueter with the gods, but also a partner with them in power. For by acting thus Diogenes and Heracleitus and those like them were deservedly divine, and were so called.

XVI.

When you see a person weeping in sorrow either when a child goes abroad or when he is dead, or when the man has lost his property, take care that the appearance do not hurry you away with it, as if he were suffering in external things. But straightway make a distinction in your own mind, and be in readiness to say, it is not that which has happened that afflicts this man, for it does not afflict another, but it is the opinion about this thing which afflicts the man. So far as words then do not be unwilling to show him sympathy, and even if it happens so, to lament with him. But take care that you do not lament internally also.

XVII.

Remember that thou art an actor in a play of such a kind as the teacher (author) may choose; if short, of a short one; if long, of a long one: if he wishes you to act the part of a poor man, see that you act the part naturally; if the part of a lame man, of a magistrate, of a private person, (do the same). For this is your duty, to act well the part that is given to you; but to select the part, belongs to another.

XVIII.

When a raven has croaked inauspiciously, let not the appearance hurry you away with it: but straightway make a distinction in your mind and say, None of these things is signified to me, but either to my poor body, or to my small property, or to my reputa-

tion, or to my children or to my wife: but to me all significations are auspicious if I choose. For whatever of these things results, it is in my power to derive benefit from it.

XIX.

You can be invincible, if you enter into no contest in which it is not in your power to conquer. Take care then when you observe a man honored before others or possessed of great power or highly esteemed for any reason, not to suppose him happy, and be not carried away by the appearance. For if the nature of the good is in our power, neither envy nor jealousy will have a place in us. But you yourself will not wish to be a general or senator or consul, but a free man: and there is only one way to this, to despise (care not for) the things which are not in our power.

XX.

Remember that it is not he who reviles you or strikes you, who insults you, but it is your opinion about these things as being insulting. When then a man irritates you, you must know that it is your own opinion which has irritated you. Therefore especially try not to be carried away by the appearance. For if you once gain time and delay, you will more easily master yourself.

XXI.

Let death and exile and every other thing which appears dreadful be daily before your eyes; but most of all death: and you will never think of anything mean nor will you desire anything extravagantly.

XXII.

If you desire philosophy, prepare

yourself from the beginning to be ridiculed, to expect that many will sneer at you, and say, He has all at once returned to us as a philosopher; and whence does he get this supercilious look for us? Do you not show a supercilious look; but hold on to the things which seem to you best as one appointed by God to this station. And remember that if you abide in the same principles, these men who first ridiculed will afterward admire you: but if you shall have been overpowered by them, you will bring on yourself double ridicule.

XXIII.

If it should ever happen to you to be turned to externals in order to please some person, you must know that you have lost your purpose in life. Be satisfied then in everything with being a philosopher; and if you wish to seem also to any person to be a philosopher, appear so to yourself, and you will be able to do this.

XXIV.

Let not these thoughts afflict you, I shall live unhonored and be nobody nowhere. For if want of honor (ἀτιμία) is an evil, you cannot be in evil through the means (fault) of another any more than you can be involved in anything base. Is it then your business to obtain the rank of magistrate, or to be received at a banquet? By no means. How then can this be want of honor (dishonor)? And how will you be nobody nowhere, when you ought to be somebody in those things only which are in your power, in which indeed it is permitted to you to be a man of the greatest worth? But your friends will be without assistance! What do you mean by being without assistance? They will not receive money from you, nor will

you make them Roman citizens. Who then told you that these are among the things which are in our power, and not in the power of others? And who can give to another what he has not himself? Acquire money then, your friends say, that we also may have something. If I can acquire money and also keep myself modest, and faithful and magnanimous, point out the way, and I will acquire it. But if you ask me to lose the things which are good and my own, in order that you may gain the things which are not good, see how unfair and silly you are. Besides, which would you rather have, money or a faithful and modest friend? For this end then rather help me to be such a man, and do not ask me to do this by which I shall lose that character. But my country, you say, as far as it depends on me, will be without my help. I ask again, what help do you mean? It will not have porticoes or baths through you. And what does this mean? For it is not furnished with shoes by means of a smith, nor with arms by means of a shoemaker. But it is enough if every man fully discharges the work that is his own: and if you provided it with another citizen faithful and modest, would you not be useful to it? Yes. Then you also cannot be useless to it. What place then, you say, shall I hold in the city? Whatever you can, if you maintain at the same time your fidelity and modesty. But if when you wish to be useful to the state, you shall lose these qualities, what profit could you be to it, if you were made shameless and faithless?

XXV.

Has any man been preferred before you at a banquet, or in being saluted, or in being invited to a consultation? If these things are good, you ought to rejoice that he has obtained them: but if bad, be not grieved because you have not obtained them; and remember that you cannot, if you do not the same things in order to obtain what is not in our power, be considered worthy of the same (equal) things. For how can a man obtain an equal share with another when he does not visit a man's doors as that other man does, when he does not attend him when he goes abroad, as the other man does; when he does not praise (flatter) him as another does? You will be unjust then and insatiable, if you do not part with the price, in return for which those things are sold, and if you wish to obtain them for nothing. Well, what is the price of lettuces? An obolus perhaps. If then a man gives up the obolus, and receives the lettuces, and if you do not give up the obolus and do not obtain the lettuces, do not suppose that you receive less than he who has got the lettuces; for as he has the lettuces, so you have the obolus which you did not give. In the same way then in the other matter also you have not been invited to a man's feast, for you did not give to the host the price at which the supper is sold; but he sells it for praise (flattery), he sells it for personal attention. Give then the price, if it is for your interest, for which it is sold. But if you wish both not to give the price and to obtain the things, you are insatiable and silly. Have you nothing then in place of the supper? You have indeed, you have the not flattering of him, whom you did not choose to flatter; you have the not enduring of the man when he enters the room.

XXVI.

We may learn the wish (will) of nature from the things in which we do not differ from one another; for instance, when your neighbor's slave has broken his cup, or anything else, we are ready to say forthwith, that it is one of the things which happen. You must know then that when your cup also is broken, you ought to think as you did when your neighbor's cup was broken. Transfer this reflection to greater things also. Is another man's child or wife dead? There is no one who would not say, this is an event incident to man. But when a man's own child or wife is dead, forthwith he calls out, Woe to me, how wretched I am. But we ought to remember how we feel when we hear that it has happened to others.

XXVII.

As a mark is not set up for the purpose of missing the aim, so neither does the nature of evil exist in the world.

XXVIII.

If any person was intending to put your body in the power of any man whom you fell in with on the way, you would be vexed: but that you put your understanding in the power of any man whom you meet, so that if he should revile you, it is disturbed and troubled, are you not ashamed at this?

XXIX.

In every act observe the things which come first, and those which follow it; and so proceed to the act. If you do not, at first you will approach it with alacrity, without having thought of the things which will follow; but afterward, when certain base (ugly) things have shown themselves, you will be ashamed. A man wishes to conquer at the Olympic games. I also wish indeed, for it is a fine thing. But observe both the things which come first, and the things which follow; and then begin the act. You must do everything according to rule, eat according to strict orders, abstain from delicacies, exercise yourself as you are bid at appointed times, in heat, in cold, you must not drink cold water, nor wine as you choose; in a word, you must deliver yourself up to the exercise master as you do to the physician, and then proceed to the contest. And sometimes you will strain the hand, put the ankle out of joint, swallow much dust, sometimes be flogged, and after all this be defeated. When you have considered all this, if you still choose, go to the contest: if you do not, you will behave like children, who at one time play at wrestlers, another time as flute players, again as gladiators, then as trumpeters, then as tragic actors: so you also will be at one time an athlete, at another a gladiator, then a rhetorician, then a philosopher, but with your whole soul you will be nothing at all; but like an ape you imitate everything that you see, and one thing after another pleases you. For you have not undertaken anything with consideration, nor have you surveyed it well; but carelessly and with cold desire. Thus some who have seen a philosopher and having heard one speak, as Euphrates speaks,—and who can speak as he does?—they wish to be philosophers themselves also. My man, first of all consider what kind of thing it is: and then examine your own nature, if you are able to sustain the character. Do you wish to be a pentathlete or a wrestler? Look at your arms, your thighs, examine your loins. For different men are formed by nature for different things. Do you think that if you do these things, you can eat in the same manner, drink in the same manner, and in the same manner loathe certain things? You must pass sleepless nights, endure toil, go away from your kinsmen, be despised by a slave, in everything have the inferior part, in honour, in office, in the courts of justice, in every little matter. Consider these things, if you would exchange for them, freedom from passions, liberty, tranquillity. If not, take care that, like little children, you be not now a philosopher, then a servant of the publicani, then a rhetorician, then a procurator (manager) for Cæsar. These things are not consistent. You must be one man, either good or bad. You must either cultivate your own ruling faculty, or external things; you must either exercise your skill on internal things or on external things; that is you must either maintain the position of a philosopher or that of a common person.

XXX.

Duties are universally measured by relations. Is a man a father? The precept is to take care of him, to yield to him in all things, to submit when he is reproachful, when he inflicts blows. But suppose that he is a bad father. Were you then by nature made akin to a good father? No; but to a father. Does a brother wrong you? Maintain then your own position toward him, and do not examine what he is doing, but what you must do that your will shall be conformable to nature. For another will not damage you, unless you choose: but you will be damaged then when you shall think that you are damaged. In this way then you will discover your duty from the relation of a neighbor, from that of a citizen, from that of a general, if you are accustomed to contemplate the relations.

XXXI.

As to piety toward the Gods you must know that this is the chief thing, to have right opinions about them, to think that they exist, and that they administer the All well and justly; and you must fix yourself in this principle (duty), to obey them, and yield to them in everything which happens, and voluntarily to follow it as being accomplished by the wisest intelligence. For if you do so, you will never either blame the Gods, nor will you accuse them of neglecting you. And it is not possible for this to be done in any other way than by withdrawing from the things which are not in our power, and by placing the good and the evil only in those things which are in our power. For if you think that any of the things which are not in our power is good or bad, it is absolutely necessary that, when you do not obtain what you wish, and when you fall into those things which you do not wish, you will find fault and hate those who are the cause of them; for every animal is formed by nature to this, to fly from and to turn from the things which appear harmful and the things which are the cause of the harm, but to follow and admire the things which are useful and the causes of the useful. It is impossible then for a person who thinks that he is harmed to be delighted with that which he thinks to be the cause of the harm, as it is also impossible to be pleased with the harm itself. For this reason also a father is reviled by his son, when he gives no part to his son of the things which are considered to be good: and it was this which made Polynices and Eteocles enemies, the opinion that royal power was a good. It is for this reason that the cultivator of the earth reviles the Gods, for this reason the sailor does, and the merchant, and for this reason those who lose their wives and their children. For where the useful (your interest) is, there also piety is. Consequently he who takes care to desire as he ought and to avoid as he ought, at the same time also cares after piety. But to make libations and to sacrifice and to offer first fruits according to the custom of our fathers, purely and not meanly nor carelessly nor scantily nor above our ability, is a thing which belongs to all to do.

XXXII.

When you have recourse to divination, remember that you do not know how it will turn out, but that you are come to inquire from the diviner. But of what kind it is, you know when you come, if indeed you are a philosopher. For if it is any of the things which are not in our power, it is absolutely necessary that it must be neither good nor bad. Do not then bring to the diviner desire or aversion ($\check{\epsilon}\kappa\kappa\lambda\iota\theta\iota\nu$): if you do, you will approach him with fear. But having determined in your mind that everything which shall turn out (result) is indifferent, and does not concern you, and whatever it may be, for it will be in your power to use it well, and no man will hinder this, come then with confidence to the Gods as your advisers. And then when any advice shall have been given, remember whom you have taken as advisers, and whom you will have neglected, if you do not obey them. And go to divination, as Socrates said that you ought, about those matters in which all the inquiry has reference to the result, and in which means are not given either by reason nor by any other art for knowing the thing which is the subject of the inquiry. Wherefore when we ought to share a friend's danger or that of our country, you must not consult the diviner whether you ought to share it. For even if the diviner shall tell you that the signs of the victims are unlucky, it is plain that this is a token of death or mutilation of part of the body or of exile. But reason prevails that even with these risks we should share the dangers of our friend and of our country. Therefore attend to the greater diviner, the

Pythian God, who ejected from the temple him who did not assist his friend when he was being murdered.

XXXIII.

Immediately prescribe some character and some form to yourself, which you shall observe both when you are alone and when you meet with men.

And let silence be the general rule, or let only what is necessary be said, and in few words. And rarely and when the occasion calls we shall say something; but about none of the common subjects, nor about gladiators, nor horse-races, nor about athletes, nor about eating or drinking, which are the usual subjects; and especially not about men, as blaming them or praising them, or comparing them. If then you are able, bring over by your conversation the conversation of your associates to that which is proper; but if you should happen to be confined to the company of strangers, be silent.

Let not your laughter be much, nor on many occasions, nor excessive.

Refuse altogether to take an oath, if it is possible: if it is not, refuse as far as you are able.

Avoid banquets which are given by strangers and by ignorant persons. But if ever there is occasion to join in them, let your attention be carefully fixed, that you slip not into the manners of the vulgar (the uninstructed). For you must know, that if your companion be impure, he also who keeps company with him must become impure, though he should happen to be pure.

Take (apply) the things which relate to the body as far as the bare use, as food, drink, clothing, house, and slaves: but exclude everything which is for show or luxury.

As to pleasure with women, abstain as far as you can before marriage: but if you do indulge in it, do it in the way which is conformable to custom. Do not however be disagreeable to those who indulge in these pleasures, or reprove them; and do not often boast that you do not indulge in them yourself.

If a man has reported to you, that a certain person speaks ill of you, do not make any defense (answer) to what has been told you: but reply, The man did not know the rest of my faults, for he would not have mentioned these only.

It is not necessary to go to the theaters often: but if there is ever a proper occasion for going, do not show yourself as being a partisan of any man except yourself, that is, desire only that to be done which is done, and for him only to gain the prize who gains the prize; for in this way you will meet with no hindrance. But abstain entirely from shouts and laughter at any (thing or person), or violent emotions. And when you are come away, do not talk much about what has passed on the stage, except about that which may lead to your own improvement. For it is plain, if you do talk much that you admired the spectacle (more than you ought).

Do not go to the hearing of certain persons' recitations nor visit them readily. But if you do attend, observe gravity and sedateness, and also avoid making yourself disagreeable.

When you are going to meet with any person, and particularly one of those who are considered to be in a superior condition, place before yourself what Socrates or Zeno would have done in such circumstances, and you will have no difficulty in making a proper use of the occasion.

When you are going to any of those who are in great power, place before yourself that you will not find the man at home, that you will be excluded, that the door will not be opened to you, that the man will not care about you. And if with all this it is your duty to visit him, bear what happens, and never say to yourself that it was not worth the trouble. For this is silly, and marks the character of a man who is offended by externals.

In company take care not to speak much and excessively about your own acts or dangers: for as it is pleasant to you to make mention of your dangers, it is not so pleasant to others to hear what has happened to you. Take care also not to provoke laughter; for this is a slippery way toward vulgar habits, and is also adapted to diminish the respect of your neighbors. It is a dangerous habit also to approach obscene talk. When then anything of this kind happens, if there is a good opportunity, rebuke the man who has proceeded to this talk: but if there is not an opportunity, by your silence at least, and blushing and expression of dissatisfaction by your countenance, show plainly that you are displeased at such talk.

XXXIV.

If you have received the impression of any pleasure, guard yourself against being carried away by it; but let the thing wait for you, and allow yourself a certain delay on your own part. Then think of both times, of the time when you will enjoy the pleasure, and of the time after the enjoyment of the pleasure when you will repent and will reproach yourself. And set against these things how you will rejoice if you have abstained from the pleasure, and how you will commend yourself. But if it seem to you seasonable to undertake (do) the thing, take care that the charm of it, and the pleasure, and the attraction of it shall not conquer you: but set on the other side the consideration how much better it is to be conscious that you have gained this victory.

XXXV.

When you have decided that a thing ought to be done and are doing it, never avoid being seen doing it, though the many shall form an unfavorable opinion about it. For if it is not right to do it, avoid doing the thing; but if it is right, why are you afraid of those who shall find fault wrongly?

XXXVI.

As the proposition it is either day or it is night is of great importance for the disjunctive argument, but for the conjunctive is of no value, so in a symposium (entertainment) to select the larger share is of great value for the body, but for the maintenance of the social feeling is worth nothing. When then you are eating with another, remember to look not only to the value for the body of the things set before you, but also to the value of the behavior toward the host which ought to be observed.

XXXVII.

If you have assumed a character above your strength, you have both acted in this matter in an unbecoming way, and you have neglected that which you might have fulfilled.

XXXVIII.

In walking about as you take care not to step on a nail or to sprain your foot, so take care not to damage your own ruling faculty: and if we observe this rule in every act, we shall undertake the act with more security.

XXXIX.

The measure of possession (property) is to every man the body, as the foot is of the shoe. If then you stand on this rule (the demands of the body), you will maintain the measure:

but if you pass beyond it, you must then of necessity be hurried as it were down a precipice. As also in the matter of the shoe, if you go beyond the (necessities of the) foot, the shoe is gilded, then of a purple color, then embroidered: for there is no limit to that which has once passed the true measure.

XL.

Women forthwith from the age of fourteen are called by the men mistresses (dominae). Therefore since they see that there is nothing else that they can obtain, but only the power of lying with men, they begin to decorate themselves, and to place all their hopes in this. It is worth our while then to take care that they may know that they are valued (by men) for nothing else than appearing (being) decent and modest and discreet.

XLI.

It is a mark of a mean capacity to spend much time on the things which concern the body, such as much exercise, much eating, much drinking, much easing of the body, much copulation. But these things should be done as subordinate things: and let all your care be directed to the mind.

XLII.

When any person treats you ill or speaks ill of you, remember that he does this or says this because he thinks that it is his duty. It is not possible then for him to follow that which seems right to you, but that which seems right to himself. Accordingly if he is wrong in his opinion, he is the person who is hurt, for he is the person who has been deceived; for if a man shall suppose the true conjunction to be false, it is not the conjunction which is hindered, but the man who has been deceived about it. If you proceed then from these opinions, you will be mild in temper to him who reviles you: for say on each occasion, It seemed so to him.

XLIII.

Everything has two handles, the one by which it may be borne, the other by which it may not. If your brother acts unjustly, do not lay hold of the act by that handle wherein he acts unjustly, for this is the handle which cannot be borne; but lay hold of the other, that he is your brother, that he was nurtured with you, and you will lay hold of the thing by that handle by which it can be borne.

XLIV.

These reasonings do not cohere: I am richer than you, therefore I am better than you; I am more eloquent than you, therefore I am better than you. On the contrary these rather cohere, I am richer than you, therefore my possessions are greater than yours: I am more eloquent than you, therefore my speech is superior to yours. But you are neither possession nor speech.

XLV.

Does a man bathe quickly (early)? do not say that he bathes badly, but that he bathes quickly. Does a man drink much wine? do not say that he does this badly, but say that he drinks much. For before you shall have determined the opinion, how do you know whether he is acting wrong? Thus it will not happen to you to comprehend some appearances which are capable of being comprehended, but to assent to others.

XLVI.

On no occasion call yourself a philosopher, and do not speak much among the uninstructed about theorems (philosophical rules, precepts): but do that which follows from them. For example at a banquet do not say how a man ought to eat, but eat as you ought to eat. For remember that in this way Socrates also altogether avoided ostentation: persons used to come to him and ask to be recommended by him to philosophers, and he used to take them to philosophers: so easily did he submit to being overlooked. Accordingly if any conversation should arise among uninstructed persons about any theorem, generally be silent; for there is great danger that you will immediately vomit up what you have not digested. And when a man shall say to you, that you know nothing, and you are not vexed, then be sure that you have begun the work (of philosophy). For even sheep do not vomit up their grass and show to the shepherds how much they have eaten; but when they have internally digested the pasture, they produce externally wool and milk. Do you also show not your theorems to the uninstructed, but show the acts which come from their digestion.

XLVII.

When at a small cost you are supplied with everything for the body, do not be proud of this; nor, if you drink water, say on every occasion, I drink water. But consider first how much more frugal the poor are than we, and how much more enduring of labor. And if you ever wish to exercise yourself in labor and endurance, do it for yourself, and not for others: do not embrace statues. But if you are ever very thirsty, take a draught of cold water, and spit it out, and tell no man.

XLVIII.

The condition and characteristic of an uninstructed person is this: he never expects from himself profit (advantage) nor harm, but from externals. The condition and characteristic of a philosopher is this: he expects all advantage and all harm from himself. The signs (marks) of one who is making progress are these: he censures no man, he praises no man, he blames no man, he accuses no man, he says nothing about himself as if he were somebody or knew something; when he is impeded at all or hindered, he blames himself: if a man praises him, he ridicules the praiser to himself: if a man censures him, he makes no defense: he goes about like weak persons, being careful not to move any of the things which are placed, before they are firmly fixed: he removes all desire from himself, and he transfers aversion ἐπκλιον to those things only of the things within our power which are contrary to nature: he employs a moderate movement toward everything: whether he is considered foolish or ignorant, he cares not: and in a word he watches himself as if he were an enemy and lying in ambush.

XLIX.

When a man is proud because he can understand and explain the writings of Chrysippus, say to yourself, If Chrysippus had not written obscurely, this man would have had nothing to be proud of. But what is it that I wish? To understand Nature and to follow it. I inquire therefore who is the interpreter: and when I have heard that it is Chrysippus, I come to him (the interpreter). But I do not understand what is written, and therefore I seek the interpreter. And so far there is yet nothing to be proud of. But when I shall have found the interpreter, the thing that remains is to use the precepts (the lessons). This itself is the only thing to be proud of. But if I shall admire the exposition, what else have I been made unless a grammarian instead of a philosopher? except in one thing, that I am explaining Chrysippus instead of Homer. When then any man says to me, Read Chrysippus to me, I rather blush, when I cannot show my acts like to and consistent with his words.

L.

Whatever things (rules) are proposed to you (for the conduct of life) abide by them, as if they were laws, as if you would be guilty of impiety if you transgressed any of them. And whatever any man shall say about you, do not attend to it: for this is no affair of yours. How long will you then still defer thinking yourself worthy of the best things, and in no matter transgressing the distinctive reason? Have you accepted the theorems (rules), which it was your duty to agree to, and have you agreed to them? what teacher then do you still expect that you defer to him the correction of yourself? You are no longer a youth, but already a full-grown man. If then you are negligent and slothful, and are continually making procrastination after procrastination, and proposal (intention) after proposal, and fixing day after day, after which you will attend to yourself, you will not know that you are not making improvement, but you will continue ignorant (uninstructed) both while you live and till you die. Immediately then think it right to live as a full-grown man, and one who is making proficiency, and let everything which appears to you to be the best be to you a law which must not be transgressed. And if anything laborious, or pleasant or glorious or inglorious be presented to you, remember that now is the contest, now are the Olympic games, and they cannot be deferred; and that it depends on one defeat and one giving way that progress is either lost or maintained. Socra-

tes in this way became perfect, in all things improving himself, attending to nothing except to reason. But you, though you are not yet a Socrates, ought to live as one who wishes to be a Socrates.

LI.

The first and most necessary place (part) in philosophy is the use of theorems (precepts), for instance, that we must not lie: the second part is that of demonstrations, for instance, How is it proved that we ought not to lie: the third is that which is confirmatory of these two and explanatory, for example, How is this a demonstration? For what is demonstration, what is consequence, what is contradiction, what is truth, what is falsehood? The third part (topic) is necessary on account of the second, and the second on account of the first; but the most necessary and that on which we ought to rest is the first. But we do the contrary. For we spend our time on the third topic, and all our earnestness is about it: but we entirely neglect the first. Therefore we lie; but the demonstration that we ought not to lie we have ready to hand.

LII.

In every thing (circumstance) we should hold these maxims ready to hand:

Lead me, O Zeus, and thou O Destiny,
The way that I am bid by you to go:
To follow I am ready. If I choose not,
I make myself a wretch, and still must follow.

But whoso nobly yields unto necessity,
We hold him wise, and skill'd in things divine.

And the third also: O Crito, if so it pleases the Gods, so let it be; Anytus and Melitus are able indeed to kill me, but they cannot harm me.

Saint Augustine (354—430)

Saint Augustine was born in Tagaste, a small Roman community not far from Carthage. Although his father was not a Christian, his mother was; she introduced him at an early age to the basic doctrines of Christianity, but postponed baptism, which in those days usually occurred when adulthood was reached. Augustine received a thorough training in the schools, following which, in 373, he began his career as a teacher of rhetoric. His life, as he tells us in *The Confessions*, followed the pattern of the typical Roman pagan of the period. During his teaching career his beliefs shifted as he sought satisfactory philosophical and religious doctrines. For a time he accepted the Manichaean religion, but shortly after coming to Rome to teach rhetoric, he turned to skepticism and later to Neo-Platonism. In 384 he moved to Milan. His mother Monica had devoted every effort to secure his acceptance of Christianity, and in Milan her hopes were to be realized at long last; for here he came under the influence of Saint Ambrose, from whom he eventually received the sacrament of baptism. In 391 he was ordained priest in the community of Hippo Regius, North Africa; later he became Bishop of the diocese. Augustine proved to be a remarkably able administrator in the affairs of the Church, and he played a major role in the struggles then being waged against heresies of various sorts. Augustine found time to write voluminously. *The City of God,* which was prompted by the sacking of Rome by Alaric and his Goths, is one of his major works. In it his Christian philosophy of history is elaborated. Some of his other principal works are *On Free Will, Enchiridion, On the Nature of God, On the Immortality of the Soul,* and *On Nature and Grace.*

THE ORIGIN OF EVIL [1]

Thus the true cause of the blessedness of the good angels is found to be this, that they cleave to Him who supremely is. And if we ask the cause of the misery of the bad, it occurs to us, and not unreasonably, that they are miserable because they have forsaken Him who supremely is, and have turned to themselves who have no such essence. And this vice, what else is it called than pride? For "pride is the beginning of sin." [2] They were unwilling, then, to preserve their strength for God; and as adherence to God was

[1] The City of God, Bk. xii:6-9.

[2] Eccles. x. 13.

164

the condition of their enjoying an ampler being, they diminished it by preferring themselves to Him. This was the first defect and the first impoverishment, and the first flaw of their nature, which was created, not indeed supremely existent, but finding its blessedness in the enjoyment of the Supreme Being; whilst by abandoning Him it should become, not indeed no nature at all, but a nature with a less ample existence, and therefore wretched.

If the further question be asked, What was the efficient cause of their evil will? there is none. For what is it which makes the will bad, when it is the will itself which makes the action bad? And consequently the bad will is the cause of the bad action, but nothing is the efficient cause of the bad will. For if anything is the cause, this thing either has or has not a will. If it has, the will is either good or bad. If good, who is so left to himself as to say that a good will makes a will bad? For in this case a good will would be the cause of sin; a most absurd supposition. On the other hand, if this hypothetical thing has a bad will, I wish to know what made it so; and that we may not go on for ever, I ask at once, what made the *first* evil will bad? For that is not the first which was itself corrupted by an evil will, but that is the first which was made evil by no other will. For if it were preceded by that which made it evil, that will was first which made the other evil. But if it is replied, "Nothing made it evil; it always was evil," I ask if it has been existing in some nature. For if not, then it did not exist at all; and if it did exist in some nature, then it vitiated and corrupted it, and injured it, and consequently deprived it of good. And therefore the evil will could not exist in an evil nature, but in a nature at once good and mutable, which this vice could injure. For if it did no in-

jury, it was no vice; and consequently the will in which it was, could not be called evil. But if it did injury, it did it by taking away or diminishing good. And therefore there could not be from eternity, as was suggested, an evil will in that thing in which there had been previously a natural good, which the evil will was able to diminish by corrupting it. If, then, it was not from eternity, who, I ask, made it? The only thing that can be suggested in reply is, that something which itself had no will, made the will evil. I ask, then, whether this thing was superior, inferior, or equal to it? If superior, then it is better. How, then, has it no will, and not rather a good will? The same reasoning applies if it was equal; for so long as two things have equally a good will, the one cannot produce in the other an evil will. Then remains the supposition that that which corrupted the will of the angelic nature which first sinned, was itself an inferior thing without a will. But that thing, be it of the lowest and most earthly kind, is certainly itself good, since it is a nature and being, with a form and rank of its own in its own kind and order. How, then, can a good thing be the efficient cause of an evil will? How, I say, can good be the cause of evil? For when the will abandons what is above itself, and turns to what is lower, it becomes evil — not because that is evil to which it turns, but because the turning itself is wicked. Therefore it is not an inferior thing which has made the evil, but it is itself which has become so by wickedly and inordinately desiring an inferior thing. For if two men, alike in physical and moral constitution, see the same corporal beauty, and one of them is excited by the sight to desire an illicit enjoyment, while the other stedfastly maintains a modest restraint of his will, what do we suppose brings it about, that there is an evil will in the one and not in the other? What produces it in the man in whom it exists? Not the bodily beauty, for that was presented equally to the gaze of both, and yet did not produce in both an evil will. Did the flesh of the one cause the desire as he looked? But why did not the flesh of the other? Or was it the disposition? But why not the disposition of both? For we are supposing that both were of a like temperament of body and soul. Must we, then, say that the one was tempted by a secret suggestion of the evil spirit? As if it was not by his own will that he consented to this suggestion and to any inducement whatever! This consent, then, this evil will which he presented to the evil suasive influence — what was the cause of it, we ask? For, not to delay on such a difficulty as this, if both are tempted equally, and one yields and consents to the temptation, while the other remains unmoved by it, what other account can we give of the matter than this, that the one is willing, the other unwilling, to fall away from chastity? And what causes this but their own wills, in cases at least such as we are supposing, where the temperament is identical? The same beauty was equally obvious to the eyes of both; the same secret temptation pressed on both with equal violence. However minutely we examine the case, therefore, we can discern nothing which caused the will of the one to be evil. For if we say that the man himself made his will evil, what was the man himself before his will was evil but a good nature created by God, the unchangeable good? Here are two men who, before the temptation, were alike in body and soul, and of whom one yielded to the tempter who persuaded him, while the other could not be persuaded to desire that lovely body which was equally before the eyes of both. Shall we say of the successfully tempted man that he cor-

rupted his own will, since he was certainly good before his will became bad? Then, why did he do so? Was it because his will was a nature, or because it was made of nothing? We shall find that the latter is the case. For if a nature is the cause of an evil will, what else can we say than that evil arises from good, or that good is the cause of evil? And how can it come to pass that a nature, good though mutable, should produce any evil—that is to say, should make the will itself wicked?

Let no one, therefore, look for an efficient cause of the evil will; for it is not efficient, but deficient, as the will itself is not an effecting of something, but a defect. For defection from that which supremely is to that which has less of being —this is to begin to have an evil will. Now, to seek to discover the causes of these defections,—causes, as I have said, not efficient, but deficient,—is as if someone sought to see darkness, or hear silence. Yet both of these are known by us, and the former by means only of the eye, the latter only by the ear; but not by their positive actuality,[3] but by their want of it. Let no one, then, seek to know from me what I know that I do not know; unless he perhaps wishes to learn to be ignorant of that of which all we know is, that it cannot be known. For those things which are known not by their actuality, but by their want of it, are known, if our expression may be allowed and understood, by not knowing them, that by knowing them they may be not known. For when the eyesight surveys objects that strike the sense, it nowhere sees darkness but where it begins not to see. And so no other sense but the ear can perceive silence, and yet it is only perceived by not hearing. Thus, too, our mind perceives intelligible forms

3 Specie.

by understanding them; but when they are deficent, it knows them by not knowing them; for "who can understand defects?" [4]

This I do know, that the nature of God can never, nowhere, nowise be defective, and that natures made of nothing can. These latter, however, the more being they have, and the more good they do (for then they do something positive), the more they have efficient causes; but in so far as they are defective in being, and consequently do evil (for then what is their work but vanity?), they have deficient causes. And I know likewise, that the will could not become evil, were it unwilling to become so; and therefore its failings are justly punished, being not necessary, but voluntary. For its defections are not to evil things, but are themselves evil; that is to say, are not towards things that are naturally and in themselves evil, but the defection of the will is evil, because it is contrary to the order of nature, and an abandonment of that which has supreme being for that which has less. For avarice is not a fault inherent in gold, but in the man who inordinately loves gold, to the detriment of justice, which ought to be held in incomparably higher regard than gold. Neither is luxury the fault of lovely and charming objects, but of the heart that inordinately loves sensual pleasures, to the neglect of temperance, which attaches us to objects more lovely in their spirituality, and more delectable by their incorruptibility. Nor yet is boasting the fault of human praise, but of the soul that is inordinately fond of the applause of men, and that makes light of the voice of conscience. Pride, too, is not the fault of him who delegates power, nor of power itself, but of the soul that is inordinately enamoured of its own

[4] Ps. xix. 12.

power, and despises the more just dominion of a higher authority. Consequently he who inordinately loves the good which any nature possesses, even though he obtain it, himself becomes evil in the good, and wretched because deprived of a greater good.

There is, then, no natural efficient cause, or, if I may be allowed the expression, no essential cause, of the evil will, since itself is the origin of evil in mutable spirits, by which the good of their nature is diminished and corrupted; and the will is made evil by nothing else than defection from God,—a defection of which the cause, too, is certainly deficient. But as to the good will, if we should say that there is no efficient cause of it, we must beware of giving currency to the opinion that the good will of the good angels is not created, but is co-eternal with God. For if they themselves are created, how can we say that their good will was eternal? But if created, was it created along with themselves, or did they exist for a time without it? If along with themselves, then doubtless it was created by Him who created them, and as soon as ever they were created, they attached themselves to Him who created them, with the love He created in them. And they are separated from the society of the rest, because they have continued in the same good will; while the others have fallen away to another will, which is an evil one, by the very fact of its being a falling away from the good; from which, we may add, they would not have fallen away had they been unwilling to do so. But if the good angels existed for a time without a good will, and produced it in themselves without God's interference, then it follows that they made themselves better than He made them. Away with such a thought! For without a good will, what were they but evil? Or if they were not evil, because they had not an evil will any more than a good one (for they had not fallen away from that which as yet they had not begun to enjoy), certainly they were not the same, not so good, as when they came to have a good will. Or if they could not make themselves better than they were made by Him who is surpassed by none in His work, then certainly, without His helpful operation, they could not come to possess that good will which made them better. And though their good will effected that they did not turn to themselves, who had a more stinted existence, but to Him who supremely is, and that, being united to Him, their own being was enlarged, and they lived a wise and blessed life by His communications to them, what does this prove but that the will, however good it might be, would have continued helplessly only to desire Him, had not He who had made their nature out of nothing, and yet capable of enjoying Him, first stimulated it to desire Him, and then filled it with Himself, and so made it better?

Besides, this too has to be inquired into, whether, if the good angels made their own will good, they did so with or without will? If without, then it was not their doing. If with, was the will good or bad? If bad, how could a bad will give birth to a good one? If good, then already they had a good will. And who made this will, which already they had, but He who created them with a good will, or with that chaste love by which they cleaved to Him, in one and the same act creating their nature, and endowing it with grace? And thus we are driven to believe that the holy angels never existed without a good will or the love of God. But the angels who, though created good, are yet evil now, become so by their own will. And this will was not made evil by their good nature, unless by its voluntary defection

from good; for good is not the cause of evil, but a defection from good is. These angels, therefore, either received less of the grace of the divine love than those who persevered in the same; or if both were created equally good, then, while the one fell by their evil will, the others were more abundantly assisted, and attained to that pitch of blessedness at which they became certain they should never fall from it,—as we have already shown in the preceding book.[5] We must therefore acknowledge with the praise due to the Creator, that not only of holy men, but also of the holy angels, it can be said that "the love of God is shed abroad in their hearts by the Holy Ghost, which is given unto them." [6] And that not only of men, but primarily and principally of angels it is true, as it is written, "It is good to draw near to God." [7] And those who have this good in common, have, both with Him to whom they draw near, and with one another, a holy fellowship, and form one city of God —His living sacrifice, and His living temple. And I see that, as I have now spoken of the rise of this city among the angels, it is time to speak of the origin of that part of it which is hereafter to be united to the immortal angels, and which at present is being gathered from among mortal men, and is either sojourning on earth, or, in the persons of those who have passed through death, is resting in the secret receptacles and abodes of disembodied spirits. For from one man, whom God created as the first, the whole human race descended, according to the faith of Holy Scripture, which deservedly is of wonderful authority among all nations throughout the world; since, among its other true

5 C. 13.
6 Rom. v. 5.
7 Ps. lxxiii. 28.

statements, it predicted, by its divine foresight, that all nations would give credit to it.

GOOD AND EVIL [8]

CHAPTER X

THE SUPREMELY GOOD CREATOR MADE
ALL THINGS GOOD

By the Trinity, thus supremely and equally and unchangeably good, all things were created; and these are not supremely and equally and unchangeably good, but yet they are good, even taken separately. Taken as a whole, however, they are very good, because their *ensemble* constitutes the universe in all its wonderful order and beauty.

CHAPTER XI

WHAT IS CALLED EVIL IN THE
UNIVERSE IS BUT THE ABSENCE
OF GOOD

And in the universe, even that which is called evil, when it is regulated and put in its own place, only enhances our admiration of the good; for we enjoy and value the good more when we compare it with the evil. For the Almightly God, who, as even the heathen acknowledge, has supreme power over all things, being Himself supremely good, would never permit the existence of anything evil among His works, if He were not so omnipotent and good that He can bring good even out of evil. For what is that which we call evil but the absence of good? In the bodies of animals, disease and wounds mean nothing but

[8] From *The Enchiridion*, translated by J. F. Shaw, Edinburgh, 1892.

the absence of health; for when a cure is effected, that does not mean that the evils which were present—namely, the diseases and wounds—go away from the body and dwell elsewhere: they altogether cease to exist; for the wound or disease is not a substance, but a defect in the fleshly substance—the flesh itself being a substance, and therefore something good, of which those evils—that is, privations of the good which we call health—are accidents. Just in the same way, what are called vices in the soul are nothing but privations of natural good. And when they are cured, they are not transferred elsewhere: when they cease to exist in the healthy soul, they cannot exist anywhere else.

CHAPTER XII

ALL BEINGS WERE MADE GOOD, BUT
NOT BEING MADE PERFECTLY GOOD,
ARE LIABLE TO CORRUPTION

All things that exist, therefore, seeing that the Creator of them all is supremely good, are themselves good. But because they are not, like their Creator, supremely and unchangeably good, their good may be diminished and increased. But for good to be diminished is an evil, although, however much it may be diminished, it is necessary, if the being is to continue, that some good should remain to constitute the being. For however small or of whatever kind the being may be, the good which makes it a being cannot be destroyed without destroying the being itself. An uncorrupted nature is justly held in esteem. But if, still further, it be incorruptible, it is undoubtedly considered of still higher value. When it is corrupted, however, its corruption is an evil, because it is deprived of some sort of good. For if it be deprived of no good, it receives no injury; but it does receive injury, therefore it is deprived of good. Therefore, so long as a being is in process of corruption, there is in it some good of which it is being deprived; and if a part of the being should remain which cannot be corrupted, this will certainly be an incorruptible being, and accordingly the process of corruption will result in the manifestation of this great good. But if it do not cease to be corrupted, neither can it cease to possess good of which corruption may deprive it. But if it should be thoroughly and completely consumed by corruption, there will then be no good left, because there will be no being. Wherefore corruption can consume the good only by consuming the being. Every being, therefore, is a good; a great good, if it can not be corrupted; a little good, if it can: but in any case, only the foolish or ignorant will deny that it is a good. And if it be wholly consumed by corruption, then the corruption itself must cease to exist, as there is no being left in which it can dwell.

CHAPTER XIII

THERE CAN BE NO EVIL WHERE THERE IS NO GOOD; AND AN EVIL MAN IS AN EVIL GOOD

Accordingly, there is nothing of what we call evil, if there be nothing good. But a good which is wholly without evil is a perfect good. A good, on the other hand, which contains evil is a faulty or imperfect good; and there can be no evil where there is no good. From all this we arrive at the curious result: that since every being, so far as it is a being, is good, when we say that a faulty being is an evil being, we just seem to say that what is good is evil, and that nothing but

what is good can be evil, seeing that every being is good, and that no evil can exist except in a being. Nothing then, can be evil except something which is good. And although this, when stated, seems to be a contradiction, yet the strictness of reasoning leaves us no escape from the conclusion. We must, however, beware of incurring the prophetic condemnation: "Woe unto them that call evil good, and good evil: that put darkness for light, and light for darkness: that put bitter for sweet, and sweet for bitter." [9] And yet our Lord says: "An evil man out of the evil treasure of his heart bringeth forth that which is evil." [10] Now, what is an evil man but an evil being? for a man is a being. Now, if a man is a good thing because he is a being, what is an evil man but an evil good? Yet, when we accurately distinguish these two things, we find that it is not because he is a man that he is evil, or because he is wicked that he is a good; but that he is a good because he is a man, and an evil because he is wicked. Whoever, then, says, "To be a man is an evil," or, "To be wicked is a good," falls under the prophetic denunciation: "Woe unto them that call evil good and good evil!" For he condemns the work of God, which is the man, and praises the defect of man, which is the wickedness. Therefore every being, even if it be a defective one, in so far as it is a being is good, and in so far as it is defective is evil.

CHAPTER XIV

GOOD AND EVIL ARE AN EXCEPTION TO THE RULE THAT CONTRARY ATTRIBUTES CANNOT BE PREDICATED OF THE

[9] Isa. v. 20.
[10] Luke vi. 45.

SAME SUBJECT. EVIL SPRINGS UP IN WHAT IS GOOD, AND CANNOT EXIST EXCEPT IN WHAT IS GOOD

Accordingly, in the case of these contraries which we call good and evil, the rule of the logicians, that two contraries cannot be predicated at the same time of the same thing, does not hold. No weather is at the same time dark and bright: no food or drink is at the same time sweet and bitter: no body is at the same time and in the same place black and white: none is at the same time and in the same place deformed and beautiful. And this rule is found to hold in regard to many, indeed nearly all, contraries, that they cannot exist at the same time in any one thing. But although no one can doubt that good and evil are contraries, not only can they exist at the same time, but evil cannot exist without good, or in anything that is not good. Good, however, can exist without evil. For a man or an angel can exist without being wicked; but nothing can be wicked except a man or an angel: and so far as he is a man or an angel, he is good; so far as he is wicked, he is an evil. And these two contraries are so far co-existent, that if good did not exist in what is evil, neither could evil exist; because corruption could not have either a place to dwell in, or a source to spring from, if there were nothing that could be corrupted; and nothing can be corrupted except what is good, for corruption is nothing else but the destruction of good. From what is good, then, evils arose, and except in what is good they do not exist; nor was there any other source from which any evil nature could arise. For if there were, then, in so far as this was a being, it was certainly a good: and a being which was incorruptible would be a great good; and even one which was

corruptible must be to some extent a good, for only by corrupting what was good in it could corruption do it harm.

CHAPTER XCVI

THE OMNIPOTENT GOD DOES WELL EVEN IN THE PERMISSION OF EVIL

Nor can we doubt that God does well even in the permission of what is evil. For He permits it only in the justice of His judgment. And surely all that is just is good. Although, therefore, evil, in so far as it is evil, is not a good; yet the fact that evil as well as good exists, is a good. For if it were not a good that evil should exist, its existence would not be permitted by the omnipotent God, who without doubt can as easily refuse to permit what He does not wish, as bring about what He does wish. And if we do not believe this, the very first sentence of our creed is endangered, wherein we profess to believe in God the Father Almighty. For He is not truly called Almighty if He cannot do whatsoever He pleases, or if the power of His almighty will is hindered by the will of any creature whatsoever.

CHAPTER C

THE WILL OF GOD IS NEVER DEFEATED, THOUGH MUCH IS DONE THAT IS CONTRARY TO HIS WILL

These are the great works of the Lord, sought out according to all His pleasure,[11] and so wisely sought out,

[11] Ps. cxi. 2 (LXX).

that when the intelligent creation, both angelic and human, sinned, doing not His will but their own, He used the very will of the creature which was working in opposition to the Creator's will as an instrument for carrying out His will, the supremely Good thus turning to good account even what is evil, to the condemnation of those whom in His justice He has predestined to punishment, and to the salvation of those whom in His mercy He has predestined to grace. For, as far as relates to their own consciousness, these creatures did what God wished not to be done: but in view of God's omnipotence, they could in no wise effect their purpose. For in the very fact that they acted in opposition to His will, His will concerning them was fulfilled. And hence it is that "the works of the Lord are great, sought out according to all His pleasure," because in a way unspeakably strange and wonderful, even what is done in opposition to His will does not defeat His will. For it would not be done did He not permit it (and of course His permission is not unwilling, but willing); nor would a Good Being permit evil to be done only that in His omnipotence He can turn evil into good.

CHAPTER CI

THE WILL OF GOD, WHICH IS ALWAYS GOOD, IS SOMETIMES FULFILLED THROUGH THE EVIL WILL OF MAN

Sometimes, however, a man in the goodness of his will desires something that God does not desire, even though God's will is also good, nay, much more fully and more surely good (for His will never can be evil): for example, if a good son is anxious that his father should live, when it is God's good will that he should die. Again, it is possible for a man with evil will to desire what God wills in His goodness: for example, if a bad son wishes his father to die, when this is also the will of God. It is plain that the former wishes what God does not wish, and that the latter wishes what God does wish; and yet the filial love of the former is more in harmony with the good will of God, though its desire is different from God's than the want of filial affection of the latter, though its desire is the same as God's. So necessary is it, in determining whether a man's desire is one to be approved or disapproved, to consider what it is proper for man, and what it is proper for God, to desire, and what is in each case the real motive of the will. For God accomplishes some of His purposes, which of course are all good, through the evil desires of wicked men: for example, it was through the wicked designs of the Jews, working out the good purpose of the Father, that Christ was slain; and this event was so truly good, that when the Apostle Peter expressed his unwillingness that it should take place, he was designated Satan by Him who had come to be slain.[12] How good seemed the intentions of the pious believers who were unwilling that Paul should go up to Jerusalem lest the evils which Agabus had foretold should there befall him![13] And yet it was God's purpose that he should suffer these evils for preaching the faith of Christ, and thereby become a witness for Christ. And this purpose of His, which was good, God did not fulfill through the good counsels of the Christians, but through the evil counsels of the Jews; so that those who opposed His purpose were more truly His servants than those who were the willing instruments of its accomplishment.

[12] Matt. xvi. 21–23.
[13] Acts xxi. 10–12.

THE SUPREME GOOD NOT IN THIS LIFE [14]

If, then, we be asked what . . . the supreme good and evil is, . . . [we] reply that life eternal is the supreme good, death eternal the supreme evil, and that to obtain the one and escape the other we must live rightly. And thus it is written, "The just lives by faith," [15] for we do not as yet see our good, and must therefore live by faith; neither have we in ourselves power to live rightly, but can do so only if He who has given us faith to believe in His help do help us when we believe and pray. As for those who have supposed that the sovereign good and evil are to be found in this life, and have placed it either in the soul or the body, or in both, or, to speak more explicitly, either in pleasure or in virtue, or in both; in repose or in virtue, or in both; in pleasure and repose, or in virtue, or in all combined; in the primary objects of nature, or in virtue, or in both,—all these have, with a marvellous shallowness, sought to find their blessedness in this life and in themselves. Contempt has been poured upon such ideas by the Truth, saying by the prophet, "The Lord knoweth the thoughts of men" (or, as the Apostle Paul cites the passage, "The Lord knoweth the thoughts of the *wise*") "that they are vain." [16]

For what flood of eloquence can suffice to detail the miseries of this life? Cicero, in the *Consolation* on the death of his daughter, has spent all his ability in lamentation; but how inadequate was even his ability here? For when, where, how, in this life can these primary objects of nature be possessed so that they may not be assailed by unforeseen accidents? Is the body of the wise man exempt from any pain which may dispel pleasure, from any disquietude which may banish repose? The amputation or decay of the members of the body puts an end to its integrity, deformity blights its beauty, weakness its health, lassitude its vigour, sleepiness or sluggishness its activity,—and which of these is it that may not assail the flesh of the wise man? Comely and fitting attitudes and movements of the body are numbered among the prime natural blessings; but what if some sickness makes the members tremble? what if a man suffers from curvature of the spine to such an extent that his hands reach the ground, and he goes upon all-fours like a quadruped? Does not this destroy all beauty and grace in the body, whether at rest or in motion? What shall I say of the fundamental blessings of the soul, sense and intellect, of which the one is given for the perception, and the other for the comprehension of truth? But what kind of sense is it that remains when a man becomes deaf and blind? Where are reason and intellect when disease makes a man delirious? We can scarcely, or not at all, refrain from tears, when we think of or see the actions and words of such frantic persons, and consider how different from and even opposed to their own sober judgment and ordinary conduct their present demeanour is. And what shall I say of those who suffer from demoniacal possession? Where is their own intelligence hidden and buried while the malignant spirit is using their body and soul according to his own will? And who is quite sure that no such thing can happen to the wise man in this life? Then, as to the perception of truth, what can we hope for even in this way while in the body, as we read in the true book of Wisdom, "The corruptible body weigheth down the soul, and the earthly taber-

---

[14] *The City of God*, Bk. xix, Chap. 4.
[15] Hab. ii. 4.
[16] Ps. xciv. 11, and 1 Cor. iii. 20.

nacle presseth down the mind that museth upon many things?" [17] And eagerness, or desire of action, if this is the right meaning to put upon the Greek ὁρμή, is also reckoned among the primary advantages of nature; and yet is it not this which produces those pitiable movements of the insane, and those actions which we shudder to see, when sense is deceived and reason deranged?

In fine, virtue itself, which is not among the primary objects of nature, but succeeds to them as the result of learning, though it holds the highest place among human good things, what is its occupation save to wage perpetual war with vices,—not those that are outside of us, but within; not other men's, but our own,—a war which is waged especially by that virtue which the Greeks call σωφροσύνη, and we temperance,[18] and which bridles carnal lusts, and prevents them from winning the consent of the spirit to wicked deeds? For we must not fancy that there is no vice in us, when, as the apostle says, "The flesh lusteth against the spirit;" [19] for to this vice there is a contrary virtue, when, as the same writer says, "The spirit lusteth against the flesh." "For these two," he says, "are contrary one to the other, so that you cannot do the things which you would." But what is it we wish to do when we seek to attain the supreme good, unless that the flesh should cease to lust against the spirit, and that there be no vice in us against which the spirit may lust? And as we cannot attain to this in the present life, however ardently we desire it, let us by God's help accomplish at least this, to preserve the soul from succumbing and yielding to the flesh that lusts against it, and to refuse our consent to the

perpetration of sin. Far be it from us, then, to fancy that while we are still engaged in this intestine war, we have already found the happiness which we seek to reach by victory. And who is there so wise that he has no conflict at all to maintain against his vices?

What shall I say of that virtue which is called prudence? Is not all its vigilance spent in the discernment of good from evil things, so that no mistake may be admitted about what we should desire and what avoid? And thus it is itself a proof that we are in the midst of evils, or that evils are in us; for it teaches us that it is an evil to consent to sin, and a good to refuse this consent. And yet this evil, to which prudence teaches and temperance enables us not to consent, is removed from this life neither by prudence nor by temperance. And justice, whose office it is to render to every man his due, whereby there is in man himself a certain just order of nature, so that the soul is subjected to God, and the flesh to the soul, and consequently both soul and flesh to God,—does not this virtue demonstrate that it is as yet rather labouring towards its end than resting in its finished work? For the soul is so much the less subjected to God as it is less occupied with the thought of God; and the flesh is so much the less subjected to the spirit as it lusts more vehemently against the spirit. So long, therefore, as we are beset by this weakness, this plague, this disease, how shall we dare to say that we are safe? and if not safe, then how can we be already enjoying our final beatitude? Then that virtue which goes by the name of fortitude is the plainest proof of the ills of life, for it is these ills which it is compelled to bear patiently. And this holds good, no matter though the ripest wisdom co-exists with it. And I am at a loss to understand how the Stoic philosophers can presume to say

17 Wisdom ix. 15.
18 Cicero, *Tusc. Quaest.* ii. 8.
19 Gal. v. 17.

that these are no ills, though at the same time they allow the wise man to commit suicide and pass out of this life if they become so grievous that he cannot or ought not to endure them. But such is the stupid pride of these men who fancy that the supreme good can be found in this life, and that they can become happy by their own resources, that their wise man, or at least the man whom they fancifully depict as such, is always happy, even though he become blind, deaf, dumb, mutilated, racked with pains, or suffer any conceivable calamity such as may compel him to make away with himself; and they are not ashamed to call the life that is beset with these evils happy. O happy life, which seeks the aid of death to end it! If it is happy, let the wise man remain in it; but if these ills drive him out of it, in what sense is it happy? Or how can they say that these are not evils which conquer the virtue of fortitude, and force it not only to yield, but so to rave that it in one breath calls life happy and recommends it to be given up? For who is so blind as not to see that if it were happy it would not be fled from? And if they say we should flee from it on account of the infirmities that beset it, why then do they not lower their pride and acknowledge that it is miserable? Was it, I would ask, fortitude or weakness which prompted Cato to kill himself? for he would not have done so had he not been too weak to endure Caesar's victory. Where, then, is his fortitude? It has yielded, it has succumbed, it has been so thoroughly overcome as to abandon, forsake, flee this happy life. Or was it no longer happy? Then it was miserable. How, then, were these not evils which made life miserable, and a thing to be escaped from?

And therefore those who admit that these are evils, as the Peripatetics do, and the Old Academy, the sect which Varro advocates, express a more intelligible doctrine; but theirs also is a surprising mistake, for they contend that this is a happy life which is beset by these evils, even though they be so great that he who endures them should commit suicide to escape them. "Pains and anguish of body," says Varro, "are evils, and so much the worse in proportion to their severity; and to escape them you must quit this life." What life, I pray? This life, he says, which is oppressed by such evils. Then it is happy in the midst of these very evils on account of which you say we must quit it? Or do you call it happy because you are at liberty to escape these evils by death? What, then, if by some secret judgment of God you were held fast and not permitted to die, nor suffered to live without these evils? In that case, at least, you would say that such a life was miserable. It is soon relinquished, no doubt, but this does not make it not miserable; for were it eternal, you yourself would pronounce it miserable. Its brevity, therefore, does not clear it of misery; neither ought it to be called happiness because it is a brief misery. Certainly there is a mighty force in these evils which compel a man—according to them, even a wise man—to cease to be a man that he may escape them, though they say, and say truly, that it is as it were the first and strongest demand of nature that a man cherish himself, and naturally therefore avoid death, and should so stand his own friend as to wish and vehemently aim at continuing to exist as a living creature, and subsisting in this union of soul and body. There is a mighty force in these evils to overcome this natural instinct by which death is by every means and with all a man's efforts avoided, and to overcome it so completely that what was avoided is desired, sought after, and if it cannot by any other way be obtained, is inflicted by the man on himself. There is a mighty force in these evils which make fortitude a homicide,—if, indeed, that is to be called fortitude which is so thoroughly overcome by these evils, that it not only cannot preserve by patience the man whom it undertook to govern and defend, but is itself obliged to kill him. The wise man, I admit ought to bear death with patience, but when it is inflicted by another. If, then, as these men maintain, he is obliged to inflict it on himself, certainly it must be owned that the ills which compel him to this are not only evils, but intolerable evils. The life, then, which is either subject to accidents, or environed with evils so considerable and grievous, could never have been called happy, if the men who give it this name had condescended to yield to the truth, and to be conquered by valid arguments, when they inquired after the happy life, as they yield to unhappiness, and are overcome by the overwhelming evils, when they put themselves to death, and if they had not fancied that the supreme good was to be found in this mortal life; for the very virtues of this life, which are certainly its best and most useful possessions, are all the more telling proofs of its miseries in proportion as they are helpful against the violence of its dangers, toils and woes. For if these are true virtues—and such cannot exist save in those who have true piety—they do not profess to be able to deliver the men who possess them from all miseries; for true virtues tell no such lies, but they profess that by the hope of the future world, this life, which is miserably involved in the many and great evils of this world, is happy as it is also safe. For if not yet safe, how could it be happy? And therefore the Apostle Paul, speaking not of men without prudence, temperance, fortitude, and justice, but of those whose lives were regulated by true piety, and whose virtues were therefore true, says, "For we are saved by hope: now hope which is seen is not hope; for what a man seeth, why doth he yet hope for? But if we hope for that we see not, then do we with patience wait for it." [20] As, therefore, we are saved, so we are made happy by hope. And as we do not as yet possess a present, but look for a future salvation, so is it with our happiness, and this "with patience;" for we are encompassed with evils, which we ought patiently to endure, until we come to the ineffable enjoyment of unmixed good; for there shall be no longer anything to endure. Salvation, such as it shall be in the world to come, shall itself be our final happiness. And this happiness these philosophers refuse to believe in, because they do not see it, and attempt to fabricate for themselves a happiness in this life, based upon a virtue which is as deceitful as it is proud.

EARTHLY AND HEAVENLY PEACE [21]

The whole use, then, of things temporal has a reference to this result of earthly peace in the earthly community, while in the city of God it is connected with eternal peace. And therefore, if we were irrational animals, we should desire nothing beyond the proper arrangement of the parts of the body and the satisfaction of the appetites,—nothing, therefore, but bodily comfort and abundance of pleasures, that the peace of the body might contribute to the peace of the soul. For if bodily peace be awanting, a bar is put to the peace even of the irrational

[20] Rom. viii. 24.
[21] *The City of God*, Bk. xix, Chaps. 14, 17, 25, 27.

soul, since it cannot obtain the gratification of its appetites. And these two together help out the mutual peace of soul and body, the peace of harmonious life and health. For as animals, by shunning pain, show that they love bodily peace, and, by pursuing pleasure to gratify their appetites, show that they love peace of soul, so their shrinking from death is a sufficient indication of their intense love of that peace which binds soul and body in close alliance. But, as man has a rational soul, he subordinates all this which he has in common with the beasts to the peace of his rational soul, that his intellect may have free play and may regulate his actions, and that he may thus enjoy the well-ordered harmony of knowledge and action which constitutes, as we have said, the peace of the rational soul. And for this purpose he must desire to be neither molested by pain, nor disturbed by desire, nor extinguished by death, that he may arrive at some useful knowledge by which he may regulate his life and manners. But, owing to the liability of the human mind to fall into mistakes, this very pursuit of knowledge may be a snare to him unless he has a divine Master, whom he may obey without misgiving, and who may at the same time give him such help as to preserve his own freedom. And because, so long as he is in this mortal body, he is a stranger to God, he walks by faith, not by sight; and he therefore refers all peace, bodily or spiritual or both, to that peace which mortal man has with the immortal God, so that he exhibits the well-ordered obedience of faith to eternal law. But as this divine Master inculcates two precepts,—the love of God and the love of our neighbour,—and as in these precepts a man finds three things he has to love,—God, himself, and his neighbour,—and that he who loves God loves himself thereby,

it follows that he must endeavour to get his neighbour to love God, since he is ordered to love his neighbour as himself. He ought to make this endeavour in behalf of his wife, his children, his household, all within his reach, even as he would wish his neighbour to do the same for him if he needed it; and consequently he will be at peace, or in well-ordered concord, with all men, as far as in him lies. And this is the order of this concord, that a man, in the first place, injure no one, and, in the second, do good to every one he can reach. Primarily, therefore, his own household are his care, for the law of nature and of society gives him readier access to them and greater opportunity of serving them. And hence the apostle says, "Now, if any provide not for his own, and specially for those of his own house, he hath denied the faith, and is worse than an infidel.[22] This is the origin of domestic peace, or the well-ordered concord of those in the family who rule and those who obey. For they who care for the rest rule —the husband the wife, the parents the children, the masters the servants; and they who are cared for obey —the women their husbands, the children their parents, the servants their masters. But in the family of the just man who lives by faith and is as yet a pilgrim journeying on to the celestial city, even those who rule serve those whom they seem to command; for they rule not from a love of power, but from a sense of the duty they owe to others—not because they are proud of authority, but because they love mercy.

But the families which do not live by faith seek their peace in the earthly advantages of this life; while the families which live by faith look for those eternal blessings which are promised and use as pilgrims such advantages of

[22] 1 Tim. v. 8.

time and of earth as do not fascinate and divert them from God, but rather aid them to endure with greater ease, and to keep down the number of those burdens of the corruptible body which weigh upon the soul. Thus the things necessary for this mortal life are used by both kinds of men and families alike, but each has its own peculiar and widely different aim in using them. The earthly city, which does not live by faith, seeks an earthly peace, and the end it proposes, in the well-ordered concord of civic obedience and rule, is the combination of men's wills to attain the things which are helpful to this life. The heavenly city, or rather the part of it which sojourns on earth and lives by faith, makes use of this peace only because it must, until this mortal condition which necessitates it shall pass away. Consequently, so long as it lives like a captive and a stranger in the earthly city, though it has already received the promise of redemption, and the gift of the Spirit as the earnest of it, it makes no scruple to obey the laws of the earthly city, whereby the things necessary for the maintenance of this mortal life are administered; and thus, as this life is common to both cities, so there is a harmony between them in regard to what belongs to it. But, as the earthly city has had some philosophers whose doctrine is condemned by the divine teaching, and who, being deceived either by their own conjectures or by demons, supposed that many gods must be invited to take an interest in human affairs, and assigned to each a separate function and a separate department,—to one the body, to another the soul; and in the body itself, to one the head, to another the neck, and each of the other members to one of the gods; and in like manner, in the soul, to one god the natural capacity was assigned, to another education, to another anger, to another lust; and so the various affairs of life were assigned,—cattle to one, corn to another, wine to another, oil to another, the woods to another, money to another, navigation to another, wars and victories to another, marriages to another, births and fecundity to another, and other things to other gods: and as the celestial city, on the other hand, knew that one God only was to be worshipped, and that to Him alone was due that service which the Greeks call λατρεία, and which can be given only to a god, it has come to pass that the two cities could not have common laws of religion, and that the heavenly city has been compelled in this matter to dissent, and to become obnoxious to those who think differently, and to stand the brunt of their anger and hatred and persecutions, except in so far as the minds of their enemies have been alarmed by the multitude of the Christians and quelled by the manifest protection of God accorded to them. This heavenly city, then, while it sojourns on earth, calls citizens out of all nations, and gathers together a society of pilgrims of all languages, not scrupling about diversities in the manners, laws, and institutions whereby earthly peace is secured and maintained, but recognising that, however various these are, they all tend to one and the same end of earthly peace. It therefore is so far from rescinding and abolishing these diversities, that it even preserves and adopts them, so long only as no hindrance to the worship of the one supreme and true God is thus introduced. Even the heavenly city, therefore, while in its state of pilgrimage, avails itself of the peace of earth, and, so far as it can without injuring faith and godliness desires and maintains a common agreement among men regarding the acquisition of the necessaries of life, and makes this earthly peace bear upon the peace of heaven; for this alone can be truly called and esteemed the peace of the reasonable creatures, consisting as it does in the perfectly ordered and harmonious enjoyment of God and of one another in God. When we shall have reached that peace, this mortal life shall give place to one that is eternal, and our body shall be no more this animal body which by its corruption weighs down the soul, but a spiritual body feeling no want, and in all its members subjected to the will. In its pilgrim state the heavenly city possesses this peace by faith; and by this faith it lives righteously when it refers to the attainment of that peace every good action towards God and man; for the life of the city is a social life.

For though the soul may seem to rule the body admirably, and the reason the vices, if the soul and reason do not themselves obey God, as God has commanded them to serve Him, they have no proper authority over the body and the vices. For what kind of mistress of the body and the vices can that mind be which is ignorant of the true God, and which instead of being subject to His authority, is prostituted to the corrupting influences of the most vicious demons? It is for this reason that the virtues which it seems to itself to possess, and by which it restrains the body and the vices that it may obtain and keep what it desires, are rather vices than virtues so long as there is no reference to God in the matter. For although some suppose that virtues which have a reference only to themselves, and are desired only on their own account, are yet true and genuine virtues, the fact is that even then they are inflated with pride, and are therefore to be reckoned vices rather than virtues. For as that which gives life to the flesh is not derived from flesh, but is above it, so that

which gives blessed life to man is not derived from man, but is something above him; and what I say of man is true of every celestial power and virtue whatsoever.

But the peace which is peculiar to ourselves we enjoy now with God by faith, and shall hereafter enjoy eternally with Him by sight. But the peace which we enjoy in this life whether common to all or peculiar to ourselves, is rather the solace of our misery than the positive enjoyment of felicity. Our very righteousness, too, though true in so far as it has respect to the true good, is yet in this life of such a kind that it consists rather in the remission of sins than in the perfecting of virtues. Witness the prayer of the whole city of God in its pilgrim state, for it cries to God by the mouth of all its members, "Forgive us our debts as we forgive our debtors." [23] And this prayer is efficacious not for those whose faith is "without works and dead," [24] but for those whose faith "worketh by love." [25] For as reason, though subjected to God, is yet "pressed down by the corruptible body." [26] So long as it is in this mortal condition, it has not perfect authority over vice, and therefore this prayer is needed by the righteous. For though it exercises authority, the vices do not submit without a struggle. For however well one maintains the conflict, and however thoroughly he has subdued these enemies, there steals in some evil thing, which, if it do not find ready expression in act, slips out by the lips, or insinuates itself into the thought; and therefore his peace is not full so long as he is at war with his vices. For it is a doubtful conflict he

[23] Matt. vi. 12.
[24] Jas. ii. 17.
[25] Gal. v. 6.
[26] Wisdom ix. 15.

wages with those that resist, and his victory over those that are defeated is not secure, but full of anxiety and effort. Amidst these temptations, therefore, of all which it has been summarily said in the divine oracles, "Is not human life upon earth a temptation?" [27] Who but a proud man can presume that he so lives that he has no need to say to God, "Forgive us our debts?" And such a man is not great, but swollen and puffed up with vanity, and is justly resisted by Him who abundantly gives grace to the humble. Whence it is said, "God resisteth the proud, but giveth grace to the humble." [28] In this then, consists the righteousness of a man, that he submit himself to God, his body to his soul, and his vices, even when they rebel, to his reason, which either defeats or at last resists them; and also that he beg from God grace to do his duty,[29] and the pardon of his sins, and that he render to God thanks for all the blessings he receives. But, in that final peace to which all our righteousness has reference, and for the sake of which it is maintained, as our nature shall enjoy a sound immortality and incorruption, and shall have no more vices, and as we shall experience no resistance either from ourselves or from others, it will not be necessary that reason should rule vices which no longer exist, but God shall rule the man, and the soul shall rule the body, with a sweetness and facility suitable to the felicity of a life which is done with bondage. And this condition shall there be eternal, and we shall be assured of its eternity; and thus the peace of this blessedness and the blessedness of this peace shall be the supreme good.

[27] Job vii. 1.
[28] Jas. iv. 6; 1 Pet. v. 5.
[29] *Gratia meritorum.*

THE BEATIFIC VISION AND ETERNAL FELICITY [30]

And now let us consider, with such ability as God may vouchsafe, how the saints shall be employed when they are clothed in immortal and spiritual bodies, and when the flesh shall live no longer in a fleshly but a spiritual fashion. And indeed, to tell the truth, I am at a loss to understand the nature of that employment, or, shall I rather say, repose and ease, for it has never come within the range of my bodily senses. And if I should speak of my mind or understanding, what is our understanding in comparison of its excellence? For then shall be that "peace of God which," as the apostle says, "passeth all understanding," [31] — that is to say, all human, and perhaps all angelic understanding, but certainly not the divine. That it passeth ours there is no doubt; but if it passeth that of the angels,—and he who says "*all* understanding" seems to make no exception in their favour,—then we must understand him to mean that neither we nor the angels can understand, as God understands, the peace which God Himself enjoys. Doubtless this passeth all understanding but His own. But as we shall one day be made to participate, according to our slender capacity, in His peace, both in ourselves, and with our neighbour, and with God our chief good, in this respect the angels understand the peace of God in their own measure, and men too, though now far behind them, whatever spiritual advance they have made. For we must remember how great a man he was who said, "We know in part, and we prophesy in part, until that which is perfect is come;" [32]

[30] *The City of God*, Bk. xxii: 29–30.
[31] Phil. iv. 7.
[32] I Cor. xiii. 9, 10.

and "Now we see through a glass, darkly; but then face to face." [33] Such also is now the vision of the holy angels, who are also called our angels, because we, being rescued out of the power of darkness, and receiving the earnest of the Spirit, are translated into the kingdom of Christ, and already begin to belong to those angels with whom we shall enjoy that holy and most delightful city of God of which we have now written so much. Thus, then, the angels of God are our angels, as Christ is God's and also ours. They are God's, because they have not abandoned Him: they are ours, because we are their fellow-citizens. The Lord Jesus also said, "See that ye despise not one of these little ones: for I say unto you, That in heaven their angels do always see the face of my Father which is in heaven." [34] As, then, they see, so shall we also see; but not yet do we thus see. Wherefore the apostle uses the words cited a little ago, "Now we see through a glass, darkly; but then face to face." This vision is reserved as the reward of our faith; and of it the Apostle John also says, "When He shall appear, we shall be like Him, for we shall see Him as He is." [35] By "the face" of God we are to understand His manifestation, and not a part of the body similar to that which in our bodies we call by that name.

And so, when I am asked how the saints shall be employed in that spiritual body, I do not say what I see, but I say what I believe, according to that which I read in the psalm, "I believed, therefore have I spoken." [36] I say, then, they shall in the body see God; but whether they shall see Him by means of the body, as now we see the sun, moon, stars, sea, earth, and all that is in it, that is a difficult question. For it is hard to say that the saints shall then have such bodies that they shall not be able to shut and open their eyes as they please; while it is harder still to say that every one who shuts his eyes shall lose the vision of God. For if the prophet Elisha, though at a distance, saw his servant Gehazi, who thought that his wickedness would escape his master's observation and accepted gifts from Naaman the Syrian, whom the prophet had cleansed from his foul leprosy, how much more shall the saints in the spiritual body see all things, not only though their eyes be shut, but though they themselves be at a great distance? For then shall be "that which is perfect," of which the apostle says, "We know in part, and we prophesy in part; but when that which is perfect is come, then that which is in part shall be done away." Then, that he may illustrate as well as possible, by a simile, how superior the future life is to the life now lived, not only by ordinary men, but even by the foremost of the saints, he says, "When I was a child, I understood as a child, I spake as a child, I thought as a child; but when I became a man, I put away childish things. Now we see through a glass, darkly; but then face to face: now I know in part; but then shall I know even as also I am known." [37] If, then, even in this life, in which the prophetic power of remarkable men is no more worthy to be compared to the vision of the future life than childhood is to manhood, Elisha, though distant from his servant, saw him accepting gifts, shall we say that when that which is perfect is come, and the corruptible body no longer oppresses the soul, but is incorruptible and offers no

[33] 1 Cor. xiii. 12.
[34] Matt. xviii. 10.
[35] 1 John iii. 2.
[36] Ps. cxvi. 10.

[37] 1 Cor. xiii. 11, 12.

impediment to it, the saints shall need bodily eyes to see, though Elisha had no need of them to see his servant: For, following the Septuagint version, these are the prophet's words: "Did not my heart go with thee, when the man came out of his chariot to meet thee, and thou tookest his gifts?" [38] Or, as the presbyter Jerome rendered it from the Hebrew, "Was not my heart present when the man turned from his chariot to meet thee?" The prophet said that he saw this with his heart, miraculously aided by God, as no one can doubt. But how much more abundantly shall the saints enjoy this gift when God shall be all in all? Nevertheless the bodily eyes also shall have their office and their place, and shall be used by the spirit through the spiritual body. For the prophet did not forgo the use of his eyes for seeing what was before them, though he did not need them to see his absent servant, and though he could have seen these present objects in spirit, and with his eyes shut, as he saw things far distant in a place where he himself was not. Far be it, then, from us to say that in the life to come the saints shall not see God when their eyes are shut, since they shall always see Him with the spirit.

But the question arises, whether, when their eyes are open, they shall see Him with the bodily eye? If the eyes of the spiritual body have no more power than the eyes which we now possess, manifestly God cannot be seen with them. They must be of a very different power if they can look upon that incorporeal nature which is not contained in any place, but is all in every place. For though we say that God is in heaven and on earth, as He Himself says by the prophet, "I fill heaven and earth,"[39] we do not mean

that there is one part of God in heaven and another part on earth; but He is all in heaven and all on earth, not at alternate intervals of time, but both at once, as no bodily nature can be. The eye, then, shall have a vastly superior power,—the power not of keen sight, such as is ascribed to serpents or eagles, for however keenly these animals see, they can discern nothing but bodily substances,—but the power of seeing things incorporeal. Possibly it was this great power of vision which was temporarily communicated to the eyes of the holy Job while yet in this mortal body, when he says to God, "I have heard of Thee by the hearing of the ear; but now mine eye seeth Thee: wherefore I abhor myself, and melt away, and count myself dust and ashes;" [40] although there is no reason why we should not understand this of the eye of the heart, of which the apostle says, "Having the eyes of your heart illuminated." [41] But that God shall be seen with these eyes no Christian doubts who believingly accepts what our God and Master says, "Blessed are the pure in heart: for they shall see God." [42] But whether in the future life God shall also be seen with the bodily eye, this is now our question.

The expression of Scripture, "And all flesh shall see the salvation of God," [43] may without difficulty be understood as if it were said, "And every man shall see the Christ of God." And He certainly was seen in the body, and shall be seen in the body when He judges quick and dead. And that Christ is the salvation of God, many other passages of Scripture witness, but especially the words of the venerable Simeon, who, when he had

[38] 2 Kings v. 26.
[39] Jer. xxiii. 24.

[40] Job xlii. 5, 6.
[41] Eph. i. 18.
[42] Matt. v. 8.
[43] Luke iii. 6.

received into his hands the infant Christ, said, "Now lettest Thou Thy servant depart in peace, according to Thy word: for mine eyes have seen Thy Salvation." [44] As for the words of the above-mentioned Job, as they are found in the Hebrew manuscripts, "And in my flesh I shall see God," [45] no doubt they were a prophecy of the resurrection of the flesh; yet he does not say "by the flesh." And indeed, if he had said this, it would still be possible that Christ was meant by "God"; for Christ shall be seen by the flesh in the flesh. But even understanding it of God, it is only equivalent to saying, I shall be in the flesh when I see God. Then the apostle's expression, "face to face," [46] does not oblige us to believe that we shall see God by the bodily face in which are the eyes of the body, for we shall see Him without intermission in spirit. And if the apostle had not referred to the face of the inner man, he would not have said, "But we, with unveiled face beholding as in a glass the glory of the Lord, are transformed into the same image, from glory to glory, as by the Spirit of the Lord." [47] In the same sense we understand what the Psalmist sings, "Draw near unto Him, and be enlightened: and your faces shall not be ashamed." [48] For it is by faith we draw near to God, and faith is an act of the spirit, not of the body. But as we do not know what degree of perfection the spiritual body shall attain, —for here we speak of a matter of which we have no experience, and upon which the authority of Scripture does not definitely pronounce,—it is necessary that the words of the Book of Wisdom be illustrated in us: "The

thoughts of mortal men are timid, and our forecastings uncertain." [49]

For if that reasoning of the philosophers, by which they attempt to make out that intelligible or mental objects are so seen by the mind, and sensible or bodily objects so seen by the body, that the former cannot be discerned by the mind through the body, nor the latter by the mind itself without the body,—if this reasoning were trustworthy, then it would certainly follow that God could not be seen by the eye even of a spiritual body. But this reasoning is exploded both by true reason and by prophetic authority. For who is so little acquainted with the truth as to say that God has no cognisance of sensible objects? Has He therefore a body, the eyes of which give Him this knowledge? Moreover, what we have just been relating of the prophet Elisha, does this not sufficiently show that bodily things can be discerned by the spirit without the help of the body? For when that servant received the gifts, certainly this was a bodily or material transaction, yet the prophet saw it not by the body, but by the spirit. As, therefore, it is agreed that bodies are seen by the spirit, what if the power of the spiritual body shall be so great that spirit also is seen by the body? For God is a spirit. Besides, each man recognises his own life— that life by which he now lives in the body, and which vivifies these earthly members and causes them to grow— by an interior sense, and not by his bodily eye; but the life of other men, though it is invisible, he sees with the bodily eye. For how do we distinguish between living and dead bodies, except by seeing at once both the body and the life which we cannot see save by the eye? But a life without a body we cannot see thus.

Wherefore it may very well be, and

[44] Luke ii. 29, 30.

[45] Job xix. 26.

[46] 1 Cor. xiii. 12.

[47] 2 Cor. iii. 18.

[48] Ps. xxxiv. 5.

[49] Wisd. ix. 14.

it is thoroughly credible, that we shall in the future world see the material forms of the new heavens and the new earth in such a way that we shall most distinctly recognize God everywhere present and governing all things, material as well as spiritual, and shall see Him, not as now we understand the invisible things of God, by the things which are made,[50] and see Him darkly, as in a mirror, and in part, and rather by faith than by bodily vision of material appearances, but by means of the bodies we shall wear and which we shall see wherever we turn our eyes. As we do not believe, but see that the living men around us who are exercising vital functions are alive, though we cannot see their life without their bodies, but see it most distinctly by means of their bodies, so, wherever we shall look with those spiritual eyes of our future bodies, we shall then, too, by means of bodily substances behold God, though a spirit, ruling all things. Either, therefore, the eyes shall possess some quality similar to that of the mind, by which they may be able to discern spiritual things, and among these God —a supposition for which it is difficult or even impossible to find any support in Scripture —or, which is more easy to comprehend, God will be so known by us, and shall be so much before us, that we shall see Him by the spirit in ourselves, in one another, in Himself, in the new heavens and the new earth, in every created thing which shall then exist; and also by the body we shall see Him in every body which the keen vision of the eye of the spiritual body shall reach. Our thoughts also shall be visible to all, for then shall be fulfilled the words of the apostle, "Judge nothing before the time, until the Lord come, who both will bring to light the hidden

[50] Rom. i. 20.

things of darkness, and will make manifest the thoughts of the heart, and then shall every one have praise of God." [51]

How great shall be that felicity, which shall be tainted with no evil, which shall lack no good, and which shall afford leisure for the praises of God, who shall be all in all! For I know not what other employment there can be where no lassitude shall slacken activity, nor any want stimulate to labour. I am admonished also by the sacred song, in which I read or hear the words, "Blessed are they that dwell in Thy house, O Lord; they will be still praising Thee." [52] All the members and organs of the incorruptible body, which now we see to be suited to various necessary uses, shall contribute to the praises of God; for in that life necessity shall have no place, but full, certain, secure, everlasting felicity. For all those parts[53] of the bodily harmony, which are distributed through the whole body, within and without, and of which I have just been saying that they at present elude our observation, shall then be discerned; and, along with the other great and marvellous discoveries which shall then kindle rational minds in praise of the great Artificer, there shall be the enjoyment of a beauty which appeals to the reason. What power of movement such bodies shall possess, I have not the audacity rashly to define, as I have not the ability to conceive. Nevertheless I will say that in any case, both in motion and at rest, they shall be, as in their appearance, seemly; for into that state nothing which is unseemly shall be admitted. One thing is certain, the body shall forthwith be wherever the spirit wills, and the spirit shall will nothing which

[51] 1 Cor. iv. 5.
[52] Ps. lxxxiv. 4.
[53] Numbers.

is unbecoming either to the spirit or to the body. True honour shall be there, for it shall be denied to none who is worthy, nor yielded to any unworthy; neither shall any unworthy person so much as sue for it, for none but the worthy shall be there. True peace shall be there, where no one shall suffer opposition either from himself or any other. God Himself, who is the Author of virtue, shall there be its reward; for, as there is nothing greater or better, He has promised Himself. What else was meant by His word through the prophet, "I will be your God, and ye shall be my people," [54] than, I shall be their satisfaction, I shall be all that men honourably desire,—life, and health, and nourishment, and plenty, and glory, and honour, and peace, and all good things? This, too, is the right interpretation of the saying of the apostle, "That God may be all in all." [55] He shall be the end of our desires who shall be seen without end, loved without cloy, praised without weariness. This outgoing of affection, this employment, shall certainly be, like eternal life itself, common to all.

But who can conceive, not to say describe, what degrees of honour and glory shall be awarded to the various degrees of merit? Yet it cannot be doubted that there shall be degrees. And in that blessed city there shall be this great blessing, that no inferior shall envy any superior, as now the archangels are not envied by the angels, because no one will wish to be what he has not received, though bound in strictest concord with him who has received; as in the body the finger does not seek to be the eye, though both members are harmoniously included in the complete structure of the body. And thus, along with his gift, greater or less, each shall receive this further gift of contentment to desire no more than he has.

Neither are we to suppose that because sin shall have no power to delight them, free will must be withdrawn. It will, on the contrary, be all the more truly free, because set free from delight in sinning to take unfailing delight in not sinning. For the first freedom of will which man received when he was created upright consisted in an ability not to sin, but also in an ability to sin; whereas this last freedom of will shall be superior, inasmuch as it shall not be able to sin. This, indeed, shall not be a natural ability, but the gift of God. For it is one thing to be God, another thing to be a partaker of God. God by nature cannot sin, but the partaker of God receives this inability from God. And in this divine gift there was to be observed this gradation, that man should first receive a free will by which he was able not to sin, and at last a free will by which he was not able to sin,—the former being adapted to the acquiring of merit, the latter to the enjoyment of the reward.[56] But the nature thus constituted, having sinned when it had the ability to do so, it is by a more abundant grace that it is delivered so as to reach that freedom in which it cannot sin. For as the first immortality which Adam lost by sinning consisted in his being able not to die, while the last shall consist in his not being able to die; so the first free will consisted in his being able not to sin, the last in his not being able to sin. And thus piety and justice shall be as indefeasible as happiness. For certainly by sinning we lost both piety and happiness; but when we lost happiness, we did not lose the love of it.

[54] Lev. xxvi. 12.

[55] 1 Cor. xv. 28.

[56] Or, the former to a state of probation, the latter to a state of reward.

Are we to say that God Himself is not free because He cannot sin? In that city, then, there shall be free will, one in all the citizens, and indivisible in each, delivered from all ill, filled with all good, enjoying indefeasibly the delights of eternal joys, oblivious of sins, oblivious of sufferings, and yet not so oblivious of its deliverance as to be ungrateful to its Deliverer.

The soul, then, shall have an intellectual remembrance of its past ills; but, so far as regards sensible experience, they shall be quite forgotten. For a skilful physician knows, indeed, professionally almost all the diseases; but experimentally he is ignorant of a great number which he himself has never suffered from. As, therefore, there are two ways of knowing evil things,—one by mental insight, the other by sensible experience, for it is one thing to understand all vices by the wisdom of a cultivated mind, another to understand them by the foolishness of an abandoned life,—so also there are two ways of forgetting evils. For a well-instructed and learned man forgets them one way, and he who has experimentally suffered from them forgets them another,—the former by neglecting what he has learned, the latter by escaping what he has suffered. And in this latter way the saints shall forget their past ills, for they shall have so thoroughly escaped them all, that they shall be quite blotted out of their experience. But their intellectual knowledge, which shall be great, shall keep them acquainted not only with their own past woes, but with the eternal sufferings of the lost. For if they were not to know that they had been miserable, how could they, as the Psalmist says, forever sing the mercies of God? Certainly that city shall have no greater joy than the celebration of the grace of Christ, who redeemed us by His blood. There

shall be accomplished the words of the psalm, "Be still, and know that I am God." [57] There shall be the great Sabbath which has no evening, which God celebrated among His first works, as it is written, "And God rested on the seventh day from all His works which He had made. And God blessed the seventh day, and sanctified it; because that in it He had rested from all His work which God began to make." [58] For we shall ourselves be the seventh day, when we shall be filled and replenished with God's blessing and sanctification. There shall we be still, and know that He is God; that He is that which we ourselves aspired to be when we fell away from Him, and listened to the voice of the seducer, "Ye shall be as gods," [59] and so abandoned God, who would have made us as gods, not by deserting Him, but by participating in Him. For without Him what have we accomplished, save to perish in His anger? But when we are restored by Him, and perfected with greater grace, we shall have eternal leisure to see that He is God, for we shall be full of Him when He shall be all in all. For even our good works, when they are understood to be rather His than ours, are imputed to us that we may enjoy this Sabbath rest. For if we attribute them to ourselves, they shall be servile; for it is said of the Sabbath, "Ye shall do no servile work in it." [60] Wherefore also it is said by Ezekiel the prophet, "And I gave them my Sabbaths to be a sign between me and them that they might know that I am the Lord who sanctify them." [61] This knowledge shall be perfected when

[57] Ps. xlvi. 10.
[58] Gen. ii. 2, 3.
[59] Gen. iii. 5.
[60] Deut. v. 14.
[61] Ezek. xx. 12.

we shall be perfectly at rest, and shall perfectly know that He is God.

This Sabbath shall appear still more clearly if we count the ages as days, in accordance with the periods of time defined in Scripture, for that period will be found to be the seventh. The first age, as the first day, extends from Adam to the deluge; the second from the deluge to Abraham, equalling the first, not in length of time, but in the number of generations, there being ten in each. From Abraham to the advent of Christ there are, as the evangelist Matthew calculates, three periods, in each of which are fourteen generations—one period from Abraham to David, a second from David to the captivity, a third from the captivity to the birth of Christ in the flesh. There are thus five ages in all. The sixth is now passing, and cannot be measured by any number of generations, as it has been said, "It is not for you to know the times, which the Father hath put in His own power." [62] After this period God shall rest as on the seventh day, when He shall give us (who shall be the seventh day) rest in Himself. But there is not now space to treat of these ages; suffice it to say that the seventh shall be our Sabbath, which shall be brought to a close, not by an evening, but by the Lord's day, as an eighth and eternal day, consecrated by the resurrection of Christ, and prefiguring the eternal repose not only of the spirit, but also of the body. There we shall rest and see, see and love, love and praise. This is what shall be in the end without end. For what other end do we propose to ourselves than to attain to the kingdom of which there is no end?

[62] Acts i. 7.

St. Thomas Aquinas (1225—1274)

In his own lifetime St. Thomas Aquinas was known as the Angelic Doctor. He was born near Aquino, Italy, the son of the local count. As a boy he spent a number of years in the Benedictine monastery of Monte Cassino. In 1239 he entered the University of Naples, and in 1244 he joined the Dominican order. He went to the University of Paris in 1245, but three years later he traveled to Cologne, where he studied under Albertus Magnus until 1252. He returned to the University of Paris and in 1256 became professor of theology. From 1259 to 1268 he taught in Italy, but by 1268 he was back in Paris where a form of Aristotelianism derived from the Moslem philosopher Averröes was the subject of intense debate. After three years he returned to Italy to establish a Dominican institute of studies in Naples. He died in 1274 en route to the Council of Lyon. His principal works are the *Summa Contra Gentiles* and the monumental *Summa Theologica,* an unfinished work in which Aquinas achieved a synthesis of Christian and Aristotelian doctrine. Thomas Aquinas was canonized in 1323. It is of interest to note that ten years before St. Thomas Aquinas was born Aristotle's works on metaphysics and natural philosophy were banned at the University of Paris, but that after the *Summas,* all attempts to censure Aristotelian doctrine failed. In 1879 St. Thomas Aquinas' synthesis of Aristotelianism and Christian doctrine was declared by Pope Leo XIII to be the authoritative teaching of the Roman Catholic Church.

TREATISE ON LAW [1]

QUESTION XC

On the Essence of Law
(*In Four Articles*)

We have now to consider the ex- trinsic principles of acts. Now the extrinsic principle inclining to evil is the devil, of whose temptations we have spoken in the First Part. But the extrinsic principle moving to good is God, Who both instructs us by means of His Law, and assists us by His Grace. Therefore, in the first place, we must speak of law; in the second place, of grace.

Concerning law, we must consider (1) law itself in general; (2) its parts. Concerning law in general three points offer themselves for our consideration: (1) its essence; (2) the different kinds of law; (3) the effects of law.

[1] The following selections are taken from the First Part of the Second Part of the *Summa Theologica* in the Dominican translation. From *Basic Writings of Saint Thomas Aquinas,* Anton C. Pegis, ed. © 1945 by Random House, Inc. Reprinted by permission.

Under the first head there are four points of inquiry: (1) Whether law is something pertaining to reason? (2) Concerning the end of law. (3) Its cause. (4) The promulgation of law.

FIRST ARTICLE

WHETHER LAW IS SOMETHING PERTAINING TO REASON?

We proceed thus to the First Article:

Objection 1. It would seem that law is not something pertaining to reason. For the Apostle says (*Rom.* vii. 23): *I see another law in my members,* etc. But nothing pertaining to reason is in the members, since the reason does not make use of a bodily organ. Therefore law is not something pertaining to reason.

Obj. 2. Further, in the reason there is nothing else but power, habit and act. But law is not the power itself of reason. In like manner, neither is it a habit of reason, because the habits of reason are the intellectual virtues, of which we have spoken above. Nor again is it an act of reason, because then law would cease when the act of reason ceases, for instance, while we are asleep. Therefore law is nothing pertaining to reason.

Obj. 3. Further, the law moves those who are subject to it to act rightly. But it belongs properly to the will to move to act, as is evident from what has been said above. Therefore law pertains, not to the reason, but to the will, according to the words of the Jurist: [2] *Whatsoever pleaseth the sovereign has the force of law.*

On the contrary, It belongs to the

[2] When St. Thomas speaks of "the Jurist," he is referring to the Digest of Justinian, a sixth-century compilation of excerpts from the ancient Roman jurists. "The Philosopher" is Aristotle.

law to command and to forbid. But it belongs to reason to command, as was stated above. Therefore law is something pertaining to reason.

I answer that, Law is a rule and measure of acts, whereby man is induced to act or is restrained from acting; for *lex* [law] is derived from *ligare* [to bind], because it binds one to act. Now the rule and measure of human acts is the reason, which is the first principle of human acts, as is evident from what has been stated above. For it belongs to the reason to direct to the end, which is the first principle in all matters of action, according to the Philosopher. Now that which is the principle in any genus is the rule and measure of that genus: for instance, unity in the genus of numbers, and the first movement in the genus of movements. Consequently, it follows that law is something pertaining to reason.

Reply Obj. 1. Since law is a kind of rule and measure, it may be in something in two ways. First, as in that which measures and rules; and since this is proper to reason, it follows that, in this way, law is in the reason alone. —Secondly, as in that which is measured and ruled. In this way, law is in all those things that are inclined to something because of some law; so that any inclination arising from a law may be called a law, not essentially, but by participation as it were. And thus the inclination of the members to concupiscence is called *the law of the members.*

Reply Obj. 2. Just as, in external acts, we may consider the work and the work done, for instance, the work of building and the house built, so in the acts of reason, we may consider the act itself of reason, *i.e.,* to understand and to reason, and something produced by this act. With regard to the speculative reason, this is first of all the definition; secondly, the proposition; thirdly, the syllogism or argument. And since the practical reason also makes use of the syllogism in operable matters, as we have stated above and as the Philosopher teaches, hence we find in the practical reason something that holds the same position in regard to operations as, in the speculative reason, the proposition holds in regard to conclusions. Such universal propositions of the practical reason that are directed to operations have the nature of law. And these propositions are sometimes under our actual consideration, while sometimes they are retained in the reason by means of a habit.

Reply Obj. 3. Reason has its power of moving from the will, as was stated above; for it is due to the fact that one wills the end, that the reason issues its commands as regards things ordained to the end. But in order that the volition of what is commanded may have the nature of law, it needs to be in accord with some rule of reason. And in this sense is to be understood the saying that the will of the sovereign has the force of law; or otherwise the sovereign's will would savor of lawlessness rather than of law.

SECOND ARTICLE

WHETHER LAW IS ALWAYS DIRECTED TO THE COMMON GOOD?

We proceed thus to the Second Article:

Objection 1. It would seem that law is not always directed to the common good as to its end. For it belongs to law to command and to forbid. But commands are directed to certain individual goods. Therefore the end of law is not always the common good.

Obj. 2. Further, law directs man in his actions. But human actions are concerned with particular matters. Therefore law is directed to some particular good.

Obj. 3. Further, Isidore says: *If law is based on reason, whatever is based on reason will be a law.* But reason is the foundation not only of what is ordained to the common good, but also of that which is directed to private good. Therefore law is not directed only to the good of all, but also to the private good of an individual.

On the contrary, Isidore says that *laws are enacted for no private profit, but for the common benefit of the citizens.*

I answer that, As we have stated above, law belongs to that which is a principle of human acts, because it is their rule and measure. Now as reason is a principle of human acts, so in reason itself there is something which is the principle in respect of all the rest. Hence to this principle chiefly and mainly law must needs be referred. Now the first principle in practical matters, which are the object of the practical reason, is the last end: and the last end of human life is happiness or beatitude, as we have stated above. Consequently, law must needs concern itself mainly with the order that is in beatitude. Moreover, since every part is ordained to the whole as the imperfect to the perfect, and since one man is a part of the perfect community, law must needs concern itself properly with the order directed to universal happiness. Therefore the Philosopher, in the above definition of legal matters, mentions both happiness and the body politic, since he says that we call those legal matters *just which are adapted to produce and preserve happiness and its parts for the body politic.* For the state is a perfect community, as he says in *Politics* i.

Now, in every genus, that which belongs to it chiefly is the principle of the others, and the others belong to that genus according to some order towards that thing. Thus fire, which is chief among hot things, is the cause of heat in mixed bodies, and these are said to be hot in so far as they have a share of fire. Consequently, since law is chiefly ordained to the common good, any other precept in regard to some individual work must needs be devoid of the nature of the law, save in so far as it regards the common good. Therefore every law is ordained to the common good.

Reply Obj. 1. A command denotes the application of a law to matters regulated by law. Now the order to the common good, at which law aims, is applicable to particular ends. And in this way commands are given even concerning particular matters.

Reply Obj. 2. Actions are indeed concerned with particular matters, but those particular matters are referable to the common good, not as to a common genus or species, but as to a common final cause, according as the common good is said to be the common end.

Reply Obj. 3. Just as nothing stands firm with regard to the speculative reason except that which is traced back to the first indemonstrable principles, so nothing stands firm with regard to the practical reason, unless it be directed to the last end which is the common good. Now whatever stands to reason in this sense has the nature of a law.

THIRD ARTICLE

WHETHER THE REASON OF ANY MAN IS COMPETENT TO MAKE LAWS?

We proceed thus to the Third Article:

Objection 1. It would seem that the reason of any man is competent to make laws. For the Apostle says (Rom. ii. 14) that *when the Gentiles, who have not the law, do by nature those things that are of the law, . . . they are a law to themselves.* Now he says this of all in general. Therefore anyone can make a law for himself.

Obj. 2. Further, as the Philosopher says, *the intention of the lawgiver is to lead men to virtue.* But every man can lead another to virtue. Therefore the reason of any man is competent to make laws.

Obj. 3. Further, just as the sovereign of a state governs the state, so every father of a family governs his household. But the sovereign of a state can make laws for the state. Therefore every father of a family can make laws for his household.

On the contrary, Isidore says, and the *Decretals* repeat: *A law is an ordinance of the people, whereby something is sanctioned by the Elders together with the Commonalty.* Therefore not everyone can make laws.

I answer that, A law, properly speaking, regards first and foremost the order to the common good. Now to order anything to the common good belongs either to the whole people, or to someone who is the vicegerent of the whole people. Hence the making of a law belongs either to the whole people or to a public personage who has care of the whole people; for in all other matters the directing of anything to the end concerns him to whom the end belongs.

Reply Obj. 1. As was stated above, a law is in a person not only as in one that rules, but also, by participation, as in one that is ruled. In the latter way, each one is a law to himself, in so far as he shares the direction that he receives from one who rules him. Hence the same text goes on: *Who show the work of the law written in their hearts* (*Rom.* ii. 15).

Reply Obj. 2. A private person cannot lead another to virtue efficaciously; for he can only advise, and if his advice be not taken, it has no coercive power, such as the law should have, in order to prove an efficacious inducement to virtue, as the Philosopher says. But this coercive power is vested in the whole people or in some public personage, to whom it belongs to inflict penalties, as we shall state further on. Therefore the framing of laws belongs to him alone.

Reply Obj. 3. As one man is a part of the household, so a household is a part of the state; and the state is a perfect community, according to *Politics* i. Therefore, just as the good of one man is not the last end, but is ordained to the good of a single state, which is a perfect community. Consequently, he that governs a family can indeed make certain commands or ordinances, but not such as to have properly the nature of law.

FOURTH ARTICLE

WHETHER PROMULGATION IS
ESSENTIAL TO LAW?

We proceed thus to the Fourth Article:

Objection 1. It would seem that promulgation is not essential to law. For the natural law, above all, has the character of law. But the natural law needs no promulgation. Therefore it is not essential to law that it be promulgated.

Obj. 2. Further, it belongs properly to law to bind one to do or not to do something. But the obligation of fulfilling a law touches not only those in whose presence it is promulgated, but also others. Therefore promulgation is not essential to law.

Obj. 3. Further, the binding force of law extends even to the future, since *laws are binding in matters of the future,* as the jurists say. But promulgation concerns those who are present. Therefore it is not essential to law.

On the contrary, It is laid down in the *Decretals* that *laws are established when they are promulgated.*

I answer that, As was stated above, a law is imposed on others as a rule and measure. Now a rule or measure is imposed by being applied to those who are to be ruled and measured by it. Therefore, in order that a law obtain the binding force which is proper to a law, it must needs be applied to the men who have to be ruled by it. But such application is made by its being made known to them by promulgation. Therefore promulgation is necessary for law to obtain its force.

Thus, from the four preceding articles, the definition of law may be gathered. Law is nothing else than an ordinance of reason for the common good, promulgated by him who has the care of the community.

Reply Obj. 1. The natural law is promulgated by the very fact that God instilled it into man's mind so as to be known by him naturally.

Reply Obj. 2. Those who are not present when a law is promulgated are bound to observe the law, in so far as it is made known or can be made known to them by others, after it has been promulgated.

Reply Obj. 3. The promulgation that takes place in the present extends to future time by reason of the durability of written characters, by which means it is continually promulgated. Hence Isidore says that *lex* [law] is derived from *legere* [to read] *because it is written.*

QUESTION XCI

ON THE VARIOUS KINDS OF LAW
(*In Six Articles*)

We must now consider the various kinds of law, under which head there are six points of inquiry: (1) Whether there is an eternal law? (2)

Whether there is a natural law?
(3) Whether there is a human law?
(4) Whether there is a divine law?
(5) Whether there is one divine law,
or several? (6) Whether there is a law
of sin?

FIRST ARTICLE

WHETHER THERE IS AN
ETERNAL LAW?

We proceed thus to the First Article:

Objection 1. It would seem that
there is no eternal law. For every law
is imposed on someone. But there was
not someone from eternity on whom
a law could be imposed, since God
alone was from eternity. Therefore no
law is eternal.

Obj. 2. Further, promulgation is essential to law. But promulgation could
not be from eternity, because there
was no one to whom it could be promulgated from eternity. Therefore no
law can be eternal.

Obj. 3. Further, law implies order to
an end. But nothing ordained to an
end is eternal, for the last end alone is
eternal. Therefore no law is eternal.

On the contrary, Augustine says:
That Law which is the Supreme Rea-
son cannot be understood to be other-
wise than unchangeable and eternal.

I answer that, As we have stated
above, law is nothing else but a dictate
of practical reason emanating from the
ruler who governs a perfect community. Now it is evident, granted that
the world is ruled by divine providence, as was stated in the First Part,
that the whole community of the universe is governed by the divine reason.
Therefore the very notion of the government of things in God, the ruler of
the universe, has the nature of a law.
And since the divine reason's conception of things is not subject to time, but
is eternal, according to *Prov.* viii. 23,

therefore it is that this kind of law
must be called eternal.

Reply Obj. 1. Those things that do
not exist in themselves exist in God,
inasmuch as they are known and pre-
ordained by Him, according to *Rom.*
iv. 17: *Who calls those things that are*
not, as those that are. Accordingly, the
eternal concept of the divine law bears
the character of an eternal law in so
far as it is ordained by God to the
government of things foreknown by
Him.

Reply Obj. 2. Promulgation is made
by word of mouth or in writing, and in
both ways the eternal law is promulgated, because both the divine Word
and the writing of the Book of Life are
eternal. But the promulgation cannot
be from eternity on the part of the
creature that hears or reads.

Reply Obj. 3. Law implies order to
the end actively, namely, in so far as
it directs certain things to the end; but
not passively,—that is to say, the law
itself is not ordained to the end, except
accidentally, in a governor whose end
is extrinsic to him, and to which end
his law must needs be ordained. But
the end of the divine government is
God Himself, and His law is not something other than Himself. Therefore
the eternal law is not ordained to another end.

SECOND ARTICLE

WHETHER THERE IS IN US A
NATURAL LAW?

We proceed thus to the Second Article:

Objection 1. It would seem that
there is no natural law in us. For man
is governed sufficiently by the eternal
law, since Augustine says that *the*
eternal law is that by which it is right
that all things should be most orderly.
But nature does not abound in super-
fluities as neither does she fail in neces-

saries. Therefore man has no natural law.

Obj. 2. Further, by the law man is directed, in his acts, to the end, as was stated above. But the directing of human acts to their end is not a function of nature, as is the case in irrational creatures, which act for an end solely by their natural appetite; whereas man acts for an end by his reason and will. Therefore man has no natural law.

Obj. 3. Further, the more a man is free, the less is he under the law. But man is freer than all the animals because of his free choice, with which he is endowed in distinction from all other animals. Since, therefore, other animals are not subject to a natural law, neither is man subject to a natural law.

On the contrary, the *Gloss* on *Rom.* ii. 14 (*When the Gentiles, who have not the law, do by nature those things that are of the law*) comments as follows: *Although they have no written law, yet they have the natural law, whereby each one knows, and is conscious of, what is good and what is evil.*

I answer that, As we have stated above, law, being a rule and measure, can be in a person in two ways: in one way, as in him that rules and measures; in another way, as in that which is ruled and measured, since a thing is ruled and measured in so far as it partakes of the rule or measure. Therefore, since all things subject to divine providence are ruled and measured by the eternal law, as was stated above, it is evident that all things partake in some way in the eternal law, in so far as, namely, from its being imprinted on them, they derive their respective inclinations to their proper acts and ends. Now among all others, the rational creature is subject to divine providence in a more excellent way, in so far as it itself partakes of a share of providence, by being provident both

for itself and for others. Therefore it has a share of the eternal reason, whereby it has a natural inclination to its proper act and end; and this participation of the eternal law in the rational creature is called the natural law. Hence the Psalmist, after saying (*Ps.* iv. 6): *Offer up the sacrifice of justice,* as though someone asked what the works of justice are, adds: *Many say, Who showeth us good things?* in answer to which question he says: *The light of Thy countenance, O Lord, is signed upon us.* He thus implies that the light of natural reason, whereby we discern what is good and what is evil, which is the function of the natural law, is nothing else than an imprint on us of the divine light. It is therefore evident that the natural law is nothing else than the rational creature's participation of the eternal law.

Reply Obj. 1. This argument would hold if the natural law were something different from the eternal law; whereas it is nothing but a participation thereof, as we have stated above.

Reply Obj. 2. Every act of reason and will in us is based on that which is according to nature, as was stated above. For every act of reasoning is based on principles that are known naturally, and every act of appetite in respect of the means is derived from the natural appetite in respect of the last end. Accordingly, the first direction of our acts to their end must needs be through the natural law.

Reply Obj. 3. Even irrational animals partake in their own way of the eternal reason, just as the rational creature does. But because the rational creature partakes thereof in an intellectual and rational manner, therefore the participation of the eternal law in the rational creature is properly called a law, since a law is something pertaining to reason, as was stated above. Irrational creatures, however, do not partake thereof in a rational manner, and therefore there is no participation of the eternal law in them, except by way of likeness.

WHETHER THERE IS A HUMAN LAW?

We proceed thus to the Third Article:

Objection 1. It would seem that there is not a human law. For the natural law is a participation of the eternal law, as was stated above. Now through the eternal law *all things are most orderly,* as Augustine states. Therefore the natural law suffices for the ordering of all human affairs. Consequently there is no need for a human law.

Obj. 2. Further, law has the character of a measure, as was stated above. But human reason is not a measure of things, but *vice versa,* as is stated in *Metaph.* x. Therefore no law can emanate from the human reason.

Obj. 3. Further, a measure should be most certain, as is stated in *Metaph.* x. But the dictates of the human reason in matters of conduct are uncertain, according to *Wis.* ix. 14: *The thoughts of mortal men are fearful, and our counsels uncertain.* Therefore no law can emanate from the human reason.

On the contrary, Augustine distinguishes two kinds of law, the one eternal, the other temporal, which he calls human.

I answer that, As we have stated above, a law is a dictate of the practical reason. Now it is to be observed that the same procedure takes place in the practical and in the speculative reason, for each proceeds from principles to conclusions, as was stated above. Accordingly, we conclude that, just as in the speculative reason, from naturally known indemonstrable principles we draw the conclusions of the various sciences, the knowledge of which is not imparted to us by nature, but acquired by the efforts of reason, so too it is that from the precepts of the natural law, as from common and indemonstrable principles the human reason needs to proceed to the more particular determination of certain matters. These particular determinations, devised by human reason, are called human laws, provided that the other essential conditions of law be observed, as was stated above. Therefore Tully says in his *Rhetoric* that *justice has its source in nature; thence certain things came into custom by reason of their utility; afterwards these things which emanated from nature, and were approved by custom, were sanctioned by fear and reverence for the law.*

Reply Obj. 1. The human reason cannot have a full participation of the dictate of the divine reason, but according to its own mode, and imperfectly. Consequently, just as on the part of the speculative reason, by a natural participation of divine wisdom, there is in us the knowledge of certain common principles, but not a proper knowledge of each single truth, such as that contained in the divine wisdom, so, too, on the part of the practical reason, man has a natural participation of the eternal law, according to certain common principles, but not as regards the particular determinations of individual cases, which are, however, contained in the eternal law. Hence the need for human reason to proceed further to sanction them by law.

Reply Obj. 2. Human reason is not, of itself, the rule of things. But the principles impressed on it by nature are the general rules and measures of all things relating to human conduct, of which the natural reason is the rule and measure, although it is not the measure of things that are from nature.

Reply Obj. 3. The practical reason is concerned with operable matters, which are singular and contingent, but not with necessary things, with which the speculative reason is concerned. Therefore human laws cannot have that inerrancy that belongs to the demonstrated conclusions of the sciences. Nor is it necessary for every measure to be altogether unerring and certain, but according as it is possible in its own particular genus.

FOURTH ARTICLE

WHETHER THERE WAS ANY NEED

FOR A DIVINE LAW?

We proceed thus to the Fourth Article:

Objection 1. It would seem that there was no need for a divine law. For, as was stated above, the natural law is a participation in us of the eternal law. But the eternal law is the divine law, as was stated above. Therefore there is no need for a divine law in addition to the natural law and to human laws derived therefrom.

Obj. 2. Further, it is written (*Ecclus.* xv. 14) that *God left man in the hand of his own counsel.* Now counsel is an act of reason, as was stated above. Therefore man was left to the direction of his reason. But a dictate of human reason is a human law, as was stated above. Therefore there is no need for man to be governed also by a divine law.

Obj. 3. Further, human nature is more self-sufficing than irrational creatures. But irrational creatures have no divine law besides the natural inclination impressed on them. Much less, therefore, should the rational creature have a divine law in addition to the natural law.

On the contrary, David prayed God to set His law before him, saying (*Ps.* cxviii. 33): *Set before me for a law the way of Thy justifications, O Lord.*

I answer that, Besides the natural and the human law it was necessary for the directing of human conduct to have a divine law. And this for four reasons. First, because it is by law that man is directed how to perform his proper acts in view of his last end. Now if man were ordained to no other end than that which is proportionate to his natural ability, there would be no need for man to have any further direction, on the part of his reason, in addition to the natural law and humanly devised law which is derived from it. But since man is ordained to an end of eternal happiness which exceeds man's natural ability, as we have stated above, therefore it was necessary that, in addition to the natural and the human law, man should be directed to his end by a law given by God.

Secondly, because, by reason of the uncertainty of human judgment, especially on contingent and particular matters, different people form different judgments on human acts; whence also different and contrary laws result. In order, therefore, that man may know without any doubt what he ought to do and what he ought to avoid, it was necessary for man to be directed in his proper acts by a law given by God, for it is certain that such a law cannot err.

Thirdly, because man can make laws in those matters of which he is competent to judge. But man is not competent to judge of interior movements, that are hidden, but only of exterior acts which are observable; and yet for the perfection of virtue it is necessary for man to conduct himself rightly in both kinds of acts. Consequently, human law could not sufficiently curb and direct interior acts, and it was necessary for this purpose that a divine law should supervene.

Fourthly, because, as Augustine says, human law cannot punish or forbid all evil deeds, since, while aiming at doing away with all evils, it would do away with many good things, and would hinder the advance of the common good, which is necessary for human living. In order, therefore, that no evil might remain unforbidden and unpunished, it was necessary for the divine law to supervene, whereby all sins are forbidden.

And these four causes are touched upon in *Ps.* cxviii. 8, where it is said: *The law of the Lord is unspotted, i.e.,* allowing no foulness of sin; *converting souls,* because it directs not only exterior, but also interior, acts; *the testimony of the Lord is faithful,* because of the certainty of what is true and right; *giving wisdom to little ones,* by directing man to an end supernatural and divine.

Reply Obj. 1. By the natural law the eternal law is participated proportionately to the capacity of human nature. But to his supernatural end man needs to be directed in a yet higher way. Hence the additional law given by God, whereby man shares more perfectly in the eternal law.

Reply Obj. 2. Counsel is a kind of inquiry, and hence must proceed from some principles. Nor is it enough for it to proceed from principles imparted by nature, which are the precepts of the natural law, for the reasons given above; but there is need for certain additional principles, namely, the precepts of the divine law.

Reply Obj. 3. Irrational creatures are not ordained to an end higher than that which is proportionate to their natural powers. Consequently the comparison fails.

QUESTION XCIII

The Eternal Law
(*In Six Articles*)

We must now consider each law by itself: (1) the eternal law; (2) the natural law; (3) the human law; (4) the Old Law; (5) the New Law, which is the law of the Gospel. Of the sixth law, which is the law of the 'fomes,' [3] *what we have said when treating of original sin must suffice.*

Concerning the first there are six points of inquiry: (1) What is the eternal law? (2) Whether it is known to all? (3) Whether every law is derived from it? (4) Whether necessary things are subject to the eternal law? (5) Whether natural contingents are subject to the eternal law? (6) Whether all human things are subject to it?

FIRST ARTICLE

WHETHER THE ETERNAL LAW IS A SUPREME EXEMPLAR EXISTING IN GOD?

We proceed thus to the First Article:

Objection 1. It would seem that the eternal law is not a supreme exemplar existing in God. For there is only one eternal law. But there are many exemplars of things in the divine mind, for Augustine says that God *made each thing according to its exemplar.* Therefore the eternal law does not seem to be the same as an exemplar existing in the divine mind.

Obj. 2. Further, it is of the nature of a law that it be promulgated by word,

---

[3] The word *fomes,* which in its literal sense means "spark," is used by St. Thomas to mean a kind of inner incitement to evil desire.

as was stated above. But *Word* is a Personal name in God, as was stated in the First Part, whereas *exemplar* refers to the essence. Therefore the eternal law is not the same as a divine exemplar.

Obj. 3. Further, Augustine says: *We see a law above our minds, which is called truth.* But the law which is above our minds is the eternal law. Therefore truth is the eternal law. But the notion of truth is not the same as the notion of an exemplar. Therefore the eternal law is not the same as the supreme exemplar.

On the contrary, Augustine says that *the eternal law is the supreme exemplar to which we must always conform.*

I answer that, Just as in every artificer there pre-exists an exemplar of the things that are made by his art, so too in every governor there must pre-exist the exemplar of the order of those things that are to be done by those who are subject to his government. And just as the exemplar of the things yet to be made by an art is called the art or model of the products of that art, so, too, the exemplar in him who governs the acts of his subjects bears the character of a law, provided the other conditions be present which we have mentioned above as belonging to the nature of law. Now God, by His wisdom, is the Creator of all things, in relation to which He stands as the artificer to the products of his art, as was stated in the First Part. Moreover, He governs all the acts and movements that are to be found in each single creature, as was also stated in the First Part. Therefore, just as the exemplar of the divine wisdom, inasmuch as all things are created by it, has the character of an art, a model or an idea, so the exemplar of divine wisdom, as moving all things to their due end, bears the character of law. Accordingly, the

eternal law is nothing else than the exemplar of divine wisdom, as directing all actions and movements.

Reply Obj. 1. Augustine is speaking in that passage of the ideal exemplars which refer to the proper nature of each single thing; and consequently in them there is a certain distinction and plurality, according to their different relations to things, as was stated in the First Part. But law is said to direct human acts by ordaining them to the common good, as was stated above. Now things which are in themselves diverse may be considered as one, according as they are ordained to something common. Therefore the eternal law is one since it is the exemplar of this order.

Reply Obj. 2. With regard to any sort of word, two points may be considered: viz., the word itself, and that which is expressed by the word. For the spoken word is something uttered by the mouth of man, and expresses that which is signified by the human word. The same applies to the human mental word, which is nothing else than something conceived by the mind, by which man expresses mentally the things of which he is thinking. So, too, in God, therefore, the Word conceived by the intellect of the Father is the name of a Person; but all things that are in the Father's knowledge, whether they refer to the essence or to the Persons, or to the works of God, are expressed by this Word, as Augustine declares. But among other things expressed by this Word, the eternal law itself is expressed thereby. Nor does it follow that the eternal law is a Personal name in God. Nevertheless, it is appropriated to the Son, because of the suitability of *exemplar* to *word*.

Reply Obj. 3. The exemplars of the divine intellect do not stand in the same relation to things as do the exemplars of the human intellect. For the human intellect is measured by things, so that a human concept is not true by reason of itself, but by reason of its being consonant with things, since *an opinion is true or false according as things are or are not.* But the divine intellect is the measure of things, since each thing has truth in it in so far as it is like the divine intellect, as was stated in the First Part. Consequently the divine intellect is true in itself, and its exemplar is truth itself.

SECOND ARTICLE

WHETHER THE ETERNAL LAW IS
KNOWN TO ALL?

We proceed thus to the Second Article:

Objection 1. It would seem that the eternal law is not known to all. For, as the Apostle says (I *Cor.* ii. 11), *the things that are of God no man knoweth, but the Spirit of God.* But the eternal law is an exemplar existing in the divine mind. Therefore it is unknown to all save God alone.

Obj. 2. Further, as Augustine says, *the eternal law is that by which it is right that all things should be most orderly.* But all do not know how all things are most orderly. Therefore all do not know the eternal law.

Obj. 3. Further, Augustine says that *the eternal law is not subject to the judgment of man.* But according to *Ethics* I., *any man can judge well of what he knows.* Therefore the eternal law is not known to us.

On the contrary, Augustine says that *knowledge of the eternal law is imprinted on us.*

I answer that, A thing may be known in two ways: first, in itself; secondly, in its effect, in which some likeness of that thing is found: e.g., someone, not seeing the sun in its substance, may know it by its rays. Hence we must say that no one can know the eternal law as it is in itself, except God and the blessed who see God in His essence. But every rational creature knows it according to some reflection, greater or less. For every knowledge of truth is a kind of reflection and participation of the eternal law, which is the unchangeable truth, as Augustine says. Now all men know the truth to a certain extent, at least as to the common principles of the natural law. As to the other truths, they partake of the knowledge of truth, some more, some less; and in this respect they know the eternal law in a greater or lesser degree.

Reply Obj. 1. We cannot know the things that are of God as they are in themselves; but they are made known to us in their effects, according to *Rom.* i. 20: *The invisible things of God . . . are clearly seen, being understood by the things that are made.*

Reply Obj. 2. Although each one knows the eternal law according to his own capacity, in the way explained above, yet none can comprehend it, for it cannot be made perfectly known by its effects. Therefore it does not follow that anyone who knows the eternal law, in the aforesaid way, knows also the whole order of things whereby they are most orderly.

Reply Obj. 3. To judge of a thing may be understood in two ways. First, as when a cognitive power judges of its proper object, according to *Job* xii. 11: *Doth not the ear discern words, and the palate of him that eateth, the taste?* It is to this kind of judgment that the Philosopher alludes when he says that *anyone judges well of what he knows,* by judging, namely, whether what is put forward is true. In another way, we speak of a superior judging of a subordinate by a kind of practical judgment, as to whether he should be such and such or not. And thus none can judge of the eternal law.

THIRD ARTICLE

WHETHER EVERY LAW IS DERIVED
FROM THE ETERNAL LAW?

We proceed thus to the Third Article:

Objection 1. It would seem that not every law is derived from the eternal law. For there is a law of the 'fomes,' as was stated above, which is not derived from that divine law which is the eternal law, since to it pertains the *prudence of the flesh,* of which the Apostle says (*Rom.* viii. 7) that *it cannot be subject to the law of God.* Therefore, not every law is derived from the eternal law.

Obj. 2. Further, nothing unjust can be derived from the eternal law, because, as was stated above, *the eternal law is that according to which it is right that all things should be most orderly.* But some laws are unjust according to *Isa.* x. 1: *Woe to them that make wicked laws.* Therefore, not every law is derived from the eternal law.

Obj. 3. Further, Augustine says that *the law which is framed for ruling the people rightly permits many things which are punished by the divine providence.* But the exemplar of the divine providence is the eternal law, stated above. Therefore not even every good law is derived from the eternal law.

On the contrary, divine Wisdom says (*Prov.* viii. 15): *By Me kings reign, and lawgivers decree just things.* But the exemplar of divine Wisdom is the eternal law, as was stated above. Therefore all laws proceed from the eternal law.

I answer that, As was stated above, law denotes a kind of plan directing acts towards an end. Now wherever there are movers ordained to one another, the power of the second mover must needs be derived from the power of the first mover, since the second mover does not move except in so far as it is moved by the first. Therefore we observe the same in all those who govern, namely, that the plan of government is derived by secondary governors from the governor in chief. Thus the plan of what is to be done in a state flows from the king's command to his inferior administrators; and again in things of art the plan of whatever is to be done by art flows from the chief craftsman to the under-craftsmen who work with their hands. Since, then, the eternal law is the plan of government in the Chief Governor, all the plans of government in the inferior governors must be derived from the eternal law. But these plans of inferior governors are all the other laws which are in addition to the eternal law. Therefore all laws, in so far as they partake of right reason, are derived from the eternal law. Hence Augustine says that *in temporal law there is nothing just and lawful but what man has drawn from the eternal law.*

Reply Obj. 1. The 'fomes' has the nature of law in man in so far as it is a punishment resulting from the divine justice; and in this respect it is evident that it is derived from the eternal law. But in so far as it denotes a proneness to sin, it is contrary to the divine law, and has not the nature of law, as was stated above.

Reply Obj. 2. Human law has the nature of law in so far as it partakes of right reason; and it is clear that, in this respect, it is derived from the eternal law. But in so far as it deviates from reason, it is called an unjust law, and has the nature, not of law, but of violence. Nevertheless, even an unjust law, in so far as it retains some appearance of law, through being framed by one who is in power, is derived from the eternal law; for all power is from the Lord God, according to *Rom.* xiii. 1.

Reply Obj. 3. Human law is said to permit certain things, not as approving of them, but as being unable to direct them. And many things are directed by the divine law, which human law is unable to direct, because more things are subject to a higher than to a lower cause. Hence the very fact that human law does not concern itself with matters it cannot direct comes under the ordination of the eternal law. It would be different, were human law to sanction what the eternal law condemns. Consequently, it does not follow that human law is not derived from the eternal law; what follows is rather that it is not on a perfect equality with it.

QUESTION XCIV

THE NATURAL LAW

(*In Six Articles*)

We must now consider the natural law, concerning which there are six points of inquiry: (1) What is the natural law? (2) What are the precepts of the natural law? (3) Whether all the acts of the virtues are prescribed by the natural law? (4) Whether the natural law is the same in all? (5) Whether it is changeable? (6) Whether it can be abolished from the mind of man?

FIRST ARTICLE

WHETHER THE NATURAL LAW
IS A HABIT?

We proceed thus to the First Article:

Objection 1. It would seem that the natural law is a habit. For, as the Philosopher says, *there are three things in the soul, power, habit and passion.* But the natural law is not one of the soul's powers, nor is it one of the passions, as we may see by going through them one by one. Therefore the natural law is a habit.

Obj. 2. Further, Basil says that *the conscience or synderesis is the law of our mind,* which can apply only to the natural law. But *synderesis* is a habit, as was shown in the First Part. Therefore the natural law is a habit.

Obj. 3. Further, the natural law abides in man always, as will be shown further on. But man's reason, which the law regards, does not always think about the natural law. Therefore the natural law is not an act, but a habit.

On the contrary, Augustine says that *a habit is that whereby something is done when necessary.* But such is not the natural law, since it is in infants and in the damned who cannot act by it. Therefore the natural law is not a habit.

I answer that, A thing may be called a habit in two ways. First, properly and essentially, and thus the natural law is not a habit. For it has been stated above that the natural law is something appointed by reason, just as a proposition is a work of reason. Now that which a man does is not the same as that whereby he does it, for he makes a becoming speech by the habit of grammar. Since, then, a habit is that by which we act, a law cannot be a habit properly and essentially.

Secondly, the term habit may be applied to that which we hold by a habit. Thus *faith* may mean *that which we hold by faith.* Accordingly, since the precepts of the natural law are sometimes considered by reason actually, while sometimes they are in the reason only habitually, in this way the natural law may be called a habit. So, too, in speculative matters, the indemonstrable principles are not the habit itself whereby we hold these principles; they are rather the principles of which we possess the habit.

Reply Obj. 1. The Philosopher proposes there to discover the genus of virtue; and since it is evident that virtue is a principle of action, he mentions only those things which are principles of human acts, viz., powers, habits, and passions. But there are other things in the soul besides these three: *e.g.*, acts, as *to will* is in the one that wills; again, there are things known in the knower; moreover its own natural properties are in the soul, such as immortality and the like.

Reply Obj. 2. *Synderesis* is said to be the law of our intellect because it is a habit containing the precepts of the natural law, which are the first principles of human actions.

Reply Obj. 3. This argument proves that the natural law is held habitually; and this is granted.

To the argument advanced in the contrary sense we reply that sometimes a man is unable to make use of that which is in him habitually, because of some impediment. Thus, because of sleep, a man is unable to use the habit of science. In like manner, through the deficiency of his age, a child cannot use the habit of the understanding of principles, or the natural law, which is in him habitually.

SECOND ARTICLE

WHETHER THE NATURAL LAW
CONTAINS SEVERAL PRECEPTS,
OR ONLY ONE?

We proceed thus to the Second Article:

Objection 1. It would seem that the natural law contains, not several precepts, but only one. For law is a kind of precept, as was stated above. If therefore there were many precepts of the natural law, it would follow that there are also many natural laws.

Obj. 2. Further, the natural law is consequent upon human nature. But human nature, as a whole, is one, though, as to its parts, it is manifold. Therefore, either there is but one precept of the law of nature because of the unity of nature as a whole, or there are many by reason of the number of parts of human nature. The result would be that even things relating to the inclination of the concupiscible power would belong to the natural law.

Obj. 3. Further, law is something pertaining to reason, as was stated above. Now reason is but one in man. Therefore there is only one precept of the natural law.

On the contrary, The precepts of the natural law in man stand in relation to operable matters as first principles do to matters of demonstration. But there are several first indemonstrable principles. Therefore there are also several precepts of the natural law.

I answer that, As was stated above, the precepts of the natural law are to the practical reason what the first principles of demonstrations are to the speculative reason, because both are self-evident principles. Now a thing is said to be self-evident in two ways: first, in itself; secondly, in relation to us. Any proposition is said to be self-evident in itself, if its predicate is contained in the notion of the subject; even though it may happen that to one who does not know the definition of the subject, such a proposition is not self-evident. For instance, this proposition, *Man is a rational being,* is, in its very nature, self-evident, since he who says *man,* says *a rational being;* and yet to one who does not know what a man is, this proposition is not self-evident. Hence it is that, as Boethius says, certain axioms or propositions are universally self-evident to all; and such are the propositions whose terms are known to all, as, *Every whole is greater than its part,* and, *Things equal to one and the same are equal to one another.* But some propositions are self-evident only to the wise, who understand the meaning of the terms of such propositions. Thus to one who understands that an angel is not a body, it is self-evident that an angel is not circumscriptively in a place. But this is not evident to the unlearned, for they cannot grasp it.

Now a certain order is to be found in those things that are apprehended by men. For that which first falls under apprehension is *being*, the understanding of which is included in all things whatsoever a man apprehends. Therefore the first indemonstrable principle is that *the same thing cannot be affirmed and denied at the same time*, which is based on the notion of *being* and *not-being*; and on this principle all others are based, as is stated in *Metaph.* iv. Now as *being* is the first thing that falls under the apprehension absolutely, so *good* is the first thing that falls under the apprehension of the practical reason, which is directed to action (since every agent acts for an end, which has the nature of good). Consequently, the first principle in the practical reason is one founded on the nature of good, viz., that *good is that which all things seek after.* Hence this is the first precept of law, that *good is to be done and promoted, and evil is to be avoided.* All other precepts of the natural law are based upon this; so that all the things which the practical reason naturally apprehends as man's good belong to the precepts of the natural law under the form of things to be done or avoided.

Since, however, good has the nature of an end, and evil, the nature of the contrary, hence it is that all those things to which man has a natural inclination are naturally apprehended by reason as being good, and conse-

quently as objects of pursuit, and their contraries as evil, and objects of avoidance. Therefore, the order of the precepts of the natural law is according to the order of natural inclinations. For there is in man, first of all, an inclination to good in accordance with the nature which he has in common with all substances, inasmuch, namely, as every substance seeks the preservation of its own being, according to its nature; and by reason of this inclination, whatever is a means of preserving human life, and of warding off its obstacles, belongs to the natural law. Secondly, there is in man an inclination to things that pertain to him more specially, according to that nature which he has in common with other animals; and in virtue of this inclination, those things are said to belong to the natural law *which nature has taught to all animals,* such as sexual intercourse, the education of offspring and so forth. Thirdly, there is in man an inclination to good according to the nature of his reason, which nature is proper to him. Thus man has a natural inclination to know the truth about God, and to live in society; and in this respect, whatever pertains to this inclination belongs to the natural law; *e.g.,* to shun ignorance, to avoid offending those among whom one has to live, and other such things regarding the above inclination.

Reply Obj. 1. All these precepts of the law of nature have the character of one natural law, inasmuch as they flow from one first precept.

Reply Obj. 2. All the inclinations of any parts whatsoever of human nature, *e.g.,* of the concupiscible and irascible parts, in so far as they are ruled by reason, belong to the natural law, and are reduced to one first precept, as was stated above. And thus the precepts of the natural law are many in themselves, but they are based on one common foundation.

Reply Obj. 3. Although reason is one in itself, yet it directs all things regarding man; so that whatever can be ruled by reason is contained under the law of reason.

WHETHER ALL THE ACTS OF THE VIRTUES ARE PRESCRIBED BY THE NATURAL LAW?

We proceed thus to the Third Article:

Objection 1. It would seem that not all the acts of the virtues are prescribed by the natural law. For, as was stated above, it is of the nature of law that it be ordained to the common good. But some acts of the virtues are ordained to the private good of the individual, as is evident especially in regard to acts of temperance. Therefore, not all the acts of the virtues are the subject of natural law.

Obj. 2. Further, every sin is opposed to some virtuous act. If therefore all the acts of the virtues are prescribed by the natural law, it seems to follow that all sins are against nature; whereas this applies to certain special sins.

Obj. 3. Further, those things which are according to nature are common to all. But the acts of the virtues are not common to all, since a thing is virtuous in one, and vicious in another. Therefore, not all the acts of the virtues are prescribed by the natural law.

On the contrary, Damascene says that *virtues are natural.* Therefore virtuous acts also are subject to the natural law.

I answer that, We may speak of virtuous acts in two ways: first, in so far as they are virtuous; secondly, as such and such acts considered in their proper species. If, then, we are speaking of the acts of the virtues in so far as they are virtuous, thus all virtuous acts belong to the natural law. For it has been stated that to the natural law belongs everything to which a man is inclined according to his nature. Now each thing is inclined naturally to an operation that is suitable to it according to its form: *e.g.,* fire is inclined to give heat. Therefore, since the rational soul is the proper form of man, there is in every man a natural inclination to act according to reason; and this is to act according to virtue. Consequently, considered thus, all the acts of the virtues are prescribed by the natural law, since each one's reason naturally dictates to him to act virtuously. But if we speak of virtuous acts, considered in themselves, *i.e.,* in their proper species, thus not all virtuous acts are prescribed by the natural law. For many things are done virtuously, to which nature does not primarily incline, but which, through the inquiry of reason, have been found by men to be conducive to well-living.

Reply Obj. 1. Temperance is about the natural concupiscences of food, drink and sexual matters, which are indeed ordained to the common good of nature, just as other matters of law are ordained to the moral common good.

Reply Obj. 2. By human nature we may mean either that which is proper to man, and in this sense all sins, as being against reason, are also against nature, as Damascene states; or we may mean that nature which is common to man and other animals, and in this sense, certain special sins are said to be against nature: *e.g.* contrary to sexual intercourse, which is natural to all animals, is unisexual lust, which has received the special name of the unnatural crime.

Reply Obj. 3. This argument considers acts in themselves. For it is owing to the various conditions of men that certain acts are virtuous for some, as being proportioned and becoming to them, while they are vicious for others, as not being proportioned to them.

We proceed thus to the Fourth Article:

Objection 1. It would seem that the natural law is not the same in all. For it is stated in the *Decretals* that *the natural law is that which is contained in the Law and the Gospel.* But this is not common to all men, because, as it is written (*Rom.* x. 16), *all do not obey the gospel.* Therefore the natural law is not the same in all men.

Obj. 2. Further, *Things which are according to the law are said to be just,* as is stated in *Ethics* v. But it is stated in the same book that nothing is so just for all as not to be subject to change in regard to some men. Therefore even the natural law is not the same in all men.

Obj. 3. Further, as was stated above, to the natural law belongs everything to which a man is inclined according to his nature. Now different men are naturally inclined to different things,—some to the desire of pleasures, others to the desire of honors, and other men to other things. Therefore, there is not one natural law for all.

On the contrary, Isidore says: *The natural law is common to all nations.*

I answer that, As we have stated above, to the natural law belong those things to which a man is inclined naturally; and among these it is proper to man to be inclined to act according to reason. Now it belongs to the reason to proceed from what is common to what is proper, as is stated in *Physics* i. The speculative reason, however, is differently situated, in this matter, from the practical reason. For, since the speculative reason is concerned chiefly with necessary things, which cannot be otherwise than they are, its proper conclusions, like the universal principles, contain the truth without fail. The practical reason, on the other hand, is concerned with contingent matters, which is the domain of human actions; and, consequently, although there is necessity in the common principles, the more we descend towards the particular, the more frequently we encounter defects. Accordingly, then, in speculative matters truth is the same in all men, both as to principles and as to conclusions; although the truth is not known to all as regards the conclusions, but only as regards the principles which are called *common notions.* But in matters of action, truth or practical rectitude is not the same for all as to what is particular, but only as to the common principles; and where there is the same rectitude in relation to particulars, it is not equally known to all.

It is therefore evident that, as regards the common principles whether of speculative or of practical reason, truth or rectitude is the same for all, and is equally known by all. But as to the proper conclusions of the speculative reason, the truth is the same for all, but it is not equally known to all. Thus, it is true for all that the three angles of a triangle are together equal to two right angles, although it is not known to all. But as to the proper conclusions of the practical reason, neither is the truth or rectitude the same for all, nor, where it is the same, is it equally known by all. Thus, it is right and true for all to act according to reason, and from this principle it follows, as a proper conclusion, that goods entrusted to another should be restored to their owner. Now this is true for the majority of cases. But it may happen in a particular case that it would be injurious, and therefore unreasonable, to restore goods held in trust; for instance, if they are claimed for the purpose of fighting against one's country. And this principle will be found to fail the more, according as we descend further towards the particular, e.g., if one were to say that goods held in trust should be restored with such and such a guarantee, or in such and such a way; because the greater the number of conditions added, the greater the number of ways in which the principle may fail, so that it be not right to restore or not to restore.

Consequently, we must say that the natural law, as to the first common principles, is the same for all, both as to rectitude and as to knowledge. But as to certain more particular aspects, which are conclusions, as it were, of those common principles, it is the same for all in the majority of cases, both as to rectitude and as to knowledge; and yet in some few cases it may fail, both as to rectitude, by reason of certain obstacles (just as natures subject to generation and corruption fail in some few cases because of some obstacle), and as to knowledge, since in some the reason is perverted by passion, or evil habit, or an evil disposition of nature. Thus at one time theft, although it is expressly contrary to the natural law, was not considered wrong among the Germans, as Julius Caesar relates.

Reply Obj. 1. The meaning of the sentence quoted is not that whatever is contained in the Law and the Gospel belongs to the natural law, since they contain many things that are above nature; but that whatever belongs to the natural laws is fully contained in them. Therefore Gratian, after saying that *the natural law is what is contained in the Law and the Gospel,* adds at once, by way of example, *by which everyone is commanded to do to others as he would be done by.*

Reply Obj. 2. The saying of the Philosopher is to be understood of things that are naturally just, not as common principles, but as conclusions drawn from them, having rectitude in the majority of cases, but failing in a few.

Reply Obj. 3. Just as in man reason rules and commands the other powers, so all the natural inclinations belonging to the other powers must needs be directed according to reason. Therefore it is universally right for all men that all their inclinations should be directed according to reason.

FIFTH ARTICLE

WHETHER THE NATURAL LAW
CAN BE CHANGED?

We proceed thus to the Fifth Article:

Objection 1. It would seem that the natural law can be changed. For on *Ecclus.* xvii. 9 (*He gave them instructions, and the law of life*) the *Gloss* says: *He wished the law of the letter to be written, in order to correct the law of nature.* But that which is corrected is changed. Therefore the natural law can be changed.

Obj. 2. Further, the slaying of the innocent, adultery and theft are against the natural law. But we find these things changed by God: as when God commanded Abraham to slay his innocent son (*Gen.* xxii. 2); and when He ordered the Jews to borrow and purloin the vessels of the Egyptians (*Exod.* xii. 35); and when He commanded Osee to take to himself *a wife of fornications* (*Osee* i. 2). Therefore the natural law can be changed.

Obj. 3. Further, Isidore says that *the possession of all things in common, and universal freedom, are matters of natural law.* But these things are seen to be changed by human laws. Therefore it seems that the natural law is subject to change.

On the contrary, It is said in the *Decretals: The natural law dates from the creation of the rational creature. It does not vary according to time, but remains unchangeable.*

I answer that, A change in the natural law may be understood in two ways, First, by way of addition. In this sense, nothing hinders the natural law from being changed, since many things for the benefit of human life have been added over and above the natural law, both by the divine law and by human laws.

Secondly, a change in the natural law may be understood by way of subtraction, so that what previously was according to the natural law, ceases to be so. In this sense, the natural law is altogether unchangeable in its first principles. But in its secondary principles, which, as we have said, are certain detailed proximate conclusions drawn from the first principles, the natural law is not changed so that what it prescribes be not right in most cases. But it may be changed in some particular cases of rare occurrence, through some special causes hindering the observance of such precepts, as was stated above.

Reply Obj. 1. The written law is said to be given for the correction of the natural law, either because it supplies what was wanting to the natural law, or because the natural law was so perverted in the hearts of some men, as to certain matters, that they esteemed those things good which are naturally evil; which perversion stood in need of correction.

Reply Obj. 2. All men alike, both guilty and innocent, die the death of nature; which death of nature is inflicted by the power of God because of original sin, according to 1 *Kings* ii. 6: *The Lord killeth and maketh alive.* Consequently, by the command of God, death can be inflicted on any man, guilty or innocent, without any injustice whatever.—In like manner, adultery is intercourse with another's wife; who is allotted to him by the law emanating from God. Consequently intercourse with any woman, by the command of God, is neither adultery nor fornication.—The same applies to theft, which is the taking of another's property. For whatever is taken by the command of God, to Whom all things belong, is not taken against the will of its owner, whereas it is in this that theft consists.—Nor is it only in human things that whatever is commanded by God is right; but also in natural things, whatever is done by God is, in some way, natural, as was stated in the First Part.

Reply Obj. 3. A thing is said to belong to the natural law in two ways. First, because nature inclines thereto: *e.g.,* that one should not do harm to another. Secondly, because nature did not bring with it the contrary. Thus, we might say that for man to be naked is of the natural law, because nature did not give him clothes, but art invented them. In this sense, *the possession of all things in common and universal freedom* are said to be of the natural law, because, namely, the distinction of possessions and slavery were not brought in by nature, but devised by human reason for the benefit of human life. Accordingly, the law of nature was not changed in this respect, except by addition.

WHETHER THE NATURAL LAW CAN BE ABOLISHED FROM THE HEART OF MAN?

We proceed thus to the Sixth Article:

Objection 1. It would seem that the natural law can be abolished from the heart of man. For on *Rom.* ii. 14 (*When the Gentiles who have not the law,* etc.) the *Gloss* says that *the law of justice, which sin had blotted out, is graven on the heart of man when he is restored by grace.* But the law of justice is the law of nature. Therefore the law of nature can be blotted out.

Obj. 2. Further, the law of grace is more efficacious than the law of nature. But the law of grace is blotted out by sin. Much more, therefore, can the law of nature be blotted out.

Obj. 3. Further, that which is established by law is proposed as something just. But many things are enacted by men which are contrary to the law of nature. Therefore the law of nature can be abolished from the heart of man.

On the contrary, Augustine says: *Thy law is written in the hearts of men, which iniquity itself effaces not.* But the law which is written in men's hearts is the natural law. Therefore the natural law cannot be blotted out.

I answer that, As we have stated above, there belong to the natural law, first, certain most common precepts that are known to all; and secondly, certain secondary and more particular precepts, which are, as it were, conclusions following closely from first principles. As to the common principles, the natural law, in its universal meaning, cannot in any way be blotted out from men's hearts. But it is blotted out in the case of a particular action, in so far as reason is hindered from applying the common principle to the particular action because of concupiscence or some other passion, as was stated above.—But as to the other, *i.e.,* the secondary precepts, the natural law can be blotted out from the human heart, either by evil persuasions, just as in speculative matters errors occur in respect of necessary conclusions; or by vicious customs and corrupt habits, as, among some men, theft, and even unnatural vices, as the Apostle states (*Rom.* i. 24), were not esteemed sinful.

Reply Obj. 1. Sin blots out the law of nature in particular cases, not universally, except perchance in regard to the secondary precepts of the natural law, in the way stated above.

Reply Obj. 2. Although grace is more efficacious than nature, yet nature is more essential to man, and therefore more enduring.

Reply Obj. 3. This argument is true of the secondary precepts of the natural law, against which some legislators have framed certain enactments which are unjust.

QUESTION XCV

HUMAN LAW
(*In Four Articles*)

We must now consider human law, and (1) concerning this law considered in itself; (2) its power; (3) its mutability. Under the first head there are four points of inquiry: (1) Its utility. (2) Its origin. (3) Its quality. (4) Its division.

FIRST ARTICLE

WHETHER IT WAS USEFUL FOR LAWS TO BE FRAMED BY MEN?

We proceed thus to the First Article:

Objection 1. It would seem that it

was not useful for laws to be framed by men. For the purpose of every law is that man be made good thereby, as was stated above. But men are more to be induced to be good willingly by means of admonitions, than against their will, by means of laws. Therefore there was no need to frame laws.

Obj. 2. Further, as the Philosopher says, *men have recourse to a judge as to animate justice.* But animate justice is better than inanimate justice, which is contained in laws. Therefore it would have been better for the execution of justice to be entrusted to the decision of judges than to frame laws in addition.

Obj. 3. Further, every law is framed for the direction of human actions, as is evident from what has been stated above. But since human actions are about singulars, which are infinite in number, matters pertaining to the direction of human actions cannot be taken into sufficient consideration except by a wise man, who looks into each one of them. Therefore it would have been better for human acts to be directed by the judgment of wise men, than by the framing of laws. Therefore there was no need of human laws.

On the contrary, Isidore says: *Laws were made that in fear thereof human audacity might be held in check, that innocence might be safeguarded in the midst of wickedness, and the dread of punishment might prevent the wicked from doing harm.* But these things are most necessary to mankind. Therefore it was necessary that human laws should be made.

I answer that, As we have stated above, man has a natural aptitude for virtue; but the perfection of virtue must be acquired by man by means of some kind of training. Thus we observe that a man is helped by diligence in his necessities, for instance, in food and clothing. Certain beginnings of these he has from nature, viz., his reason and his hands; but he has not the full complement, as other animals have, to whom nature has given sufficiently of clothing and food. Now it is difficult to see how man could suffice for himself in the matter of this training, since the perfection of virtue consists chiefly in withdrawing man from undue pleasures, to which above all man in inclined, and especially the young, who are more capable of being trained. Consequently a man needs to receive this training from another, whereby to arrive at the perfection of virtue. And as to those young people who are inclined to acts of virtue by their good natural disposition, or by custom, or rather by the gift of God, paternal training suffices, which is by admonitions. But since some are found to be dissolute and prone to vice, and not easily amenable to words, it was necessary for such to be restrained from evil by force and fear, in order that, at least, they might desist from evil-doing, and leave others in peace, and that they themselves, by being habituated in this way, might be brought to do willingly what hitherto they did from fear, and thus become virtuous. Now this kind of training, which compels through fear of punishment, is the discipline of laws. Therefore, in order that man might have peace and virtue, it was necessary for laws to be framed; for, as the Philosopher says, *as man is the most noble of animals if he be perfect in virtue, so he is the lowest of all, if he be severed from law and justice.* For man can use his reason to devise means of satisfying his lusts and evil passions, which other animals are unable to do.

Reply Obj. 1. Men who are well disposed are led willingly to virtue by being admonished better than by coercion; but men whose disposition is evil are not led to virtue unless they are compelled.

Reply Obj. 2. As the Philosopher says, *it is better that all things be regulated by law, than left to be decided by judges.* And this for three reasons. First, because it is easier to find a few wise men competent to frame right laws, than to find the many who would be necessary to judge rightly ot each single case.—Secondly, because those who make laws consider long beforehand what laws to make, whereas judgment on each single case has to be pronounced as soon as it arises; and it is easier for man to see what is right, by taking many instances into consideration, than by considering one solitary instance.—Thirdly, because lawgivers judge universally and about future events, whereas those who sit in judgment judge of things present, towards which they are affected by love, hatred, or some kind of cupidity; and thus their judgment becomes perverted.

Since, then, the animated justice of the judge is not found in every man, and since it can be bent, therefore it was necessary, whenever possible, for the law to determine how to judge, and for very few matters to be left to the decision of men.

Reply Obj. 3. Certain individual facts which cannot be covered by the law *have necessarily to be committed to judges,* as the Philosopher says in the same passage: *e.g., concerning something that has happened or not happened,* and the like.

SECOND ARTICLE

WHETHER EVERY HUMAN LAW

IS DERIVED FROM THE

NATURAL LAW?

We proceed thus to the Second Article:

Objection 1. It would seem that not every human law is derived from the natural law. For the Philosopher says that *the legal just is that which originally was a matter of indifference.* But those things which arise from the natural law are not matters of indifference. Therefore the enactments of human laws are not all derived from the natural law.

Obj. 2. Further, positive law is divided against natural law, as is stated by Isidore and the Philosopher. But those things which flow as conclusions from the common principles of the natural law belong to the natural law, as was stated above. Therefore that which is established by human law is not derived from the natural law.

Obj. 3. Further, the law of nature is the same for all, since the Philosopher says that *the natural just is that which is equally valid everywhere.* If therefore human laws were derived from the natural law, it would follow that they too are the same for all; which is clearly false.

Obj. 4. Further, it is possible to give a reason for things which are derived from the natural law. But *it is not possible to give the reason for all the legal enactments of the lawgivers,* as the Jurist says. Therefore not all human laws are derived from the natural law.

On the contrary, Tully says: *Things which emanated from nature, and were approved by custom, were sanctioned by fear and reverence for the laws.*

I answer that, As Augustine says, *that which is not just seems to be no law at all.* Hence the force of a law depends on the extent of its justice. Now in human affairs a thing is said to be just from being right, according to the rule of reason. But the first rule of reason is the law of nature, as is clear from what has been stated above. Consequently, every human law has just so much of the nature of law as it is derived from the law of nature. But if in any point it departs from the law of nature, it is no longer a law but a perversion of law.

But it must be noted that something may be derived from the natural law in two ways: first, as a conclusion from principles; secondly, by way of a determination of certain common notions. The first way is like to that by which, in the sciences, demonstrated conclusions are drawn from the principles; while the second is likened to that whereby, in the arts, common forms are determined to some particular. Thus, the craftsman needs to determine the common form of a house to the shape of this or that particular house. Some things are therefore derived from the common principles of the natural law by way of conclusions: e.g., that *one must not kill* may be derived as a conclusion from the principle that *one should do harm to no man;* while some are derived therefrom by way of determination: e.g., the law of nature has it that the evildoer should be punished, but that he be punished in this or that way is a determination of the law of nature.

Accordingly, both modes of derivation are found in the human law. But those things which are derived in the first way are contained in human law, not as emanating therefrom exclusively, but as having some force from the natural law also. But those things which are derived in the second way have no other force than that of human law.

Reply Obj. 1. The Philosopher is speaking of those enactments which are by way of determination or specification of the precepts of the natural law.

Reply Obj. 2. This argument holds for those things that are derived from the natural law by way of conclusion.

Reply Obj. 3. The common principles of the natural law cannot be applied to all men in the same way

because of the great variety of human affairs; and hence arises the diversity of positive laws among various people.

Reply Obj. 4. These words of the Jurist are to be understood as referring to the decisions of rulers in determining particular points of the natural law; and to these determinations the judgment of expert and prudent men is related as to its principles, in so far, namely, as they see at once what is the best thing to decide. Hence the Philosopher says that, in such matters, *we ought to pay as much attention to the undemonstrated sayings and opinions of persons who surpass us in experience, age, and prudence, as to their demonstrations.*

QUESTION XCVI

On the Power of Human Law

FOURTH ARTICLE

WHETHER HUMAN LAW BINDS A MAN IN CONSCIENCE?

We proceed thus to the Fourth Article:

Objection 1. It would seem that human law does not bind a man in conscience. For an inferior power cannot impose its law on the judgment of a higher power. But the power of man, which frames human law, is beneath the divine power. Therefore human law cannot impose its precept on a divine judgment, such as is the judgment of conscience.

Obj. 2. Further, the judgment of conscience depends chiefly on the commandments of God. But sometimes God's commandments are made void by human laws, according to *Matt.* xv. 6: *You have made void the commandment of God for your tradition.* Therefore human law does not bind a man in conscience.

Obj. 3. Further, human laws often bring loss of character and injury on man, according to *Isa.* x. 1, 2: *Woe to them that make wicked laws, and when they write, write injustice; to oppress the poor in judgment, and do violence to the cause of the humble of My people.* But it is lawful for anyone to avoid oppression and violence. Therefore human laws do not bind man in conscience.

On the contrary, It is written (I *Pet.* ii. 19): *This is thanksworthy, if for conscience . . . a man endure sorrows, suffering wrongfully.*

I answer that, Laws framed by man are either just or unjust. If they be just, they have the power of binding in conscience from the eternal law whence they are derived, according to *Prov.* viii. 15: *By Me kings reign, and lawgivers decree just things.* Now laws are said to be just, both from the end (when, namely, they are ordained to the common good), from their author (that is to say, when the law that is made does not exceed the power of the lawgiver), and from their form (when, namely, burdens are laid on the subjects according to an equality of proportion and with a view to the common good). For, since one man is a part of the community, each man, in all that he is and has, belongs to the community; just as a part, in all that it is, belongs to the whole. So, too, nature inflicts a loss on the part in order to save the whole; so that for this reason such laws as these, which impose proportionate burdens, are just and binding in conscience, and are legal laws.

On the other hand, laws may be unjust in two ways: first, by being contrary to human good, through being opposed to the things mentioned above:—either in respect of the end, as when an authority imposes on his subjects burdensome laws, conducive, not to the common good, but rather to his own cupidity or vain-glory; or in respect of the author, as when a man makes a law that goes beyond the power committed to him; or in respect of the form, as when burdens are imposed unequally on the community, although with a view to the common good. Such are acts of violence rather than laws, because, as Augustine says, *a law that is not just seems to be no law at all.* Therefore, such laws do not bind in conscience, except perhaps in order to avoid scandal or disturbance, for which cause a man should even yield his right, according to *Matt.* v. 40, 41: *If a man . . . take away thy coat, let go thy cloak also unto him; and whosoever will force thee one mile, go with him another two.*

Secondly, laws may be unjust through being opposed to the divine good. Such are the laws of tyrants inducing to idolatry, or to anything else contrary to the divine law. Laws of this kind must in no way be observed, because, as is stated in *Acts* v. 29, *we ought to obey God rather than men.*

Reply Obj. 1. As the Apostle says (*Rom.* xiii. 1, 2), all human power is from God . . . *therefore he that resisteth the power,* in matters that are within its scope, *resisteth the ordinance of God;* so that he becomes guilty in conscience.

Reply Obj. 2. This argument is true of laws that are contrary to the commandments of God, which is beyond the scope of [human] power. Therefore in such matters human law should not be obeyed.

Reply Obj. 3. This argument is true of a law that inflicts an unjust burden on its subjects. Furthermore, the power that man holds from God does not extend to this. Hence neither in such matters is man bound to obey the law, provided he avoid giving scandal or inflicting a more grievous injury.

We proceed thus to the Fifth Article:

Objection 1. It would seem that not all are subject to the law. For those alone are subject to a law for whom a law is made. But the Apostle says (I *Tim.* 1. 9): *The law is not made for the just man.* Therefore the just are not subject to human law.

Obj. 2. Further, Pope Urban says (this is also found in the *Decretals*): *He that is guided by a private law need not for any reason be bound by the public law.* Now all spiritual men are led by the private law of the Holy Ghost, for they are the sons of God, of whom it is said (*Rom.* viii, 14): *Whosoever are led by the Spirit of God, they are the sons of God.* There-fore not all men are subject to human law.

Obj. 3. Further, the Jurist says that *the sovereign is exempt from the laws.* But he that is exempt from the law is not bound thereby. Therefore not all are subject to law.

On the contrary, The Apostle says (*Rom.* xiii, 1): *Let every soul be sub-ject to the higher powers.* But subjec-tion to a power seems to imply subjec-tion to the laws framed by that power. Therefore all men should be subject to law.

I answer that, As was stated above, the notion of law contains two things: first, that it is a rule of human acts; secondly, that it has coercive power. Therefore a man may be subject to law in two ways. First, as the regu-lated is subject to the regulator; and whoever is subject to a power in this way is subject to the law framed by that power. But it may happen in two ways that one is not subject to a power. In one way, by being alto-gether free from its authority. And so it happens that the subjects of one city or kingdom are not bound by the laws of the sovereign of another city or kingdom, since they are not subject to his authority. In another way, by being under a yet higher law. Thus the subject of a proconsul should be ruled by his command, but not in those matters in which the subject re-ceives his orders from the emperor; for in these matters he is not bound by the mandate of the lower authority, since he is directed by that of a higher. In this way, one who is sub-ject absolutely to a law may not be subject thereto in certain matters, in respect of which he is ruled by a higher law.

Secondly, a man is said to be sub-ject to a law as the coerced is subject to the coercer. In this way the virtu-ous and righteous are not subject to law, but only the wicked. For coercion and violence are contrary to the will; but the will of the good is in harmony with law, whereas the will of the wicked is discordant from it. There-fore in this sense the good are not subject to law, but only the wicked.

Reply Obj. 1. This argument is true of subjection by way of coercion, for, in this way, *the law is not made for the just men,* because *they are a law to themselves,* since they *show the work of the law written in their hearts,* as the Apostle says (*Rom.* ii. 14, 15). Consequently law does not coerce them in the way that it does the wicked.

Reply Obj. 2. The law of the Holy Ghost is above all law framed by man, and therefore spiritual men, in so far as they are led by the law of the Holy Ghost, are not subject to the law in those matters that are inconsistent with the guidance of the Holy Ghost. Nevertheless, it is an effect of the guidance of the Holy Ghost that spir-itual men are subject to human laws, according to I *Pet.* ii. 13: *Be ye sub-ject . . . to every human creature for God's sake.*

Reply Obj. 3. The sovereign is said to be *exempt from the law,* as to its coercive power, since, properly speak-ing, no man is coerced by himself, and law has no coercive power save from the authority of the sovereign. Thus is the sovereign said to be exempt from the law because none is competent to pass sentence on him, if he acts against the law. Therefore on *Ps.* 1. 6 (*To Thee only have I sinned*) the *Gloss* says that *there is no man who can judge the deeds of a king.* But as to the directive force of law, the sov-ereign is subject to the law by his own will, according to the statement that *whatever law a man makes for another, he should keep himself.* And the authority of a wise man says: *Obey the law that thou makest thyself.* Moreover the Lord reproaches those who *say and do not; and who bind heavy burdens and lay them on men's shoulders, but with a finger of their own they will not move them* (*Matt.* xxiii. 3, 4). Hence, in the judgment of God, the sovereign is not exempt from the law, as to its directive force; but he should fulfill it voluntarily, and not of constraint. Again, the sovereign is above the law, in so far as, when it is expedient, he can change the law, and rule within it according to time and place.

ON THE MORAL PRECEPTS OF THE OLD LAW [4]

FIRST ARTICLE

WHETHER ALL THE MORAL PRECEPTS OF THE OLD LAW BELONG TO THE LAW OF NATURE?

[4] This selection is from Question C, the *Summa Theologica,* in the Dominican translation, from The *Basic Writings of*

We proceed thus to the First Article:

Objection 1. It would seem that not all the moral precepts belong to the law of nature. For it is written (*Ecclus.* xvii. 9): *Moreover He gave them instructions, and the law of life for an inheritance.* But instruction is in contradistinction to the law of na-ture, since the law of nature is not learned, but possessed by natural in-stinct. Therefore not all the moral pre-cepts belong to the natural law.

Obj. 2. Further, the divine law is more perfect than human law. But hu-man law adds certain things concern-ing good morals to those that belong to the law of nature; as is evidenced by the fact that the natural law is the same in all men, while these moral institutions are various for various peo-ple. Much more reason therefore there why the divine law should add to the law of nature ordinances per-taining to good morals.

Obj. 3. Further, just as natural rea-son leads to good morals in certain matters, so does faith. Hence it is writ-ten (*Gal.* v. 6) that faith *worketh by charity.* But faith is not included in the law of nature, since that which is of faith is above nature. Therefore not all the moral precepts of the divine law belong to the law of nature.

On the contrary, The Apostle says (*Rom.* ii. 14) that *the Gentiles, who have not the Law, do by nature those things that are of the Law;* which must be understood of things pertaining to good morals. Therefore all the moral precepts of the Law belong to the law of nature.

I answer that, The moral precepts are distinct from the ceremonial and judicial precepts, for they are about things pertaining of their very nature to good morals. Now since human morals depend on their relation to rea-

Saint Thomas Aquinas, ed. by Anton C. Pegis. © by Random House, Inc. Re-printed by permission.

son, which is the proper principle of human acts, those morals are called good which accord with reason, and those are called bad which are discordant from reason. And as every judgment of the speculative reason proceeds from the natural knowledge of first principles, so every judgment of the practical reason proceeds from naturally known principles . . . . From these principles one may proceed in various ways to judge of various matters. For some matters connected with human actions are so evident, that after very little consideration one is able at once to approve or disapprove of them by means of these common first principles; while other matters cannot be the subject of judgment without much consideration of the various circumstances. Not all are able to do this carefully, but only those who are wise; just as it is not possible for all to consider the particular conclusions of the sciences, but only for those who are philosophers. Lastly, there are some matters of which man cannot judge unless he be helped by divine instruction: *e.g.*, matters of faith.

It is therefore evident that since the moral precepts are about matters which concern good morals; and since good morals are such as are in accord with reason; and since every judgment of human reason must needs be derived in some way from natural reason,—it follows, of necessity, that all the moral precepts belong to the law of nature, but not all in the same way. For there are certain things which the natural reason of every man, of its own accord and at once, judges to be done or not to be done: *e.g.*, *Honor thy father and thy mother*, and, *Thou shalt not kill, Thou shalt not steal* (*Exod.* xx. 12, 13, 15); and these belong to the law of nature absolutely. And there are certain things which, after a more careful consideration, wise men deem obligatory. Such belong to the law of nature, yet so that they need to be inculcated, the wiser teaching the less wise: *e.g.*, *Rise up before the hoary head, and honor the person of the aged man* (*Levit.* xix. 32), and the like.—And there are some things, to judge of which human reason needs divine instruction, whereby we are taught about the things of God: *e.g.*, *Thou shalt not make to thyself a graven thing, nor the likeness of anything; Thou shalt not take the name of the Lord thy God in vain* (*Exod.* xx. 4, 7).

This suffices for the Replies to the Objections.

WHETHER THE MORAL PRECEPTS OF THE LAW ARE ABOUT ALL THE ACTS OF THE VIRTUES?

We proceed thus to the Second Article:

Objection 1. It would seem that the moral precepts of the Law are not about all the acts of the virtues. For the observance of the precepts of the Old Law is called justification, according to *Ps.* cxviii. 8: *I will keep Thy justifications.* But justification is the execution of justice. Therefore the moral precepts are only about acts of justice.

Obj. 2. Further, that which comes under a precept has the character of a duty. But the character of duty belongs to justice alone and to none of the other virtues, for the proper act of justice consists in rendering to each one his due. Therefore the precepts of the moral law are not about the acts of the other virtues, but only about the acts of justice.

Obj. 3. Further, every law is made for the common good, as Isidore says. But of all the virtues justice alone regards the common good, as the Philosopher says.[5] Therefore the moral pre-

[5] *Eth.*, V, 1 (1130a 4).

cepts are only about the acts of justice.

On the contrary, Ambrose says that *a sin is a transgression of the divine law, and a disobedience to the commandments of heaven.*[6] But there are sins contrary to all the acts of virtue. Therefore it belongs to the divine law to direct all the acts of virtue.

I answer that, Since the precepts of the Law are ordained to the common good . . . the precepts of the Law must needs be diversified according to the various kinds of community. Hence the Philosopher teaches that the laws which are made in a state that is ruled by a king must be different from the laws of a state that is ruled by the people, or by a few powerful men in the state.[7] Now human law is ordained for one kind of community, and the divine law for another kind. For human law is ordained for the civil community, which men have in relation to one another; and men are ordained to one another by outward acts, whereby men live in communion with one another. This life in common of man with man pertains to justice, whose proper function consists in directing the human community. Therefore human law makes precepts only about acts of justice; and if it commands acts of the other virtues, this is only in so far as they assume the nature of justice, as the Philosopher explains.[8]

But the community for which the divine law is ordained is that of men in relation to God, either in this life or in the life to come. Therefore the divine law proposes precepts about all those matters whereby men are well ordered in their relations to God. Now man is united to God by his reason or mind, in which is God's image. Therefore the divine law proposes precepts about all those matters whereby hu-

man reason is well ordered. But this is effected by the acts of all the virtues, since the intellectual virtues set in good order the acts of the reason in themselves, while the moral virtues set in good order the acts of the reason in reference to interior passions and exterior actions. It is therefore evident that the divine law fittingly proposes precepts about the acts of all the virtues, and yet in such a way that certain matters, without which the order of virtue, which is the order of reason, cannot even exist, come under an obligation of precept, while other matters, which pertain to the well-being of perfect virtue, come under an admonition of counsel.

Reply Obj. 1. The fulfillment of the commandments of the Law, even of those which are about the acts of the other virtues, has the character of justification, inasmuch as it is just that man should obey God; or, again, inasmuch as it is just that all that belongs to man should be subject to reason.

Reply Obj. 2. Justice, properly so called, regards the duty of one man to another; but all the other virtues regard the duty of the lower powers to reason. It is in relation to this latter duty that the Philosopher speaks of a kind of metaphorical justice.[9]

The Reply to the Third Objection is clear from what has been said about the different kinds of community.

THIRD ARTICLE

WHETHER ALL THE MORAL PRECEPTS OF THE OLD LAW ARE REDUCIBLE TO THE TEN PRECEPTS OF THE DECALOGUE?

We proceed thus to the Third Article:

Objection 1. It would seem that not all the moral precepts of the Old Law

---

[6] *De Parad.,* VIII (PL 14, 309).
[7] *Polit.,* IV, 1 (1289a 11; a. 22).
[8] *Eth.,* V, 1 (1129b 23).

[9] *Eth.,* V, 11 (1138b 5).

are reducible to the ten precepts of the decalogue. For the first and principal precepts of the Law are, *Thou shalt love the Lord thy God,* and, *Thou shalt love thy neighbor,* as is stated in *Matt.* xxii. 37, 39. But these two are not contained in the precepts of the decalogue. Therefore not all the moral precepts are contained in the precepts of the decalogue.

Obj. 2. Further, the moral precepts are not reducible to the ceremonial precepts, but rather *vice versa.* But among the precepts of the decalogue, one is ceremonial, viz., *Remember that thou keep holy the Sabbath-day* (*Exod.* xx. 8). Therefore the moral precepts are not reducible to all the precepts of the decalogue.

Obj. 3. Further, the moral precepts are about all the acts of the virtues. But among the precepts of the decalogue are only such as regard acts of justice, as may be seen by going through them all. Therefore the precepts of the decalogue do not include all the moral precepts.

On the contrary, The *Gloss* on *Matt.* v. 11 (*Blessed are ye when they shall revile you,* etc.) says that *Moses, after propounding the ten precepts, set them out in detail.*[10] Therefore all the precepts of the Law are so many parts of the precepts of the decalogue.

I answer that, The precepts of the decalogue differ from the other precepts of the Law in the fact that God Himself is said to have given the precepts of the decalogue; whereas He gave the other precepts to the people through Moses. Therefore the decalogue includes those precepts the knowledge of which man has immediately from God. Such are those which, with but slight reflection, can be gathered at once from the first common principles, and those also which become known to man immediately through divinely infused faith. Conse-

quently, two kinds of precepts are not reckoned among the precepts of the decalogue: viz., the first common principles, for they need no further promulgation after being once imprinted on the natural reason to which they are self-evident, as, for instance, that one should do evil to no man, and other similar principles;—and again those which the careful reflection of wise men shows to be in accord with reason, for the people receive these principles from God, through the teaching of wise men. Nevertheless, both kinds of precepts are contained in the precepts of the decalogue, but in different ways. For the first common principles are contained in them, as principles in their proximate conclusions; while those which are known through wise men are contained, conversely, as conclusions in their principles.

Reply Obj. 1. These two principles are the first common principles of the natural law, and are self-evident to human reason, either through nature or through faith. Therefore all the precepts of the decalogue are referred to these as conclusions to common principles.

Reply Obj. 2. The precept of the Sabbath observance is moral in one respect, in so far as it commands man to give some time to the things of God, according to *Ps.* xlv. 11: *Be still and see that I am God.* In this respect it is placed among the precepts of the decalogue; but not as to the fixing of the time, in which respect it is a ceremonial precept.

Reply Obj. 3. The notion of duty is not so patent in the other virtues as it is in justice. Hence the precepts about the acts of the other virtues are not so well known to the people as are the precepts about acts of justice. Therefore the acts of justice especially come under the precepts of the decalogue, which are the primary elements of the Law.

[10] *Glossa ordin.* (V, 19B).

Thomas Hobbes (1588—1679)

Few men sought more earnestly than Hobbes to win friends and admirers and failed more abjectly. A late and self-developed interest in mathematics led him to the claim that he had squared the circle, and the conceit he exhibited in the controversies it occasioned alienated the best minds of the time. A naturalist (more specifically a materialist who sought to found the principles of psychology, politics, and morals upon the principles of bodies in motion), he was, none the less, a rationalist; and he criticized the Royal Society of London for what he considered its exaggerated attention to empirical details. In politics he succeeded, at one time or another, in offending all parties to the dispute between king and parliament. He advocated political absolutism in order to forestall a ruinous civil strife, but while he won the support of the courtiers, he offended the constitutionalists. Upon Charles' exile, however, his failure to defend the principle of the divine right of kings, and his subsequent willingness to accommodate his own views to the interests of the de facto sovereignty of the constitutionalists, alienated the party of the king but did not succeed wholly in removing all suspicion from the minds of the other party. In religion, he succeeded in arousing the ire of ecclesiastics by his apparent atheism and his subordination of church to state. Hobbes' principal works are *De Cive* (1642), in which appeared a revised version of his controversial *The Elements of Law* (widely circulated in unpublished form in 1640), *Leviathan* (1651), *De Corpore* (1655), and *De Homine* (1658).

LEVIATHAN [1]

Or the Matter, Form, and Power of a Commonwealth, Ecclesiastical and Civil The First Part, of Man

CHAPTER VI

OF THE INTERIOR BEGINNINGS OF

[1] Reprinted from the Molesworth edition, London, 1841.

VOLUNTARY MOTIONS; COMMONLY CALLED THE PASSIONS

There be in animals, two sorts of *motions* peculiar to them: one called *vital;* begun in generation, and continued without interruption through their whole life; such as are the *course* of the *blood,* the *pulse,* the *breathing,* the *concoction, nutrition, excretion,* &c., to which motions there needs no help of imagination: the other is *animal motion,* otherwise called *voluntary motion;* as to *go,* to *speak,* to *move* any of our limbs in such manner as is first fancied in our minds. That sense of motion in the organs and interior parts of man's body, caused by the action of the things we see, hear, &c.; and that fancy is but the relics of the same motion, remaining after sense, has been already said in the first and second chapters. And because *going, speaking,* and the like voluntary motions, depend always upon a precedent thought of *whither, which way,* and *what,* it is evident that the imagination is the first internal beginning of all voluntary motion. And although unstudied men do not conceive any motion at all to be there, where the thing moved is invisible; or the space it is moved in is, for the shortness of it, insensible; yet that does not hinder but that such motions are. For let a space be never so little, that which is moved over a greater space, whereof that little one is part, must first be moved over that. These small beginnings of motion, within the body of man, before they appear in walking, speaking, striking, and other visible actions, are commonly called EN-DEAVOUR.

This endeavour, when it is toward something which causes it, is called APPETITE, or DESIRE; the latter being the general name; and the other oftentimes restrained to signify the desire of food, namely *hunger* and *thirst.* And when the endeavour is fromward something, it is generally called AVERSION. These words, *appetite* and *aversion,* we have from the Latins, and they both of them signify the motions, one of approaching, the other of retiring. So also do the Greek works for the same, which are ὁρμή and ἀφορμή. For nature itself does often press upon men those truths, which afterwards, when they look for somewhat beyond nature, they stumble at. For the Schools find in mere appetite to

go, or move, no actual motion at all: but because some motion they must acknowledge, they call it metaphorical motion; which is but an absurd speech; for though words may be called metaphorical, bodies and motions cannot.

That which men desire, they are also said to LOVE, and to HATE those things for which they have aversion. So that desire and love are the same thing; save that by desire, we always signify the absence of the object; by love, most commonly the presence of the same. So also by aversion, we signify the absence; and by hate, the presence of the object.

Of appetites and aversions, some are born with men; as appetite of food, appetite of excretion, and exoneration, which may also and more properly be called aversions, from somewhat they feel in their bodies; and some other appetites, not many. The rest, which are appetites of particular things, proceed from experience, and trial of their effects upon themselves or other men. For of things we know not at all, or believe not to be, we can have no further desire than to taste and try. But aversion we have for things, not only which we know have hurt us, but also that we do not know whether they will hurt us, or not.

Those things which we neither desire, nor hate, we are said to *contemn;* CONTEMPT being nothing else but an immobility, or contumacy of the heart, in resisting the action of certain things; and proceeding from that the heart is already moved otherwise, by other more potent objects; or from want of experience of them.

And because the constitution of a man's body is in continual mutation, it is impossible that all the same things should always cause in him the same appetites and aversions; much less can all men consent, in the desire of almost any one and the same object.

But whatsoever is the object of any man's appetite or desire, that is it which he for his part calleth *good:* and the object of his hate and aversion, *evil;* and of his contempt, *vile* and *inconsiderable.* For these words of good, evil, and contemptible, are ever used with relation to the person that useth them: there being nothing simply and absolutely so; nor any common rule of good and evil, to be taken from the nature of the objects themselves; but from the person of the man, where there is no Commonwealth; or, in a Commonwealth, from the person that representeth it; or from an arbitrator or judge, whom men disagreeing shall by consent set up, and make his sentence the rule thereof.

The Latin tongue has two words, whose significations approach to those of good and evil; but they are not precisely the same; and those are *pulchrum* and *turpe.* Whereof the former signifies that, which by some apparent signs promiseth good; and the latter, that which promiseth evil. But in our tongue we have not so general names to express them by. But for *pulchrum* we say in some things, *fair;* in others, *beautiful,* or *handsome,* or *gallant,* or *honourable,* or *comely,* or *amiable;* and for *turpe, foul, deformed, ugly, base, nauseous,* and the like, as the subject shall require; all which words, in their proper places, signify nothing else but the *mien* or countenance, that promiseth good and evil. So that of good there be three kinds; good in the promise, that is *pulchrum;* good in effect, as the end desired, which is called *jucundum, delightful;* and good as the means, which is called *utile, profitable;* and as many of evil: for *evil* in promise, is that they call *turpe;* evil in effect, and end, is *molestum, unpleasant, troublesome;* and evil in the means, *inutile, unprofitable, hurtful.*

As, in sense, that which is really within us, is, as I have said before, only motion, caused by the action of external objects, but in appearance; to the sight, light and colour; to the ear, sound; to the nostril, odour, etc.; so, when the action of the same object is continued from the eyes, ears, and other organs to the heart, the real effect there is nothing but motion, or endeavour; which consisteth in appetite, or aversion, to or from the object moving. But the apparence, or sense of that motion, is that we either call *delight* or *trouble of mind.*

This motion, which is called appetite, and for the apparence of it *delight* and *pleasure,* seemeth to be a corroboration of vital motion, and a help thereunto; and therefore such things as caused delight were not improperly called *jucunda, a juvando,* from helping or fortifying; and the contrary *molesta, offensive,* from hindering, and troubling the motion vital.

Pleasure, therefore, or *delight* is the apparence, or sense of good; and *molestation* or *displeasure,* the apparence or sense of evil. And consequently all appetite, desire, and love, is accompanied with some delight more or less; and all hatred and aversion, with more or less displeasure and offence.

Of pleasure or delights, some arise from the sense of an object present; and those may be called *pleasures of sense;* the word *sensual,* as it is used by those only that condemn them, having no place till there be laws. Of this kind are all onerations and exonerations of the body; as also all that is pleasant, in the *sight, hearing, smell, taste,* or *touch.* Others arise from the expectation, that proceeds from foresight of the end, or consequence of things; whether those things in the sense please or displease. And these are *pleasures of the mind* of him that draweth those consequences, and are generally called JOY. In the like manner, displeasures are some in the sense, and called PAIN; others in the expectation of consequences, and are called GRIEF.

.   .   .

CHAPTER XI

OF THE DIFFERENCE OF MANNERS

By manners I mean not here decency of behaviour; as how one should salute another, or how a man should wash his mouth, or pick his teeth before company, and such other points of the 'small morals'; but those qualities of mankind that concern their living together in peace and unity. To which end we are to consider that the felicity of this life consisteth not in the repose of a mind satisfied. For there is no such *finis ultimus,* utmost aim, nor *summum bonum,* greatest good, as is spoken of in the books of the old moral philosophers. Nor can a man any more live, whose desires are at an end, than he whose senses and imaginations are at a stand. Felicity is a continual progress of the desire, from one object to another, the attaining of the former being still but the way to the latter. The cause whereof is that the object of man's desire is not to enjoy once only, and for one instant of time, but to assure for ever the way of his future desire. And therefore the voluntary actions and inclinations of all men, tend not only to the procuring, but also to the assuring of a contented life; and differ only in the way which ariseth partly from the diversity of passions in divers men; and partly from the difference of the knowledge or opinion each one has of the causes which produce the effect desired.

So that in the first place, I put for a general inclination of all mankind, a perpetual and restless desire of power after power, that ceaseth only in death. And the cause of this is not always that a man hopes for a more intensive delight than he has already attained to, or that he cannot be content with a moderate power; but because he cannot assure the power and means to live well, which he hath present, without the acquisition of more. And from hence it is that kings, whose power is greatest, turn their endeavours to the assuring it at home by laws, or abroad by wars; and when that is done, there succeedeth a new desire; in some, of fame from new conquest; in others, of ease and sensual pleasure; in others, of admiration, or being flattered for excellence in some art, or other ability of the mind.

Competition of riches, honour, command, or other power, inclineth to contention, enmity, and war; because the way of one competitor, to the attaining of his desire, is to kill, subdue, supplant, or repel the other. Particularly, competition of praise, inclineth to a reverence of antiquity. For men contend with the living, not with the dead; to these ascribing more than due, that they may obscure the glory of the other.

Desire of ease, and sensual delight, disposeth men to obey a common power, because by such desires a man doth abandon the protection that might be hoped for from his own industry and labour. Fear of death, and wounds, disposeth to the same, and for the same reason. On the contrary, needy men, and hardy, not contented with their present condition, as also all men that are ambitious of military command, are inclined to continue the causes of war; and to stir up trouble and sedition, for there is no honour military but by war, nor any such hope to mend an ill game, as by causing a new shuffle.

Desire of knowledge, and arts of peace, inclineth men to obey a common power: for such desire, containeth a desire of leisure; and consequently protection from some other power than their own.

. . .

CHAPTER XIII

OF THE NATURAL CONDITION OF
MANKIND AS CONCERNING THEIR
FELICITY AND MISERY

Nature hath made men so equal, in the faculties of the body, and mind; as that though there be found one man sometimes manifestly stronger in body, or of quicker mind than another, yet when all is reckoned together, the difference between man and man, is not so considerable, as that one man can thereupon claim to himself any benefit to which another may not pretend, as well as he. For as to the strength of body, the weakest has strength enough to kill the strongest, either by secret machination, or by confederacy with others, that are in the same danger with himself.

And as to the faculties of the mind, setting aside the arts grounded upon words, and especially that skill of proceeding upon general and infallible rules, called science; which very few have, and but in few things; as being not a native faculty born with us; nor attained, as prudence, while we look after somewhat else, I find yet a greater equality amongst men than that of strength. For prudence, is but experience; which equal time, equally bestows on all men, in those things they equally apply themselves unto. That which may perhaps make such equality incredible, is but a vain conceit of one's own wisdom, which almost all men think they have in a greater degree than the vulgar; that is, than all men but themselves, and a few others, whom by fame, or for concurring with themselves, they ap-

prove. For such is the nature of men, that howsoever they may acknowledge many others to be more witty, or more eloquent, or more learned; yet they will hardly believe there be many so wise as themselves; for they see their own wit at hand, and other men's at a distance. But this proveth rather that men are in that point equal, than unequal. For there is not ordinarily a greater sign of the equal distribution of anything, than that every man is contented with his share.

From this equality of ability, ariseth equality of hope in the attaining of our ends. And therefore if any two men desire the same thing, which nevertheless they cannot both enjoy, they become enemies; and in the way to their end, which is principally their own conservation, and sometimes their delectation only, endeavour to destroy or subdue one another. And from hence it comes to pass, that where an invader hath no more to fear, than another man's single power; if one plant, sow, build, or possess a convenient seat, others may probably be expected to come prepared with forces united, to dispossess, and deprive him, not only of the fruit of his labour, but also of his life or liberty. And the invader again is in the like danger of another.

And from this diffidence of one another, there is no way for any man to secure himself, so reasonable as anticipation; that is, by force, or wiles, to master the persons of all men he can, so long, till he see no other power great enough to endanger him: and this is no more than his own conservation requireth, and is generally allowed. Also because there be some, that taking pleasure in contemplating their own power in the acts of conquest, which they pursue farther than their security requires; if others, that otherwise would be glad to be at ease within modest bounds, should not by invasion increase their power, they would not be able, long time, by standing only on their defence, to subsist. And by consequence, such augmentation of dominion over men being necessary to a man's conservation, it ought to be allowed him.

Again, men have no pleasure, but on the contrary a great deal of grief, in keeping company, where there is no power able to overawe them all. For every man looketh that his companion should value him, at the same rate he sets upon himself: and upon all signs of contempt, or undervaluing, naturally endeavours as far as he dares (which amongst them that have no common power to keep them in quiet, is far enough to make them destroy each other), to extort a greater value from his contemners, by damage; and from others, by the example.

So that in the nature of man, we find three principal causes of quarrel. First, competition; secondly, diffidence; thirdly, glory.

The first maketh men invade for gain; the second, for safety; and the third, for reputation. The first use violence, to make themselves masters of other men's persons, wives, children, and cattle; the second, to defend them; the third, for trifles, as a word, a smile, a different opinion, and any sign of undervalue, either direct in their persons, or by reflection in their kindred, their friends, their nation, their profession, or their name.

Hereby it is manifest, that during the time men live without a common power to keep them all in awe, they are in that condition which is called WAR; and such a war, as is of every man, against every man. For WAR, consisteth not in battle only, or the act of fighting; but in a tract of time, wherein the will to contend by battle is sufficiently known: and therefore the notion of *time*, is to be considered in the nature of war, as it is in the nature of weather. For as the nature of foul weather, lieth not in a shower or two of rain, but in an inclination thereto of many days together; so the nature of war, consisteth not in actual fighting, but in the known disposition thereto, during all the time there is no assurance to the contrary. All other time is PEACE.

Whatsoever therefore is consequent to a time of war, where every man is enemy to every man, the same is consequent to the time wherein men live without other security, than what their own strength, and their own invention shall furnish them withal. In such condition, there is no place for industry, because the fruit thereof is uncertain, and consequently no culture of the earth; no navigation, nor use of the commodities that may be imported by sea; no commodious building; no instruments of moving, and removing, such things as require much force; no knowledge of the face of the earth; no account of time; no arts; no letters; no society; and, which is worst of all, continual fear, and danger of violent death; and the life of man, solitary, poor, nasty, brutish, and short.

It may seem strange to some man, that has not well weighed these things, that Nature should thus dissociate, and render men apt to invade and destroy one another; and he may therefore, not trusting to this inference made from the passions, desire perhaps to have the same confirmed by experience. Let him therefore consider with himself, when taking a journey, he arms himself, and seeks to go well accompanied; when going to sleep he locks his doors; when even in his house, he locks his chest; and this when he knows there be laws, and public officers, armed, to revenge all injuries shall be done him; what opinion he has of his fellow-subjects, when he rides armed; of his fellow-citizens, when he locks his doors; and of his children and servants, when he locks his chests. Does he not there as much accuse mankind by his actions, as I do by my words? But neither of us accuse man's nature in it. The desires, and other passions of man, are in themselves no sin. No more are the actions, that proceed from those passions, till they know a law that forbids them: which till laws be made they cannot know, nor can any law be made, till they have agreed upon the person that shall make it.

It may peradventure be thought, there was never such a time nor condition of war as this; and I believe it was never generally so, over all the world: but there are many places where they live so now. For the savage people in many places of America, except the government of small families, the concord whereof dependeth on natural lust, have no government at all, and live at this day in that brutish manner, as I said before. However, it may be perceived what manner of life there would be, where there were no common power to fear, by the manner of life, which men that have formerly lived under a peaceful government, use to degenerate into, in a civil war.

But though there had never been any time, wherein particular men were in a condition of war one against another; yet in all times, kings, and persons of sovereign authority, because of their independency, are in continual jealousies, and in the state and posture of gladiators; having their weapons pointing, and their eyes fixed on one another; that is, their forts, garrisons, and guns upon the frontiers of their kingdoms; and continual spies upon their neighbours; which is a posture of war. But because they uphold thereby the industry of their subjects; there does not follow from it that misery, which accompanies the liberty of particular men.

To this war of every man, against every man, this also is consequent; that nothing can be unjust. The notions of right and wrong, justice and injustice, have there no place. Where there is no common power, there is no law: where no law, no injustice. Force, and fraud, are in war the two cardinal virtues. Justice, and injustice are none of the faculties neither of the body nor mind. If they were, they might be in a man that were alone in the world, as well as his senses, and passions. They are qualities, that relate to men in society, not in solitude. It is consequent also to the same condition, that there be no propriety, no dominion, no *mine* and *thine* distinct; but only that to be every man's, that he can get; and for so long, as he can keep it. And thus much for the ill condition, which man by mere nature is actually placed in: though with a possibility to come out of it, consisting partly in the passions, partly in his reason.

The passions that incline men to peace, are fear of death; desire of such things as are necessary to commodious living; and a hope by their industry to obtain them. And reason suggesteth convenient articles of peace, upon which men may be drawn to agreement. These articles, are they, which otherwise are called the Laws of Nature: whereof I shall speak more particularly, in the two following chapters.

CHAPTER XIV

OF THE FIRST AND SECOND NATURAL LAWS, AND OF CONTRACTS

The RIGHT OF NATURE, which writers commonly call *jus naturale*, is the liberty each man hath, to use his own power, as he will himself, for the preservation of his own nature; that is to say, of his own life; and consequently, of doing anything which in his own judgement and reason he shall conceive to be the aptest means thereunto.

By LIBERTY, is understood, according to the proper signification of the word, the absence of external impediments: which impediments, may take away part of a man's power to do what he would; but cannot hinder him from using the power left him, according as his judgment and reason shall dictate to him.

A LAW OF NATURE, *lex naturalis*, is a precept or general rule, found out by reason, by which a man is forbidden to do that, which is destructive of his life, or taketh away the means of preserving the same; and to omit that, by which he thinketh it may be best preserved. For though they that speak of this subject use to confound *jus* and *lex*, *right* and *law*: yet they ought to be distinguished; because RIGHT consisteth in liberty to do, or to forbear; whereas LAW, determineth, and bindeth to one of them: so that law, and right, differ as much as obligation, and liberty; which in one and the same matter are inconsistent.

And because the condition of man, as hath been declared in the precedent chapter, is a condition of war of every one against every one; in which case every one is governed by his own reason; and there is nothing he can make use of, that may not be a help unto him in preserving his life against his enemies; it followeth, that in such a condition, every man has a right to everything; even to one another's body. And therefore, as long as this natural right of every man to everything endureth, there can be no security to any man, how strong or wise soever he be, of living out the time which Nature ordinarily alloweth men to live. And consequently it is a precept, or general rule of reason, *that every man ought to endeavor peace,*

as far as he has hope of obtaining it; and when he cannot obtain it, that he may seek, and use, all helps and advantages of war. The first branch of which rule containeth the first, and fundamental law of Nature; which is *to seek peace, and follow it.* The second, the sum of the right of Nature; which is, *by all means we can, to defend ourselves.*

From this fundamental law of Nature, by which men are commanded to endeavour peace, is derived this second law; *that a man be willing, when others are so too, as far-forth, as for peace, and defence of himself he shall think it necessary to lay down this right to all things; and be contented with so much liberty against other men as he would allow other men against himself.* For as long as every man holdeth this right of doing anything he liketh; so long are all men in the condition of war. But if other men will not lay down their right as well as he; then there is no reason for any one to divest himself of his: for that were to expose himself to prey, which no man is bound to, rather than to dispose himself to peace. This is that law of the Gospel; *whatsoever you require that others should do to you, that do ye to them.* And that law of all men, *quod tibi fieri non vis, alteri ne feceris.*

To *lay down* a man's *right* to any thing, is to *divest* himself of the *liberty*, of hindering another of the benefit of his own right to the same. For he that renounceth or passeth away his right, giveth not to any other man a right which he had not before; because there is nothing to which every man had not right by nature: but only standeth out of his way, that he may enjoy his own original right, without hindrance from him, not without hindrance from another. So that the effect which redoundeth to one man, by another man's defect of right, is but so much diminution of impediments to the use of his own right original.

Right is laid aside, either by simply renouncing it, or by transferring it to another. By *simply renouncing*, when he cares not to whom the benefit thereof redoundeth. By *transferring*, when he intendeth the benefit thereof to some certain person or persons. And when a man hath in either manner abandoned or granted away his right; then is he said to be *obliged*, or bound, not to hinder those to whom such right is granted or abandoned, from the benefit of it; and that he *ought*, and it is his *duty*, not to make void that voluntary act of his own; and that such hindrance is *injustice*, and *injury*, as being *sine jure*; the right being before renounced, or transferred. So that injury, or injustice, in the controversies of the world, is somewhat like to that, which in the disputations of scholars is called *absurdity*. For as it is there called an absurdity to contradict what one maintained in the beginning; so in the world, it is called injustice, and injury, voluntarily to undo that which from the beginning he had voluntarily done. The way by which a man either simply renounceth, or transferreth his right, is a declaration, or signification, by some voluntary and sufficient sign or signs, that he doth so renounce or transfer, or hath so renounced or transferred the same, to him that accepteth it. And these signs are either words only, or actions only, or, as it happeneth most often, both words and actions. And the same are the *bonds*, by which men are bound and obliged —bonds that have their strength, not from their own nature, for nothing is more easily broken than a man's word, but from fear of some evil consequence upon the rupture.

Whensoever a man transferreth his right, or renounceth it; it is either in consideration of some right reciprocally transferred to himself, or for some other good he hopeth for thereby. For it is a voluntary act; and of the voluntary acts of every man, the object is some *good to himself*. And therefor there be some rights which no man can be understood by any words, or other signs, to have abandoned or transferred. As first a man cannot lay down the right of resisting them that assault him by force, to take away his life; because he cannot be understood to aim thereby, at any good to himself. The same may be said of wounds, and chains, and imprisonment: both because there is no benefit consequent to such patience, as there is to the patience of suffering another to be wounded or imprisoned; as also because a man cannot tell, when he seeth men proceed against him by violence, whether they intend his death or not. And lastly the motive, and end for which this renouncing and transferring of right is introduced, is nothing else but the security of a man's person, in his life, and in the means of so preserving life as not to be weary of it. And therefore if a man by words, or other signs, seem to despoil himself of the end for which those signs were intended, he is not to be understood as if he meant it, or that it was his will, but that he was ignorant of how such words and actions were to be interpreted.

The mutual transferring of right, is that which men call *contract*.

· · ·

CHAPTER XV

OF OTHER LAWS OF NATURE

From that law of Nature, by which we are obliged to transfer to another, such rights, as being retained, hinder the peace of mankind, there followeth a third; which is this, *that men perform their covenants made*: without which, covenants are in vain, and but empty words; and the right of all men to all things remaining, we are still in the condition of war.

And in this law of Nature, consisteth the fountain and original of JUSTICE. For where no covenant hath preceded, there hath no right been transferred, and every man has right to everything; and consequently, no action can be unjust. But when a covenant is made, then to break it is *unjust*: and the definition of INJUSTICE, is no other than *the not performance of covenant*. And whatsoever is not unjust, is *just*.

But because covenants of mutual trust, where there is a fear of not performance on either part, as hath been said in the former chapter, are invalid; though the original of justice be the making of covenants; yet injustice actually there can be none, till the cause of such fear be taken away; which while men are in the natural condition of war, cannot be done. Therefore before the names of just, and unjust can have place, there must be some coercive power, to compel men equally to the performance of their covenants, by the terror of some punishment, greater than the benefit they expect by the breach of their covenant; and to make good that propriety, which by mutual contract men acquire, in recompense of the universal right they abandon: and such power there is none before the erection of a commonwealth. And this is also to be gathered out of the ordinary definition of justice in the Schools: for they say, that *justice is the constant will of giving to every man his own*. And therefore where there is no *own*, that is no propriety, there is no injustice; and where there is no coercive power erected, that is, where there is no Commonwealth, there is no propriety; all men having right to all things: therefore where there is no Common-

wealth, there nothing is unjust. So that the nature of justice, consisteth in keeping of valid covenants: but the validity of covenants begins not but with the constitution of a civil power, sufficient to compel men to keep them; and then it is also that propriety begins.

. . .

As justice dependeth on antecedent covenant; so does GRATITUDE depend on antecedent grace; that is to say, antecedent free gift: and is the fourth law of Nature; which may be conceived in this form, *that a man which receiveth benefit from another of mere grace, endeavour that he which giveth it, have no reasonable cause to repent him of his good will*. For no man giveth, but with intention of good to himself; because gift is voluntary and of all voluntary acts, the object is to every man his own good; of which if men see they shall be frustrated, there will be no beginning of benevolence, or trust, nor consequently of mutual help; nor of reconciliation of one man to another; and therefore they are to remain still in the condition of *war*; which is contrary to the first and fundamental law of Nature, which commandeth men to *seek peace*. The breach of this law is called *ingratitude*; and hath the same relation to grace, that injustice hath to obligation by covenant.

A fifth law of Nature is COMPLAISANCE; that is to say, *that every man strive to accommodate himself to the rest*. For the understanding whereof, we may consider, that there is in men's aptness to society, a diversity of nature, rising from their diversity of affections; not unlike to that we see in stones brought together for building of an edifice. . . . For seeing every man, not only by right, but also by necessity of nature, is supposed to endeavour all he can, to obtain that which is necessary for his conservation; he that shall oppose himself against it, for things superfluous, is guilty of the war that thereupon is to follow; and therefore doth that, which is contrary to the fundamental law of Nature, which commandeth *to seek peace.* The observers of this law, may be called SOCIABLE, the Latins call them *commodi;* the contrary, *stubborn, insociable, forward, intractable.*

A sixth law of Nature is this, *that upon caution of the future time, a man ought to pardon the offences past of them that repenting, desire it.* For PARDON, is nothing but granting of peace; which though granted to them that persevere in their hostility, be not peace, but fear; yet not granted to them that give caution of the future time, is sign of an aversion to peace; and therefore contrary to the law of Nature.

A seventh is, *that in revenges,* that is, retribution of evil for evil, *men look not at the greatness of the evil past, but the greatness of the good to follow.* Whereby we are forbidden to inflict punishment with any other design, than for correction of the offender, or direction of others. For this law is consequent to the next before it, that commandeth pardon, upon security of the future time. Besides, revenge, without respect to the example, and profit to come, is a triumph or glorying in the hurt of another, tending to no end; for the end is always somewhat to come; and glorying to no end, is vain-glory, and contrary to reason, and to hurt without reason, tendeth to the introduction of war which is against the law of Nature; and is commonly styled by the name of *cruelty.*

And because all signs of hatred, or contempt, provoke to fight; insomuch as most men choose rather to hazard their life, than not to be revenged; we may in the eighth place, for a law of nature, set down this precept, *that no man by deed, word, countenance,* *or gesture, declare hatred, or contempt of another.* The breach of which law is commonly called *contumely.*

The question who is the better man, has no place in the condition of mere nature; where, as has been shown before, all men are equal. The inequality that now is, has been introduced by the laws civil. I know that Aristotle in the first book of his *Politics,* for a foundation of his doctrine, maketh men by nature, some more worthy to command, meaning the wiser sort, such as he thought himself to be for his philosophy; others to serve, meaning those that had strong bodies, but were not philosophers as he; as if master and servant were not introduced by consent of men, but by difference of wit; which is not only against reason, but also against experience. For there are very few so foolish, that had not rather govern themselves, than be governed by others: nor when the wise in their own conceit, contend by force, with them who distrust their own wisdom, do they always, or often, or almost at any time, get the victory. If Nature therefore have made them equally, that equality is to be acknowledged: or if nature have made men unequal; yet because men that think themselves equal, will not enter into conditions of peace, but upon equal terms, such equality must be admitted. And therefore for the ninth law of Nature, I put this, *that every man acknowledge another for his equal by nature.* The breach of this precept is *pride.*

On this law dependeth another, *that at the entrance into conditions of peace, no man require to reserve to himself any right, which he is not content should be reserved to every one of the rest.* As it is necessary for all men that seek peace, to lay down certain rights of nature; that is to say, not to have liberty to do all they list: so is it necessary for man's life, to retain some, as right to govern their own bodies; enjoy air, water, motion, ways to go from place to place; and all things else, without which a man cannot live, or not live well. If in this case, at the making of peace, men require for themselves that which they would not have to be granted to others, they do contrary to the precedent law, that commandeth the acknowledgment of natural equality, and therefore also against the law of Nature. The observers of this law are those we call *modest*, and the breakers *arrogant* men. The Greeks call the violation of this law πλεονεξία, that is, a desire of more than their share.

Also if a man be trusted to judge between man and man, it is a precept of the law of nature, *that he deal equally between them*. For without that, the controversies of men cannot be determined but by war. He therefore that is partial in judgment, doth what in him lies, to deter men from the use of judges and arbitrators, and consequently against the fundamental law of nature, is the cause of war.

The observance of this law, from the equal distribution to each man, of that which in reason belongeth to him, is called *equity*, and, as I have said before, distributive justice; the violation, *acception of persons*, προσωποληψία.

And from this followeth another law, *that such things as cannot be divided, be enjoyed in common, if it can be; and if the quantity of the thing permit, without stint; otherwise proportionably to the number of them that have right*. For otherwise the distribution is unequal, and contrary to equity.

But some things there be, that can neither be divided, nor enjoyed in common. Then, the law of nature, which prescribeth equity, requireth *that the entire right, or else, making the use alternate, the first possession, be determined by lot*. For equal distribution is of the law of nature, and other means of equal distribution cannot be imagined.

Of *lots* there be two sorts, *arbitrary* and *natural*. Arbitrary is that which is agreed on by the competitors; natural is either *primo-geniture*, which the Greek calls κληρονομία, which signifies, given by lot; or *first seizure*.

And therefore those things which cannot be enjoyed in common, nor divided, ought to be adjudged to the first possessor; and in some cases to the first born, as acquired by lot.

It is also a law of nature, *that all men that mediate peace, be allowed safe conduct*. For the law that commandeth peace, as the *end*, commandeth intercession, as the *means*; and to intercession the means is safe conduct.

And because, though men be never so willing to observe these laws, there may nevertheless arise questions concerning a man's action; first, whether it were done, or not done; secondly, if done, whether against the law, or not against the law; the former whereof is called a question of *fact*, the latter a question of *right*: therefore unless the parties to the question covenant mutually to stand to the sentence of another, they are as far from peace as ever. This other to whose sentence they submit is called an *arbitrator*. And therefore it is of the law of nature, *that they that are at controversy, submit their right to the judgment of an arbitrator*.

And seeing every man is presumed to do all things in order to his own benefit, no man is a fit arbitrator in his own cause; and if he were never so fit, yet equity allowing to each party equal benefit, if one be admitted to be judge, the other is to be admitted also; and so the controversy, that is, the cause of war, remains, against the law of nature.

For the same reason no man in any cause ought to be received for arbitrator, to whom greater profit or honor or pleasure apparently ariseth out of the victory of one party than of the other: for he hath taken, though an unavoidable bribe, yet a bribe; and no man can be obliged to trust him. And thus also the controversy and the condition of war remaineth, contrary to the law of nature.

And in a controversy of *fact*, the judge being to give more credit to one than to the other, if there be no other arguments must give credit to a third, or to a third and fourth, or more: for else the question is undecided, and left to force, contrary to the law of nature.

These are the laws of Nature, dictating peace, for a means of the conservation of men in multitudes; and which only concern the doctrine of civil society. There be other things tending to the destruction of particular men; as drunkenness, and all other parts of intemperance; which may therefore also be reckoned amongst those things which the law of Nature hath forbidden; but are not necessary nor pertinent enough here to be mentioned.

And though this may seem too subtle a deduction of the laws of Nature to be taken notice of by all men; whereof the most part are too busy in getting food, and the rest too negligent to understand; yet to leave all men inexcusable, they have been contracted into one easy sum, intelligible even to the meanest capacity; and that is, *Do not that to another, which thou wouldst not have done to thyself;* which sheweth him, that he has no more to do in learning the laws of nature, but, when weighing the actions of other men with his own, they seem too heavy, to put them into the other part of the balance, and his own into their place, that his own passions, and self-love, may add nothing to the weight; and then there is none of these

laws of Nature that will not appear unto him very reasonable.

The laws of Nature oblige *in foro interno*; that is to say, they bind to a desire they should take place: but *in foro externo*; that is, to the putting them in act, not always. For he that should be modest, and tractable, and perform all he promises, in such time and place where no man else should do so, should but make himself a prey to others, and procure his own certain ruin, contrary to the ground of all laws of Nature, which tend to nature's preservation. And again, he that having sufficient security, that others shall observe the same laws towards him, observes them not himself, seeketh not peace, but war; and consequently the destruction of his nature by violence.

And whatsoever laws bind *in foro interno*, may be broken, not only by a fact contrary to the law, but also by a fact according to it, in case a man think it contrary. For though his action in this case be according to the law, yet his purpose was against the law; which, where the obligation is *in foro interno*, is a breach.

The laws of Nature are immutable and eternal; for injustice, ingratitude, arrogance, pride, iniquity, acception of persons, and the rest, can never be made lawful. For it can never be that war shall preserve life, and peace destroy it.

The same laws, because they oblige only to a desire and endeavour, I mean an unfeigned and constant endeavour, are easy to be observed. For in that they require nothing but endeavour, he that endeavoureth their performance, fulfilleth them; and he that fulfilleth the law, is just.

And the science of them is the true and only moral philosophy. For moral philosophy is nothing else but the science of what is *good*, and *evil*, in the conversation and society of mankind. *Good*, and *evil*, are names that signify our appetites, and aversions; which in different tempers, customs, and doctrines of men, are different: and divers men, differ not only in their judgment, on the senses of what is pleasant, and unpleasant to the taste, smell, hearing, touch, and sight; but also of what is conformable or disagreeable to reason, in the actions of common life. Nay, the same man, in divers times, differs from himself; and one time praiseth, that is, calleth good, what another time he dispraiseth, and calleth evil: from whence arise disputes, controversies, and at last war. And therefore so long as a man is in the condition of mere nature, which is a condition of war, as private appetite is the measure of good and evil: and consequently all men agree on this, that peace is good, and therefore also the way or means of peace, which, as I have shewed before, are *justice, gratitude, modesty, equity, mercy,* and the rest of the laws of Nature, are good; that is to say, *moral virtues;* and their contrary *vices,* evil. Now the science of virtue and vice, is moral philosophy; and therefore the true doctrine of the laws of Nature is the true moral philosophy. But the writers of moral philosophy, though they acknowledge the same virtues and vices; yet not seeing wherein consisted their goodness; nor that they come to be praised, as the means of peaceable, sociable, and comfortable living, place them in a mediocrity of passions: as if not the cause, but the degree of daring, made fortitude; or not the cause, but the quantity of a gift, made liberality.

These dictates of reason, men used to call by the name of laws, but improperly: for they are but conclusions, or theorems concerning what conduceth to the conservation and defence of themselves; whereas law, properly, is the word of him that by right hath command over others. But yet if we consider the same theorems, as delivered in the word of God, that by right commandeth all things; then are they properly called laws.

Joseph Butler (1692—1752)

The *Sermons*, from which the present readings are taken, were first published in 1726 and, if we accept Butler's own account, consist of an accidental selection from the many sermons delivered by him during his eight years as preacher at the Rolls Chapel in London. The life of Butler is unmarked by dramatic events. Bishop of Bristol, Dean of St. Paul's, and, during the last two years of his life, Bishop of Durham, Butler sought earnestly and intelligently to rescue religion from the low state to which it had fallen in his day and to ground morals in a conception of human nature acceptable to reasonable men. In ethics his influence has been of the first importance, particularly in England down to the present day. His refutation of psychological egoism, against which he uttered the famous protest "Everything is what it is, and not another thing," is a lasting achievement to which nothing essential has been added since his time and a monument to the sagacity that characterizes his thinking on morals. Although Butler's most significant work is the *Sermons*, his ethical views are also to be found in his *Analogy* and *The Dissertation of the Nature of Virtue*.

SERMONS [1]

PREFACE

· · ·

There are two ways in which the subject of morals may be treated. One begins from inquiring into the abstract relations of things; the other from matter of fact, namely, what the particular nature of man is, its several parts, their economy or constitution; from whence it proceeds to determine what course of life it is, which is correspondent to this whole nature.

In the former method the conclusion is expressed thus, that vice is contrary to the nature and reason of things; in the latter, that it is a violation or breaking in upon our own nature. Thus they both lead us to the same thing, our obligations to the practice of virtue; and thus they exceedingly strengthen and enforce each other. The first seems the most direct formal proof, and in some respects the least liable to cavil and dispute; the latter is in a peculiar manner adapted to satisfy a fair mind, and is more easily applicable to the several particular relations and circumstances in life.

The following Discourses proceed chiefly in this latter method. The first three wholly. They were intended to

[1] From Joseph Butler's *Fifteen Sermons upon Human Nature*, London, 1726; 2nd ed., 1729.

explain what is meant by the nature of man, when it is said that virtue consists in following, and vice in deviating from it; and by explaining to show that the assertion is true. That the ancient moralists had some inward feeling or other; which they chose to express in this manner, that man is born to virtue, that it consists in the following nature, and that vice is more contrary to this nature than tortures or death, their works in our hands are instances. Now a person who found no mystery in this way of speaking of the ancients; who, without being very explicit with himself, kept to his natural feeling, went along with them, and found within himself a full conviction, that what they laid down was just and true; such an one would probably wonder to see a point, in which he never perceived any difficulty, so laboured as this is, in the second and third Sermons; insomuch perhaps as to be at a loss for the occasion, scope, and drift of them. But it need not be thought strange that this manner of expression, though familiar with them, and, if not usually carried so far, yet not uncommon amongst ourselves, should want explaining; since there are several perceptions daily felt and spoken of, which yet it may not be very easy at first view to explicate, to distinguish from all others, and ascertain exactly what the idea or perception is. The many treatises upon the passions are a proof of this; since so many would never have undertaken to unfold their several complications, and trace and resolve them into their principles, if they had thought, what they were endeavouring to shew was obvious to every one, who felt and talked to those passions. Thus, though there seems no ground to doubt, but that the generality of mankind have the inward perception expressed so commonly in that manner by the ancient moralists, more than to doubt

whether they have those passions; yet it appeared of use to unfold that inward conviction, and lay it open in a more explicit manner, than I had seen done; especially when there were not wanting persons, who manifestly mistook the whole thing, and so had great reason to express themselves dissatisfied with it. A late author of great and deserved reputation says, that to place virtue in following nature, is at best a loose way of talk. And he has reason to say this, if what I think he intends to express, though with great decency, be true, that scarce any other sense can be put upon those words, but acting as any of the several parts, without distinction, of a man's nature happened most to incline him.[2]

Whoever thinks it worth while to consider this matter thoroughly, should begin with stating to himself exactly the idea of a system, economy, or constitution, of any particular nature, or particular anything; and he will, I suppose, find, that it is an one or a whole, made up of several parts; but yet that the several parts, even considered as a whole, do not complete the idea, unless in the notion of a whole you include the relations and respects which those parts have to each other. Every work, both of nature and of art, is a system: and as every particular thing, both natural and artificial, is for some use or purpose out of and beyond itself, one may add to what has been already brought into the idea of a system, its conduciveness to this one or more ends. Let us instance in a watch: Suppose the several parts of it taken to pieces, and placed apart from each other; let a man have ever so exact a notion of these several parts, unless he considers the respect and relations which they have to each other, he will not have

[2] *Rel. of Nature Delin.*, Par. I, art. ix. pp. 22, 23, edit. 1725.

anything like the idea of a watch. Suppose these several parts brought together and any how united: neither will he yet, be the union ever so close, have an idea which will bear any resemblance to that of a watch. But let him view those several parts put together, or consider them as to be put together in the manner of a watch; let him form a notion of the relations which those several parts have to each other—all conducive, in their respective ways, to this purpose, showing the hour of the day; and then he has the idea of a watch. Thus it is with regard to the inward frame of man. Appetites, passions, affections, and the principle of affection, considered merely as the several parts of our inward nature, do not at all give us an idea of the system or constitution of this nature: because the constitution is formed by somewhat not yet taken into consideration, namely, by the relations which these several parts have to each other; the chief of which is the authority of reflection or conscience. It is from considering the relations which the several appetites and passions in the inward frame have to each other, and, above all, the supremacy of reflection or conscience, that we get the idea of the system or constitution of human nature. And from the idea itself it will as fully appear, that this our nature, i. e., constitution, is adapted to virtue, as from the idea of a watch it appears, that its nature, i. e., constitution or system, is adapted to measure time. What in fact or event commonly happens, is nothing to this question. Every work of art is apt to be out of order; but this is so far from being according to its system, that let the disorder increase, and it will totally destroy it. This is merely by way of explanation, what an economy, system, or constitution is. And thus far the cases are perfectly parallel. It we go further, there is indeed a difference, nothing to the present purpose, but too important an one ever to be omitted. A machine is inanimate and passive: but we are agents. Our constitution is put in our power; we are charged with it, and therefore are accountable for any disorder or violation of it.

Thus nothing can possibly be more contrary to nature than vice; meaning by nature not only the *several parts* of our internal frame, but also the *constitution* of it. Misery and injustice are indeed equally contrary to some different parts of our nature taken singly: but injustice is moreover contrary to the whole constitution of the nature.

If it can be asked whether this constitution be really what those philosophers meant, and whether they would have explained themselves in this manner; the answer is the same, as if it should be asked, whether a person, who had often used the word *resentment*, and felt the thing, would have explained this passion exactly in the same manner, in which it is done in one of these Discourses. As I have no doubt, but that this is a true account of that passion, which he referred to and intended to express by the word *resentment;* so I have no doubt, but that this is the true account of the ground of that conviction which they referred to, when they said, vice was contrary to nature. And though it should be thought that they meant no more than that vice was contrary to the higher and better part of our nature; even this implies such a constitution as I have endeavoured to explain. For the very terms, higher and better, imply a relation or respect of parts to each other; and these relative parts, being in one and the same nature, form a constitution, and are the very idea of it. They had a perception that injustice was contrary to their nature, and that pain was so also. They observed these two perceptions totally different, not in degree, but in kind: and the reflecting upon each of them, as they thus stood in their nature, wrought a full intuitive conviction, that more was due and of right belonged to one of these inward perceptions, than to the other; that it demanded in all cases to govern such a creature as man. So that, upon the whole, this is a fair and true account of what was the ground of their conviction; of what they intended to refer to, when they said, virtue consisted in following nature: a manner of speaking not loose and undeterminate, but clear and distinct, strictly just and true.

Though I am persuaded the force of this conviction is felt by almost every one; yet since, considered as an argument and put in words, it appears somewhat abstruse, and since the connexion of it is broken in the three first Sermons, it may not be amiss to give the reader the whole argument here in one view.

Mankind has various instincts and principles of action, as brute creatures have; some leading most directly and immediately to the good of the community, and some more directly to private good.

Man has several which brutes have not; particularly reflection or conscience, an approbation of some principles or actions, and disapprobation of others.

Brutes obey their instincts or principles of action, according to certain rules; suppose the constitution of their body, and the objects around them.

The generality of mankind also obey their instincts and principles, all of them; those propensions we call good, as well as the bad, according to the same rules; namely, the constitution of their body, and the external circumstances which they are in. (Therefore it is not a true representation of mankind to affirm, that they are wholly governed by self-love, the love of power and sensual appetites: since, as on the one hand they are often actuated by these, without any regard to right or wrong; so on the other it is manifest fact, that the same persons, the generality, are frequently influenced by friendship, compassion, gratitude; and even a general abhorrence of what is base, and liking of what is fair and just, takes its turn amongst the other motives of action. This is the partial inadequate notion of human nature treated of in the first Discourse: and it is by this nature, if one may speak so, that the world is in fact influenced, and kept in that tolerable order, in which it is.)

Brutes in acting according to the rules before mentioned, their bodily constitution and circumstances, act suitably to their whole nature. (It is however to be distinctly noted, that the reason why we affirm this is not merely that brutes in fact act so; for this alone, however universal, does not at all determine, whether such course of action be correspondent to their whole nature: but the reason of the assertion is, that as in acting thus they plainly act conformably to somewhat in their nature, so, from all observations we are able to make upon them, there does not appear the least ground to imagine them to have any thing else in their nature, which requires a different rule or course of action.)

Mankind also in acting thus would act suitably to their whole nature, if no more were to be said of man's nature than what has been now said; if that, as it is a true, were also a complete, adequate account of our nature.

But that is not a complete account of man's nature. Somewhat further must be brought in to give us an adequate notion of it; namely, that one of those principles of action, conscience or reflection, compared with the rest as they all stand together in the nature of man, plainly bears upon it marks of authority over all the rest, and claims the absolute direction of them all, to allow or forbid their gratification: a disapprobation of reflection being in itself a principle manifestly superior to a mere propension. And the conclusion is, that to allow no more to this superior principle or part of our nature, than to other parts; to let it govern and guide only occasionally in common with the rest, as its turn happens to come, from the temper and circumstances one happens to be in; this is not to act conformably to the constitution of man: neither can any human creature be said to act conformably to his constitution of nature, unless he allows to that superior principle the absolute authority which is due to it. And this conclusion is abundantly confirmed from hence, that one may determine what course of action the economy of man's nature requires without so much as knowing in what degrees of *strength* the several principles prevail, or which of them have actually the greatest influence.

The practical reason of insisting so much upon this natural authority of the principle of reflection or conscience is, that it seems in great measure overlooked by many, who are by no means the worse sort of men. It is thought sufficient to abstain from gross wickedness, and to be humane and kind to such as happen to come in their way. Whereas in reality the very constitution of our nature requires, that we bring our whole conduct before this superior faculty; wait its determination; enforce upon ourselves its authority, and make it the business of our lives, as it is absolutely the whole business of a moral agent, to conform ourselves to it. This is the true meaning of that ancient precept, *Reverence thyself.*

The not taking into consideration this authority, which is implied in the idea of reflex approbation or disapprobation, seems a material deficiency or omission in Lord Shaftesbury's *Inquiry concerning Virtue.* He has shewn beyond all contradiction, that virtue is naturally the interest or happiness, and vice the misery, of such a creature as man, placed in the circumstances which we are in this world. But suppose there are particular exceptions; a case which this author was unwilling to put, and yet surely it is to be put: or suppose a case which he has put and determined, that of a sceptic not convinced of this happy tendency of virtue, or being of a contrary opinion. His determination is, that it would be *without remedy.*[3] One may say more explicitly, that leaving out the authority of reflex approbation or disapprobation, such an one would be under an obligation to act viciously; since interest, one's own happiness, is a manifest obligation, and there is not supposed to be any other obligation in the case. 'But does it much mend the matter, to take in that natural authority of reflection? There indeed would be an obligation to virtue; but would not the obligation from supposed interest on the side of vice remain?' If it should, yet to be under two contrary obligations, i. e. under none at all, would not be exactly the same, as to be under a formal obligation to be vicious, or to be in circumstances in which the constitution of man's nature plainly required that vice should be preferred. But the obligation on the side of interest really does not remain. For the natural authority of the principle of reflection is an obligation the most near and intimate, the most certain and known: whereas the contrary obligation can at the utmost appear no more than probable; since no man can be *certain* in any circumstances that vice is his interest in the present world,

[3] 'Inquiry,' B.i. part 3, § 3.

much less can he be certain against another: and thus the certain obligation would entirely supersede and destroy the uncertain one; which yet would have been of real force without the former.

In truth, the taking in this consideration totally changes the whole state of the case; and shews, what this author does not seem to have been aware of, that the greatest degree of scepticism which he thought possible will still leave men under the strictest moral obligations, whatever their opinion be concerning the happiness of virtue. For that mankind upon reflection felt an approbation of what was good, and disapprobation of the contrary, he thought a plain matter of fact, as it undoubtedly is, which none could deny, but from mere affectation. Take in then that authority and obligation, which is a constituent part of this reflex approbation, and it will undeniably follow, though a man should doubt of everything else, yet, that he would still remain under the nearest and most certain obligation to the practice of virtue; and obligation implied in the very idea of virtue, in the very idea of reflex approbation.

And how little influence soever this obligation alone can be expected to have in fact upon mankind, yet one may appeal even to interest and self-love, and ask, since from man's nature, condition, and the shortness of life, so little, so very little indeed, can possibly in any case be gained by vice; whether it be so prodigious a thing to sacrifice that little to the most intimate of all obligations; and which a man cannot transgress without being self-condemned, and, unless he has corrupted his nature, without real self-dislike: this question, I say, may be asked, even upon supposition that the prospect of a future life were ever so uncertain.

The observation, that man is thus by his very nature a law to himself, pursued to its just consequences, is of the utmost importance; because from it will follow, that though men should, through stupidity or speculative scepticism, be ignorant of, or disbelieve, any authority in the universe to punish the violation of this law; yet, if there should be such authority, they would be as really liable to punishment, as though they had been beforehand convinced, that such punishment would follow. For in whatever sense we understand justice, even supposing, what I think would be very presumptuous to assert, that the end of divine punishment is no other than that of civil punishment, namely, to prevent future mischief; upon this bold supposition, ignorance or disbelief of the sanction would by no means exempt even from this justice: because it is not foreknowledge of the punishment which renders us obnoxious to it; but merely violating a known obligation.

And here it comes in one's way to take notice of a manifest error or mistake in the author now cited, unless perhaps he has incautiously expressed himself so as to be misunderstood: namely, that *it is malice only and not goodness, which can make us afraid.* Whereas in reality, goodness is the natural and just object of the greatest fear to an ill man. Malice may be appeased or satiated; humour may change, but goodness is a fixed, steady, immovable principle of action. If either of the former holds the sword of justice, there is plainly ground for the greatest of crimes to hope for impunity: but if it be goodness, there can be no possible hope, whilst the reasons of things, or the ends of government, call for punishment. Thus every one sees how much greater chance of impunity an ill man has in a partial administration, than in a just and upright one. It is said, that *the interest or good of the whole must be the interest of the universal Being, and that he can have no other.* Be it so. This author has proved, that vice is naturally the misery of mankind in this world. Consequently it was for the good of the whole that it should be so. What shadow of reason then is there to assert, that this may not be the case hereafter? Danger of future punishment (and if there be danger, there is ground of fear) no more supposes malice, than the present feeling of punishment does.

. . .

The chief design of the eleventh Discourse is to state the notion of self-love and disinterestedness, in order to shew that benevolence is not more unfriendly to self-love, than any other particular affection whatever. There is a strange affectation in many people of explaining away all particular affections, and representing the whole of life as nothing but one continued exercise of self-love. Hence arises that surprising confusion and perplexity in the Epicureans [4] of old, Hobbes, the author of *Reflexions, Sentences, et Maximes Morales,* and this whole set of writers; the confusion of calling actions interested which are done in con-

[4] One need only look into Torquatus's account of the Epicurean system, in Cicero's first book *De Finibus,* to see in what a surprising manner this was done by them. Thus the desire of praise, and of being beloved, he explains to be no other than desire of safety: regard to our country, even in the most virtuous character, to be nothing but regard to ourselves. The author of *Reflexions & Morales,* says, Curiosity proceeds from interest or pride; which pride also would doubtless have been explained to be self-love. Page 85, ed. 1725. As if there were no such passions in mankind as desire of esteem, or of being beloved, or of knowledge. Hobbes's account of the affections of good-will and pity are instances of the same kind.

tradiction to the most manifest known interest, merely for the gratification of a present passion. Now all this confusion might easily be avoided, by stating to ourselves wherein the idea of self-love in general consists, as distinguished from all particular movements towards particular external objects; the appetites of sense, resentment, compassion, curiosity, ambition, and the rest. When this is done, if the words *selfish* and *interested* cannot be parted with, but must be applied to every thing; yet, to avoid such total confusion of all language, let the distinction be made by epithets: and the first may be called cool or settled selfishness, and the other passionate or sensual selfishness. But the most natural way of speaking plainly is, to call the first only, self-love, and the actions proceeding from it, interested: and to say of the latter, that they are love to ourselves, but movements towards somewhat external: honour, power, the harm or good of another: and that the pursuit of these external objects, so far as it proceeds from these movements, (for it may proceed from self-love,) is no otherwise interested, than as every action of every creature must, from the nature of the thing, be; for no one can act but from a desire, or choice, or preference of his own.

Self-love and any particular passion may be joined together; and from this complication, it becomes impossible in numberless instances to determine precisely, how far an action, perhaps even of one's own, has for its principle general self-love, or some particular passion. But this need create no confusion in the ideas themselves of self-love and particular passions. We distinctly discern what one is, and what the other are: though we may be uncertain how far one or the other influences us. And though, from this uncertainty, it cannot but be that there will be different opinions concerning mankind, as more or less governed by interest; and some will ascribe actions to self-love, which others will ascribe to particular passions: yet it is absurd to say that mankind are wholly actuated by either; since it is manifest that both have their influence. For as, on the one hand, men form a general notion of interest, some placing it in one thing, and some in another, and have a considerable regard to it throughout the course of their life, which is owing to self-love; so, on the other hand, they are often set on work by the particular passions themselves, and a considerable part of life is spent in the actual gratification of them, i. e. is employed, not by self-love, but by the passions.

Besides, the very idea of an interested pursuit necessarily presupposes particular passions or appetites; since the very idea of interest or happiness consists in this, that an appetite or affection enjoys its object. It is not because we love ourselves that we find delight in such and such objects, but because we have particular affections towards them. Take away these affections, and you leave self-love absolutely nothing at all to employ itself about; no end or object for it to pursue, excepting only that of avoiding pain. Indeed the Epicureans, who maintained that absence of pain was the highest happiness, might, consistently with themselves, deny all affection, and, if they had so pleased, every sensual appetite too; but the very idea of interest or happiness other than absence of pain implies particular appetites or passions; these being necessary to constitute that interest or happiness.

The observation, that benevolence is no more disinterested than any of the common particular passions, seems in itself worth being taken notice of; but is insisted upon to obviate that scorn, which one sees rising upon the faces of people who are said to know the world, when mention is made of a disinterested, generous, or public-spirited action. The truth of that observation might be made appear in a more formal manner of proof: for whoever will consider all the possible respects and relations which any particular affection can have to self-love and private interest, will, I think, see demonstrably, that benevolence is not in any respect more at variance with self-love, than any other particular affection whatever, but that it is in every respect, as friendly to it.

If the observation be true, it follows, that self-love and benevolence, virtue and interest, are not to be opposed, but only to be distinguished from each other; in the same way as virtue and any other particular affection, love of arts, suppose, are to be distinguished. Every thing is what it is, and not another thing. The goodness or badness of actions does not arise from hence, that the epithet, interested or disinterested, may be applied to them, any more than that any other indifferent epithet, suppose inquisitive or jealous, may or may not be applied to them; not from their being attended with present or future pleasure or pain; but from their being what they are; namely, what becomes such creatures as we are, what the state of the case requires, or the contrary. Or in other words, we may judge and determine, that an action is morally good or evil, before we so much as consider, whether it be interested or disinterested. This consideration no more comes in to determine whether an action be virtuous, than to determine whether it be resentful. Self-love in its due degree is as just and morally good, as any affection whatever. Benevolence towards particular persons may be to a degree of weakness, and so be blamable: and disinterestedness is so far from being in itself commendable, that the utmost possible depravity which we can in imagination conceive, is that of disinterested cruelty.

Neither does there appear any reason to wish self-love were weaker in the generality of the world than it is. The influence which it has seems plainly owing to its being constant and habitual, which it cannot but be, and not to the degree or strength of it. Every caprice of the imagination, every curiosity of the understanding, every affection of the heart, is perpetually shewing its weakness, by prevailing over it. Men daily, hourly sacrifice the greatest known interest, to fancy, inquisitiveness, love, or hatred, any vagrant inclination. The thing to be lamented is, not that men have so great regard to their own good or interest in the present world, for they have not enough; but that they have so little to the good of others. And this seems plainly owing to their being so much engaged in the gratification of particular passions unfriendly to benevolence, and which happen to be most prevalent in them, much more than to self-love. As a proof of this may be observed, that there is no character more void of friendship, gratitude, natural affection, love to their country, common justice, or more equally and uniformly hard-hearted, than the *abandoned* in, what is called, the *way* of pleasure — hard-hearted and totally without feeling in behalf of others; except when they cannot escape the sight of distress, and so are interrupted by it in their pleasures. And yet it is ridiculous to call such an abandoned course of pleasure interested, when the person engaged in it knows before hand, and goes on under the feeling and apprehension, that it will be as ruinous to himself, as to those who depend upon him.

Upon the whole, if the generality of mankind were to cultivate within themselves the principle of self-love; if they were to accustom themselves often to set down and consider, what was the greatest happiness they were capable of attaining for themselves in this life, and if self-love were so strong and prevalent, as that they would uniformly pursue this their supposed chief temporal good, without being diverted from it by any particular passion; it would manifestly prevent numberless follies and vices. This was in a great measure the Epicurean system of philosophy. It is indeed by no means the religious or even moral institution of life. Yet, with all the mistakes men would fall into about interest, it would be less mischievous than the extravagances of mere appetite, will, and pleasure: for certainly self-love, though confined to the interest of this life, is, of the two, a much better guide than passion, which has absolutely no bound or measure, but what is set to it by this self-love, or moral considerations.

From the distinction above made between self-love, and the several particular principles or affections in our nature, we may see how good ground there was for that assertion, maintained by the several ancient schools of philosophy against the Epicureans, namely, that virtue is to be pursued as an end, eligible in and for itself. For, if there be any principles or affections in the mind of man distinct from self-love, that the things those principles tend towards, or that the objects of those affections are, each of them, in themselves eligible, to be pursued upon its own account, and to be rested in as an end, is implied in the very idea of such principle or affection. They indeed asserted much higher things of virtue, and with very good reason; but to say thus much of it, that it is to be pursued for itself, is to say no more of it, than may truly be said of the object of every natural affection whatever.

The question, which was a few years ago disputed in France concerning *the love of God,* which was there called enthusiasm, as it will everywhere by the generality of the world; this question, I say, answers in religion to that old one in morals now mentioned. And both of them are, I think, fully determined by the same observation, namely, that the very nature of affection, the idea itself, necessarily implies resting in its object as an end.

. . .

SERMON I

UPON THE SOCIAL NATURE OF MAN

For as we have many members in one body, and all members have not the same office: so we being many are one body in Christ, and every one members one of another.—ROM. xii. 4, 5.

. . .

The relation which the several parts or members of the natural body have to each other and to the whole body, is here compared to the relation which each particular person in society has to other particular persons and to the whole society; and the latter is intended to be illustrated by the former. And if there be a likeness between these two relations, the consequence is obvious: that the latter shows us we were intended to do good to others, as the former shows us that the several members of the natural body were intended to be instruments of good to each other and to the whole body. But as there is scarce any ground for a comparison between society and the mere material body, this without the mind being a dead unactive thing; much less can the comparison be carried to any length. And since the apostle speaks of the several members as having distinct offices, which im-

plies the mind; it cannot be thought an unallowable liberty; instead of the *body* and *its members,* to substitute the *whole nature of man,* and *all the variety of internal principles which belong to it.* And then the comparison will be between the nature of man as respecting self, and tending to private good, his own preservation and happiness; and the nature of man as having respect to society, and tending to promote public good, the happiness of that society. These ends do indeed perfectly coincide; and to aim at public and private good are so far from being inconsistent, that they mutually promote each other: yet in the following discourse they must be considered as entirely distinct; otherwise the nature of man as tending to one, or as tending to the other cannot be compared. There can no comparison be made, without considering the things compared as distinct and different.

From this review and comparison of the nature of man as respecting self, and as respecting society, it will plainly appear, that *there are as real and the same kind of indications in human nature, that we were made for society and to do good to our fellow-creatures, as that we were intended to take care of our own life and health and private good: and that the same objections lie against one of these assertions, as against the other.* For,

First, There is a natural principle of *benevolence* [5] in man; which is in

[5] Suppose a man of learning to be writing a grave book upon human nature, and to show in several parts of it that he had an insight into the subject he was considering; amongst other things, the following one would require to be accounted for: the appearance of benevolence or good-will in men towards each other in the instances of natural relation, and in others. (Hobbes, *On Human Nature,* c. ix. § 17.) Cautious of being deceived with outward show, he retires within himself, to see exactly what that is

some degree to *society*, what *self-love* is to the *individual*. And if there be in mankind any disposition to friendship; if there be any such thing as compassion, for compassion is momentary love; if there be any such thing as the paternal or filial affections; if there be any affection in human nature, the object and end of which is the good of another, this is itself benevolence, or the love of another. Be it ever so short, be it in ever so low a degree, or ever so unhappily confined; it proves the assertion, and

in the mind of man from whence this appearance proceeds; and, upon deep reflection, asserts the principle in the mind to be only the love of power, and delight in the exercise of it. Would not everybody think here was a mistake of one word for another? That the philosopher was contemplating and accounting for some other human actions, some other behaviour of man to man? And could any one be thoroughly satisfied, that what is commonly called benevolence or good-will was really the affection meant, but only by being made to understand that this learned person had a general hypothesis, to which the appearance of good-will could no otherwise be reconciled? That what has this appearance, is often nothing but ambition; that delight in superiority often (suppose always) mixes itself with benevolence, only makes it more specious to call it ambition than hunger, of the two: but in reality that passion does no more account for the whole appearance of good-will than this appetite does. Is there not often the appearance of one man's wishing that good to another, which he knows himself unable to procure him; and rejoicing in it, though bestowed by a third person? And can love of power any way possibly come in to account for this desire or delight? Is there not often the appearance of men's distinguishing between two or more persons, preferring one before another, to do good to, in cases where love of power cannot in the least account for the distinction and preference? For this principle can no otherwise distinguish between objects, than as it is a greater instance and exertion of power to do good to one rather than to another. Again, suppose good-will in the mind of man to be nothing but delight in the exercise of power; men might indeed be restrained by distant and accidental considerations; but these restraints being removed, they would have a disposition to, and delight in mischief, as an exercise and proof of power: And this disposition and delight would arise from, or be the same principle in the mind, as a disposition to, and delight in charity. Thus cruelty, as distinct from envy and resentment, would be exactly the same in the mind of man as good-will: That one tends to the happiness, the other to the misery of our fellow creatures, is, it seems, merely an accidental circumstance, which the mind has not the least regard to. These are the absurdities which even men of capacity run into, when they have occasion to belie their nature, and will perversely disclaim that image of God which was originally stamped upon it; the traces of which, however faint, are plainly discernible upon the mind of man.

If any person can in earnest doubt, whether there be such a thing as good-will in one man towards another, (for the question is not concerning either the degree or extensiveness of it, but concerning the affection itself), let it be observed, that *whether man be thus or otherwise constituted, what is the inward frame in this particular*, is a mere question of fact or natural history, not provable immediately by reason. It is therefore to be judged of and determined in the same way other facts or matters of natural history are: By appealing to the external senses, or inward perceptions, respectively, as the matter under consideration is cognizable by one or the other: By arguing from acknowledged facts and actions; for a great number of actions of the same kind in different circumstances, and respecting different objects, will prove, to certainty, what principles they do not, and, to the greatest probability, what principles they do proceed from: And, lastly, by the testimony of mankind. Now, that there is some degree of benevolence amongst points out what we were designed for, as really as though it were in a higher degree and more extensive. I must, however, remind you that though benevolence and self-love are different; though the former tends most directly to public good, and the latter to private: yet they are so perfectly coincident that the greatest satisfactions to ourselves depend upon our having benevolence in a due degree; and that self-love is one chief security of our right behaviour towards society. It may be added, that their mutual coinciding, so that we can scarce promote one without the other, is equally a proof that we were made for both.

Secondly, This will further appear, from observing that the *several passions* and *affections,* which are distinct,[6] both from benevolence and self-love, do in general contribute and lead us to *public* good as really as to *private.* It might be thought too minute and particular, and would carry us too great a length, to distinguish between and compare together the several passions or appetites distinct from benevolence, whose primary use and intention is the security and good of

---

men, may be as strongly and plainly proved in all these ways as it could possibly be proved, supposing there was this affection in our nature. And should any one think fit to assert, that resentment in the mind of man was absolutely nothing but reasonable concern for our own safety, the falsity of this, and what is the real nature of that passion, could be shown in no other ways than those in which it may be shown, that there is such a thing, in *some degree,* as *real* good-will in man towards man. It is sufficient that the seeds of it be implanted in our nature by God. There is, it is owned, much left for us to do upon our own heart and temper; to cultivate, to improve, to call it forth, to exercise it in a steady uniform manner. This is our work: this is Virtue and Religion.

[6] Everybody makes a distinction between self-love, and the several particular passions, appetites, and affections; and yet they are often confounded again. That they are totally different, will be seen by any one who will distinguish between the passions and appetites *themselves* and *endeavoring* after the means of their gratification. Consider the appetite of hunger, and the desire of esteem; these being the occasion both of pleasure and pain, the coolest *self-love,* as well as the appetites and passions themselves, may put us upon making use of the *proper methods of obtaining* that pleasure, and avoiding that pain; but the *feelings themselves,* the pain of hunger and shame, and the delight from esteem,

are no more self-love than they are anything in the world. Though a man hated himself, he would as much feel the pain of hunger as he would that of the gout; and it is plainly supposable, there may be creatures with self-love in them to the highest degree who may be quite insensible and indifferent (as men in some cases are), to the contempt and esteem of those upon whom their happiness depends not in some further respects depend. And as self-love and the several particular passions and appetites are in themselves totally different, so that some actions proceed from one and some from the other, will be manifest to any who will observe the two following very supposable cases:—One man rushes upon certain ruin for the gratification of a present desire; nobody will call the principle of this action self-love. Suppose another man to go through some laborious work, upon promise of a great reward, without any distinct knowledge what the reward would be; this course of action cannot be ascribed to any particular passion. The former of these actions is plainly to be imputed to some particular passion or affection, the latter as plainly to the general affection or principle of self-love. That there are some particular pursuits or actions concerning which we cannot determine how far they are owing to one, and how far to the other, proceeds from this, that the two principles are frequently mixed together, and run into each other. The distinction is further explained in the eleventh sermon.

society; and the passions distinct from self-love, whose primary intention and design is the security and good of the individual.[7] It is enough to the present argument, that desire of esteem from others, contempt and esteem of them, love of society as distinct from affection to the good of it, indignation against successful vice, that these are public affections or passions; have an immediate respect to others, naturally lead us to regulate our behaviour in such a manner as will be of service to our fellow-creatures. If any or all of these may be considered likewise as private affections, as tending to private good; this does not hinder them from being public affections too, or destroy the good influence of them upon society, and their tendency to public good. It may be added, that as persons without any conviction from reason of the desirableness of life, would yet of course preserve it merely from the appetite of hunger; so by acting merely from regard (suppose) to reputation, without any consideration of the good of others, men often contribute to public good. In both these instances they are plainly

[7] If any desire to see this distinction and comparison made in a particular instance, the appetite and passion now mentioned may serve for one. Hunger is to be considered as a private appetite; because the end for which it was given us is the preservation of the individual. Desire of esteem is a public passion; because the end for which it was given us is to regulate our behaviour towards society. The respect which this has to private good is as remote as the respect that it has to public good; and the appetite is no more self-love, than the passion is benevolence. The object and end of the former is merely food; the object and end of the latter is merely esteem: but the latter can no more be gratified, without contributing to the good of society, than the former can be gratified, without contributing to the preservation of the individual.

instruments in the hands of another, in the hands of Providence, to carry on ends, the preservation of the individual and good of society, which they themselves have not in their view or intention. The sum is, men have various appetites, passions, and particular affections, quite distinct both from self-love and from benevolence: all of these have a tendency to promote both public and private good, and may be considered as respecting others and ourselves equally and in common: but some of them seem most immediately to respect others, or tend to public good; others of them most immediately to respect self, or tend to private good: as the former are not benevolence, so the latter are not self-love: neither sort are instances of our love either to ourselves or others; but only instances of our Maker's care and love both of the individual and the species, and proofs that he intended we should be instruments of good to each other, as well as that we should be so to ourselves.

Thirdly, There is a principle of reflection in men, by which they distinguish between, approve, and disapprove their own actions. We are plainly constituted such sort of creatures as to reflect upon our own nature. The mind can take a view of what passes within itself, its propensions, aversions, passions, affections, as respecting such objects, and in such degrees; and of the several actions consequent thereupon. In this survey it approves of one, disapproves of another, and towards a third is affected in neither of these ways, but is quite indifferent. This principle in man, by which he approves or disapproves his heart, temper, and actions, is conscience; for this is the strict sense of the word, though sometimes it is used so as to take in more. And that this faculty tends to restrain men from doing mischief to each other, and leads them to do good, is too manifest to need being insisted upon. Thus a parent has the affection of love to his children: this leads him to take care of, to educate, to make due provision for them: the natural affection leads to this; but the reflection that it is his proper business, what belongs to him, that it is right and commendable so to do, this added to the affection becomes a much more settled principle, and carries him on through more labour and difficulties for the sake of his children, then he would undergo from that affection alone, if he thought it, and the course of action it led to, either indifferent or criminal. This indeed is impossible, to do that which is good and not to approve of it; for which reason they are frequently not considered as distinct, though they really are; for men often approve of the actions of others, which they will not imitate, and likewise do that which they approve not. It cannot possibly be denied that there is this principle of reflection or conscience in human nature. Suppose a man to relieve an innocent person in great distress; suppose the same man afterwards, in the fury of anger, to do the greatest mischief to a person who had given no just cause of offence; to aggravate the injury, add the circumstances of former friendship, and obligation from the injured person; let the man who is supposed to have done these two different actions, coolly reflect upon them afterwards, without regard to their consequences to himself: to assert that any common man would be affected in the same way towards these different actions, that he would make no distinction between them, but approve or disapprove them equally, is too glaring a falsity to need being confuted. There is therefore this principle of reflection or conscience in mankind. It is needless to compare the respect it has to private good, with the respect it has to public; since it plainly tends as much to the latter as to the former, and is commonly thought to tend chiefly to the latter. This faculty is now mentioned merely as another part in the inward frame of man, pointing out to us in some degree what we are intended for, and as what will naturally and of course have some influence. The particular place assigned to it by nature, what authority it has, and how great influence it ought to have, shall be hereafter considered.

From this comparison of benevolence and self-love, of our public and private affections, of the courses of life they lead to, and of the principle of reflection or conscience as respecting each of them, it is as manifest, that *we were made for society, and to promote the happiness of it, as that we were intended to take care of our own life, and health, and private good.*

And from this whole review must be given a different draught of human nature from what we are often presented with. Mankind are by nature so closely united, there is such a correspondence between the inward sensations of one man and those of another, that disgrace is as much avoided as bodily pain, and to be the object of esteem and love as much desired as any external goods: and in many particular cases persons are carried on to do good to others, as the end their affection tends to and rests in; and manifest that they find real satisfaction and enjoyment in this course of behaviour. There is such a natural principle of attraction in man towards man, that having trod the same tract of land, having breathed in the same climate, barely having been born in the same artificial district or division, becomes the occasion of contracting acquaintances and familiarities many years after: for anything may serve the purpose. Thus relations merely nominal are sought and invented, not by governors, but by the lowest of the people, which are found sufficient to hold mankind together in little fraternities and copartnerships; weak ties indeed, and what may afford fund enough for ridicule, if they are absurdly considered as the real principles of that union; but they are in truth merely the occasions, as anything may be of anything upon which our nature carries us on according to its own previous bent and bias; which occasions therefore would be nothing at all, were there not this prior disposition and bias of nature. Men are so much one body, that in a peculiar manner they feel for each other shame, sudden danger, resentment, honour, prosperity, distress; one or another, or all of these, from the social nature in general, from benevolence, upon the occasion of natural relation, acquaintance, protection, dependence; each of these being distinct cements of society. And therefore to have no restraint from, no regard to others in our behaviour, is the speculative absurdity of considering ourselves as single and independent, as having nothing in our nature which has respect to our fellow-creatures, reduced to action and practice. And this is the same absurdity, as to suppose a hand, or any part to have no natural respect to any other, or to the whole body.

But allowing all this, it may be asked, "Has not man dispositions and principles within, which lead him to do evil to others, as well as to do good? Whence come the many miseries else, which men are the authors and instruments of to each other?" These questions, so far as they relate to the foregoing discourse, may be answered by asking, Has not man also dispositions and principles within, which lead him to do evil to himself, as well as good? Whence come the many miseries else, sickness, pain, and death, which men are instruments and authors of to themselves?

It may be thought more easy to answer one of these questions than the other, but the answer to both is really the same; that mankind have ungoverned passions which they will gratify at any rate, as well to the injury of others, as in contradiction to known private interest; but that as there is no such thing as self-hatred, so neither is there any such thing as ill-will in one man towards another, emulation and resentment being away, whereas there is plainly benevolence or good-will; there is no such thing as love of injustice, oppression, treachery, ingratitude, but only eager desires after such and such external goods; which, according to a very ancient observation, the most abandoned would choose to obtain by innocent means, if they were as easy, and as effectual to their end; that even emulation and resentment, by any one who will consider what these passions really are in nature,[8] will be found nothing to the purpose of this objection: and that the principles and passions in the mind of man, which are distinct both from self-

[8] Emulation is merely the desire and hope of equality with, or superiority over others, with whom we compare ourselves. There does not appear to be any *other* grief in the natural passion, but only *that want* which is implied in desire. However, this may be so strong as to be the occasion of great *grief*. To desire the attainment of this equality, or superiority, by the *particular means* of others being brought down to our own level, or below it, is, I think, the distinct notion of envy. From whence it is easy to see, that the real end which the natural passion, emulation, and which the unlawful one, envy, aims at, is exactly the same; namely, that equality or superiority; and, consequently, that to do mischief is not the end of envy, but merely the means it makes use of to attain its end. As to resentment, see the eighth sermon.

love and benevolence, primarily and most directly lead to right behaviour with regard to others as well as himself, and only secondarily and accidentally to what is evil. Thus though men, to avoid the shame of one villainy, are sometimes guilty of a greater, yet it is easy to see, that the original tendency of shame is to prevent the doing of shameful actions; and its leading men to conceal such actions when done, is only in consequence of their being done; *i. e.* of the passion's not having answered its first end.

If it be said, that there are persons in the world, who are in great measure without the natural affections towards their fellow-creatures: there are likewise instances of persons without the common natural affections to themselves: but the nature of man is not to be judged of by either of these, but by what appears in the common world, in the bulk of mankind.

I am afraid it would be thought very strange, if to confirm the truth of this account of human nature, and make out the justness of the foregoing comparison, it should be added, that, from what appears, men in fact as much and as often contradict that *part* of their nature which respects *self*, and which leads them to their *own private* good and happiness, as they contradict that *part* of it which respects *society*, and tends to *public* good, that there are as few persons, who attain the greatest satisfaction and enjoyment which they might attain in the present world; as who do the greatest good to others which they might do; nay, that there are as few who can be said really and in earnest to aim at one, as at the other. Take a survey of mankind: the world in general, the good and bad, almost without exception, equally are agreed, that were religion out of the case, the happiness of the present life would consist in a manner wholly in riches, honours, sexual gratifications; insomuch that one scarce hears a reflection made upon prudence, life, conduct, but upon this supposition. Yet on the contrary, that persons in the greatest affluence of fortune are no happier than such as have only a competency; that the cares and disappointments of ambition for the most part far exceed the satisfactions of it; as also the miserable intervals of intemperance and excess, and the many untimely deaths occasioned by a dissolute course of life: these things are all seen, acknowledged, by every one acknowledged; but are thought no objections against, though they expressly contradict, this universal principle, that the happiness of the present life consists in one or other of them. Whence is all this absurdity and contradiction? Is not the middle way obvious? Can any thing be more manifest, than that the happiness of life consists in these possessed and enjoyed only to a certain degree; that to pursue them beyond this degree, is always attended with more inconvenience than advantage to a man's self, and often with extreme misery and unhappiness? Whence then, I say, is all this absurdity and contradiction? Is it really the result of consideration in mankind, how they may become most easy to themselves, most free from care, and enjoy the chief happiness attainable in this world? Or is it not manifestly owing either to this, that they have not cool and reasonable concern enough for themselves to consider wherein their chief happiness in the present life consists; or else, if they do consider it, that they will not act conformably to what is the result of that consideration: *i. e.* reasonable concern for themselves, or cool self-love is prevailed over by passion and appetite. So that from what appears, there is no ground to assert that those principles in the nature of man, which most directly lead to promote the good of our fellow-creatures, are more generally or in a greater degree violated, than those, which most directly lead us to promote our own private good and happiness.

The sum of the whole is plainly this. The nature of man considered in his single capacity, and with respect only to the present world, is adapted and leads him to attain the greatest happiness he can for himself in the present world. The nature of man considered in his public or social capacity leads him to a right behaviour in society, to that course of life which we call virtue. Men follow or obey their nature in both these capacities and respects to a certain degree but not entirely: their actions do not come up to the whole of what their nature leads them to in either of these capacities or respects: and they often violate their nature in both, i. e. as they neglect the duties they owe to their fellow-creatures, to which their nature leads them; and are injurious, to which their nature is abhorrent; so there is a manifest negligence in men of their real happiness or interest in the present world, when that interest is inconsistent with a present gratification; for the sake of which they negligently, nay, even knowingly, are the authors and instruments of their own misery and ruin. Thus they are as often unjust to themselves as to others, and for the most part are equally so to both by the same actions.

SERMON II, III

UPON THE NATURAL SUPREMACY
OF CONSCIENCE

For when the Gentiles, which have not the law, do by nature the things contained in the law, these, having not the law, are a law unto themselves.—ROM. ii. 14.

As speculative truth admits of different kinds of proof, so likewise moral obligations may be shown by different methods. If the real nature of any creature leads him and is adapted to such and such purposes only, or more than to any other; this is a reason to believe the author of that nature intended it for those purposes. Thus there is no doubt the eye was intended for us to see with. And the more complex any constitution is, and the greater variety of parts there are which thus tend to some one end, the stronger is the proof that such end was designed. However, when the inward frame of man is considered as any guide in morals, the utmost caution must be used that none make peculiarities in their own temper, or any thing which is the effect of particular customs, though observable in several, the standard of what is common to the species, and above all, that the highest principle be not forgot or excluded, that to which belongs the adjustment and correction of all other inward movements and affections: which principle will of course have some influence, but which being in nature supreme, as shall now be shown, ought to preside over and govern all the rest. The difficulty of rightly observing the two former cautions; the appearance there is of some small diversity amongst mankind with respect to this faculty, with respect to their natural sense of moral good and evil; and the attention necessary to survey with any exactness what passes within, have occasioned that it is not so much agreed what is the standard of the internal nature of man, as of his external form. Neither is this last exactly settled. Yet we understand one another when we speak of the shape of a human body; so likewise we do when we speak of the heart and inward principles, how far soever the standard is from being exact or precisely fixed. There is therefore ground for an attempt of showing men to themselves, of showing them what course of life and behaviour their real nature points out and would lead them to. Now obligations of virtue shown, and motives to the practice of it enforced, from a review of the nature of man, are to be considered as an appeal to each particular person's heart and natural conscience; as the external senses are appealed to for the proof of things cognizable by them. Since then our inward feelings, and the perceptions we receive from our external senses, are equally real; to argue from the former to life and conduct is as little liable to exception, as to argue from the latter to absolutely speculative truth. A man can as little doubt whether his eyes were given him to see with, as he can doubt of the truth of the science of *optics,* deduced from ocular experiments. And allowing the inward feeling, shame; a man can as little doubt whether it was given him to prevent his doing shameful actions, as he can doubt whether his eyes were given him to guide his steps. And as to these inward feelings themselves; that they are real, that man has in his nature passions and affections, can no more be questioned, than that he has external senses. Neither can the former be wholly mistaken; though to a certain degree liable to greater mistakes than the latter.

There can be no doubt but that several propensions or instincts, several principles in the heart of man, carry him to society, and to contribute to the happiness of it, in a sense and a manner in which no inward principle leads him to evil. These principles, propensions, or instincts which lead him to do good, are approved of by a certain faculty within, quite distinct from

these propensions themselves. All this hath been fully made out in the foregoing discourse.

But it may be said, "What is all this, though true, to the purpose of virtue and religion? these require, not only that we do good to others when we are led this way, by benevolence or reflection, happening to be stronger than other principles, passions, or appetites; but likewise that the *whole* character be formed upon thought and reflection; that *every* action be directed by some determinate rule, some other rule than the strength and prevalency of any principle or passion. What sign is there in our nature (for the inquiry is only about what is to be collected from thence) that this was intended by its Author? Or how does so various and fickle a temper as that of man appear adapted thereto? It may indeed be absurd and unnatural for men to act without any reflection; nay, without regard to that particular kind of reflection which you call conscience; because this does belong to our nature. For as there never was a man but who approved one place, prospect, building, before another, so it does not appear that there ever was a man who would not have approved an action of humanity rather than of cruelty; interest and passion being quite out of the case. But interest and passion do come in, and are often too strong for and prevail over reflection and conscience. Now as brutes have various instincts, by which they are carried on to the end the Author of their nature intended them for: is not man in the same condition; with this difference only, that to his instincts (*i.e.* appetites and passions) is added the principle of reflection or conscience? And as brutes act agreeably to their nature, in following that principle or particular instinct which for the present is strongest in them; does not man likewise act agreeably to his nature, or obey the law of his creation, by following that principle, be it passion or conscience, which for the present happens to be strongest in him? Thus different men are by their particular nature hurried on to pursue honour or riches or pleasure: there are also persons whose temper leads them in an uncommon degree to kindness, compassion, doing good to their fellow-creatures: as there are others who are given to suspend their judgment, to weigh and consider things, and to act upon thought and reflection. Let every one then quietly follow his nature; as passion, reflection, appetite, the several parts of it, happen to be strongest: but let not the man of virtue taken upon him to blame the ambitious, the covetous, the dissolute; since these equally with him obey and follow their nature. Thus, as in some cases we follow our nature in doing the works *contained in the law,* so in other cases we follow nature in doing contrary."

Now all this licentious talk entirely goes upon a supposition, that men follow their nature in the same sense, in violating the known rules of justice and honesty for the sake of a present gratification, as they do in following those rules when they have no temptation to the contrary. And if this were true, that could not be so which St. Paul asserts, that men are *by nature a law to themselves.* If by following nature were meant only acting as we please, it would indeed be ridiculous to speak of nature as any guide in morals: nay the very mention of deviating from nature would be absurd; and the mention of following it, when spoken by way of distinction, would absolutely have no meaning. For did ever any one act otherwise than as he pleased? And yet the ancients speak of deviating from nature as vice; and of following nature so much as a distinction, that according to them the

perfection of virtue consists therein. So that language itself should teach people another sense to the words *following nature,* than barely acting as we please. Let it however be observed, that though the words *human nature* are to be explained, yet the real question of this discourse is not concerning the meaning of words, any other than as the explanation of them may be needful to make out and explain the assertion, that *every man is naturally a law to himself,* that *every one may find within himself the rule of right, and obligations to follow it.* This St. Paul affirms in the words of the text, and this the foregoing objection really denies by seeming to allow it. And the objection will be fully answered, and the text before us explained, by observing that *nature* is considered in different views, and the word used in different senses; and by showing in what view it is considered, and in what sense the word is used, when intended to express and signify that which is the guide of life, that by which men are a law to themselves. I say, the explanation of the term will be sufficient, because from thence it will appear, that in some senses of the word *nature* cannot be, but that in another sense it manifestly is, a law to us.

I. By nature is often meant no more than some principle in man, without regard either to the kind or degree of it. Thus the passion of anger, and the affection of parents to their children, would be called equally *natural.* And as the same person hath often contrary principles, which at the same time draw contrary ways, he may by the same action both follow and contradict his nature in this sense of the word; he may follow one passion and contradict another.

II. *Nature* is frequently spoken of as consisting in those passions which are strongest, and most influence the actions; which being vicious ones mankind is in this sense naturally vicious, or vicious by nature. Thus St. Paul says of the Gentiles, *who were dead in trespasses and sins, and walked according to the spirit of disobedience, that they were by nature the children of wrath.*[9] They could be no otherwise *children of wrath* by nature, than they were vicious by nature.

Here then are two different senses of the word *nature,* in neither of which men can at all be said to be a law unto themselves. They are mentioned only to be excluded; to prevent their being confounded, as the latter is in the objection, with another sense of it, which is now to be inquired after and explained.

III. The apostle asserts, that the Gentiles *do by* NATURE *the things contained in the law.* Nature is indeed here put by way of distinction from revelation, but yet it is not a mere negative. He intends to express more than that by which they *did not,* that by which they *did* the works of the law; namely, by *nature.* It is plain the meaning of the word is not the same in this passage as in the former, where it is spoken of as evil; for in this latter it is spoken of as good; as that by which they acted, or might have acted virtuously. What that is in man by which he is *naturally a law to himself,* is explained in the following words: *Which show the work of the law written in their hearts, their consciences also bearing witness, and their thoughts the mean while accusing or else excusing one another.* If there be a distinction to be made between the *works written in their hearts,* and the *witness of conscience;* by the former must be meant the natural disposition to kindness and compassion, to do what is of good report, to which this apostle often refers, that part of the nature of man, treated of in the fore-going discourse, which with very little reflection and of course leads him to society, and by means of which he naturally acts a just and good part in it, unless other passions or interest lead him astray. Yet since other passions, and regards to private interest, which lead us (though indirectly, yet they lead us) astray, are themselves in a degree equally natural, and often most prevalent; and since we have no method of seeing the particular degrees in which one or the other is placed in us by nature; it is plain the former, considered merely as natural, good and right as they are, can no more be a law to us than the latter. But there is a superior principle of reflection or conscience in every man, which distinguishes between the internal principles of his heart, as well as his external actions; which passes judgment upon himself and them; pronounces determinately some actions to be in themselves just, right, good; others to be in themselves evil, wrong, unjust; which, without being consulted, without being advised with, magisterially exerts itself, and approves or condemns him the doer of them accordingly; and which, if not forcibly stopped, naturally and always of course goes on to anticipate a higher and more effectual sentence, which shall hereafter second and affirm its own. But this part of the office of conscience is beyond my present design explicitly to consider. It is by this faculty, natural to man, that he is a moral agent, that he is a law to himself; but this faculty, I say, is not to be considered merely as a principle in his heart, which is to have some influence as well as others; but considered as a faculty in kind and in nature supreme over all others, and which bears its own authority of being so.

This *prerogative,* this *natural supremacy,* of the faculty which surveys, approves or disapproves the several

[9] Ephes. ii. 3.

affections of our mind and actions of our lives, being that by which men *are a law to themselves*, their conformity or disobedience to which law of our nature renders their actions, in the highest and most proper sense, natural or unnatural; it is fit it be further explained to you: and I hope it will be so, if you will attend to the following reflections.

Man may act according to that principle or inclination which for the present happens to be strongest, and yet act in a way disproportionate to, and violate his real proper nature. Suppose a brute creature by any bait to be allured into a snare, by which he is destroyed. He plainly followed the bent of his nature, leading him to gratify his appetite; there is an entire correspondence between his whole nature and such an action: such action therefore is natural. But suppose a man, foreseeing the same danger of certain ruin, should rush into it for the sake of a present gratification; he in this instance would follow his strongest desire, as did the brute creature: but there would be as manifest a disproportion, between the nature of a man and such an action, as between the meanest work of art and the skill of the greatest master in that art: which disproportion arises, not from considering the action singly in *itself*, or in its *consequences*; but from *comparison* of it with the nature of the agent. And since such an action is utterly disproportionate to the nature of man, it is in the strictest and most proper sense unnatural; this word expressing that disproportion. Therefore instead of the words *disproportionate to his nature*, the word *unnatural* may now be put; this being more familiar to us: but let it be observed, that it stands for the same thing precisely.

Now what is it which renders such a rash action unnatural? Is it that he went against the principle of reasonable and cool self-love, considered *merely* as a part of his nature? No: for if he had acted the contrary way, he would equally have gone against a principle, or part of his nature, namely, passion or appetite. But to deny a present appetite, from foresight that the gratification of it would end in immediate ruin or extreme misery, is by no means an unnatural action; whereas to contradict or go against cool self-love for the sake of such gratification, is so in the instance before us. Such an action then being unnatural; and its being so not arising from a man's going against a principle or desire barely, nor in going against that principle or desire which happens for the present to be strongest; it necessarily follows, that there must be some other difference or distinction to be made between these two principles, passion and cool self-love, than what I have yet taken notice of. And this difference, not being a difference in strength or degree, I call a difference in *nature* and in *kind*. And since, in the instance still before us, if passion prevails over self-love, the consequent action is unnatural; but if self-love prevails over passion, the action is natural: it is manifest that self-love is in human nature a superior principle to passion. This may be contradicted without violating that nature; but the former cannot. So that, if we will act conformably to the economy of man's nature, reasonable self-love must govern. Thus, without particular consideration of conscience, we may have a clear conception of the *superior nature* of one inward principle to another; and see that there really is this natural superiority, quite distinct from degrees of strength and prevalency.

Let us now take a view of the nature of man, as consisting partly of various appetites, passions, affections, and partly of the principle of reflection or conscience; leaving quite out all consideration of the different degrees of strength, in which either of them prevail, and it will further appear that there is this natural superiority of one inward principle to another, and that it is even part of the idea of reflection or conscience.

Passion or appetite implies a direct simple tendency towards such and such objects, without distinction of the means by which they are to be obtained. Consequently it will often happen there will be a desire of particular objects, in cases where they cannot be obtained without manifest injury to others. Reflection or conscience comes in, and disapproves the pursuit of them in these circumstances; but the desire remains. Which is to be obeyed, appetite or reflection? Cannot this question be answered, from the economy and constitution of human nature merely, without saying which is strongest? Or need this at all come into consideration? Would not the question be *intelligibly* and fully answered by saying, that the principle of reflection or conscience being compared with the various appetites, passions, and affections in men, the former is manifestly superior and chief, without regard to strength? And how often soever the latter happens to prevail, it is mere *usurpation:* the former remains in nature and in kind its superior; and every instance of such prevalence of the latter is an instance of breaking in upon and violation of the constitution of man.

All this is no more than the distinction, which everybody is acquainted with, between *mere power* and *authority:* only instead of being intended to express the difference between what is possible, and what is lawful in civil government; here it has been shown applicable to the several principles in the mind of man. Thus that principle, by which we survey, and either approve or disapprove our own heart, temper, and actions, is not only to be considered as what is in its turn to have some influence; which may be said of every passion, of the lowest appetites; but likewise as being superior; as from its very nature manifestly claiming superiority over all others: insomuch that you cannot form a notion of this faculty, conscience, without taking in judgment, direction, superintendency. This is a constituent part of the idea, that is, of the faculty itself: and, to preside and govern, from the very economy and constitution of man, belongs to it. Had it strength, as it had right; had it power, as it had manifest authority, it would absolutely govern the world.

This gives us a further view of the nature of man; shows us what course of life we were made for: not only that our real nature leads us to be influenced in some degree by reflection and conscience; but likewise in what degree we are to be influenced by it, if we will fall in with, and act agreeably to the constitution of our nature: that this faculty was placed within to be our proper governor; to direct and regulate all under principles, passions, and motives of action. This is its right and office: thus sacred is its authority. And how often soever men violate and rebelliously refuse to submit to it, for supposed interest which they cannot otherwise obtain, or for the sake of passion which they cannot otherwise gratify; this makes no alteration as to the *natural right* and *office* of conscience.

Let us now turn this whole matter another way, and suppose there was no such thing at all as this natural supremacy of conscience; that there was no distinction to be made between one inward principle and another, but only that of strength; and see what would be the consequence.

Consider then what is the latitude

and compass of the actions of man with regard to himself, his fellow-creatures, and the Supreme Being? What are their bounds, besides that of our natural power? With respect to the two first, they are plainly no other than these: no man seeks misery as such for himself: and no one unprovoked does mischief to another for its own sake. For in every degree within these bounds, mankind knowingly from passion or wantonness bring ruin and misery upon themselves and others. And impiety and profaneness, I mean, what every one would call so who believes the being of God, have absolutely no bounds at all. Men blaspheme the Author of nature, formally and in words renounce their allegiance to their Creator. Put an instance then with respect to any one of these three. Though we should suppose profane swearing, and in general that kind of impiety now mentioned, to mean nothing, yet it implies wanton disregard and irreverence towards an infinite Being, our Creator; and is this as suitable to the nature of man, as reverence and dutiful submission of heart towards that Almighty Being? Or suppose a man guilty of parricide, with all the circumstances of cruelty which such an action can admit of. This action is done in consequence of its principle being for the present strongest; and if there be no difference between inward principles, but only that of strength; the strength being given, you have the whole nature of the man given, so far as it relates to this matter. The action plainly corresponds to the principle, the principle being in that degree of strength it was; it therefore corresponds to the whole nature of the man. Upon comparing the action and the whole nature, there arises no disproportion, there appears no unsuitableness between them. Thus the *murder of a father* and the *nature of man* correspond to each other, as

the same nature and an act of filial duty. If there be no difference between inward principles, but only that of strength; we can make no distinction between these two actions considered as the actions of such a creature; but in our coolest hours must approve or disapprove them equally: than which nothing can be reduced to a greater absurdity.

SERMON III

The natural supremacy of reflection or conscience being thus established; we may from it form a distinct notion of what is meant by *human nature*, when virtue is said to consist in following it, and vice in deviating from it.

As the idea of a civil constitution implies in it united strength, various subordinations, under one direction, that of the supreme authority; the different strength of each particular member of the society not coming into the idea; whereas, if you leave out the subordination, the union, and the one direction, you destroy and lose it: so reason, several appetites, passions, and affections, prevailing in different degrees of strength, is not *that* idea or notion of *human nature;* but *that nature* consists in these several principles considered as having a natural respect to each other, in the several passions being naturally subordinate to the one superior principle of reflection or conscience. Every bias, instinct, propension within, is a natural part of our nature, but not the whole: add to these the superior faculty, whose office it is to adjust, manage, and preside over them, and take in this its natural superiority, and you complete the idea of human nature. And as in civil government the constitution is broken in upon and violated by power and strength prevailing over authority; so the constitution of man is broken in upon and violated by the lower faculties or principles within prevailing over that which is in its nature supreme over them all. Thus, when it is said by ancient writers, that tortures and death are not so contrary to human nature as injustice; by this to be sure is not meant, that the aversion to the former in mankind is less strong and prevalent than their aversion to the latter; but that the former is only contrary to our nature considered in a partial view, and which takes in only the lowest part of it, that which we have in common with the brutes; whereas the latter is contrary to our nature, considered in a higher sense, as a system and constitution contrary to the whole economy of man.[10]

And from all these things put to-gether, nothing can be more evident, than that, exclusive of revelation, man cannot be considered as a creature left by his Maker to act at random, and live at large up to the extent of his natural power, as passion, humour, wilfulness, happen to carry him; which is the condition brute creatures are in: but that *from his make, constitution, or nature, he is in the strictest and most proper sense a law to himself.* He hath the rule of right within: what is wanting is only that he honestly attends to it.

The inquiries which have been made by men of leisure after some general rule, the conformity to, or disagreement from which, should denominate our actions good or evil, are in many respects of great service. Yet

---

[10] Every man, in his physical nature is one individual single agent. He has likewise properties and principles, each of which may be considered separately, and without regard to the respects which they have to each other. Neither of these are the nature we are taking a view of. But it is the inward frame of man, considered as a *system or constitution;* whose several parts are united, not by a physical principle of individuation, but by the respects they have to each other; the chief of which is the subjection which the appetites, passions, and particular affections have to the one supreme principle of reflection or conscience. The system, or constitution, is formed by, and consists in these respects and this subjection. Thus, the body is a *system or constitution;* so is a tree; so is every machine. Consider all the several parts of a tree, without the natural respects they have to each other, and you have not at all the idea of a tree; but add these respects, and this gives you the idea. The body may be impaired by sickness, a tree may decay, a machine be out of order, and yet the system and constitution of them not totally dissolved. There is plainly somewhat which answers to all this in the moral constitution of man. Whoever will consider his own nature will see, that the several appetites, passions, and particular affections, have different respects among themselves. They are restraints upon, and are in proportion to each other. This proportion is just and perfect, when all those under principles are perfectly co-incident with conscience, so far as their nature permits, and, in all cases, under its absolute and entire direction. The least excess or defect, the least alteration of the due proportions amongst themselves, or of their coincidence with conscience, though not proceeding into action, is some degree of disorder in the moral constitution. But perfection, though plainly intelligible and supposable, was never attained by any man. If the higher principle of reflection maintains its place, and, as much as it can, corrects that disorder, and hinders it from breaking out into action, that is all that can be expected in such a creature as man. And though the appetites and passions have not their exact due proportion to each other; though they often strive for mastery with judgment or reflection; yet, since the superiority of this principle to all others is the chief respect which forms the constitution, so far as this superiority is maintained, the character, the man, is good, worthy, virtuous.

let any plain honest man, before he
engages in any course of action, ask
himself, Is this I am going about right,
or is it wrong? Is it good, or is it evil?
I do not in the least doubt, but that
this question would be answered
agreeably to truth and virtue, by almost any fair man in almost any circumstance. Neither do there appear
any cases which look like exceptions
to this; but those of superstition, and
of partiality to ourselves. Superstition
may perhaps be somewhat of an exception: but partiality to ourselves is
not; this being itself dishonesty. For
a man to judge that to be the equitable, the moderate, the right part for
him to act, which he would see to be
hard, unjust, oppressive in another;
this is plain vice, and can proceed only
from great unfairness of mind.

But allowing that mankind hath the
rule of right within himself, yet it may
be asked, "What obligations are we
under to attend to and follow it?" I
answer: it has been proved that man
by his nature is a law to himself, without the particular distinct consideration of the positive sanctions of that
law; the rewards and punishments
which we feel, and those which from
the light of reason we have ground to
believe, are annexed to it. The question then carries its own answer along
with it. Your obligation to obey this
law, is its being the law of your nature.
That your conscience approves of and
attests to such a course of action, is
itself alone an obligation. Conscience
does not only offer itself to show us
the way we should walk in, but it likewise carries its own authority with it,
that it is our natural guide; the guide
assigned us by the Author of our nature: it therefore belongs to our condition of being, it is our duty to walk in
that path, and follow this guide, without looking about to see whether we
may not possibly forsake them with
impunity.

However, let us hear what is to be
said against obeying this law of our
nature. And the sum is no more than
this: "Why should we be concerned
about anything out of and beyond ourselves? If we do find within ourselves
regards to others, and restraints of we
know not how many different kinds;
yet these being embarrassments, and
hindering us from going the nearest
way to our own good, why should we
not endeavor to suppress and get over
them?"

Thus people go on with words,
which, when applied to human nature,
and the condition in which it is placed
in this world, have really no meaning.
For does not all this kind of talk go
upon the supposition, that our happiness in this world consists in somewhat
quite distinct from regard to others;
and that it is the privilege of vice to
be without restraint or confinement?
Whereas, on the contrary, the enjoyments, in a manner all the common
enjoyments of life, even the pleasures
of vice, depend upon these regards of
one kind or another to our fellow-
creatures. Throw off all regards to
others, and we should be quite indifferent to infamy and to honour;
there could be no such thing at all as
ambition; and scarce any such thing
as covetousness; for we should likewise be equally indifferent to the disgrace of poverty, the several neglects
and kinds of contempt which accompany this state; and to the reputation
of riches, the regard and respect they
usually procure. Neither is restraint
by any means peculiar to one course
of life; but our very nature, exclusive
of conscience and our condition, lays
us under an absolute necessity of it.
We cannot gain any end whatever
without being confined to the proper
means, which is often the most painful
and uneasy confinement. And in numberless instances a present appetite
cannot be gratified without such ap-

parent and immediate ruin and misery, that the most dissolute man in the world chooses to forego the pleasure, rather than endure the pain.

Is the meaning then, to indulge those regards to our fellow-creatures, and submit to those restraints, which upon the whole are attended with more satisfaction than uneasiness, and get over only those which bring more uneasiness and inconvenience than satisfaction? "Doubtless this was our meaning." You have changed sides then. Keep to this; be consistent with yourselves; and you and the men of virtue are *in general* perfectly agreed. But let us take care and avoid mistakes. Let it not be taken for granted that the temper of envy, rage, resentment, yields greater delight than meekness, forgiveness, compassion, and good-will; especially when it is acknowledged that rage, envy, resentment, are in themselves mere misery; and the satisfaction arising from the indulgence of them is little more than relief from that misery; whereas the temper of compassion and benevolence is itself delightful; and the indulgence of it, by doing good, affords new positive delight and enjoyment. Let it not be taken for granted, that the satisfaction arising from the reputation of riches and power, however obtained, and from the respect paid to them, is greater than the satisfaction arising from the reputation of justice, honesty, charity, and the esteem which is universally acknowledged to be their due. And if it be doubtful which of these satisfactions is the greatest, as there are persons who think neither of them very considerable, yet there can be no doubt concerning ambition and covetousness, virtue and a good mind, considered in themselves, and as leading to different courses of life; there can, I say, be no doubt, which temper and which course is attended with most peace and tranquillity of mind,

which with most perplexity, vexation, and inconvenience. And both the virtues and vices which have been now mentioned, do in a manner equally imply in them regards of one kind or another to our fellow-creatures. And with respect to restraint and confinement: whoever will consider the restraints from fear and shame, the dissimulation, mean arts of concealment, servile compliances, one or other of which belong to almost every course of vice, will soon be convinced that the man of virtue is by no means upon a disadvantage in this respect. How many instances are there in which men feel and own and cry aloud under the chains of vice with which they are enthralled, and which yet they will not shake off! How many instances, in which persons manifestly go through more pains and self-denial to gratify a vicious passion, than would have been necessary to the conquest of it! To this is to be added, that when virtue is become habitual, when the temper of it is acquired, what was before confinement ceases to be so, by becoming choice and delight. Whatever restraint and guard upon ourselves may be needful to unlearn any unnatural distortion or odd gesture; yet, in all propriety of speech, natural behaviour must be the most easy and unrestrained. It is manifest that, in the common course of life, there is seldom any inconsistency between our duty and what is *called* interest; it is much seldomer that there is an inconsistency between duty and what is really our present interest; meaning by interest, happiness and satisfaction. Self-love then, though confined to the interest of the present world, does in general perfectly coincide with virtue; and leads us to one and the same course of life. But, whatever exceptions there are to this, which are much fewer than they are commonly thought, all shall be set right at the final distributions of things. It is a manifest absurdity to suppose evil prevailing finally over good, under the conduct and administration of a perfect mind.

The whole argument, which I have been now insisting upon, may be thus summed up, and given you in one view. The nature of man is adapted to some course of action or other. Upon comparing some actions with this nature, they appear suitable and correspondent to it; from comparison of other actions with the same nature, there arises to our view some unsuitableness or disproportion. The correspondence of actions to the nature of the agent renders them natural: their disproportion to it, unnatural. That an action is correspondent to the nature of the agent, does not arise from its being agreeable to the principle which happens to be the strongest; for it may be so, and yet be quite disproportionate to the nature of the agent. The correspondence therefore, or disproportion, arises from somewhat else. This can be nothing but a difference in nature and kind, altogether distinct from strength, between the inward principles. Some then are in nature and kind superior to others. And the correspondence arises from the action being conformable to the higher principle; and the unsuitableness from its being contrary to it. Reasonable self-love and conscience are the chief or superior principles in the nature of man, because an action may be suitable to this nature, though all other principles be violated; but becomes unsuitable, if either of those are. Conscience and self-love, if we understand our true happiness, always lead us the same way. Duty and interest are perfectly coincident; for the most part in this world, but entirely, and in every instance, if we take in the future, and the whole; this being implied in the notion of a good and perfect administration of things. Thus, they

who have been so wise in their generation, as to regard only their own supposed interest, at the exense and to the injury of others, shall at last find, that he who has given up all the advantages of the present world, rather than violate his conscience and the relations of life, has infinitely better provided for himself, and secured his own interest and happiness.

SERMON XI

UPON THE LOVE OF OUR NEIGHBOUR
(PREACHED ON ADVENT SUNDAY)

And if there be any other command-ment, it is briefly comprehended in this saying, namely, Thou shalt love thy neighbour as thyself.—ROMANS xiii. 9.

It is commonly observed that there is a disposition in men to complain of the viciousness and corruption of the age in which they live, as greater than that of former ones; which is usually followed with this further observation that mankind has been in that respect much the same in all times. Now, not to determine whether this last be not contradicted by the accounts of history, thus much can scarce be doubted —that vice and folly takes different turns, and some particular kinds of it are more open and avowed in some ages than in others; and I suppose it may be spoken of as very much the distinction of the present to profess a contracted spirit and greater regards to self-interest than appears to have been done formerly. Upon this account it seems worth while to inquire whether private interest is likely to be promoted in proportion to the degree in which self-love engrosses us, and prevails over all other principles, or whether the contracted affection may not possibly be so prevalent as to disappoint itself, and even contradict its own end, private good.

And since, further, there is generally thought to be some peculiar kind of contrariety between self-love and the love of our neighbor, between the pursuit of public and of private good, insomuch that when you are recommending one of these, you are supposed to be speaking against the other; and from hence arises a secret prejudice against and frequently open scorn of all talk of public spirit and real goodwill to our fellow creatures; it will be necessary to inquire what respect benevolence hath to self-love, and the pursuit of private interest to the pursuit of public; or whether there be anything of that peculiar inconsistency and contrariety between them, over and above what there is between self-love and other passions and particular affections, and their respective pursuits.

These inquiries, it is hoped, may be favorably attended to; for there shall be all possible concessions made to the favorite passion, which hath so much allowed to it, and whose cause is so universally pleaded: it shall be treated with the utmost tenderness and concern for its interests.

In order to this, as well as to determine the forementioned questions, it will be necessary to consider the nature, the object, and end of that self-love, as distinguished from other principles or affections in the mind and their respective objects.

Every man hath a general desire of his own happiness; and likewise a variety of particular affections, passions, and appetites, to particular external objects. The former proceeds from, or is, self-love, and seems inseparable from all sensible creatures, who can reflect upon themselves and their own interest or happiness, so as to have that interest an object to their minds:

what is to be said of the latter is, that they proceed from, or together make up, that particular nature, according to which man is made. The object the former pursues is somewhat internal, our own happiness, enjoyment, satisfaction; whether we have or have not a distinct particular perception what it is, or wherein it consists: the objects of the latter are this or that particular external thing, which the affections tend towards, and of which it hath always a particular idea or perception. The principle we call self-love never seeks anything external for the sake of the thing, but only as a means of happiness or good: particular affections rest in the external things themselves. One belongs to man as a reasonable creature reflecting upon his own interest or happiness; the other, though quite distinct from reason, are as much a part of human nature.

That all particular appetites and passions are towards *external things themselves*, distinct from the *pleasure arising from them*, is manifested from hence, that there could not be this pleasure, were it not for that prior suitableness between the object and the passion: there could be no enjoyment or delight for one thing more than another, from eating food more than from swallowing a stone, if there were not an affection or appetite to one thing more than another.

Every particular affection, even the love of our neighbour, is as really our own affection, as self-love; and the pleasure arising from its gratification is as much my own pleasure, as the pleasure self-love would have from knowing I myself should be happy some time hence, would be my own pleasure. And if, because every particular affection is a man's own, and the pleasure arising from its gratification his own pleasure, or pleasure to himself, such particular affection must be called self-love. According to this way of speaking, no creature whatever can possibly act but merely from self-love; and every action and every affection whatever is to be resolved up into this one principle. But then this is not the language of mankind: or, if it were, we should want words to express the difference between the principle of an action, proceeding from cool consideration that it will be to my own advantage; and an action, suppose of revenge, or of friendship by which a man runs upon certain ruin, to do evil or good to another. It is manifest the principles of these actions are totally different, and so want different words to be distinguished by: all that they agree in is, that they both proceed from, and are done to gratify an inclination in a man's self. But the principle or inclination in one case is self-love; in the other, hatred, or love of another. There is then a distinction between the cool principle of self-love, or general desire of our own happiness, as one part of our nature, and one principle of action; and the particular affections towards particular external objects, as another principle of action. How much soever, therefore, is to be allowed to self-love, yet it cannot be allowed to be the whole of our inward constitution; because, you see, there are other parts or principles which come into it.

Further, private happiness or good is all which self-love can make us desire or be concerned about. In having this consists its gratification; it is an affection to ourselves—a regard to our own interest, happiness, and private good: and in the proportion a man hath this, he is interested, or a lover of himself. Let this be kept in mind, because there is commonly, as I shall presently have occasion to observe, another sense put upon these words. On the other hand, particular affections tend towards particular ex-ternal things; these are their objects; having these is their end; in this consists their gratification: no matter whether it be, or be not, upon the whole, our interest or happiness. An action, done from the former of these principles, is called an interested action. An action, proceeding from any of the latter, has its denomination of passionate, ambitious, friendly, revengeful, or any other, from the particular appetite or affection from which it proceeds. Thus self-love, as one part of human nature, and the several particular principles as the other part, are themselves, their objects, and ends, stated and shown.

From hence it will be easy to see how far, and in what ways, each of these can contribute and be subservient to the private good of the individual. Happiness does not consist in self-love. The desire of happiness is no more the thing itself, than the desire of riches is the possession or enjoyment of them. People may love themselves with the most entire and unbounded affection, and yet be extremely miserable. Neither can self-love any way help them out, but by setting them on work to get rid of the causes of their misery, to gain or make use of those objects which are by nature adapted to afford satisfaction. Happiness or satisfaction consists only in the enjoyment of those objects which are by nature suited to our several particular appetites, passions, and affections. So that if self-love wholly engrosses us, and leaves no room for any other principle, there can be absolutely no such thing at all as happiness or enjoyment of any kind whatever; since happiness consists in the gratification of particular passions, which supposes the having of them. Self-love then does not constitute *this* or *that* to be our interest or good; but our interest or good being constituted by nature and supposed self-love, only puts us upon obtaining and securing it. Therefore, if it be possible that self-love may prevail and exert itself in a degree or manner which is not subservient to this end, then it will not follow that our interest will be promoted in proportion to the degree in which that principle engrosses us, and prevails over others. Nay, further, the private and contracted affection, when it is not subservient to this end, private good, may, for anything that appears, have a direct contrary tendency and effect. And if we will consider the matter, we shall see that it often really has. Disengagement is absolutely necessary to enjoyment; and a person may have so steady and fixed an eye upon his own interest, whatever he places it in, as may hinder him from attending to many gratifications within his reach, which others have their minds free and open to. Overfondness for a child is not generally thought to be for its advantage; and, if there be any guess to be from appearances, surely that character we call *selfish* is not the most promising for happiness. Such a temper may plainly be, and exert itself in a degree and manner which may give unnecessary and useless solicitude and anxiety, in a degree and manner which may prevent obtaining the means and materials of enjoyment, as well as the making use of them. Immoderate self-love does very ill consult its own interest; and how much soever a paradox it may appear, it is certainly true, that, even from self-love, we should endeavour to get over all inordinate regard to, and consideration of, ourselves. Every one of our passions and affections hath its natural stint and bound, which may easily be exceeded; whereas our enjoyments can possibly be but in a determinate measure and degree. Therefore such excess of the affection, since it cannot procure any enjoyment, must in all cases be useless, but is generally attended with inconveniences, and often is down-right pain and misery. This holds as much with regard to self-love as to all other affections. The natural degree of it, so far as it sets us on work to gain and make use of the materials of satisfaction, may be to our real advantage; but beyond or beside this, it is in several respects an inconvenience and disadvantage. Thus it appears that private interest is so far from being likely to be promoted in proportion to the degree in which self-love engrosses us, and prevails over all other principles, that *the contracted affection may be so prevalent as to disappoint itself and even contradict its own end, private good.*

"But who, except the most sordidly covetous, ever thought there was any rivalship between the love of greatness, honour, power, or between sensual appetites, and self-love? No; there is a perfect harmony between them. It is by means of these particular appetites and affections that self-love is gratified in enjoyment, happiness, and satisfaction. The competition and rivalship is between self-love and the love of our neighbour. That affection which leads us out of ourselves, makes us regardless of our own interest, and substitute that of another in its stead." Whether then there be any peculiar competition and contrariety in this case, shall now be considered.

Self-love and interestedness was stated to consist in or be an affection to ourselves, a regard to our own private good: it is, therefore, distinct from benevolence, which is an affection to the good of our fellow-creatures. But that benevolence is distinct from, that is, not the same thing with self-love, is no reason for its being looked upon with any peculiar suspicion, because every principle whatever, by means of which self-love is gratified, is distinct from it. And all things, which are distinct from each other, are equally so. A man has an affection or aversion to another: that one of these tends to, and is gratified by doing good, that the other tends to, and is gratified by doing harm, does not in the least alter the respect which either one or the other of these inward feelings has to self-love. We use the word *property* so as to exclude any other persons having an interest in that, of which we say a particular man has the property: and we often use the word *selfish* so as to exclude in the same manner all regards to the good of others. But the cases are not parallel: for though that exclusion is really part of the idea of property, yet such positive exclusion, or bringing this peculiar disregard to the good of others into the idea of self-love, is in reality adding to the idea, or changing it from what it was before stated to consist in, namely, in an affection to ourselves. This being the whole idea of self-love, it can no otherwise exclude good-will or love of others, than merely by not including it, no otherwise than it excludes love of arts, or reputation, or of anything else. Neither, on the other hand, does benevolence, any more than love of arts or of reputation, exclude self-love. Love of our neighbour, then has just the same respect to, is no more distant from self-love, than hatred of our neighbour, or than love and hatred of anything else. Thus the principles, from which men rush upon certain ruin for the destruction of an enemy, and for the preservation of a friend, have the same respect to the private affection, are equally interested, or equally disinterested: and it is of no avail, whether they are said to be one or the other. Therefore, to those who are shocked to hear virtue spoken of as disinterested, it may be allowed, that it is indeed absurd to speak thus of it; unless hatred, several particular instances of vice, and all the common affections and aversions in mankind, are acknowledged to be disinterested too. Is there any less inconsistence between the love of inanimate things, or of creatures merely sensitive, and self-love, than between self-love, and the love of our neighbour? Is desire of, and delight in the happiness of another any more a diminution of self-love, than desire of and delight in the esteem of another? They are both equally desire of and delight in somewhat external to ourselves: either both or neither are so. The object of self-love is expressed in the term self: and every appetite of sense, and every particular affection of the heart, are equally interested or disinterested, because the objects of them all are equally self or somewhat else. Whatever ridicule, therefore, the mention of a disinterested principle or action may be supposed to lie open to, must, upon the matter being thus stated, relate to ambition, and every appetite and particular affection, as much as to benevolence. And indeed all the ridicule, and all the grave perplexity, of which this subject hath had its full share, is merely from words. The most intelligible way of speaking of it seems to be this: that self-love, and the actions done in consequence of it, (for these will presently appear to be the same as to this question) are interested; that particular affections towards external objects, and the actions done in consequence of those affections, are not so. But every one is at liberty to use words as he pleases. All that is here insisted upon is, that ambition, revenge, benevolence, all particular passions whatever, and the actions they produce, are equally interested or disinterested.

Thus it appears, that there is no peculiar contrariety between self-love and benevolence; no greater competition between these, than between any other particular affections and self-love. This relates to the affections themselves. Let us now see whether there be any peculiar contrariety between the respective courses of life which these affections lead to; whether there be any greater competition between the pursuit of private and of public good, than between any other particular pursuits and that of private good.

There seems no other reason to suspect that there is any such peculiar contrariety, but only that the course of action which benevolence leads to, has a more direct tendency to promote the good of others, than that course of action, which love of reputation, suppose, or any other particular affection, leads to. But that any affection tends to the happiness of another, does not hinder its tending to one's own happiness too. That others enjoy the benefit of the air and the light of the sun, does not hinder but that these are as much one's own private advantage now, as they would be if we had the property of them exclusive of all others. So a pursuit which tends to promote the good of another, yet may have as great tendency to promote private interest, as a pusuit which does not tend to the good of another at all, or which is mischievous to him. All particular affections whatever, resentment, benevolence, love of the arts, equally lead to a course of action for their own gratification, i. e., the gratification of ourselves: and the gratification of each gives delight: so far, then, it is manifest they have all the same respect to private interest. Now, take into consideration further, concerning these three pursuits, that the end of the first is the harm; of the second, the good of another; of the last, somewhat indifferent: and is there any necessity, that these additional considerations should alter the respect

which we before saw these three pursuits had to private interest; or render any one of them less conducive to it than any other? Thus, one man's affection is to honour, as his end; in order to obtain which, he thinks no pains too great. Suppose another, with such a singularity of mind, as to have the same affection to public good, as his end, which he endeavours with the same labour to obtain. In case of success, surely the man of benevolence hath as great enjoyment as the man of ambition; they both equally having the end, their affections, in the same degree, tended to; but in case of disappointment, the benevolent man has clearly the advantage; since endeavouring to do good, considered as a virtuous pursuit, is gratified by its own consciousness, i. e., is in a degree its own reward.

And as to these two, or benevolence and any other particular passions whatever, considered in a further view, is forming a general temper, which more or less disposes us for enjoyment of all the common blessings of life, distinct from their own gratification: is benevolence less the temper of tranquility and freedom, than ambition or covetousness? Does the benevolent man appear less easy with himself, from his love to his neighbour? Does he less relish his being? Is there any peculiar gloom seated on his face? Is his mind less open to entertainment, or to any particular gratification? Nothing is more manifest, than that being in good humour, which is benevolence whilst it last, is itself the temper of satisfaction and enjoyment.

Suppose, then, a man sitting down to consider how he might become most easy to himself, and attain the greatest pleasure he could; all that which is his real natural happiness; this can only consist in the enjoyment of those objects which are by nature adapted to our several faculties. These particular enjoyments make up the sum total of our happiness; and they are supposed to arise from riches, honours, and the gratification of sensual appetites. Be it so: yet none profess themselves so completely happy in these enjoyments, but that there is room left in the mind for others, if they were presented to them. Nay, these, as much as they engage us, are not thought so high, but that human nature is capable even of greater. Now there have been persons in all ages, who have professed that they found satisfaction in the exercise of charity, in the love of their neighbour, in endeavouring to promote the happiness of all they had to do with, and in the pursuit of what is just, and right, and good, as the general bent of their mind and end of their life; and that doing an action of baseness or cruelty, would be as great violence to *their* self, as much breaking in upon their nature, as any external force. Persons of this character would add, if they might be heard, that they consider themselves as acting in the view of an infinite Being, who is in a much higher sense the object of reverence and of love, than all the world besides; and, therefore, they could have no more enjoyment from a wicked action done under his eye, than the persons to whom they are making their apology could, if all mankind were the spectators of it; and that the satisfaction of approving themselves to his unerring judgment, to whom they thus refer all their actions, is a more continued settled satisfaction than any this world can afford; as also that they have, no less than others, a mind free and open to all the common innocent gratifications of it such as they are. And, if we go no further, does there appear any absurdity in this? Will any one take upon him to say, that a man cannot find his account in this general

course of life, as much as in the most unbounded ambition, or the excesses of pleasure? Or that such a person has not consulted so well for himself, for the satisfaction and peace of his own mind, as the ambitious or dissolute man? And though the consideration, that God himself will in the end justify their taste, and support their cause, is not formally to be insisted upon here; yet thus much comes in, that all enjoyments whatever are much more clear and unmixed, from the assurance that they will end well. Is it certain, then, that there is nothing in these pretensions to happiness, especially when there are not wanting persons, who have supported themselves with satisfactions of this kind in sickness, poverty, disgrace, and in the very pangs of death? whereas, it is manifest all other enjoyments fail in these circumstances. This surely looks suspicious of having somewhat in it. Self-love, methinks, should be alarmed. May she not possibly pass over greater pleasures, than those she is so wholly taken up with?

The short of the matter is no more than this. Happiness consists in the gratification of certain affections, appetites, passions, with objects which are by nature adapted to them. Self-love may indeed set us on work to gratify these: but happiness or enjoyment has no immediate connexion with self-love, but arises from such gratification alone. Love of our neighbour is one of those affections. This, considered as a virtuous principle, is gratified by a consciousness of endeavouring to promote the good of others: but considered as a natural affection, its gratification consists in the actual accomplishment of this endeavour. Now, indulgence or gratification of this affection, whether in that consciousness, or this accomplishment, has the same respect to interest, as indulgence of any other affection; they equally proceed from, or do not proceed from, self-love; they equally include or equally exclude, this principle. Thus it appears, that "benevolence and the pursuit of public good have at least as great respect to self-love and the pursuit of private good, as any other particular passions, and their respective pursuits."

Neither is covetousness, whether as a temper or pursuit, any exception to this. For if by covetousness is meant the desire and pursuit of riches for their own sake, without any regard to or consideration of the uses of them; this hath as little to do with self-love, as benevolence hath. But by this word is usually meant, not such madness and total distraction of mind, but immoderate affection to and pursuit of riches as possessions, in order to some further end; namely, satisfaction, interest, or good. This, therefore, is not a particular affection, or particular pursuit, but it is the general principle of self-love, and the general pursuit of our own interest; for which reason, the word *selfish* is by every one appropriated to this temper and pursuit. Now, as it is ridiculous to assert that self-love and the love of our neighbour are the same; so neither is it asserted that following these different affections hath the same tendency and respect to our own interest. The comparison is not between self-love and the love of our neighbour; between pursuit of our own interest, and the interest of others; but between the several particular affections in human nature towards external objects, as one part of the comparison; and the one particular affection to the good of our neighbour, as the one part of it: and it has been shown, that all these have the same respect to self-love and private interest.

There is indeed frequently an inconsistence, or interfering between self-love or private interest, and the several particular appetites, passions, affections, or the pursuits they lead to. But this competition or interfering is merely accidental, and happens much oftener between pride, revenge, sensual gratifications, and private interest, than between private interest and benevolence. For nothing is more common than to see men give themselves up to a passion or an affection to their known prejudice and ruin, and in direct contradiction to manifest and real interest, and the loudest calls of self-love: whereas the seeming competitions and interfering between benevolence and private interest, relate much more to the materials or means of enjoyment, than to enjoyment itself. There is often an interfering in the former, where there is none in the latter. Thus, as to riches: so much money as a man gives away, so much less will remain in his possession. Here is a real interfering. But though a man cannot possibly give without lessening his fortune, yet there are multitudes might give without lessening their own enjoyment; because they may have more than they can turn to any real use or advantage to themselves. Thus, the more thought and time any one employs about the interests and good of others, he must necessarily have less to attend his own; but he may have so ready and large a supply of his own wants, that such thought might be really useless to himself, though of great service and assistance to others.

The general mistake, that there is some greater inconsistence between endeavouring to promote the good of another and self-interest, than between self-interest and pursuing anything else, seems, as hath already been hinted to arise from our notions of property; and to be carried on by this property's being supposed to be itself our happiness or good. People are so very much taken up with this one subject, that they seem from it to have formed a general way of thinking, which they apply to other things that they have nothing to do with. Hence, in a confused and slight way, it might well be taken for granted, that another's having no interest in an affection (*i. e.*, his good not being the object of it,) renders, as one may speak, the proprietor's interest in it greater; and that if another had an interest in it, this would render his less, or occasion that such affection could not be so friendly to self-love, or conducive to private good, as an affection or pursuit which has not a regard to the good of another. This, I say, might be taken for granted, whilst it was not attended to, that the object of every particular affection is equally somewhat external to ourselves: and whether it be the good of another person, or whether it be any other external thing, makes no alteration with regard to its being one's own affection, and the gratification of it one's own private enjoyment. And so far as it is taken for granted, that barely having the means and materials of enjoyment is what constitutes interest and happiness; that our interest and good consists in possessions themselves, in having the property of riches, houses, lands, gardens, not in the enjoyment of them; so far it will even more strongly be taken for granted, in the way already explained, that an affection's conducing to the good of another, must even necessarily occasion it to conduce less to private good, if not to be positively detrimental to it. For, if property and happiness are one and the same thing, as by increasing the property of another, you lessen your own property, so by promoting the happiness of another, you must lessen your own happiness. But whatever occasioned the mistake, I hope it has been fully proved to be one; as it has been proved, that there is no peculiar rivalship or competition between self-love and benevolence; that as there may be a competition between these two, so there may also between any particular affection whatever and self-love; that every particular affection, benevolence among the rest, is subservient to self-love, by being the instrument of private enjoyment; and that in one respect benevolence contributes more to private interest, *i. e.*, enjoyment or satisfaction, than any other of the particular common affections, as it is in a degree its own gratification.

And to all these things may be added, that religion, from whence arises our strongest obligation to benevolence, is so far from disowning the principle of self-love, that it often addresses itself to that very principle, and always to the mind in that state when reason presides; and there can no access be had to the understanding, but by convincing men, that the course of life we would persuade them to is not contrary to their interest. It may be allowed, without any prejudice to the cause of virtue and religion, that our ideas of happiness and misery are, of all our ideas, the nearest and most important to us; that they will, nay, if you please, that they ought to prevail over those of order, and beauty, and harmony, and proportion, if there should ever be, as it is impossible there ever should be, any inconsistency between them; though these last, too, as expressing the fitness of action, are real as truth itself. Let it be allowed, though virtue or moral rectitude does indeed consist in affection to and pursuit of what is right and good, as such: yet that, when we sit down in a cool hour, we can neither justify to ourselves this or any other pursuit, till we are convinced that it will be for our happiness, or at least not contrary to it.

A DISSERTATION UPON THE NATURE OF VIRTUE [11]

That which renders beings capable of moral government is their having a moral nature and moral faculties of perception and of action. Brute creatures are impressed and actuated by various instincts and propensions; so also are we. But additional to this, we have a capacity of reflecting upon actions and characters, and making them an object to our thought; and in doing this, we naturally and unavoidably approve some actions, under the peculiar view of their being virtuous and of good desert, and disapprove others as vicious and of ill desert. That we have this moral approving and disapproving [12] faculty is certain from our experiencing it in ourselves, and recognizing it in each other. It appears from our exercising it unavoidably, in the approbation and disapprobation even of feigned characters; from the words "right" and "wrong," "odious" and "amiable," "base" and "worthy," with many others of like signification in all languages applied to actions and char-

[11] From *The Analogy of Religion*, London, 1736.

[12] This way of speaking is taken from Epictetus, (Arr. Epict., lib. i. cap. I), and is made use of as seeming the most full, and least liable to cavil. And the moral faculty may be understood to have these two epithets δοκιμαστικὴ and ἀποδοκιμαστικη, upon a double account; because, upon a survey of actions, whether before or after they are done, it determines them to be good or evil; and also because it determines itself to be the guide of action and life, in contradistinction from all other faculties, or natural principles of action, in the very same manner as speculative reason *directly* and naturally judges of speculative truth and falsehood; and at the same time is attended with a consciousness upon *reflection* that the natural right to judge of them belong to it.

acters; from the many written systems of morals which suppose it, since it cannot be imagined that all these authors, throughout all these treatises, had absolutely no meaning at all to their words, or a meaning merely chimerical; from our natural sense of gratitude, which implies a distinction between merely being the instrument of good and intending it; from the like distinction every one makes between injury and mere harm, which Hobbes says is peculiar to mankind, and between injury and just punishment, a distinction plainly natural, prior to the consideration of human laws. It is manifest great part of common language, and of common behavior over the world, is formed upon supposition of such a moral faculty, whether called conscience, moral reason, moral sense, or divine reason; whether considered as a sentiment of the understanding or as a perception of the heart, or, which seems the truth, as including both. Nor is it at all doubtful in the general what course of action this faculty, or practical discerning power within us, approves and what it disapproves. For, as much as it has been disputed wherein virtue consists, or whatever ground for doubt there may be about particulars, yet in general, there is in reality an universally acknowledged standard of it. It is that which all ages and all countries have made profession of in public; it is that which every man you meet puts on the show of; it is that which the primary and fundamental laws of all civil constitutions over the face of the earth make it their business and endeavor to enforce the practice of upon mankind, namely, justice, veracity and regard to common good. It being manifest then, in general, that we have such a faculty or discernment as this, it may be of use to remark some things more distinctly concerning it.

First, it ought to be observed that

the object of this faculty is actions,[13] comprehending under that name active or practical principles — those principles from which men would act if occasions and circumstances gave them power; and which, when fixed and habitual in any person, we call his character. It does not appear that brutes have the least reflex sense of actions, as distinguished from events, or that will and design, which constitute the very nature of actions as such, are at all an object to their perception. But to ours they are; and they are the object, and the only one, of the approving and disapproving faculty. Acting, conduct, behavior, abstracted from all regard to what is in fact and event the consequence of it, is itself the natural object of the moral discernment, as speculative truth and falsehood is of speculative reason. Intention of such and such consequences, indeed, is always included, for it is part of the action itself; but though the intended good or bad consequences do not follow, we have exactly the same sense of the action as if they did. In like manner we think well or ill of characters, abstracted from all consideration of the good or the evil, which persons of such characters have it actually in their power to do. We never, in the moral way, applaud or blame either ourselves or others for what we enjoy or what we suffer, or for having impressions made upon us, which we consider as altogether out of our power, but only for what we do or would have done had it been in our power; or for what we leave undone, which we might have done or would have left undone, though we could have done it.

Secondly, our sense or discernment

of actions as morally good or evil implies in it a sense or discernment of them as of good or ill desert. It may be difficult to explain this perception so as to answer all the questions which may be asked concerning it; but everyone speaks of such and such actions as deserving punishment; and it is not, I suppose, pretended that they have absolutely no meaning at all to the expression. Now the meaning plainly is not that we conceive it for the good of society that the doer of such actions should be made to suffer. For if, unhappily, it were resolved that a man who, by some innocent action, was infected with the plague should be left to perish lest, by other people's coming near him, the infection should spread, no one would say he deserved this treatment. Innocence and ill desert are inconsistent ideas. Ill desert always supposes guilt; and if one be no part of the other, yet they are evidently and naturally connected in our mind. The sight of a man in misery raises our compassion toward him, and, if this misery be inflicted on him by another, our indignation against the author of it. But when we are informed that the sufferer is a villain and is punished only for his treachery or cruelty, our compassion exceedingly lessens, and in many instances our indignation wholly subsides. Now what produces this effect is the conception of that in the sufferer which we call ill desert. Upon considering then, or viewing together, our notion of vice and that of misery, there results a third—that of ill desert. And thus there is in human creatures an association of the two ideas, natural and moral evil, wickedness and punishment. If this association were merely artificial or accidental, it were nothing; but being most unquestionably natural, it greatly concerns us to attend to it, instead of endeavoring to explain it away.

[13] "Οὐδὲ ἡ ἀρετὴ καὶ κακία — ἐν πείσει, ἀλλὰ ἐνεργεία," M. Anton., lib. ix. 16; "*Virtutis laus omnis in actione consistit,*" Cic.. *Off.*, lib. i. cap. 6.

It may be observed further, concerning our perception of good and of evil desert, that the former is very weak with respect to common instances of virtue. One reason of which may be that it does not appear to a spectator, how far such instances of virtue proceed from a virtuous principle, or in what degree this principle is prevalent; since a very weak regard to virtue may be sufficient to make men act well in many common instances. And on the other hand, our perception of ill desert in vicious actions lessens, in proportion to the temptations men are thought to have had to such vices. For vice in human creatures consisting chiefly in the abscence or want of the virtuous principle, though a man be overcome, suppose, by tortures, it does not from thence appear to what degree the virtuous principle was wanting. All that appears is that he had it not in such a degree as to prevail over the temptation; but possibly he had it in a degree which would have rendered him proof against common temptations.

Thirdly, our perception of vice and ill desert arises from, and is the result of, a comparison of actions with the nature and capacities of the agent. For the mere neglect of doing what we ought to do would, in many cases, be determined by all men to be in the highest degree vicious. And his determination must arise from such comparison, and be the result of it; because such neglect would not be vicious in creatures of other natures and capacities, as brutes. And it is the same also with respect to positive vices, or such as consist in doing what we ought not. For every one has a different sense of harm done by an idiot, madman, or child, and by one of mature and common understanding, though the action of both, including the intention, which is part of the

action, be the same; as it may be, since idiots and madmen, as well as children, are capable not only of doing mischief, but also of intending it. Now this difference must arise from somewhat discerned in the nature or capacities of one, which renders the action vicious; and the want of which, in the other, renders the same action innocent or less vicious; and this plainly supposes a comparison, whether reflected upon or not, between the action and capacities of the agent, previous to our determining an action to be vicious. And hence arises a proper application of the epithets "incongruous," "unsuitable," "disproportionate," "unfit" to actions which our moral faculty determines to be vicious.

Fourthly, it deserves to be considered whether men are more at liberty, in point of morals, to make themselves miserable without reason than to make other people so, or dissolutely to neglect their own greater good, for the sake of a present lesser gratification, than they are to neglect the good of others whom nature has committed to their care. It should seem that a due concern about our own interest or happiness, and a reasonable endeavor to secure and promote it, which is, I think, very much the meaning of the word "prudence" in our language —it should seem that this is virtue, and the contrary behavior faulty and blameable, since, in the calmest way of reflection, we approve of the first, and condemn the other conduct, both in ourselves and others. This approbation and disapprobation are altogether different from mere desire of our own or of their happiness, and from sorrow upon missing it. For the object or occasion of this last kind of perception is satisfaction or uneasiness, whereas the object of the first is active behavior. In one case, what our thoughts fix upon is our condition, in the other, our conduct. It is true, indeed, that nature has not given us so sensible a disapprobation of imprudence and folly, either in *ourselves* or *others*, as of falsehood, injustice and cruelty; I suppose, because that constant habitual sense of private interest and good, which we always carry about with us, renders such sensible disapprobation less necessary, less wanting, to keep us from imprudently neglecting our own happiness and foolishly injuring ourselves, than it is necessary and wanting to keep us from injuring others to whose good we cannot have so strong and constant a regard; and also because imprudence and folly appearing to bring its own punishment more immediately and constantly than injurious behavior, it less needs the additional punishment which would be inflicted upon it by others had they the same sensible indignation against it as against injustice and fraud and cruelty. Besides, unhappiness being in itself the natural object of compassion, the unhappiness which people bring upon themselves, though it be willfully, excites in us some pity for them; and this, of course, lessens our displeasure against them. But still it is matter of experience that we are formed so as to reflect very severely upon the greater instances of imprudent neglect and foolish rashness, both in ourselves and others. In instances of this kind, men often say of themselves with remorse, and of others with some indignation, that they deserved to suffer such calamities because they brought them upon themselves and would not take warning. Particularly when persons come to poverty and distress by a long course of extravagance and after frequent admonitions, though without falsehood or injustice; we plainly do not regard such people as alike objects of compassion with those who are brought into the same condition by unavoidable accidents. From these things it

appears that prudence is a species of virtue, and folly of vice, meaning by "folly" somewhat quite different from mere incapacity—a thoughtless want of that regard and attention to our own happiness which we had capacity for. And this the word properly includes, and, as it seems, in its usual acceptation, for we scarcely apply it to brute creatures.

However, if any person be disposed to dispute the matter, I shall very willingly give him up the words "virtue" and "vice," as not applicable to prudence and folly, but must beg leave to insist that the faculty within us, which is the judge of actions, approves of prudent actions, and disapproves imprudent ones; I say prudent and imprudent *actions* as such, and considered distinctly from the happiness or misery which they occasion. And, by the way, this observation may help to determine what justness there is in that objection against religion, that it teaches us to be interested and selfish.

Fifthly, without inquiring how far, and in what sense, virtue is resolvable into benevolence, and vice into the want of it, it may be proper to observe that benevolence and the want of it, singly considered, are in no sort the whole of virtue and vice. For if this were the case, in the review of one's own character, or that of others, our moral understanding and moral sense would be indifferent to everything but the degrees in which benevolence prevailed, and the degrees in which it was wanting. That is, we should neither approve of benevolence to some persons rather than to others, nor disapprove injustice and falsehood upon any other account than merely as an overbalance of happiness was foreseen likely to be produced by the first, and of misery by the second. But now, on the contrary, suppose two men competitors for anything whatever, which would be of equal advantage to each of them; though nothing indeed would be more impertinent than for a stranger to busy himself to get one of them preferred to the other, yet such endeavor would be virtue, in behalf of a friend or benefactor, abstracted from all consideration of distant consequences, as that examples of gratitude, and the cultivation of friendship, would be of general good to the world. Again, suppose one man should, by fraud or violence, take from another the fruit of his labor, with intent to give it to a third who he thought would have as much pleasure from it as would balance the pleasure which the first possessor would have had in the enjoyment, and his vexation in the loss of it; suppose also that no bad consequences would follow, yet such an action would surely be vicious. Nay further, were treachery, violence and injustice not otherwise vicious than as foreseen likely to produce an overbalance of misery to society, then, if in any case a man could procure to himself as great advantage by an act of injustice as the whole foreseen inconvenience, likely to be brought upon others by it, would amount to, such a piece of injustice would not be faulty or vicious at all; because it would be no more than, in any other case, for a man to prefer his own satisfaction to another's in equal degrees. The fact then appears to be that we are constituted so as to condemn falsehood, unprovoked violence, injustice, and to approve of benevolence to some, preferably to others, abstracted from all consideration which conduct is likeliest to produce an overbalance of happiness or misery. And therefore, were the Author of Nature to propose nothing to himself as an end but the production of happiness, were his moral character merely that of benevolence, yet ours is not so. Upon that supposition, indeed, the only reason of

his giving us the above-mentioned approbation of benevolence to some persons rather than others, and disapprobation of falsehood, unprovoked violence, and injustice, must be that he foresaw this constitution of our nature would produce more happiness than forming us with a temper of mere general benevolence. But still, since this is our constitution, falsehood, violence, injustice must be vice in us, and benevolence to some, preferably to others, virtue, abstracted from all consideration of the overbalance of evil or good, which they may appear likely to produce.

Now if human creatures are endued with such a moral nature as we have been explaining, or with a moral faculty the natural object of which is actions, moral government must consist in rendering them happy and unhappy, in rewarding and punishing them as they follow, neglect or depart from, the moral rule of action interwoven in their nature, or suggested and enforced by this moral faculty—in rewarding and punishing them upon account of their so doing.

I am not sensible that I have, in this fifth observation, contradicted what any author designed to assert. But some of great and distinguished merit have, I think, expressed themselves in a manner which may occasion some danger to careless readers, of imagining the whole of virtue to consist in singly aiming, according to the best of their judgment, at promoting the happiness of mankind in the present state; and the whole of vice in doing what they foresee, or might foresee, is likely to produce an overbalance of unhappiness in it; than which mistakes, none can be conceived more terrible. For it is certain that some of the most shocking instances of injustice, adultery, murder, perjury, and even of persecution, may, in many supposable cases, not have the appearance of being likely to produce an overbalance of misery in the present state; perhaps sometimes may have the contrary appearance. For this reflection might easily be carried on, but I forbear. The happiness of the world is the concern of him who is the Lord and the Proprietor of it; nor do we know what we are about when we endeavor to promote the good of mankind in any ways but those which he has directed—that is indeed in all ways not contrary to veracity and justice. I speak thus upon supposition of persons really endeavoring, in some sort, to do good without regard to these. But the truth seems to be that such supposed endeavors proceed, almost always, from ambition, the spirit of the party, or some indirect principle, concealed perhaps in great measure from persons themselves. And though it is our business and our duty to endeavor, within the bounds of veracity and justice, to contribute to the ease, convenience, and even cheerfulness and diversion of our fellow creatures, yet, from our short views, it is greatly uncertain whether this endeavor will in particular instances produce an overbalance of happiness upon the whole, since so many and distant things must come into the account. And that which makes it our duty is that there is some appearance that it will, and no positive appearance sufficient to balance this, on the contrary side; and also, that such benevolent endeavor is a cultivation of that most excellent of all virtuous principles, the active principle of benevolence.

However, though veracity as well as justice is to be our rule of life, it must be added, otherwise a snare will be laid in the way of some plain men, that the use of common forms of speech, generally understood, cannot be falsehood; and in general, that there can be no designed falsehood without designing to deceive. It must likewise be observed that, in numberless cases, a man may be under the strictest obligations to what he foresees will deceive, without his intending it. For it is impossible not to foresee that the words and actions of men, in different ranks and employments, and of different educations, will perpetually be mistaken by each other; and it cannot but be so whilst they will judge with the utmost carelessness, as they daily do, of what they are not, perhaps, enough informed to be competent judges of, even though they considered it with great attention.

David Hume (1711—1776)

In his own day abused by many of his contemporaries and refused a longed-for appointment to a professorship at the university in his native Edinburgh because of his reputed skepticism and heterodoxy, David Hume, ironically, was mainly admired by his contemporaries not for his enormous philosophical achievements but rather for the pedestrian *History of England* that he began during the five years he had the post of librarian of the Advocates' Library in Edinburgh from 1752 to 1757. His *Treatise of Human Nature*, first published in three volumes in 1739 and 1740, is subtitled "An Attempt to introduce the experimental Method of Reasoning into Moral Subjects"; it attempts to provide a systematic account of the theory of knowledge, the passions, and morals based upon an empirical study of human nature. The fact that, where noticed, it was received with hostility and that, in general, it fell as he put it, "dead born from the press" led him to spend many years in rewriting its sections and even to refer disparagingly to the Treatise in the Author's Advertisement of *An Enquiry Concerning the Principles of Morals* (1751) as a "juvenile work," "projected before he left College" containing "negligencies in . . . reasoning and more in expression." Nevertheless, there is no essential modification of doctrine in this work, as he himself elsewhere acknowledged. In 1748 Hume had published his *Enquiry Concerning the Human Understanding*, and, subsequently, in 1757, his dissertation *Of the Passions*, which was one of four included in *The Natural History of Religion*. His *Essays on Moral and Political Subjects* appeared in 1741 and 1742. Finally, the *Dialogues Concerning Natural Religion*, written toward the close of his life, was published posthumously in 1779. The last work alone would have insured Hume's permanent place in the history of philosophy.

AN ENQUIRY CONCERNING THE PRINCIPLES OF MORALS [1]

SECTION I

OF THE GENERAL PRINCIPLES OF MORALS

Disputes with men, pertinaciously obstinate in their principles, are, of all others, the most irksome; except,

[1] From the edition of 1777.

perhaps, those with persons, entirely disingenuous, who really do not believe the opinions they defend, but engage in the controversy, from affectation, from a spirit of opposition, or from a desire of showing wit and ingenuity, superior to the rest of mankind. The same blind adherence to their own arguments is to be expected in both; the same contempt of their antagonists; and the same passionate vehemence, in inforcing sophistry and falsehood. And as reasoning is not the source, whence either disputant derives his tenets; it is in vain to expect, that any logic, which speaks not to the affections, will ever engage him to embrace sounder principles.

Those who have denied the reality of moral distinctions, may be ranked among the disingenuous disputants; nor is it conceivable, that any human creature could ever seriously believe, that all characters and actions were alike entitled to the affection and regard of everyone. The difference, which nature has placed between one man and another, is so wide, and this difference is still so much farther widened, by education, example, and habit, that, where the opposite extremes come at once under our apprehension, there is no scepticism so scrupulous, and scarce any assurance so determined, as absolutely to deny all distinction between them. Let a man's insensibility be ever so great, he must often be touched with the images of Right and Wrong; and let his prejudices be ever so obstinate, he must observe, that others are susceptible of like impressions. The only way, therefore, of converting an antagonist of this kind, is to leave him to himself. For, finding that nobody keeps up the controversy with him, it is probable he will, at last, of himself, from mere weariness, come over to the side of common sense and reason.

There has been a controversy started of late, much better worth examination, concerning the general foundation of Morals; whether they be derived from Reason, or from Sentiment; whether we attain the knowledge of them by a chain of argument and induction, or by an immediate feeling and finer internal sense; whether, like all sound judgement of truth and falsehood, they should be the same to every rational intelligent being; or whether, like the perception of beauty and deformity, they be founded entirely on the particular fabric and constitution of the human species.

The ancient philosophers, though they often affirm, that virtue is nothing but conformity to reason, yet, in general, seem to consider morals as deriving their existence from taste and sentiment. On the other hand, our modern enquirers, though they also talk much of the beauty of virtue, and deformity of vice, yet have commonly endeavoured to account for these distinctions by metaphysical reasonings, and by deductions from the most abstract principles of the understanding. Such confusion reigned in these subjects, that an opposition of the greatest consequence could prevail between one system and another, and even in the parts of almost each individual system; and yet nobody, till very lately, was ever sensible of it. The elegant Lord Shaftesbury, who first gave occasion to remark this distinction, and who, in general, adhered to the principles of the ancients, is not, himself, entirely free from the same confusion.

It must be acknowledged, that both sides of the question are susceptible of specious arguments. Moral distinctions, it may be said, are discernible by pure *reason:* else, whence the many disputes that reign in common life, as well as in philosophy, with regard to this subject: the long chain of proofs often produced on both sides; the examples cited, the authorities appealed to, the analogies employed, the fallacies detected, the inferences drawn, and the several conclusions adjusted to their proper principles. Truth is disputable; not taste: what exists in the nature of things is the standard of our judgement; what each man feels within himself is the standard of sentiment. Propositions in geometry may be proved, systems in physics may be controverted; but the harmony of verse, the tenderness of passion, the brilliancy of wit, must give immediate pleasure. No man reasons concerning another's beauty; but frequently concerning the justice or injustice of his actions. In every criminal trial the first object of the prisoner is to disprove the facts alleged, and deny the actions imputed to him: the second to prove, that, even if these actions were real, they might be justified, as innocent and lawful. It is confessedly by deductions of the understanding, that the first point is ascertained: how can we suppose that a different faculty of the mind is employed in fixing the other?

On the other hand, those who would resolve all moral determinations into *sentiment,* may endeavour to show, that it is impossible for reason ever to draw conclusions of this nature. To virtue, say they, it belongs to be *amiable,* and vice *odious.* This forms their very nature or essence. But can reason or argumentation distribute these different epithets to any subjects, and pronounce beforehand, that this must produce love, and that hatred? Or what other reason can we ever assign for these affections, but the original fabric and formation of the human mind, which is naturally adapted to receive them?

The end of all moral speculations is to teach us our duty; and, by proper representations of the deformity of vice and beauty of virtue, beget correspondent habits, and engage us to avoid the one, and embrace the other. But is this ever to be expected from inferences and conclusions of the understanding, which of themselves have no hold of the affections or set in motion the active powers of men? They discover truths: but where the truths which they discover are indifferent, and beget no desire or aversion, they can have no influence on conduct and behaviour. What is honourable, what is fair, what is becoming, what is noble, what is generous, takes possession of the heart, and animates us to

embrace and maintain it. What is intelligible, what is evident, what is probable, what is true, procures only the cool assent of the understanding; and gratifying a speculative curiosity, puts an end to our researches.

Extinguish all the warm feelings and prepossessions in favour of virtue, and all disgust or aversion to vice: render men totally indifferent towards these distinctions; and morality is no longer a practical study, nor has any tendency to regulate our lives and actions.

These arguments on each side (and many more might be produced) are so plausible, that I am apt to suspect, they may, the one as well as the other, be solid and satisfactory, and that *reason* and *sentiment* concur in almost all moral determinations and conclusions. The final sentence, it is probable, which pronounces characters and actions amiable or odious, praiseworthy or blameable; that which stamps on them the mark of honour or infamy, approbation or censure; that which renders morality an active principle and constitutes virtue our happiness, and vice our misery; it is probable, I say, that this final sentence depends on some internal sense or feeling, which nature has made universal in the whole species. For what else can have an influence of this nature? But in order to pave the way for such a sentiment, and give a proper discernment of its object, it is often necessary, we find, that much reasoning should precede, that nice distinctions be made, just conclusions drawn, distant comparisons formed, complicated relations examined, and general facts fixed and ascertained. Some species of beauty, especially the natural kinds, on their first appearance, command our affection and approbation; and where they fail of this effect, it is impossible for any reasoning to redress their influence, or adapt them better to our taste and sentiment. But in many orders of beauty, particularly those of the finer arts, it is requisite to employ much reasoning, in order to feel the proper sentiment; and a false relish may frequently be corrected by argument and reflection. There are just grounds to conclude, that moral beauty partakes much of this latter species, and demands the assistance of our intellectual faculties, in order to give it a suitable influence on the human mind.

But though this question, concerning the general principles of morals, be curious and important, it is needless for us, at present, to employ farther care in our researches concerning it. For if we can be so happy, in the course of this enquiry, as to discover the true origin of morals, it will then easily appear how far either sentiment or reason enters into all determinations of this nature.[2] In order to attain this purpose, we shall endeavour to follow a very simple method: we shall analyse that complication of mental qualities, which form what, in common life, we call Personal Merit: we shall consider every attribute of the mind, which renders a man an object either of esteem and affection, or of hatred and contempt; every habit or sentiment or faculty, which, if ascribed to any person, implies either praise or blame, and may enter into any panegyric or satire of his character and manners. The quick sensibility, which, on this head, is so universal among mankind, gives a philosopher sufficient assurance, that he can never be considerably mistaken in framing the catalogue, or incur any danger of misplacing the objects of his contemplation: he needs only enter into his own breast for a moment, and consider whether or not he should desire to have this or that quality ascribed to him, and whether such or such an imputation would proceed

2 See Appendix i, p. 281.

from a friend or an enemy. The very nature of language guides us almost infallibly in forming a judgement of this nature; and as every tongue possesses one set of words which are taken in a good sense, and another in the opposite, the least acquaintance with the idiom suffices, without any reasoning, to direct us in collecting and arranging the estimable or blameable qualities of men. The only object of reasoning is to discover the circumstances on both sides, which are common to these qualities; to observe that particular in which the estimable qualities agree on the one hand, and the blameable on the other; and thence to reach the foundation of ethics, and find those universal principles, from which all censure or approbation is ultimately derived. As this is a question of fact, not of abstract science, we can only expect success, by following the experimental method, and deducing general maxims from a comparison of particular instances. The other scientific method, where a general abstract principle is first established, and is afterwards branched out into a variety of inferences and conclusions, may be more perfect in itself, but suits less the imperfection of human nature, and is a common source of illusion and mistake in this as well as in other subjects. Men are now cured of their passion for hypotheses and systems in natural philosophy, and will hearken to no arguments but those which are derived from experience. It is full time they should attempt a like reformation in all moral disquisitions; and reject every system of ethics, however subtle or ingenious, which is not founded on fact and observation.

We shall begin our enquiry on this head by the consideraton of the social virtues, Benevolence and Justice. The explication of them will probably give us an opening by which the others may be accounted for.

SECTION II

OF BENEVOLENCE

PART I

It may be esteemed, perhaps, a superfluous task to prove, that the benevolent or softer affections are estimable; and wherever they appear, engage the approbation and good-will of mankind. The epithets *sociable, good-natured, humane, merciful, grateful, friendly, generous, beneficent,* or their equivalents, are known in all languages, and universally express the highest merit, which *human nature* is capable of attaining. Where these amiable qualities are attended with birth and power and eminent abilities, and display themselves in the good government or useful instruction of mankind, they seem even to raise the possessors of them above the rank of *human nature,* and make them approach in some measure to the divine. Exalted capacity, undaunted courage, prosperous success; these may only expose a hero or politician to the envy and ill-will of the public: but as soon as the praises are added of humane and beneficent; when instances are displayed of lenity, tenderness or friendship; envy itself is silent, or joins the general voice of approbation and applause.

When Pericles, the great Athenian statesman and general, was on his death-bed, his surrounding friends, deeming him now insensible, began to indulge their sorrow for their expiring patron, by enumerating his great qualities and successes, his conquests and victories, the unusual length of his administration, and his nine trophies erected over the enemies of the republic. *You forget,* cries the dying hero, who had heard all, *you forget the most eminent of my praises, while you dwell so much on those vulgar advantages, in which fortune had a principal share. You have not observed that no citizen has ever yet worne mourning on my account.*[3]

In men of more ordinary talents and capacity, the social virtues become, if possible, still more essentially requisite; there being nothing eminent, in that case, to compensate for the want of them, or preserve the person from our severest hatred, as well as contempt. A high ambition, an elevated courage, is apt, says Cicero, in less perfect characters, to degenerate into a turbulent ferocity. The more social and softer virtues are there chiefly to be regarded. These are always good and amiable.[4]

The principal advantage, which Juvenal discovers in the extensive capacity of the human species, is that it renders our benevolence also more extensive, and gives us larger opportunities of spreading our kindly influence than what are indulged to the inferior creation.[5] It must, indeed, be confessed, that by doing good only, can a man truly enjoy the advantages of being eminent. His exalted station, of itself but the more exposes him to danger and tempest. His sole prerogative is to afford shelter to inferiors, who repose themselves under his cover and protection.

But I forget, that it is not my present business to recommend generosity and benevolence, or to paint, in their true colours, all the genuine charms of the social virtues. These, indeed, sufficiently engage every heart, on the first apprehension of them; and it is difficult to abstain from some sally of panegyric, as often as they occur in discourse or reasoning. But our object here being more the speculative, than the practical part of morals, it will suffice to remark, (what will readily,

---

3 Plut. in Pericle.
4 Cic. de Officiis, lib. i.
5 Sat. xv. 139 and seq.

I believe, be allowed) that no qualities are more intitled to the general good-will and approbation of mankind than beneficence and humanity, friendship and gratitude, natural affection and public spirit, or whatever proceeds from a tender sympathy with others, and a generous concern for our kind and species. These wherever they appear seem to transfuse themselves, in a manner, into each beholder, and to call forth, in their own behalf, the same favourable and affectionate sentiments, which they exert on all around.

PART II

We may observe that, in displaying the praises of any humane, beneficent man, there is one circumstance which never fails to be amply insisted on, namely, the happiness and satisfaction, derived to society from his intercourse and good offices. To his parents, we are apt to say, he endears himself by his pious attachment and duteous care still more than by the connexions of nature. His children never feel his authority, but when employed for their advantage. With him, the ties of love are consolidated by beneficence and friendship. The ties of friendship approach, in a fond observance of each obliging office, to those of love and inclination. His domestics and dependants have in him a sure resource; and no longer dread the power of fortune, but so far as she exercises it over him. From him the hungry receive food, the naked clothing, the ignorant and slothful skill and industry. Like the sun, an inferior minister of providence he cheers, invigorates, and sustains the surrounding world.

If confined to private life, the sphere of his activity is narrower; but his influence is all benign and gentle. If exalted into a higher station, mankind and posterity reap the fruit of his labours.

As these topics of praise never fail to be employed, and with success, where we would inspire esteem for any one; may it not thence be concluded, that the utility, resulting from the social virtues, forms, at least, a *part* of their merit, and is one source of that approbation and regard so universally paid to them?

. . .

Upon the whole, then, it seems undeniable, *that* nothing can bestow more merit on any human creature than the sentiment of benevolence in an eminent degree; and *that* a *part*, at least, of its merit arises from its tendency to promote the interests of our species, and bestow happiness on human society. We carry our view into the salutary consequences of such a character and disposition; and whatever has so benign an influence, and forwards so desirable an end, is beheld with complacency and pleasure. The social virtues are never regarded without their beneficial tendencies, nor viewed as barren and unfruitful. The happiness of mankind, the order of society, the harmony of families, the mutual support of friends, are always considered as the result of their gentle dominion over the breasts of men. How considerable a *part* of their merit we ought to ascribe to their utility, will better appear from future disquisitions; [6] as well as the reason, why this circumstance has such a command over our esteem and approbation.[7]

SECTION III

Of Justice

PART I

That Justice is useful to society, and consequently that *part* of its merit, at

[6] Sect. iii. and iv.
[7] Sect. v.

least, must arise from that consideration, it would be a superfluous undertaking to prove. That public utility is the *sole* origin of justice, and that reflections on the beneficial consequences of this virtue are the *sole* foundation of its merit; this proposition, being more curious and important, will better deserve our examination and enquiry.

Let us suppose that nature has bestowed on the human race such profuse *abundance* of all *external* conveniencies, that, without any uncertainty in the event, without any care or industry on our part, every individual finds himself fully provided with whatever his most voracious appetites can want, or luxurious imagination wish or desire. His natural beauty, we shall suppose, surpasses all acquired ornaments: the perpetual clemency of the seasons renders useless all clothes or covering: the raw herbage affords him the most delicious fare; the clear fountain, the richest beverage. No laborious occupation required: no tillage: no navigation. Music, poetry, and contemplation form his sole business: conversation, mirth, and friendship his sole amusement.

It seems evident that, in such a happy state, every other social virtue would flourish, and receive tenfold increase; but the cautious, jealous virtue of justice would never once have been dreamed of. For what purpose make a partition of goods, where every one has already more than enough? Why give rise to property, where there cannot possibly be any injury? Why call this object *mine*, when upon the seizing of it by another, I need but stretch out my hand to possess myself to what is equally valuable? Justice, in that case, being totally useless, would be an idle ceremonial, and could never possibly have place in the catalogue of virtues.

We see, even in the present necessitous condition of mankind, that, wherever any benefit is bestowed by nature in an unlimited abundance, we leave it always in common among the whole human race, and make no subdivisions of right and property. Water and air, though the most necessary of all objects, are not challenged as the property of individuals; nor can any man commit injustice by the most lavish use and enjoyment of these blessings. In fertile extensive countries, with few inhabitants, land is regarded on the same footing. And no topic is so much insisted on by those, who defend the liberty of the seas, as the unexhausted use of them in navigation. Were the advantages, procured by navigation, as inexhaustible, these reasoners had never had any adversaries to refute; nor had any claims ever been advanced of a separate, exclusive dominion over the ocean.

It may happen, in some countries, at some periods, that there be established a property in water, none in land; [8] if the latter be in greater abundance than can be used by the inhabitants, and the former be found, with difficulty, and in very small quantities.

Again; suppose, that, though the necessities of human race continue the same as at present, yet the mind is so enlarged, and so replete with friendship and generosity, that every man has the utmost tenderness for every man, and feels no more concern for his own interest than for that of his fellows; it seems evident, that the use of justice would, in this case, be suspended by such an extensive benevolence, nor would the divisions and barriers of property and obligation have ever been thought of. Why should I bind another, by a deed or promise, to do me any good office, when I know that he is already

[8] Genesis, chaps. xiii and xxi.

prompted, by the strongest inclination, to seek my happiness, and would, of himself, perform the desired service; except the hurt, he thereby receives, be greater than the benefit accruing to me? in which case, he knows, that, from my innate humanity and friendship, I should be the first to oppose myself to his impudent generosity. Why raise land marks between my neighbour's field and mine, when my heart has made no division between our interests; but shares all his joys and sorrows with the same force and vivacity as if originally my own? Every man, upon this supposition, being a second self to another, would trust all his interests to the discretion of every man; without jealousy, without partition, without distinction. And the whole human race would form only one family; where all would lie in common, and be used freely, without regard to property; but cautiously too, with as entire regard to the necessities of each individual, as if our own interests were most intimately concerned.

In the present disposition of the human heart, it would, perhaps, be difficult to find complete instances of such enlarged affections; but still we may observe, that the case of families approaches towards it; and the stronger the mutual benevolence is among the individuals, the nearer it approaches; till all distinction of property be, in a great measure, lost and confounded among them. Between married persons, the cement of friendship is by the laws supposed so strong as to abolish all division of possessions; and has often, in reality, the force ascribed to it. And it is observable, that, during the ardour of new enthusiasms, when every principle is inflamed into extravagance, the community of goods has frequently been attempted; and nothing but experience of its inconveniencies, from the returning or disguised selfishness of men, could make the imprudent fanatics adopt anew the ideas of justice and of separate property. So true is it, that this virtue derives its existence entirely from its necessary *use* to the intercourse and social state of mankind.

To make this truth more evident, let us reverse the foregoing suppositions; and carrying everything to the opposite extreme, consider what would be the effect of these new situations. Suppose a society to fall into such want of all common necessaries, that the utmost frugality and industry cannot preserve the greater number from perishing, and the whole from extreme misery; it will readily, I believe, be admitted, that the strict laws of justice are suspended, in such a pressing emergence, and give place to the stronger motives of necessity and self-preservation. Is it any crime, after a shipwreck, to seize whatever means or instrument of safety one can lay hold of, without regard to former limitations of property? Or if a city besieged were perishing with hunger; can we imagine, that men will see any means of preservation before them, and lose their lives, from a scrupulous regard to what, in other situations, would be the rules of equity and justice? The use and tendency of that virtue is to procure happiness and security, by preserving order in society: but where the society is ready to perish from extreme necessity, no greater evil can be dreaded from violence and injustice; and every man may now provide for himself by all the means, which prudence can dictate, or humanity permit. The public, even in less urgent necessities, opens granaries, without the consent of proprietors; as justly supposing, that the authority of magistracy may, consistent with equity, extend so far: but were any number of men to assemble, without the tie of laws or civil jurisdiction;

would an equal partition of bread in a famine, though effected by power and even violence, be regarded as criminal or injurious?

Suppose likewise, that it should be a virtuous man's fate to fall into the society of ruffians, remote from the protection of laws and government; what conduct must he embrace in that melancholy situation? He sees such a desperate rapaciousness prevail; such a disregard to equity, such contempt of order, such stupid blindness to future consequences, as must immediately have the most tragical conclusion, and must terminate in destruction to the greater number, and in a total dissolution of society to the rest. He, meanwhile, can have no other expedient than to arm himself, to whomever the sword he seizes, or the buckler, may belong: To make provision of all means of defence and security: And his particular regard to justice being no longer of use to his own safety or that of others, he must consult the dictates of self-preservation alone, without concern for those who no longer merit his care and attention.

When any man, even in political society, renders himself by his crimes, obnoxious to the public, he is punished by the laws in his goods and person; that is, the ordinary rules of justice are, with regard to him, suspended for a moment, and it becomes equitable to inflict on him, for the *benefit* of society, what otherwise he could not suffer without wrong or injury.

The rage and violence of public war; what is it but a suspension of justice among the warring parties, who perceive, that this virtue is now no longer of any *use* or advantage to them? The laws of war, which then succeed to those of equity and justice, are rules calculated for the *advantage* and *utility* of that particular state, in which men are now placed. And were a civilized nation engaged with bar-

barians, who observed no rules even of war, the former must also suspend their observance of them, where they no longer serve to any purpose; and must render every action or rencounter as bloody and pernicious as possible to the first aggressors.

Thus, the rules of equity or justice depend entirely on the particular state and condition in which men are placed, and owe their origin and existence to that utility, which results to the public from their strict and regular observance. Reverse, in any considerable circumstance, the condition of men: Produce extreme abundance or extreme necessity: Implant in the human breast perfect moderation and humanity, or perfect rapaciousness and malice: By rendering justice totally *useless*, you thereby totally destroy its essence, and suspend its obligation upon mankind.

The common situation of society is a medium amidst all these extremes. We are naturally partial to ourselves, and to our friends; but are capable of learning the advantage resulting from a more equitable conduct. Few enjoyments are given us from the open and liberal hand of nature; but by art, labour, and industry, we can extract them in great abundance. Hence the ideas of property become necessary in all civil society: Hence justice derives its usefulness to the public: And hence alone arises its merit and moral obligation.

These conclusions are so natural and obvious, that they have not escaped even the poets, in their descriptions of the felicity attending the golden age or the reign of Saturn. The seasons, in that first period of nature, were so temperate, if we credit these agreeable fictions, that there was no necessity for men to provide themselves with clothes and houses, as a security against the violence of heat and cold: The rivers flowed with wine and milk: The oaks yielded honey; and nature spontaneously produced her greatest delicacies. Nor were these the chief advantages of that happy age. Tempests were not alone removed from nature; but those more furious tempests were unknown to human breasts, which now cause such uproar, and engender such confusion. Avarice, ambition, cruelty, selfishness, were never heard of: Cordial affection, compassion, sympathy, were the only movements with which the mind was yet acquainted. Even the punctilious distinction of *mine* and *thine* was banished from among the happy race of mortals, and carried with it the very notion of property and obligation, justice and injustice.

This *poetical* fiction of the *golden age,* is in some respects, of a piece with the *philosophical* fiction of the *state of nature;* only that the former is represented as the most charming and most peaceable condition, which can possibly be imagined; whereas the latter is painted out as a state of mutual war and violence, attended with the most extreme necessity. On the first origin of mankind, we are told, their ignorance and savage nature were so prevalent, that they could give no mutual trust, but must each depend upon himself and his own force or cunning for protection and security. No law was heard of: No rule of justice known: No distinction of property regarded: Power was the only measure of right; and a perpetual war of all against all was the result of men's untamed selfishness and barbarity.[9]

[9] This fiction of a state of nature, as a state of war, was not first started by Mr. Hobbes, as is commonly imagined. Plato endeavors to refute an hypothesis very like it in the second, third, and fourth books de republica. Cicero, on the contrary, supposes it certain and universally acknowledged in the following passage. 'Quis enim vestrum, judices, ignorat, ita

Whether such a condition of human nature could ever exist, or if it did, could continue so long as to merit the appellation of a *state,* may justly be doubted. Men are necessarily born in a family-society, at least; and are trained up by their parents to some rule of conduct and behaviour. But this must be admitted, that, if such a state of mutual war and violence was ever real, the suspension of all laws of justice, from their absolute inutility, is a necessary and infallible consequence.

The more we vary our views of human life, and the newer and more unusual the lights are in which we survey it, the more shall we be convinced, that the origin here assigned for the virtue of justice is real and satisfactory.

Were there a species of creatures intermingled with men, which, though rational, were possessed of such inferior strength, both of body and mind,

naturam rerum tulisse, ut quodam tempore homines, nondum neque naturali neque civili jure descripto, fusi per agros ac dispersi vagarentur tantumque haberent quantum manu ac viribus, per caedem ac vulnera, aut eripere aut retinere potuissent? Qui igitur primi virtute & consilio praestanti extiterunt, ii perspecto genere humanae docilitatis atque ingenii, dissipatos unum in locum congregarunt, eosque ex feritate illa ad justitiam ac mansuetudinem transduxerunt. Tum res ad communem utilitatem, quas publicas appellamus, tum conventicula hominum quae postea civitates nominatae sunt, tum domicilia conjuncta, quas urbes dicamus, invento & divino & humano jure moenibus sepserunt. Atque inter hanc vitam, per politam humanitate, & illam immanem, nihil tam interest quam JUS atque VIS. Horum utro uti nolimus, altero est utendum. Vim volumus extingui. Jus valeat necesse est, id est, judicia, quibus omne jus continetur. Judicia displicent, aut nulla sunt. Vis dominetur necesse est. Haec vident omnes.' *Pro Sext.* § 42.

that they were incapable of all resistance, and could never, upon the highest provocation, make us feel the effects of their resentment; the necessary consequence, I think, is that we should be bound by the laws of humanity to give gentle usage to these creatures, but should not, properly speaking, lie under any restraint of justice with regard to them, nor could they possess any right or property, exclusive of such arbitrary lords. Our intercourse with them could not be called society, which supposes a degree of equality; but absolute command on the one side, and servile obedience on the other. What we covet, they must instantly resign: Our permission is the only tenure, by which they hold their possessions: Our compassion and kindness the only check, by which they curb our lawless will: And as no inconvenience ever results from the exercise of a power, so firmly established in nature, the restraints of justice and property, being totally *useless*, would never have place in so unequal a confederacy.

This is plainly the situation of men, with regard to animals; and how far these may be said to possess reason, I leave it to others to determine. The great superiority of civilized Europeans above barbarous Indians, tempted us to imagine ourselves on the same footing with regard to them, and made us throw off all restraints of justice, and even of humanity, in our treatment of them. In many nations, the female sex are reduced to like slavery, and are rendered incapable of all property, in opposition to their lordly masters. But though the males, when united, have in all countries bodily force sufficient to maintain this severe tyranny, yet such are the insinuation, address, and charms of their fair companions, that women are commonly able to break the confederacy, and share with the other sex in all the rights and privileges of society.

Were the human species so framed by nature as that each individual possessed within himself every faculty, requisite both for his own preservation and for the propagation of his kind: Were all society and intercourse cut off between man and man, by the primary intention of the supreme Creator: It seems evident, that so solitary a being would be as much incapable of justice, as of social discourse and conversation. Where mutual regards and forbearance serve to no manner of purpose, they would never direct the conduct of any reasonable man. The headlong course of the passions would be checked by no reflection on future consequences. And as each man is here supposed to love himself alone, and to depend only on himself and his own activity for safety and happiness, he would, on every occasion, to the utmost of his power, challenge the preference above every other being, to none of which he is bound by any ties, either of nature or of interest.

But suppose the conjunction of the sexes to be established in nature, a family immediately arises; and particular rules being found requisite for its subsistence, these are immediately embraced; though without comprehending the rest of mankind within their prescriptions. Suppose that several families unite together into one society, which is totally disjoined from all others, the rules, which preserve peace and order, enlarge themselves to the utmost extent of that society; but becoming then entirely useless, lose their force when carried one step farther. But again suppose, that several distinct societies maintain a kind of intercourse for mutual convenience and advantage, the boundaries of justice still grow larger, in proportion to the largeness of men's views, and the force of their mutual connexions. History, experience, reason sufficiently instruct us in this natural progress of human sentiments, and in the gradual enlargement of our regards to justice, in proportion as we become acquainted with the extensive utility of that virtue.

PART II

If we examine the *particular* laws, by which justice is directed, and property determined; we shall still be presented with the same conclusion. The good of mankind is the only object of all these laws and regulations. Not only is it requisite, for the peace and interest of society, that men's possessions should be separated; but the rules, which we follow, in making the separation, are such as can best be contrived to serve farther the interests of society.

We shall suppose that a creature, possessed of reason, but unacquainted with human nature, deliberates with himself what rules of justice or property would best promote public interest, and establish peace and security among mankind: His most obvious thought would be, to assign the largest possessions to the most extensive virtue, and give every one the power of doing good, proportioned to his inclination. In a perfect theocracy, where a being, infinitely intelligent, governs by particular volitions, this rule would certainly have place, and might serve to the wisest purposes: But were mankind to execute such a law; so great is the uncertainty of merit, both from its natural obscurity, and from the self-conceit of each individual, that no determinate rule of conduct would ever result from it; and the total dissolution of society must be the immediate consequence. Fanatics may suppose, *that dominion is founded on grace*, and *that saints alone inherit the earth;* but the civil

magistrate very justly puts these sublime theorists on the same footing with common robbers, and teaches them by the severest discipline, that a rule, which, in speculation, may seem the most advantageous to society, may yet be found, in practice, totally pernicious and destructive.

That there were *religious* fanatics of this kind in England, during the civil wars, we learn from history; though it is probable, that the obvious *tendency* of these principles excited such horror in mankind, as soon obliged the dangerous enthusiasts to renounce, or at least conceal their tenets. Perhaps the *levellers*, who claimed an equal distribution of property, were a kind of *political* fanatics, which arose from the religious species, and more openly avowed their pretensions; as carrying a more plausible appearance, of being practicable in themselves, as well as useful to human society.

It must, indeed, be confessed, that nature is so liberal to mankind, that, were all her presents equally divided among the species, and improved by art and industry, every individual would enjoy all the necessaries, and even most of the comforts of life; nor would ever be liable to any ills but such as might accidentally arise from the sickly frame and constitution of his body. It must also be confessed, that, wherever we depart from this equality, we rob the poor of more satisfaction than we add to the rich, and that the slight gratification of a frivolous vanity, in one individual, frequently costs more than bread to many families, and even provinces. It may appear withal, that the rule of equality, as it would be highly *useful,* is not altogether *impracticable;* but has taken place, at least in an imperfect degree, in some republics; particularly that of Sparta; where it was attended, it is said, with the most beneficial consequences. Not to mention that the Agrarian laws, so frequently claimed in Rome, and carried into execution in many Greek cities, proceeded, all of them, from a general idea of the utility of this principle.

But historians, and even common sense, may inform us, that, however specious these ideas of *perfect* equality may seem, they are really, at bottom, *impracticable;* and were they not so, would be extremely *pernicious* to human society. Render possessions ever so equal, men's different degrees of art, care, and industry will immediately break that equality. Or if you check these virtues, you reduce society to the most extreme indigence; and instead of preventing want and beggary in a few, render it unavoidable to the whole community. The most rigorous inquisition too is requisite to watch every inequality on its first appearance; and the most severe jurisdiction, to punish and redress it. But besides, that so much authority must soon degenerate into tyranny, and be exerted with great partialities; who can possibly be possessed of it, in such a situation as is here supposed? Perfect equality of possessions, destroying all subordination, weakens extremely the authority of magistracy, and must reduce all power nearly to a level, as well as property.

We may conclude, therefore, that, in order to establish laws for the regulation of property, we must be acquainted with the nature and situation of man; must reject appearances, which may be false, though specious; and must search for those rules, which are, on the whole, most *useful* and *beneficial.* Vulgar sense and slight experience are sufficient for this purpose; where men give not way to too selfish avidity, or too extensive enthusiasm.

Who sees not, for instance, that whatever is produced or improved by a man's art or industry ought, for ever, to be secured to him, in order to give encouragement to such *useful* habits and accomplishments? That the property ought also to descend to children and relations, for the same *useful* purpose? That it may be alienated by consent, in order to beget that commerce and intercourse, which is so *beneficial* to human society? And that all contracts and promises ought carefully to be fulfilled, in order to secure mutual trust and confidence, by which the general *interest* of mankind is so much promoted?

Examine the writers on the laws of nature; and you will always find, that, whatever principles they set out with, they are sure to terminate here at last, and to assign, as the ultimate reason for every rule which they establish, the convenience and necessities of mankind. A concession thus extorted, in opposition to systems, has more authority than if it had been made in prosecution of them. What other reason, indeed, could writers ever give, why this must be *mine* and that *yours;* since uninstructed nature surely never made any such distinction? The objects which receive those appellations are, of themselves, foreign to us; they are totally disjoined and separated from us; and nothing but the general interests of society can form the connexion.

Sometimes the interests of society may require a rule of justice in a particular case; but may not determine any particular rule, among several, which are all equally beneficial. In that case, the slightest *analogies* are laid hold of, in order to prevent that indifference and ambiguity, which would be the source of perpetual dissension. Thus possession alone, and first possession, is supposed to convey property, where no body else has any preceding claim and pretension. Many of the reasonings of lawyers are of this analogical nature, and depend on very slight connexions of the imagination.

Does any one scruple, in extraordinary cases, to violate all regard to the private property of individuals, and sacrifice to public interest a distinction which had been established for the sake of that interest? The safety of the people is the supreme law: All other particular laws are subordinate to it, and dependent on it: And if, in the *common* course of things, they be followed and regarded; it is only because the public safety and interest *commonly* demand so equal and impartial an administration.

Sometimes both *utility* and *analogy* fail, and leave the laws of justice in total uncertainty. Thus, it is highly requisite, that prescription or long possession should convey property; but what number of days or months or years should be sufficient for that purpose, it is impossible for reason alone to determine. *Civil laws* here supply the place of the natural *code,* and assign different terms for prescription, according to the different *utilities,* proposed by the legislator. Bills of exchange and promissory notes, by the laws of most countries, prescribe sooner than bonds, and mortgages, and contracts of a more formal nature.

In general we may observe that all questions of property are subordinate to the authority of civil laws, which extend, restrain, modify, and alter the rules of natural justice, according to the particular *convenience* of each community. The laws have, or ought to have, a constant reference to the constitution of government, the manners, the climate, the religion, the commerce, the situation of each society. A late author of genius, as well as learning, has prosecuted this subject at large, and has established, from these principles, a system of political knowledge, which abounds in inge-nious and brilliant thoughts, and is not wanting in solidity.[10]

What is man's property? Anything which it is lawful for him, and for him alone, to use. *But what rule have we, by which we can distinguish these objects?* Here we must have recourse to statutes, customs, precedents, analogies, and a hundred other circumstances; some of which are constant and inflexible, some variable and arbitrary. But the ultimate point, in which they all professedly terminate, is the interest and happiness of human society. Where this enters not into consideration, nothing can appear more whimsical, unnatural, and even superstitious, than all or most of the laws of justice and of property.

Those who ridicule vulgar superstitions, and expose the folly of particular regards to meats, days, places, postures, apparel, have an easy task;

[10] The author of *L'Esprit des Loix.* This illustrious writer, however, sets out with a different theory, and supposes all right to be founded on certain *rapports* or relations; which is a system, that, in my opinion, never will be reconciled with true philosophy. Father Malebranche, as far as I can learn, was the first that started this abstract theory of morals, which was afterwards adopted by Cudworth, Clarke, and others; and as it excludes all sentiment, and pretends to found everything on reason, it has not wanted followers in this philosophic age. See Section I, Appendix I. With regard to justice, the virtue here treated of, the inference against this theory seems short and conclusive. Property is allowed to be dependent on civil laws; civil laws are allowed to have no other object, but the interest of society: This therefore must be allowed to be the sole foundation of property and justice. Not to mention, that our obligation itself to obey the magistrate and his laws is founded on nothing but the interests of society.

If the ideas of justice, sometimes, do not follow the dispositions of civil law;

while they consider all the qualities and relations of the objects, and discover no adequate cause for that affection or antipathy, veneration of horror, which have so mighty an influence over a considerable part of mankind. A Syrian would have starved rather than taste pigeon: an Egyptian would not have approached bacon: But if these species of food be examined by the senses of sight, smell, or taste, or scrutinized by the sciences of chemistry, medicine, or physics, no difference is ever found between them and any other species, nor can that precise circumstance be pitched on, which may afford a just foundation for the religious passion. A fowl on Thursday is lawful food; on Friday abominable: Eggs in this house and in this diocese, are permitted during Lent; a hundred paces farther, to

---

we shall find, that these cases, instead of objections, are confirmations of the theory delivered above. Where a civil law is so perverse as to cross all the interests of society, it loses all its authority, and men judge by the ideas of natural justice, which are conformable to those interests. Sometimes also civil laws, for useful purposes, require a ceremony or form to any deed; and where that is wanting, their decrees run contrary to the usual tenour of justice; but one who takes advantage of such chicanes, is not commonly regarded as an honest man. Thus, the interests of society require, that contracts be fulfilled; and there is not a more material article either of natural or civil justice: But the omission of a trifling circumstance will often, by law, invalidate a contract, *in foro humano,* but not *in foro conscientiae,* as divines express themselves. In these cases, the magistrate is supposed only to withdraw his power of enforcing the right, not to have altered the right. Where his intention extends to the right, and is conformable to the interests of society; it never fails to alter the right; a clear proof of the origin of justice and of property, as assigned above.

eat them is a damnable sin. This earth or building, yesterday was profane; to-day, by the muttering of certain words, it has become holy and sacred. Such reflections as these, in the mouth of a philosopher, one may safely say, are too obvious to have any influence; because they must always, to every man, occur at first sight; and where they prevail not, of themselves, they are surely obstructed by education, prejudice, and passion, not by ignorance or mistake.

It may appear to a careless view, or rather a too abstracted reflection, that there enters a like superstition into all the sentiments of justice; and that, if a man expose its object, or what we call property, to the same scrutiny of sense and science, he will not, by the most accurate enquiry, find any foundation for the difference made by moral sentiment. I may lawfully nourish myself from this tree; but the fruit of another of the same species, ten paces off, it is criminal for me to touch. Had I worn this apparel an hour ago, I had merited the severest punishment; but a man, by pronouncing a few magical syllables, has now rendered it fit for my use and service. Were this house placed in the neighbouring territory, it had been immoral for me to dwell in it; but being built on this side the river, it is subject to a different municipal law, and by its becoming mine I incur no blame or censure. The same species of reasoning it may be thought, which so successfully exposes superstition, is also applicable to justice; nor is it possible, in the one case more than in the other, to point out, in the object, that precise quality or circumstance, which is the foundation of the sentiment.

But there is this material difference between *superstition* and *justice,* that the former is frivolous, useless, and burdensome; the latter is absolutely requisite to the well-being of mankind and existence of society. When we abstract from this circumstance (for it is too apparent ever to be overlooked) it must be confessed, that all regards to right and property, seem entirely without foundation, as much as the grossest and most vulgar superstition. Were the interests of society nowise concerned, it is as unintelligible why another's articulating certain sounds implying consent, should change the nature of my actions with regard to a particular object, as why the reciting of a liturgy by a priest, in a certain habit and posture, should dedicate a heap of brick and timber, and render it, thenceforth and for ever, sacred.[11]

These reflections are far from weakening the obligations of justice, or diminishing anything from the most sacred attention to property. On the contrary, such sentiments must acquire new force from the present reasoning. For what stronger foundation can be desired or conceived for any duty, than to observe, that human society, or even human nature, could not subsist without the establishment of it; and will still arrive at greater degrees of happiness and perfection, the more inviolable the regard is, which is paid to that duty?

The dilemma seems obvious: As justice evidently tends to promote public utility and to support civil society, the sentiment of justice is either derived from our reflecting on that tendency, or like hunger, thirst, and other appetites, resentment, love of

---

[11] It is evident, that the will or consent alone never transfers property, nor causes the obligation of a promise (for the same reasoning extends to both), but the will must be expressed by words or signs, in order to impose a tie upon any man. The expression being once brought in as subservient to the will, soon becomes the principal part of the promise; nor will a man be less bound by his word, though he secretly give a different direction to his intention, and withhold the assent of his mind. But though the expression makes, on most occasions, the whole of the promise, yet it does not always so; and one who should make use of any expression, of which he knows not the meaning, and which he uses without any sense of the consequences, would not certainly be bound by it. Nay, though he know its meaning, yet if he use it in jest only, and with such signs as evidently show, that he has no serious intention of binding himself, he would not lie under any obligation of performance; but it is necessary, that the words be a perfect expression of the will, without any contrary signs. Nay, even this we must not carry so far as to imagine, that one, whom, by our quickness of understanding, we conjecture, from certain signs, to have an intention of deceiving us, is not bound by his expression or verbal promise, if we accept of it; but must limit this conclusion to those cases where the signs are of a different nature from those of deceit. All these contradictions are easily accounted for, if justice arise entirely from its usefulness to society; but will never be explained on any other hypothesis.

It is remarkable that the moral decisions of the *Jesuits* and other relaxed casuists, were commonly formed in prosecution of some such subtilties of reasoning as are here pointed out, and proceed as much from the habit of scholastic refinement as from any corruption of the heart, if we follow the authority of Mons. Bayle. See his Dictionary, article Loyola. And why has the indignation of mankind risen so high against these casuists, but because every one perceived, that human society could not subsist were such practices authorized, and that morals must always be handled with a view to public interest, more than philosophical regularity? If the secret direction of the intention, said every man of sense, could invalidate a contract; where is our security? And yet a metaphysical schoolman might think, that, where an intention was supposed to be requisite, if that intention really had not place, no

life, attachment to offspring, and other passions, arises from a simple original instinct in the human breast, which nature has implanted for like salutary purposes. If the latter be the case, it follows, that property, which is the object of justice, is also distinguished by a simple original instinct, and is not ascertained by any argument or reflection. But who is there that ever heard of such an instinct? Or is this a subject in which new discoveries can be made? We may as well expect to discover, in the body, new senses, which had before escaped the observation of all mankind.

But farther, though it seems a very simple proposition to say, that nature, by an instinctive sentiment, distinguishes property, yet in reality we

---

consequence ought to follow, and no obligation be imposed. The casuistical subtilties may not be greater than the subtilties of lawyers, hinted at above; but as the former are *pernicious,* and the latter *innocent* and even *necessary,* this is the reason of the very different reception they meet with from the world.

It is a doctrine of the Church of Rome, that the priest, by a secret direction of his intention, can invalidate any sacrament. This position is derived from a strict and regular prosecution of the obvious truth, that empty words alone, without any meaning or intention in the speaker, can never be attended with any effect. If the same conclusion be not admitted in reasonings concerning civil contracts, where the affair is allowed to be of so much less consequence than the eternal salvation of thousands, it proceeds entirely from men's sense of the danger and inconvenience of the doctrine in the former case: And we may thence observe, that however positive, arrogant, and dogmatical any superstition may appear, it never can convey any thorough persuasion of the reality of its objects, or put them, in any degree, on a balance with the common incidents of life, which we learn from daily observation and experimental reasoning.

shall find, that there are required for that purpose ten thousand different instincts, and these employed about objects of the greatest intricacy and nicest discernment. For when a definition of *property* is required, that relation is found to resolve itself into any possession acquired by occupation, by industry, by prescription, by inheritance, by contract, &c. Can we think that nature, by an original instinct, instructs us in all these methods of acquisition?

These words too, inheritance and contract, stand for ideas infinitely complicated; and to define them exactly, a hundred volumes of laws, and a thousand volumes of commentators, have not been found sufficient. Does nature, whose instincts in men are all simple, embrace such complicated and artificial objects, and create a rational creature, without trusting anything to the operation of his reason?

But even though all this were admitted, it would not be satisfactory. Positive laws can certainly transfer property. It is by another original instinct, that we recognize the authority of kings and senates, and mark all the boundaries of their jurisdiction? Judges too, even though their sentence be erroneous and illegal, must be allowed, for the sake of peace and order, to have decisive authority, and ultimately to determine property. Have we original innate ideas of praetors and chancellors and juries? Who sees not, that all these institutions arise merely from the necessities of human society?

All birds of the same species in every age and country, built their nests alike: In this we see the force of instinct. Men, in different times and places, frame their houses differently: Here we perceive the influence of reason and custom. A like inference may be drawn from comparing the instinct of generation and the institution of property.

How great soever the variety of municipal laws, it must be confessed, that their chief outlines pretty regularly concur; because the purposes, to which they tend, are everywhere exactly similar. In like manner, all houses have a roof and walls, windows and chimneys; though diversified in their shape, figure, and materials. The purposes of the latter, directed to the conveniencies of human life, discover not more plainly their origin from reason and reflection, than do those of the former, which points all to a like end.

I need not mention the variations, which all the rules of property receive from the finer turns and connexions of the imagination, and from the subtilties and abstractions of law-topics and reasonings. There is no possibility of reconciling this observation to the notion of original instincts.

What alone will beget a doubt concerning the theory, on which I insist, is the influence of education and acquired habits, by which we are so accustomed to blame injustice, that we are not, in every instance, conscious of any immediate reflection on the pernicious consequences of it. The views the most familiar to us are apt, for that very reason, to escape us; and what we have very frequently performed from certain motives, we are apt likewise to continue mechanically, without recalling, on every occasion, the reflections, which first determined us. The convenience, or rather necessity, which leads to justice is so universal, and everywhere points so much to the same rules, that the habit takes place in all societies; and it is not without some scrutiny, that we are able to ascertain its true origin. The matter, however, is not so obscure, but that even in common life we have every moment recourse to the principle of public utility, and ask, *What must become of the world, if such practices prevail? How could society subsist under such disorders?* Were the distinction or separation of possessions entirely useless, can any one conceive, that it ever should have obtained in society?

Thus we seem, upon the whole, to have attained a knowledge of the force of that principle here insisted on, and can determine what degree of esteem or moral approbation may result from reflections on public interest and utility. The necessity of justice to the support of society is the sole foundation of that virtue; and since no moral excellence is more highly esteemed, we may conclude that this circumstance of usefulness has, in general, the strongest energy, and most entire command over our sentiments. It must, therefore, be the source of a considerable part of the merit ascribed to humanity, benevolence, friendship, public spirit, and other social virtues of that stamp; as it is the sole source of the moral approbation paid to fidelity, justice, veracity, integrity, and those other estimable and useful qualities and principles. It is entirely agreeable to the rules of philosophy, and even of common reason; where any principle has been found to have a great force and energy in one instance, to ascribe to it a like energy in all similar instances. This indeed is Newton's chief rule of philosophizing.[12]

SECTION V

Why Utility Pleases

PART I

It seems so natural a thought to ascribe to their utility the praise, which we bestow on the social virtues, that

[12] Principia, Lib. iii.

one would expect to meet with this principle everywhere in moral writers, as the chief foundation of their reasoning and enquiry. In common life, we may observe, that the circumstance of utility is always appealed to; nor is it supposed, that a greater eulogy can be given to any man, than to display his usefulness to the public, and enumerate the services, which he has performed to mankind and society. What praise, even of an inanimate form, if the regularity and elegance of its parts destroy not its fitness for any useful purpose! And how satisfactory an apology for any disproportion or seeming deformity, if we can show the necessity of that particular construction for the use intended! A ship appears more beautiful to an artist, or one moderately skilled in navigation, where its prow is wide and swelling beyond its poop, than if it were framed with a precise geometrical regularity, in contradiction to all the laws of mechanics. A building, whose doors and windows were exact squares, would hurt the eye by that very proportion; as ill adapted to the figure of a human creature, for whose service the fabric was intended. What wonder then, that a man, whose habits and conduct are hurtful to society, and dangerous or pernicious to every one who has an intercourse with him, should, on that account, be an object of disapprobation, and communicate to every spectator the strongest sentiment of disgust and hatred.[13]

[13] We ought not to imagine because an inanimate object may be useful as well as a man, that therefore it ought also, according to this system, to merit the appellation of *virtuous*. The sentiments, excited by utility, are, in the two cases, very different; and the one is mixed with affection, esteem, approbation, &c., and not the other. In like manner, an inanimate object may have good colour and proportions as well as a human figure.

But perhaps the difficulty of accounting for these effects of usefulness, or its contrary, has kept philosophers from admitting them into their systems of ethics, and has induced them rather to employ any other principle, in explaining the origin of moral good and evil. But it is no just reason for rejecting any principle, confirmed by experience, that we cannot give a satisfactory account of its origin, nor are able to resolve it into other more general principles. And if we would employ a little thought on the present subject, we need be at no loss to account for the influence of utility, and to deduce it from principles, the most known and avowed in human nature.

From the apparent usefulness of the social virtues, it has readily been inferred by sceptics, both ancient and modern, that all moral distinctions arise from education, and were, at first, invented, and afterwards encouraged, by the art of politicians, in order to

---

But can we ever be in love with the former? There are a numerous set of passions and sentiments, of which thinking rational beings are, by the original constitution of nature, the only proper objects; and though the very same qualities be transferred to an insensible, inanimate being, they will not excite the same sentiments. The beneficial qualities of herbs and minerals are, indeed, sometimes called their *virtues;* but this is an effect of the caprice of language, which ought not to be regarded in reasoning. For though there be a species of approbation attending even inanimate objects, when beneficial, yet this sentiment is so weak, and so different from that which is directed to beneficent magistrates or statesmen; that they ought not be ranked under the same class or appellation.

A very small variation of the object, even where the same qualities are preserved, will destroy a sentiment. Thus, the same beauty, transferred to a different sex, excites no amorous passion, where nature is not extremely perverted.

render men tractable, and subdue their natural ferocity and selfishness, which incapacitated them for society. This principle, indeed, of precept and education, must so far be owned to have a powerful influence, that it may frequently increase or diminish, beyond their natural standard, the sentiments of approbation or dislike; and may even, in particular instances, create, without any natural principle, a new sentiment of this kind; as is evident in all superstitious practices and observances: But that *all* moral affection or dislike arises from this origin, will never surely be allowed by any judicious enquirer. Had nature made no such distinction, founded on the original constitution of the mind, the words, *honourable* and *shameful*, *lovely* and *odious*, *noble* and *despicable*, had never had place in any language; nor could politicians, had they invented these terms, ever have been able to render them intelligible, or make them convey any idea to the audience. So that nothing can be more superficial than this paradox of the sceptics; and it were well, if, in the abstruser studies of logic and metaphysics, we could as easily obviate the cavils of that sect, as in the practical and more intelligible sciences of politics and morals.

The social virtues must, therefore, be allowed to have a natural beauty and amiableness, which, at first, antecedent to all precept or education, recommends them to the esteem of uninstructed mankind, and engages their affections. And as the public utility of these virtues is the chief circumstance, whence they derive their merit, it follows, that the end, which they have a tendency to promote, must be some way agreeable to us, and take hold of some natural affection. It must please, either from considerations of self-interest, or from more generous motives and regards.

It has often been asserted, that, as every man has a strong connexion with society, and perceives the impossibility of his solitary subsistence, he becomes, on that account, favourable to all those habits or principles, which promote order in society, and insure to him the quiet possession of so inestimable a blessing. As much as we value our own happiness and welfare, as much must we applaud the practice of justice and humanity, by which alone the social confederacy can be maintained, and every man reap the fruits of mutual protection and assistance.

This deduction of morals from self-love, or a regard to private interest, is an obvious thought, and has not arisen wholly from the wanton sallies and sportive assaults of the sceptics. To mention no others, Polybius, one of the gravest and most judicious, as well as most moral writers of antiquity, has assigned this selfish origin to all our sentiments of virtue.[14] But though the solid practical sense of that author, and his aversion to all vain subtilties, render his authority on the present subject very considerable; yet is not this an affair to be decided by authority, and the voice of nature and experience seems plainly to oppose the selfish theory.

We frequently bestow praise on virtuous actions, performed in very

[14]Undutifulness to parents is disapproved of by mankind, προορωμένους τὸ μέλλον, καὶ συλλογιζομένους ὅτι τὸ παραπλήσιον ἑκάστοις αὐτῶν συγκυρήσει. Ingratitude for a like reason (though he seems there to mix a more generous regard συναγανακτοῦντας μὲν τῷ πέλας, ἀναφέροντας δ' ἐπ' αὑτοὺς τὸ παραπλήσιον, ἐξ ὧν ὑπογίγνεταί τις ἔννοια παρ' ἑκάστῳ τῆς τοῦ καθήκοντος δυνάμεως καὶ θεωρίας-Lib. vi cap 4. Ed. Gronorius.) Perhaps the historian only meant, that our sympathy and humanity was more enlivened, by our considering the similarity of our case with that of the person suffering: which is a just sentiment.

distant ages and remote countries; where the utmost subtilty of imagination would not discover any appearance of self-interest, or find any connexion of our present happiness and security with events so widely separated from us.

A generous, a brave, a noble deed, performed by an adversary, commands our approbation; while in its consequences it may be acknowledged prejudicial to our particular interest.

Where private advantage concurs with general affection for virtue, we readily perceive and avow the mixture of these distinct sentiments, which have a very different feeling and influence on the mind. We praise, perhaps, with more alacrity, where the generous humane action contributes to our particular interest: But the topics of praise, which we insist on, are very wide of this circumstance. And we may attempt to bring over others to our sentiments, without endeavouring to convince them, that they reap any advantage from the actions which we recommend to their approbation and applause.

Frame the model of a praiseworthy character, consisting of all the most amiable moral virtues: Give instances, in which these display themselves after an eminent and extraordinary manner: You readily engage the esteem and approbation of all your audience, who never so much as enquire in what age and country the person lived, who possessed these noble qualities: A circumstance, however, of all others, the most material to self-love, or a concern for our own individual happiness.

Once on a time, a statesman, in the shock and contest of parties, prevailed so far as to procure, by his eloquence, the banishment of an able adversary; whom he secretly followed, offering him money for his support during his exile, and soothing him with topics of consolation in his misfortunes. *Alas!* cries the banished statesman, *with what regret must I leave my friends in this city, where even enemies are so generous!* Virtue, though in an enemy, here pleased him: And we also give it the just tribute of praise and approbation; nor do we retract these sentiments, when we hear, that the action passed at Athens, about two thousand years ago, and that the persons' names were Eschines and Demosthenes.

What is that to me? There are few occasions, when this question is not pertinent: And had it that universal, infallible influence supposed, it would turn into ridicule every composition, and almost every conversation, which contain any praise or censure of men and manners.

It is but a weak subterfuge, when pressed by these facts and arguments, to say, that we transport ourselves, by the force of imagination, into distant ages and countries, and consider the advantage, which we should have reaped from these characters, had we been contemporaries, and had any commerce with the persons. It is not conceivable, how a *real* sentiment or passion can ever arise from a known *imaginary* interest; especially when our *real* interest is still kept in view, and is often acknowledged to be entirely distinct from the imaginary, and even sometimes opposite to it.

A man, brought to the brink of a precipice, cannot look down without trembling; and the sentiment of *imaginary* danger actuates him, in opposition to the opinion and belief of *real* safety. But the imagination is here assisted by the presence of a striking object; and yet prevails not, except it be also aided by novelty, and the unusual appearance of the object. Custom soon reconciles us to heights and precipices, and wears off these false and delusive terrors. The reverse is observable in the estimates which we form of characters and manners; and the more we habituate ourselves to an accurate scrutiny of morals, the more delicate feeling do we acquire of the most minute distinctions between vice and virtue. Such frequent occasion, indeed, have we, in common life, to pronounce all kinds of moral determinations, that no object of this kind can be new or unusual to us; nor could any *false* views or prepossessions maintain their ground against an experience, so common and familiar. Experience being chiefly what forms the associations of ideas, it is impossible that any association could establish and support itself, in direct opposition to that principle.

Usefulness is agreeable, and engages our approbation. This is a matter of fact, confirmed by daily observation. But, *useful?* For what? For somebody's interest, surely. Whose interest then? Not our own only: For our approbation frequently extends farther. It must, therefore, be the interest of those, who are served by the character or action approved of; and these we may conclude, however remote, are not totally indifferent to us. By opening up this principle, we shall discover one great source of moral distinctions.

PART II

Self-love is a principle in human nature of such extensive energy, and the interest of each individual is, in general, so closely connected with that of the community, that those philosophers were excusable, who fancied that all our concern for the public might be resolved into a concern for our own happiness and preservation. They saw every moment, instances of approbation or blame, satisfaction or displeasure towards characters and actions; they denominated the objects of

these sentiments, *virtues,* or *vices;* they observed, that the former had a tendency to increase the happiness, and the latter the misery of mankind; they asked, whether it were possible that we could have any general concern for society, or any disinterested resentment of the welfare or injury of others; they found it simpler to consider all these sentiments as modifications of self-love; and they discovered a pretence, at least, for this unity of principle, in that close union of interest, which is so observable between the public and each individual.

But notwithstanding this frequent confusion of interests, it is easy to attain what natural philosophers, after Lord Bacon, have affected to call the *experimentum crucis,* or that experiment which points out the right way in any doubt or ambiguity. We have found instances, in which private interest was separate from public; in which it was even contrary: And yet we observed the moral sentiment to continue, notwithstanding this disjunction of interests. And wherever these distinct interests sensibly concurred, we always found a sensible increase of the sentiment, and a more warm affection to virtue, and detestation of vice, or what we properly call, *gratitude* and *revenge.* Compelled by these instances, we must renounce the theory, which accounts for every moral sentiment by the principle of self-love. We must adopt a more public affection, and allow, that the interests of society are not, even on their own account, entirely indifferent to us. Usefulness is only a tendency to a certain end; and it is a contradiction in terms, that anything pleases as means to an end, where the end itself no wise affects us. If usefulness, therefore, be a source of moral sentiment, and if this usefulness be not always considered with a reference to self; it follows, that everything, which contributes to the happiness of society, recommends itself directly to our approbation and good-will. Here is a principle, which accounts, in great part, for the origin of morality: And what need we seek for abstruse and remote systems, when there occurs one so obvious and natural? [15]

Have we any difficulty to comprehend the force of humanity and benevolence? Or to conceive, that the very aspect of happiness, joy, prosperity, gives pleasure; that of pain, suffering, sorrow, communicates uneasiness? The human countenance, says Horace,[16] borrows smiles or tears from the human countenance. Reduce a person to solitude, and he loses all enjoyment, except either of the sensual or speculative kind; and that because the movements of his heart are not forwarded by correspondent movements in his fellow-creatures. The signs of sorrow and mourning, though arbitrary, affect us with melancholy; but the natural symptoms, tears and cries and groans, never fail to infuse

[15] It is needless to push our researches so far as to ask, why we have humanity or a fellow-feeling with others. It is sufficient, that this is experienced to be a principle in human nature. We must stop somewhere in our examination of causes; and there are, in every science, some general principles, beyond which we cannot hope to find any principle more general. No man is absolutely indifferent to the happiness and misery of others. The first has a natural tendency to give pleasure; the second, pain. This every one may find in himself. It is not probable, that these principles can be resolved into principles more simple and universal, whatever attempts may have been made to that purpose. But if it were possible, it belongs not to the present subject; and we may here safely consider these principles as original; happy, if we can render all the consequences sufficiently plain and perspicuous!

[16] 'Uti ridentibus arrident, ita flentibus adflent. Humani vultus.'—Hor.

compassion and uneasiness. And if the effects of misery touch us in so lively a manner; can we be supposed altogether insensible or indifferent towards its causes; when a malicious or treacherous character and behaviour are presented to us?

We enter, I shall suppose, into a convenient, warm, well-contrived apartment: We necessarily receive a pleasure from its very survey; because it presents us with the pleasing ideas of ease, satisfaction, and enjoyment. The hospitable, good-humoured, humane landlord appears. This circumstance surely must embellish the whole; nor can we easily forbear reflecting, with pleasure, on the satisfaction which results to every one from his intercourse and good-offices.

His whole family, by the freedom, ease, confidence, and calm enjoyment, diffused over their countenances, sufficiently express their happiness. I have a pleasing sympathy in the prospect of so much joy, and can never consider the source of it, without the most agreeable emotions.

He tells me, that an oppressive and powerful neighbour had attempted to dispossess him of his inheritance, and had long disturbed all his innocent and social pleasures. I feel an immediate indignation arise in me against such violence and injury.

But it is no wonder, he adds, that a private wrong should proceed from a man, who had enslaved provinces, depopulated cities, and made the field and scaffold stream with human blood. I am struck with horror at the prospect of so much misery, and am actuated by the strongest antipathy against its author.

In general, it is certain, that, wherever we go, whatever we reflect on or converse about, everything still presents us with the view of human happiness or misery, and excites in our breast a sympathetic movement of pleasure or uneasiness. In our serious occupations, in our careless amusements, this principle still exerts its active energy.

. . .

If any man from a cold insensibility, or narrow selfishness of temper, is unaffected with the images of human happiness or misery, he must be equally indifferent to the images of vice and virtue: As, on the other hand, it is always found, that a warm concern for the interests of our species is attended with a delicate feeling of all moral distinctions; a strong resentment of injury done to men; a lively approbation of their welfare. In this particular, though great superiority is observable of one man above another; yet none are so entirely indifferent to the interest of their fellow-creatures, as to perceive no distinctions of moral good and evil, in consequence of the different tendencies of actions and principles. How, indeed, can we suppose it possible in any one, who wears a human heart, that if there be subjected to his censure, one character or system of conduct, which is beneficial, and another which is pernicious to his species or community, he will not so much as give a cool preference to the former, or ascribe to it the smallest merit or regard? Let us suppose such a person ever so selfish; let private interest have ingrossed ever so much his attention; yet in instances, where that is not concerned, he must unavoidably feel *some* propensity to the good of mankind, and make it an object of choice, if everything else be equal. Would any man, who is walking along, tread as willingly on another's gouty toes, whom he has no quarrel with, as on the hard flint and pavement? There is here surely a difference in the case. We surely take into consideration the happiness and misery of others, in weighing the several motives of action, and incline to the former, where no private regards draw us to seek our own promotion or advantage by the injury of our fellow-creatures. And if the principles of humanity are capable, in many instances, of influencing our actions, they must, at all times, have *some* authority over our sentiments, and give us a general approbation of what is useful to society, and blame of what is dangerous or pernicious. The degrees of these sentiments may be the subject of controversy; but the reality of their existence, one should think, must be admitted in every theory or system.

. . .

The more we converse with mankind, and the greater social intercourse we maintain, the more shall we be familiarized to these general preferences and distinctions, without which our conversation and discourse could scarcely be rendered intelligible to each other. Every man's interest is peculiar to himself, and the aversions and desires, which result from it, cannot be supposed to affect others in a like degree. General language, therefore, being formed for general use, must be moulded on some more general views, and must affix the epithets of praise or blame, in conformity to sentiments, which arise from the general interests of the community. And if these sentiments, in most men, be not so strong as those, which have a reference to private good; yet still they must make some distinction, even in persons the most depraved and selfish; and must attach the notion of good to a beneficent conduct, and of evil to the contrary. Sympathy, we shall allow, is much fainter than our concern for ourselves, and sympathy with persons remote from us much fainter than that with persons near and contiguous; but for this very reason it is necessary for us, in our calm judgments and discourse concerning the characters of men, to neglect all these differences, and render our sentiments more public and social. Besides, that we ourselves often change our situation in this particular, we every day meet with persons who are in a situation different from us, and who could never converse with us were we to remain constantly in that position and point of view, which is peculiar to ourselves. The intercourse of sentiments, therefore, in society and conversation, makes us form some general unalterable standard, by which we may approve or disapprove of characters and manners. And though the heart takes not part entirely with those general notions, nor regulates all its love and hatred by the universal abstract differences of vice and virtue, without regard to self, or the persons with whom we are more intimately connected; yet have these moral differences a considerable influence, and being sufficient, at least for discourse, serve all our purposes in company, in the pulpit, on the theatre, and in the schools.[17]

Thus, in whatever light we take this subject, the merit, ascribed to the social virtues, appears still uniform, and arises chiefly from that regard, which the natural sentiment of benevolence engages us to pay to the interests of mankind and society. If we con-

[17] It is wisely ordained by nature, that private connexions should commonly prevail over universal views and considerations; otherwise our affections and actions would be dissipated and lost, for want of a proper limited object. Thus a small benefit done to ourselves, or our near friends, excites more lively sentiments of love and approbation than a great benefit done to a distant commonwealth: But still we know here, as in all the senses, to correct these inequalities by reflection, and retain a general standard of vice and virtue, founded chiefly on general usefulness.

sider the principles of the human make, such as they appear to daily experience and observation, we must, *a priori*, conclude it impossible for such a creature as man to be totally indifferent to the well or ill-being of his fellow-creatures, and not readily, of himself, to pronounce, where nothing gives him any particular bias, that what promotes their happiness is good, what tends to their misery is evil, without any farther regard or consideration. Here then are the faint rudiments, at least, or outlines, of a *general* distinction between actions; and in proportion as the humanity of the person is supposed to encrease, his connexion with those who are injured or benefited, and his lively conception of their misery or happiness; his consequent censure or approbation acquires proportionable vigour. There is no necessity, that a generous action, barely mentioned in an old history or remote gazette, should communicate any strong feelings of applause and admiration. Virtue, placed at such a distance, is like a fixed star, which, though to the eye of reason it may appear as luminous as the sun in his meridian, is so infinitely removed as to affect the senses, neither with light nor heat. Bring this virtue nearer, by our acquaintance or connexion with the persons, or even by an eloquent recital of the case; our hearts are immediately caught, our sympathy enlivened, and our cool approbation converted into the warmest sentiments of friendship and regard. These seem necessary and infallible consequences of the general principles of human nature, as discovered in common life and practice.

Again; reverse these views and reasonings: Consider the matter *a posteriori;* and weighing the consequences, enquire if the merit of social virtue be not, in a great measure, derived from the feelings of humanity, with which it affects the spectators. It appears to be matter of fact, that the circumstance of *utility*, in all subjects, is a source of praise and approbation: That it is constantly appealed to in all moral decisions concerning the merit and demerit of actions: That it is the *sole* source of that high regard paid to justice, fidelity, honour, allegiance, and chastity: That it is inseparable from all the other social virtues, humanity, generosity, charity, affability, lenity, mercy, and moderation: And, in a word, that it is a foundation of the chief part of morals, which has a reference to mankind and our fellow-creatures.

It appears also, that, in our general approbation of characters and manners, the useful tendency of the social virtues moves us not by any regards to self-interest, but has an influence much more universal and extensive. It appears that a tendency to public good, and to the promoting of peace, harmony, and order in society, does always, by affecting the benevolent principles of our frame, engage us on the side of the social virtues. And it appears, as an additional confirmation, that these principles of humanity and sympathy enter so deeply into all our sentiments, and have so powerful an influence, as may enable them to excite the strongest censure and applause. The present theory is the simple result of all these inferences, each of which seems founded on uniform experience and observation.

Were it doubtful, whether there were any such principle in our nature as humanity or a concern for others, yet when we see, in numberless instances, that whatever has a tendency to promote the interests of society, is so highly approved of, we ought thence to learn the force of the benevolent principle; since it is impossible for anything to please as means to an end, where the end is totally indifferent. On the other hand, were it doubtful, whether there were, implanted in our nature, any general principle of moral blame and approbation, yet when we see, in numberless instances, the influence of humanity, we ought hence to conclude, that it is impossible, but that everything which promotes the interest of society must communicate pleasure, and what is pernicious give uneasiness. But when these different reflections and observations concur in establishing the same conclusion, must they not bestow an undisputed evidence upon it?

It is however hoped, that the progress of this argument will bring a farther confirmation of the present theory, by showing the rise of other sentiments of esteem and regard from the same or like principles.

SECTION VI

OF QUALITIES USEFUL TO OURSELVES

PART I

It seems evident, that where a quality or habit is subjected to our examination, if it appear in any respect prejudicial to the person possessed of it, or such as incapacitates him for business and action, it is instantly blamed, and ranked among his faults and imperfections. Indolence, negligence, want of order and method, obstinacy, fickleness, rashness, credulity; these qualities were never esteemed by any one indifferent to a character; much less, extolled as accomplishments or virtues. The prejudice, resulting from them, immediately strikes our eye, and gives us the sentiment of pain and disapprobation.

No quality, it is allowed, is absolutely either blameable or praiseworthy. It is all according to its degree. A due medium, says the Peripatetics, is the characteristic of virtue. But this medium is chiefly determined by utility. A proper celerity, for instance, and dispatch in business, is commendable. When defective, no progress is ever made in the execution of any purpose: When excessive, it engages us in precipitate and ill-concerted measures and enterprises: By such reasonings, we fix the proper and commendable mediocrity in all moral and prudential disquisitions; and never lose view of the advantages, which result from any character or habit.

Now as these advantages are enjoyed by the person possessed of the character, it can never be *self-love* which renders the prospect of them agreeable to us, the spectators, and prompts our esteem and approbation. No force of imagination can convert us into another person, and make us fancy, that we, being that person, reap benefit from those valuable qualities, which belong to him. Or if it did, no celerity of imagination could immediately transport us back, into ourselves, and make us love and esteem the person, as different from us. Views and sentiments, so opposite to known truth and to each other, could never have place, at the same time, in the same person. All suspicion, therefore, of selfish regards, is here totally excluded. It is a quite different principle, which actuates our bosom, and interests us in the felicity of the person whom we contemplate. Where his natural talents and acquired abilities give us the prospect of elevation, advancement, a figure in life, prosperous success, a steady command over fortune, and the execution of great or advantageous undertakings; we are struck with such agreeable images, and feel a complacency and regard immediately arise towards him. The ideas of happiness, joy, triumph, prosperity, are connected with every circumstance of his character, and diffuse over our minds a pleasing sentiment of sympathy and humanity.[18]

Let us suppose a person originally framed so as to have no manner of concern for his fellow-creatures, but to regard the happiness and misery of all sensible beings with greater indifference than even two contiguous shades of the same colour. Let us suppose, if the prosperity of nations were laid on the one hand, and their ruin on the other, and he were desired to choose; that he would stand like the schoolman's ass, irresolute and undetermined, between equal motives; or rather, like the same ass between two pieces of

[18] One may venture to affirm, that there is no human creature, to whom the appearance of happiness (where envy or revenge has no place) does not give pleasure, that of misery, uneasiness. This seems inseparable from our make and constitution. But they are only the more generous minds, that are thence prompted to seek zealously the good of others, and to have a real passion for their welfare. With men of narrow and ungenerous spirits, this sympathy goes not beyond a slight feeling of the imagination, which serves only to excite sentiments of complacency or censure, and makes them apply to the object either honourable or dishonourable appellations. A griping miser, for instance, praises extremely *industry* and *frugality* even in others, and sets them, in his estimation, above all the other virtues. He knows the good that results from them, and feels that species of happiness with a more lively sympathy, than any other you could represent to him; though perhaps he would not part with a shilling to make the fortune of the industrious man, whom he praises so highly.

wood or marble, without any inclination or propensity to either side. The consequence, I believe, must be allowed just, that such a person, being absolutely unconcerned, either for the public good of a community or the private utility of others, would look on every quality, however pernicious, or however beneficial, to society, or to its possessor, with the same indifference as on the most common and uninteresting object.

But if, instead of this fancied monster, we suppose a *man* to form a judgment or determination in the case, there is to him a plain foundation of preference, where everything else is equal; and however cool his choice may be, if his heart be selfish, or if the persons interested be remote from him; there must still be a choice or distinction between what is useful, and what is pernicious. Now this distinction is the same in all its parts, with the *moral distinction,* whose foundation has been so often, and so much in vain, enquired after. The same endowments of the mind, in every circumstance, are agreeable to the sentiment of morals and to that of humanity; the same temper is susceptible of high degrees of the one sentiment and of the other; and the same alteration in the objects, by their nearer approach or by connexions, enlivens the one and the other. By all the rules of philosophy, therefore, we must conclude, that these sentiments are originally the same; since, in each particular, even the most minute, they are governed by the same laws, and are moved by the same objects.

.   .   .

In this kingdom, such continued ostentation, of late years, has prevailed among men in *active* life with regard to *public spirit,* and among those in *speculative* with regard to *benevolence;* and so many false pretentions

to each have been, no doubt, detected, that men of the world are apt, without any bad intention, to discover a sullen incredulity on the head of those moral endowments, and even sometimes absolutely to deny their existence and reality. In like manner I find, that, of old, the perpetual cant of the *Stoics* and *Cynics* concerning *virtue,* their magnificent professions and slender performances, bred a disgust in mankind; and Lucian, who, though licentious with regard to pleasure, is yet in other respects a very moral writer, cannot sometimes talk of virtue, so much boasted without betraying symptoms of spleen and irony. But surely this peevish delicacy, whence-ever it arises can never be carried so far as to make us deny the existence of every species of merit, and all distinction of manners and behaviour. Besides *discretion, caution, enterprise, industry, assiduity, frugality, economy, good-sense, prudence, discernment;* besides these endowments, I say, whose very names force an avowal of their merit, there are many others, to which the most determined scepticism cannot for a moment refuse the tribute of praise and approbation. *Temperance, sobriety, patience, constancy, perseverance, forethought, considerateness, secrecy, order, insinuation, address, presence of mind, quickness of conception, facility of expression,* these, and a thousand more of the same kind, no man will ever deny to be excellencies and perfections. As their merit consists in their tendency to serve the person, possessed of them, without any magnificent claim to public and social desert, we are the less jealous of their pretensions, and readily admit them into the catalogue of laudable qualities. We are not sensible that, by this concession, we have paved the way for all the other moral excellencies, and cannot consistently hesitate any longer, with regard to disinterested benevolence, patriotism, and humanity.

It seems, indeed, certain, that first appearances are here, as usual, extremely deceitful, and that it is more difficult, in a speculative way, to resolve into self-love the merit which we ascribe to the selfish virtues above mentioned, than that even of the social virtues, justice and beneficence. For this latter purpose, we need but say, that whatever conduct promotes the good of the community is loved, praised, and esteemed by the community, on account of that utility and interest, of which every one partakes; and though this affection and regard be, in reality, gratitude, not self-love, yet a distinction, even of this obvious nature, may not readily be made by superficial reasoners; and there is room, at least, to support the cavil and dispute for a moment. But as qualities, which tend only to the utility of their possessor, without any reference to us, or to the community, are yet esteemed and valued; by what theory or system can we account for this sentiment from self-love, or deduce it from that favourite origin? There seems here a necessity for confessing that the happiness and misery of others are not spectacles entirely indifferent to us; but that the view of the former, whether in its causes or effects, like sunshine or the prospect of well-cultivated plains (to carry our pretensions no higher), communicates a secret joy and satisfaction; the appearance of the latter, like a lowering cloud or barren landscape, throws a melancholy damp over the imagination. And this concession being once made, the difficulty is over; and a natural unforced interpretation of the phenomena of human life will afterwards, we may hope, prevail among all speculative enquirers.

PART I

It may justly appear surprising that any man in so late an age, should find it requisite to prove, by elaborate reasoning, that Personal Merit consists altogether in the possession of mental qualities, *useful* or *agreeable* to the *person himself* or to *others*. It might be expected that this principle would have occurred even to the first rude, unpractised enquirers concerning morals, and been received from its own evidence, without any argument or disputation. Whatever is valuable in any kind, so naturally classes itself under the division of *useful* or *agreeable*, the *utile* or the *dulce*, that it is not easy to imagine why we should ever seek further, or consider the question as a matter of nice research or inquiry. And as every thing useful or agreeable must possess these qualities with regard either to the *person himself* or to *others*, the complete delineation or description of merit seems to be performed as naturally as a shadow is cast by the sun, or any image is reflected upon water. If the ground, on which the shadow is cast, be not broken and uneven; nor the surface from which the image is reflected, disturbed and confused; a just figure is immediately presented, without any art or attention. And it seems a reasonable presumption, that systems and hypotheses have perverted our natural understanding, when a theory, so simple and obvious, could so long have escaped the most elaborate examination.

But however the case may have fared with philosophy, in common life these principles are still implicitly maintained; nor is any other topic of praise or blame ever recurred to, when we employ any panegyric or satire, any applause or censure of human action and behaviour. If we observe men, in every intercourse of business or pleasure, in every discourse and conversation, we shall find them nowhere, except in the schools, at any loss upon this subject. What so natural, for instance, as the following dialogue? You are very happy, we shall suppose one, to say, addressing himself to another, that you have given your daughter to Cleanthes. He is a man of honour and humanity. Every one, who has any intercourse with him, is sure of *fair* and *kind* treatment.[19] I congratulate you too, says another, on the promising expectations of this son-in-law; whose assiduous application to the study of the laws, whose quick penetration and early knowledge both of men and business, prognosticate the greatest honours and advancement.[20] You surprise me, replies a third, when you talk of Cleanthes as a man of business and application. I met him lately in a circle of the gayest company, and he was the very life and soul of our conversation: so much wit with good manners; so much gallantry without affectation; so much ingenious knowledge so genteelly delivered, I have never before observed in any one.[21] You would admire him still more, says a fourth, if you knew him more familiarly. That cheerfulness, which you might remark in him, is not a sudden flash struck out by company: it runs through the whole tenor of his life, and preserves a perpetual serenity on his countenance, and tranquillity in his soul. He has met with severe trials, misfortunes as well as dangers; and by his greatness of mind, was still superior to all of them.[22] The image, gentlemen, which you have here delineated of Cleanthes, cried I, is that of accomplished merit. Each of you has given a stroke of the pencil to his figure; and you have unawares exceeded all the pictures drawn by Gratian or Castiglione. A philosopher might select this character as a model of perfect virtue.

And as every quality which is useful or agreeable to ourselves or others is, in common life, allowed to be a part of personal merit; so no other will ever be received, where men judge of things by their natural, unprejudiced reason, without the delusive glosses of superstition and false religion. Celibacy, fasting, penance, mortification, self-denial, humility, silence, solitude, and the whole train of monkish virtues; for what reason are they everywhere rejected by men of sense, but because they serve to no manner of purpose; neither advance a man's fortune in the world, nor render him a more valuable member of society; neither qualify him for the entertainment of company, nor increase his power of self-enjoyment? We observe, on the contrary, that they cross all these desirable ends; stupify the understanding and harden the heart, obscure the fancy and sour the temper. We justly, therefore, transfer them to the opposite column, and place them in the catalogue of vices; nor has any superstition force sufficient among men of the world, to pervert entirely these natural sentiments. A gloomy, hair-brained enthusiast, after his death, may have a place in the calendar; but will scarcely ever be admitted, when alive, into intimacy and society, except by those who are as delirious and dismal as himself.

It seems a happiness in the present theory, that it enters not into that vul-

---

[19] Qualities useful to others.

[20] Qualities useful to the person himself.

[21] Qualities immediately agreeable to others.

[22] Qualities immediately agreeable to the person himself.

gar dispute concerning the *degrees* of benevolence or self-love, which prevail in human nature; a dispute which is never likely to have any issue, both because men, who have taken part, are not easily convinced, and because the phenomena, which can be produced on either side, are so dispersed, so uncertain, and subject to so many interpretations, that it is scarcely possible accurately to compare them, or draw from them any determinate inference or conclusion. It is sufficient for our present purpose, if it be allowed, what surely, without the greatest absurdity cannot be disputed, that there is some benevolence, however small, infused into our bosom; some spark of friendship for human kind; some particle of the dove kneaded into our frame, along with the elements of the wolf and serpent. Let these generous sentiments be supposed ever so weak; let them be insufficient to move even a hand or finger of our body, they must still direct the determinations of our mind, and where everything else is equal, produce a cool preference of what is useful and serviceable to mankind, above what is pernicious and dangerous. A *moral distinction*, therefore, immediately arises; a general sentiment of blame and approbation; a tendency, however faint, to the objects of the one, and a proportionable aversion to those of the other. Nor will those reasoners, who so earnestly maintain the predominant selfishness of human kind, be any wise scandalized at hearing of the weak sentiments of virtue implanted in our nature. On the contrary, they are found as ready to maintain the one tenet as the other; and their spirit of satire (for such it appears, rather than of corruption) naturally gives rise to both opinions; which have, indeed, a great and almost an indissoluble connexion together.

Avarice, ambition, vanity, and all passions vulgarly, though improperly, comprised under the denomination of *self-love*, are here excluded from our theory concerning the origin of morals, not because they are too weak, but because they have not a proper direction for that purpose. The notion of morals implies some sentiment common to all mankind, which recommends the same object to general approbation, and makes every man, or most men, agree in the same opinion or decision concerning it. It also implies some sentiment, so universal and comprehensive as to extend to all mankind, and render the actions and conduct, even of the persons the most remote, an object of applause or censure, according as they agree or disagree with that rule of right which is established. These two requisite circumstances belong alone to the sentiment of humanity here insisted on. The other passions produce in every breast, many strong sentiments of desire and aversion, affection and hatred; but these neither are felt so much in common, nor are so comprehensive, as to be the foundation of any general system and established theory of blame or approbation.

When a man denominates another his *enemy*, his *rival*, his *antagonist*, his *adversary*, he is understood to speak the language of self-love, and to express sentiments, peculiar to himself, and arising from his particular circumstances and situation. But when he bestows on any man the epithets of *vicious* or *odious* or *depraved*, he then speaks another language and expresses sentiments, in which he expects all his audience to concur with him. He must here, therefore, depart from his private and particular situation, and must choose a point of view, common to him with others; he must move some universal principle of the human frame, and touch a string to which all mankind have an accord and symphony. If he mean, therefore, to express that this man possesses qualities, whose tendency is pernicious to society, he has chosen this common point of view, and has touched the principle of humanity, in which every man, in some degree, concurs. While the human heart is compounded of the same elements as at present, it will never be wholly indifferent to public good, nor entirely unaffected with the tendency of characters and manners. And though this affection of humanity may not generally be esteemed so strong as vanity or ambition, yet, being common to all men, it can alone be the foundation of morals, or of any general system of blame or praise. One man's ambition is not another's ambition, nor will the same event or object satisfy both; but the humanity of one man is the humanity of every one, and the same object touches this passion in all human creatures.

But the sentiments, which arise from humanity, are not only the same in all human creatures, and produce the same approbation or censure; but they also comprehend all human creatures; nor is there any one whose conduct or character is not, by their means, an object to every one of censure or approbation. On the contrary, those other passions, commonly denominated selfish, both produce different sentiments in each individual, according to his particular situation; and also contemplate the greater part of mankind with the utmost indifference and unconcern. Whoever has a high regard and esteem for me flatters my vanity; whoever expresses contempt mortifies and displeases me; but as my name is known but to a small part of mankind, there are few who come within the sphere of this passion, or excite, on its account, either my affection or disgust But if you represent a tyrannical, insolent, or barbarous behaviour, in any country or in any age of the world, I soon carry my eye to the pernicious tendency of such a conduct, and feel the sentiment of repugnance and displeasure towards it. No character can be so remote as to be, in this light, wholly indifferent to me. What is beneficial to society or to the person himself must still be preferred. And every quality or action, of every human being, must, by this means, be ranked under some class or denomination, expressive of general censure or applause.

What more, therefore, can we ask to distinguish the sentiments, dependent on humanity, from those connected with any other passion, or to satisfy us, why the former are the origin of morals, not the latter? Whatever conduct gains my approbation, by touching my humanity, procures also the applause of all mankind, by affecting the same principle in them; but what serves my avarice or ambition pleases these passions in me alone, and affects not the avarice and ambition of the rest of mankind. There is no circumstance of conduct in any man, provided it have a beneficial tendency, that is not agreeable to my humanity, however remote the person; but every man, so far removed as neither to cross nor serve my avarice and ambition, is regarded as wholly indifferent by those passions. The distinction, therefore, between these species of sentiment being so great and evident, language must soon be moulded upon it, and must invent a peculiar set of terms, in order to express those universal sentiments of censure or approbation, which arise from humanity, or from views of general usefulness and its contrary. Virtue and Vice become then known; morals are recognized; certain general ideas are framed of human conduct and behaviour; such measures are expected from men in such situations. This action is determined to be conformable to our abstract rule; that other, contrary. And by such universal principles are the particular sentiments of self-love frequently controlled and limited.[23]

From instances of popular tumults, seditions, factions, panics, and of all passions, which are shared with a multitude, we may learn the influence of society in exciting and supporting any emotion; while the most ungovernable disorders are raised, we find, by that means, from the slightest and most frivolous occasions. Solon was no very cruel, though, perhaps, an unjust legislator, who punished neuters in civil

[23] It seems certain, both from reason and experience, that a rude, untaught savage regulates chiefly his love and hatred by the ideas of private utility and injury, and has but faint conceptions of a general rule or system of behaviour. The man who stands opposite to him in battle, he hates heartily, not only for the present moment, which is almost unavoidable, but for ever after; nor is he satisfied without the most extreme punishment and vengeance. But we, accustomed to society, and to more enlarged reflections, consider, that this man is serving his own country and community; that any man, in the same situation, would do the same; that we ourselves, in like circumstances, observe a like conduct; that, in general, human society is best supported on such maxims: and by these suppositions and views, we correct, in some measure, our ruder and narrower passions. And though much of our friendship and enmity be still regulated by private considerations of benefit and harm, we pay, at least, this homage to general rules, which we are accustomed to respect, that we commonly pervert our adversary's conduct, by imputing malice or injustice to him, in order to give vent to those passions, which arise from self-love and private interest. When the heart is full of rage, it never wants pretences of this nature; though sometimes as frivolous, as those from which Horace, being almost crushed by the fall of a tree, affects to accuse of parricide the first planter of it.

wars; and few, I believe, would, in such cases, incur the penalty, were their affection and discourse allowed sufficient to absolve them. No selfishness, and scarce any philosophy, have there force sufficient to support a total coolness and indifference; and he must be more or less than man, who kindles not in the common blaze. What wonder then, that moral sentiments are found of such influence in life; though springing from principles, which may appear, at first sight, somewhat small and delicate? But these principles, we must remark, are social and universal; they form, in a manner, the *party* of humankind against vice or disorder, its common enemy. And as the benevolent concern for others is diffused, in a greater or less degree, over all men, and is the same in all, it occurs more frequently in discourse, is cherished by society and conversation, and the blame and approbation, consequent on it, are thereby roused from that lethargy into which they are probably lulled, in solitary and uncultivated nature. Other passions, though perhaps originally stronger, yet being selfish and private, are often overpowered by its force, and yield the dominion of our breast to those social and public principles.

Another spring of our constitution, that brings a great addition of force to moral sentiments, is the love of fame; which rules, with such uncontrolled authority, in all generous minds, and is often the grand object of all their designs and undertakings. By our continual and earnest pursuit of a character, a name, a reputation in the world, we bring our own deportment and conduct frequently in review, and consider how they appear in the eyes of those who approach and regard us. This constant habit of surveying ourselves, as it were, in reflection, keeps alive all the sentiments of right and wrong, and begets, in noble natures, a certain reverence for themselves as well as others, which is the surest guardian of every virtue. The animal conveniencies and pleasures sink gradually in their value; while every inward beauty and moral grace is studiously acquired, and the mind is accomplished in every perfection, which can adorn or embellish a rational creature.

Here is the most perfect morality with which we are acquainted: here is displayed the force of many sympathies. Our moral sentiment is itself a feeling chiefly of that nature, and our regard to a character with others seems to arise only from a care of preserving a character with ourselves; and in order to attain this end, we find it necessary to prop our tottering judgment on the correspondent approbation of mankind.

But, that we may accommodate matters, and remove if possible every difficulty, let us allow all these reasonings to be false. Let us allow that, when we resolve the pleasure, which arises from views of utility, into the sentiments of humanity and sympathy, we have embraced a wrong hypothesis. Let us confess it necessary to find some other explication of that applause, which is paid to objects, whether inanimate, animate, or rational, if they have a tendency to promote the welfare and advantage of mankind. However difficult it be to conceive that an object is approved of on account of its tendency to a certain end, while the end itself is totally indifferent: let us swallow this absurdity, and consider what are the consequences. The preceding delineation or definition of Personal Merit must still retain its evidence and authority: it must still be allowed that every quality of the mind, which is *useful* or *agreeable* to the *person himself* or to *others*, communicates a pleasure to the spectator, engages his esteem, and is admitted under the honourable denomination of virtue or merit. Are not justice, fidelity, honour, veracity, allegiance, chastity, esteemed solely on account of their tendency to promote the good of society? Is not that tendency inseparable from humanity, benevolence, lenity, generosity, gratitude, moderation, tenderness, friendship, and all the other social virtues? Can it possibly be doubted that industry, discretion, frugality, secrecy, order, perseverance, forethought, judgement, and this whole class of virtues and accomplishments, of which many pages would not contain the catalogue; can it be doubted, I say, that the tendency of these qualities to promote the interest and happiness of their possessor, is the sole foundation of their merit? Who can dispute that a mind, which supports a perpetual serenity and cheerfulness, a noble dignity and undaunted spirit, a tender affection and good-will to all around; as it has more enjoyment within itself, is also a more animating and rejoicing spectacle, than if dejected with melancholy, tormented with anxiety, irritated with rage, or sunk into the most abject baseness and degeneracy? And as to the qualities, immediately *agreeable to others,* they speak sufficiently for themselves; and he must be unhappy, indeed, either in his own temper, or in his situation and company, who has never perceived the charms of a facetious wit or flowing affability, of a delicate modesty or decent genteelness of address and manner.

I am sensible, that nothing can be more unphilosophical than to be positive or dogmatical on any subject; and that, even if *excessive* scepticism could be maintained, it would not be more destructive to all just reasoning and inquiry. I am convinced that, where men are the most sure and arrogant, they are commonly the most mistaken, and have there given reins to passion, without that proper deliberation and suspense, which can alone secure them from the grossest absurdities. Yet, I must confess, that this enumeration puts the matter in so strong a light, that I cannot, *at present*, be more assured of any truth, which I learn from reasoning and argument, than that personal merit consists entirely in the usefulness or agreeableness of qualities to the person himself possessed of them, or to others, who have any intercourse with him. But when I reflect that, though the bulk and figure of the earth have been measured and delineated, though the motions of the tides have been accounted for, the order and economy of the heavenly bodies subjected to their proper laws, and Infinite itself reduced to calculation; yet men still dispute concerning the foundation of their moral duties. When I reflect on this, I say, I fall back into diffidence and scepticism, and suspect that an hypothesis, so obvious, had it been a true one, would, long ere now, have been received by the unanimous suffrage and consent of mankind.

APPENDIX I

CONCERNING MORAL SENTIMENT

If the foregoing hypothesis be received, it will now be easy for us to determine the question first started,[24] concerning the general principles of morals; and though we postponed the decision of that question, lest it should then involve us in intricate speculations, which are unfit for moral discourses, we may resume it at present, and examine how far either *reason* or *sentiment* enters into all decisions of praise or censure.

One principal foundation of moral praise being supposed to lie in the usefulness of any quality or action, it is evident that *reason* must enter for a considerable share in all decisions of this kind; since nothing but that faculty can instruct us in the tendency of qualities and actions, and point out their beneficial consequences to society and to their possessor. In many cases this is an affair liable to great controversy: doubts may arise; opposite interests may occur; and a preference must be given to one side, from very nice views, and a small overbalance of utility. This is particularly remarkable in questions with regard to justice; as is, indeed, natural to suppose, from that species of utility which attends this virtue.[25] Were every single instance of justice, like that of benevolence, useful to society; this would be a more simple state of the case, and seldom liable to great controversy. But as single instances of justice are often pernicious in their first and immediate tendency, and as the advantage to society results only from the observance of the general rule, and from the concurrence and combination of several persons in the same equitable conduct; the case here becomes more intricate and involved. The various circumstances of society; the various consequences of any practice; the various interests which may be proposed; these, on many occasions, are doubtful, and subject to great discussion and inquiry. The object of municipal laws is to fix all the questions with regard to justice: the debates of civilians; the reflections of politicians; the precedents of history and public records, are all directed to the same purpose. And a very accurate *reason* or *judgement* is often requisite, to give the true determination, amidst such intricate doubts arising from obscure or opposite utilities.

But though reason, when fully as-

[24] Sect. I.

[25] See App. III.

sisted and improved, be sufficient to instruct us in the pernicious or useful tendency of qualities and actions; it is not alone sufficient to produce any moral blame or approbation. Utility is only a tendency to a certain end; and were the end totally indifferent to us, we should feel the same indifference towards the means. It is requisite a *sentiment* should here display itself, in order to give a preference to the useful above the pernicious tendencies. This sentiment can be no other than a feeling for the happiness of mankind, and a resentment of their misery; since these are the different ends which virtue and vice have a tendency to promote. Here therefore *reason* instructs us in the several tendencies of actions, and *humanity* makes a distinction in favour of those which are useful and beneficial.

This partition between the faculties of understanding and sentiment, in all moral decisions, seems clear from the preceding hypothesis. But I shall suppose that hypothesis false: it will then be requisite to look out for some other theory that may be satisfactory; and I dare venture to affirm that none such will ever be found, so long as we suppose reason to be the sole source of morals. To prove this, it will be proper to weigh the five following considerations.

I. It is easy for a false hypothesis to maintain some appearance of truth, while it keeps wholly in generals, makes use of undefined terms, and employs comparisons, instead of instances. This is particularly remarkable in that philosophy, which ascribes the discernment of all moral distinctions to reason alone, without the concurrence of sentiment. It is impossible that, in any particular instance, this hypothesis can so much as be rendered intelligible, whatever specious figure it may make in general declamations and discourses. Examine the crime of *ingratitude*, for instance; which has place, wherever we observe good-will, expressed and known, together with good-offices performed, on the other side, and a return of ill-will or indifference, with ill-offices or neglect on the other: anatomize all these circumstances, and examine, by your reason alone, in what consists the demerit or blame. You never will come to any issue or conclusion.

Reason judges either of *matter of fact* or of *relations*. Enquire then, *first*, where is that matter of fact which we here call *crime*; point it out; determine the time of its existence; describe its essence or nature; explain the sense or faculty to which it discovers itself. It resides in the mind of the person who is ungrateful. He must, therefore, feel it, and be conscious of it. But nothing is there, except the passion of ill-will or absolute indifference. You can not say that these, of themselves, always and in all circumstances, are crimes. No, they are only crimes when directed towards persons who have before expressed and displayed good-will towards us. Consequently, we may infer, that the crime of ingratitude is not any particular individual *fact;* but arises from a complication of circumstances, which, being presented to the spectator, excites the *sentiment* of blame, by the particular structure and fabric of his mind.

This representation, you say, is false. Crime, indeed, consists not in a particular *fact*, of whose reality we are assured by *reason;* but it consists in certain *moral relations*, discovered by reason, in the same manner as we discover by reason the truths of geometry or algebra. But what are the relations, I ask, of which you here talk? In the case stated above, I see first good-will and good-offices in one person; then ill-will and ill-offices in the other. Between these, there is a relation of *contrariety*. Does the crime consist in that relation? But suppose a person bore me ill-will or did me ill-offices; and I, in return, were indifferent towards him, or did him good offices. Here is the same relation of *contrariety;* and yet my conduct is often highly laudable. Twist and turn this matter as much as you will, you can never rest the morality on relations; but must have recourse to the decisions of sentiment.

When it is affirmed that two and three are equal to the half of ten, this relation of equality I understand perfectly. I conceive, that if ten be divided into two parts, of which one has as many units as the other; and if any of these parts be compared to two added to three, it will contain as many units as that compound number. But when you draw thence a comparison to moral relations, I own that I am altogether at a loss to understand you. A moral action, a crime, such as ingratitude, is a complicated object. Does the morality consist in the relation of its parts to each other? How? After what manner? Specify the relation: be more particular and explicit in your propositions, and you will easily see their falsehood.

No, say you, the morality consists in the relation of actions to the rule of right; and they are denominated good or ill, according as they agree or disagree with it. What then is this rule of right? In what does it consist? How is it determined? By reason, you say, which examines the moral relations of actions. So that moral relations are determined by the comparison of action to a rule. And that rule is determined by considering the moral relations of objects. Is not this fine reasoning?

All this is metaphysics, you cry. That is enough; there needs nothing more to give a strong presumption of falsehood. Yes, reply I, here are metaphysics surely; but they are all on your side, who advance an abstruse hypothesis, which can never be made intelligible, nor quadrate with any particular instance or illustration. The hypothesis which we embrace is plain. It maintains that morality is determined by sentiment. It defines virtue to be *whatever mental action or quality gives to a spectator the pleasing sentiment of approbation;* and vice the contrary. We then proceed to examine a plain matter of fact, to wit, what actions have this influence. We consider all the circumstances in which these actions agree, and thence endeavor to extract some general observations with regard to these sentiments. If you call this metaphysics, and find anything abstruse here, you need only conclude that your turn of mind is not suited to the moral sciences.

II. When a man, at any time, deliberates concerning his own conduct (as, whether he had better, in a particular emergence, assist a brother or a benefactor), he must consider these separate relations, with all the circumstances and situations of the persons, in order to determine the superior duty and obligation; and in order to determine the proportion of lines in any triangle, it is necessary to examine the nature of that figure, and the relation which its several parts bear to each other. But notwithstanding this appearing similarity in the two cases, there is, at bottom, an extreme difference between them. A speculative reasoner concerning triangles or circles considers the several known and given relations of the parts of these figures; and thence infers some unknown relation, which is dependent on the former. But in moral deliberations we must be acquainted beforehand with all the objects, and all their relations to each other and from a comparison of the whole, fix our choice or approbation. No new fact to be ascertained; no new relation to be discovered. All the circumstances of the case are supposed to be laid before us, ere we can fix any sentence of blame or approbation. If any material circumstance be yet unknown or doubtful, we must first employ our inquiry or intellectual faculties to assure us of it; and must suspend for a time all moral decision or sentiment. While we are ignorant whether a man were aggressor or not, how can we determine whether the person who killed him be criminal or innocent? But after every circumstance, every relation is known, the understanding has no further room to operate, nor any object on which it could employ itself. The approbation or blame which then ensues, cannot be the work of the judgement, but of the heart; and is not a speculative proposition or affirmation, but an active feeling or sentiment. In the disquisitions of the understanding, from known circumstances and relations, we infer some new and unknown. In moral decisions, all the circumstances and relations must be previously known; and the mind, from the contemplation of the whole, feels some new impression of affection or disgust, esteem or contempt, approbation or blame.

Hence the great difference between a mistake of *fact* and one of *right;* and hence the reason why the one is commonly criminal and not the other. When Oedipus killed Laius, he was ignorant of the relation, and from circumstances, innocent and involuntary, formed erroneous opinions concerning the action which he committed. But when Nero killed Agrippina, all the relations between himself and the person, and all the circumstances of the fact, were previously known to him; but the motive of revenge, or fear, or interest, prevailed in his savage heart over the sentiments of duty and humanity. And when we express that

detestation against him to which he himself, in a little time, became insensible, it is not that we see any relations, of which he was ignorant; but that, for the rectitude of our disposition, we feel sentiments against which he was hardened from flattery and a long perseverance in the most enormous crimes. In these sentiments, then, not in a discovery of relations of any kind, do all moral determinations consist. Before we can pretend to form any decision of this kind, everything must be known and ascertained on the side of the object or action. Nothing remains but to feel, on our part, some sentiment of blame or approbation; whence we pronounce the action criminal or virtuous.

III. This doctrine will become still more evident, if we compare moral beauty with natural, to which in many particulars it bears so near a resemblance. It is on the proportion, relation, and position of parts, that all natural beauty depends; but it would be absurd thence to infer, that the perception of beauty, like that of truth in geometrical problems, consists wholly in the perception of relations, and was performed entirely by the understanding or intellectual faculties. In all the sciences, our mind from the known relations investigates the unknown. But in all decisions of taste or external beauty, all the relations are beforehand obvious to the eye; and we thence proceed to feel a sentiment of complacency or disgust, according to the nature of the object, and disposition of our organs.

Euclid has fully explained all the qualities of the circle; but has not in any proposition said a word of its beauty. The reason is evident. The beauty is not a quality of the circle. It lies not in any part of the line, whose parts are equally distant from a common centre. It is only the effect which that figure produces upon the mind, whose peculiar fabric of structure renders it susceptible of such sentiments. In vain would you look for it in the circle, or seek it, either by your senses or by mathematical reasoning, in all the properties of that figure.

. . .

IV. Inanimate objects may bear to each other all the same relations which we observe in moral agents; though the former can never be the object of love or hatred, nor are consequently susceptible of merit or iniquity. A young tree, which over-tops and destroys its parent, stands in all the same relations with Nero, when he murdered Agrippina; and if morality consisted merely in relations, would no doubt be equally criminal.

V. It appears evident that the ultimate ends of human actions can never, in any case, be accounted for by *reason*, but recommend themselves entirely to the sentiments and affections of mankind, without any dependance on the intellectual faculties. Ask a man *why he uses exercise;* he will answer, *because he desires to keep his health.* If you then enquire, *why he desires health,* he will readily reply, *because sickness is painful.* If you push your enquiries farther, and desire a reason *why he hates pain,* it is impossible he can ever give any. This is an ultimate end, and is never referred to any other object.

Perhaps to your second question, *why he desires health,* he may also reply, that *it is necessary for the exercise of his calling.* If you ask, *why he is anxious on that head,* he will answer, *because he desires to get money.* If you demand *Why? It is the instrument of pleasure,* says he. And beyond this it is an absurdity to ask for a reason. It is impossible there can be a progress *in infinitum;* and that one thing can always be a reason why another is desired. Something must be desirable on its own account, and be-

cause of its immediate accord or agreement with human sentiment and affection.

Now as virtue is an end, and is desirable on its own account, without fee and reward, merely for the immediate satisfaction which it conveys; it is requisite that there should be some sentiment which it touches, some internal taste or feeling, or whatever you may please to call it, which distinguishes moral good and evil, and which embraces the one and rejects the other.

Thus the distinct boundaries and offices of *reason* and of *taste* are easily ascertained. The former conveys the knowledge of truth and falsehood: the latter gives the sentiment of beauty and deformity, vice and virtue. The one discovers objects as they really stand in nature, without addition and diminution: the other has a productive faculty, and gilding or staining all natural objects with the colours, borrowed from internal sentiment, raises in a manner a new creation. Reason being cool and disengaged, is no motive to action, and directs only the impulse received from appetite or inclination, by showing us the means of attaining happiness or avoiding misery: Taste, as it gives pleasure or pain, and thereby constitutes happiness or misery, becomes a motive to action, and is the first spring or impulse to desire and volition. From circumstances and relations, known or supposed, the former leads us to the discovery of the concealed and unknown: after all circumstances and relations are laid before us, the latter makes us feel from the whole a new sentiment of blame or approbation. The standard of the one, being founded on the nature of things, is eternal and inflexible, even by the will of the Supreme Being: the standard of the other arising from the eternal frame and constitution of animals, is ultimately derived from that Supreme Will, which bestowed on each being its peculiar nature, and arranged the several classes and orders of existence.

APPENDIX III

SOME FARTHER CONSIDERATIONS WITH REGARD TO JUSTICE

The intention of this Appendix is to give some more particular explication of the origin and nature of Justice, and to mark some differences between it and the other virtues.

The social virtues of humanity and benevolence exert their influence immediately by a direct tendency or instinct, which chiefly keeps in view the simple object, moving the affections, and comprehends not any scheme or system, nor the consequences resulting from the concurrence, imitation, or example of others. A parent flies to the relief of his child; transported by that natural sympathy which actuates him, and which affords no leisure to reflect on the sentiments or conduct of the rest of mankind in like circumstances. A generous man cheerfully embraces an opportunity of serving his friend; because he then feels himself under the dominion of the beneficent affections, nor is he concerned whether any other person in the universe were ever before actuated by such noble motives, or will ever afterwards prove their influence. In all these cases the social passions have in view a single individual object, and pursue the safety or happiness alone of the person loved and esteemed. With this they are satisfied: in this they acquiesce. And as the good, resulting from their benign influence, is in itself complete and entire, it also excites the moral sentiment of approbation, without any reflection on farther consequences, and without any more enlarged views of the concurrence or imitation of the other members of society. On the contrary, were the generous friend or disinterested patriot to stand alone in the practice of beneficence, this would rather inhance his value in our eyes, and join the praise of rarity and novelty to his other more exalted merits.

The case is not the same with the social virtues of justice and fidelity. They are highly useful, or indeed absolutely necessary to the well-being of mankind: but the benefit resulting from them is not the consequence of every individual single act; but arises from the whole scheme or system concurred in by the whole, or the greater part of the society. General peace and order are the attendants of justice or a general abstinence from the possessions of others; but a particular regard to the particular right of one individual citizen may frequently, considered in itself, be productive of pernicious consequences. The result of the individual acts is here, in many instances, directly opposite to that of the whole system of actions; and the former may be extremely hurtful, while the latter is, to the highest degree, advantageous. Riches, inherited from a parent, are, in a bad man's hand, the instrument of mischief. The right of succession may, in one instance, be hurtful. Its benefit arises only from the observance of the general rule; and it is sufficient, if compensation be thereby made for all the ills and inconveniences which flow from particular characters and situations.

Cyrus, young and unexperienced, considered only the individual case before him, and reflected on a limited fitness and convenience, when he assigned the long coat to the tall boy, and the short coat to the other of smaller size. His governor instructed him better, while he pointed out more enlarged views and consequences, and informed his pupil of the general, inflexible rules, necessary to support general peace and order in society.

The happiness and prosperity of mankind, arising from the social virtue of benevolence and its subdivisions, may be compared to a wall, built by many hands, which still rises by each stone that is heaped upon it, and receives increase proportional to the diligence and care of each workman. The same happiness, raised by the social virtue of justice and its subdivisions, may be compared to the building of a vault, where each individual stone would, of itself, fall to the ground; nor is the whole fabric supported but by the mutual assistance and combination of its corresponding parts.

All the laws of nature, which regulate property, as well as all civil laws, are general, and regard alone some essential circumstances of the case, without taking into consideration the characters, situations, and connexions of the person concerned, or any particular consequences which may result from the determination of these laws in any particular case which offers. They deprive, without scruple, a beneficent man of all his possessions, if acquired by mistake, without a good title; in order to bestow them on a selfish miser, who has already heaped up immense stores of superfluous riches. Public utility requires that property should be regulated by general inflexible rules; and though such rules are adopted as best serve the same end of public utility, it is impossible for them to prevent all particular hardships, or make beneficial consequences result from every individual case. It is sufficient, if the whole plan or scheme be necessary to the support of civil society, and if the balance of good, in the main, do thereby preponderate much above that of evil. Even the general laws of the universe, though planned by infinite wisdom, cannot exclude all evil or inconvenience in every particular operation.

It has been asserted by some, that justice arises from Human Conventions, and proceeds from the voluntary choice, consent, or combination of mankind. If by *convention* be here meant a *promise* (which is the most usual sense of the word) nothing can be more absurd than this position. The observance of promises is itself one of the most considerable parts of justice, and we are not surely bound to keep our word because we have given our word to keep it. But if by convention be meant a sense of common interest, which sense each man feels in his own breast, which he remarks in his fellows, and which carries him, in concurrence with others, into a general plan or system of actions, which tends to public utility; it must be owned, that, in this sense, justice arises from human conventions. For if it be allowed (what is, indeed, evident) that the particular consequences of a particular act of justice may be hurtful to the public as well as to individuals; it follows that every man, in embracing the virtue, must have an eye to the whole plan or system, and must expect the concurrence of his fellows in the same conduct and behaviour. Did all his views terminate in the consequences of each act of his own, his benevolence and humanity, as well as his self-love, might often prescribe to him measures of conduct very different from those which are agreeable to the strict rules of right and justice.

Thus, two men pull the oars of a boat by common convention for common interest, without any promise or contract: thus gold and silver are made the measures of exchange; thus speech and words and language are fixed by human convention and agreement. Whatever is advantageous to two or more persons, if all perform their part; but what loses all advantage if only one perform, can arise from no other principle. There would otherwise be no motive for any one of them to enter into that scheme of conduct.

The word *natural* is commonly taken in so many senses and is of so loose a signification, that it seems vain to dispute whether justice be natural or not. If self-love, if benevolence be natural to man; if reason and forethought be also natural; then may the same epithet be applied to justice, order, fidelity, property, society. Men's inclination, their necessities, lead them to combine; their understanding and experience tell them that this combination is impossible where each governs himself by no rule, and pays no regard to the possessions of others: and from these passions and reflections conjoined, as soon as we observe like passions and reflections in others, the sentiment of justice, throughout all ages, has infallibly and certainly had place to some degree or other in every individual of the human species. In so sagacious an animal, what necessarily arises from the exertion of his intellectual faculties may justly be esteemed natural.[26]

Among all civilized nations it has

[26] Natural may be opposed, either to what is *unusual, miraculous* or *artificial.* In the two former senses, justice and property are undoubtedly natural. But as they suppose reason, forethought, design, and a social union and confederacy among men, perhaps that epithet cannot strictly, in the last sense, be applied to them. Had men lived without society, property had never been known, and neither justice nor injustice had ever existed. But society among human creatures had been impossible without reason and forethought. Inferior animals, that unite, are guided by instinct, which supplies the place of reason. But all these disputes are merely verbal.

been the constant endeavour to remove everything arbitrary and partial from the decision of property, and to fix the sentence of judges by such general views and considerations as may be equal to every member of society. For besides, that nothing could be more dangerous than to accustom the bench, even in the smallest instance, to regard private friendship or enmity; it is certain, that men, where they imagine that there was no other reason for the preference of their adversary but personal favour, are apt to entertain the strongest ill-will against the magistrates and judges. When natural reason, therefore, points out no fixed view of public utility by which a controversy of property can be decided, positive laws are often framed to supply its place, and direct the procedure of all courts of judicature. When these too fail, as often happens, precedents are called for; and a former decision, though given itself without any sufficient reason, justly becomes a sufficient reason for new decision. If direct laws and precedents be wanting, imperfect and indirect ones are brought in aid; and the controverted case is ranged under them by analogical reasonings and comparisons, and similitudes, and correspondencies, which are often more fanciful than real. In general, it may safely be affirmed that jurisprudence is, in this respect, different from all the sciences; and that in many of its nicer questions, there cannot properly be said to be truth or falsehood on either side. If one pleader bring the case under any former law or precedent, by a refined analogy or comparison; the opposite pleader is not at a loss to find an opposite analogy or comparison: and the preference given by the judge is often founded more on taste and imagination than on any solid argument. Public utility is the general object of all courts of judicature; and this utility too requires a stable rule in all controversies: but where several rules, nearly equal and indifferent, present themselves, it is a very slight turn of thought which fixes the decision in favour of either party.[27]

We may just observe, before we conclude this subject, that after the laws of justice are fixed by views of general utility, the injury, the hardship, the harm, which result to any

individual from a violation of them, enter very much into consideration, and are a great source of that universal blame which attends every wrong or iniquity. By the laws of society, this coat, this horse is mine, and *ought* to remain perpetually in my possession: I reckon on the secure enjoyment of it: by depriving me of it, you disappoint my expectations,

---

[27] That there be a separation or distinction of possessions, and that this separation be steady and constant; this is absolutely required by the interests of society, and hence the origin of justice and property. What possessions are assigned to particular persons; this is, generally speaking, pretty indifferent; and is often determined by very frivolous views and considerations. We shall mention a few particulars.

Were a society formed among several independent members, the most obvious rule, which could be agreed on, would be to annex property to *present* possession, and leave every one a right to what he at present enjoys. The relation of possession, which takes place between the person and the object, naturally draws on the relation of property.

For a like reason, occupation or first possession becomes the foundation of property.

Where a man bestows labour and industry upon any object, which before belonged to no body; as in cutting down and shaping a tree, in cultivating a field, &c., the alterations, which he produces, causes a relation between him and the object, and naturally engages us to annex it to him by the new relation of property. This cause here concurs with the public utility, which consists in the encouragement given to industry and labour.

Perhaps too, private humanity towards the possessor concurs, in this instance, with the other motives, and engages us to leave with him what he has acquired by sweat and labour; and what he has flattered himself in the constant enjoyment of. For though private humanity can, by no means, be the origin of justice; since the latter virtue so often contradicts

the former; yet when the rule of separate and constant possession is once formed by the indispensable necessities of society, private humanity, and an aversion to the doing a hardship to another, may, in a particular instance, give rise to a particular rule of property.

I am much inclined to think, that the right succession or inheritance much depends on those connexions of the imagination, and that the relation to a former proprietor begetting a relation to the object, is the cause why the property is transferred to a man after the death of his kinsman. It is true; industry is more encouraged by the transference of possession to children or near relations: but this consideration will only have place in a cultivated society; whereas the right of succession is regarded even among the greatest Barbarians.

Acquisition of property by *accession* can be explained no way but by having recourse to the relations and connexions of the imaginations.

The property of rivers, by the laws of most nations, and by the natural turn of our thoughts, is attributed to the proprietors of their banks, excepting such vast rivers as the Rhine or the Danube, which seem too large to follow as an accession to the property of the neighbouring fields. Yet even these rivers are considered as the property of that nation, through whose dominions they run; the idea of a nation being of a suitable bulk to correspond with them, and bear them such a relation in the fancy.

The accessions, which are made to land, bordering upon rivers, follow the land, say the civilians, provided it be made by what they call *alluvion*, that is, insensibly and imperceptibly; which and doubly displease me, and offend every bystander. It is a public wrong, so far as the rules of equity are violated: it is a private harm, so far as an individual is injured. And though the second consideration could have no place, were not the former previously established: for otherwise the distinction of *mine* and *thine* would be unknown in society: yet there is no question but the regard to general good is much enforced by the respect to particular. What injures the community, without hurting any individual, is often more lightly thought of. But where the greatest public wrong is also conjoined with a considerable private one, no wonder the highest disapprobation attends so iniquitous a behaviour.

---

are circumstances, that assist the imagination in the conjunction.

Where there is any considerable portion torn at once from one bank and added to another, it becomes not *his* property, whose land it falls on, till it unite with the land, and till the trees and plants have spread their roots into both. Before that, the thought does not sufficiently join them.

In short, we must ever distinguish between the necessity of a separation and constancy in men's possession, and the rules, which assign particular objects to particular persons. The first necessity is obvious, strong, and invincible: the latter may depend on a public utility more light and frivolous, on the sentiment of private humanity and aversion to private hardship, on positive laws, on precedents, analogies, and very fine connexions and turns of the imagination.

Immanuel Kant (1724—1804)

Immanuel Kant was born in Königsberg, East Prussia, the son of a fairly prosperous saddler. Both his parents were devout Pietists. At the age of ten, Kant entered the Pietistic Collegium Fredericianum; his chief interests during this period were theology and the classics. At sixteen, he enrolled in the University of Königsberg to study theology, but his interests turned to natural science and philosophy. The death of his father forced him, in 1746, to work as a private tutor. In 1755, Kant was enabled, through the generosity of a friend, to complete his university studies. Late in the same year he was appointed *Privatdocent* and, in 1770, full Professor in the philosophical faculty of the University of Königsberg. Kant's outward life was wholly uneventful. He never traveled more than forty miles from his birthplace in the eighty years of his life, and his townspeople would set their watches as he came into view during his daily constitutional. Kant's early works covered a wide variety of topics in natural science, the most important of these being his *General Natural History and Theory of the Heavens* (1755) in which he anticipated Laplace's nebular hypothesis. In 1781 appeared the work that made Kant famous and altered profoundly the course of all subsequent philosophy, the *Critique of Pure Reason*. This was followed by the *Prolegomena* (1783), *The Foundations of the Metaphysics of Morals* (1785), the *Critique of Practical Reason* (1788), the *Critique of Judgment* (1790), *Religion Within the Limits of Bare Reason* (1794)—which occasioned, almost immediately, the issuance of a royal mandate prohibiting Kant from all further writing on and teaching of theology, and *Perpetual Peace* (1795). In politics and morals, Kant was profoundly influenced by Rousseau; it is well to remind those who hold Kant's Pietistic background responsible for an alleged sterile formalism in ethics that Pietism began late in the 17th Century as a protest against clerical despotism and empty formalism and that Kant's reaction to the appearance of these symptoms in the Collegium he attended was one of loathing and disgust. A liberal and a democrat, he sympathized with the French Revolution but was horrified by the resulting Reign of Terror. His devotion to the principle that human beings are to be treated as ends and never merely as means is central in his ethics and politics, and nothing seemed more dreadful to this man than that any person should be degraded by the tyranny of another man's will.

FOUNDATIONS OF THE METAPHYSICS OF MORALS [1]

PREFACE

Ancient Greek philosophy was divided into three sciences: physics, ethics, and logic. This division conforms perfectly to the nature of the subject, and one need improve on it perhaps only by supplying its principle in order both to insure its exhaustiveness and to define correctly the necessary subdivisions.

All rational knowledge is either material, and observes some object, or formal, and is occupied merely with the form of understanding and reason itself and with the universal rules of thinking without regard to distinctions between objects. Formal philosophy is called logic. Material philosophy, however, which has to do with definite objects and the laws to which they are subject, is itself divided into two parts. This is because these laws are either laws of nature or laws of freedom. The science of the former is called physics and that of the latter, ethics. The former is also called theory of nature and the latter, theory of morals.

Logic can have no empirical part—a part in which universal and necessary laws of thinking would rest upon grounds taken from experience. For in that case it would not be logic, i. e., a canon for understanding or reason which is valid for all thinking and which must be demonstrated. But, on the other hand, natural and moral phi-

losophy can each have its empirical part. The former must do so, for it must determine the laws of nature as an object of experience, and the latter because it must determine the human will so far as it is affected by nature. The laws of the former are laws according to which everything happens; those of the latter are laws according to which everything should happen, but allow for conditions under which what should happen often does not.

All philosophy, so far as it is based on experience, may be called empirical; but, so far as it presents its doctrines solely on the basis of a priori principles, it may be called pure philosophy. The latter, when merely formal, is logic; when limited to definite objects of understanding, it is metaphysics.

In this way there arises the idea of a twofold metaphysics—a metaphysics of nature and a metaphyics of morals. Physics, therefore, will have an empirical and also a rational part, and ethics likewise. In ethics, however, the empirical part may be called more specifically practical anthropology; the rational part, morals proper.

All crafts, handiworks, and arts have gained by the division of labor, for when one person does not do everything, but each limits himself to a particular job which is distinguished from all the others by the treatment it requires, he can do it with greater perfection and with more facility. Where work is not thus differentiated and divided, where everyone is a jack-of-all-trades, the crafts remain at a barbaric level. It might be worth considering whether pure philosophy in each of its parts does not require a man particularly devoted to it, and whether it would not be better for the learned profession as a whole to warn those who are in the habit of catering to the taste of the public by mixing up the empirical with the rational in all sorts

[1] Reprinted with the permission of the publisher from the *Critique of Practical Reason and Other Writings in Moral Philosophy*, by Immanuel Kant, translated and edited by Lewis White Beck, University of Chicago Press, 1949. Material added by the translator is enclosed in square brackets.

of proportions which they do not themselves know and who call themselves independent thinkers (giving the name of speculator to those who apply themselves to the merely rational part). This warning would be that they should not at one and the same time carry on two employments which differ widely in the treatment they require, and for each of which perhaps a special talent is required, since the combination of these talents in one person produces only bunglers. I only ask whether the nature of the science does not require that a careful separation of the empirical from the rational part be made, with a metaphysics of nature put before real (empirical) physics and a metaphysics of morals before practical anthropology. These prior sciences [2] must be carefully purified of everything empirical so that we can know how much pure reason can accomplish in each case and from what sources it creates its a priori teaching, whether the latter inquiry be conducted by all moralists (whose name is legion) or only by some who feel a calling to it.

Since my purpose here is directed to moral philosophy, I narrow the proposed question to this: Is it not of the utmost necessity to construct a pure moral philosophy which is completely freed from everything which may be only empirical and thus belong to anthropology? That there must be such a philosophy is self-evident from the common idea of duty and moral laws. Everyone must admit that a law, if it is to hold morally, i. e., as a ground of obligation, must imply absolute necessity; he must admit that the command, "Thou shalt not lie," does not apply to men only, as if other rational beings had no need to observe it. The same is true for all other moral laws properly so called. He must concede that the ground of obligation here must not be sought in the nature of man or in the circumstances in which he is placed but sought a priori solely in the concepts of pure reason, and that every other precept which rests on principles of mere experience, even a precept which is in certain respects universal, so far as it leans in the least on empirical grounds (perhaps only in regard to the motive involved), may be called a practical rule but never a moral law.

Thus, not only are moral laws together with their principles essentially different from all practical knowledge in which there is anything empirical, but all moral philosophy rests solely on its pure part. Applied to man, it borrows nothing from knowledge of him (anthropology) but gives him, as a rational being, a priori laws. No doubt these laws require a power of judgment sharpened by experience partly in order to decide in what cases they apply and partly to procure for them an access to man's will and an impetus to their practice. For man is affected by so many inclinations that, though he is capable of the idea of a practical pure reason, he is not so easily able to make it concretely effective in the conduct of his life.

A metaphysics of morals is therefore indispensable, not merely because of motives to speculate concerning the source of the a priori practical principles which lie in our reason, but also because morals themselves remain subject to all kinds of corruption so long as the guide and supreme norm of their correct estimation is lacking. For it is not sufficient to that which should be morally good that it conform to the law; it must be done for the sake of the law. Otherwise the conformity is merely contingent and spurious, because, though the unmoral ground may indeed now and then produce

2 [Reading the plural with the Academy ed.]

lawful actions, more often it brings forth unlawful ones. But the moral law can be found in its purity and genuineness (which is the central concern in the practical) nowhere else than in a pure philosophy; therefore, this (i. e., metaphysics) must lead the way, and without it there can be no moral philosophy. Philosophy which mixes pure principles with empirical ones does not deserve the name, for what distinguishes philosophy from common rational knowledge is its treatment in separate sciences of what is confusedly comprehended in such knowledge. Much less does it deserve the name of moral philosophy, since by this confusion it spoils the purity of morals themselves and works contrary to its own end.

It should not be thought that what is here required is already present in the celebrated Wolff's propaedeutic to his moral philosophy, i. e., in what he calls universal practical philosophy, and that it is not an entirely new field that is to be opened. Precisely because his work was to be universal practical philosophy, it deduced no will of any particular kind, such as one determined without any empirical motives but completely by a priori principles; in a word, it had nothing which could be called a pure will, since it considered only volition in general with all the actions and conditions which pertain to it in this general sense. Thus his propaedeutic differs from a metaphysics of morals in the same way that general logic is distinguished from transcendental philosophy, the former expounding the actions and rules of thinking in general, and the latter presenting the particular actions and rules of pure thinking, i. e., of thinking by which objects are known completely a priori. For the metaphysics of morals is meant to investigate the idea and principles of a possible pure will and not the actions and conditions of the human volition as such, which are for the most part drawn from psychology.

That in general practical philosophy laws and duty are discussed (though improperly) is no objection to my assertion. For the authors of this science remain even here true to their idea of it: They do not distinguish the motives which are presented completely a priori by reason alone, and which are thus moral in the proper sense of the word, from the empirical motives which the understanding by comparing experiences elevates to universal concepts. Rather, they consider motives without regard to the difference in their source but only with reference to their greater or smaller number (as they are considered to be all of the same kind); they thus formulate their concept of obligation, which is anything but moral, but which is all that can be desired in a philosophy which does not decide whether the origin of all possible practical concepts is a priori or only a posteriori.

As a preliminary to a metaphysics of morals which I intend someday to publish, I issue these *Foundations*. There is, to be sure, no other foundation for such a metaphysics than a critical examination of a pure practical reason, just as there is no other foundation for metaphysics than the already published critical examination of the pure speculative reason. But, in the first place, a critical examination of pure practical reason is not of such extreme importance as that of the speculative reason, because the human reason, even in the commonest mind, can easily be brought to a high degree of correctness and completeness in moral matters, while, on the other hand, in its theoretical but pure use it is entirely dialectical. In the second place, I require of a critical examination of a pure practical reason, if it is to be complete, that its unity with the speculative be subject to presentation under a common principle, because in the final analysis there can be but one and the same reason which must be differentiated only in application. But I could not bring this to such a completeness without bringing in observations of an altogether different kind and without thereby confusing the reader. For these reasons I have employed the title, *Foundations of the Metaphyics of Morals*, instead of *Critique of Pure Practical Reason*.

Because, in the third place, a metaphysics of morals, in spite of its forbidding title, is capable of a high degree of popularity and adaptation to common understanding, I find it useful to separate this preliminary work of laying the foundation, in order not to have to introduce unavoidable subtleties into the later, more comprehensible work.

The present foundations, however, are nothing more than the search for and establishment of the supreme principle of morality. This constitutes a task altogether complete in its intention and one which should be kept separate from all other moral inquiry. My conclusions concerning this important question, which has not yet been discussed nearly enough, would, of course, be clarified by application of the principle to the whole system of morality, and it would receive much confirmation by the adequacy which it would everywhere show. But I must forego this advantage which would in the final analysis be more privately gratifying than commonly useful, because ease of use and apparent adequacy of a principle are not any sure proof of its correctness but rather awaken a certain partiality which prevents a rigorous investigation and evaluation of it for itself without regard to consequences.

I have adopted in this writing the method which is, I think, most suitable if one wishes to proceed analytically from common knowledge to the determination of its supreme principle, and then synthetically from the examination of this principle and its sources back to common knowledge where it finds its application. The division is therefore as follows:

1. First Section. Transition from the Common Rational Knowledge of Morals to the Philosophical
2. Second Section. Transition from the Popular Moral Philosophy to the Metaphysics of Morals
3. Third Section. Final Step from the Metaphysics of Morals to the Critical Examination of Pure Practical Reason

FIRST SECTION

Transition From the Common Rational Knowledge of Morals to the Philosophical

Nothing in the world—indeed nothing even beyond the world—can possibly be conceived which could be called good without qualification except a *good will*. Intelligence, wit, judgment, and the other talents of the mind, however they may be named, or courage, resoluteness, and perseverance as qualities of temperament are doubtless in many respects good and desirable. But they can become extremely bad and harmful if the will, which is to make use of these gifts of nature and which in its special constitution is called character, is not good. It is the same with the gifts of fortune. Power, riches, honor, even health, general well-being, and the contentment with one's condition which is called happiness make for pride and even arrogance if there is not a good will to correct their influence on the mind and on its principles of action, so as to make it universally conformable to its end. It need hardly be mentioned that the sight of a being adorned with no feature of a pure and good will yet enjoying uninterrupted prosperity can never give pleasure to a rational impartial observer. Thus the good will seems to constitute the indispensable condition even of worthiness to be happy.

Some qualities seem to be conducive to this good will and can facilitate its action, but, in spite of that, they have no intrinsic unconditional worth. They rather presuppose a good will, which limits the high esteem which one otherwise rightly has for them and prevents their being held to be absolutely good. Moderation in emotions and passions, self-control, and calm deliberation not only are good in many respects but even seem to constitute a part of the inner worth of the person. But however unconditionally they were esteemed by the ancients, they are far from being good without qualification. For, without the principles of a good will, they can become extremely bad, and the coolness of a villain makes him not only far more dangerous but also more directly abominable in our eyes than he would have seemed without it.

The good will is not good because of what it effects or accomplishes or because of its adequacy to achieve some proposed end; it is good only because of its willing, i. e., it is good of itself. And, regarded for itself, it is to be esteemed incomparably higher than anything which could be brought about by it in favor of any inclination or even of the sum total of all inclinations. Even if it should happen that, by a particularly unfortunate fate or by the niggardly provision of a stepmotherly nature, this will should be

wholly lacking in power to accomplish its purpose, and if even the greatest effort should not avail it to achieve anything of its end, and if there remained only the good will (not as a mere wish but as the summoning of all the means in our power), it would sparkle like a jewel with its own light, as something that had its full worth in itself. Usefulness or fruitlessness can neither diminish nor augment this worth. Its usefulness would be only its setting, as it were, so as to enable us to handle it more conveniently in commerce or to attract the attention of those who are not yet connoisseurs, but not to recommend it to those who are experts or to determine its worth.

But there is something so strange in this idea of the absolute worth of the will alone, in which no account is taken of any use, that, notwithstanding the agreement even of common sense, the suspicion must arise that perhaps only high-flown fancy is its hidden basis, and that we may have misunderstood the purpose of nature in its appointment of reason as the ruler of our will. We shall therefore examine this idea from this point of view.

In the natural constitution of an organized being, i. e., one suitably adapted to life, we assume as an axiom that no organ will be found for any purpose which is not the fittest and best adapted to that purpose. Now if its preservation, welfare—in a word, its happiness—were the real end of nature in a being having reason and will, then nature would have hit upon a very poor arrangement in appointing the reason of the creature to be the executor of this purpose. For all the actions which the creature has to perform with this intention, and the entire rule of its conduct, would be dictated much more exactly by instinct, and that end would be far more certainly attained by instinct than it ever could be by reason. And if, over and above this, reason should have been granted to the favored creature, it would have served only to let it contemplate the happy constitution of its nature, to admire it, to rejoice in it, and to be grateful for it to its beneficent cause. But reason would not have been given in order that the being should subject its faculty of desire to that weak and delusive guidance and to meddle with the purpose of nature. In a word, nature would have taken care that reason did not break forth into practical use nor have the presumption, with its weak insight, to think out for itself the plan of happiness and the means of attaining it. Nature would have taken over not only the choice of ends but also that of the means and with wise foresight would have intrusted both to instinct alone.

And, in fact, we find that the more a cultivated reason deliberately devotes itself to the enjoyment of life and happiness, the more the man falls short of true contentment. From this fact there arises in many persons, if only they are candid enough to admit it, a certain degree of misology, hatred of reason. This is particularly the case with those who are most experienced in its use. After counting all the advantages which they draw—I will not say from the invention of the arts of common luxury—from the sciences (which in the end seem to them to be also a luxury of the understanding), they nevertheless find that they have actually brought more trouble on their shoulders instead of gaining in happiness; they finally envy, rather than despise, the common run of men who are better guided by mere natural instinct and who do not permit their reason much influence on their conduct. And we must at least admit that a morose attitude or ingratitude to the goodness with which the world is governed is by no means always found among those who temper or refute the boasting eulogies which are given of the advantages of happiness and contentment with which reason is supposed to supply us. Rather their judgment is based on the idea of another and far more worthy purpose of their existence for which, instead of happiness, their reason is properly intended, this purpose, therefore, being the supreme condition to which the private purposes of men must for the most part defer.

Reason is not, however, competent to guide the will safely with regard to its objects and the satisfaction of all our needs (which it in part multiplies), and to this end an innate instinct would have led with far more certainty. But reason is given to us as a practical faculty, i. e., one which is meant to have an influence on the will. As nature has elsewhere distributed capacities suitable to the functions they are to perform, reason's proper function must be to produce a will good in itself and not one good merely as a means, for to the former reason is absolutely essential. This will must indeed not be the sole and complete good but the highest good and the condition of all others, even of the desire for happiness. In this case it is entirely compatible with the wisdom of nature that the cultivation of reason, which is required for the former unconditional purpose, at least in this life restricts in many ways—indeed can reduce to less than nothing—the achievement of the latter conditional purpose, happiness. For one perceives that nature here does not proceed unsuitably to its purpose, because reason, which recognizes its highest practical vocation in the establishment of a good will, is capable only of a contentment of its own kind, i. e., one that springs from the attainment of a purpose, which in turn is determined by reason, even though this injures the ends of inclination.

We have, then, to develop the concept of a will which is to be esteemed as good of itself without regard to anything else. It dwells already in the natural sound understanding and does not need so much to be taught as only to be brought to light. In the estimation of the entire worth of our actions it always takes first place and is the condition of everything else. In order to show this, we shall take the concept of duty. It contains that of a good will, though with certain subjective restrictions and hindrances; but these are far from concealing it and making it unrecognizable, for they rather bring it out by contrast and make it shine forth all the brighter.

I here omit all actions which are recognized as opposed to duty, even though they may be useful in one respect or another, for with these the question does not arise at all as to whether they may be done *from* duty, since they conflict with it. I also pass over the actions which are really in accordance with duty and to which one has no direct inclination, rather doing them because impelled to do so by another inclination. For it is easily decided whether an action in accord with duty is done from duty or for some selfish purpose. It is far more difficult to note this difference when the action is in accordance with duty and, in addition, the subject has a direct inclination to do it. For example, it is in fact in accordance with duty that a dealer should not overcharge an inexperienced customer, and wherever there is much business the prudent merchant does not do so, having a fixed price for everyone, so that a child may buy of him as cheaply as any other. Thus the customer is honestly served. But this is far from sufficient to justify the belief that the merchant has behaved in this way from duty and principles of honesty. His own advantage required this be-

havior; but it cannot be assumed that over and above that he had a direct inclination to the purchaser and that, out of love, as it were, he gave none an advantage in price over another. Therefore the action was done neither from duty nor from direct inclination but only for a selfish purpose.

On the other hand, it is a duty to preserve one's life, and moreover everyone has a direct inclination to do so. But, for that reason, the often anxious care which most men take of it has no intrinsic worth, and the maxim of doing so has no moral import. They preserve their lives according to duty, but not from duty. But if adversities and hopeless sorrow completely take away the relish for life; if an unfortunate man, strong in soul, is indignant rather than despondent or dejected over his fate and wishes for death, and yet preserves his life without loving it and from neither inclination nor fear but from duty—then his maxim has a moral import.

To be kind where one can is duty, and there are, moreover, many persons so sympathetically constituted that without any motive or vanity or selfishness they find an inner satisfaction in spreading joy and rejoice in the contentment of others which they have made possible. But I say that, however dutiful and amiable it may be, that kind of action has no true moral worth. It is on a level with other inclinations, such as the inclination to honor, which, if fortunately directed to what in fact accords with duty and is generally useful and thus honorable, deserve praise and encouragement but no esteem. For the maxim lacks the moral import of an action done not from inclination but from duty. But assume that the mind of that friend to mankind was clouded by a sorrow of his own which extinguished all sympathy with the lot of others and that he still had the power to benefit others in distress, but that their need left him untouched because he was preoccupied with his own need. And now suppose him to tear himself, unsolicited by inclination, out of this dead insensibility and to do this action only from duty and without any inclination—then for the first time his action has genuine moral worth. Furthermore, if nature has put little sympathy in the heart of a man, and if he, though an honest man, is by temperament cold and indifferent to the sufferings of others perhaps because he is provided with special gifts of patience and fortitude, and expects or even requires that others should have the same—and such a man would certainly not be the meanest product of nature —would not he find in himself a source from which to give himself a far higher worth than he could have got by having a good-natured temperament? This is unquestionably true even though nature did not make him philanthropic, for it is just here that the worth of the character is brought out, which is morally and incomparably the highest of all: he is beneficent not from inclination but from duty.

To secure one's own happiness is at least indirectly a duty, for discontent with one's condition under pressure from many cares and amid unsatisfied wants could easily become a great temptation to transgress duties. But, without any view to duty, all men have the strongest and deepest inclination to happiness, because in this idea all inclinations are summed up. But the precept of happiness is often so formulated that it definitely thwarts some inclinations, and men can make no definite and certain concept of the sum of satisfaction of all inclinations, which goes under the name of happiness. It is not to be wondered at, therefore, that a single inclination, definite as to what it promises and as to the time at which it can be satisfied, can outweigh a fluctuating idea, and that, for example, a man with the gout can choose to enjoy what he likes and to suffer what he may, because according to his calculations at least on this occasion he has not sacrificed the enjoyment of the present moment to a perhaps groundless expectation of a happiness supposed to lie in health. But, even in this case, if the universal inclination to happiness did not determine his will, and if health were not at least for him a necessary factor in these calculations, there yet would remain, as in all other cases, a law that he ought to promote his happiness, not from inclination but from duty. Only from this law would his conduct have true moral worth.

It is in this way, undoubtedly, that we should understand those passages of Scripture which command us to love our neighbor and even our enemy, for love as an inclination cannot be commanded. But beneficence from duty, also when no inclination impels it and even when it is opposed by a natural and unconquerable aversion, is practical love, not pathological love; it resides in the will and not in the propensities of feeling, in principles of action and not in tender sympathy; and it alone can be commanded.

[Thus the first proposition of morality is that to have moral worth an action must be done from duty.] The second proposition is: An action done from duty does not have its moral worth in the purpose which is to be achieved through it but in the maxim by which it is determined. Its moral value, therefore, does not depend on the reality of the object of the action but merely on the principle of volition by which the action is done without any regard to the objects of the faculty of desire. From the preceding discussion it is clear that the purposes we may have for our actions and their effects as ends and incentives of the will cannot give the actions any unconditional and moral worth. Wherein, then, can this worth lie, if it is not in the will in relation to its hoped-for effect? It can lie nowhere else than in the principle of the will irrespective of the ends which can be realized by such action. For the will stands, as it were, at the crossroads halfway between its a priori principle which is formal and its a posteriori incentive which is material. Since it must be determined by something, if it is done from duty, it must be determined by the formal principle of volition as such, since every material principle has been withdrawn from it.

The third principle, as a consequence of the two preceding, I would express as follows: Duty is the necessity of an action done from respect for the law. I can certainly have an inclination to the object as an effect of the proposed action, but I can never have respect for it precisely because it is a mere effect and not an activity of a will. Similarly, I can have no respect for any inclination whatsoever, whether my own or that of another; in the former case I can at most approve of it and in the latter I can even love it, i. e., see it as favorable to my own advantage. But that which is connected with my will merely as a ground and not as consequence, that which does not serve my inclination but overpowers it or at least excludes it from being considered in making a choice—in a word, the law itself—can be an object of respect and thus a command. Now as an act from duty wholly excludes the influence of inclination and therewith every object of the will, nothing remains which can determine the will objectively except the law and subjectively except pure respect for this practical law. This subjective element is the maxim [3] that I should follow such a law even if it thwarts all my inclinations.

Thus the moral worth of an action does not lie in the effect which is expected from it or in any principle of action which has to borrow its motive from this expected effect. For all these effects (agreeableness of condition, indeed even the promotion of the happiness of others) could be brought about through other causes and would not require the will of a rational being, while the highest and unconditional good can be found only in such a will. Therefore, the pre-eminent good can consist only in the conception of the law in itself (which can be present only in a rational being) so far as this conception and not the hoped-for effect is the determining ground of the will. This pre-eminent good, which we call moral, is already present in the person who acts according to this conception, and we do not have to expect it first in the result. [4]

[3] A maxim is the subjective principle of volition. The objective principle (i.e., that which would serve all rational beings also subjectively as a practical principle if reason had full power over the faculty of desire) is the practical law.

[4] It might be objected that I seek to take refuge in an obscure feeling behind the word "respect," instead of clearly resolving the question with a concept of reason. But though respect is a feeling, it is not one received through any [outer] influence but is self-wrought by a rational concept; thus it differs specifically from all feelings of the former kind which may be referred to inclination or fear. What I recognize directly as a law for myself I recognize with respect, which means merely the consciousness of the submission of my will to a law without the intervention of other influences on my mind. The direct determination of the will by the law and the consciousness of this determination is respect; thus respect can be regarded as the effect of the law on the subject and not as the

But what kind of a law can that be, the conception of which must determine the will without reference to the expected result? Under this condition alone the will can be called absolutely good without qualification. Since I have robbed the will of all impulses which could come to it from obedience to any law, nothing remains to serve as a principle of the will except universal conformity of its action to law as such. That is, I should never act in such a way that I could not will that my maxim should be a universal law. Mere conformity to law as such (without assuming any particular law applicable to certain actions) serves as the principle of the will, and it must serve as such a principle if duty is not to be a vain delusion and chimerical concept. The common reason of mankind in its practical judgments is in perfect agreement with this and has this principle constantly in view.

Let the question, for example, be: May I, when in distress, make a promise with the intention not to keep it?

---

cause of the law. Respect is properly the conception of a worth which thwarts my self-love. Thus it is regarded as an object neither of inclination nor of fear, though it has something analogous to both. The only object of respect is the law, and indeed only the law which we impose on ourselves and yet recognize as necessary in itself. As a law we are subject to it without consulting self-love; as imposed on us by ourselves, it is conseqence of our will. In the former respect it is analogous to fear and in the latter to inclination. All respect for a person is only respect for the law (of righteousness, etc.) of which the person provides an example. Because we see the improvement of our talents as a duty, we think of a person of talents as the example of a law, as it were (the law that we should by practice become like him in his talents), and that constitutes our respect. All so-called moral interest consists solely in respect for the law.

I easily distinguish the two meanings which the question can have, viz., whether it is prudent to make a false promise, or whether it conforms to my duty. Undoubtedly the former can often be the case, though I do see clearly that it is not sufficient merely to escape from the present difficulty by this expedient, but that I must consider whether inconveniences much greater than the present one may not later spring from this lie. Even with all my supposed cunning, the consequences cannot be so easily foreseen. Loss of credit might be far more disadvantageous than the misfortune I now seek to avoid, and it is hard to tell whether it might not be more prudent to act according to a universal maxim and to make it a habit not to promise anything without intending to fulfil it. But it is soon clear to me that such a maxim is based only on an apprehensive concern with consequences.

To be truthful from duty, however, is an entirely different thing from being truthful out of fear of disadvantageous consequences, for in the former case the concept of the action itself contains a law for me, while in the latter I must first look about to see what results for me may be connected with it. For to deviate from the principle of duty is certainly bad, but to be unfaithful to my maxim of prudence can sometimes be very advantageous to me, though it is certainly safer to abide by it. The shortest but most infallible way to find the answer to the question as to whether a deceitful promise is consistent with duty is to ask myself: Would I be content that my maxim (of extricating myself from difficulty by a false promise) should hold as a universal law for myself as well as for others? And could I say to myself that everyone may make a false promise when he is in a difficulty from which he otherwise cannot escape? I immediately see that I could will the lie but not a universal law to lie. For with such a law there would be no promises at all inasmuch as it would be futile to make a pretense of my intention in regard to future actions to those who would not believe this pretense or—if they overhastily did so—who would pay me back in my own coin. Thus my maxim would necessarily destroy itself as soon as it was made a universal law.

I do not, therefore, need any penetrating acuteness in order to discern what I have to do in order that my volition may be morally good. Inexperienced in the course of the world, incapable of being prepared for all its contingencies, I only ask myself: Can I will that my maxim become a universal law? If not, it must be rejected, not because of any disadvantage accruing to myself or even to others, but because it cannot enter as a principle into a possible universal legislation, and reason extorts from me an immediate respect for such legislation. I do not as yet discern on what it is grounded (a question the philosopher may investigate), but I at least understand that it is an estimation of the worth which far outweighs all the worth of whatever is recommended by the inclinations, and that the necessity of my actions from pure respect for the practical law constitutes duty. To duty every other motive must give place, because duty is the condition of a will good in itself, whose worth transcends everything.

Thus within the moral knowledge of common human reason we have attained its principle. To be sure, common human reason does not think it abstractly in such a universal form, but it always has it in view and uses it as the standard of its judgments. It would be easy to show how common human reason, with this compass, knows well how to distinguish what is good, what

is bad, and what is consistent or inconsistent with duty. Without in the least teaching common reason anything new, we need only to draw its attention to its own principle, in the manner of Socrates, thus showing that neither science nor philosophy is needed in order to know what one has to do in order to be honest and good, and even wise and virtuous. We might have conjectured beforehand that the knowledge of what everyone is obliged to do and thus also to know would be within the reach of everyone, even the most ordinary man. Here we cannot but admire the great advantages which the practical faculty of judgment has over the theoretical in ordinary human understanding. In the theoretical, if ordinary reason ventures to go beyond the laws of experience and perceptions of the senses, it falls into sheer inconceivabilities and self-contradictions, or at least into a chaos of uncertainty, obscurity, and instability. In the practical, on the other hand, the power of judgment first shows itself to advantage when common understanding excludes all sensuous incentives from practical laws. It then becomes even subtle, quibbling with its own conscience or with other claims to what should be called right, or wishing to determine correctly for its own instruction the worth of certain actions. But the most remarkable thing about ordinary reason in its practical concern is that it may have as much hope as any philosopher of hitting the mark. In fact, it is almost more certain to do so than the philosopher, because he has no principle which the common understanding lacks, while his judgment is easily confused by a mass of irrelevant considerations, so that it easily turns aside from the correct way. Would it not, therefore, be wiser in moral matters to acquiesce in the common rational judgment, or at most to call in philosophy in order to make the system of morals more complete and comprehensible and its rules more convenient for use (especially in disputation) than to steer the common understanding from its happy simplicity in practical matters and to lead it through philosophy into a new path of inquiry and instruction?

Innocence is indeed a glorious thing, but, on the other hand, it is very sad that it cannot well maintain itself, being easily led astray. For this reason, even wisdom—which consists more in acting than in knowing—needs science, not so as to learn from it but to secure admission and permanence to its precepts. Man feels in himself a powerful counterpoise against all commands of duty which reason presents to him as so deserving of respect; this counterpoise is his needs and inclinations, the complete satisfaction of which he sums up under the name of happiness. Now reason issues inexorable commands without promising anything to the inclinations. It disregards, as it were, and holds in contempt those claims which are so impetuous and yet so plausible, and which will not allow themselves to be abolished by any command. From this a natural dialectic arises, i. e., a propensity to argue against the stern laws of duty and their validity, or at least to place their purity and strictness in doubt and, where possible, to make them more accordant with our wishes and inclinations. This is equivalent to corrupting them in their very foundations and destroying their dignity— a thing which even common practical reason cannot ultimately call good.

In this way common human reason is impelled to go outside its sphere and to take a step into the field of practical philosophy. But it is forced to do so not by any speculative need, which never occurs to it so long as it is satisfied to remain merely healthy

reason; rather, it is so impelled on practical grounds in order to obtain information and clear instruction respecting the source of its principle and the correct determination of this principle in its opposition to the maxims which are based on need and inclination. It seeks this information in order to escape from the perplexity of opposing claims and to avoid the danger of losing all genuine moral principles through the equivocation in which it is easily involved. Thus when practical common reason cultivates itself, a dialectic surreptitiously ensues, which forces it to seek aid in philosophy, just as the same thing happens in the theoretical use of reason. In this case, as in the theoretical, it will find rest only in a thorough critical examination of our reason.

SECOND SECTION

Transition from the Popular Moral Philosophy to the Metaphysics of Morals

If we have derived our earlier concept of duty from the common use of our practical reason, it is by no means to be inferred that we have treated it as an empirical concept. On the contrary, if we attend to our experience of the way men act, we meet frequent and, as we ourselves confess, justified complaints that we cannot cite a single sure example of the disposition to act from pure duty. There are also justified complaints that, though much may be done that accords with what duty commands, it is nevertheless always doubtful whether it is done from duty, and thus whether it has moral worth. There have always been philosophers who for this reason have absolutely denied the reality of this disposition in human actions, attributing everything to more or less refined self-love. They have done so without questioning the correctness of the concept of morality. Rather they spoke with sincere regret of the frailty and corruption of human nature, which is noble enough to take as its precept an idea so worthy of respect but which at the same time is too weak to follow it, employing reason, which should legislate for human nature, only to provide for the interest of the inclinations either singly or, at best, in their greatest possible harmony with one another.

It is in fact absolutely impossible by experience to discern with complete certainty a single case in which the maxim of an action, however much it may conform to duty, rested solely on moral grounds and on the conception of one's duty. It sometimes happens that in the most searching self-examination we can find nothing except the moral ground of duty which could have been powerful enough to move us to this or that good action and to such great sacrifice. But from this we cannot by any means conclude with certainty that a secret impulse of self-love, falsely appearing as the idea of duty, was not actually the true determining cause of the will. For we like to flatter ourselves with a pretended nobler motive, while in fact even the strictest examination can never lead us entirely behind the secret incentives, for, when moral worth is in question, it is not a matter of actions which one sees but of their inner principles which one does not see.

Moreover, one cannot better serve the wishes of those who ridicule all morality as a mere phantom of human imagination overreaching itself through self-conceit than by conceding to them that the concepts of duty must be derived only from experience (for they are ready to believe from indolence that this is true of all other concepts too). For, by this concession, a sure triumph is prepared for them. Out of love for humanity I am willing to admit that most of our actions are in accordance with duty; but, if we look closer at our thoughts and aspirations, we everywhere come upon the dear self, which is always salient, and it is this instead of the stern command of duty (which would often require self-denial) which supports our plans. One need not be an enemy of virtue, but only a cool observer who does not mistake even the liveliest aspiration for the good with its reality, to be doubtful sometimes whether true virtue can really be found anywhere in the world. This is especially true as one's years increase and the power of judgment is made wiser by experience and more acute in observation. This being so, nothing can secure us against the complete abandonment of our ideas of duty and preserve in us a well-founded respect for its law except the clear conviction that, even if there never were actions springing from such pure sources, our concern is not whether this or that was done but that reason of itself and independently of all appearances commands what ought to be done. Our concern is with actions of which perhaps the world has never had an example, with actions whose feasibility might be seriously doubted by those who base everything on experience, and yet with actions inexorably commanded by reason. For example, pure sincerity in friendship can be demanded of every man, and this demand is not in the least diminished if a sincere friend has never existed, because this duty, as duty in general, prior to all experience lies in the idea of a reason which determines the will by a priori grounds.

It is clear that no experience can give occasion for inferring the possibility of such apodictic laws. This is especially clear when we add that, unless we wish to deny all truth to the concept of morality and renounce its application to any possible object, we cannot refuse to admit that the law of this concept is of such broad significance that it holds not merely for men but for all rational beings as such; we must grant that it must be valid with absolute necessity and not merely under contingent conditions and with exceptions. For with what right could we bring into unlimited respect something that might be valid only under contingent human conditions? And how could laws of the determination of our will be held to be laws of the determination of the will of a rational being in general and of ourselves in so far as we are rational beings, if they were merely empirical and did not have their origin completely a priori in pure, but practical, reason?

Nor could one give poorer counsel to morality than to attempt to derive it from examples. For each example of morality which is exhibited to me must itself have been previously judged according to principles of morality to see whether it is worthy to serve as an original example, i. e., as a model. By no means could it authoritatively furnish the concept of morality. Even the Holy One of the Gospel must be compared with our ideal of moral perfection before He is recognized as such; even He says of Himself, "Why call ye Me (Whom you see) good? None is good (the archetype of the good) except God only (Whom you do not see)." But whence do we have the concept of God as the highest good? Solely from the idea of moral perfection which reason formulates a priori and which it inseparably connects with the concept of a free will. Imitation has no place in moral matters, and examples serve only for encouragement. That is, they put

beyond question the practicability of what the law commands, and they make visible that which the practical rule expresses more generally. But they can never justify our guiding ourselves by examples and our setting-aside their true original which lies in reason.

If there is thus no genuine supreme principle of morality which does not rest merely on pure reason independently of all experience, I do not believe it is necessary even to ask whether it is well to exhibit these concepts generally (in abstracto), which, together with the principles belonging to them, are established a priori. At any rate, this question need not be asked if knowledge which establishes this is to be distinguished from ordinary knowledge and called philosophical. But in our times this question may perhaps be necessary. For if we collected votes as to whether pure rational knowledge separated from all experience, i. e., metaphysics of morals, or popular practical philosophy is to be preferred, it is easily guessed on which side the majority would stand.

This condescension to popular notions is certainly very commendable once the ascent to the principles of pure reason has been satisfactorily accomplished. That would mean the prior establishment of the doctrine of morals on metaphysics and then, when it is established, to procure a hearing for it through popularization. But it is extremely absurd to want to achieve popularity in the first investigation, where everything depends on the correctness of the fundamental principles. Not only can this procedure never make claim to that rarest merit of true philosophical popularity, since there is really no art in being generally comprehensible if one thereby renounces all basic insight; but it produces a disgusting jumble of patched-up observations and half-reasoned principles.

Shallow pates enjoy this, for it is very useful in everyday chitchat, while the more sensible feel confused and dissatisfied without being able to help themselves. They turn their eyes away, even though philosophers, who see very well through the delusion, find little audience when they call men away for a time from this pretended popularization in order that they may rightly appear popular after they have attained a definite insight.

One need only look at the essays on morality which that popular taste favors. One will sometimes meet with the particular vocation of human nature (but occasionally also the idea of a rational nature in general), sometimes perfection, and sometimes happiness, here moral feeling, there fear of God, a little of this and a little of that in a marvelous mixture. However, it never occurs to the authors to ask whether the principles of morality are, after all, to be sought anywhere in knowledge of human nature (which we can derive only from experience). And if this is not the case, if the principles are completely a priori, free from everything empirical, and found exclusively in pure rational concepts and not at all in any other place, they never ask whether they should undertake this investigation as a separate inquiry, i. e., as pure practical philosophy or (if one may use a name so decried) a metaphysics [5] of morals.

[5] If one wishes, the pure philosophy of morals (metaphysics) can be distinguished from the applied (i e., applied to human nature), just as pure mathematics and pure logic are distinguished from applied mathematics and applied logic. By this designation one is immediately reminded that moral principles are not founded on the peculiarities of human nature but must stand of themselves a priori, and that from such principles practical rules for every rational nature, and accordingly for man, must be derivable.

They never think of dealing with it alone and bringing it by itself to completeness and of requiring the public, which desires popularization, to await the outcome of this undertaking.

But a completely isolated metaphysics of morals, mixed with no anthropology, no theology, no physics or hyperphysics, and even less with occult qualities (which might be called hypophysical), is not only an indispensable substrate of all theoretically sound and definite knowledge of duties; it is also a desideratum of the highest importance to the actual fulfilment of its precepts. For the pure conception of duty and of the moral law generally, with no admixture of empirical inducements, has an influence on the human heart so much more powerful than all other incentives [6] which may be derived from the

[6] I have a letter from the late excellent Sulzer [*] in which he asks me why the theories of virtue accomplish so little even though they contain so much that is convincing to reason. My answer was delayed in order that I might make it complete. The answer is only that the teachers themselves have not completely clarified their concepts, and when they wish to make up for this by hunting in every quarter for motives to the morally good so as to make their physic right strong, they spoil it. For the commonest observation shows that if we imagine an act of honesty performed with a steadfast soul and sundered from all view to any advantage in this or another world and even under the greatest temptations of need or allurement, it far surpasses and eclipses any similar action which was affected in the least by any foreign incentive; it elevates the soul and arouses the wish to be able to act in this way. Even moderately young children feel this impression, and one should never represent duties to them in any other way.

[*] [Johann Georg Sulzer (1720-79), an important figure at the court and in literary circles in Berlin. Cf. Allgemeine deutsche Biographie, XXXVII, 144-47.]

empirical field that reason, in the consciousness of its dignity, despises them and gradually becomes master over them. It has this influence only through reason, which thereby first realizes that it can of itself be practical. A mixed theory of morals which is put together both from incentives of feelings and inclinations and from rational concepts must, on the other hand, make the mind vacillate between motives which cannot be brought under any principle and which can lead only accidentally to the good and often to the bad.

From what has been said it is clear that all moral concepts have their seat and origin entirely a priori in reason. This is just as much the case in the most ordinary reason as in reason which is speculative to the highest degree. It is obvious that they can be abstracted from no empirical and hence merely contingent cognitions. In the purity of their origin lies their worthiness to serve us as supreme practical principles, and to the extent that something empirical is added to them, just this much is subtracted from their genuine influence and from the unqualified worth of actions. Furthermore, it is evident that it is not only of the greatest necessity in a theoretical point of view when it is a question of speculation but also of the utmost practical importance to derive the concepts and laws of morals from pure reason and to present them pure and unmixed, and to determine the scope of this entire practical but pure rational knowledge (the entire faculty of pure practical reason) without making the principles depend upon the particular nature of human reason, as speculative philosophy may permit and even sometimes find necessary. But since moral laws should hold for every rational being as such, the principles must be derived from the universal concept of a rational being generally. In this manner all morals, which

need anthropology for their application to men, must be completely developed first as pure philosophy, i. e., metaphysics, independently of anthropology (a thing which is easily done in such distinct fields of knowledge). For we know well that if we are not in possession of such a metaphysics, it is not merely futile to define accurately for the purposes of speculative judgment the moral element of duty in all actions which accord with duty, but impossible to base morals on legitimate principles for merely ordinary and practical use, especially in moral instruction; and it is only in this manner that pure moral dispositions can be produced and engrafted on men's minds for the purpose of the highest good in the world.

In this study we do not advance merely from the common moral judgment (which here is very worthy of respect) to the philosophical, as this has already been done, but we advance by natural stages from a popular philosophy (which goes no further than it can grope by means of examples) to metaphysics (which is not held back by anything empirical and which, as it must measure out the entire scope of rational knowledge of this kind, reaches even ideas, where examples fail us). In order to make this advance, we must follow and clearly present the practical faculty of reason from its universal rules of determination to the point where the concept of duty arises from it.

Everything in nature works according to laws. Only a rational being has the capacity of acting according to the conception of laws, i. e., according to principles. This capacity is will. Since reason is required for the derivation of actions from laws, will is nothing else than practical reason. If reason infallibly determines the will, the actions which such a being recognizes as objectively necessary are also subjectively necessary. That is, the will is a faculty of choosing only that which reason, independently of inclination, recognizes as practically necessary, i.e., as good. But if reason of itself does not sufficiently determine the will, and if the will is subjugated to subjective conditions (certain incentives) which do not always agree with objective conditions; in a word, if the will is not of itself in complete accord with reason (the actual case of men), then the actions which are recognized as objectively necessary are subjectively contingent, and the determination of such a will according to objective laws is constraint. That is, the relation of objective laws to a will which is not completely good is conceived as the determination of the will of a rational being by principles of reason to which this will is not by nature necessarily obedient.

The conception of an objective principle, so far as it constrains a will, is a command (of reason), and the formula of this command is called an *imperative.*

All imperatives are expressed by an "ought" and thereby indicate the relation of an objective law of reason to a will which is not in its subjective constitution necessarily determined by this law. This relation is that of constraint. Imperatives say that it would be good to do or to refrain from doing something, but they say it to a will which does not always do something simply because it is presented to it as a good thing to do. Practical good is what determines the will by means of the conception of reason and hence not by subjective causes but, rather, objectively, i. e., on grounds which are valid for every rational being as such. It is distinguished from the pleasant, as that which has an influence on the will only by means of a sensation from merely subjective causes, which hold only for the senses of this or that per-

son and not as a principle of reason which holds for everyone.[7]

A perfectly good will, therefore, would be equally subject to objective laws (of the good), but it could not be conceived as constrained by them to act in accord with them, because, according to its own subjective constitution, it can be determined to act only through the conception of the good. Thus no imperatives hold for the divine will or, more generally, for a holy will. The "ought" is here out of place, for the volition of itself is necessarily in unison with the law. Therefore imperatives are only formulas expressing the relation of objective laws of volition in general to the subjective imperfection of the will of this or that rational being, e. g., the human will.

All imperatives command either hy-

---

[7] The dependence of the faculty of desire on sensations is called inclination, and inclination always indicates a need. The dependence of a contingently determinable will on principles of reason, however, is called interest. An interest is present only in a dependent will which is not of itself always in accord with reason; in the divine will we cannot conceive of an interest. But the human will can take an interest in something without thereby acting from interest. The former means the practical interest in the action; the latter, the pathological interest in the object of the action. The former indicates only the dependence of the will on principles of reason in themselves, while the latter indicates dependence on the principles of reason for the purpose of inclination, since reason gives only the practical rule by which the needs of inclination are to be aided. In the former case the action interests me, and in the latter the object of the action (so far as it is pleasant for me) interests me. In the first section we have seen that, in the case of an action done from duty, no regard must be given to the interest in the object, but merely in the action itself and its principle in reason (i.e., the law).

pothetically or categorically. The former present the practical necessity of a possible action as a means to achieving something else which one desires (or which one may possibly desire). The categorical imperative would be one which presented an action as of itself objectively necessary, without regard to any other end.

Since every practical law presents a possible action as good and thus as necessary for a subject practically determinable by reason, all imperatives are formulas of the determination of action which is necessary by the principle of a will which is in any way good. If the action is good only as a means to something else, the imperative is hypothetical; but if it is thought of as good in itself, and hence as necessary in a will which of itself conforms to reason as the principle of this will, the imperative is categorical.

The imperative thus says what action possible to me would be good, and it presents the practical rule in relation to a will which does not forthwith perform an action simply because it is good, in part because the subject does not always know that the action is good and in part (when it does know it) because his maxims can still be opposed to the objective principles of practical reason.

The hypothetical imperative, therefore, says only that the action is good to some purpose, possible or actual. In the former case it is a problematical,[8] in the latter an assertorical, practical principle. The categorical imperative, which declares the action to be of itself objectively necessary without making any reference to a purpose, i. e., without having any other end, holds as an apodictical (practical) principle.

We can think of that which is possible through the mere powers of some rational being as a possible purpose of any will. As a consequence, the principles of action, in so far as they are thought of as necessary to attain a possible purpose which can be achieved by them, are in reality infinitely numerous. All sciences have some practical part which consists of problems of some end which is possible for us and of imperatives as to how it can be reached. These can therefore generally be called imperatives of skill. Whether the end is reasonable and good is not in question at all, for the question is only of what must be done in order to attain it. The precepts to be followed by a physician in order to cure his patient and by a

8 [The *First Introduction to the Critique of Judgment* says: "This is the place to correct an error into which I fell in the *Foundations of the Metaphysics of Morals*. After I had stated that the imperatives of prudence commanded only conditionally, and indeed only under the condition of merely possible, i.e., problematic, ends, I called that kind of practical precept 'problematic imperatives.' But there is certainly a contradiction in this expression. I should have called them 'technical imperatives,' i.e., imperatives of art. The pragmatic imperatives, or rules of prudence which command under the condition of an actual and even subjectively necessary end, belong also among the technical imperatives. (For what is prudence but the skill to use free men and even the natural dispositions and inclinations of oneself for one's own designs?) Only the fact that the end to which we submit ourselves and others, namely, our own happiness, does not belong to the merely arbitrary ends [which we may or may not have] justifies a special name for these imperatives, because the problem does not require merely a mode of reaching the end, as is the case with technical imperatives, but also requires a definition of what constitutes this end itself (happiness). The end must be presupposed as known in the case of technical imperatives" (Cassirer ed., V, 183 n.).]

poisoner in order to bring about certain death are of equal value in so far as each does that which will perfectly accomplish his purpose. Since in early youth we do not know what ends may occur to us in the course of life, parents seek to let their children learn a great many things and provide for skill in the use of means to all sorts of arbitrary ends, among which they cannot determine whether any one of them may later become an actual purpose of their pupil, though it is possible that he may someday have it as his actual purpose. And this anxiety is so great that they commonly neglect to form and correct their judgment on the worth of things which they may make their ends.

There is one end, however, which we may presuppose as actual in all rational beings so far as imperatives apply to them, i. e., so far as they are dependent beings; there is one purpose not only which they *can* have but which we can presuppose that they all *do* have by a necessity of nature. This purpose is happiness. The hypothetical imperative which represents the practical necessity of action as means to the promotion of happiness is an assertorical imperative. We may not expound it as merely necessary to an uncertain and a merely possible purpose, but as necessary to a purpose which we can a priori and with assurance assume for everyone because it belongs to his essence. Skill in the choice of means to one's own highest welfare can be called prudence [9] in the narrowest sense. Thus the imperative which refers to the choice of means to one's own happiness, i. e., the precept of prudence, is still only hypothetical; the action is not absolutely commanded but commanded only as a means to another end.

Finally, there is one imperative which directly commands a certain conduct without making its condition some purpose to be reached by it. This imperative is categorical. It concerns not the material of the action and its intended result but the form and the principle from which it results. What is essentially good in it consists in the intention, the result being what it may. This imperative may be called the imperative of morality. *CI or I of M*

Volition according to these three principles is plainly distinguished by dissimilarity in the constraint to which they subject the will. In order to clarify this dissimilarity, I believe that they are most suitably named if one says that they are either rules of skill, counsels of prudence, or commands (laws) of morality, respectively. For law alone implies the concept of an unconditional and objective and hence universally valid necessity, and commands are laws which must be obeyed, even against inclination. Counsels do indeed involve necessity, but a necessity that can hold only under a subjectively contingent condition, i. e., whether this or that man counts this or that as part of his happiness; but the categorical imperative, on the other hand, is restricted by no condition. As absolutely, though practically, necessary it can be called a command in the strict sense. We could also call the first imperative technical (belonging to art), the sec-

---

[9] The word "prudence" may be taken in two senses, and it may bear the name of prudence with reference to things of the world and private prudence. The former sense means the skill of a man in having an influence on others so as to use them for his own purposes. The latter is the ability to unite all these purposes to his own lasting advantage. The worth of the first is finally reduced to the latter, and of one who is prudent in the former sense but not in the latter we might better say that he is clever and cunning yet, on the whole, imprudent.

ond pragmatic [10] (belonging to welfare), and the third moral (belonging to free conduct as such, i.e, to morals).

The question now arises: How are all these imperatives possible? This question does not require an answer as to how the action which the imperative commands can be performed but merely as to how the constraint of the will, which the imperative expresses in the problem, can be conceived. How an imperative of skill is possible requires no particular discussion. Whoever wills the end, so far as reason has decisive influence on his action, wills also the indispensably necessary means to it that lie in his power. This proposition, in what concerns the will, is analytical; for, in willing an object as my effect, my causality as an [11] acting subject, i. e., the use of the means, is already thought, and the imperative derives the concept of necessary actions to this end from the concept of willing this end. Synthetical propositions undoubtedly are necessary in determining the means to a proposed end, but they do not concern the ground, the act of the will, but only the way to make the object real. Mathematics teaches, by synthetical propositions only, that in order to bisect a line according to an infallible principle, I must make two intersecting arcs from each of its extremities; but if I know

10 It seems to me that the proper meaning of the word "pragmatic" could be most accurately defined in this way. For sanctions which properly flow not from the law of states as necessary statutes but from provision for the general welfare are called pragmatic. A history is pragmatically composed when it teaches prudence, i.e., instructs the world how it could provide for its interest better than, or at least as well as, has been done in the past.

11 [Reading handelnde with the Academy ed.; the Cassirer ed. has: "my causality as that of an acting subject."]

the proposed result can be obtained only by such an action, then it is an analytical proposition that, if I fully will the effect, I must also will the action necessary to produce it. For it is one and the same thing to conceive of something as an effect which is in a certain way possible through me and to conceive of myself as acting in this way.

If it were only easy to give a definite concept of happiness, the imperatives of prudence would completely correspond to those of skill and would be likewise analytical. For it could be said in this case as well as in the former that whoever wills the end wills also (necessarily according to reason) the only means to it which are in his power. But it is a misfortune that the concept of happiness is such an indefinite concept that, although each person wishes to attain it, he can never definitely and self-consistently state what it is he really wishes and wills. The reason for this is that all elements which belong to the concept of happiness are empirical, i. e., they must be taken from experience, while for the idea of happiness an absolute whole, a maximum, of well-being is needed in my present and in every future condition. Now it is impossible even for a most clear-sighted and omnipotent but finite being to form here a definite concept of that which he really wills. If he wills riches, how much anxiety, envy, and intrigues might he not thereby draw upon his shoulders! If he wills much knowledge and vision, perhaps it might become only an eye that much sharper to show him as more dreadful the evils which are now hidden from him and which are yet unavoidable or to burden his desires—which already sufficiently engage him —with even more needs! If he wills a long life, who guarantees that it will not be long misery? If he wills at least health, how often has not the discomfort of the body restrained him from excesses into which perfect health would have led him? In short, he is not capable, on any principle and with complete certainty, of ascertaining what would make him truly happy; omniscience would be needed for this. He cannot, therefore, act according to definite principles so as to be happy, but only according to empirical counsels, e. g., those of diet, economy, courtesy, restraint, etc., which are shown by experience best to promote welfare on the average. Hence the imperatives of prudence cannot, in the strict sense, command, i. e., present actions objectively as practically necessary; thus they are to be taken as counsels (consilia) rather than as commands (praecepta) of reason, and the task of determining infallibly and universally what action will promote the happiness of a rational being is completely unsolvable. There can be no imperative which would, in the strict sense, command us to do what makes for happiness, because happiness is an ideal not of reason but of imagination,[12] depending only on empirical grounds which one would expect in vain to determine an action through which the totality of consequences—which is in fact infinite—could be achieved. Assuming that the means to happiness could be infallibly stated, this imperative of prudence would be an analytical prop-

12 [The distinction between happiness and pleasure, which Kant says the followers of Epicurus confused, is explained in a fragment dating back to about 1775: "Happiness is not something sensed but something thought. Nor is it a thought which can be taken from experience but a thought which only makes its experience possible. Not as if one had to know happiness in all its elements, but [one must know] the a priori condition by which alone one can be capable of happiness" (Lose Blätter [Reicke ed.], trans. Schilpp, in Kant's Precritical Ethics, p. 129).]

osition, for it differs from the imperative of skill only in that its end is given while in the latter case it is merely possible. Since both, however, only command the means to that which one presupposes, the imperative which commands the willing of the means to him who wills the end are both analytical. There is, consequently, no difficulty in seeing the possibility of such an imperative.

To see how the imperative of morality is possible is, then, without doubt the only question needing an answer. It is not hypothetical, and thus the objectively conceived necessity cannot be supported by any presupposition, as was the case with the hypothetical imperatives. But it must not be overlooked that it cannot be shown by any example (i. e., it cannot be empirically shown) whether or not there is such an imperative; it is rather to be suspected that all imperatives which appear to be categorical be yet hypothetical, but in a hidden way. For instance, when it is said, "Thou shalt not make a false promise," we assume that the necessity of this avoidance is not a mere counsel for the sake of escaping of some other evil, so that it would read, "Thou shalt not make a false promise so that, if it comes to light, thou ruinest thy credit;" we assume rather that an action of this kind must be regarded as of itself bad and that the imperative of the prohibition is categorical. But we cannot show with certainty by any example that the will is here determined by the law alone without any other incentives, even though this appears to be the case. For it is always possible that secretly fear of disgrace, and perhaps also obscure apprehension of other dangers, may have had an influence on the will. Who can prove by experience the nonexistence of a cause when experience shows us only that we do not perceive the cause? But in such a case the so-called moral imperative, which as such appears to be categorical and unconditional, would be actually only a pragmatic concept which makes us attentive to our own advantage and teaches us to consider it.

Thus we shall have to investigate purely a priori the possibility of a categorical imperative, for we do not have the advantage that experience would give us the reality of this imperative, so that the [demonstration of its] possibility would be necessary only for its explanation and not for its establishment. In the meantime, this much may at least be seen: the categorical imperative alone can be taken as a practical *law,* while all the others may be called principles of the will but not laws. This is because what is necessary merely for the attainment of an arbitrary purpose can be regarded as itself contingent, and we get rid of the precept once we give up the purpose, where as the unconditional command leaves the will no freedom to choose the opposite. Thus it alone implies the necessity which we require of a law.

Secondly, in the case of the categorical imperative or law of morality, the cause of difficulty in discerning its possibility is very weighty. This imperative is an a priori synthetical practical proposition,[13] and, since to discern the possibility of propositions of this sort is so difficult in theoretical

knowledge, it may well be gathered that it will be no less difficult in the practical.

In attacking this problem, we will first inquire whether the mere concept of a categorical imperative does not also furnish the formula containing the proposition which alone can be a categorical imperative. For even when we know the formula of the imperative, to learn how such an absolute law is possible will require difficult and special labors which we shall postpone to the last section.

If I think of a hypothetical imperative as such, I do not know what it will contain until the condition is stated [under which it is an imperative]. But if I think of a categorical imperative, I know immediately what it contains. For since the imperative contains besides the law only the necessity of the maxim [14] of acting in accordance with this law, while the law contains no condition to which it is restricted, there is nothing remaining in it except the universality of law as such to which the maxim of the action should conform; and in effect this conformity alone is represented as necessary by the imperative.[15]

There is, therefore, only one categorical imperative. It is: Act only according to that maxim by which you can at the same time will that it should become a universal law.

Now if all imperatives of duty can be derived from this one imperative as

---

[13] I connect a priori the will, without a presupposed condition resulting from an inclination, with the action (though I do so only objectively, i.e., under the idea of a reason which would have complete power over all subjective motives). This is, therefore, a practical proposition which does not analytically derive the willing of an action from some other volition already presupposed (for we do not have such a perfect will); it rather connects it directly with the concept of the will of a rational being as something which is not contained within it.

[14] A maxim is the subjective principle of acting and must be distinguished from the objective principle, i.e., the practical law. The former contains the practical rule which reason determines according to the conditions of the subject (often its ignorance or inclinations) and is thus the principle according to which the subject acts. The law, on the other hand, is the objective principle valid for every rational being, and the principle by which it ought to act, i.e., an imperative.

[15] [Following reading of Cassirer ed.]

a principle, we can at least show what we understand by the concept of duty and what it means, even though it remain undecided whether that which is called duty is an empty concept or not.

The universality of law according to which effects are produced constitutes what is properly called nature in the most general sense (as to form), i. e., the existence of things so far as it is determined by universal laws. [By analogy], then, the universal imperative of duty can be expressed as follows: Act as though the maxim of your action were by your will to become a universal law of nature.

We shall now enumerate some duties, adopting the usual division of them into duties to ourselves and to others and into perfect and imperfect duties.[16]

1. A man who is reduced to despair by a series of evils feels a weariness with life but is still in possession of his reason sufficiently to ask whether it would not be contrary to his duty to himself to take his own life. Now he asks whether the maxim of his action could become a universal law of nature. His maxim, however, is: For love of myself, I make it my principle to shorten my life when by a longer duration it threatens more evil than satisfaction. But it is questionable whether this principle of self-love could become a universal law of na-

[16] It must be noted here that I reserve the division of duties for a future *Metaphysics of Morals* and that the division here stands as only an arbitrary one (chosen in order to arrange my examples). For the rest, by a perfect duty I here understand a duty which permits no exception in the interest of inclination; thus I have not merely outer but also inner perfect duties. This runs contrary to the usage adopted in the schools, but I am not disposed to defend it here because it is all one to my purpose whether this is conceded or not.

ture. One immediately sees a contradiction in a system of nature, whose law would be to destroy life by the feeling whose special office is to impel the improvement of life. In this case it would not exist as nature; hence that maxim cannot obtain as a law of nature, and thus it wholly contradicts the supreme principle of all duty.

2. Another man finds himself forced by need to borrow money. He well knows that he will not be able to repay it, but he also sees that nothing will be loaned him if he does not firmly promise to repay it at a certain time. He desires to make such a promise, but he has enough conscience to ask himself whether it is not improper and opposed to duty to relieve his distress in such a way. Now, assuming he does decide to do so, the maxim of his action would be as follows: When I believe myself to be in need of money, I will borrow money and promise to repay it, although I know I shall never do so. Now this principle of self-love or of his own benefit may very well be compatible with his whole future welfare, but the question is whether it is right. He changes the pretension of self-love into a universal law and then puts the question: How would it be if my maxim became a universal law? He immediately sees that it could never hold as a universal law of nature and be consistent with itself; rather it must necessarily contradict itself. For the universality of a law which says that anyone who believes himself to be in need could promise what he pleased with the intention of not fulfilling it would make the promise itself and the end to be accomplished by it impossible; no one would believe what was promised to him but would only laugh at any such assertion as vain pretense.

3. A third finds in himself a talent which could, by means of some cultivation, make him in many respects a

useful man. But he finds himself in comfortable circumstances and prefers indulgence in pleasure to troubling himself with broadening and improving his fortunate natural gifts. Now, however, let him ask whether his maxim of neglecting his gifts, besides agreeing with his propensity to idle amusement, agrees also with what is called duty. He sees that a system of nature could indeed exist in accordance with such a law, even though man (like the inhabitants of the South Sea Islands) should let his talents rust and resolve to devote his life merely to idleness, indulgence, and propagation—in a word, to pleasure. But he cannot possibly will that this should become a universal law of nature or that it should be implanted in us by a natural instinct. For, as a rational being, he necessarily wills that all his faculties should be developed, inasmuch as they are given to him for all sorts of possible purposes.

4. A fourth man, for whom things are going well, sees that others (whom he could help) have to struggle with great hardships, and he asks, "What concern of mine is it? Let each one be as happy as heaven wills, or as he can make himself; I will not take anything from him or even envy him but to his welfare or to his assistance in time of need I have no desire to contribute." If such a way of thinking were a universal law of nature, certainly the human race could exist, and without doubt even better than in a state where everyone talks of sympathy and good will or even exerts himself occasionally to practice them while, on the other hand, he cheats when he can and betrays or otherwise violates the rights of man. Now although it is possible that a universal law of nature according to that maxim could exist, it is nevertheless impossible to will that such a principle should hold everywhere as a law of

nature. For a will which resolved this would conflict with itself, since instances can often arise in which he would need the love and sympathy of others, and in which he would have robbed himself, by such a law of nature springing from his own will, of all hope of the aid he desires.

The foregoing are a few of the many actual duties, or at least of duties we hold to be real, whose derivation from the one stated principle is clear. We must be able to will that a maxim of our action become a universal law; this is the canon of the moral estimation of our action generally. Some actions are of such a nature that their maxim cannot even be *thought* as a universal law of nature without contradiction, far from it being possible that one could will that it should be such. In others this internal impossibility is not found, though it is still impossible to *will* that their maxim should be raised to the universality of a law of nature, because such a will would contradict itself. We easily see that the former maxim conflicts with the stricter or narrower (imprescriptible) duty, the latter with broader (meritorious) duty. Thus all duties, so far as the kind of obligation (not the object of their action) is concerned, have been completely exhibited by these examples in their dependence on the one principle.

When we observe ourselves in any transgression of a duty, we find that we do not actually will that our maxim should become a universal law. That is impossible for us; rather, the contrary of this maxim should remain as a law generally, and we only take the liberty of making an exception to it for ourselves or for the sake of our inclination, and for this one occasion. Consequently, if we weighed everything from one and the same standpoint, namely, reason, we would come upon a contradiction in our own will, viz., that a certain principle is objectively necessary as a universal law and yet subjectively does not hold universally but rather admits exceptions. However, since we regard our action at one time from the point of view of a will wholly conformable to reason and then from that of a will affected by inclinations, there is actually no contradiction, but rather an opposition of inclination to the precept of reason (antagonismus). In this the universality of the principle (universalitas) is changed into mere generality (generalitas), whereby the practical principle of reason meets the maxim halfway. Although this cannot be justified in our own impartial judgment, it does show that we actually acknowledge the validity of the categorical imperative and allow ourselves (with all respect to it) only a few exceptions which seem to us to be unimportant and forced upon us.

We have thus at least established that if duty is a concept which is to have significance and actual legislation for our actions, it can be expressed only in categorical imperatives and not at all in hypothetical ones. For every application of it we have also clearly exhibited the content of the categorical imperative which must contain the principle of all duty (if there is such). This is itself very much. But we are not yet advanced far enough to prove a priori that that kind of imperative really exists, that there is a practical law which of itself commands absolutely and without any incentives, and that obedience to this law is duty.

With a view to attaining this, it is extremely important to remember that we must not let ourselves think that the reality of this principle can be derived from the particular constitution of human nature. For duty is practical unconditional necessity of action; it must, therefore, hold for all rational beings (to which alone an imperative can apply), and only for that reason can it be a law for all human wills. Whatever is derived from the particular natural situation of man as such, or from certain feelings and propensities, or, even, from a particular tendency of the human reason which might not hold necessarily for the will of every rational being (if such a tendency is possible) can give a maxim valid for us but not a law; that is, it can give a subjective principle by which we may act but not an objective principle by which we would be directed to act even if all our propensity, inclination, and natural tendency were opposed to it. This is so far the case that the sublimity and intrinsic worth of the command is the better shown in a duty the fewer subjective causes there are for it and the more they are against it; the latter do not weaken the constraint of the law or diminish its validity.

Here we see philosophy brought to what is, in fact, a precarious position, which should be made fast even though it is supported by nothing in either heaven or earth. Here philosophy must show its purity, as the absolute sustainer of its laws, and not as the herald of those which an implanted sense or who knows what tutelary nature whispers to it. Those may be better than no laws at all, but they can never afford fundamental principles, which reason alone dictates. These fundamental principles must originate entirely a priori and thereby obtain their commanding authority; they can expect nothing from the inclination of men but everything from the supremacy of the law and due respect for it. Otherwise they condemn man to self-contempt and inner abhorrence.

Thus everything empirical is not only wholly unworthy to be an ingredient in the principle of morality but is even highly prejudicial to the purity of moral practices themselves. For, in morals, the proper and inestimable worth of an absolutely good will consists precisely in the freedom of the principle of action from all influences from contingent grounds which only experience can furnish. We cannot too much or too often warn against the lax or even base manner of thought which seeks principles among empirical motives and laws, for human reason in its weariness is glad to rest on this pillow. In a dream of sweet illusions (in which it embraces not Juno but a cloud), it substitutes for morality a bastard patched up from limbs of very different parentage, which looks like anything one wishes to see in it, but not like virtue to anyone who has ever beheld her in her true form.[17]

The question then is: Is it a necessary law for all rational beings that they should always judge their actions by such maxims that they themselves could will to serve as universal laws? If it is such a law, it must be connected (wholly a priori) with the concept of the will of a rational being as such. But in order to discover this connection, we must, however reluctantly, take a step into metaphysics, although into a region of it different from speculative philosophy, i.e., the metaphysics of morals. In a practical philosophy it is not a question of assuming grounds for what happens but of assuming laws of what ought to happen even though it may never happen, that is to say, objective, practical laws. Hence in practical philoso-

phy we need not inquire into the reasons why something pleases or displeases, how the pleasure of mere feeling differs from taste, and whether this is distinct from a general satisfaction of reason. Nor need we ask on what the feeling of pleasure or displeasure rests, how desires and inclinations arise, and how, finally, maxims arise from desires and inclination under the co-operation of reason. For all these matters belong to an empirical psychology, which would be the second part of physics, if we consider it as philosophy of nature so far as it rests on empirical laws. But here it is a question of objectively practical laws and thus of the relation of a will to itself so far as it determines itself only by reason; for everything which has a relation to the empirical automatically falls away, because if reason of itself alone determines conduct, it must necessarily do so a priori. The possibility of reason's thus determining conduct must now be investigated.

The will is thought of as a faculty of determining itself to action in accordance with the conception of certain laws. Such a faculty can be found only in rational beings. That which serves the will as the objective ground of its self-determination is an end, and if it is given by reason alone, it must hold alike for all rational beings. On the other hand, that which contains the ground of the possibility of the action, whose result is an end, is called the means. The subjective ground of desire is the incentive,[18] while the objective ground of volition is the motive. Thus arises the distinction between subjective ends, which rest on incentives, and objective ends,

---

[17] To behold virtue in her proper form is nothing else than to exhibit morality stripped of all admixture of sensuous things and of every spurious adornment of reward or self-love. How much she then eclipses everything which appears charming to the senses can easily be seen by everyone with the least effort of his reason, if it be not spoiled for all abstraction.

[18] [*Triebfeder* in contrast to *Bewegungsgrund*. Abbott translates the former as "spring," but "urge" might better convey the meaning. I follow Greene and Hudson's excellent usage in their translation of the *Religion*.]

which depend on motives valid for every rational being. Practical principles are formal when they disregard all subjective ends; they are material when they have subjective ends, and thus certain incentives, as their basis. The ends which a rational being arbitrarily proposes to himself as consequences of his action are material ends and are without exception only relative, for only their relation to a particularly constituted faculty of desire in the subject gives them their worth. And this worth cannot, therefore, afford any universal principles for all rational beings or valid and necessary principles for every volition. That is, they cannot give rise to any practical laws. All these relative ends, therefore, are grounds for hypothetical imperatives only.

But suppose that there were something the existence of which in itself had absolute worth, something which, as an end in itself, could be a ground of definite laws. In it and only in it could lie the ground of a possible categorical imperative, i. e., of a practical law.

Now, I say, man and, in general, every rational being exists as an end in himself and not merely as a means to be arbitrarily used by this or that will. In all his actions, whether they are directed to himself or to other rational beings, he must always be regarded at the same time as an end. All objects of inclinations have only a conditional worth, for if the inclinations and the needs founded on them did not exist, their object would be without worth. The inclinations themselves as the sources of needs, however, are so lacking in absolute worth that the universal wish of every rational being must be indeed to free themselves completely from them. Therefore, the worth of any objects to be obtained by our actions is at all times conditional. Beings whose

existence does not depend on our will but on nature, if they are not rational beings, have only a relative worth as means and are therefore called "things"; on the other hand, rational beings are designated "persons," because their nature indicates that they are ends in themselves, i. e., things which may not be used merely as means. Such a being is thus an object of respect and, so far, restricts all [arbitrary] choice. Such beings are not merely subjective ends whose existence as a result of our action has a worth for us but are objective ends, i. e., beings whose existence in itself is an end. Such an end is one for which no other end can be substituted, to which these beings should serve merely as means. For, without them, nothing of absolute worth could be found, and if all worth is conditional and thus contingent, no supreme practical principle for reason could be found anywhere.

Thus if there is to be a supreme practical principle and a categorical imperative for the human will, it must be one that forms an objective principle of the will from the conception of that which is necessarily an end for everyone because it is an end in itself. Hence this objective principle can serve as a universal practical law. The ground of this principle is: rational nature exists as an end in itself. Man necessarily thinks of his own existence in this way; thus far it is a subjective principle of human actions. Also every other rational being thinks of his existence by means of the same rational ground which holds also for myself;[19] thus it is at the same time an objective principle from which, as a supreme practical ground, it must be possible to derive all laws of the will. The practical imperative,

[19] Here I present this proposition as a postulate, but in the last section grounds for it will be found.

therefore, is the following: Act so that you treat humanity, whether in your own person or in that of another, always as an end and never as a means only. Let us now see whether this can be achieved.

To return to our previous examples: First, according to the concept of necessary duty to one's self, he who contemplates suicide will ask himself whether his action can be consistent with the idea of humanity as an end in itself. If, in order to escape from burdensome circumstances, he destroys himself, he uses a person merely as a means to maintain a tolerable condition up to the end of life. Man, however, is not a thing, and thus not something to be used merely as a means; he must always be regarded in all his actions as an end in himself. Therefore, I cannot dispose of man in my own person so as to mutilate, corrupt, or kill him. (It belongs to ethics proper to define more accurately this basic principle so as to avoid all misunderstanding, e. g., as to the amputation of limbs in order to preserve myself, or to exposing my life to danger in order to save it; I must, therefore, omit them here.)

Secondly, as concerns necessary or obligatory duties to others, he who intends a deceitful promise to others sees immediately that he intends to use another man merely as a means, without the latter containing the end in himself at the same time. For he whom I want to use for my own purposes by means of such a promise cannot possibly assent to my mode of acting against him and cannot contain the end of this action in himself. This conflict against the principle of other men is even clearer if we cite examples of attacks on their freedom and property. For then it is clear that he who transgresses the rights of men intends to make use of the person of others merely as a means, without

considering that, as rational beings, they must always be esteemed at the same time as ends, i. e., only as beings who must be able to contain in themselves the end of the very same action.[20]

Thirdly, with regard to contingent (meritorious) duty to one's self, it is not sufficient that the action not conflict with humanity in our person as an end in itself; it must also harmonize with it. Now in humanity there are capacities for greater perfection which belong to the end of nature with respect to humanity in our own person; to neglect these might perhaps be consistent with the preservation of humanity as an end in itself but not with the furtherance of that end.

Fourthly, with regard to meritorious duty to others, the natural end which all men have is their own happiness. Humanity might indeed exist if no one contributed to the happiness of others, provided he did not intentionally detract from it; but this harmony with humanity as an end in itself is only negative rather than positive if everyone does not also endeavor, so far as he can, to further the ends of others. For the ends of any person, who is an end in himself, must as far as possible also be my end, if that con-

[20] Let it not be thought that the banal "quod tibi non vis fieri, etc." could here serve as quide or principle, for it is only derived from the principle and is restricted by various limitations. It cannot be a universal law, because it contains the ground neither of duties to one's self nor of the benevolent duties to others (for many a man would gladly consent that others should not benefit him, provided only that he might be excused from showing benevolence to them). Nor does it contain the ground of obligatory duties to another, for the criminal would argue on this ground against the judge who sentences him. And so on.

ception of an end in itself is to have its full effect on me.

This principle of humanity and of every rational creature as an end in itself is the supreme limiting condition on freedom of the actions of each man. It is not borrowed from experience, first, because of its universality, since it applies to all rational beings generally, and experience does not suffice to determine anything about them; and, secondly, because in experience humanity is not thought of (subjectively) as the end of men, i. e., as an object which we ourselves really make our end. Rather it is thought of as the objective end which should constitute the supreme limiting condition of all subjective ends, whatever they may be. Thus this principle must arise from pure reason. Objectively the ground of all practical legislation lies (according to the first principle) in the rule and in the form of universality, which makes it capable of being a law (at most a natural law); subjectively, it lies in the end. But the subject of all ends is every rational being as an end in itself (by the second principle); from this there follows the third practical principle of the will as the supreme condition of its harmony with universal practical reason, viz., the idea of the will of every rational being as making universal law.[21]

By this principle all maxims are rejected which are not consistent with the universal lawgiving of will. The will is thus not only subject to the law but subject in such a way that it must be regarded also as legislative and only for this reason as being subject to the law (of which it can regard itself as the author).

In the foregoing mode of conception, in which imperatives are conceived universally either as conformity to law by actions—a conformity which is similar to a natural order—or as the prerogative of rational beings as such, the imperatives exclude from their legislative authority all admixture of any interest as an incentive. They do so because they were conceived as categorical. They were only assumed to be categorical, however, because we had to make such an assumption if we wished to explain the concept of duty. But that there were practical propositions which commanded categorically could not here be proved independently, just as little as it can be proved anywhere in this section. One thing, however, might have been done: to indicate in the imperative itself, by some determination which it contained, that in volition from duty the renunciation of all interest is the specific mark of the categorical imperative, distinguishing it from the hypothetical. And this is now being done in the third formulation of the principle, i. e., in the idea of the will of every rational being as a will giving universal law. A will which stands under laws can be bound to this law by an interest. But if we think of a will giving universal laws, we find that a supreme legislating will cannot possibly depend on any interest, for such a dependent will would itself need still another law which would restrict the interest of its self-love to the condition that [the maxims of this will] should be valid as universal law.

Thus the principle of every human will as a will giving universal laws in all its maxims [22] is very well adapted to being a categorical imperative, provided it is otherwise correct. Because of the idea of universal law-

---

[21] [Following the suggestion of Paton. Cf. *The Categorical Imperative*, p. 180.]

[22] I may be excused from citing examples to elucidate this principle, for those which have already illustrated the categorical imperative and its formula can here serve the same purpose.

giving, it is based on no interest, and, thus of all possible imperatives, it alone can be unconditional. Or, better, converting the proposition: if there is a categorical imperative (a law for the will of every rational being), it can only command that everything be done from the maxim of its will as one which could have as its object only itself considered as giving universal laws. For only in this case are the practical principle and the imperative which the will obeys unconditional, because the will can have no interest as its foundation.

If we now look back upon all previous attempts which have ever been undertaken to discover the principle of morality, it is not to be wondered at that they all had to fail. Man was seen to be bound to laws by his duty, it was not seen that he is subject only to his own, yet universal, legislation, and that he is only bound to act in accordance with his own will, which is, however, designed by nature to be a will giving universal laws. For if one thought of him as subject only to a law (whatever it may be), this necessarily implied some interest as a stimulus or compulsion to obedience because the law did not arise from his will. Rather, his will was constrained by something else according to a law to act in a certain way. By this strictly necessary consequence, however, all the labor of finding a supreme ground for duty was irrevocably lost, and one never arrived at duty but only at the necessity of action from a certain interest. This might be his own interest or that of another, but in either case the imperative always had to be conditional and could not at all serve as a moral command. This principle I will call the principle of *autonomy* of the will in contrast to all other principles which I accordingly count under *heteronomy.*

The concept of each rational being as a being that must regard itself as giving universal law through all the maxims of its will, so that it may judge itself and its actions from this standpoint, leads to a very fruitful concept, namely, that of a *realm of ends.*

By "realm" I understand the systematic union of different rational beings through common laws. Because laws determine ends with regard to their universal validity, if we abstract from the personal difference of rational beings and thus from all content of their private ends, we can think of a whole of all ends in systematic connection, a whole of rational beings as ends in themselves as well as of the particular ends which each may set for himself. This is a realm of ends, which is possible on the aforesaid principles. For all rational beings stand under the law that each of them should treat himself and all others never merely as means but in every case also as an end in himself. Thus there arises a systematic union of rational beings through common objective laws. This is a realm which may be called a realm of ends (certainly only an ideal), because what these laws have in view is just the relation of these beings to each other as ends and means.

A rational being belongs to the realm of ends as a member when he gives universal laws in it while also himself subject to these laws. He belongs to it as sovereign when he, as legislating, is subject to the will of no other. The rational being must regard himself always as legislative in a realm of ends possible through the freedom of the will, whether he belongs to it as member or as sovereign. He cannot maintain the latter position merely through the maxims of his will but only when he is a completely independent being without need and with power adequate to his will.

Morality, therefore, consists in the

relation of every action to that legislation through which alone a realm of ends is possible. This legislation, however, must be found in every rational being. It must be able to arise from his will, whose principle then is to do no action according to any maxim which would be inconsistent with its being a universal law and thus to act only so that the will through its maxims could regard itself at the same time as universally lawgiving. If now the maxims do not by their nature already necessarily conform to this objective principle of rational beings as universally lawgiving, the necessity of acting according to that principle is called practical constraint, i. e., duty. Duty pertains not to the sovereign in the realm of ends, but rather to each member, and to each in the same degree.

The practical necessity of acting according to this principle, i. e., duty, does not rest at all on feelings, impulses, and inclinations; it rests merely on the relation of rational beings to one another, in which the will of a rational being must always be regarded as legislative, for otherwise it could not be thought of as an end in itself. Reason, therefore, relates every maxim of the will as giving universal laws to every other will and also to every action toward itself; it does so not for the sake of any other practical motive or future advantage but rather from the idea of the dignity of a rational being, which obeys no law except that which he himself also gives.

In the realm of ends, everything has either a *price* or a *dignity*. Whatever has a price can be replaced by something else as its equivalent; on the other hand, whatever is above all price, and therefore admits of no equivalent, has a dignity.

That which is related to general human inclinations and needs has a market price. That which, without presupposing any need, accords with a certain taste, i. e., with pleasure in the mere purposeless play of our faculties, has an *affective price*. But that which constitutes the condition under which alone something can be an end in itself does not have mere relative worth, i. e., a price, but an intrinsic worth, i. e., dignity.

Now morality is the condition under which alone a rational being can be an end in itself, because only through it is it possible to be a legislative member in the realm of ends. Thus morality and humanity, so far as it is capable of morality, alone have dignity. Skill and diligence in work have a market value; wit, lively imagination, and humor have an affective price; but fidelity in promises and benevolence on principle (not from instinct) have intrinsic worth. Nature and likewise art contain nothing which could replace their lack, for their worth consists not in effects which flow from them, nor in advantage and utility which they procure; it consists only in intentions, i. e., maxims of the will, which are ready to reveal themselves in this manner through actions even though success does not favor them. These actions need no recommendation from any subjective disposition or taste in order that they may be looked upon with immediate favor and satisfaction, nor do they have need of any immediate propensity or feeling directed to them. They exhibit the will which performs them as the object of an immediate respect, since nothing but reason is required in order to impose them on the will. The will is not to be cajoled into them, for this, in the case of duties, would be a contradiction. This esteem lets the worth of such a turn of mind be recognized as dignity and puts it infinitely beyond any price, with which it cannot in the least be brought into competition or comparison without, as it were, violating its holiness.

And what is it that justifies the morally good disposition or virtue in making such lofty claims? It is nothing less than the participation it affords the rational being in giving universal laws. He is thus fitted to be a member in a possible realm of ends to which his own nature already destined him. For, as an end in himself, he is destined to be legislative in the realm of ends, free from all laws of nature and obedient only to those which he himself gives. Accordingly, his maxims can belong to a universal legislation to which he is at the same time also subject. A thing has no worth other than that determined for it by the law. The legislation which determines all worth must therefore have a dignity, i. e., unconditional and incomparable worth. For the esteem, which a rational being must have for it, only the word "respect" supplies a suitable expression. Autonomy is thus the basis of the dignity of both human nature and every rational nature.

The three aforementioned ways of presenting the principle of morality are fundamentally only so many formulas of the very same law, and each of them unites the others in itself. There is, nevertheless, a difference in them, but the difference is more subjectively than objectively practical, for it is intended to bring an idea of reason closer to intuition (by means of a certain analogy) and thus nearer to feeling. All maxims have:

1. A form, which consists in universality; and in this respect the formula of the moral imperative requires that the maxims be chosen as though they should hold as universal laws of nature.

2. A material, i. e., an end; in this respect the formula says that the rational being, as by its nature an end and thus as an end in itself, must serve in every maxim as the condition restricting all merely relative and arbitrary ends.

3. A complete determination of all maxims by the formula that all maxims which stem from autonomous legislation ought to harmonize with a possible realm of ends as with a realm of nature.[23]

There is a progression here like that through the categories of the unity of the form of the will (its universality), the plurality of material (the objects, i. e., the ends), and the all-comprehensiveness or totality of the system of ends. But it is better in moral evaluation to follow the rigorous method and to make the universal formula of the categorical imperative the basis: Act according to the maxim which can at the same time make itself a universal law. But if one wishes to gain a hearing for the moral law, it is very useful to bring one and the same action under the three stated principles and thus, so far as possible, to bring it nearer to intuition.

We can now end where we started, with the concept of an unconditionally good will. That will is absolutely good which cannot be bad, and thus it is a will whose maxims, when made a universal law, can never conflict with itself. Thus this principle is also its supreme law: Always act according to that maxim whose universality as a law you can at the same time will. This is the only condition under which a will can never come into conflict with itself, and such an imperative is categorical. Because the validity of the

[23] Teleology considers nature as a realm of ends; morals regards a possible realm of ends as a realm of nature. In the former the realm of ends is a theoretical idea for the explanation of what actually is. In the latter it is a practical idea for bringing about that which is not actually real but which can become real through our conduct, and which is in accordance with this idea.

will, as a universal law for possible actions, has an analogy with the universal connection of the existence of things under universal laws, which is the formal element of nature in general, the categorical imperative can also be expressed as follows: Act according to maxims which can at the same time have themselves as universal laws of nature as their object. Such, then, is the formula of an absolutely good will.

Rational nature is distinguished from others in that it proposes an end to itself. This end would be the material of every good will. Since, however, in the idea of an absolutely good will without any limiting condition of the attainment of this or that end, every end to be effected must be completely abstracted (as any particular end would make each will only relatively good), the end here is not conceived as one to be effected but as an independent end and thus merely negatively. It is that which must never be acted against, and which must consequently never be valued as merely a means but in every volition also as an end. Now this end can never be other than the subject of all possible ends themselves, because this is at the same time the subject of a possible will which is absolutely good; for the latter cannot be made secondary to any other object without contradiction. The principle: Act with reference to every rational being (whether yourself or another) so that it is an end in itself in your maxim, is thus basically identical with the principle: Act by a maxim which involves its own universal validity for every rational being.

That in the use of means to every end I should restrict my maxim to the condition of its universal validity as a law for every subject is tantamount to saying that the subject of ends, i. e., the rational being itself, must be made the basis of all maxims of actions and

thus be treated never as a mere means but as the supreme limiting condition in the use of all means, i. e., as an end at the same time.

It follows incontestably that every rational being must be able to regard himself as an end in himself with reference to all laws to which he may be subject, whatever they may be, and thus as giving universal laws. For it is just the fitness of his maxims to a universal legislation that indicates that he is an end in himself. It also follows that his dignity (his prerogative) over all merely natural beings entails that he must take his maxims from the point of view which regards himself, and hence also every other rational being, as legislative. (The rational beings are, on this account, called persons.) In this way, a world of rational beings (mundus intelligibilis) is possible as a realm of ends, because of the legislation belonging to all persons as members. Consequently, every rational being must act as if he, by his maxims, were at all times a legislative member in the universal realm of ends. The formal principle of these maxims is: So act as if your maxims should serve at the same time as the universal law (of all rational beings). A realm of ends is thus possible only by analogy with a realm of nature. The former, however, is possible only by maxims, i. e., self-imposed rules, while the latter is possible by laws of efficient causes of things externally necessitated. Regardless of this difference, by analogy we call the natural whole a realm of nature so far as it is related to rational beings as its end; we do so even though the natural whole is looked at as a machine. Such a realm of ends would actually be realized through maxims whose rule is prescribed to all rational beings by the categorical imperative, if they were universally obeyed. But a rational being, though he scrupulously follow this maxim, cannot for that reason expect every other rational being to be true to it; nor can he expect the realm of nature and its orderly design to harmonize with him as a fitting member of a realm of ends which is possible through himself. That is, he cannot count on its favoring his expectation of happiness. Still the law: Act according to the maxims of a universally legislative member of a merely potential realm of ends, remains in full force, because it commands categorically. And just in this lies the paradox that merely the dignity of humanity as rational nature without any end or advantage to be gained by it, and thus respect for a mere idea, should serve as the inflexible precept of the will. There is the further paradox that the sublimity and worthiness of every rational subject to be a legislative member in the realm of ends consists precisely in independence of maxims from all such incentives. Otherwise he would have to be viewed as subject only to the natural law of his needs.[24] Although the realm of nature as well as that of ends would be thought of as united under a sovereign, so that the latter would no longer remain a mere idea but would receive true reality, the realm of ends would undoubtedly gain a strong urge in its favor, but its intrinsic worth would not be augmented. Regardless of this, even the one and only absolute legislator would still have to be conceived as judging the worth of rational beings only by the disinterested conduct which they prescribe to themselves merely from the idea [of dignity]. The essence of things is not changed by their external relations, and without reference to these relations a man must be judged only by what constitutes his absolute worth; and this is true whoever his judge is, even if it be the Supreme Being. Morality is thus the re-

24 [Reading plural with Vorländer.]

lation of actions to the autonomy of the will, i. e., to possible universal lawgiving by maxims of the will. The action which can be compatible with the autonomy of the will is permitted; that which does not agree with it is prohibited. The will whose maxims necessarily are in harmony with the laws of autonomy is a holy will or an absolutely good will. The dependence of a will not absolutely good on the principle of autonomy (moral constraint) is *obligation*. Hence obligation cannot be applied to a holy will. The objective necessity of an action from obligation is called *duty*.

From what has just been said, it can easily be explained how it happens that, although in the concept of duty we think of subjection to law, we do nevertheless ascribe a certain sublimity and dignity to the person who fulfils all his duties. For though there is no sublimity in him in so far as he is subject to the moral law, yet he is sublime in so far as he is legislative with reference to the law and subject to it only for this reason. We have also shown above how neither fear of nor inclination to the law is the incentive which can give a moral worth to action; only respect for it can do so. Our own will, so far as it would act only under the condition of a universal legislation rendered possible by its maxims — this will ideally possible for us is the proper object of respect, and the dignity of humanity consists just in its capacity of giving universal laws, although with the condition that it is itself subject to this same legislation.

THE AUTONOMY OF THE WILL AS THE SUPREME PRINCIPLE OF MORALITY

Autonomy of the will is that property of it by which it is a law to itself independently of any property of objects of volition. Hence the principle of autonomy is: Never choose except in such a way that the maxims of the choice are comprehended in the same volition as a universal law. That this practical rule is an imperative, that is, that the will of every rational being is necessarily bound to it as a condition, cannot be proved by a mere analysis of the concepts occurring in it, because it is a synthetical proposition. To prove it, we would have to go beyond the knowledge of objects to a critical examination of the subject, i.e., of the pure practical reason, for this synthetical proposition which commands apodictically must be susceptible of being known completely a priori. This matter, however, does not belong in the present section. But that the principle of autonomy, which is now in question, is the sole principle of morals can be readily shown by mere analysis of concepts of morality; for by this analysis we find that its principle must be a categorical imperative and that the imperative commands neither more nor less than this very autonomy.

THE HETERONOMY OF THE WILL AS THE SOURCE OF ALL SPURIOUS PRINCIPLES OF MORALITY

If the will seeks the law which is to determine it anywhere else than in the fitness of its maxims to its own universal legislation, and if it thus goes outside itself and seeks this law in the property of any of its objects, heteronomy always results. For then the will does not give itself the law, but the object through its relation to the will gives the law to it. This relation, whether it rests on inclination or on conceptions of reason, only admits of hypothetical imperatives: I should do

something for the reason that I will something else. The moral, and therewith categorical, imperative, on the other hand, says I should act this or that way even though I will nothing else. For example, the former says I should not lie if I wish to keep my reputation. The latter says I should not lie even though it would not cause me the least injury. The latter, therefore, must disregard every object to such an extent that it has absolutely no influence on the will, so that practical reason (will) not merely may minister to an interest not its own but rather may show its commanding authority as the supreme legislation. Thus, for instance, I should seek to further the happiness of others, not as though its realization was any concern of mine (whether because of direct inclination or of some satisfaction related to it indirectly through reason); I should do so merely because the maxim which excludes it from my duty cannot be comprehended as a universal law in one and the same volition.

CLASSIFICATION OF ALL POSSIBLE PRINCIPLES OF MORALITY FOLLOWING FROM THE ASSUMED PRINCIPLE OF HETERONOMY

Here as everywhere in the pure use of reason so long as a critical examination of it is lacking, human reason at first tries all possible wrong ways before it succeeds in finding the one true way.

All principles which can be taken in this point of view are either empirical or rational. The former, drawn from the principle of happiness, are based on physical or moral feeling; the latter, drawn from the principle of perfection, are based either on the rational concept of perfection as a possible result or on the concept of an independent perfection (the will of God) as the determining cause of our will.

Empirical principles are not at all suited to serve as the basis of moral laws. For if the basis of the universality by which they should be valid for all rational beings without distinction (the unconditional practical necessity which is thereby imposed upon them) is derived from a particular tendency of human nature or the particular circumstance in which it is found, that universality is lost. But the principle of one's own happiness is the most objectionable of all. This is not merely because it is false and because experience contradicts the supposition that well-being is always proportional to good conduct, nor yet because this principle contributes nothing to the establishment of morality, inasmuch as it is a very different thing to make a man happy from making him good, and to make him prudent and farsighted for his own advantage is far from making him virtuous. Rather, it is because this principle supports morality with incentives which undermine it and destroy all its sublimity, for it puts the motives to virtue and those to vice in the same class, teaching us only to make a better calculation while obliterating the specific difference between them. On the other hand, there is the alleged special sense,[25] the moral feeling. The appeal to it is

[25] I count the principle of moral feeling under that of happiness, because every empirical interest promises to contribute to our well-being by the agreeableness that a thing affords, either directly and without a view to future advantage or with a view to it. We must likewise, with Hutcheson, count the principle of sympathy with the happiness of others under the moral sense which he assumed.

superficial, since those who cannot think expect help from feeling, even with respect to that which concerns universal laws; they do so even though feelings naturally differ so infinitely in degree that they are incapable of furnishing a uniform standard of the good and bad, and also in spite of the fact that one cannot validly judge for others by means of his own feeling. Nevertheless, the moral feeling is nearer to morality and its dignity, inasmuch as it pays virtue the honor of ascribing the satisfaction and esteem for her directly to morality, and does not, as it were, say to her face that it is not her beauty but only our advantage which attaches us to her.

Among the rational principles of morality, there is the ontological concept of perfection. It is empty, indefinite, and consequently useless for finding in the immeasurable field of possible reality the greatest possible sum which is suitable to us; and, in specifically distinguishing the reality which is here in question from all other reality, it inevitably tends to move in a circle and cannot avoid tacitly presupposing the morality which it ought to explain. Nevertheless, it is better than the theological concept, which derives morality from a most perfect divine will. It is better not merely because we cannot intuit its perfection, having rather to derive it only from our own concepts of which morality itself is foremost, but also because if we do not so derive it (and to do so would involve a most flagrant circle in explanation), the only remaining concept of the divine will is made up of the attributes of desire for glory and dominion combined with the awful conceptions of might and vengeance, and any system of ethics based on them would be directly opposed to morality.

But if I had to choose between the concept of the moral sense and that of perfection in general (neither of which at any rate weakens morality, although they are not capable of serving as its foundations), I would decide for the latter, because it preserves the indefinite idea (of a will good in itself) free from corruption until it can be more narrowly defined. It at least withdraws the decision of the question from sensibility and brings it to the court of pure reason, although it does not even here decide the question.

For the rest, I think that I may be excused from a lengthy refutation of all these doctrines. It is so easy, and presumably so well understood even by those whose office requires them to decide for one of these theories (since the hearers would not tolerate suspension of judgment), that such a refutation would be only superfluous work. What interests us more, however, is to know that all these principles set up nothing other than the heteronomy of the will as the first ground of morality and thus necessarily miss their aim.

In every case in which an object of the will must be assumed as prescribing the rule which is to determine the will, the rule is nothing else but heteronomy. The imperative in this case is conditional, stating that if or because one wills this object, one should act thus or so. Therefore the imperative can never command morally, that is, categorically. The object may determine the will by means of inclination, as in the principle of one's own happiness, or by means of reason directed to objects of our possible volition in general, as in the principle of perfection; but the will in these cases never determines itself directly by the conception of the action itself but only by the incentive which the foreseen result of the action incites in the will — that is, "I ought to do something because I will something else." And here still another law

must be assumed in my person as the basis of this imperative; it would be a law by which I would necessarily will that other thing; but this law would again require an imperative to restrict this maxim. Since the conception of an object commensurate to our power incites in the will an impulse according to the natural characteristic of our person, this impulse belongs to the nature of the subject (either to the sensibility, i.e., inclination and taste, or to understanding and reason which faculties, according to the particular constitution of their nature, take pleasure in exercising themselves on an object). It follows that it would be really nature that would give the law. As a law of nature, known and proved by experience, it would be contingent and therefore unfit to be an apodictical practical rule such as the moral rule must be. Such a law always represents heteronomy of the will; the will does not give itself the law, but an external impulse gives it to the will according to the nature of the subject which is adapted to receive it.

The absolutely good will, the principle of which must be a categorical imperative, is thus undetermined with reference to any objects. It contains only the form of volition in general, and this form is autonomy. This is, the capability of the maxims of every good will to make themselves universal laws is itself the sole law which the will of every rational being imposes on itself, and it does not need to support this on any incentive or interest.

How such a synthetical practical a priori proposition is possible and why it is necessary is a problem whose solution does not lie within the boundaries of the metaphysics of morals. Moreover, we have not here affirmed its truth, and even less professed to command a proof of it. We showed only through the development of the universally received concept of morals that autonomy of the will is unavoidably connected with it, or rather that it is its foundation. Whoever, therefore, holds morality to be something real and not a chimerical idea without truth must also concede its principle which has been adduced here. Consequently, this section was merely analytical, like the first. To prove that morality is not a mere phantom of the mind — and if the categorical imperative, and with it the autonomy of the will, is true and absolutely necessary as an a priori principle, it follows that it is no phantom — requires that a synthetical use of pure practical reason is possible. But we must not venture on this proof without first making a critical examination of this faculty of reason. In the last section we shall give the principal features of such an examination that will be sufficient for our purpose.

THIRD SECTION

Transition from the Metaphysics of Morals to the Critical Examination of Pure Practical Reason

THE CONCEPT OF FREEDOM IS THE KEY TO THE EXPLANATION OF THE AUTONOMY OF THE WILL

As will is a kind of causality of living beings so far as they are rational, freedom would be that property of this causality by which it can be effective independently of foreign causes determining it, just as natural necessity is the property of the causality of all irrational beings by which they are determined to activity by the influence of foreign causes.

The preceding definition of freedom is negative and therefore affords no insight into its essence. But a positive concept of freedom flows from it which is so much the richer and more fruitful. Since the concept of a causality entails that of laws according to which something, i.e., the effect, must be established through something else which we call cause, it follows that freedom is by no means lawless even though it is not a property of the will according to laws of nature. Rather, it must be a causality according to immutable laws, but of a peculiar kind. Otherwise a free will would be an absurdity. Natural necessity is, as we have seen, a heteronomy of efficient causes, for every effect is possible only according to the law that something else determines the efficient cause to its causality. What else, then, can the freedom of the will be but autonomy, i. e., the property of the will to be a law to itself? The proposition that the will is a law to itself in all its actions, however, only expresses the principle that we should act according to no other maxim than that which can also have itself as a universal law for its object. And this is just the formula of the categorical imperative and the principle of morality. Therefore a free will and a will under moral laws are identical.

Thus if freedom of the will is presupposed, morality together with its principle follows from it by the mere analysis of its concept. But the principle is nevertheless a synthetical proposition; an absolutely good will is one whose maxim can always include itself as a universal law. It is synthetical because by analysis of the concept of an absolutely good will that property of the maxim cannot be found. Such synthetical propositions, however, are possible only by the fact that both cognitions are connected through their union with a third in which both of them are to be found. The positive concept of freedom furnishes this third cognition, which cannot be, as in the case of physical causes, the nature of the sensuous world, in the concept of which we find conjoined the concepts of something as cause in relation to something else as effect. We cannot yet show directly what this third cognition is to which freedom directs us and of which we have an a priori idea, nor can we explain the deduction of the concept of freedom from pure practical reason and therewith the possibility of a categorical imperative. For this some further preparation is needed.

FREEDOM MUST BE PRESUPPOSED AS THE PROPERTY OF THE WILL OF ALL RATIONAL BEINGS

It is not enough to ascribe freedom to our will, on any grounds whatever, if we do not also have sufficient grounds for attributing it to all rational beings. For since morality serves as a law for us only as rational beings, morality must hold valid for all rational beings, and since it must be derived exclusively from the property of freedom, freedom as the property of the will of all rational beings must be demonstrated. And it does not suffice to prove it from certain alleged experiences of human nature (which is indeed impossible, as it can be proved only a priori), but we must prove it as belonging generally to the activity of rational beings endowed with a will. Now I say that every being which cannot act otherwise than under the idea of freedom is thereby really free in a practical respect. That is to say, all laws which are inseparably bound

with freedom hold for it just as if its will were proved free in itself by theoretical philosophy.[26] Now I affirm that we must necessarily grant that every rational being who has a will also has the idea of freedom and that it acts only under this idea. For in such a being we think of a reason which is practical, i.e., a reason which has causality with respect to its objects. Now we cannot conceive of a reason which consciously responds to a bidding from the outside with respect to its judgments, for then the subject would attribute the determination of its power of judgment not to reason but to an impulse. Reason must regard itself as the author of its principles, independently of foreign influences; consequently, as practical reason or as the will of a rational being, it must regard itself as free. That is to say, the will of a rational being can be a will of its own only under the idea of freedom, and therefore in a practical point of view such a will must be ascribed to all rational beings.

OF THE INTEREST ATTACHING TO THE IDEAS OF MORALITY

We have finally reduced the definite concept of morality to the idea of freedom, but we could not prove freedom to be real in ourselves and in

[26] I follow this method of assuming that freedom only ideally assumed by rational beings as the basis of their actions is sufficient to our purpose, because I wish to avoid having to prove freedom also in its theoretical aspect. For if the latter is left unproved, the laws which would obligate a being who was really free would hold for a being who cannot act except under the idea of his own freedom. Thus we can escape here from the onus which presses on the theory.

human nature. We only saw that we must presuppose it if we would think of a being as rational and conscious of his causality with respect to actions, that is, as endowed with a will; and so we find that on the very same grounds we must ascribe to each being endowed with reason and will the property of determining himself to action under the idea of freedom.

From presupposing this idea [of freedom] there followed also consciousness of a law to act so that the subjective principles of actions, i. e., maxims, in every instance must be so chosen that they can hold also as objective, i. e., universal, principles, and thus can serve as principles for the universal laws we give. But why should I subject myself as a rational being, and thereby all other beings endowed with reason, to this law? I will admit that no interest impels me to do so, for that would then give no categorical imperative. But I must nevertheless take an interest in it and see how it comes about, for this "ought" is properly a "would" that is valid for every rational being provided reason is practical for him without hindrance [i. e., exclusively determined his action]. For beings who like ourselves are affected by the senses as incentives different from reason and who do not always do that which reason for itself alone would have done, that necessity of action is expressed only as an "ought." The subjective necessity is thus distinguished from the objective.

It therefore seems that the moral law, i. e., the principle of the autonomy of the will, is, properly speaking, only presupposed in the idea of freedom, as if we could not prove its reality and objective necessity by itself. Even if that were so, we would have still gained something because we would at least have defined the genuine principle more accurately

than had been done before. But with regard to its validity and to the practical necessity of subjection to it, we would not have advanced a single step, for we could give no satisfactory answer to anyone who asked us why the universality of our maxim as of a law had to be the restricting condition of our action. We could not tell on what is based the worth we ascribe to actions of this kind — a worth so great that there can be no higher interest, nor could we tell how it happens that man believes it is only through this that he feels his own personal worth, in contrast to which the worth of a pleasant or unpleasant condition is to be regarded as nothing.

We do find sometimes that we can take an interest in a personal quality which involves no [personal] interest in any [external] condition, provided only that [possession of] this quality makes us capable of participating in the [desired] condition in case reason were to effect the allotment of it. That is, mere worthiness to be happy even without the motive of participating in it can interest of itself. But this judgment is in fact only the effect of the already assumed importance of moral laws (if by the idea of freedom we detach ourselves from every empirical interest). But that we ought to detach ourselves, i. e., regard ourselves as free in acting and yet as subject to certain laws, in order to find a worth merely in our person which would compensate for the loss of everything which makes our situation desirable — how this is possible and hence on what grounds the moral law obligates us we still cannot see in this way.

We must openly confess that there is a kind of circle here from which it seems that there is no escape. We assume that we are free in the order of efficient causes so that we can conceive of ourselves as subject to moral laws in the order of ends. And then we think of ourselves as subject to these laws because we have ascribed freedom of the will to ourselves. This is circular because freedom and self-legislation of the will are both autonomy and thus are reciprocal concepts, and for that reason one of them cannot be used to explain the other and to furnish a ground for it. At most they can be used for the logical purpose of bringing apparently different conceptions of the same object under a single concept (as we reduce different fractions of the same value to the lowest common terms).

One recourse, however, remains open to us, namely, to inquire whether we do not assume a different standpoint when we think of ourselves as causes a priori efficient through freedom from that which we occupy when we conceive of ourselves in the light of our actions as effects which we see before our eyes.

The following remark requires no subtle reflection, and we may suppose that even the commonest understanding can make it, though it does so, after its fashion, by an obscure discernment of judgment which it calls feeling: all conceptions, like those of the senses, which come to us without our choice enable us to know the objects only as they affect us, while what they are in themselves remains unknown to us; therefore, as regards this kind of conception, even with the closest attention and clearness which understanding may ever bring to them we can attain only to knowledge of appearances and never to knowledge of things in themselves. As soon as this distinction is once made (perhaps merely because of a noticed difference between conceptions which are given to us from somewhere else and to which we are passive and those which we produce only from ourselves and in which we show our own activity), it follows of itself that we must as-

sume behind the appearances something else which is not appearance, namely, things-in-themselves; we do so although we must admit that we cannot approach them more closely and can never know what they are in themselves, since they can never be known by us except as they affect us. This must furnish a distinction, though a crude one, between a world of sense and a world of understanding. The former, by differences in the sensuous faculties, can be very different among various observers, while the latter, which is its foundation, remains always the same. A man may not presume to know even himself as he really is by knowing himself through inner sensation. For since he does not, as it were, produce himself or derive his concept of himself a priori but only empirically, it is natural that he obtains his knowledge of himself through inner sense and consequently only through the appearance of his nature and the way in which his consciousness is affected. But beyond the characteristic of his own subject which is compounded of these mere appearances, he necessarily assumes something else as its basis, namely, his ego as it is in itself. Thus in respect to mere perception and receptivity to sensations he must count himself as belonging to the world of sense; but in respect to that which may be pure activity in himself (i. e., in respect to that which reaches consciousness directly and not by affecting the senses) he must reckon himself as belonging to the intellectual world. But he has no further knowledge of that world.

To such a conclusion the thinking man must come with respect to all things which may present themselves to him. Presumably it is to be met with in the commonest understanding which, as is well known, is very much inclined to expect behind the objects of the senses something else invisible and acting of itself. But such an understanding soon spoils it by trying to make the invisible again sensuous, i. e., to make it an object of intuition. Thus common understanding becomes not in the least wiser.

Now man really finds in himself a faculty by which he distinguishes himself from all other things, even from himself so far as he is affected by objects. This faculty is reason. As a pure spontaneous activity it is even elevated above understanding. For though the latter is also a spontaneous activity and does not, like sense, merely contain conceptions which arise only when one is affected by things, being passive, it nevertheless cannot produce by its activity any other concepts than those which serve to bring the sensuous conceptions under rules and thereby to unite them in one consciousness. Without this use of sensibility it would not think at all, while, on the other hand, reason shows such a pure spontaneity in the case of ideas that it [27] far transcends everything that sensibility can give to consciousness [27] and shows its chief occupation in distinguishing the world of sense from the world of understanding, thereby prescribing limits to the understanding itself.

For this reason a rational being must regard himself as intelligence (and not from the side of his lower powers), as belonging to the world of understanding and not to that of the senses. Thus he has two standpoints from which he can consider himself and recognize the laws of the

[27] [Kant wrote *er . . . . ihm,* which gives no tenable meaning. Adickes suggested *sie . . . . ihr* = reason . . . . *to reason.* But as sensibility does not give material to reason, at least directly, Vorländer and the Cassirer ed. read *sie . . . . ihm,* and they are followed here.]

employment of his powers and consequently of all his actions: first, as belonging to the world of sense, under laws of nature (heteronomy), and, second, as belonging to the intelligible world under laws which, independent of nature, are not empirical but founded only on reason.

As a rational being and thus as belonging to the intelligible world, man cannot think of the causality of his own will except under the idea of freedom, for independence from the determining causes of the world of sense (an independence which reason must always ascribe to itself) is freedom. The concept of autonomy is inseparably connected with the idea of freedom, and with the latter there is inseparably bound the universal principle of morality, which ideally is the ground of all actions of rational beings, just as natural law is the ground of all appearances.

Now we have removed the suspicion which we raised that there might be a hidden circle in our reasoning from freedom to autonomy and from the latter to the moral law. This suspicion was that we laid down the idea of freedom for the sake of the moral law in order later to derive freedom from it, and that we were thus unable to give any ground for the law, presenting it only as a *petitio principii* that well-disposed minds would gladly allow us but which we could never advance as a demonstrable proposition. But we now see that, if we think of ourselves as free, we transport ourselves into the intelligible world as members of it and know the autonomy of the will together with its consequence, morality; while, if we think of ourselves as obligated, we consider ourselves as belonging both to the world of sense and at the same time to the intelligible world.

HOW IS A CATEGORICAL IMPERATIVE
POSSIBLE?

The rational being counts himself, *qua* intelligence, as belonging to the intelligible world, and only as an efficient cause belonging to it does he call his causality a will. On the other side, however, he is conscious of himself as a part of the world of sense in which his actions are found as mere appearances of that causality. But we do not discern how they are possible on the basis of that causality which we do not know; rather, those actions must be regarded as determined by other appearances, namely, desires and inclinations, belonging to the world of sense. As a mere member of the intelligible world, all my actions would completely accord with the principle of the autonomy of the pure will, and as a part only of the world of sense would they have to be assumed to conform wholly to the natural law of desires and inclinations and thus to the heteronomy of nature. (The former actions would rest on the supreme principle of morality, and the latter on that of happiness.) But since the intelligible world contains the ground of the world of sense and hence of its laws, the intelligible world is (and must be conceived as) directly legislative for my will, which belongs wholly to the intelligible world. Therefore I recognize myself *qua* intelligence as subject to the law of the world of understanding and to the autonomy of the will. That is, I recognize myself as subject to the law of reason which contains in the idea of freedom the law of the intelligible world, while at the same time I must acknowledge that I am a being which belongs to the world of sense. Therefore I must regard the laws of the intelligible world as imperatives for me, and actions in accord with this principle as duties.

Thus categorical imperatives are possible because the idea of freedom makes me a member of an intelligible world. Consequently, if I were a member of only that world, all my actions *would* always be in accordance with the autonomy of the will. But since I intuit myself at the same time as a member of the world of sense, my actions *ought* to conform to it, and this categorical ought presents a synthetic a priori proposition, since besides my will affected by my sensuous desires there is added the idea of the will as pure, practical of itself, and belonging to the intelligible world, which according to reason contains the supreme condition of the former [sensuously affected] will. It is similar to the manner in which concepts of the understanding, which of themselves mean nothing but lawful form in general, are added to the intuitions of the sensuous world, thus rendering possible a priori synthetic propositions, on which all knowledge of a system of nature rests.

The practical use of common human reason confirms the correctness of this deduction. When we present examples of honesty of purpose, of steadfastness in following good maxims, and of sympathy and general benevolence even with great sacrifice of advantages and comfort, there is no man, not even the most malicious villain (provided he is otherwise accustomed to using his reason), who does not wish that he also might have these qualities. But because of his inclinations and impulses he cannot bring this about, yet at the same time he wishes to be free from such inclinations which are burdensome even to himself. He thus proves that, with a will free from all impulses of sensibility, he in thought transfers himself into an order of things altogether different from that of his desires in the field of sensibility. He cannot expect to obtain by that wish any gratification of desires nor any condition which would satisfy his real or even imagined inclinations, for the idea itself, which elicits this wish from him, would lose its pre-eminence if he had any such expectation. He can expect only a greater inner worth of his person. He imagines himself to be this better person when he transfers himself to the standpoint of a member of the intelligible world to which he is involuntarily impelled by the idea of freedom, i. e., independence from the determining causes of the world of sense; and from this standpoint he is conscious of a good will, which on his own confession constitutes the law for his bad will as a member of the world of sense. He acknowledges the authority of this law even while transgressing it. The moral ought is therefore his own volition as a member of the intelligible world, and it is conceived by him as an ought only in so far as he regards himself at the same time as a member of the world of sense.

ON THE EXTREME LIMIT OF ALL
PRACTICAL PHILOSOPHY

In respect to their will, all men think of themselves as free. Hence arise all judgments of actions as being such as ought to have been done, although they were not done. But this freedom is not an empirical concept and cannot be such, for it still remains even though experience shows the contrary of the demands which are necessarily conceived as consequences of the supposition of freedom. On the other hand, it is equally necessary that everything which happens should be inexorably determined by natural laws,

and this natural necessity is likewise no empirical concept, because it implies the concept of necessity and thus of a priori knowledge. But this concept of a system of nature is confirmed by experience, and it is inevitably presupposed if experience, which is knowledge of the objects of the senses interconnected by universal laws, is to be possible. Therefore freedom is only an idea of reason whose objective reality in itself is doubtful, while nature is a concept of the understanding which shows and necessarily must show its reality by examples of experience.

There now arises a dialectic of reason, since the freedom ascribed to the will seems to stand in contradiction to natural necessity. At this parting of the ways reason in its speculative purpose finds the way of natural necessity more well-beaten and usable than that of freedom; but in its practical purpose the footpath of freedom is the only one on which it is possible to make use of reason in our conduct. Hence it is as impossible for the subtlest philosophy as for the commonest reasoning to argue freedom away. Philosophy must therefore assume that no true contradiction will be found between freedom and natural necessity in the same human actions, for it cannot give up the concept of nature any more than that of freedom.

Hence even if we should never be able to conceive how freedom is possible, at least this apparent contradiction must be convincingly eradicated. For if even the thought of freedom contradicts itself or nature, which is equally necessary, it would have to be surrendered in competition with natural necessity.

But it would be impossible to escape this contradiction if the subject, which seems to himself free, thought of himself in the same sense or in the same relationship when he calls himself free as when he assumes that in the same action he is subject to natural law. Therefore it is an inescapable task of speculative philosophy to show at least that its illusion about the contradiction rests in the fact that we [do not][28] think of man in a different sense and relationship when we call him free from that in which we consider him as a part of nature and subject to its laws. It must show not only that they can very well coexist but also that they must be thought of as necessarily united in one and the same subject; for otherwise no ground could be given why we should burden reason with an idea which, though it may without contradiction be united with another that is sufficiently established, nevertheless involves us in a perplexity which sorely embarrasses reason in its speculative use. This duty is imposed only on speculative philosophy, so that it may clear the way for practical philosophy. Thus the philosopher has no choice as to whether he will remove the apparent contradiction or leave it untouched, for in the latter case the theory of it would be *bonum vacans,* into the possession of which the fatalist can rightly enter and drive all morality from its alleged property as occupying it without title.

Yet we cannot say here that we have reached the beginnings of practical philosophy. For the settlement of the controversy does not belong to practical philosophy, as the latter only demands from speculative reason that it put an end to the discord in which it entangles itself in theoretical questions, so that practical reason may have rest and security from outer attacks which could dispute it the ground on which it desires to erect its edifice.

The title to freedom of the will claimed by common reason is based

[28] [Following the suggestion of R. F. A. Hoernlé, *Mind,* XLV (new ser., 1936), 127-28.]

on the consciousness and the conceded presupposition of the independence of reason from merely subjectively determining causes which together constitute what belongs only to sensation, being comprehended under the general name of sensibility. Man, who in this way regards himself as intelligence, puts himself in a different order of things and in a relationship to determining grounds of an altogether different kind when he thinks of himself as intelligence with a will and thus as endowed with causality, compared with that other order of things and that other set of determining grounds which become relevant when he perceives himself as a phenomenon in the world of sense (as he really is also) and submits his causality to external determination according to natural laws. Now he soon realizes that both can subsist together — indeed, that they must. For there is not the least contradiction between a thing in appearance (as belonging to the world of sense) being subject to certain laws from which it is independent as a thing or a being in itself. That it must think of itself in this twofold manner rests, with regard to the first, on the consciousness of itself as an object affected through the senses, and, with regard to what is required by the second, on the consciousness of itself as intelligence, i. e., as independent from sensuous impressions in the use of reason and thus as belonging to the intelligible world.

This is why man claims to possess a will which does not let him become accountable for what belongs merely to his desires and inclinations, but thinks of actions, which can be done only by disregarding all desires and sensuous attractions, as possible and indeed necessary for him. The causality of these actions lies in him as an intelligence and in effects and actions in accordance with principles of an intelligible world, of which he knows only that reason alone and indeed pure reason independent of sensibility gives the law in it. Moreover, since it is only as intelligence that he is his proper self (being as man only appearance of himself), he knows that those laws apply to him directly and categorically, so that that to which inclinations and impulses and hence the entire nature of the world of sense incite him cannot in the least impair the laws of his volition as an intelligence. He does not even hold himself responsible for these inclinations and impulses or attribute them to his proper self, i. e., his will, though he does ascribe to his will the indulgence which he may grant to them when he permits them an influence on his maxims to the detriment of the rational laws of his will.

When practical reason thinks itself into an intelligible world, it does in no way transcend its limits. It would do so, however, if it tried to intuit or feel itself into it. The intelligible world is only a negative thought with respect to the world of sense, which does not give reason any laws for determining the will. It is positive only in the single point that freedom as negative determination is at the same time connected with a positive faculty and even a causality of reason. This causality we call a will to act so that the principle of actions will accord with the essential characteristic of a rational cause, i. e., with the condition of universal validity of a maxim as a law. But if it were to borrow an object of the will, i. e., a motive, from the intelligible world, it would overstep its boundaries and pretend to be acquainted with something of which it knows nothing. The concept of a world of understanding is therefore only a standpoint which reason sees itself forced to take outside appearances, in order to think of itself as

practical. If the influences of sensibility were determining for man, this would not be possible; but it is necessary unless he is to be denied the consciousness of himself as an intelligence, and thus as a rational and rationally active cause, i. e., a cause acting in freedom. This thought certainly implies the idea of an order and legislation different from that of natural mechanism which applies to the world of sense; and it makes necessary the concept of an intelligible world, the whole of rational beings as things-in-themselves. But it does not give us the least occasion to think of it other than according to its formal condition only, i.e., the universality of the maxim of the will as law and thus the autonomy of the will, which alone is consistent with freedom. All laws, on the other hand, which are directed to an object make for heteronomy, which only belongs to natural laws and which can apply only to the world of sense.

But reason would overstep all its bounds if it undertook to explain how pure reason can be practical, which is the same problem as explaining how freedom is possible.

For we can explain nothing but what we can reduce to laws whose object can be given in some possible experience. But freedom is a mere idea, the objective reality of which can in no way be shown according to natural laws or in any possible experience. Since no example in accordance with any analogy can support it, it can never be comprehended or even imagined. It holds only as the necessary presupposition of reason in a being that believes itself conscious of a will, i. e., of a faculty different from the mere faculty of desire, or a faculty of determining itself to act as intelligence and thus according to laws of reason independently of natural instincts. But where determination according to natural laws comes to an end, there too all explanation ceases, and nothing remains but defense, i. e., refutation of the objections of those who pretend to have seen deeper into the essence of things and therefore boldly declare freedom to be impossible. We can only show them that the supposed contradiction they have discovered lies nowhere else than in their necessarily regarding man as appearance in order to make natural law valid with respect to human actions. And now when we require them to think of him *qua* intelligence as a thing-in-itself, they still persist in considering him as appearance. Obviously, then, the separation of his causality (his will) from all natural laws of the world of sense in one and the same subject is a contradiction, but this disappears when they reconsider and confess, as is reasonable, that behind the appearances things-in-themselves must stand as their hidden ground and that we cannot expect the laws of the activity of these grounds to be the same as those under which their appearances stand.

The subjective impossibility of explaining the freedom of the will is the same as the impossibility of discovering and explaining an interest [29] which man can take in moral laws. Nevertheless, he does actually take an interest in them, and the foundation in us of this interest we call the moral feeling. This moral feeling has been erroneously construed by some as the standard for our moral judgment, whereas it must rather be regarded as the subjective effect which the law has upon the will to which reason alone gives objective grounds.

In order to will that which reason alone prescribes to the sensuously affected rational being as that which he ought to will, certainly there is required a power of reason to instil a feeling of pleasure or satisfaction in the fulfilment of duty, and hence there must be a causality of reason to determine the sensibility in accordance with its own principles. But it is wholly impossible to discern, i. e., to make a priori conceivable, how a mere thought containing nothing sensuous is to produce a sensation of pleasure or displeasure. For that is a particular kind of causality of which, as of all causality, we cannot determine anything a priori but must consult experience only. But since experience can exemplify the relation of cause to effect only as subsisting between two objects of experience, while here pure reason by mere ideas (which furnish no object for experience) is to be the cause of an effect which does lie in experience, an explanation of how and why the universality of the maxim as law (and hence morality) interests us is completely impossible for us men. Only this much is certain: that it is valid for us not because it interests us (for that is heteronomy and dependence of practical reason on sensibility,

29 Interest is that by which reason becomes practical, i.e., a cause determining the will. We therefore say only of a rational being that he takes an interest in something; irrational creatures feel only sensuous impulses. A direct interest in the action is taken by reason only if the universal validity of its maxim is a sufficient determining ground of the will. Only such an interest is pure. But if reason can determine the will only by means of another object of desire or

under the presupposition of a particular feeling of the subject, reason takes merely an indirect interest in the action, and since reason for itself alone without experience can discover neither objects of the will nor a particular feeling which lies at its root, that indirect interest would be only empirical and not a pure interest of reason. The logical interest of reason in advancing its insights is never direct but rather presupposes purposes for which they are to be used.

i. e., on a basic feeling, and thus it could never be morally legislative) but that it interests us because it is valid for us as men, inasmuch as it has arisen from our will as intelligence and hence from our proper self; but what belongs to mere appearance is necessarily subordinated by reason to the nature of the thing-in-itself.

Thus the question, "How is a categorical imperative possible?" can be answered to this extent: We can cite the only presupposition under which it is alone possible. This is the idea of freedom, and we can discern the necessity of this presupposition which is sufficient to the practical use of reason, i. e., to the conviction of the validity of this imperative and hence also of the moral law. But how this presupposition itself is possible can never be discerned by any human reason. However, on the presupposition of freedom of the will of an intelligence, its autonomy as the formal condition under which alone it can be determined is a necessary consequence. To presuppose the freedom of the will is not only quite possible, as speculative philosophy itself can prove, for it does not involve itself in a contradiction with the principle of natural necessity in the interconnection of appearances in the world of sense. But, it is also unconditionally necessary that a rational being conscious of his causality through reason and thus conscious of a will different from desires should practically presuppose it, i. e., presuppose it in the idea as the fundamental condition of all his voluntary actions. Yet how pure reason, without any other incentives, wherever they may be derived, can by itself be practical, i. e., how the mere principle of the universal validity of all its maxims as laws (which would certainly be the form of a pure practical reason), without any material (object) of the will in

which we might in advance take some interest, can itself furnish an incentive and produce an interest which would be called purely moral; or, in other words, how pure reason can be practical—to explain this, all human reason is wholly incompetent, and all the pains and work of seeking an explanation of it are wasted.

It is just the same as if I sought to find out how freedom itself as causality of a will is possible; for, in so doing, I would leave the philosophical basis of explanation behind, and I have no other. Certainly I could revel in the intelligible world, the world of intelligences, which still remains to me; but although I have a well-founded idea of it, still I do not have the least knowledge of it, nor can I ever attain to it by all the exertions of my natural capacity of reason. This intelligible world signifies only a something which remains when I have excluded from the determining grounds of my will everything belonging to the world of sense in order to withhold the principle of motives from the field of sensibility. I do so by limiting it and showing that it does not contain absolutely everything in itself but that outside it there is still more; but this more I do not further know. After banishing all material, i. e., knowledge of objects, from pure reason which formulates this ideal, there remain to me only the form, the practical law of universal validity of maxims, and, in conformity with this, reason in relation to a pure intelligible world as a possible effective cause, i. e., as determining the will. An incentive must here be totally absent unless this idea of an intelligible world itself be the incentive or that in which reason primarily takes an interest. But to make this conceivable is precisely the problem we cannot solve.

Here is, then, the supreme limit

of all moral inquiry. To define it is very important, both in order that reason may not seek around, on the one hand, in the world of sense, in a way harmful to morals, for the supreme motive and for a comprehensible but empirical interest; and so that it will not, on the other hand, impotently flap its wings in the space (for it, an empty space) of transcendent concepts which we call the intelligible world, without being able to move from its starting-point and losing itself amid phantoms. Furthermore, the idea of a pure intelligible world as a whole of all intelligences to which we ourselves belong as rational beings (though on the other side we are at the same time members of the world of sense) is always a useful and permissible idea for the purpose of a rational faith. This is so even though all knowledge terminates at its boundary, for through the glorious ideal of a universal realm of ends-in-themselves (rational beings) a lively interest in the moral law can be awakened in us. To that realm we can belong as members only when we carefully conduct ourselves according to maxims of freedom as if they were laws of nature.

CONCLUDING REMARK

The speculative use of reason with respect to nature leads to the absolute necessity of some supreme cause of the world. The practical use of reason with respect to freedom leads also to an absolute necessity, but to the necessity only of laws of actions of a rational being as such. Now it is an essential principle of all use of reason to push its knowledge to a consciousness of its necessity, for otherwise it would not be rational knowledge. But it is also an equally essential restriction of this very same reason that it cannot discern the necessity of what is or what occurs or what ought to be done, unless a condition under which it is or occurs or ought to be done is presupposed. In this way, however, the satisfaction of reason is only further and further postponed by the constant inquiry after the condition. Therefore, reason restlessly seeks the unconditionally necessary and sees itself compelled to assume it, though it has no means by which to make it comprehensible and is happy enough if it can only discover the concept which is consistent with this presupposition. It is therefore no objection to our deduction of the supreme principle of morality, but a reproach which we must make to human reason generally, that it cannot render comprehensible the absolute necessity of an unconditional practical law (such as the categorical imperative must be). Reason cannot be blamed for being unwilling to explain it by a condition, i. e., by making some interest its basis, for the law would then cease to be moral, i. e., a supreme law of freedom. And so we do not indeed comprehend the practical unconditional necessity of the moral imperative; yet we do comprehend its incomprehensibility, which is all that can be fairly demanded of a philosophy which in its principles strives to reach the limit of human reason.

Jeremy Bentham (1748 – 1832)

A person of unusually tender sentiments, Bentham was disturbed by the social evils of his time and repelled by the current varieties of moral, legal, and political theory that condoned or, at best, ignored these evils. A reading of Hume's *Treatise of Human Nature,* possibly before his graduation from Oxford at the age of 15, served as a dramatic turning point in the intellectual development of the precocious Bentham. Hume's principle of utility was transformed with an unwavering consistency into "the greatest happiness" principle, according to which virtue is measured solely by purely quantitative determinations of pleasure and pain. The doctrine, so achieved, served as an effective philosophical basis for social reform. In addition to *The Principles of Morals and Legislation* (1789), from which the selections that follow are taken, Bentham's most important writings are *A Fragment on Government* (1776), the historically important *A Defence of Usury* (1787), *Theory of Legislation* (1802), and *Principles of the Constitutional Code* (1830, 1843).

AN INTRODUCTION TO THE PRINCIPLES OF MORALS AND LEGISLATION [1]

CHAPTER I

OF THE PRINCIPLE OF UTILITY

Mankind governed by pain and pleasure.

I. Nature has placed mankind under the governance of two sovereign masters, *pain* and *pleasure.* It is for them alone to point out what we ought to do, as well as to determine what we shall do. On the one hand the standard of right and wrong, on the other the chain of causes and effects, are fastened to their throne. They govern us in all we do, in all we say, in all we think; every effort we can make to throw off our subjection, will serve but to demonstrate and confirm it. In words a man may pretend to abjure their empire: but in reality he

[1] First printed, London, 1780; first published, *ib.* 1789; corr. ed. *ib.* 1823.

367

will remain subject to it all the while. The *principle of utility* [2] recognizes the subjection, and assumes it for the foundation of that system, the object of which is to rear the fabric of felicity by the hands of reason and of law. Systems which attempt to question it, deal in sounds instead of sense, in caprice instead of reason, in darkness instead of light.

But enough of metaphor and declamation: it is not by such means that moral science is to be improved.

II. The principle of utility is the foundation of the present work; it will be proper therefore at the outset to give an explicit and determinate account of what is meant by it. By the principle [3] of utility is meant that principle which approves or disapproves of every action whatsoever, according to the tendency which it appears to have to augment or diminish the happiness of the party whose interest is in question; or, what is the same thing in other words, to promote or to oppose that happiness. I say of every action whatsoever; and therefore not only of every action of a private individual, but of every measure of government.

Principle of utility, what.

III. By utility is meant that property in any object, whereby it tends to produce benefit, advantage, pleasure, good, or happiness, (all this in the present case comes to the same thing) or (what comes again to the same thing) to prevent the happening of mischief, pain, evil, or unhappiness to the party whose interest is considered: if that party be the community in general, then the happiness of the community: if a particular individual, then the happiness of that individual.

Utility what.

[2] Note by the Author, July, 1812.

To this denomination has of late been added, or substituted, the *greatest happiness or greatest felicity* principle: this for shortness, instead of saying at length *that principle* which states the greatest happiness of all those whose interest is in question, as being the right and proper, and only right and proper and universally desirable, end of human action: of human action in every situation, and in particular in that of a functionary or set of functionaries exercising the powers of government. The word *utility* does not so clearly point to the ideas of *pleasure* and *pain* as the words *happiness* and *felicity* do: nor does it lead us to the consideration of the *number*, of the interests affected; to the *number*, as being the circumstance, which contributes, in the largest proportion, to the formation of the standard here in question; the *standard of right and wrong*, by which alone the propriety of human conduct, in every situation, can with propriety be tried. This want of a sufficiently manifest connexion between the ideas of *happiness* and *pleasure* on the one hand, and the idea of *utility* on the other, I have every now and then found operating, and with but too much efficiency, as a bar to the acceptance, that might otherwise have been given, to this principle.

A principle, what.

[3] The word principle is derived from the Latin principium: which seems to be compounded of the two words *primus*, first, or chief, and *cipium*, a termination which seems to be derived from *capio*, to take, as in *mancipium, municipium;* to which are analo

IV. The interest of the community is one of the most general expressions that can occur in the phraseology of morals: no wonder that the meaning of it is often lost. When it has a meaning, it is this. The community is a fictitious *body*, composed of the individual persons who are considered as constituting as it were its *members*. The interest of the community then is, what?—the sum of the interests of the several members who compose it.

V. It is in vain to talk of the interest of the community, without understanding what is the interest of the individual.[4] A thing is said to promote the interest, or to be *for* the interest, of an individual, when it tends to add to the sum total of his pleasures: or, what comes to the same thing, to diminish the sum total of his pains.

VI. An action then may be said to be conformable to the principle of utility, or, for shortness' sake, to utility, (meaning with respect to the community at large) when the tendency it has to augment the happiness of the community is greater than any it has to diminish it.

VII. A measure of government (which is but a particular kind of action, performed by a particular person or persons) may be said to be conformable to or dictated by the principle of utility, when in like manner the tendency which it has to augment the happiness of the community is greater than any which it has to diminish it.

VIII. When an action, or in particular a measure of government, is supposed by a man to be conformable to the principle of utility, it may be convenient, for the purposes of discourse, to imagine a kind of law or dictate, called a law or dictate of utility: and to speak of the action in question, as being conformable to such law or dictate.

IX. A man may be said to be a partizan of the principle of utility, when the approbation or disapprobation he annexes to any action, or to any measure, is determined by and proportioned to the tendency which he conceives it to have to augment or to diminish the happiness of the community: or in other words, to its conformity or unconformity to the laws or dictates of utility.

---

gous, *auceps, forceps,* and others. It is a term of very vague and very extensive signification: it is applied to any thing which is conceived to serve as a foundation or beginning to any series of operations: in some cases, of physical operations; but of mental operations in the present case.

The principle here in question may be taken for an act of the mind; a sentiment; a sentiment of approbation; a sentiment which, when applied to an action, approves of its utility, as that quality of it by which the measure of approbation or disapprobation bestowed upon it ought to be governed.

[4] Interest is one of those words, which not having any superior *genus*, cannot in the ordinary way be defined.

Ought, ought not, right and wrong, &c., how to be understood.

X. Of an action that is conformable to the principle of utility, one may always say either that it is one that ought to be done, or at least that it is not one that ought not to be done. One may say also, that it is right it should be done; at least that it is not wrong it should be done: that it is a right action; at least that it is not a wrong action. When thus interpreted, the words *ought*, and *right* and *wrong*, and others of that stamp, have a meaning: when otherwise, they have none. *righteousness*

To prove the rectitude of this principle is at once unnecessary and impossible.

XI. Has the rectitude of this principle been ever formally contested? It should seem that it had, by those who have not known what they have been meaning. Is it susceptible of any direct proof? It should seem not, for that which is used to prove everything else, cannot itself be proved; a chain of proofs must have their commencement somewhere. To give such proof is as impossible as it is needless.

It has seldom, however, as yet been consistently pursued.

XII. Not that there is or ever has been that human creature breathing, however stupid or perverse, who has not on many, perhaps on most occasions of his life, deferred to it. By the natural constitution of the human frame, on most occasions of their lives men in general embrace this principle, without thinking of it; if not for the ordering of their own actions, yet for the trying of their own actions, as well as of those of other men. There have been, at the same time, not many, perhaps, even of the most intelligent, who have been disposed to embrace it purely and without reserve. There are even few who have not taken some occasion or other to quarrel with it, either on account of their not understanding always how to apply it, or on account of some prejudice or other which they were afraid to examine into, or could not bear to part with. For such is the stuff that man is made of: in principle and in practice, in a right track and in a wrong one, the rarest of all human qualities is consistency.

It can never be consistently combated.

XIII. When a man attempts to combat the principle of utility, it is with reason drawn, without his being aware of it, from that very principle itself. [5] His arguments, if they

[5] 'The principle of utility, (I have heard it said) is a dangerous principle: it is dangerous on certain occasions to consult it.' This is as much as to say, what? that it is not consonant to utility, to consult utility: in short, that it is *not* consulting it, to consult it.

Addition by the Author, July 1822.

Not long after the publication of the Fragment on Government, anno 1776, in which, in the character of an all-comprehensive and all-commanding principle, the principle of utility was brought to view, one person by whom observation to the above effect was made was *Alexander Wedderburn*, at that time Attorney or Solicitor General, afterwards successively Chief Justice of the Common Pleas, and Chancellor of England, under the successive titles of Lord Loughborough and Earl of Rosslyn. It was made—not indeed in my hearing, but in the hearing of a person by whom it prove anything, prove not that the principle is *wrong*, but that, according to the applications he supposes to be made of it, it is *misapplied*. Is it possible for a man to move the earth? Yes; but he must first find out another earth to stand upon.

Courses to be taken for surmounting prejudices that may have been entertained against it.

XIV. To disapprove the propriety of it by arguments is impossible; but, from the causes that have been mentioned, or from some confused or partial view of it, a man may happen to be disposed not to relish it. Where this is the case, if he thinks the settling of his opinions on such a subject worth the trouble, let him take the following steps, and at length, perhaps, he may come to reconcile himself to it.

1. Let him settle with himself, whether he would wish to discard this principle altogether; if so, let him consider what it is that all his reasonings (in matters of politics especially) can amount to?

2. If he would, let him settle with himself, whether he

---

was almost immediately communicated to me. So far from being self-contradictory, it was a shrewd and perfectly true one. By that distinguished functionary, the state of the Government was thoroughly understood: by the obscure individual, at that time not so much as supposed to be so: his disquisitions had not been as yet applied, with any thing like a comprehensive view, to the field of Constitutional Law, nor therefore to those features of the English Government, by which the greatest happiness of the ruling *one* with or without that of a favoured few, are now so plainly seen to be the only ends to which the course of it has at any time been directed. The *principle of utility* was an appellative, at that time employed—employed by me, as it had been by others, to designate that which, in a more perspicuous and instructive manner, may, as above, be designated by the name of the *greatest happiness principle*. 'This principle (said Wedderburn) is a dangerous one.' Saying so, he said that which, to a certain extent, is strictly true: a principle, which lays down, as the only *right* and justifiable end of Government, the greatest happiness of the greatest number— how can it be denied to be a dangerous one? dangerous it unquestionably is, to every government which has for its *actual* end or object, the greatest happiness of a certain *one,* with or without the addition of some comparatively small number of others, whom it is matter of pleasure or accommodation to him to admit, each of them, to a share in the concern, on the footing of so many junior partners. *Dangerous* it therefore really was, to the interest—the sinister interest—of all those functionaries, himself included, whose interest it was, to maximize delay, vexation, and expense, in judicial and other modes of procedure, for the sake of the profit, extractible out of the expense. In a Government which had for its end in view the greatest happiness of the greatest number, Alexander Wedderburn might have been Attorney General and then Chancellor: but he would not have been Attorney General with £15,000 a year, nor Chancellor, with a peerage with a veto upon all justice, with £25,000 a year, and with 500 sinecures at his disposal, under the name of Ecclesiastical Benefices, besides *et caeteras.*

would judge and act without any principle, or whether there is any other he would judge and act by?

3. If there be, let him examine and satisfy himself whether the principle he thinks he has found is really any separate intelligible principle; or whether it be not a mere principle in words, a kind of phrase, which at bottom expresses neither more nor less than the mere averment of his own unfounded sentiments; that is, what in another person he might be apt to call caprice?—sudden, unmotivated notion or action

4. If he is inclined to think that his own approbation or disapprobation, annexed to the idea of an act, without any regard to its consequences, is a sufficient foundation for him to judge and act upon, let him ask himself whether his sentiment is to be a standard of right and wrong, with respect to every other man, or whether every man's sentiment has the same privilege of being a standard to itself?

5. In the first case, let him ask himself whether his principle is not despotical, and hostile to all the rest of the human race?

6. In the second case, whether it is not anarchical, and whether at this rate there are not as many different standards of right and wrong as there are men? and whether even to the same man, the same thing, which is right today, may not (without the least change in its nature) be wrong tomorrow? and whether the same thing is not right and wrong in the same place at the same time? and in either case, whether all argument is not at an end? and whether, when two men have said, "I like this," and "I don't like it," they can (upon such principle) have anything more to say?

7. If he should have said to himself, No: for that the sentiment which he proposes as a standard must be grounded on reflection, let him say on what particulars the reflection is to turn? if on particulars having relation to the utility of the act, then let him say whether this is not deserting his own principle, and borrowing assistance from that very one in opposition to which he sets it up: or if not on those particulars, on what other particulars?

8. If he should be for compounding the matter, and adopting his own principle in part, and the principle of utility in part, let him say how far he will adopt it?

9. When he has settled with himself where he will stop, then let him ask himself how he justifies to himself the adopting it so far? and why he will not adopt it any farther?

10. Admitting any other principle than the principle of utility to be a right principle, a principle that it is right for a man to pursue; admitting (what is not true) that the word *right* can have a meaning without reference to utility, let him say whether there is any such thing as a *motive* that a man

can have to pursue the dictates of it: if there is, let him say what that motive is, and how it is to be distinguished from those which enforce the dictates of utility: if not, then lastly let him say what it is this other principle can be good for?

CHAPTER II

OF PRINCIPLES ADVERSE TO THAT OF UTILITY

I. If the principle of utility be a right principle to be governed by, and that in all cases, it follows from what has been just observed, that whatever principle differs from it in any case must necessarily be a wrong one. To prove any other principle, therefore, to be a wrong one, there needs no more than just to show it to be what it is, a principle of which the dictates are in some point or other different from those of the principle of utility: to state it is to confute it.

II. A principle may be different from that of utility in two ways; 1. By being constantly opposed to it: this is the case with a principle which may be termed the principle of *asceticism*.[6] 2. By being sometimes opposed to it, and sometimes not, as it may happen: this is the case with another, which may be termed the principle of *sympathy* and *antipathy*.

III. By the principle of asceticism I mean that principle, which, like the principle of utility, approves or disapproves of any action, according to the tendency which it appears to

[6] Ascetic is a term that has been sometimes applied to Monks. It comes from a Greek word which signifies *exercise*. The practice by which Monks sought to distinguish themselves from other men were called their Exercises. These exercises consisted in so many contrivances they had for tormenting themselves. By this they thought to ingratiate themselves with the Deity. For the Deity, said they, is a Being of infinite benevolence: now a Being of the most ordinary benevolence is pleased to see others make themselves as happy as they can: therefore to make ourselves as unhappy as we can is the way to please the Deity. If any body asked them, what motive they could find for doing all this? Oh! said they, you are not to imagine that we are punishing ourselves for nothing: we know very well what we are about. You are to know, that for every grain of pain it costs us now, we are to have a hundred grains of pleasure by and by. The case is, that God loves to see us torment ourselves at present: indeed he has as good as told us so. But this is done only to try us, in order just to see how we should behave: which it is plain he could not know, without making the experiment. Now then, from the satisfaction it gives him to see us make ourselves as unhappy as we can make ourselves in this present life, we have a sure proof of the satisfaction it will give him to see us as happy as he can make us in a life to come.

have to augment or diminish the happiness of the party whose interest is in question; but in an inverse manner: approving of actions in as far as they tend to diminish his happiness; disapproving of them in as far as they tend to augment it.

*   *   *

The principle of asceticism, in its origin, was but that of utility misapplied.

IX. The principle of asceticism seems originally to have been the reverie of certain hasty speculators, who having perceived, or fancied, that certain pleasures, when reaped in certain circumstances, have, at the long run, been attended with pains more than equivalent to them, took occasion to quarrel with everything that offered itself under the name of pleasure. Having then got thus far, and having forgot the point which they set out from, they pushed on, and went so much further as to think it meritorious to fall in love with pain. Even this, we see, is at bottom but the principle of utility misapplied.

It can never be consistently pursued.

X. The principle of utility is capable of being consistently pursued; and it is but tautology to say, that the more consistently it is pursued, the better it must ever be for human-kind. The principle of asceticism never was, or ever can be, consistently pursued by any living creature. Let but one tenth part of the inhabitants of this earth pursue it consistently, and in a day's time they will have turned it into a hell.

The principle of sympathy and antipathy, what.

XI. Among principles adverse to that of utility, that which at this day seems to have most influence in matters of government, is what may be called the principle of sympathy and antipathy. By the principle of sympathy and antipathy, I mean that principle which approves or disapproves of certain actions, not on account of their tending to augment the happiness, nor yet on account of their tending to diminish the happiness of the party whose interest is in question, but merely because a man finds himself disposed to approve or disapprove of them: holding up that approbation or disapprobation as a sufficient reason for itself, and disclaiming the necessity of looking out for any extrinsic ground. Thus far in the general department of morals; and in the particular department of politics, measuring out the quantum (as well as determining the ground) of punishment, by the degree of the disapprobation.

This is rather the negation of all principle, than any thing positive.

XII. It is manifest, that this is rather a principle in name than in reality; it is not a positive principle of itself, so much as a term employed to signify the negation of all principle. What one expects to find in a principle is something that points out some external consideration, as a means of warranting and guiding the internal sentiments of approbation and disapprobation; this expectation is but ill fulfilled by a proposition, which does neither more nor less than hold up each of those sentiments as a ground and standard for itself.

Sentiments of a partizan of

XIII. In looking over the catalogue of human actions (says a partizan of this principle) in order to determine which of

the principle
of antipathy.

them are to be marked with the seal of disapprobation, you need but to take counsel of your own feelings: whatever you find in yourself a propensity to condemn, is wrong for that very reason. For the same reason it is also meet for punishment: what proportion it is adverse to utility, or whether it be adverse to utility at all, is a matter that makes no difference. In that same *proportion* also is it meet for punishment; if you hate much, punish much; if you hate little, punish little; punish as you hate. If you hate not at all, punish not at all; the fine feelings of the soul are not to be overborne and tyrannized by the harsh and rugged dictates of political utility.

The systems
that have
been formed
concerning
the standard
of right and
wrong, are all
reducible to
this principle.

XIV. The various systems that have been formed concerning the standard of right and wrong, may all be reduced to the principle of sympathy and antipathy. One account may serve for all of them. They consist all of them in so many contrivances for avoiding the obligation of appealing to any external standard, and for prevailing upon the reader to accept of the author's sentiment or opinion as a reason for itself. The phrases different, but the principle the same. [7]

Various phrases
that have
served as the
characteristic
marks of so
many pre-
tended systems.

[7] It is curious enough to observe the variety of inventions men have hit upon, and the variety of phrases they have brought forward, in order to conceal from the world, and, if possible, from themselves, this very general and therefore very pardonable self-sufficiency.

1. Moral Sense.

1. One man says, he has a thing made on purpose to tell him what is right and what is wrong; and that it is called a *moral sense*: and then he goes to work at his ease, and says, such a thing is right, and such a thing is wrong—why? "because my moral sense tells me it is."

2. Common
Sense.

2. Another man comes and alters the phrase: leaving out *moral*, and putting in *common*, in the room of it. He then tells you, that his common sense teaches him what is right and wrong, as surely as the other's moral sense did: meaning by common sense, a sense of some kind or other, which, he says, is possessed by all mankind: the sense of those, whose sense is not the same as the author's, being struck out of the account as not worth taking. This contrivance does better than the other; for a moral sense, being a new thing, a man may feel about him a good while without being able to find it out: but common sense is as old as the creation; and there is no man but would be ashamed to be thought not to have as much of it as his neighbours. It has another great advantage: by appearing to share power, it lessens envy: for when a man gets up upon this ground, in order to anathematize those who differ from him, it is not by a *sic volo sic jubeo*, but by a *velitis jubeatis*.

3. Under-
standing.

3. Another man comes, and says, that as to a moral sense indeed, he cannot find that he has any such thing: that however he has an *understanding*, which will do quite as well. This understanding, he says, is the standard of right and wrong: it tells him so and so. All good and wise men understand as he does: if other men's understandings differ in any point from his, so much the worse for them: it is a sure sign they are either defective or corrupt.

4. Rule of Right.

4. Another man says, that there is an eternal and immutable Rule of Right: that that rule of right dictates so and so: and then he begins giving you his sentiments upon anything that comes uppermost: and these sentiments (you are to take for granted) are so many branches of the eternal rule of right.

5. Fitness of Things

5. Another man, or perhaps the same man (it's no matter) says, that there are certain practices conformable, and others repugnant to the Fitness of Things; and then he tells you, at his leisure, what practices are conformable and what repugnant: just as he happens to like a practice or dislike it.

6. Law of Nature.

6. A great multitude of people are continually talking of the Law of Nature; and then they go on giving you their sentiments about what is right and what is wrong: and these sentiments, you are to understand, are so many chapters and sections of the Law of Nature.

7. Law of Reason, Right Reason, Natural Justice, Natural Equity, Good Order.

7. Instead of the phrase, Law of Nature, you have sometimes, Law of Reason, Right Reason, Natural Justice, Natural Equity, Good Order. Any of them will do equally well. This latter is most used in politics. The last three are much more tolerable than the others, because they do not very explicitly claim to be anything more than phrases; they insist but feebly upon the being looked upon as so many positive standards of themselves, and seem content to be taken, upon occasion, for phrases expressive of the conformity of the thing in question to the proper standard, whatever that may be. On most occasions, however, it will be better to say *utility: utility* is clearer, as referring more explicitly to pain and pleasure.

8. Truth.

8. We have one philosopher, who says, there is no harm in anything in the world but in telling a lie: and that if, for example, you were to murder your own father, this would only be a particular way of saying, he was not your father. Of course, when this philosopher sees anything that he does not like, he says, it is a particular way of telling a lie. It is saying, that the act ought to be done, or may be done, when, *in truth*, it ought not to be done.

9. Doctrine of Election.

9. The fairest and openest of them all is that sort of man who speaks out, and says, I am of the number of the Elect: now God himself takes care to inform the Elect what is right: and that with so good effect, that let them strive ever so, they cannot help not only knowing it but practising it. If therefore a man wants to know what is right and what is wrong, he has nothing to do but to come to me.

Repugnancy to Nature.

It is upon the principle of antipathy that such and such acts are often reprobated on the score of their being *unnatural:* the practice of exposing children, established among the Greeks and Romans, was an unnatural practice. Unnatural, when it means any thing, means unfrequent: and there it means something; although nothing to the present purpose. But here it means no such thing: for the frequency of such acts is perhaps the great complaint. It therefore means nothing; nothing, I mean, which there is in the act itself. All it can serve to express is, the disposition of the person who is talking of it: the disposition he is in to be angry at the thoughts of it. Does it merit his anger? Very likely it may: but whether it does or no is a question, which to be answered rightly, can only be answered upon the principle of utility.

Unnatural, is as good a word as moral sense, or common sense; and would be as good a foundation for a system. Such an act is unnatural; that is, repugnant to nature: for I do not like to practise it: and, consequently, do not practise it. It is therefore repugnant to what ought to be the nature of everybody else.

Mischief they produce.

This mischief common to all these ways of thinking and arguing (which, in truth, as we have seen, are but one and the same method, couched in different forms of words) is their serving as a cloke, and pretence, and aliment, to despotism: if not a despotism in practice, a despotism however in disposition: which is but too apt, when pretence and power offer, to show itself in practice. The consequence is, that with intentions very commonly of the purest kind, a man becomes a torment either to himself or his fellow-creatures. If he be of the melancholy cast, he sits in silent grief, bewailing their blindness and depravity: if of the irascible, he declaims with fury and virulence against all who differ from him; blowing up the coals of fanaticism, and branding with the charge of corruption and insincerity, every man who does not think, or profess to think, as he does.

[margin note: a system w/ a ruler who has absolute authority]

If such a man happens to possess the advantages of style, his book may do a considerable deal of mischief before the nothingness of it is understood.

These principles, if such they can be called, it is more frequent to see applied to morals than to politics: but their influence extends itself to both. In politics, as well as morals, a man will be at least equally glad of a pretence for deciding any question in the manner that best pleases him, without the trouble of inquiry. If a man is an infallible judge of what is right and wrong in the actions of private individuals, why not in the measures to be observed by public men in the direction of those actions? accordingly (not to mention other chimeras) I have more than once known the pretended law of nature set up in legislative debates, in opposition to arguments derived from the principle of utility.

Whether utility is actually the sole ground of all the approbation we ever bestow, is a different consideration.

'But is it never, then, from any other considerations than those of utility, that we derive our notions of right and wrong?' I do not know: I do not care. Whether a moral sentiment can be originally conceived from any other source than a view of utility, is one question: whether upon examination and reflection it can, in point of fact, be actually persisted in and justified on any other ground, by a person reflecting within himself, is another: whether in point of right it can properly be justified on any other ground, by a person addressing himself to the community, is a third. The two first are questions of speculation: it matters not, comparatively speaking, how they are decided. The last is a question of practice: the decision of it is of as much importance as that of any can be.

'I feel in myself,' (say you) 'a disposition to approve of such or such an action in a moral view: but this is not owing to any notions I have of its being a useful one to the community. I do not pretend to know whether it be an useful one or not: it may be, for aught I know, a mischievous one.' 'But is it then,' (say I) 'a mischievous one? examine; and if you can make yourself sensible that it is so, then, if duty means any thing, that is, moral duty, it is your *duty* at least to abstain from it: and more than that, if it is what lies in your power, and can be done without too great a sacrifice, to endeavour to prevent it. It is not your cherish-

XV. It is manifest, that the dictates of this principle will frequently coincide with those of utility, though perhaps without intending any such thing. Probably more frequently than not: and hence it is that the business of penal justice is carried on upon that tolerable sort of footing upon which we see it carried on in common at this day. For what more natural or more general ground of hatred to a practice can there be, than the mischievousness of such practice? What all men are exposed to suffer by, all men will be disposed to hate. It is far yet, however, from being a constant ground: for when a man suffers, it is not always that he knows what it is he suffers by. A man may suffer grievously, for instance, by a new tax, without being able to trace up the cause of his sufferings to the injustice of some neighbour, who has eluded the payment of an old one.

This principle is most apt to err on the side of severity.

XVI. The principle of sympathy and antipathy is most apt to err on the side of severity. It is for applying punishment in many cases which deserve none: in many cases which deserve some, it is for applying more than they deserve. There is no incident imaginable, be it ever so trivial, and so remote from mischief, from which this principle may not extract a ground of punishment. Any difference in taste: any difference in opinion: upon one subject as well as upon another. No disagreement so trifling which perseverance and altercation will not render serious. Each becomes in the other's eyes an enemy, and, if laws permit, a criminal. [8] This is one of

---

ing the notion of it in your bosom, and giving it the name of virtue, that will excuse you.'

'I feel in myself,' (say you again) 'a disposition to detest such or such an action in a moral view; but this is not owing to any notions I have of its being a mischievous one to the community. I do not pretend to know whether it be a mischievous one or not: it may be not a mischievous one: it may be, for aught I know, an useful one.'—'May it indeed,' (say I) 'an useful one? but let me tell you then, that unless duty, and right and wrong, be just what you please to make them, if it really be not a mischievous one, and any body has a mind to do it, it is no duty of yours, but, on the contrary, it would be very wrong in you, to take upon you to prevent him: detest it within yourself as much as you please; that may be a very good reason (unless it be also a useful one) for your not doing it yourself: but if you go about, by word or deed, to do any thing to hinder him, or make him suffer for it, it is you, and not he, that have done wrong: it is not your setting yourself to blame his conduct, or branding it with the name of vice, that will make him culpable, or you blameless. Therefore, if you can make yourself content that he shall be of one mind, and you of another, about that matter, and so continue, it is well: but if nothing will serve you, but that you and he must needs be of the same mind, I'll tell you what you have to do: it is for you to get the better of your antipathy, not for him to truckle to it.'

[8] King James the First of England had conceived a violent anti-

the circumstances by which the human race is distinguished (not much indeed to its advantage) from the brute creation.

But errs in some instances, on the side of lenity.

XVII. It is not, however, by any means unexampled for this principle to err on the side of lenity. A near and perceptible mischief moves antipathy. A remote and imperceptible mischief, though not less real, has no effect. Instances in proof of this will occur in numbers in the course of the work. [9] It would be breaking in upon the order of it to give them here.

The theological principle, what— not a separate principle.

XVIII. It may be wondered, perhaps, that in all this while no mention has been made of the *theological* principle; meaning that principle which professes to recur for the standard of right and wrong to the will of God. But the case is, this is not in fact a distinct principle. It is never anything more or less than one or other of the three before-mentioned principles presenting itself under another shape. The *will* of God here meant cannot be his revealed will, as contained in the sacred writings: for that is a system which nobody ever thinks of recurring to at this time of day, for the details of political

---

pathy against Arians: two of whom he burnt.[*] This gratification he procured himself without much difficulty: the notions of the times were favourable to it. He wrote a furious book against Vorstius, for being what was called an Arminian: for Vorstius was at a distance. He also wrote a furious book called 'A Counterblast to Tobacco,' against the use of that drug, which Sir Walter Raleigh had then lately introduced. Had the notions of the times cooperated with him, he would have burnt the Anabaptist and the smoker of tobacco in the same fire. However he had the satisfaction of putting Raleigh to death afterwards, though for another crime.

Disputes concerning the comparative excellence of French and Italian music have occasioned very serious bickerings at Paris. One of the parties would not have been sorry (says Mr. D'Alembert[†]) to have brought government into the quarrel. Pretences were sought after and urged. Long before that, a dispute of like nature, and of at least equal warmth, had been kindled at London upon the comparative merits of two composers at London; where riots between the approvers and disapprovers of a new play are, at this day, not unfrequent. The ground of quarrel between the Big-endians and the Little-endians in the fable, was not more frivolous than many an one which has laid empires desolate. In Russia, it is said, there was a time when some thousands of persons lost their lives in a quarrel, in which the government had taken part, about the number of fingers to be used in making the sign of the cross. This was in days of yore: the ministers of Catherine II. are better *instructed* [§] than to take any other part in such disputes, than that of preventing the parties concerned from doing one another a mischief.

[*] Hume's *Hist.* vol. 6.
[†] Melanges' *Essai sur la Liberté de la Musique.*
[§] See ch. xvi. (Division), par. 42, 44.

[9] Instruct. art. 474, 475, 476.

administration: and even before it can be applied to the details of private conduct, it is universally allowed, by the most eminent divines of all persuasions, to stand in need of pretty ample interpretations; else to what use are the works of those divines? And for the guidance of these interpretations, it is also allowed, that some other standard must be assumed. The will then which is meant on this occasion, is that which may be called the *presumptive* will: that is to say, that which is presumed to be his will on account of the conformity of its dictates to those of some other principle. What then may be this other principle? it must be one or other of the three mentioned above; for there cannot, as we have seen, be any more. It is plain, therefore, that, setting revelation out of the question, no light can ever be thrown upon the standard of right and wrong, by anything that can be said upon the question, what is God's will. We may be perfectly sure, indeed, that whatever is right is conformable to the will of God; but so far is that from answering the purpose of showing us what is right, that it is necessary to know first whether a thing is right, in order to know from thence whether it be conformable to the will of God. [10]

Antipathy, let the actions it dictates be ever so right, is never of itself a right ground of action.

XIX. There are two things which are very apt to be confounded, but which it imports us carefully to distinguish:— the motive or cause, which, by operating on the mind of an individual, is productive of any act. and the ground or reason which warrants a legislator, or other bystander, in regarding that act with an eye of approbation. When the act happens, in the particular instance in question, to be productive of effects which we approve of, much more if we happen to observe that the same motive may frequently be productive, in other instances, of the like effects, we are apt to transfer

The principle of theology, how reducible to one or another of the other three principles.

[10] The principle of theology refers every thing to God's pleasure. But what is God's pleasure? God does not, he confessedly does not now, either speak or write to us. How then are we to know what is his pleasure? By observing what is our own pleasure, and pronouncing it to be his. Accordingly, what is called the pleasure of God, is and must necessarily be (revelation apart) neither more nor less than the good pleasure of the person, whoever he be, who is pronouncing what he believes, or pretends, to be God's pleasure. How know you it to be God's pleasure that such or such an act should be abstained from? whence come you even to suppose as much? 'Because the engaging in it would, I imagine, be prejudicial upon the whole to the happiness of mankind;' says the partizan of the principle of utility: 'Because the commission of it is attended with a gross and sensual, or at least with a trifling and transient satisfaction;' says the partizan of the principle of asceticism: 'Because I detest the thoughts of it; and I cannot, neither ought I to be called upon to tell why;' says he who proceeds upon the principle of antipathy. In the words of one or other of these must that person necessarily answer (revelation apart) who professes to take for his standard the will of God.

our approbation to the motive itself, and to assume, as the just ground for the approbation we bestow on the act, the circumstance of its originating from that motive. It is in this way that the sentiment of antipathy has often been considered as a just ground of action. Antipathy, for instance, in such or such a case, is the cause of an action which is attended with good effects; but this does not make it a right ground of action in that case, any more than in any other. Still farther. Not only the effects are good, but the agent sees beforehand that they will be so. This may make the action indeed a perfectly right action: but it does not make antipathy a right ground for action. For the same sentiment of antipathy, if implicitly deferred to, may be, and very frequently is, productive of the very worst effects. Antipathy, therefore, can never be a right ground of action. No more, therefore, can resentment, which, as will be seen more particularly hereafter, is but a modification of antipathy. The only right ground of action, that can possibly subsist, is, after all, the consideration of utility, which, if it is a right principle of action, and of approbation, in any one case, is so in every other. Other principles in abundance, that is, other motives, may be the reasons why such and such an act *has* been done, that is, the reasons or causes of its being done; but it is this alone that can be the reason why it might or ought to have been done. Antipathy or resentment requires always to be regulated, to prevent its doing mischief: to be regulated by what? always by the principle of utility. The principle of utility neither requires nor admits of any other regulator than itself.

CHAPTER III

OF THE FOUR SANCTIONS OR SOURCES OF PAIN AND PLEASURE

Connexion of this chapter with the preceding.

I. It has been shown that the happiness of the individuals, of whom a community is composed, that is their pleasures and their security, is the end and the sole end which the legislator ought to have in view: the sole standard, in conformity to which each individual ought, as far as depends upon the legislator, to be *made* to fashion his behaviour. But whether it be this or anything else that is to be *done*, there is nothing by which a man can ultimately be *made* to do it, but either pain or pleasure. Having taken a general view of these two grand objects (*viz.* pleasure, and what comes to the same thing, immunity from pain) in the character of *final* causes; it will be necessary to take a view of pleasure and pain itself, in the character of *efficient* causes or means.

Four sanctions or sources of pleasure and pain.

II. There are four distinguishable sources from which pleasure and pain are in use to flow: considered separately, they may be termed the *physical,* the *political,* the *moral,* and the *religious:* and inasmuch as the pleasures and pains belonging to each of them are capable of giving a binding force to any law or rule of conduct, they may all of them be termed *sanctions.* [11]

1. The physical sanction.

III. If it be in the present life, and from the ordinary course of nature not purposely modified by the interposition of the will of any human being, nor by any extraordinary interposition of any superior invisible being, that the pleasure or the pain takes place or is expected, it may be said to issue from or to belong to the *physical sanction.*

2. The political.

IV. If at the hands of a *particular* person or set of persons in the community, who under names correspondent to that of *judge,* are chosen for the particular purpose of dispensing it, according to the will of the sovereign or supreme ruling power in the state, it may be said to issue from the *political sanction.*

3. The moral or popular.

V. If at the hands of such *chance* persons in the community as the party in question may happen in the course of his life to have concerns with, according to each man's spontaneous disposition, and not according to any settled or concerted rule, it may be said to issue from the *moral* or *popular sanction.* [12]

[11] Sanctio, in Latin, was used to signify the *act of binding,* and, by a common grammatical transition, *any thing which serves to bind a man:* to wit, to the observance of such or such a mode of conduct. According to a Latin grammarian,° the import of the word is derived by rather a far-fetched process (such as those commonly are, and in great measure indeed must be, by which intellectual ideas are derived from sensible ones) from the word *sanguis,* blood: because, among the Romans, with a view to inculcate into the people a persuasion that such or such a mode of conduct would be rendered obligatory upon a man by the force of what I call the religious sanction (that is, that he would be made to suffer by the extraordinary interposition of some superior being, if he failed to observe the mode of conduct in question) certain ceremonies were contrived by the priests: in the course of which ceremonies the blood of victims was made use of.

A Sanction then is a source of obligatory powers or *motives:* that is, of *pains* and *pleasures;* which, according as they are connected with such or such modes of conduct, operate, and are indeed the only things which can operate, *as motives.* See Chap. x. (Motives).

° Servius. See Ainsworth's Dict. ad verbum *Sanctio.*

[12] Better termed *popular,* as more directly indicative of its constituent cause; as likewise of its relation to the more common phrase *public opinion,* in French *opinion publique,* the name there

The pleasures
and pains
which belong
to the religious
sanction, may
regard either
the present life,
or a future.

Those which
regard the
present life,
from which-
soever source
they flow,
differ only in
the circum-
stances of
their
production.

VI. If from the immediate hand of a superior invisible being, either in the present life, or in a future, it may be said to issue from the *religious sanction*.

VII. Pleasures or pains which may be expected to issue from the *physical, political,* or *moral* sanctions, must all of them be expected to be experienced, if ever, in the *present* life: those which may be expected to issue from the *religious* sanction, may be expected to be experienced either in the *present* life or in a *future*.

VIII. Those which can be experienced in the present life, can of course be no others than such as human nature in the course of the present life is susceptible of: and from each of these sources may flow all the pleasures or pains of which, in the course of the present life, human nature is susceptible. With regard to these then, (with which alone we have in this place any concern) those of them which belong to any one of those sanctions, differ not ultimately in kind from those which belong to any one of the other three: the only difference there is among them lies in the circumstances that accompany their production. A suffering which befalls a man in the natural and spontaneous course of things, shall be styled, for instance, a *calamity;* in which case, if it be supposed to befall him through any imprudence of his, it may be styled a punishment issuing from the physical sanction. Now this same suffering, if inflicted by the law, will be what is commonly called a *punishment;* if incurred for want of any friendly assistance, which the misconduct, or supposed misconduct, of the sufferer has occasioned to be withholden, a punishment issuing from the *moral* sanction; if through the immediate interposition of a particular providence, a punishment issuing from the religious sanction.

Example.

IX. A man's goods, or his person, are consumed by fire. If this happened to him by what is called an accident, it was a calamity; if by reason of his own imprudence, (for instance, from his neglecting to put his candle out) it may be styled a punishment of the physical sanction; if it happened to him by the sentence of the political magistrate, a punishment belonging to the political sanction; that is, what is commonly called a punishment, if for want of any assistance which his *neighbour* withheld from him out of some dislike to his *moral* character, a punishment of the *moral* sanction; if by an immediate act of *God's* displeasure, manifested on account of some *sin* committed by him, or through any distraction of

given to that tutelary power, of which of late so much is said, and by which so much is done. The latter appellation is however unhappy and inexpressive; since if *opinion* is material, it is only in virtue of the influence it exercises over action, through the medium of the affections and the will.

Those which
regard a
future life are
not specifically
known.

mind, occasioned by the dread of such displeasure, a punishment of the *religious* sanction. [13]

X. As to such of the pleasures and pains belonging to the
religious sanction, as regard a future life, of what kind these
may be we cannot know. These lie not open to our observation. During the present life they are matter only of expectation: and, whether that expectation be derived from natural
or revealed religion, the particular kind of pleasure or pain,
if it be different from all those which lie open to our observation, is what we can have no idea of. The best ideas we
can obtain of such pains and pleasures are altogether un-
liquidated in point of quality. In what other respects our
ideas of them *may* be liquidated will be considered in another
place. [14]

The physical
sanction
included in
each of the
other three.

XI. Of these four sanctions the physical is altogether, we
may observe, the ground-work of the political and the moral:
so is it also of the religious, in as far as the latter bears relation to the present life. It is included in each of those other
three. This may operate in any case, (that is, any of the
pains or pleasures belonging to it may operate) independently
of *them:* none of *them* can operate but by means of this. In
a word, the powers of nature may operate of themselves; but
neither the magistrate, nor men at large, *can* operate, nor is
God in the case in question *supposed* to operate, but through
the powers of nature.

Use of this
chapter.

XII. For these four objects, which in their nature have
so much in common, it seemed of use to find a common
name. It seemed of use, in the first place, for the convenience
of giving a name to certain pleasures and pains, for which a
name equally characteristic could hardly otherwise have been
found: in the second place, for the sake of holding up the
efficacy of certain moral forces, the influence of which is apt
not to be sufficiently attended to. Does the political sanction
exert an influence over the conduct of mankind? The moral,
the religious sanctions do so too. In every inch of his career
are the operations of the political magistrate liable to be
aided or impeded by these two foreign powers: who, one or
other of them, or both, are sure to be either his rivals or his
allies. Does it happen to him to leave them out in his calculations? he will be sure almost to find himself mistaken in
the result. Of all this we shall find abundant proofs in the
sequel of this work. It behoves him, therefore, to have them
continually before his eyes; and that under such a name as
exhibits the relation they bear to his own purposes and
designs.

[13] A suffering conceived to befall a man by the immediate act of
God, as above, is often, for shortness' sake, called a *judgment:*
instead of saying, a suffering inflicted on him in consequence of
a special judgment formed, and resolution thereupon taken, by
the Deity.

[14] See ch. xiii. (Cases unmeet) par. 2. note.

CHAPTER IV

VALUE OF A LOT OF PLEASURE OR PAIN,
HOW TO BE MEASURED

Use of this
chapter.

I. Pleasures then, and the avoidance of pains, are the *ends* which the legislator has in view: it behoves him therefore to understand their *value*. Pleasures and pains are the *instruments* he has to work with: it behoves him therefore to understand their force, which is again, in other words, their value.

Circumstances
to be taken
into account
in estimating
the value of
a pleasure or
pain considered
with reference
to a single
person, and
by itself.

II. To a person considered *by himself*, the value of a pleasure or pain considered *by itself*, will be greater or less, according to the four following circumstances. [15]

1. Its *intensity*.
2. Its *duration*.
3. Its *certainty* or *uncertainty*.
4. Its *propinquity* or *remoteness*.

closeness, proximity

—considered
as connected
with other
pleasures
or pains.

III. These are the circumstances which are to be considered in estimating a pleasure or a pain considered each of them by itself. But when the value of any pleasure or pain is considered for the purpose of estimating the tendency of any *act* by which it is produced, there are two other circumstances to be taken into the account; these are,

fruitfulness

5. Its *fecundity*, or the chance it has of being followed by sensations of the *same* kind: that is, pleasures, if it be a pleasure: pains, if it be a pain.

6. Its *purity*, or the chance it has of *not* being followed by sensations of the *opposite* kind: that is, pains, if it be a pleasure: pleasures, if it be a pain.

These two last, however, are in strictness scarcely to be deemed properties of the pleasures or the pain itself; they are not, therefore, in strictness to be taken into the account of the value of that pleasure or that pain. They are in strictness

[15] These circumstances have since been denominated *elements* or *dimensions* of *value* in a pleasure or a pain.

Not long after the publication of the first edition, the following memoriter verses were framed, in the view of lodging more effectually, in the memory, these points, on which the whole fabric of morals and legislation may be seen to rest:

> *Intense, long, certain, speedy, fruitful, pure*—
> Such marks in *pleasures* and in *pains* endure.
> Such pleasures seek, if *private* be thy end:
> If it be *public*, wide let them *extend*.
> Such *pains* avoid, whichever be thy view:
> If pains *must* come, let them *extend* to few.

to be deemed properties only of the act, or other event, by which such pleasure or pain has been produced; and accordingly are only to be taken into the account of the tendency of such act or such event.

IV. To a *number* of persons, with reference to each of whom the value of a pleasure or a pain is considered, it will be greater or less, according to seven circumstances: to wit, the six preceding ones; *viz.*

1. Its *intensity*.
2. Its *duration*.
3. Its *certainty* or *uncertainty*.
4. Its *propinquity* or *remoteness*.
5. Its *fecundity*.
6. Its *purity*.

And one other; to wit:

7. Its *extent;* that is, the number of persons to whom it *extends;* or (in other words) who are affected by it.

V. To take an exact account then of the general tendency of any act, by which the interests of a community are affected, proceed as follows. Begin with any one person of those whose interests seem most immediately to be affected by it: and take an account,

1. Of the value of each distinguishable *pleasure* which appears to be produced by it in the *first* instance.

2. Of the value of each *pain* which appears to be produced by it in the *first* instance.

3. Of the value of each pleasure which appears to be produced by it *after* the first. This constitutes the *fecundity* of the first *pleasure* and the *impurity* of the first *pain*.

4. Of the value of each *pain* which appears to be produced by it after the first. This constitutes the *fecundity* of the first *pain*, and the *impurity* of the first pleasure.

5. Sum up all the values of all the *pleasures* on the one side, and those of all the pains on the other. The balance, if it be on the side of pleasure, will give the *good* tendency of the act upon the whole, with respect to the interests of that *individual* person; if on the side of pain, the *bad* tendency of it upon the whole.

6. Take an account of the *number* of persons whose interests appear to be concerned; and repeat the above process with respect to each. *Sum up* the numbers expressive of the degrees of *good* tendency, which the act has, with respect to each individual, in regard to whom the tendency of it is *good* upon the whole: do this again with respect to each individual, in regard to whom the tendency of it is *bad* upon the whole. Take the *balance;* which, if on the side of *pleasure,* will give the general *good tendency* of the act, with respect to the total number of community of individuals concerned; if on the side of pain the general *evil tendency,* with respect to the same community.

VI. It is not to be expected that this process should be

foregoing
process.

strictly pursued previously to every moral judgment, or to every legislative or judicial operation. It may, however, be always kept in view: and as near as the process actually pursued on these occasions approaches to it, so near will such process approach to the character of an exact one.

The same
process applicable to
good and
evil, profit
and mischief,
and all other
modifications
of pleasure
and pain.

VII. The same process is alike applicable to pleasure and pain in whatever shape they appear: and by whatever denomination they are distinguished: to pleasure, whether it be called *good* (which is properly the cause or instrument of pleasure), or *profit* (which is distant pleasure, or the cause or instrument of distant pleasure), or *convenience*, or *advantage, benefit, emolument, happiness,* and so forth: to pain, whether it be called *evil* (which corresponds to *good*), or *mischief,* or *inconvenience,* or *disadvantage,* or *loss,* or *unhappiness,* and so forth.

Conformity
of men's
practice to
this theory.

VIII. Nor is this a novel and unwarranted, any more than it is a useless theory. In all this there is nothing but what the practice of mankind, wheresoever they have a clear view of their own interest, is perfectly conformable to. An article of property, an estate in land, for instance, is valuable, on what account? On account of the pleasures of all kinds which it enables a man to produce, and what comes to the same thing, the pains of all kinds which it enables him to avert. But the value of such an article of property is universally understood to rise or fall according to the length or shortness of the time which a man has in it: the certainty or uncertainty of its coming into possession: and the nearness or remoteness of the time at which, if at all, it is to come into possession. As to the *intensity* of the pleasures which a man may derive from it, this is never thought of, because it depends upon the use which each particular person may come to make of it; which cannot be estimated till the particular pleasures he may come to derive from it, or the particular pains he may come to exclude by means of it, are brought to view. For the same reason, neither does he think of the *fecundity* or *purity* of those pleasures.

. . .

CHAPTER X

MOTIVES

§ 2. NO MOTIVES EITHER CONSTANTLY GOOD, OR

CONSTANTLY BAD

Nothing can
act of itself
as a motive
but the ideas
of pleasure
or pain.

IX. In all this chain of motives, the principle or original link seems to be the last internal motive in prospect; it is to this that all the other motives in prospect owe their materiality; and the immediately acting motive its existence. This motive in prospect, we see, is always some pleasure, or some pain; some pleasure, which the act in question is expected to be a means of continuing or producing: some pain which it is expected to be a means of discontinuing or preventing. A motive is substantially nothing more than pleasure or pain, operating in a certain manner.

No sort of motive is in itself a bad one.

X. Now, pleasure is in *itself* a good: nay, even setting aside immunity from pain, the only good: pain is in itself an evil; and, indeed, without exception, the only evil; or else the words good and evil have no meaning. And this is alike true of every sort of pain, and of every sort of pleasure. It follows, therefore, immediately and incontestably, that *there is no such thing as any sort of motive that is in itself a bad one.* [16]

Inaccuracy of expressions in which *good* or *bad* are applied to motives.

XI. It is common, however, to speak of actions as proceeding from *good* or *bad* motives: in which case the motives meant are such as are internal. The expression is far from being an accurate one; and as it is apt to occur in the consideration of almost every kind of offence, it will be requisite to settle the precise meaning of it, and observe how far it quadrates with the truth of things.

Any sort of motive may give birth to any sort of act.

XII. With respect to goodness and badness, as it is with everything else that is not itself either pain or pleasure, so is it with motives. If they are good or bad, it is only on account of their effects: good, on account of their tendency to produce pleasure, or avert pain: bad, on account of their tendency to produce pain, or avert pleasure. Now the case is, that from one and the same motive, and from every kind of motive, may proceed actions that are good, others that are bad, and others that are indifferent. This we shall proceed to show with respect to all the different kinds of motives, as determined by the various kinds of pleasures and pains.

Difficulties which stand in the way of an analysis of this sort.

XIII. Such an analysis, useful as it is, will be found to be a matter of no small difficulty; owing, in great measure, to a certain perversity of structure which prevails more or less throughout all languages. To speak of motives, as of anything else, one must call them by their names. But the misfortune is that it is rare to meet with a motive of which the name expresses that and nothing more. Commonly along with the very name of the motive, is tacitly involved a proposition imputing to it a certain quality; a quality which, in many cases, will appear to include that very goodness or badness, concerning which we are here inquiring whether, properly speaking, it be or be not imputable to motives. To

---

[16] Let a man's motive be ill-will; call it even malice, envy, cruelty; it is still a kind of pleasure that is his motive: the pleasure he takes at the thought of the pain which he sees, or expects to see, his adversary undergo. Now even this wretched pleasure, taken by itself, is good: it may be faint; it may be short: it must at any rate be impure: yet while it lasts, and before any bad consequences arrive, it is good as any other that is not more intense. See ch. iv. (Value).

use the common phrase, in most cases, the name of the motive is a word which is employed either only in a *good sense*, or else only in a *bad sense*. Now, when a word is spoken of as being used in a good sense, all that is necessarily meant is this: that in conjunction with the idea of the object it is put to signify, it conveys an idea of *approbation*: that is, of a pleasure or satisfaction, entertained by the person who employs the term at the thoughts of such object. In like manner, when a word is spoken of as being used in a bad sense, all that is necessarily meant is this: that, in conjunction with the idea of the object it is put to signify, it conveys an idea of *disapprobation:* that is, of a displeasure entertained by the person who employs the term at the thoughts of such object. Now, the circumstance on which such approbation is grounded, will, as naturally as any other, be the opinion of the *goodness* of the object in question, as above explained: such, at least, it must be, upon the principle of utility: so, on the other hand, the circumstance on which any such disapprobation is grounded, will, as naturally as any other, be the opinion of the *badness* of the object: such, at least, it must be, in as far as the principle of utility is taken for the standard.

Now there are certain motives which, unless in a few particular cases, have scarcely any other name to be expressed by but such a word as is used only in a good sense. This is the case, for example, with the motives of piety and honour. The consequence of this is, that if, in speaking of such a motive, a man should have occasion to apply the epithet bad to any actions which he mentions as apt to result from it, he must appear to be guilty of a contradiction in terms. But the names of motives which have scarcely any other name to be expressed by, but such a word as is used only in a bad sense, are many more.[17] This is the case, for example, with the motives of lust and avarice. And, accordingly, if in speaking of any such motive, a man should have occasion to apply the epithets good or indifferent to any actions which he mentions as apt to result from it, he must here also appear to be guilty of a similar contradiction. [18]

[17] For the reason, see chap. xi. (Dispositions), par. xvii. note.

[18] To this imperfection of language, and nothing more, are to be attributed, in great measure, the violent clamours that have from time to time been raised against those ingenious moralists, who, travelling out of the beaten tract of speculation, have found more or less difficulty in disentangling themselves from the shackles of ordinary language: such as Rochefoucault, Mandeville and Helvetius. To the unsoundness of their opinions, and, with still greater injustice, to the corruption of their hearts, was often imputed, what was most commonly owing either to a want of skill, in matters of language on the part of the author, or a want of discernment, possibly now and then in some instances a want of probity, on the part of the commentator.

This perverse association of ideas cannot, it is evident, but throw great difficulties in the way of the inquiry now before us. Confining himself to the language most in use, a man can scarce avoid running, in appearance, into perpetual contradictions. His propositions will appear, on the one hand, repugnant to truth; and on the other hand, adverse to utility. As parodoxes, they will excite contempt: as mischievous paradoxes, indignation. For the truths he labours to convey, however important, and however salutary, his reader is never the better: and he himself is much the worse. To obviate this inconvenience, completely, he has but this one unpleasant remedy; to lay aside the old phraseology and invent a new one. Happy the man whose language is ductile enough to permit him this resource. To palliate the inconvenience, where that method of obviating it is impracticable, he has nothing left for it but to enter into a long discussion, to state the whole matter at large, to confess, that for the sake of promoting the purposes, he has violated the established laws of language, and to throw himself upon the mercy of his readers. [19]

[19] Happily, language is not always so intractable, but that by making use of two words instead of one, a man may avoid the inconvenience of fabricating words that are absolutely new. Thus instead of the word lust, by putting together two words in common use, he may frame the neutral expression, sexual desire: instead of the word avarice, by putting together two other words also in common use, he may frame the neutral expression, pecuniary interest. This, accordingly, is the course which I have taken. In these instances, indeed, even the combination is not novel: the only novelty there is consists in the steady adherence to the one neutral expression, rejecting altogether the terms, of which the import is infected by adventitious and unsuitable ideas.

In the catalogue of motives, corresponding to the several sorts of pains and pleasures, I have inserted such as have occurred to me. I cannot pretend to warrant it complete. To make sure of rendering it so, the only way would be, to turn over the dictionary from beginning to end: an operation which, in a view to perfection, would be necessary for more purposes than this.

John Stuart Mill (1806—1873)

John Stuart Mill was brought up by his father and Jeremy Bentham in strictest Utilitarian orthodoxy. He was subjected to a stupendous plan of studies that saw him learning mathematics and Greek at the age of three, logic and political economy at twelve. An enthusiastic Benthamite at first, he suffered a nervous breakdown at the age of twenty-one from which he emerged slowly with a new appreciation, which his earlier training had wholly neglected, of the emotional side of experience, and a hatred of sectarianism coupled with a willingness to understand and accommodate other points of view. In his moral philosophy the effect was a utilitarianism which, despite his protestations to the contrary, departs from the doctrine of Bentham on fundamental issues. Mill was the intellectual spokesman for the liberalism of his time. His most important writings are, in addition to such philosophical treatises as *System of Logic* (1843) and *Examination of Sir William Hamilton's Philosophy* (1865), the *Principles of Political Economy* (1848), *On Liberty* (1859), *Considerations on Representative Government* (1861), *Subjection of Women* (1869), and his *Autobiography,* published posthumously in 1873.

UTILITARIANISM [1]

CHAPTER 1

GENERAL REMARKS

There are few circumstances among those which make up the present condition of human knowledge more unlike what might have been expected, or more significant of the backward state in which speculation on the most important subjects still lingers, than the little progress which has been

[1] London, 1863.

made in the decision of the controversy respecting the criterion of right and wrong. From the dawn of philosophy, the question concerning the *summum bonum,* or, what is the same thing, concerning the foundation of morality, has been accounted the main problem in speculative thought, has occupied the most gifted intellects and divided them into sects and schools, carrying on a vigorous warfare against one another. And after more than two thousand years the same discussions continue, philosophers are still ranged under the same contending banners, and neither thinkers nor mankind at large seem nearer to being unanimous on the subject than when the youth Socrates listened to the old Protagoras, and asserted (if Plato's dialogue be grounded on a real conversation) the theory of utilitarianism against the popular morality of the so-called sophist.

It is true that similar confusion and uncertainty and, in some cases, similar discordance exist respecting the first principles of all the sciences, not excepting that which is deemed the most certain of them—mathematics, without much impairing, generally indeed without impairing at all, the trustworthiness of the conclusions of those sciences. An apparent anomaly, the explanation of which is that the detailed doctrines of a science are not usually deduced from, nor depend for their evidence upon, what are called its first principles. Were it not so, there would be no science more precarious, or whose conclusions were more insufficiently made out, than algebra, which derives none of its certainty from what are commonly taught to learners as its elements, since these, as laid down by some of its most eminent teachers, are as full of fictions as English law, and of mysteries as theology. The truths which are ultimately accepted as the first principles of a science are really the last results of metaphysical analysis, practised on the elementary notions with which the science is conversant; and their relation to the science is not that of foundations to an edifice, but of roots to a tree, which may perform their office equally well though they be never dug down to and exposed to light. But though in science the particular truths precede the general theory, the contrary might be expected to be the case with a practical art, such as morals or legislation. All action is for the sake of some end, and rules of action, it seems natural to suppose, must take their whole character and color from the end to which they are subservient. When we engage in a pursuit, a clear and precise conception of what we are pursuing would seem to be the first thing we need, instead of the last we are to look forward to. A test of right and wrong must be the means, one would think, of ascertaining what is right or wrong, and not a consequence of having already ascertained it.

The difficulty is not avoided by having recourse to the popular theory of a natural faculty, a sense or instinct, informing us of right and wrong. For —besides that the existence of such a moral instinct is itself one of the matters in dispute—those believers in it who have any pretensions to philosophy have been obliged to abandon the idea that it discerns what is right or wrong in the particular case in hand, as our other senses discern the sight or sound actually present. Our moral faculty, according to all those of its interpreters who are entitled to the name of thinkers, supplies us only with the general principles of moral judgments; it is a branch of our reason, not of our sensitive faculty; and must be looked to for the abstract doctrines of morality, not for perception of it in the concrete. The intuitive, no less than what may be termed the inductive, school of ethics insists on the necessity of general laws. They both agree that the morality of an individual action is not a question of direct perception, but of the application of a law to an individual case. They recognize also, to a great extent, the same moral laws, but differ as to their evidence and the source from which they derive their authority. According to the one opinion, the principles of morals are evident a priori, requiring nothing to command assent except that the meaning of the terms be understood.

According to the other doctrine, right and wrong, as well as truth and falsehood, are questions of observation and experience. But both hold equally that morality must be deduced from principles; and the intuitive school affirm as strongly as the inductive that there is a science of morals. Yet they seldom attempt to make out a list of the *a priori* principles which are to serve as the premises of the science; still more rarely do they make any effort to reduce those various principles to one first principle, or common ground of obligation. They either assume the ordinary precepts of morals as of *a priori* authority, or they lay down as the common groundwork of those maxims, some generality much less obviously authoritative than the maxims themselves, and which has never succeeded in gaining popular acceptance. Yet to support their pretensions there ought either to be some one fundamental principle or law at the root of all morality, or, if there be several, there should be a determinate order of precedence among them; and the one principle, or the rule for deciding between the various principles when they conflict, ought to be self-evident.

To inquire how far the bad effects of this deficiency have been mitigated in practice, or to what extent the moral beliefs of mankind have been vitiated or made uncertain by the absence of any distinct recognition of an ultimate standard, would imply a complete survey and criticism of past and present ethical doctrine. It would, however, be easy to show that whatever steadiness or consistency these moral beliefs have attained has been mainly due to the tacit influence of a standard not recognized. Although the non-existence of an acknowledged first principle has made ethics not so much a guide as a consecration of men's actual sentiments, still, as men's sentiments, both in favor and of aversion, are greatly influenced by what they suppose to be the effect of things upon their happiness, the principle of utility, or, as Bentham latterly called it, the greatest happiness principle, has had a large share in forming the moral doctrines even of those who most scornfully reject its authority. Nor is there any school of thought which refuses to admit that the influence of actions on happiness is a most material and even predominant consideration in many of the details of morals, however unwilling to acknowledge it as the fundamental principle of morality and the source of moral obligation. I might go much further and say that to all those *a priori* moralists who deem it necessary to argue at all, utilitarian arguments are indispensable. It is not my present purpose to criticize these thinkers; but I cannot help referring, for illustration, to a systematic treatise by one of the most illustrious of them, the *Metaphysics of Ethics* by Kant. This remarkable man, whose system of thought will long remain one of the landmarks in the history of philosophical speculation, does, in the treatise in question, lay down a universal first principle as the origin and ground of moral obligation; it is this: "So act that the rule on which thou actest would admit of being adopted as a law by all rational beings." But when he begins to deduce from this precept any of the actual duties of morality, he fails, almost grotesquely, to show that there would be any contradiction, any logical (not to say physical) impossibility, in the adoption by all rational beings of the most outrageously immoral rules of conduct. All he knows is that the *consequences* of their universal adoption would be such as no one would choose to incur.

On the present occasion, I shall, without further discussion of the other theories, attempt to contribute something towards the understanding and appreciation of the "utilitarian" or "happiness" theory, and towards such proof as it is susceptible of. It is evident that this cannot be proof in the ordinary and popular meaning of the term. Questions of ultimate ends are not amenable to direct proof. Whatever can be proved to be good must be so by being shown to be a means to something admitted to be good without proof. The medical art is proved to be good by its conducing to health; but how is it possible to prove that health is good? The art of music is good, for the reason, among others, that it produces pleasure; but what proof is it possible to give that pleasure is good? If, then, it is asserted that there is a comprehensive formula, including all things which are in themselves good, and that whatever else is good is not so as an end but as a means, the formula may be accepted or rejected, but is not a subject of what is commonly understood by proof. We are not, however, to infer that its acceptance or rejection must depend on blind impulse, or arbitrary choice. There is a larger meaning of the word "proof," in which this question is as amenable to it as any other of the disputed questions of philosophy. The subject is within the cognizance of the rational faculty; and neither does that faculty deal with it solely in the way of intuition. Considerations may be presented capable of determining the intellect either to give or withhold its assent to the doctrine; and this is equivalent to proof.

We shall examine presently of what nature are these considerations; in what manner they apply to the case, and what rational grounds, therefore, can be given for accepting or rejecting the utilitarian formula. But it is a preliminary condition of rational acceptance or rejection that the formula should be correctly understood. I believe that the very imperfect notion ordinarily formed of its meaning is the chief obstacle which impedes its reception, and that, could it be cleared even from only the grosser misconceptions the question would be greatly simplified and a large proportion of its difficulties removed. Before, therefore, I attempt to enter into the philosophical grounds which can be given for assenting to the utilitarian standard, I shall offer some illustrations of the doctrine itself, with the view of showing more clearly what it is, distinguishing it from what it is not, and disposing of such of the practical objections to it as either originate in, or are closely connected with, mistaken interpretation of its meaning. Having thus prepared the ground, I shall afterwards endeavor to throw such light as I can call upon the question considered as one of philosophical theory.

CHAPTER II

WHAT UTILITARIANISM IS

A passing remark is all that needs be given to the ignorant blunder of supposing that those who stand up for utility as the test of right and wrong use the term in that restricted and merely colloquial sense in which utility is opposed to pleasure. An apology is due to the philosophical opponents of utilitarianism, for even the momentary appearance of confounding them with anyone capable of so absurd a misconception; which is the more extraordinary, inasmuch as the contrary accusation, of referring everything to pleasure, and that, too, in its grossest form, is another of the common charges against utilitarianism: and, as has been pointedly remarked by an able writer, the same sort of persons, and often the very same persons, denounce the theory "as impracticably dry when the word 'utility' precedes the word 'pleasure,' and as too practically voluptuous when the word 'pleasure' precedes the word 'utility'." Those who know anything about the matter are aware that every writer, from Epicurus to Bentham, who maintained the theory of utility, meant by it, not something to be contradistinguished from pleasure, but pleasure itself, together with exemption from pain; and instead of opposing the useful to the agreeable or the ornamental, have always declared that the useful means these, among other things. Yet the common herd, including the herd of writers, not only in newspapers and periodicals, but in books of weight and pretension, are perpetually falling into this shallow mistake. Having caught up the word "utilitarian," while knowing nothing whatever about it but its sound, they habitually express by it the rejection or the neglect of pleasure in some of its forms: of beauty, of ornament, or of amusement. Nor is the term thus ignorantly misapplied solely in disparagement, but occasionally in compliment, as though it implied superiority to frivolity and the mere pleasures of the moment. And this perverted use is the only one in which the word is popularly known, and the one from which the new generation are acquiring their sole notion of its meaning. Those who introduced the word, but who had for many years discontinued it as a distinctive appellation, may well feel themselves called upon to resume it if by doing so they can hope to contribute anything towards rescuing it from this utter degradation.[2]

[2] The author of this essay has reason for believing himself to be the first person who brought the word "utilitarian"

The creed which accepts as the foundation of morals "utility" or the "greatest happiness principle" holds that actions are right in proportion as they tend to promote happiness, wrong as they tend to produce the reverse of happiness. By happiness is intended pleasure, and the absence of pain; by unhappiness, pain, and the privation of pleasure. To give a clear view of the moral standard set up by the theory, much more requires to be said; in particular, what things it includes in the ideas of pain and pleasure; and to what extent this is left an open question. But these supplementary explanations do not affect the theory of life on which this theory of morality is grounded—namely, that pleasure and freedom from pain are the only things desirable as ends; and that all desirable things (which are as numerous in the utilitarian as in any other scheme) are desirable either for the pleasure inherent in themselves, or as means to the promotion of pleasure and the prevention of pain.

Now such a theory of life excites in many minds, and among them in some of the most estimable in feeling and purpose, inveterate dislike. To suppose that life has (as they express it) no higher end than pleasure—no better and nobler object of desire and pursuit—they designate as utterly mean and groveling; as a doctrine worthy only of swine, to whom the followers

into use. He did not invent it, but adopted it from a passing expression in Mr. Galt's *Annals of the Parish*. After using it as a designation for several years, he and others abandoned it from a growing dislike to anything resembling a badge or watchword of sectarian distinction. But as a name for one single opinion, not a set of opinions—to denote the recognition of utility as a standard, not any particular way of applying it—the term supplies a want in the language, and offers, in many cases, a convenient mode of avoiding tiresome circumlocution.

of Epicurus were, at a very early period, contemptuously likened; and modern holders of the doctrine are occasionally made the subject of equally polite comparisons by its German, French, and English assailants.

When thus attacked, the Epicureans have always answered that it is not they, but their accusers, who represent human nature in a degrading light, since the accusation supposes human beings to be capable of no pleasures except those of which swine are capable. If this supposition were true, the charge could not be gainsaid, but would then be no longer an imputation; for if the sources of pleasure were precisely the same to human beings and to swine, the rule of life which is good enough for the one would be good enough for the other. The comparison of the Epicurean life to that of beasts is felt as degrading, precisely because a beast's pleasures do not satisfy a human being's conceptions of happiness. Human beings have faculties more elevated than the animal appetites and, when once made conscious of them, do not regard anything as happiness which does not include their gratification. I do not, indeed, consider the Epicureans to have been by any means faultless in drawing out their scheme of consequences from the utilitarian principle. To do this in any sufficient manner, many Stoic, as well as Christian, elements require to be included. But there is no known Epicurean theory of life which does not assign to the pleasures of the intellect, of the feelings and imagination, and of the moral sentiments, a much higher value of pleasures than to those of mere sensation. It must be admitted, however, that utilitarian writers in general have placed the superiority of mental over bodily pleasures chiefly in the greater permanency, safety, uncostliness, etc., of the

former—that is, in their circumstantial advantages rather than in their intrinsic nature. And on all these points utilitarians have fully proved their case; but they might have taken the other and, as it may be called, higher ground with entire consistency. It is quite compatible with the principle of utility to recognize the fact that some kinds of pleasure are more desirable and more valuable than others. It would be absurd that, while, in estimating all other things, quality is considered as well as quantity, the estimation of pleasures should be supposed to depend on quantity alone.

If I am asked what I mean by difference of quality in pleasures, or what makes one pleasure more valuable than another, merely as a pleasure, except its being greater in amount, there is but one possible answer. Of two pleasures, if there be one to which all or almost all who have experience of both give a decided preference, irrespective of a feeling of moral obligation to prefer it, that is the more desirable pleasure. If one of the two is, by those who are competently acquainted with both, placed so far above the other that they prefer it, even though knowing it to be attended with a greater amount of discontent, and would not resign it for any quantity of the other pleasure which their nature is capable of, we are justified in ascribing to the preferred enjoyment a superiority in quality so far outweighing quantity as to render it, in comparison, of small account.

Now it is an unquestionable fact that those who are equally acquainted with and equally capable of appreciating and enjoying both, do give a most marked preference to the manner of existence which employs their higher faculties. Few human creatures would consent to be changed into any of the lower animals for a promise of the fullest allowance of a beast's pleasures; no intelligent human being would consent to be a fool, no instructed person would be an ignoramus, no person of feeling and conscience would be selfish and base, even though they should be persuaded that the fool, the dunce, or the rascal is better satisfied with his lot than they are with theirs. They would not resign what they possess more than he for the most complete satisfaction of all the desires which they have in common with him. If they ever fancy they would, it is only in cases of unhappiness so extreme that to escape from it they would exchange their lot for almost any other, however undesirable in their own eyes. A being of higher faculties requires more to make him happy, is capable probably of more acute suffering, and certainly accessible to it at more points, than one of an inferior type; but in spite of these liabilities, he can never really wish to sink into what he feels to be a lower grade of existence. We may give what explanation we please of this unwillingness; we may attribute it to pride, a name which is given indiscriminately to some of the most and to some of the least estimable feelings of which mankind are capable: we may refer it to the love of liberty and personal independence, an appeal to which was with the Stoics one of the most effective means for the inculcation of it; to the love of power or to the love of excitement, both of which do really enter into and contribute to it; but its most appropriate appellation is a sense of dignity, which all human beings possess in one form or other, and in some, though by no means in exact, proportion to their higher faculties, and which is so essential a part of the happiness of those in whom it is strong that nothing which conflicts with it could be otherwise than mo-

mentarily an object of desire to them. Whoever supposes that this preference takes place at a sacrifice of happiness—that the superior being, in anything like equal circumstances, is not happier than the inferior—confounds the two very different ideas of happiness and content. It is indisputable that the being whose capacities of enjoyment are low has the greatest chance of having them fully satisfied; and a highly endowed being will always feel that any happiness which he can look for, as the world is constituted, is imperfect. But he can learn to bear its imperfections, if they are at all bearable; and they will not make him envy the being who is indeed unconscious of the imperfections, but only because he feels not at all the good which those imperfections qualify. It is better to be a human being dissatisfied than a pig satisfied; better to be Socrates dissatisfied than a fool satisfied. And if the fool, or the pig, are of a different opinion, it is because they only know their own side of the question. The other party to the comparison knows both sides.

It may be objected that many who are capable of the higher pleasures occasionally, under the influence of temptation, postpone them to the lower. But this is quite compatible with a full appreciation of the intrinsic superiority of the higher. Men often, from infirmity of character, make their election for the nearer good, though they know it to be the less valuable; and this no less when the choice is between two bodily pleasures than when it is between bodily and mental. They pursue sensual indulgences to the injury of health, though perfectly aware that health is the greater good. It may be further objected that many who begin with youthful enthusiasm for everything noble, as they advance in years, sink into indolence and selfishness.

[handwritten marginal note:] what Util. says to an Epicurean

But I do not believe that those who undergo this very common change voluntarily choose the lower description of pleasures in preference to the higher. I believe that, before they devote themselves exclusively to the one, they have already become incapable of the other. Capacity for the nobler feelings is in most natures a very tender plant, easily killed, not only by hostile influences, but by mere want of sustenance; and in the majority of young persons it speedily dies away if the occupations to which their position in life has devoted them, and the society into which it has tł rown them, are not favorable to k eping that higher capacity in exercis . Men lose their high aspirations as they lose their intellectual tastes, because they have not time or opportunity for indulging them; and they addict themselves to inferior pleasures, not because they deliberately prefer them, but because they are either the only ones to which they have access, or the only ones which they are any longer capable of enjoying. It may be questioned whether any one who has remained equally susceptible to both classes of pleasures, ever knowingly and calmly preferred the lower, though many, in all ages, have broken down in an ineffectual attempt to combine both.

From this verdict of the only competent judges, I apprehend there can be no appeal. On a question which is the best worth having of two pleasures, or which of two modes of existence is the most grateful to the feelings, apart from its moral attributes and from its consequences, the judgment of those who are qualified by knowledge of both, or, if they differ, that of the majority of them, must be admitted as final. And there needs be the less hesitation to accept this judgment respecting the quality of pleasures, since there is no other tribunal to be referred to even on the question of quantity. What means are there of determining which is the acutest of two pains, or the intensest of two pleasurable sensations, except the general suffrage of those who are familiar with both? Neither pains nor pleasures are homogeneous, and pain is always heterogeneous with pleasure. What is there to decide whether a particular pleasure is worth purchasing at the cost of a particular pain, except the feelings and judgment of the experienced? When, therefore, those feelings and judgment declare the pleasures derived from the higher faculties to be preferable *in kind*, apart from the question of intensity, to those of which the animal nature, disjoined from the higher faculties, is susceptible, they are entitled on this subject to the same regard.

I have dwelt on this point, as being a necessary part of a perfectly just conception of utility or happiness considered as the directive rule of human conduct. But it is by no means an indispensable condition to the acceptance of the utilitarian standard; for that standard is not the agent's own greatest happiness, but the greatest amount of happiness altogether; and if it may possibly be doubted whether a noble character is always the happier for its nobleness, there can be no doubt that it makes other people happier, and that the world in general is immensely a gainer by it. Utilitarianism, therefore, could only attain its end by the general cultivation of nobleness of character, even if each individual were only benefited by the nobleness of others, and his own, so far as happiness is concerned, were a sheer deduction from the benefit. But the bare enunciation of such an absurdity as this last renders refutation superfluous.

According to the greatest happiness principle, as above explained, the ultimate end, with reference to and for the sake of which all other things are desirable—whether we are considering our own good or that of other people—is an existence exempt as far as possible from pain, and as rich as possible in enjoyments, both in point of quantity and quality; the test of quality and the rule for measuring it against quantity being the preference felt by those who, in their opportunities of experience, to which must be added their habits of self-consciousness and self-observation, are best furnished with the means of comparison. This, being, according to the utilitarian opinion, the end of human action, is necessarily also the standard of morality, which may accordingly be defined "the rules and precepts for human conduct," by the observance of which an existence such as has been described might be, to the greatest extent possible, secured to all mankind; and not to them only, but, so far as the nature of things admits, to the whole sentient creation.

Against this doctrine, however, arises another class of objectors who say that happiness, in any form, cannot be the rational purpose of human life and action; because, in the first place, it is unattainable; and they contemptuously ask, What right hast thou to be happy?—a question which Mr. Carlyle clenches by the addition, What right, a short time ago, hadst thou even *to be*? Next they say that men can do *without* happiness; that all noble human beings have felt this, and could not have become noble but by learning the lesson of *Entsagen*, or renunciation; which lesson, thoroughly learnt and submitted to, they affirm to be the beginning and necessary condition of all virtue.

The first of these objections would go to the root of the matter were it well founded; for if no happiness is to be had at all by human beings, the attainment of it cannot be the end of morality or of any rational conduct. Though, even in that case, something might still be said for the utilitarian theory, since utility includes not solely the pursuit of happiness, but the prevention or mitigation of unhappiness; and if the former aim be chimerical, there will be all the greater scope and more imperative need for the latter, so long at least as mankind think fit to live, and do not take refuge in the simultaneous act of suicide recommended under certain conditions by Novalis. When, however, it is thus positively asserted to be impossible that human life should be happy, the assertion, if not something like a verbal quibble, is at least an exaggeration. If by happiness be meant a continuity of highly pleasurable excitement, it is evident enough that this is impossible. A state of exalted pleasure lasts only moments or in some cases, and with some intermissions, hours or days, and is the occasional brilliant flash of enjoyment, not its permanent and steady flame. Of this the philosophers who have taught that happiness is the end of life were as fully aware as those who taunt them. The happiness which they meant was not a life of rapture; but moments of such, in an existence made up of few and transitory pains, many and various pleasures, with a decided predominance of the active over the passive, and having as the foundation of the whole not to expect more from life than it is capable of bestowing. A life thus composed, to those who have been fortunate enough to obtain it, has always appeared worthy of the name of happiness. And such an existence is even now the lot of many, during some considerable portion of their lives. The present wretched education and wretched social arrangements are the only real hindrance to its being attainable by almost all.

The objectors perhaps may doubt whether human beings, if taught to consider happiness as the end of life, would be satisfied with such a moderate share of it. But great numbers of mankind have been satisfied with much less. The main constituents of a satisfied life appear to be two, either of which by itself is often found sufficient for the purpose: tranquility and excitement. With much tranquility, many find that they can be content with very little pleasure; with much excitement, many can reconcile themselves to a considerable quantity of pain. There is assuredly no inherent impossibility of enabling even the mass of mankind to unite both, since the two are so far from being incompatible that they are in natural alliance, the prolongation of either being a preparation for, and exciting a wish for, the other. It is only those in whom indolence amounts to a vice that do not desire excitement after an interval of repose; it is only those in whom the need of excitement is a disease that feel the tranquility which follows excitement dull and insipid, instead of pleasurable in direct proportion to the excitement which preceded it. When people who are tolerably fortunate in their outward lot do not find in life sufficient enjoyment to make it valuable to them, the cause generally is caring for nobody but themselves. To those who have neither public nor private affections, the excitements of life are much curtailed, and in any case dwindle in value as the time approaches when all selfish interests must be terminated by death; while those who leave after them objects of personal affection, and especially those who have also cultivated a fellow-feeling with the collective interests of mankind, retain as lively an interest in life on the eve of death as in the vigor of youth and health. Next to selfishness, the principal cause which makes life unsatisfactory is want of mental cultivation. A cultivated mind — I do not mean that of a philosopher, but any mind to which the fountains of knowledge have been opened, and which has been taught, in any tolerable degree, to exercise its faculties—finds sources of inexhaustible interest in all that surrounds it: in the objects of nature, the achievements of art, the imaginations of poetry, the incidents of history, the ways of mankind, past and present, and their prospects in the future. It is possible, indeed, to become indifferent to all this, and that too without having exhausted a thousandth part of it, but only when one has had from the beginning no moral or human interest in these things, and has sought in them only the gratification of curiosity.

Now there is absolutely no reason in the nature of things why an amount of mental culture sufficient to give an intelligent interest in these objects of contemplation should not be the inheritance of every one born in a civilized country. As little is there an inherent necessity that any human being should be a selfish egotist, devoid of every feeling or care but those which center in his own miserable individuality. Something far superior to this is sufficiently common even now, to give ample earnest of what the human species may be made. Genuine private affections and a sincere interest in the public good are possible, though in unequal degrees, to every rightly brought up human being. In a world in which there is so much to interest, so much to enjoy, and so much also to correct and improve, every one who has this moderate amount of moral and intellectual requisites is capable of an existence which may be called enviable; and unless such a person, through bad laws or subjection to the will of others, is denied the liberty to use the sources of happiness within his reach, he will not fail to find this enviable existence, if he escape the positive evils of life, the great sources of physical and mental suffering—such as indigence, disease, and the unkindness, worthlessness, or premature loss of objects of affection. The main stress of the problem lies, therefore, in the contest with these calamities from which it is a rare good fortune entirely to escape; which, as things now are, cannot be obviated, and often cannot be in any material degree mitigated. Yet no one whose opinion deserves a moment's consideration can doubt that most of the great positive evils of the world are in themselves removable, and will, if human affairs continue to improve, be in the end reduced within narrow limits. Poverty, in any sense implying suffering, may be completely extinguished by the wisdom of society combined with the good sense and providence of individuals. Even that most intractable of enemies, disease, may be indefinitely reduced in dimensions by good physical and moral education and proper control of noxious influences, while the progress of science holds out a promise for the future of still more direct conquests over this detestable foe. And every advance in that direction relieves us from some, not only of the chances which cut short our own lives, but, what concerns us still more, which deprive us of those in whom our happiness is wrapt up. As for vicissitudes of fortune and other disappointments connected with worldly circumstances, these are principally the effect either of gross imprudence, of ill-regulated desires, or of bad or imperfect social institutions. All the grand sources, in short, of human suffering are in a great degree, many of them almost entirely, conquerable by human care and effort; and though their removal

is grievously slow— though a long succession of generations will perish in the breach before the conquest is completed, and this world becomes all that, if will and knowledge were not wanting, it might easily be made—yet every mind sufficiently intelligent and generous to bear a part, however small and inconspicuous, in the endeavour will draw a noble enjoyment from the contest itself, which he would not for any bribe in the form of selfish indulgence consent to be without.

And this leads to the true estimation of what is said by the objectors concerning the possibility and the obligation of learning to do without happiness. Unquestionably it is possible to do without happiness; it is done involuntarily by nineteen-twentieths of mankind, even in those parts of our present world which are least deep in barbarism; and it often has to be done voluntarily by the hero or the martyr, for the sake of something which he prizes more than his individual happiness. But this something, what is it, unless the happiness of others or some of the requisites of happiness? It is noble to be capable of resigning entirely one's own portion of happiness, or chances of it; but, after all, this self-sacrifice must be for some end; it is not its own end; and if we are told that its end is not happiness but virtue, which is better than happiness, I ask, would the sacrifice be made if the hero or martyr did not believe that it would earn for others immunity from similar sacrifices? Would it be made if he thought that his renunciation of happiness for himself would produce no fruit for any of his fellow creatures, but to make their lot like his, and place them also in the condition of persons who have renounced happiness? All honor to those who can abnegate for themselves the personal enjoyment of life when by such renunciation they contribute worthily to increase the amount of happiness in the world; but he who does it or professes to do it for any other purpose is no more deserving of admiration than the ascetic mounted on his pillar. He may be an inspiriting proof of what men *can* do, but assuredly not an example of what they *should*.

Though it is only in a very imperfect state of the world's arrangements that any one can best serve the happiness of others by the absolute sacrifice of his own, yet, so long as the world is in that imperfect state, I fully acknowledge that the readiness to make such a sacrifice is the highest virtue which can be found in man. I will add that in this condition of the world, paradoxical as the assertion may be, the conscious ability to do without happiness gives the best prospect of realizing such happiness as is attainable. For nothing except that consciousness can raise a person above the chances of life, by making him feel that, let fate and fortune do their worst, they have not power to subdue him; which, once felt, frees him from excess of anxiety concerning the evils of life, and enables him, like many a Stoic in the worst times of the Roman Empire, to cultivate in tranquility the sources of satisfaction accessible to him, without concerning himself about the uncertainty of their duration any more than about their inevitable end.

Meanwhile, let utilitarians never cease to claim the morality of self-devotion as a possession which belongs by as good a right to them as either to the Stoic or to the Transcendentalist. The utilitarian morality does recognize in human beings the power of sacrificing their own greatest good for the good of others. It only refuses to admit that the sacrifice is itself a good. A sacrifice which does not increase or tend to increase the sum total of happiness, it considers as wasted. The only self-renunciation which it applauds is devotion to the happiness, or to some of the means of happiness, of others, either of mankind collectively or of individuals within the limits imposed by the collective interests of mankind.

I must again repeat what the assailants of utilitarianism seldom have the justice to acknowledge, that the happiness which forms the utilitarian standard of what is right in conduct is not the agent's own happiness but that of all concerned. As between his own happiness and that of others, utilitarianism requires him to be as strictly impartial as a disinterested and benevolent spectator. In the golden rule of Jesus of Nazareth, we read the complete spirit of the ethics of utility. "To do as you would be done by," and "to love your neighbor as yourself," constitute the ideal perfection of utilitarian morality. As the means of making the nearest approach to this ideal, utility would enjoin, first, that laws and social arrangements should place the happiness or (as, speaking practically, it may be called) the interest of every individual as nearly as possible in harmony with the interest of the whole; and, secondly, that education and opinion, which have so vast a power over human character, should so use that power as to establish in the mind of every individual an indissoluble association between his own happiness and the good of the whole, especially between his own happiness and the practice of such modes of conduct, negative and positive, as regard for the universal happiness prescribes; so that not only he may be able to conceive the possibility of happiness to himself, consistently with conduct opposed to the general good, but also that a direct impulse to promote the general good may be in every individual one of the habitual motives of action, and the sentiments connected therewith may fill a large and prominent place in every human being's sentient existence. If the impugners of the utilitarian morality represented it to their own minds in this its true character, I know not what recommendation possessed by any other morality they could possibly affirm to be wanting to it; what more beautiful or more exalted developments of human nature any other ethical system can be supposed to foster, or what springs of action, not accessible to the utilitarian, such systems rely on for giving effect to their mandates.

The objectors to utilitarianism cannot always be charged with representing it in a discreditable light. On the contrary, those among them who entertain anything like a just idea of its disinterested character sometimes find fault with its standard as being too high for humanity. They say it is exacting too much to require that people shall always act from the inducement of promoting the general interests of society. But this is to mistake the very meaning of a standard of morals, and confound the rule of action with the motive of it. It is the business of ethics to tell us what are our duties, or by what test we may know them; but no system of ethics requires that the sole motive of all we do shall be a feeling of duty; on the contrary, ninety-nine hundredths of all our actions are done from other motives, and rightly so done if the rule of duty does not condemn them. It is the more unjust to utilitarianism that this particular misapprehension should be made a ground of objection to it, inasmuch as utilitarian moralists have gone beyond almost all others in affirming that the motive has nothing to do with the morality of the action, though much with the worth of the agent. He who saves a fellow creature from drowning does what is morally right, whether his motive be duty or the hope of being paid for his trouble; he who betrays the friend that trusts him is guilty of a crime, even if his object be to serve another friend to whom he is under greater obligations. But to speak only of actions done from the motive of duty, and in direct obedience to principle: it is a misapprehension of the utilitarian mode of thought to conceive it as implying that people should fix their minds upon so wide a generality as the world, or society at large. The great majority of good actions are intended not for the benefit of the world, but for that of individuals, of which the good of the world is made up; and the thoughts of the most virtuous man need not on these occasions travel beyond the particular persons concerned, except so far as is necessary to assure himself that in benefiting them he is not violating the rights, that is, the legitimate and authorized expectations, of any one else. The multiplication of happiness is, according to the utilitarian ethics, the object of virtue: the occasions on which any person (except one in a thousand) has it in his power to do this on an extended scale, in other words, to be a public benefactor, are but exceptional; and on these occasions alone is he called on to consider public utility; in every other case, private utility, the interest or happiness of some few persons, is all he has to attend to. Those alone the influence of whose actions extends to society in general need concern themselves habitually about so large an object. In the case of abstinences indeed— of things which people forbear to do from moral considerations, though the consequences in the particular case might be beneficial—it would be unworthy of an intelligent agent not to be consciously aware that the action is of a class which, if practiced generally, would be generally injurious, and that this is the ground of the obligation to abstain from it. The amount of regard for the public interest implied in this recognition is no greater than is demanded by every system of morals, for they all enjoin to abstain from whatever is manifestly pernicious to society.

The same considerations dispose of another reproach against the doctrine of utility, founded on a still grosser misconception of the purpose of a standard of morality, and of the very meaning of the words "right" and "wrong." It is often affirmed that utilitarianism renders men cold and unsympathizing; that it chills their moral feelings towards individuals; that it makes them regard only the dry and hard consideration of the consequences of actions, not taking into their moral estimate the qualities from which those actions emanate. If the assertion means that they do not allow their judgment respecting the rightness or wrongness of an action to be influenced by their opinion of the qualities of the person who does it, this is a complaint not against utilitarianism, but against any standard of morality at all; for certainly no known ethical standard decides an action to be good or bad because it is done by a good or a bad man, still less because done by an amiable, a brave, or a benevolent man, or the contrary. These considerations are relevant, not to the estimation of actions, but of persons; and there is nothing in the utilitarian theory inconsistent with the fact that there are other things which interest us in persons besides the rightness and wrongness of their actions. The Stoics, indeed, with the paradoxical misuse of language which was part of their system, and by which they strove to raise themselves above all concern about anything but virtue, were fond of saying that he who has that has everything; that he, and only he, is rich, is beautiful, is a king. But no claim of this description is made for the virtuous man by the utilitarian doctrine. Utilitarians are quite aware that there are other desirable possessions and qualities besides virtue, and are perfectly willing to allow to all of them their full worth. They are also aware that a right action does not necessarily indicate a virtuous character, and that actions which are blamable often proceed from qualities entitled to praise. When this is apparent in any particular case, it modifies their estimation, not certainly of the act, but of the agent. I grant that they are, notwithstanding, of opinion that in the long run the best proof of a good character is good actions; and resolutely refuse to consider any mental disposition as good of which the predominant tendency is to produce bad conduct. This makes them unpopular with many people; but it is an unpopularity which they must share with every one who regards the distinction between right and wrong in a serious light; and the reproach is not one which a conscientious utilitarian need be anxious to repel.

If no more be meant by the objection than that many utilitarians look on the morality of actions, as measured by the utilitarian standards, with too exclusive a regard, and do not lay sufficient stress upon the other beauties of character which go towards making a human being lovable or admirable, this may be admitted. Utilitarians who have cultivated their moral feelings, but not their sympathies, nor their artistic perceptions, do fall into this mistake; and so do all other moralists under the same conditions. What can be said in excuse for other moralists is equally available for them, namely, that, if there is to be any error, it is better that it should be on that side. As a matter of fact, we may affirm that among utilitarians, as among adherents of other systems, there is every imaginable degree of rigidity and of laxity in the application of their standard; some are even puritanically rigorous, while others are as indulgent as can possibly be desired by sinner or by sentimentalist. But on the whole, a doctrine which brings prominently forward the interest that mankind have in the repression and prevention of conduct which violates the moral law, is likely to be inferior to no other in turning the sanctions of opinion against such violations. It is true, the question, "What does violate the moral law?" is one on which those who recognize different standards of morality are likely now and then to differ. But difference of opinion on moral questions was not first introduced into the world by utilitarianism, while that doctrine does supply, if not always an easy, at all events a tangible and intelligible, mode of deciding such differences.

It may not be superfluous to notice a few more of the common misapprehensions of utilitarian ethics, even those which are so obvious and gross that it might appear impossible for any person of candor and intelligence to fall into them; since persons, even of considerable mental endowment, often give themselves so little trouble to understand the bearings of any opinion against which they entertain a prejudice, and men are in general so little conscious of this voluntary ignorance as a defect, that the vulgarest misunderstandings of ethical doctrines are continually met with in the deliberate writings of persons of the greatest pretensions both to high principle and to philosophy. We not uncommonly hear the doctrine of utility inveighed against as a *godless* doctrine. If it be necessary to say anything at all against so mere an assumption, we may say that the question depends upon what idea we have formed of the moral character of the Deity. If it be a true belief that God desires, above all things, the happiness of his creatures, and that this was his purpose in their creation, utility is not only not a godless doctrine, but more profoundly religious than any other. If it be meant that utilitarianism does not recognize the revealed will of God as the supreme law of morals, I answer that a utilitarian who believes in the perfect goodness and wisdom of God necessarily believes that whatever God has thought fit to reveal on the subject of morals must fulfil the requirements of utility in a supreme degree. But others besides utilitarians have been of opinion that the Christian revelation was intended, and is fitted, to inform the hearts and minds of mankind with a spirit which should enable them to find for themselves what is right, and incline them to do it when found, rather than to tell them, except in a very general way, what it is; and that we need a doctrine of ethics, carefully followed out, to *interpret* to us the will of God. Whether this opinion is correct or not, it is superfluous here to discuss; since whatever aid religion, either natural or revealed, can afford to ethical investigation, is as open to the utilitarian moralist as to any other. He can use it as the testimony of God to the usefulness or hurtfulness of any given course of action, by as good a right as others can use it for the indication of a transcendental law, having no connection with usefulness or with happiness.

Again, utility is often summarily stigmatized as an immoral doctrine by giving it the name of "expediency," and taking advantage of the popular use of that term to contrast it with principle. But the expedient, in the sense in which it is opposed to the right, generally means that which is expedient for the particular interest of the agent himself; as when a minister sacrifices the interests of his country to keep himself in place. When it means anything better than this, it means that which is expedient for some immediate object, some temporary purpose, but which violates a rule whose observance is expedient in a much higher degree. The expedient, in this sense, instead of being the same thing with the useful, is a branch of the hurtful. Thus it would often be expedient, for the purpose of getting over some momentary embarrassment, or attaining some object immediately useful to ourselves or others, to tell a lie. But inasmuch as the cultivation in ourselves of a sensitive feeling on the subject of veracity is one of the most useful, and the enfeeblement of that feeling one of the most hurtful, things to which our conduct can be instrumental; and inasmuch as any, even unintentional, deviation from truth does that much towards weakening the trustworthiness of human assertion, which is not only the principal support of all present social well-being but the insufficiency of which does more than any one thing that can be named to keep back civilization, virtue, everything on which human happiness on the largest scale depends—we feel that the violation, for a present advantage, of a rule of such transcendent expediency is not expedient, and that he who, for the sake of convenience to himself or to some other individual, does what depends on him to deprive mankind of the good, and inflict upon them the evil, involved in the greater or less reliance which they can place in each other's word, acts the part of one of their worst enemies. Yet

that even this rule, sacred as it is, admits of possible exceptions is acknowledged by all moralists; the chief of which is when the withholding of some fact (as of information from a malefactor, or of bad news from a person dangerously ill) would save an individual (especially an individual other than oneself) from great and unmerited evil, and when the withholding can only be effected by denial. But in order that the exception may not extend itself beyond the need, and may have the least possible effect in weakening reliance on veracity, it ought to be recognized and, if possible, its limits defined; and, if the principle of utility is good for anything, it must be good for weighing these conflicting utilities against one another, and marking out the region within which one or the other preponderates.

Again, defenders of utility often find themselves called upon to reply to such objections as this—that there is not time, previous to action, for calculating and weighing the effects of any line of conduct on the general happiness. This is exactly as if any one were to say that it is impossible to guide our conduct by Christianity because there is not time, on every occasion on which anything has to be done, to read through the Old and New Testaments. The answer to the objection is that there has been ample time, namely, the whole past duration of the human species. During all that time, mankind have been learning by experience the tendencies of actions; on which experience all the prudence, as well as all the morality, of life are dependent. People talk as if the commencement of this course of experience had hitherto been put off, and as if, at the moment when some man feels tempted to meddle with the property or life of another, he had to begin considering for the first time whether murder and theft are injurious to human happiness. Even then I do not think that he would find the question very puzzling; but, at all events, the matter is now done to his hand. It is truly a whimsical supposition that, if mankind were agreed in considering utility to be the test of morality, they would remain without any agreement as to what *is* useful, and would take no measures for having their notions on the subject taught to the young, and enforced by law and opinion. There is no difficulty in proving any ethical standard whatever to work ill if we suppose universal idiocy to be conjoined with it; but on any hypothesis short of that, mankind must by this time have acquired positive beliefs as to the effects of some actions on their happiness; and the beliefs which have thus come down are the rules of morality for the multitude, and for the philosopher until he has succeeded in finding better. That philosophers might easily do this, even now, on many subjects; that the received code of ethics is by no means of divine right; and that mankind have still much to learn as to the effects of actions on the general happiness, I admit or rather earnestly maintain. The corollaries from the principle of utility, like the precepts of every practical art, admit of indefinite improvement, and, in a progressive state of the human mind, their improvement is perpetually going on. But to consider the rules of morality as improvable is one thing; to pass over the intermediate generalization entirely and endeavor to test each individual action directly by the first principle is another. It is a strange notion that the acknowledgment of a first principle is inconsistent with the admission of secondary ones. To inform a traveller respecting the place of his ultimate destination is not to forbid the use of landmarks and direction-posts on the way. The proposition that happiness is the end and aim of morality does not mean that no road ought to be laid down to that goal, or that persons going thither should not be advised to take one direction rather than another. Men really ought to leave off talking a kind of nonsense on this subject, which they would neither talk nor listen to on other matters of practical concernment. Nobody argues that the art of navigation is not founded on astronomy because sailors cannot wait to calculate the Nautical Almanac. Being rational creatures, they go to sea with it ready calculated; and all rational creatures go out upon the sea of life with their minds made up on the common questions of right and wrong, as well as on many of the far more difficult questions of wise and foolish. And this, as long as foresight is a human quality, it is to be presumed they will continue to do. Whatever we adopt as the fundamental principle of morality, we require subordinate principles to apply it by; the impossibility of doing without them, being common to all systems, can afford no argument against any one in particular; but gravely to argue as if no such secondary principles could be had, and as if mankind had remained till now, and always must remain, without drawing any general conclusions from the experience of human life, is as high a pitch, I think, as absurdity has ever reached in philosophical controversy.

The remainder of the stock arguments against utilitarianism mostly consist in laying to its charge the common infirmities of human nature, and the general difficulties which embarrass conscientious persons in shaping their course through life. We are told that a utilitarian will be apt to make his own particular case an exception to moral rules, and, when under temptation, will see a utility in the breach of a rule, greater than he will see in its observance. But is utility the only creed which is able to furnish us with excuses for evil doing, and means of cheating our own conscience? They are afforded in abundance by all doctrines which recognize as a fact in morals the existence of conflicting considerations, which all doctrines do that have been believed by sane persons. It is not the fault of any creed, but of the complicated nature of human affairs, that rules of conduct cannot be so framed as to require no exceptions, and that hardly any kind of action can safely be laid down as either always obligatory or always condemnable. There is no ethical creed which does not temper the rigidity of its laws by giving a certain latitude, under the moral responsibility of the agent, for accommodation to peculiarities of circumstances; and under every creed, at the opening thus made, self-deception and dishonest casuistry get in. There exists no moral system under which there do not arise unequivocal cases of conflicting obligation. These are the real difficulties, the knotty points both in the theory of ethics and in the conscientious guidance of personal conduct. They are overcome practically, with greater or with less success, according to the intellect and virtue of the individual; but it can hardly be pretended than anyone will be the less qualified for dealing with them, from possessing an ultimate standard to which conflicting rights and duties can be referred. If utility is the ultimate source of moral obligations, utility may be invoked to decide between them when their demands are incompatible. Though the application of the standard may be difficult, it is better than none at all; while in other systems the moral laws all claiming independent authority, there is no common umpire entitled to

interfere between them; their claims to precedence one over another rest on little better than sophistry, and, unless determined, as they generally are, by the unacknowledged influence of consideration of utility, afford a free scope for the action of personal desires and partialities. We must remember that only in these cases of conflict between secondary principles is it requisite that first principles should be appealed to. There is no case of moral obligation in which some secondary principle is not involved; and if only one, there can seldom be any real doubt which one it is, in the mind of any person by whom the principle itself is recognized.

CHAPTER III

OF THE ULTIMATE SANCTION OF THE
PRINCIPLE OF UTILITY

The question is often asked, and properly so, in regard to any supposed moral standard—What is its sanction? what are the motives to obey? or more specifically, what is the source of its obligation? whence does it derive its binding force? It is a necessary part of moral philosophy to provide the answer to this question, which, though frequently assuming the shape of an objection to the utilitarian morality, as if it had some special applicability to that above others, really arises in regard to all standards. It arises, in fact, whenever a person is called on to *adopt* a standard, or refer morality to any basis on which he has not been accustomed to rest it. For the customary morality, that which education and opinion have consecrated is the only one which presents itself to the mind with the feeling of being *in itself* obligatory; and when a person is asked to believe that this morality *derives* its obligation from some general principle round which custom has not thrown the same halo, the assertion is to him a paradox; the supposed corollaries seem to have a more binding force than the original theorem; the superstructure seems to stand better without than with what is represented as its foundation. He says to himself, I feel that I am bound not to rob or murder, betray or deceive; but why am I bound to promote the general happiness? If my own happiness lies in something else, why may I not give that the preference?

If the view adopted by the utilitarian philosophy of the nature of the moral sense be correct, this difficulty will always present itself until the influences which form moral character have taken the same hold of the principle which they have taken of some of the consequences—until, by the improvement of education, the feeling of unity with our fellow creatures shall be (what it cannot be denied that Christ intended it to be) as deeply rooted in our character, and to our own consciousness as completely a part of our nature, as the horror of crime is in an ordinarily well brought up young person. In the meantime, however, the difficulty has no peculiar application to the doctrine of utility, but is inherent in every attempt to analyze morality and reduce it to principles; which, unless the principle is already in men's minds invested with as much sacredness as any of its applications, always seems to divest them of a part of their sanctity.

The principle of utility either has, or there is no reason why it might not have, all the sanctions which belong to any other system of morals. Those sanctions are either external or internal. Of the external sanctions it is not necessary to speak at any length. They are the hope of favor and the fear of displeasure from our fellow creatures or from the Ruler of the universe, along with whatever we may have of sympathy or affection for them, or of love and awe of Him, inclining us to do His will independently of selfish consequences. There is evidently no reason why all these motives for observance should not attach themselves to the utilitarian morality as completely and as powerfully as to any other. Indeed, those of them which refer to our fellow creatures are sure to do so, in proportion to the amount of general intelligence; for whether there be any other ground of moral obligation than the general happiness or not, men do desire happiness; and however imperfect may be their own practice, they desire and commend all conduct in others towards themselves by which they think their happiness is promoted. With regard to the religious motive, if men believe, as most profess to do, in the goodness of God, those who think that conduciveness to the general happiness is the essence or even only the criterion of good must necessarily believe that it is also that which God approves. The whole force therefore of external reward and punishment, whether physical or moral, and whether proceeding from God or from our fellow men, together with all that the capacities of human nature admit of disinterested devotion to either, become available to enforce the utilitarian morality, in proportion as that morality is recognized; and the more powerfully, the more the appliances of education and general cultivation are bent to the purpose.

So far as to external sanctions. The internal sanction of duty, whatever our standard of duty may be, is one and the same—a feeling in our own mind; a pain, more or less intense, attendant on violation of duty, which in properly cultivated moral natures rises, in the more serious cases, into shrinking from it as an impossibility. This feeling, when disinterested and connecting it-

self with the pure idea of duty, and
not with some particular form of it,
or with any of the merely accessory
circumstances, is the essence of conscience; though in that complex phenomenon as it actually exists, the
simple fact is in general all encrusted
over with collateral associations derived from sympathy, from love, and
still more from fear; from all the forms
of religious feeling; from the recollec-
tions of childhood and of all our past
life; from self-esteem, desire of the
esteem of others, and occasionally
even self-abasement. This extreme
complication is, I apprehend, the
origin of the sort of mystical character
which, by a tendency of the human
mind of which there are many other
examples, is apt to be attributed to
the idea of moral obligation, and
which leads people to beleive that the
idea cannot possibly attach itself to
any other objects than those which,
by a supposed mysterious law, are
found in our present experience to
excite it. Its binding force, however,
consists in the existence of a mass of
feeling which must be broken through
in order to do what violates our
standard of right, and which, if we
do nevertheless violate that standard,
will probably have to be encountered
afterwards in the form of remorse.
Whatever theory we have of the nature or origin of conscience, this is
what essentially constitutes it.

The ultimate sanction, therefore,
of all morality (external motives
apart) being a subjective feeling in
our own minds, I see nothing em-
barrassing to those whose standard is
utility in the question, What is the
sanction of that particular standard?
We may answer, the same as of all
other moral standards — the conscientious feelings of mankind. Undoubtedly this sanction has no binding
efficacy on those who do not possess
the feelings it appeals to; but neither

will these persons be more obedient
to any other moral principle than to
the utilitarian one. On them morality
of any kind has no hold but through
the external sanctions. Meanwhile the
feelings exist, a fact in human nature,
the reality of which, and the great
power with which they are capable of
acting on those in whom they have
been duly cultivated, are proved by
experience. No reason has ever been
shown why they may not be cultivated
to as great intensity in connection
with the utilitarian, as with any other
rule of morals.

There is, I am aware, a disposition
to believe that a person who sees in
moral obligation a transcendental fact,
an objective reality belonging to the
province of "things in themselves," is
likely to be more obedient to it than
one who believes it to be entirely subjective, having its seat in human consciousness only. But whatever a person's opinion may be on this point of
ontology, the force he is really urged
by is his own subjective feeling, and
is exactly measured by its strength.
No one's belief that duty is an objective reality is stronger than the belief
that God is so; yet the belief in God,
apart from the expectation of actual
reward and punishment, only operates
on conduct through, and in proportion
to, the subjective religious feeling.
The sanction, so far as it is disinterested, is always in the mind itself; and
the notion, therefore, of the transcendental moralists must be that this
sanction will not exist in the mind
unless it is believed to have its root
out of the mind; and that if a person
is able to say to himself, "This which
is restraining me and which is called
my conscience is only a feeling in my
own mind," he may possibly draw the
conclusion that when the feeling
ceases the obligation ceases, and that
if he find the feeling inconvenient, he
may disregard it and endeavor to get

rid of it. But is this danger confined to the utilitarian morality? Does the belief that moral obligation has its seat outside the mind make the feeling of it too strong to be got rid of? The fact is so far otherwise that all moralists admit and lament the ease with which, in the generality of minds, conscience can be silenced or stifled. The question, "Need I obey my conscience?" is quite as often put to themselves by persons who never heard of the principle of utility, as by its adherents. Those whose conscientious feelings are so weak as to allow of their asking this question, if they answer it affirmatively, will not do so because they believe in the transcendental theory, but because of the external sanctions.

It is not necessary, for the present purpose, to decide whether the feeling of duty is innate or implanted. Assuming it to be innate, it is an open question to what objects it naturally attaches itself; for the philosophic supporters of that theory are now agreed that the intuitive perception is of principles of morality and not of the details. If there be anything innate in the matter, I see no reason why the feeling which is innate should not be that of regard to the pleasures and pains of others. If there is any principle of morals which is intuitively obligatory, I should say it must be that. If so, the intuitive ethics would coincide with the utilitarian, and there would be no further quarrel between them. Even as it is, the intuitive moralists, though they believe that there are other intuitive moral obligations, do already believe this to be one; for they unanimously hold that a large *portion* of morality turns upon the consideration due to the interests of our fellow creatures. Therefore, if the belief in the transcendental origin of moral obligation gives any additional efficacy to the internal sanction, it appears to me that the utilitarian principle has already the benefit of it.

On the other hand, if, as is my own belief, the moral feelings are not innate but acquired, they are not for that reason the less natural. It is natural to man to speak, to reason, to build cities, to cultivate the ground, though these are acquired faculties. The moral feelings are not indeed a part of our nature, in the sense of being in any perceptible degree present in all of us; but this, unhappily, is a fact admitted by those who believe the most strenuously in their transcendental origin. Like the other acquired capacities above referred to, the moral faculty, if not a part of our nature, is a natural outgrowth from it; capable, like them, in a certain, small degree, of springing up spontaneously; and susceptible of being brought by cultivation to a high degree of development. Unhappily it is also susceptible, by a sufficient use of the external sanctions and of the force of early impressions, of being cultivated in almost any direction, so that there is hardly anything so absurd or so mischievous that it may not, by means of these influences, be made to act on the human mind with all the authority of conscience. To doubt that the same potency might be given by the same means to the principle of utility, even if it had no foundation in human nature, would be flying in the face of all experience.

But moral associations which are wholly of artificial creation, when intellectual culture goes on, yield by degrees to the dissolving force of analysis; and if the feeling of duty, when associated with utility, would appear equally arbitrary; if there were no leading department of our nature, no powerful class of sentiments, with which that association would harmonize, which would make us feel it congenial and incline us not only to it in others (for which we have lant interested motives), but ⸺ to cherish it in ourselves — if there were not, in short, a natural basis of sentiment for utilitarian morality, it might well happen that this association also, even after it had been implanted by education, might be analyzed away.

But there *is* this basis of powerful natural sentiment; and this it is which, when once the general happiness is recognized as the ethical standard, will constitute the strength of the utilitarian morality. This firm foundation is that of the social feelings of mankind; the desire to be in unity with our fellow creatures, which is already a powerful principle in human nature, and happily one of those which tend to become stronger, even without express inculcation, from the influences of advancing civilization. The social state is at once so natural, so necessary, and so habitual to man, that, except in some unusual circumstances or by an effort of voluntary abstraction, he never conceives himself otherwise than as a member of a body; and this association is riveted more and more, as mankind are further removed from the state of savage independence. Any condition, therefore, which is essential to a state of society, becomes more and more an inseparable part of every person's conception of the state of things which he is born into, and which is the destiny of a human being. Now society between human beings, except in the relation of master and slave, is manifestly impossible on any other footing than that the interests of all are to be consulted. Society between equals can only exist on the understanding that the interests of all are to be regarded equally. And since in all states of civilization, every person, except an absolute monarch, has equals, everyone is obliged to live on

these terms with somebody; and in every age some advance is made towards a state in which it will be impossible to live permanently on other terms with anybody. In this way people grow up unable to conceive as possible to them a state of total disregard of other people's interests. They are under a necessity of conceiving themselves as at least abstaining from all the grosser injuries, and (if only for their own protection) living in a state of constant protest against them. They are also familiar with the fact of co-operating with others, and proposing to themselves a collective, not an individual, interest as the aim (at least for the time being) of their actions. So long as they are co-operating, their ends are identified with those of others; there is at least a temporary feeling that the interests of others are their own interests. Not only does all strengthening of social ties, and all healthy growth of society, give to each individual a stronger personal interest in practically consulting the welfare of others, it also leads him to identify his *feelings* more and more with their good, or at least with an even greater degree of practical consideration for it. He comes, as though instinctively, to be conscious of himself as a being who *of course* pays regard to others. The good of others becomes to him a thing naturally and necessarily to be attended to, like any of the physical conditions of our existence. Now, whatever amount of this feeling a person has, he is urged by the strongest motive both of interest and of sympathy to demonstrate it, and to the utmost of his power encourage it in others; and even if he has none of it himself, he is as greatly interested as any one else that others should have it. Consequently the smallest germs of the feeling are laid hold of and nourished by the contagion of sympathy and the influences of education; and a complete web of corroborative association is woven round it, by the powerful agency of the external sanctions. This mode of conceiving ourselves and human life, as civilization goes on, is felt to be more and more natural. Every step in political improvement renders it more so, by removing the sources of opposition of interest and levelling those inequalities of legal privilege between individuals or classes, owing to which there are large portions of mankind whose happiness it is still practicable to disregard. In an improving state of the human mind, the influences are constantly on the increase which tend to generate in each individual a feeling of unity with all the rest; which, if perfect, would make him never think of, or desire, any beneficial condition for himself, in the benefits of which they are not included. If we now suppose this feeling of unity to be taught as a religion, and the whole force of education, of institutions, and of opinion, directed, as it once was in the case of religion, to make every person grow up from infancy surrounded on all sides both by the profession and the practice of it, I think that no one who can realize this conception will feel any misgiving about the sufficiency of the ultimate sanction for the happiness morality. To any ethical student who finds the realization difficult, I recommend, as a means of facilitating it, the second of M. Comte's two principal works, the *Traité de politique positive.* I entertain the strongest objections to the system of politics and morals set forth in that treatise; but I think it has superabundantly shown the possibility of giving to the service of humanity, even without the aid of belief in a Providence, both the psychological power and the social efficacy of a religion, making it take hold of human life, and color all thought, feeling, and action, in a manner of which the greatest ascendancy ever exercised by any religion may be but a type and foretaste; and of which the danger is, not that it should be insufficient, but that it should be so excessive as to interfere unduly with human freedom and individuality.

Neither is it necessary to the feeling which constitutes the binding force of the utilitarian morality on those who recognize it, to wait for those social influences which would make its obligation felt by mankind at large. In the comparatively early state of human advancement in which we now live, a person cannot, indeed, feel that entireness of sympathy with all others, which would make any real discordance in the general direction of their conduct in life impossible, but already a person in whom the social feeling is at all developed cannot bring himself to think of the rest of his fellow creatures as struggling rivals with him for the means of happiness, whom he must desire to see defeated in their object in order that he may succeed in his. The deeply rooted conception which every individual even now has of himself as a social being tends to make him feel it one of his natural wants that there should be harmony between his feelings and aims and those of his fellow creatures. If differences of opinion and of mental culture make it impossible for him to share many of their actual feelings—perhaps make him denounce and defy those feelings—he still needs to be conscious that his real aim and theirs do not conflict; that he is not opposing himself to what they really wish for, namely, their own good, but is, on the contrary, promoting it. This feeling in most individuals is much inferior in strength to their selfish feelings, and is often wanting altogether. But to those who have it, it possesses all the characters of a natural feeling. It does not present itself to their minds as a superstition of education, or a law despotically imposed by the power of society, but as an attribute which it would not be well for them to be without. This conviction is the ultimate sanction of the greatest happiness morality. This it is which makes any mind of well-developed feelings work with, and not against, the outward motives to care for others, afforded by what I have called the external sanctions; and, when those sanctions are wanting, or act in an opposite direction, constitutes in itself a powerful internal binding force, in proportion to the sensitiveness and thoughtfulness of the character; since few but those whose mind is a moral blank could bear to lay out their course of life on the plan of paying no regard to others except so far as their own private interest compels.

CHAPTER IV

OF WHAT SORT OF PROOF THE
PRINCIPLE OF UTILITY IS SUSCEPTIBLE

It has already been remarked that questions of ultimate ends do not admit of proof, in the ordinary acceptation of the term. To be incapable of proof by reasoning is common to all first principles, to the first premises of our knowledge, as well as to those of our conduct. But the former, being matters of fact, may be the subject of a direct appeal to the faculties which judge of fact—namely, our senses and our internal consciousness. Can an appeal be made to the same faculties on questions of practical ends? Or by what other faculty is cognizance taken of them?

Questions about ends are, in other words, questions what things are desirable. The utilitarian doctrine is that happiness is desirable, and the only thing desirable, as an end; all other things being only desirable as means to that end. What ought to be required of this doctrine, what conditions is it requisite that the doctrine should fulfill—to make good its claim to be believed?

The only proof capable of being given that an object is visible is that people actually see it. The only proof that a sound is audible is that people hear it; and so of the other sources of our experience. In like manner, I apprehend, the sole evidence it is possible to produce that anything is desirable is that people do actually desire it. If the end which the utilitarian doctrine proposes to itself were not, in theory and in practice, acknowledged to be an end, nothing could ever convince any person that it was so. No reason can be given why the general happiness is desirable, except that each person, so far as he believes it to be attainable, desires his own happiness. This, however, being a fact, we have not only all the proof which the case admits of, but all which it is possible to require, that happiness is a good; that each person's happiness is a good to that person, and the general happiness, therefore, a good to the aggregate of all persons. Happiness has made out its title as *one* of the ends of conduct, and consequently one of the criteria of morality.

But it has not, by this alone, proved itself to be the sole criterion. To do that, it would seem, by the same rule, necessary to show, not only that people desire happiness, but that they never desire anything else. Now it is palpable that they do desire things which, in common language, are decidedly distinguished from happiness. They desire, for example, virtue and the absence of vice, no less really than pleasure and the absence of pain. The desire of virtue is not as universal, but it is as authentic a fact as the desire of happiness. And hence the opponents of the utilitarian standard deem that they have a right to infer that there are other ends of human action besides happiness, and that happiness is not the standard of approbation and disapprobation.

But does the utilitarian doctrine deny that people desire virtue, or maintain that virtue is not a thing to be desired? The very reverse. It maintains not only that virtue is to be desired, but that it is to be desired distinterestedly, for itself. Whatever may be the opinion of utilitarian moralists as to the original conditions by which virtue is made virtue, however they may believe (as they do) that actions and dispositions are only virtuous because they promote another end than virtue, yet this being granted, and it having been decided, from considerations of this description, what *is* virtuous, they not only place virtue at the very head of the things which are good as means to the ultimate end, but they also recognize as a psychological fact the possibility of its being, to the individual, a good in itself, without looking to any end beyond it; and hold that the mind is not in a right state, not in a state conformable to utility, not in the state most conducive to the general happiness, unless it does love virtue in this manner—as a thing desirable in itself, even although, in the individual instance, it should not produce those other desirable consequences which it tends to produce, and on account of which it is held to be virtue. This opinion is not, in the smallest degree, a departure from the happiness principle. The ingredients of happiness are very various, and each of them is desirable in itself, and not merely when considered as swelling an aggregate. The principle of utility does not mean that any given pleasure, as music, for instance, or any given exemption from pain, as for example health, is to be looked upon as means to a collective something termed happiness, and to be desired on that account. They are desired and desirable in and for themselves; besides being means, they are a part of the end. Virtue, according to the utilitarian doctrine, is not naturally and originally part of the end, but it is capable of becoming so; and in those who love it disinterestedly it has become so, and is desired and cherished, not as a means to happiness, but as a part of their happiness.

To illustrate this further, we may remember that virtue is not the only thing originally a means, and which if it were not a means to anything else would be and remain indifferent, but which by association with what it is a means to comes to be desired for itself, and that too with the utmost intensity. What, for example, shall we say of the love of money? There is nothing originally more desirable about money than about any heap of glittering pebbles. Its worth is solely that of the things which it will buy; the desires for other things than itself, which it is a means of gratifying. Yet the love of money is not only one of the strongest moving forces of human life, but money is, in many cases, desired in and for itself; the desire to possess it is often stronger than the desire to use it, and goes on increasing when all the desires which point to ends beyond it, to be compassed by it, are falling off. It may, then, be said truly that money is desired not for the sake of an end, but as part of the end. From being a means to happiness, it has come to be itself a principal ingredient of the individual's conception of happiness. The same may be said of the majority of the great objects of human life: power, for example, or fame, except that to each of these there is a certain amount of immediate pleasure annexed, which has at least the semblance of being naturally inherent in them—a thing which cannot be said of money. Still, however, the strongest natural attraction, both of power and of fame, is the immense aid they give to the attainment of our other wishes; and it is the strong association thus generated between them and all our objects of desire which gives to the direct desire of them the intensity it often assumes, so as in some characters to surpass in strength all other desires. In these cases the means have become a part of the end, and a more important part of it than any of the things which they are means to. What was once desired as an instrument for the attainment of happiness has come to be desired for its own sake. In being desired for its own sake it is, however, desired as *part* of happiness. The person is made, or thinks he would be made, happy by its mere possession; and is made unhappy by failure to obtain it. The desire of it is not a different thing from the desire of happiness any more than the love of music or the desire of health. They are included in happiness. They are some of the elements of which the desire of happiness is made up. Happiness is not an abstract idea but a concrete whole; and these are some of its parts. And the utilitarian standard sanctions and approves their being so. Life would be a poor thing, very ill provided with sources of happiness, if there were not this provision of nature by which things originally indifferent, but conducive to, or otherwise associated with, the satisfaction of our primitive desires, become in themselves sources of pleasure more valuable than the primitive pleasures,

both in permanency, in the space of human existence that they are capable of covering, and even in intensity.

Virtue, according to the utilitarian conception, is a good of this description. There was no original desire of it, or motive to it, save its conduciveness to pleasure, and especially to protection from pain. But through the association thus formed it may be felt a good in itself, and desired as such with as great intensity as any other good; and with this difference between it and the love of money, of power, or of fame, that all of these may, and often do, render the individual noxious to the other members of the society to which he belongs, whereas there is nothing which makes him so much a blessing to them as the cultivation of the disinterested love of virtue. And consequently, the utilitarian standard, while it tolerates and approves those other acquired desires, up to the point beyond which they would be more injurious to the general happiness than promotive of it, enjoins and requires the cultivation of the love of virtue up to the greatest strength possible, as being above all things important to the general happiness.

It results from the preceding considerations that there is in reality nothing desired except happiness. Whatever is desired otherwise than as a means to some end beyond itself, and ultimately to happiness, is desired as itself a part of happiness, and is not desired for itself until it has become so. Those who desire virtue for its own sake desire it either because the consciousness of it is a pleasure, or because the consciousness of being without it is a pain, or for both reasons united; as in truth the pleasure and pain seldom exist separately, but almost always together— the same person feeling pleasure in the degree of virtue attained, and pain in not having attained more. If one of these gave him no pleasure, and the other no pain, he would not love or desire virtue, or would desire it only for the other benefits which it might produce to himself or to persons whom he cared for.

We have now, then, an answer to the question, of what sort of proof the principle of utility is susceptible. If the opinion which I have now stated is psychologically true—if human nature is so constituted as to desire nothing which is not either a part of happiness or a means of happiness, we can have no other proof, and we require no other, that these are the only things desirable. If so, happiness is the sole end of human action, and the promotion of it the test by which to judge of all human conduct; from whence it necessarily follows that it must be the criterion of morality, since a part is included in the whole.

And now to decide whether this is really so, whether mankind do desire nothing for itself but that which is a pleasure to them, or of which the absence is a pain, we have evidently arrived at a question of fact and experience, dependent, like all similar questions, upon evidence. It can only be determined by practised self-consciousness and self-observation, assisted by observation of others. I believe that these sources of evidence, impartially consulted, will declare that desiring a thing and finding it pleasant, aversion to it and thinking of it as painful, are phenomena entirely inseparable or rather two parts of the same phenomenon; in strictness of language, two different modes of naming the same psychological fact; that to think of an object as desirable (unless for the sake of its consequences) and to think of it as pleasant are one and the same thing; and that to desire anything except in proportion as the idea of it is pleasant, is a physical and metaphysical impossibility.

So obvious does this appear to me that I expect it will hardly be disputed; and the objection made will be, not that desire can possibly be directed to anything ultimately except pleasure and exemption from pain, but that the will is a different thing from desire; that a person of confirmed virtue or any other person whose purposes are fixed carries out his purposes without any thought of the pleasure he has in contemplating them or expects to derive from their fulfilment, and persists in acting on them, even though these pleasures are much diminished by changes in his character or decay of his passive sensibilities, or are outweighed by the pains which the pursuit of the purposes may bring upon him. All this I fully admit and have stated it elsewhere as positively and emphatically as anyone. Will, the active phenomenon, is a different thing from desire, the state of passive sensibility, and, though originally an offshoot from it, may in time take root and detach itself from the parent stock, so much so that in the case of an habitual purpose, instead of willing the thing because we desire it, we often desire it only because we will it. This, however, is but an instance of that familiar fact, the power of habit, and is nowise confined to the case of virtuous actions. Many indifferent things which men originally did from a motive of some sort, they continue to do from habit. Sometimes this is done unconsciously; the consciousness coming only after the action; at other times with conscious volition, but volition which has become habitual and is put in operation by the force of habit, in opposition perhaps to the deliberate preference, as often happens with those who have contracted habits of vicious or hurtful indulgence. Third and last comes the case in which the habitual act of will in the individual instance is not in contradiction to the general intention prevailing at other times, but in fulfilment of it; as in the case of the person of confirmed virtue and of all who pursue deliberately and consistently any determinate end. The distinction between will and desire thus understood is an authentic and highly important psychological fact; but the fact consists solely in this—that will, like all other parts of our constitution, is amenable to habit, and that we may will from habit what we no longer desire for itself, or desire only because we will it. It is not the less true that will, in the beginning, is entirely produced by desire; including in that term the repelling influence of pain as well as the attractive one of pleasure. Let us take into consideration no longer the person who has a confirmed will to do right, but him in whom that virtuous will is still feeble, conquerable by temptation, and not to be fully relied on; by what means can it be strengthened? How can the will to be virtuous, where it does not exist in sufficient force, be implanted or awakened? Only by making the person *desire* virtue—by making him think of it in a pleasurable light, or of its absence in a painful one. It is by associating the doing right with pleasure, or the doing wrong with pain, or by eliciting and impressing and bringing home to the person's experience the pleasure naturally involved in the one or the pain in the other, that it is possible to call forth that will to be virtuous which, when confirmed, acts without any thought of either pleasure or pain. Will is the child of desire, and passes out of the dominion of its parent only to come under that of habit. That which is the result of habit affords no presumption of being intrinsically good; and there would be no reason

for wishing that the purpose of virtue should become independent of pleasure and pain were it not that the influence of the pleasurable and painful associations which prompt to virtue is not sufficiently to be depended on for unerring constancy of action until it has acquired the support of habit. Both in feeling and in conduct, habit is the only thing which imparts certainty; and it is because of the importance to others of being able to rely absolutely on one's feelings and conduct, and to oneself of being able to rely on one's own, that the will to do right ought to be cultivated into this habitual independence. In other words, this state of the will is a means to good, not intrinsically a good; and does not contradict the doctrine that nothing is a good to human beings but in so far as it is either itself pleasurable or a means of attaining pleasure or averting pain.

But if this doctrine be true, the principle of utility is proved. Whether it is so or not, must now be left to the consideration of the thoughtful reader.

ON THE CONNECTION BETWEEN JUSTICE AND UTILITY

In all ages of speculation one of the strongest obstacles to the reception of the doctrine that utility or happiness is the criterion of right and wrong has been drawn from the idea of justice. The powerful sentiment and apparently clear perception which that word recalls with a rapidity and certainty resembling an instinct have seemed to the majority of thinkers to point to an inherent quality in things; to show that the just must have an existence in nature as something absolute, generically distinct from every variety of the expedient and, in idea, opposed to it, though (as is commonly acknowledged) never, in the long run, disjoined from it in fact.

In the case of this, as of our other moral sentiments, there is no necessary connection between the question of its origin and that of its binding force. That a feeling is bestowed on us by nature does not necessarily legitimate all its promptings. The feeling of justice might be a peculiar instinct, and might yet require, like our other instincts, to be controlled and enlightened by a higher reason. If we have intellectual instincts leading us to judge in a particular way, as well as animal instincts that prompt us to act in a particular way, there is no necessity that the former should be more infallible in their sphere than the latter in theirs; it may as well happen that wrong judgments are occasionally suggested by those, as wrong actions by these. But though it is one thing to believe that we have natural feelings of justice, and another to acknowledge them as an ultimate criterion of conduct, these two opinions are very closely connected in point of fact. Mankind are always predisposed to believe that any subjective feeling, not otherwise accounted for, is a revelation of some objective reality. Our present object is to determine whether the reality to which the feeling of justice corresponds is one which needs any such special revelation, whether the justice or injustice of an action is a thing intrinsically peculiar and distinct from all its other qualities or only a combination of certain of those qualities presented under a peculiar aspect. For the purpose of this inquiry it is practically important to consider whether the feeling itself, of justice and injustice, is *sui generis* like our sensations of color and taste or a derivative feeling formed by a combination of others. And this it is the more

essential to examine, as people are in general willing enough to allow that objectively the dictates of justice coincide with a part of the field of general expediency; but inasmuch as the subjective mental feeling of justice is different from that which commonly attaches to simple expediency, and, except in the extreme cases of the latter, is far more imperative in its demands, people find it difficult to see in justice only a particular kind or branch of general utility, and think that its superior binding force requires a totally different origin.

To throw light upon this question, it is necessary to attempt to ascertain what is the distinguishing character of justice, or of injustice; what is the quality, or whether there is any quality, attributed in common to all modes of conduct designated as unjust (for justice, like many other moral attributes, is best defined by its opposite), and distinguishing them from such modes of conduct as are disapproved, but without having that particular epithet of disapprobation applied to them. If in everything which men are accustomed to characterize as just or unjust some one common attribute or collection of attributes is always present, we may judge whether this particular attribute or combination of attributes would be capable of gathering round it a sentiment of that peculiar character and intensity by virtue of the general laws of our emotional constitution, or whether the sentiment is inexplicable and requires to be regarded as a special provision of nature. If we find the former to be the case, we shall, in resolving this question, have resolved also the main problem; if the latter, we shall have to seek for some other mode of investigating it.

To find the common attributes of a variety of objects, it is necessary to begin by surveying the objects themselves in the concrete. Let us therefore advert successively to the various modes of action and arrangements of human affairs which are classed, by universal or widely spread opinion, as just or as unjust. The things well known to excite the sentiments associated with those names are of a very multifarious character. I shall pass them rapidly in review, without studying any particular arrangement.

In the first place, it is mostly considered unjust to deprive anyone of his personal liberty, his property, or any other thing which belongs to him by law. Here, therefore, is one instance of the application of the terms "just" and "unjust" in a perfectly definite sense, namely, that it is just to respect, unjust to violate, the *legal rights* of anyone. But this judgment admits of several exceptions, arising from the other forms in which the notions of justice and injustice present themselves. For example, the person who suffers the deprivation may (as the phrase is) have *forfeited* the rights which he is so deprived of—a case to which we shall return presently. But also—

Secondly, the legal rights of which he is deprived may be rights which *ought* not to have belonged to him; in other words, the law which confers on him these rights may be a bad law. When it is so or when (which is the same thing for our purpose) it is supposed to be so, opinions will differ as to the justice or injustice of infringing it. Some maintain that no law, however bad, ought to be disobeyed by an individual citizen; that his opposition to it, if shown at all, should only be shown in endeavoring to get it altered by competent authority. This opinion (which condemns many of the most illustrious benefactors of mankind, and would often protect pernicious institutions against the only weapons which, in the state of things

existing at the time, have any chance of succeeding against them) is defended by those who hold it on grounds of expediency, principally on that of the importance to the common interest of mankind, of maintaining inviolate the sentiment of submission to law. Other persons, again, hold the directly contrary opinion that any law, judged to be bad, may blamelessly be disobeyed, even though it be not judged to be unjust but only inexpedient, while others would confine the license of disobedience to the case of unjust laws; but, again, some say that all laws which are inexpedient are unjust, since every law imposes some restriction on the natural liberty of mankind, which restriction is an injustice unless legitimated by tending to their good. Among these diversities of opinion it seems to be universally admitted that there may be unjust laws, and that law, consequently, is not the ultimate criterion of justice, but may give to one person a benefit, or impose on another an evil, which justice condemns. When, however, a law is thought to be unjust, it seems always to be regarded as being so in the same way in which a breach of law is unjust, namely, by infringing somebody's right, which, as it cannot in this case be a legal right, receives a different appellation and is called a moral right. We may say, therefore, that a second case of injustice consists in taking or withholding from any person that to which he has a *moral right.*

Thirdly, it is universally considered just that each person should obtain that (whether good or evil) which he *deserves,* and unjust that he should obtain a good or be made to undergo an evil which he does not deserve. This is, perhaps, the clearest and most emphatic form in which the idea of justice is conceived by the general mind. As it involves the notion of desert, the question arises what constitutes desert? Speaking in a general way, a person is understood to deserve good if he does right, evil if he does wrong; and in a more particular sense, to deserve good from those to whom he does or has done good, and evil from those to whom he does or has done evil. The precept of returning good for evil has never been regarded as a case of the fulfillment of justice, but as one in which the claims of justice are waived, in obedience to other considerations.

Fourthly, it is confessedly unjust to *break faith* with anyone: to violate an engagement, either express or implied, or disappoint expectations raised by our own conduct, at least if we have raised those expectations knowingly and voluntarily. Like the other obligations of justice already spoken of, this one is not regarded as absolute, but as capable of being overruled by a stronger obligation of justice on the other side, or by such conduct on the part of the person concerned as is deemed to absolve us from our obligation to him and to constitute a *forfeiture* of the benefit which he has been led to expect.

Fifthly, it is, by universal admission, inconsistent with justice to be *partial*—to show favor or preference to one person over another in matters to which favor and preference do not properly apply. Impartiality, however, does not seem to be regarded as a duty in itself, but rather as instrumental to some other duty; for it is admitted that favor and preference are not always censurable, and, indeed, the cases in which they are condemned are rather the exception than the rule. A person would be more likely to be blamed than applauded for giving his family or friends no superiority in good offices over strangers when he could do so without violating any other duty; and no one

thinks it unjust to seek one person in preference to another as a friend, connection, or companion. Impartiality where rights are concerned is of course obligatory, but this is involved in the more general obligation of giving to everyone his right. A tribunal, for example, must be impartial because it is bound to award, without regard to any other consideration, a disputed object to the one of two parties who has the right to it. There are other cases in which impartiality means being solely influenced by desert, as with those who, in the capacity of judges, preceptors, or parents, administer reward and punishment as such. There are cases, again, in which it means being solely influenced by consideration for the public interest, as in making a selection among candidates for a government employment. Impartiality, in short, as an obligation of justice, may be said to mean being exclusively influenced by the considerations which it is supposed ought to influence the particular case in hand, and resisting solicitation of any motives which prompt to conduct different from what those considerations would dictate.

Nearly allied to the idea of impartiality is that of *equality*, which often enters as a component part both into the conception of justice and into the practice of it, and, in the eyes of many persons, constitutes its essence. But in this, still more than in any other case, the notion of justice varies in different persons, and always conforms in its variations to their notion of utility. Each person maintains that equality is the dictate of justice, except where he thinks that expediency requires inequality. The justice of giving equal protection to the rights of all is maintained by those who support the most outrageous inequality in the rights themselves. Even in slave countries it is theoretically admitted that the rights of the slave, such as they are, ought to be as sacred as those of the master, and that a tribunal which fails to enforce them with equal strictness is wanting in justice; while, at the same time, institutions which leave to the slave scarcely any rights to enforce are not deemed unjust because they are not deemed inexpedient. Those who think that utility requires distinctions of rank do not consider it unjust that riches and social privileges should be unequally dispensed; but those who think this inequality inexpedient think it unjust also. Whoever thinks that government is necessary sees no injustice in as much inequality as is constituted by giving to the magistrate powers not granted to other people. Even among those who hold leveling doctrines, there are differences of opinion about expediency. Some communists consider it unjust that the produce of the labor of the community should be shared on any other principle than that of exact equality; others think it just that those should receive most whose wants are greatest; while others hold that those who work harder, or who produce more, or whose services are more valuable to the community, may justly claim a larger quota in the division of the produce. And the sense of natural justice may be plausibly appealed to in behalf of every one of these opinions.

Among so many diverse applications of the term "justice," which yet is not regarded as ambiguous, it is a matter of some difficulty to seize the mental link which holds them together, and on which the moral sentiment adhering to the term essentially depends. Perhaps, in this embarrassment, some help may be derived from the history of the word, as indicated by its etymology.

In most if not in all languages, the etymology of the word which corresponds to "just" points distinctly to an origin connected with the ordinances of law. *Justum* is a form of *jussum*, that which has been ordered. *Dikaion* comes directly from *dike*, a suit at law. *Recht*, from which came *right* and *righteous*, is synonymous with law. The courts of justice, the administration of justice, are the courts and the administration of law. *La justice*, in French, is the established term for judicature. I am not committing the fallacy, imputed with some show of truth to Horne Tooke, of assuming that a word must still continue to mean what it originally meant. Etymology is slight evidence of what the idea now signified is, but the very best evidence of how it sprang up. There can, I think, be no doubt that the *idée mère*, the primitive element, in the formation of the notion of justice was conformity to law. It constituted the entire idea among the Hebrews, up to the birth of Christianity; as might be expected in the case of a people whose laws attempted to embrace all subjects on which precepts were required, and who believed those laws to be a direct emanation from the Supreme Being. But other nations, and in particular the Greeks and Romans, who knew that their laws had been made originally, and still continued to be made, by men, were not afraid to admit that those men might make bad laws; might do, by law, the same things, and from the same motives, which if done by individuals without the sanction of law would be called unjust. And hence the sentiment of injustice came to be attached, not to all violations of law, but only to violations of such laws as *ought* to exist, including such as ought to exist but do not, and to laws themselves if supposed to be contrary to what ought to be law. In this manner the idea of law and of its injunctions was still predominant in the notion of justice, even when the laws actually in force ceased to be accepted as the standard of it.

It is true that mankind consider the idea of justice and its obligations as applicable to many things which neither are, nor is it desired that they should be, regulated by law. Nobody desires that laws should interfere with the whole detail of private life; yet everyone allows that in all daily conduct a person may and does show himself to be either just or unjust. But even here, the idea of the breach of what ought to be law still lingers in a modified shape. It would always give us pleasure, and chime in with our feelings of fitness, that acts which we deem unjust should be punished, though we do not always think it expedient that this should be done by the tribunals. We forego that gratification on account of incidental inconveniences. We should be glad to see just conduct enforced and injustice repressed, even in the minutest details, if we were not, with reason, afraid of trusting the magistrate with so unlimited an amount of power over individuals. When we think that a person is bound in justice to do a thing, it is an ordinary form of language to say that he ought to be compelled to do it. We should be gratified to see the obligation enforced by anybody who had the power. If we see that its enforcement by law would be inexpedient, we lament the impossibility, we consider the impunity given to injustice as an evil, and strive to make amends for it by bringing a strong expression of our own and the public disapprobation to bear upon the offender. Thus the idea of legal constraint is still the generating idea of the notion of justice, though undergoing several transformations before that notion as it exists in an advanced state of society becomes complete.

The above is, I think, a true account, as far as it goes, of the origin and progressive growth of the idea of justice. But we must observe that it contains as yet nothing to distinguish that obligation from moral obligation in general. For the truth is that the idea of penal sanction, which is the essence of law, enters not only into the conception of injustice, but into that of any kind of wrong. We do not call anything wrong unless we mean to imply that a person ought to be punished in some way or other for doing it—if not by law, by the opinion of his fellow creatures; if not by opinion, by the reproaches of his own conscience. This seems the real turning point of the distinction between morality and simple expediency. It is a part of the notion of duty in every one of its forms that a person may rightfully be compelled to fulfill it. Duty is a thing which may be *exacted* from a person, as one exacts a debt. Unless we think that it may be exacted from him, we do not call it his duty. Reasons of prudence, or the interest of other people, may militate against actually exacting it, but the person himself, it is clearly understood, would not be entitled to complain. There are other things, on the contrary, which we wish that people should do, which we like or admire them for doing, perhaps dislike or despise them for not doing, but yet admit that they are not bound to do; it is not a case of moral obligation; we do not blame them, that is, we do not think that they are proper objects of punishment. How we come by these ideas of deserving and not deserving punishment will appear, perhaps, in the sequel; but I think there is no doubt that this distinction lies at the bottom of the notions of right and wrong; that we call any conduct wrong, or employ, instead, some other term of dislike or disparagement, according as we think that the person ought, or ought not, to be punished for it; and we say it would be right to do so and so, or merely that it would be desirable or laudable, according as we would wish to see the person whom it concerns compelled, or only persuaded and exhorted, to act in that manner.[2]

This, therefore, being the characteristic difference which marks off, not justice, but morality in general from the remaining provinces of expediency and worthiness, the character is still to be sought which distinguishes justice from other branches of morality. Now it is known that ethical writers divide moral duties into two classes, denoted by the ill-chosen expressions, duties of perfect and of imperfect obligation; the latter being those in which, though the act is obligatory, the particular occasions of performing it are left to our choice, as in the case of charity or beneficence, which we are indeed bound to practice but not toward any definite person, nor at any prescribed time. In the more precise language of philosophic jurists, duties of perfect obligation are those duties in virtue of which a correlative *right* resides in some person or persons; duties of imperfect obligation are those moral obligations which do not give birth to any right. I think it will be found that this distinction exactly coincides with that which exists between justice and the other obligations of morality. In our survey of the various popular acceptations of justice, the term appeared generally to involve the idea of a personal right—a claim on the part of one or more individuals, like that which the law gives when it confers a proprietary or

[2] See this point enforced and illustrated by Professor Bain, in an admirable chapter (entitled "The Ethical Emotions, or the Moral Sense"), of the second of the two treatises composing his elaborate and profound work on the Mind.

other legal right. Whether the injustice consists in depriving a person of a possession, or in breaking faith with him, or in treating him worse than he deserves, or worse than other people who have no greater claims—in each case the supposition implies two things: a wrong done, and some assignable person who is wronged. Injustice may also be done by treating a person better than others; but the wrong in this case is to his competitors, who are also assignable persons. It seems to me that this feature in the case—a right in some person, correlative to the moral obligation—constitutes the specific difference between justice and generosity or beneficence. Justice implies something which it is not only right to do, and wrong not to do, but which some individual person can claim from us as his moral right. No one has a moral right to our generosity or beneficence because we are not morally bound to practice those virtues toward any given individual. And it will be found with respect to this as to every correct definition that the instances which seem to conflict with it are those which most confirm it. For if a moralist attempts, as some have done, to make out that mankind generally, though not any given individual, have a right to all the good we can do them, he at once, by that thesis, includes generosity and beneficence within the category of justice. He is obliged to say that our utmost exertions are *due* to our fellow creatures, thus assimilating them to a debt; or that nothing less can be a sufficient *return* for what society does for us, thus classing the case as one of gratitude; both of which are acknowledged cases of justice, and not of the virtue of beneficence; and whoever does not place the distinction between justice and morality in general, where we have now placed it, will be found to make no distinction between them at all, but to merge all morality in justice.

Having thus endeavored to determine the distinctive elements which enter into the composition of the idea of justice, we are ready to enter on the inquiry whether the feeling which accompanies the idea is attached to it by a special dispensation of nature, or whether it could have grown up, by any known laws, out of the idea itself; and, in particular, whether it can have originated in considerations of general expediency.

I conceive that the sentiment itself does not arise from anything which would commonly or correctly be termed an idea of expediency, but that, though the sentiment does not, whatever is moral in it does.

We have seen that the two essential ingredients in the sentiment of justice are the desire to punish a person who has done harm and the knowledge or belief that there is some definite individual or individuals to whom harm has been done.

Now it appears to me that the desire to punish a person who has done harm to some individual is a spontaneous outgrowth from two sentiments, both in the highest degree natural and which either are or resemble instincts: the impulse of self-defense and the feeling of sympathy.

It is natural to resent and to repel or retaliate any harm done or attempted against ourselves or against those with whom we sympathize. The origin of this sentiment it is not necessary here to discuss. Whether it be an instinct or a result of intelligence, it is, we know, common to all animal nature; for every animal tries to hurt those who have hurt, or who it thinks are about to hurt, itself or its young. Human beings, on this point, only differ from other animals in two particulars. First, in being capable of sympathizing, not solely with their offspring, or, like some of the more noble animals, with some superior animal who is kind to them, but with all human, and even with all sentient, beings; secondly, in having a more developed intelligence, which gives a wider range to the whole of their sentiments, whether self-regarding or sympathetic. By virtue of his superior intelligence, even apart from his superior range of sympathy, a human being is capable of apprehending a community of interest between himself and the human society of which he forms a part, such that any conduct which threatens the security of the society generally is threatening to his own, and calls forth his instinct (if instinct it be) of self-defense. The same superiority of intelligence, joined to the power of sympathizing with human beings generally, enables him to attach himself to the collective idea of his tribe, his country, or mankind in such a manner that any act hurtful to them raises his instinct of sympathy and urges him to resistance.

The sentiment of justice, in that one of its elements which consists of the desire to punish, is thus, I conceive, the natural feeling of retaliation or vengeance, rendered by intellect and sympathy applicable to those injuries, that is, to those hurts, which wound us through, or in common with, society at large. This sentiment, in itself, has nothing moral in it; what is moral is the exclusive subordination of it to the social sympathies, so as to wait on and obey their call. For the natural feeling would make us resent indiscriminately whatever anyone does that is disagreeable to us; but, when moralized by the social feeling, it only acts in the directions conformable to the general good: just persons resenting a hurt to society, though not otherwise a hurt to themselves, and not resenting a hurt to themselves, however painful, unless it be of the kind which society has a common interest with them in the repression of.

It is no objection against this doctrine to say that, when we feel our sentiment of justice outraged, we are not thinking of society at large or of any collective interest, but only of the individual case. It is common enough, certainly, though the reverse of commendable, to feel resentment merely because we have suffered pain; but a person whose resentment is really a moral feeling, that is, who considers whether an act is blamable before he allows himself to resent it—such a person, though he may not say expressly to himself that he is standing up for the interest of society, certainly does feel that he is asserting a rule which is for the benefit of others as well as for his own. If he is not feeling this, if he is regarding the act solely as it affects him individually, he is not consciously just; he is not concerning himself about the justice of his actions. This is admitted even by anti-utilitarian moralists. When Kant (as before remarked) propounds as the fundamental principle of morals, "So act that thy rule of conduct might be adopted as a law by all rational beings," he virtually acknowledges that the interest of mankind collectively, or at least of mankind indiscriminately, must be in the mind of the agent when conscientiously deciding on the morality of the act. Otherwise he uses words without a meaning; for that a rule even of utter selfishness could not *possibly* be adopted by all rational beings—that there is any insuperable obstacle in the nature of things to its adoption—cannot be even plausibly maintained. To give any meaning to Kant's principle, the sense put upon it must be that we ought to shape our conduct by a rule which all rational beings might adopt *with benefit to their collective interest.*

To recapitulate: the idea of justice supposes two things—a rule of conduct and a sentiment which sanctions the rule. The first must be supposed common to all mankind and intended for their good. The other (the sentiment) is a desire that punishment may be suffered by those who infringe the rule. There is involved, in addition, the conception of some definite person who suffers by the infringement, whose rights (to use the expression appropriated to the case) are violated by it. And the sentiment of justice appears to me to be the animal desire to repel or retaliate a hurt or damage to oneself or to those with whom one sympathizes, widened so as to include all persons, by the human capacity of enlarged sympathy and the human conception of intelligent self-interest. From the latter elements the feeling derives its morality; from the former, its peculiar impressiveness and energy of self-assertion.

I have, throughout, treated the idea of a *right* residing in the injured person and violated by the injury, not as a separate element in the composition of the idea and sentiment, but as one of the forms in which the other two elements clothe themselves. These elements are a hurt to some assignable person or persons, on the one hand, and a demand for punishment, on the other. An examination of our own minds, I think, will show that these two things include all that we mean when we speak of violation of a right. When we call anything a person's right, we mean that he has a valid claim on society to protect him in the possession of it, either by the force of law or by that of education and opinion. If he has what we consider a sufficient claim, on whatever account, to have something guaranteed to him by society, we say that he has a right to it. If we desire to prove that anything does not belong to him by right, we think this done as soon as it is admitted that society ought not to take measures for securing it to him, but should leave him to chance or to his own exertions. Thus a person is said to have a right to what he can earn in fair professional competition, because society ought not to allow any other person to hinder him from endeavoring to earn in that manner as much as he can. But he has not a right to three hundred a year, though he may happen to be earning it; because society is not called on to provide that he shall earn that sum. On the contrary, if he owns ten thousand pounds three-per-cent stock, he *has* a right to three hundred a year because society has come under an obligation to provide him with an income of that amount.

To have a right, then, is, I conceive, to have something which society ought to defend me in the possession of. If the objector goes on to ask why it ought, I can give him no other reason than general utility. If that expression does not seem to convey a sufficient feeling of the strength of the obligation, nor to account for the peculiar energy of the feeling, it is because there goes to the composition of the sentiment, not a rational only but also an animal element—the thirst for retaliation; and this thirst derives its intensity, as well as its moral justification, from the extraordinarily important and impressive kind of utility which is concerned. The interest involved is that of security, to everyone's feelings the most vital of all interests. All other earthly benefits are needed by one person, not needed by another; and many of them can, if necessary, be cheerfully foregone or replaced by something else; but security no human being can possibly do without; on it we depend for all our immunity from evil and for the whole value of all and every good, beyond

the passing moment, since nothing but the gratification of the instant could be of any worth to us if we could be deprived of everything the next instant by whoever was momentarily stronger than ourselves. Now this most indispensable of all necessaries, after physical nutriment, cannot be had unless the machinery for providing it is kept unintermittedly in active play. Our notion, therefore, of the claim we have on our fellow creatures to join in making safe for us the very groundwork of our existence gathers feelings around it so much more intense than those concerned in any of the more common cases of utility that the difference in degree (as is often the case in psychology) becomes a real difference in kind. The claim assumes that character of absoluteness, that apparent infinity and incommensurability with all other considerations which constitute the distinction between the feeling of right and wrong and that of ordinary expediency and inexpediency. The feelings concerned are so powerful, and we count so positively on finding a responsive feeling in others (all being alike interested) that *ought* and *should* grow into *must,* and recognized indispensability becomes a moral necessity, analogous to physical, and often not inferior to it in binding force.

If the preceding analysis, or something resembling it, be not the correct account of the notion of justice—if justice be totally independent of utility, and be a standard *per se,* which the mind can recognize by simple introspection of itself—it is hard to understand why that internal oracle is so ambiguous, and why so many things appear either just or unjust, according to the light in which they are regarded.

We are continually informed that utility is an uncertain standard, which every different person interprets differently, and that there is no safety but in the immutable, ineffaceable, and unmistakable dictates of justice, which carry their evidence in themselves and are independent of the fluctuations of opinion. One would suppose from this that on questions of justice there could be no controversy; that, if we take that for our rule, its application to any given case could leave us in as little doubt as a mathematical demonstration. So far is this from being the fact that there is as much difference of opinion, and as much discussion, about what is just as about what is useful to society. Not only have different nations and individuals different notions of justice, but in the mind of one and the same individual, justice is not some one rule, principle, or maxim, but many which do not always coincide in their dictates, and, in choosing between which, he is guided either by some extraneous standard or by his own personal predilections.

For instance, there are some who say that is it unjust to punish anyone for the sake of example to others, that punishment is just only when intended for the good of the sufferer himself. Others maintain the extreme reverse, contending that to punish persons who have attained years of discretion, for their own benefit, is despotism and injustice, since, if the matter at issue is solely their own good, no one has a right to control their own judgment of it; but that they may justly be punished to prevent evil to others, this being the exercise of the legitimate right of self-defense. Mr. Owen,[3] again, affirms that it is unjust to punish at all, for the criminal did not make his own character; his education and the circumstances which sur-

[3] [The utopian reformer, Robert Owen (1771-1858)]

rounded him have made him a criminal, and for these he is not responsible. All these opinions are extremely plausible; and so long as the question is argued as one of justice simply, without going down to the principles which lie under justice and are the source of its authority, I am unable to see how any of these reasoners can be refuted. For in truth every one of the three builds upon rules of justice confessedly true. The first appeals to the acknowledged injustice of singling out an individual and making him a sacrifice, without his consent, for other people's benefit. The second relies on the acknowledged justice of self-defense and the admitted injustice of forcing one person to conform to another's notions of what constitutes his good. The Owenite invokes the admitted principle that it is unjust to punish anyone for what he cannot help. Each is triumphant so long as he is not compelled to take into consideration any other maxims of justice than the one he has selected; but as soon as their several maxims are brought face to face, each disputant seems to have exactly as much to say for himself as the others. No one of them can carry out his own notion of justice without trampling upon another equally binding. These are difficulties; they have always been felt to be such; and many devices have been invented to turn rather than to overcome them. As a refuge from the last of the three, men imagined what they called the freedom of the will—fancying that they could not justify punishing a man whose will is in a thoroughly hateful state unless it be supposed to have come into that state through no influence of anterior circumstances. To escape from the other difficulties, a favorite contrivance has been the fiction of a contract whereby at some unknown period all the members of society engaged to obey the laws and consented to be punished for any dis-obedience to them, thereby giving to their legislators the right, which it is assumed they would not otherwise have had, of punishing them, either for their own good or for that of society. This happy thought was con-sidered to get rid of the whole dif-ficulty and to legitimate the infliction of punishment, in virtue of another received maxim of justice, *volenti non fit injuria*—that is not unjust which is done with the consent of the person who is supposed to be hurt by it. I need hardly remark that, even if the consent were not a mere fiction, this maxim is not superior in authority to the others which it is brought in to supersede. It is, on the contrary, an instructive specimen of the loose and irregular manner in which supposed principles of justice grow up. This particular one evidently came into use as a help to the coarse exigencies of courts of law, which are sometimes obliged to be content with very uncer-tain presumptions, on account of the greater evils which would often arise from any attempt on their part to cut finer. But even courts of law are not able to adhere consis*ent*ly to the maxim, for they allow voluntary en-gagements to be set aside on the ground of fraud, and sometimes on that of mere mistake or misinforma-tion.

Again, when the legitimacy of in-flicting punishment is admitted, how many conflicting conceptions of jus-tice come to light in discussing the proper apportionment of punishments to offenses. No rule on the subject recommends itself so strongly to the primitive and spontaneous sentiment of justice as the *lex talionis*, an eye for an eye and a tooth for a tooth. Though this principle of the Jewish and of the Mohammedan law has been generally abandoned in Europe as a practical maxim, there is, I

suspect, in most minds, a secret hankering after it; and when retribu-tion accidentally falls on an offender in that precise shape, the general feeling of satisfaction evinced bears witness how natural is the sentiment to which this repayment in kind is acceptable. With many, the test of justice in penal infliction is that the punishment should be proportioned to the offense, meaning that it should be exactly measured by the moral guilt of the culprit (whatever be their standard for measuring moral guilt), the consideration what amount of punishment is necessary to deter from the offense having nothing to do with the question of justice, in their estima-tion; while there are others to whom that consideration is all in all, who maintain that it is not just, at least for man, to inflict on a fellow creature, whatever may be his offenses, any amount of suffering beyond the least that will suffice to prevent him from repeating, and others from imitating, his misconduct.

To take another example from a subject already once referred to. In co-operative industrial association, is it just or not that talent or skill should give a title to superior remuneration? On the negative side of the question it is argued that whoever does the best he can deserves equally well, and ought not in justice to be put in a position of inferiority for no fault of his own; that superior abilities have already advantages more than enough, in the admiration they excite, the per-sonal influence they command, and the internal sources of satisfaction at-tending them, without adding to these a superior share of the world's goods; and that society is bound in justice rather to make compensation to the less favored for this unmerited ine-quality of advantages than to ag-gravate it. On the contrary side it is contended that society receives more from the more efficient laborer; that, his services being more useful, society owes him a larger return for them; that a greater share of the joint result is actually his work, and not to allow his claim to it is a kind of robbery; that, if he is only to receive as much as others, he can only be justly required to produce as much, and to give a smaller amount of time and exertion, proportioned to his superior efficiency. Who shall decide between these appeals to conflicting principles of justice? Justice has in this case two sides to it, which it is impossible to bring into harmony, and the two disputants have chosen opposite sides; the one looks to what it is just that the individual should receive, the other to what it is just that the community should give. Each, from his own point of view, is unanswerable; and any choice between them, on grounds of justice, must be perfectly arbitrary. Social utility alone can decide the preference.

How many, again, and how irreconcilable are the standards of justice to which reference is made in discussing the repartition of taxation. One opinion is that payment to the state should be in numerical proportion to pecuniary means. Others think that justice dictates what they term graduated taxation—taking a higher percentage from those who have more to spare. In point of natural justice a strong case might be made for disregarding means altogether, and taking the same absolute sum (whenever it could be got) from everyone; as the subscribers to a mess or to a club all pay the same sum for the same privileges, whether they can all equally afford it or not. Since the protection (it might be said) of law and government is afforded to and is equally required by all, there is no injustice in making all buy it at the same price. It is reckoned justice, not injustice, that a dealer should charge to all customers the same price for the same article, not a price varying according to their means of payment. This doctrine, as applied to taxation, finds no advocates because it conflicts so strongly with man's feelings of humanity and of social expediency; but the principle of justice which it invokes is as true and as binding as those which can be appealed to against it. Accordingly it exerts a tacit influence on the line of defense employed for other modes of assessing taxation. People feel obliged to argue that the state does more for the rich man than for the poor, as a justification for its taking more from them, though this is in reality not true, for the rich would be far better able to protect themselves, in the absence of law or government, than the poor, and indeed would probably be successful in converting the poor into their slaves. Others, again, so far defer to the same conception of justice as to maintain that all should pay an equal capitation tax for the protection of their persons (these being of equal value to all), and an unequal tax for the protection of their property, which is unequal. To this others reply that the all of one man is as valuable to him as the all of another. From these confusions there is no other mode of extrication than the utilitarian.

Is, then, the difference between the just and the expedient a merely imaginary distinction? Have mankind been under a delusion in thinking that justice is a more sacred thing than policy, and that the latter ought only to be listened to after the former has been satisfied? By no means. The exposition we have given of the nature and origin of the sentiment recognizes a real distinction; and no one of those who profess the most sublime contempt for the consequences of actions as an element in their morality attaches more importance to the distinction than I do. While I dispute the pretensions of any theory which sets up an imaginary standard of justice not grounded on utility, I account the justice which is grounded on utility to be the chief part, and incomparably the most sacred and binding part, of all morality. Justice is a name for certain classes of moral rules which concern the essentials of human well-being more nearly, and are therefore of more absolute obligation, than any other rules for the guidance of life; and the notion which we have found to be of the essence of the idea of justice—that of a right residing in an individual—implies and testifies to this more binding obligation.

The moral rules which forbid mankind to hurt one another (in which we must never forget to include wrongful interference with each other's freedom) are more vital to human well-being than any maxims, however important, which only point out the best mode of managing some department of human affairs. They have also the peculiarity that they are the main element in determining the whole of the social feelings of mankind. It is their observance which alone preserves peace among human beings; if obedience to them were not the rule, and disobedience the exception, everyone would see in everyone else an enemy against whom he must be perpetually guarding himself. What is hardly less important, these are the precepts which mankind have the strongest and the most direct inducements for impressing upon one another. By merely giving to each other prudential instruction or exhortation, they may gain, or think they gain, nothing; in inculcating on each other the duty of positive beneficence, they have an unmistakable interest, but far less in degree; a person may possibly not need the benefits of others, but he always needs that they should not do him hurt. Thus the moralities which protect every individual from being harmed by others, either directly or by being hindered in his freedom of pursuing his own good, are at once those which he himself has most at heart and those which he has the strongest interest in publishing and enforcing by word and deed. It is by a person's observance of these that his fitness to exist as one of the fellowship of human beings is tested and decided; for on that depends his being a nuisance or not to those with whom he is in contact. Now it is these moralities primarily which compose the obligations of justice. The most marked cases of injustice, and those which give the tone to the feeling of repugnance which characterizes the sentiment, are acts of wrongful aggression or wrongful exercise of power over someone; the next are those which consist in wrongfully withholding from him something which is his due—in both cases inflicting on him a positive hurt, either in the form of direct suffering or of the privation of some good which he had reasonable ground, either of a physical or of a social kind, for counting upon.

The same powerful motives which command the observance of these primary moralities enjoin the punishment of those who violate them; and as the impulses of self-defense, of defense of others, and of vengeance are all called forth against such persons, retribution, or evil for evil, becomes closely connected with the sentiment of justice, and is universally included in the idea. Good for good is also one of the dictates of justice; and this, though its social utility is evident, and though it carries with it a natural human feeling, has not at first sight that obvious connection with hurt or injury which, existing in the most elementary cases of just and unjust, is the source of the characteristic intensity of the sentiment. But the connection, though less obvious, is not less real. He who accepts benefits and denies a return of them when needed inflicts a real hurt by disappointing one of the most natural and reasonable of expectations, and one which he must at least tacitly have encouraged, otherwise the benefits would seldom have been conferred. The important rank, among human evils and wrongs, of the disappointment of expectation is shown in the fact that it constitutes the principal criminality of two such highly immoral acts as a breach of friendship and a breach of promise. Few hurts which human beings can sustain are greater, and none wound more, then when that on which they habitually and with full assurance relied fails them in the hour of need; and few wrongs are greater than this mere withholding of good; none excite more resentment, either in the person suffering or in a sympathizing spectator. The principle, therefore, of giving to each what they deserve, that is, good for good as well as evil for evil, is not only included within the idea of justice as we have defined it, but is a proper object of that intensity of sentiment which places the just in human estimation above the simply expedient.

Most of the maxims of justice current in the world, and commonly appealed to in its transactions, are simply instrumental to carrying into effect the principles of justice which we have now spoken of. That a person is only responsible for what he has done voluntarily, or could voluntarily have avoided, that it is unjust to condemn any person unheard; that the punishment ought to be proportioned to the offense, and the like, are maxims intended to prevent the just principle of evil for evil from being perverted to the infliction of evil without that

justification. The greater part of these common maxims have come into use from the practice of courts of justice, which have been naturally led to a more complete recognition and elaboration than was likely to suggest itself to others, of the rules necessary to enable them to fulfill their double function—of inflicting punishment when due, and of awarding to each person his right.

That first of judicial virtues, impartiality, is an obligation of justice, partly for the reason last mentioned, as being a necessary condition of the fulfillment of other obligations of justice. But this is not the only source of the exalted rank, among human obligations, of those maxims of equality and impartiality, which, both in popular estimation and in that of the most enlightened, are included among he precepts of justice. In one point of view, they may be considered as corollaries from the principles already laid down. If it is a duty to do to each according to his deserts, returning good for good, as well as repressing evil by evil, it necessarily follows that we should treat all equally well (when no higher duty forbids) who have deserved equally well of *us*, and that society should treat all equally well who have deserved equally well of *it*, that is, who have deserved equally well absolutely. This is the highest abstract standard of social and distributive justice, toward which all institutions and the efforts of all virtuous citizens should be made in the utmost possible degree to converge. But this great moral duty rests upon a still deeper foundation, being a direct emanation from the first principle of morals, and not a mere logical corollary from secondary or derivative doctrines. It is involved in the very meaning of utility, or the greatest happiness principle. That principle is a mere form of words without rational signification unless one person's happiness, supposed equal in degree (with the proper allowance made for kind), is counted for exactly as much as another's. Those conditions being supplied, Bentham's dictum, "everybody to count for one, nobody for more than one," might be written under the principle of utility as an explanatory commentary.[4] The equal

[4] This implication, in the first principle of the utilitarian scheme, of perfect impartiality between persons is regarded by Mr. Herbert Spencer (in his *Social Statics*) as a disproof of the pretensions of utility to be a sufficient guide to right; since (he says) the principle of utility presupposes the anterior principle that everybody has an equal right to happiness. It may be more correctly described as supposing that equal amounts of happiness are equally desirable, whether felt by the same or different persons. This, however, is not a *pre*supposition, not a premise needful to support the principle of utility, but the very principle itself; for what is the principle of utility if it be not that "happiness" and "desirable" are synonymous terms? If there is any anterior principle implied, it can be no other than this, that the truths of arithmetic are applicable to the valuation of happiness, as of all other measurable quantities.

(Mr. Herbert Spencer, in a private communication on the subject of the preceding note, objects to being considered an opponent of utilitarianism and states that he regards happiness as the ultimate end of morality; but deems that end only partially attainable by empirical generalizations from the observed results of conduct, and completely attainable only by deducing, from the laws of life and the conditions of existence, what kinds of action necessarily tend to produce happiness, and what kinds to produce unhappiness. With the exception of the word "necessarily," I have no dissent to express from this doctrine; and (omitting that

claim of everybody to happiness, in the estimation of the moralist and of the legislator, involves an equal claim to all the means of happiness except in so far as the inevitable conditions of human life and the general interest in which that of every individual is included set limits to the maxim; and those limits ought to be strictly construed. As every other maxim of justice, so this is by no means applied or held applicable universally; on the contrary, as I have already remarked, it bends to every person's ideas of social expediency. But in whatever case it is deemed applicable at all, it is held to be the dictate of justice. All persons are deemed to have a *right* to equality of treatment, except when some recognized social expediency requires the reverse. And hence all social inequalities which have ceased to be considered expedient assume the character, not of simple inexpediency, but of injustice, and appear so tyrannical that people are apt to wonder how

word) I am not aware that any modern advocate of utilitarianism is of a different opinion. Bentham, certainly, to whom in the *Social Statics* Mr. Spencer particularly referred, is, least of all writers, chargeable with unwillingness to deduce the effect of actions on happiness from the laws of human nature and the universal conditions of human life. The common charge against him is of relying too exclusively upon such deductions and declining altogether to be bound by the generalizations from specific experience which Mr. Spencer thinks that utilitarians generally confine themselves to. My own opinion (and, as I collect, Mr. Spencer's) is that in ethics, as in all other branches of scientific study, the consilience of the results of both these processes, each corroborating and verifying the other, is requisite to give to any general proposition the kind and degree of evidence which constitutes scientific proof.)

they ever could have been tolerated—forgetful that they themselves, perhaps, tolerate other inequalities under an equally mistaken notion of expediency, the correction of which would make that which they approve seem quite as monstrous as what they have at last learned to condemn. The entire history of social improvement has been a series of transitions by which one custom or institution after another, from being a supposed primary necessity of social existence, has passed into the rank of a universally stigmatized injustice and tyranny. So it has been with the distinctions of slaves and freemen, nobles and serfs, patricians and plebeians; and so it will be, and in part already is, with the aristocracies of color, race, and sex.

It appears from what has been said that justice is a name for certain moral requirements which, regarded collectively, stand higher in the scale of social utility, and are therefore of more paramount obligation, than any others, though particular cases may occur in which some other social duty is so important as to overrule any one of the general maxims of justice. Thus, to save a life, it may not only be allowable, but a duty, to steal or take by force the necessary food or medicine, or to kidnap and compel to officiate the only qualified medical practitioner. In such cases, as we do not call anything justice which is not a virtue, we usually say, not that justice must give way to some other moral principle, but that what is just in ordinary cases is, by reason of that other principle, not just in the particular case.

By this useful accommodation of language, the character of indefeasibility attributed to justice is kept up, and we are saved from the necessity of maintaining that there can be laudable injustice.

The considerations which have now been adduced resolve, I conceive, the only real difficulty in the utilitarian theory of morals. It has always been evident that all cases of justice are also cases of expediency; the difference is in the peculiar sentiment which attaches to the former, as contradistinguished from the latter. If this characteristic sentiment has been sufficiently accounted for; if there is no necessity to assume for it any peculiarity of origin; if it is simply the natural feeling of resentment, moralized by being made co-extensive with the demands of social good; and if this feeling not only does but ought to exist in all the classes of cases to which the idea of justice corresponds —that idea no longer presents itself as a stumbling block to the utilitarian ethics. Justice remains the appropriate name for certain social utilities which are vastly more important, and therefore more absolute and imperative, than any others are as a class (though not more so than others may be in particular cases); and which, therefore, ought to be, as well as naturally are, guarded by a sentiment, not only different in degree, but also in kind; distinguished from the milder feeling which attaches to the mere idea of promoting human pleasure or convenience at once by the more definite nature of its commands and by the sterner character of its sanctions.

Friedrich Nietzsche (1844—1900)

Friedrich Nietzsche, the son of a Lutheran minister, was brought up by his mother, grandmother, and maiden aunt. He studied at Bonn, received his doctorate at Leipzig, and was appointed professor of classical philology at Basel. Poor health forced him to retire in 1879 after ten years of teaching. For a time he served as medical orderly in the Franco-Prussian War. During the next ten years he wrote prolifically until he sank into the mental illness in 1889 that put an end to his creative labors. Among the thirteen books that Nietzsche published during his lifetime are *Beyond Good and Evil, Thus Spake Zarathustra, The Birth of Tragedy, The Geneology of Morals, The Antichrist, The Use and Abuse of History*. His sister published *The Will to Power*, a two-volume collection of his notes and sketches, ten years after his death.

THOUGHTS ON THE PHILOSOPHY OF MORALS [1]

I

The Chemistry of Our Opinions and Sentiments. At present in almost all matters, philosophical problems assume the same form of questioning as they did two thousand years ago:

How can something arise from its opposite? For instance, the reasonable from the reasonless, the sentient from the dead, the logical from the alogical, disinterested contemplation from selfish desire, altruism from egoism, truth

---

[1] The selections included here have been translated specifically for this volume by Professors Fred Hagen and Ursula Mahlendorf. I acknowledge gratefully, in addition, their assistance in selecting these materials from the writings of Nietzsche. The translations were made from Friedrich Nietzsche's *Werke in drei Bänden*, edited by Karl Schlechta (Carl Hauser Verlag, Munchen, 2nd edition, 1960). The sections, here published under the title given by the editor, are derived from the following works of Nietzsche:

1. *Menschliches, Allzumenschliches. Erster Band,* section 1; Schlechta edition, I, 447–48.
2. *Menschliches, Allzumenschliches. Erster Band,* section 2; Schlechta edition, I, 448.
3. *Morgenröte,* section 112, Schlechta edition, I, 1084–85.
4. *Menschliches, Allzumenschliches. Erster Band,* section 96, Schlechta edition, I, 504–5.
5. *Menschliches, Allzumenschliches. Erster Band,* section 97, Schlechta edition, I, 505.
6. *Morgenröte,* section 106, Schlechta edition, I, 1078–79.
7. *Morgenröte,* section 107, Schlechta edition, I, 1079–80.

436   Thoughts on the Philosophy of Morals

from error? Hitherto traditional metaphysics overcame this difficulty by

8. *Die Fröhliche Wissenschaft. Drittes
   Buch,* section 116, Schlechta edition,
   II, 121–22.
9. *Die Fröhliche Wissenschaft. Drittes
   Buch,* section 117, Schlechta edition,
   II, 122.
10. *Morgenröte,* section 534, Schlechta
    edition, I, 1257–58.
11. *Menschliches, Allzumenschliches. Er-
    ster Band,* section 56, Schlechta edi-
    tion, I, 489–90.
12. *Morgenröte,* section 103, Schlechta
    edition, I, 1076–77.
13. *Morgenröte,* section 104, Schlechta
    edition, I, 1077.
14. *Morgenröte,* section 116, Schlechta
    edition, I, 1090–92.
15. *Menschliches, Allzumenschliches. Er-
    ster Band,* section 39, Schlechta edi-
    tion, I, 479–81.
16. *Menschliches, Allzumenschliches. Er-
    ster Band,* section 107, Schlechta edi-
    tion, I, 513–15.
17. *Morgenröte,* section 146, Schlechta
    edition, I, 1115–16.
18. *Morgenröte,* section 147, Schlechta
    edition, I, 1116.
19. *Menschliches, Allzumenschliches.
    Zweiter Band,* section 350, Schlechta
    edition, I, 1006.
20. *Menschliches, Allzumenschliches. Er-
    ster Band,* section 95, Schlechta edi-
    tion, I, 503–4.
21. *Menschliches, Allzumenschliches. Er-
    ster Band,* section 292, Schlechta edi-
    tion, I, 623–24.

The translators offer the following explanatory note: "We have consulted the
standard translation into English: *The
Complete Works of Friedrich Nietzsche,*
ed. by Oscar Levy, XVIII vols. (Russell
and Russell, New York, 1909–1911, re-
issued 1964). Although we found this
translation of Nietzsche's works outdated,
we found ourselves in many instances in
agreement with Mr. J. M. Kennedy's
translation of *The Dawn.*"

denying the origin of the one from
the other; it assumed a miraculous
origin for more highly valued things,
coming immediately from the essential
core of the "thing-in-itself." The
youngest of all philosophical methods,
historical philosophy, on the other
hand, which is no longer to be thought
of as separate from the natural
sciences, has ascertained in particular
cases (and presumably this will be its
findings in all cases) that the alleged
opposites do not exist except as the
usual exaggerations of popular metaphysics and that a fallacy underlies
such thinking in terms of opposites:
According to historical explanation
there is, strictly speaking, neither a
purely altruistic act nor a completely
disinterested contemplation; both are
only sublimations in which the basic
element seems to have almost disap-
peared and which is discernible only
by the keenest observation. All that
we need, and that can be given us at
the present advance of the different
sciences, is a chemistry of the moral,
religious, aesthetic opinions and sentiments, as also a chemistry of those
emotions which we personally experience in the great and small ways of
cultural and social communication, indeed even in solitude. But what if this
investigation were to conclude that, in
this sphere also, the most beautiful
colors are obtained from base, even
despised materials? Will many be inclined to pursue such investigations?
Men prefer to ignore questions as to
origin and beginning; must one not be
almost inhuman to feel inclined to
such an investigation?

II

*Traditional Mistakes of Philoso-
phers.* All philosophers make the
common mistake of starting from
contemporary man and believe that
they prove their points by analyzing

him. Involuntarily, they imagine "man" to be an *aeterna veritas*, as static in the midst of flux as the fixed measure of things. But everything that the philosopher says about man is really nothing more than a testimony about the man of a *very limited* period of time. The traditional error of all philosophers is their lack of historical perspective. Many even unwittingly take the most recent type of man as formed through the influence of particular religious and political conditions as the permanent type from which one is to begin his analysis. They do not want to acknowledge that man has developed, that even his cognitive faculty has developed; indeed, some would fabricate the whole world from this very cognitive faculty. The *essentials* of human development, however, took place in prehistoric times, long before the four thousand years of which we have some limited knowledge; during this time, man probably did not change significantly. But the philosopher observes "instincts" in the present-day man and supposes that these are immutable facts about mankind, and that they will provide him with a key to the understanding of the world. The foundation of this whole teleology is the assumption that man of the last four thousand years is an *eternal* being towards whom all things from their very beginning had a nisus. But everything has evolved; there are *no eternal facts* as there are no absolute truths. Therefore, *historical philosophising* is henceforth necessary and with it the virtue of humility before the facts.

III

On the Natural History of Duty and Right. Our duties are the claims which others have upon us. How did they acquire these claims? They acquired them by regarding us as capable of making and keeping contracts and of securing reprisals; they took us for their equals and therefore they trusted, educated, censured, and supported us. We do our duty: . . . We justify that conception of our power for the sake of which all these things were done for us; we repay them measure for measure. Therefore, it is our pride which summons us to our duty. We wish to restore our self-determination when we do something for them in return for something that was done for us; for by helping us, they [have] intruded upon our sphere of power and would take permanent abode there if we did not retaliate by assuming "duties," whereby we make inroads into their sphere of power. The rights of others relate only to what is within our power; it would be unreasonable for them to demand of us something which is not ours. To put the matter more precisely, their rights can only relate to what they believe to be in our power, provided that it is something that we ourselves consider as being in our power. Both sides may easily be mistaken. One's sense of duty depends upon sharing the beliefs of others as to the extent of our power, i.e., our belief that we can promise certain things with the *ability* to discharge the obligation ("free will").

My rights are that part of my power which others have not only conceded to me, but which they wish to preserve for me. Why do they do so? On the one hand, they are motivated by prudence and fear and precaution. It may be that they expect us to reciprocate (namely, in the protection of their rights), it may be that they consider a conflict with us as dangerous or pointless, or it may be that they deem any diminution of our power to be to their disadvantage, because then we would be an ill-equipped ally in a conflict with a hostile third power. On the other hand, they grant us our rights freely or they delegate them to us. In the latter case, the others have not only sufficient power, but a super-abundance of it so that they can give up part of it and guarantee it to the person to whom they give it: In so doing they assume an inferior feeling of power in the person who accepts the grant. This is the origin of rights: They are recognized and guaranteed gradations of power. When the balance of power shifts radically, old rights expire and new ones develop. The relationship between the rights of nations shows such a continual decline of old rights and development of new ones. If our power decreases radically, then the attitude of those who guaranteed our rights changes; they deliberate [on] whether or not they can restore our power in full measure and if they feel incapable of doing so, they disavow our rights "from that time on." Likewise, when our power increases markedly, the attitude of those who until now recognized our power and whose recognition we no longer need changes. They will probably attempt to reduce us to our earlier position of power, and they will want to interfere in our affairs, justifying their interference by an appeal to their "duty." But this is merely useless word-quibbling. Where right dominates, a certain state and degree of power is maintained, and all attempts at its augmentation and diminution are resisted. The right of others is the concession of our feeling of power to their feeling of power. When our power is profoundly shaken and broken, our rights cease: On the other hand, when we have become very powerful, the rights of others as we have admitted them hitherto cease to exist for us. The "equitable" man must himself possess a delicate scale of justice attuned to the varying degrees of might and right which, given the transitoriness of human things, are in balance only for short intervals of time, but for the most part they either sink or rise. To be equitable, therefore, is difficult and requires much practice, good will, and sound judgment.

IV

Custom and Morality. To be moral, well-mannered, and virtuous means to be obedient to an entrenched law or tradition. It is immaterial whether we submit to them grudgingly or willingly; it suffices that we do so. We call him "good" who, because of good breeding, easily and gladly does what is virtuous as if it were the natural thing, however moral may be defined by custom (for example, he takes revenge if taking revenge, as among Greeks, is morally right). He is called good because he is good "for some end"; because generosity, compassion, and the like were felt to be useful and purposeful, we persist to this day in calling the generous and compassionate man a "good man" in spite of subsequent changes in manners and customs. To be evil is to be "not moral" (asocial), to practice immorality, to resist tradition, however reasonable or stupid it may be. But to injure one's neighbor has always been felt as eminently harmful in all moral laws of all ages so that we think of the intentional injury of one's fellow man when we now hear the word "evil." What brought men to differentiate between the moral and immoral, good and evil, was not the basic contrast between egoism and altruism, but rather the distinction between adherence to traditions (law) and disobedience to them. It is indifferent how tradition *originated;* in any case it did not originate with respect to good and evil or any immanent categorical imperative, but did so above all for the purpose of preserving a *community,* a people; any superstitious taboo which originated because of some misconstrued accident creates a tradition which it is moral to obey: To disobey it is dangerous, but more dangerous for the *community* than for the individual (because the Deity punishes the community, and the individual only as a member of the community, for any sacrilege and any violation of its rights). Every tradition grows continually more venerable, the more distant its origin and the more its beginning has been forgotten; the veneration of such a tradition increases from generation to generation, the tradition at last becomes holy and inspires awe. In any case, the morality of piety is much older than that of altruistic actions.

v

Pleasure in Traditional Custom. An important kind of pleasure, and therewith one source of morality, arises from habit. Man does the habitual more easily, better, and therefore more gladly. He feels pleasure in doing it and knows from experience that the habitual has proven itself and is therefore useful; a custom with which one can live has shown itself to be beneficial and rewarding in contrast to all untested innovations. Custom therefore continues the pleasurable and the useful; moreover, obeying it requires no deliberation. As soon as man can coerce others, he does so in order to introduce and enforce his *customs*, for in his eyes they are the proven wisdom of life. In similar fashion a community of individuals forces the same customs upon each member. Here is the misconception: Because one feels comfortable in doing the customary or at least because the customary enables one to prevail in his existence, this custom is viewed as necessary, for it is deemed to be the *only* possibility for giving comfort; the comforts of life seem to grow from it alone. This way

of regarding the conventional as a precondition of living extends to the smallest details of custom; since primitive peoples and cultures have very limited insight into actual causality, they are superstitiously concerned to preserve the traditional routine. Even when customs are severe, exacting, and burdensome, they are retained because of their presumed utility. Such peoples do not know that the same degree of well-being can also exist with other customs, and that even higher degrees can be achieved. But we certainly observe that all customs, even the most exacting, become more congenial as we grow inured to them and that even the most austere way of life may become second nature and consequently pleasurable.

VI

Against Definitions of Moral Aims. Everywhere men now give the following rough definition of the *objective* of morality: It is said to be the preservation and advancement of humanity, but that means no more than that one wants to have a formula. One must immediately counter: Preservation *in what state?* Advancement *to what state?* Does not the formula omit the most essential point, namely the answers to the questions wherein and whereto? Does this formula contribute anything to the explication of moral precepts which we do not already acknowledge tacitly and unreflectively? Does it guide us sufficiently in determining whether or not we should seek to prolong mankind's existence as long as possible? Or should we seek the greatest possible de-animalization of man? How different the means, i.e., practical morality, would have to be in the two cases! Let us suppose that we wanted to bestow upon mankind the highest reasonableness of which it is capable: This certainly would not guarantee the longest possible existence for them! Or let us suppose that we thought their "greatest happiness" to be the state to be attained: Does one mean then the highest degree of happiness which individual men can achieve gradually, or does one mean an incalculable, though finally attainable, average state of happiness for all? But why should morality be the only road that leads to it? By and large, is not morality the source of so much displeasure that one might rather argue that every refinement of morality until now has made men more *dissatisfied* with themselves, their fellows, and their lot? Did not until now the most moral of men believe that the *profoundest unhappiness* is the only proper condition of man as a moral being?

VII

Our Right to Our Folly. How ought we to act? For what end ought we to act? These questions are easily enough answered so far as the immediate and most basic needs of the individual are concerned; but as one rises to the subtler, more comprehensive and important domains of action, the answers will become more doubtful and consequently more arbitrary. But precisely in this domain there ought not to be arbitrary decisions!—thus the authority of morality demands. An obscure anxiety and awe should guide man instantly just in those very actions, the purpose and means of which he can least of all make out *immediately*. This authority of morality rules out any thinking in those situations where it could be dangerous to think *wrongly;* in this manner, morality usually justifies itself before its accusers. Wrongly . . . here [means] dangerously, but dangerous to whom? Authoritarian moralists do not usually consider the danger to the person who acts, but

much rather the danger to *themselves,* to their possible loss of power and prestige as soon as this right to act is conceded to all, regardless of whether or not these "all" act arbitrarily and foolishly according to individual lesser or greater judgment. The authoritarians on their part make unhesitating use of their right to arbitrariness and folly: They even command others to act even in situations when it is scarcely possible or very difficult to answer the questions, "How ought I to act, for what end ought I to act?" And if the *reason* of mankind grows with such extraordinary slowness that it has often been denied in the course of the development of humanity, what is more to blame than this solemn presence, indeed omnipresence, of moral commands which forbid us to question *as individuals* the purpose and the how? Have we not been trained to *become sentimental* and to retreat into obscurity just when our judgment should be keen and detached—i.e., in all higher and more important concerns?

VIII

Herd-Instinct. Wherever we find a morality we encounter an evaluation and a ranking of human instincts and actions. These valuations and rankings are always the expression of the needs of a community and a herd. The chief criterion for the value of every individual is his usefulness to his society —there is a first, second, and third degree of usefulness. By means of morality the individual is trained to become a function of the herd and to value himself only as a function. Since there were great differences in the conditions for the preservation of different communities, there were therefore very different moralities; and in respect to the future essential transformations of herds and communities, states and societies, one can prophesy that very divergent moralities will come into existence. Morality is the herd-instinct in the individual.

IX

The Herd's Sting of Conscience. In the earliest and remotest ages of mankind the sting of conscience differed completely from what it is today. Today we feel responsible only for what we intend and do, and we take pride only in what lies within ourselves. All our jurists consider this feeling of self-esteem and pleasure in our individuality and power to be the eternal source of Right. But during the longest period of human development nothing inspired more terror in man than to feel this individuality in himself. To be alone, to feel individually, neither to obey nor to rule, to be an individual—at that time this was no pleasure, but a punishment; one was condemned "to be an individual." Freedom of thought was regarded as anguish personified. Whereas we feel law and subordination to be a restraint and an inhibition, people once felt egoism to be distressing, indeed to be distress itself. For a person to be himself, to value himself according to his own measure and weight . . . was then quite distasteful. An inclination in that direction would have been felt to be madness because every misery and terror was associated with solitude. At that time "free will" was the nearest neighbor to a bad conscience. Man esteemed himself all the more moral the less independently he acted, the more the herd-instinct and not personality was expressed in his actions. At that time everything that injured the herd, whether the individual had intended the injury or not, caused him a sting of conscience: His neighbor felt it too, indeed the whole herd felt

it! It is in this respect that we have most changed our mode of thinking.

X

Small Doses. If a transformation is to be as profound as possible, then one should administer the remedy in minute doses, but continuously over long periods. Can something great be created in *a single stroke?* Thus we want to be careful not to exchange the familiar conditions of morality for a new valuation of things precipitately and violently—no, we want to continue living in the old way for a long, long time until, probably at a very late date, we come to realize that the *new valuation* has become the prevailing power within us and that its small doses, *to which we must from now on become accustomed*, have endowed us with a new nature. We now begin to understand that the last attempt at a great transvaluation of values—that which concerns politics (the "great revolution")—was nothing but a rhapsodic and bloody *piece of quackery* which, by means of *sudden* crises, knew how to inspire a credulous Europe with the hope of a sudden recovery and thereby made all political invalids *impatient* and *dangerous* up to this very moment.

XI

Victory of Knowledge Over Radical Evil. He who wishes to become wise will obtain rich profit from having entertained for a time the idea that man is basically evil and corrupt; the idea is wrong just as its opposite is, but during long periods of time it held sway and its roots have taken a firm and subtle hold on us. In order to understand *ourselves* we must understand this idea, and then in order to mount higher we must surmount it. Then we will realize that there are neither sins nor virtues in the metaphysical sense; we will realize that the entire province of moral ideas is constantly wavering and that there are higher and lower conceptions of good and evil, of moral and immoral. He who desires little more from things than knowledge of them easily makes peace with his soul and will perhaps make a wrong move (or commit a sin, as the world calls it), in ignorance, but hardly from passion. He will no longer want to slander and exterminate his appetites, but his single-minded goal will be to *know* as well as possible at all times, and that will make him detached and will tame the wildness in his disposition. Moreover, freed from a number of tormenting conceptions, he will no longer feel anything at the mention of "punishments of hell," "sinfulness," "incapacity for goodness." He knows them to be the fleeting distorted shadows of the world and of life.

XII

There Are Two Classes of People Who Deny Morality. "To deny morality" can mean, *in the first place,* to deny that the moral motives which men *cite* for their actions have really prompted them. This amounts to saying that morality consists of empty words and is part of that gross and yet subtle deception (especially self-deception) practiced by men and perhaps most adeptly practiced by those famous for their virtues. *In the second place,* it can mean the denial that moral judgments are founded on truths. One admits on this view that they are really motives of the actions, but insists that *error* lies at the foundation of moral judgments prompting men to their moral actions. This is *my* point of view; yet I should be far from denying that in *very many cases* a lingering distrust based on the first

point of view—in the spirit of La Rochefoucauld—is also justifiable and, in any case, is of the highest general utility. Therefore I deny morality in the same way as I deny alchemy; i.e., I deny its presuppositions, but I do not deny that there have been alchemists who believed in these presuppositions and based their actions upon them. I also deny immorality: not that innumerable people *feel* themselves to be immoral, but I do deny that there is any *justifying reason* for them to feel so. I should not, of course, deny—unless I were a fool—that many actions which are called immoral should be avoided and combated, and likewise that many which are called moral should be performed and encouraged. But I believe this about these two kinds of action *for reasons different* from those that have been given up to the present. We must transform our ideas so that we, perhaps much later, may achieve even more: namely, *to transform our feelings and attitudes.*

XIII

Our Evaluations. All actions spring from evaluations and all evaluations are either one's own or adopted, the latter being by far the most numerous. Why do we adopt them? From fear—i.e., we consider it more advisable to pretend that these evaluations are also our own, and we get so accustomed to this pretence that it finally is our nature. Personal evaluation is something extremely rare for it means that we must appraise a matter according to the extent it pleases or displeases only us and no one else. But must not *we* determine the worth of our fellows which then in turn provides us in most cases with the motive for adopting their evaluations? No doubt [we must], but then we make these initial evaluations during our childhood, and we seldom learn to alter them. Most of us remain during our whole lifetime the dupes of our childish and habitual judgments in our manner of appraising our fellow men (their minds, rank, morality, exemplariness, and reprehensibility), and we find it necessary to pay homage to their valuations.

XIV

The Unknown World of the "Subject." From the most ancient times to the present, men have found it hardest to grasp the extent of their ignorance about themselves not only with respect to good and evil, but also with respect to something far more essential. The ancient illusion still lives on that we know, and know percisely in each case, what makes human beings act. Not only "God, who looks into the heart," not only the man who acts and reflects on his action, but indeed no one else doubts that he understands the essential features of action in everyone else. "I know what I want and what I have done, I am free and responsible for my actions, and I hold others responsible for theirs; I can name all moral possibilities and all inner impulses which precede an act—you may act as you will; I know myself and therefore all others." Everyone thought so in the past, and almost everyone thinks so today. Socrates and Plato, who in this respect were great skeptics and admirable innovators, were nevertheless naively credulous in regard to that fatal prejudice, that profoundest error, which is that "Right knowledge *must* be followed by right action." In holding this principle they were still heirs to the common folly and presumption that there is such a thing as knowledge concerning the essence of an action.

"It would indeed be *dreadful* if insight into what constitutes a right action were not followed by that right action": This is the only way in which these great men deemed it necessary to prove this idea—that the opposite seemed to them to be unthinkable and mad. Nevertheless the opposite is precisely the naked reality which has been demonstrated daily and hourly from time immemorial. Is it not a "dreadful" truth that all that we know about an act is *never* sufficient to accomplish it, that the bridge connecting knowledge with the action until now has not been built in even a single case? Acts are *never* simply what they seem to us to be. We have been at great pains to learn that the external world is not quite as it appears to us. Well! It is the same with the inner world. We cannot say more than that moral actions are in truth "something different," all actions are essentially unknown. The opposite was and is the common belief. The most ancient realism is against us. Up to the present humanity has thought, "An action is simply what it appears to be to us." (In rereading these words a very expressive passage from Schopenhauer occurs to me which I will quote as a proof that even he, without the slightest scruple, continued to adhere to this moral realism: "Each one of us is in reality a competent and perfect moral judge, exactly knowing good and evil, sanctified by loving good and abhoring evil; this applies to every one of us in so far as not his own, but the actions of others are scrutinized, and he must merely approve and disapprove while the burden of performing the action falls on the shoulders of others. Everyone is therefore justified in replacing God by himself in the role of father confessor.")

XV

The Fable of Noumenal Freedom. The history of those sentiments through which we hold someone accountable, i.e., the so-called moral sentiments, has the following principal phases. In the beginning, one calls individual actions good or evil without considering their motives, but only [taking into account] their useful or harmful consequences. But one soon forgets the origin of these designations and assumes that the attributes "good" or "evil" inhere in the actions themselves without regard to their consequences . . . . Next, the goodness or evilness is transferred to the motives, and the actions in themselves are regarded as morally ambiguous. Then one goes beyond that and no longer applies the predicates "good" or "evil" to particular motives, but to the whole character of a man out of whom the motive is presumed to grow as the plant grows out of the earth. Thus successively, man is held responsible for the consequences of his actions, then for his actions, then for his motives, and finally for his character. Finally one discovers that character cannot be responsible in so far as it is a necessary consequence, an outgrowth of past and present elements and influences: Therefore that a man cannot be held responsible for anything, neither for his character, nor his motives, nor his actions, nor the consequences of his actions. At that point, one comes to realize that the history of moral sentiments is the history of a fiction, the fiction of responsibility which in turn reposes upon the fiction of the freedom of the will. Schopenhauer argued the following: Since certain actions have as a consequence *ill humor* ("sense of guilt"), there must be responsibility. There would be *no reason* for this ill humor if all human actions were done of necessity (which is actually the case and also the belief of this philosopher), and if, in addition, man acquired precisely the *character* that he has

with the same necessity as that by which he acts (which Schopenhauer denies). From the existence of this ill humor Schopenhauer believes he can infer a freedom which man must somehow have had, not with regard to his actions, but with regard to his character: freedom, therefore, *to be* this or that, but not *to act* thus or otherwise. According to his opinion, the *esse*, the sphere of freedom and responsibility, results in the *operari*, the sphere of strict causality, necessity, and nonresponsibility. This ill humor is seemingly directed to the *operari*,—in so far it strays from its real target which is the *esse*, the deed of a free will, the original cause of the existence of an individual. Man becomes that which he *wills* to become; willing precedes existence. Schopenhauer fallaciously deduces the reasonableness and justifiability of ill humor from its mere existence, and having made this fallacious deduction he arrives at his fantastic conclusion about the so-called noumenal (intelligible) freedom. But the ill humor after the deed need not be reasonable at all; indeed it certainly is not, for it arises from our mistaken assumption that the action was *not* necessitated. Therefore, it is only because man *believes* himself to be free, not because he is free, that he experiences remorse and stings of conscience. Moreover, this ill humor can be overcome; in many people it is entirely absent in connection with actions where others experience it. The feeling is very protean; it is connected with the development of customs and culture, and probably has existed only for a relatively short time in world history. Nobody is responsible for his actions, nobody for his character; to judge is equivalent to being unjust. This also holds when an individual judges himself. This proposition is as clear as day, and yet everyone, fearing the consequences, prefers to retreat into darkness and illusion.

XVI

Nonliability and Innocence. The fact that man is accountable for neither his actions nor his character is the bitterest pill which the inquirer must swallow if he has been accustomed to regard responsibility and duty as mankind's patent letter of nobility. All his valuations, approbations, and disapprobations are thereby devaluated and become counterfeit. The deepest feeling with which he regarded the sufferer and the hero was sustained by a fiction; he may no longer either praise or blame, for it is absurd to praise and blame blind nature and necessity. Just as he loves a fine work of art but does not commend it for creating itself, just as he regards a plant, so must he regard his own actions and those of mankind. He can admire the forcefulness, beauty, and plenitude of actions, but he must not attribute merit to them. Chemical processes, the strife of elements, [and] the torments of the invalid who thirsts for recovery are no less meritorious than those struggles of the soul and states of distress in which we are torn hither and thither by different motives until, as we say, we finally decide for the most powerful one (in truth, however, it is the strongest motive which decides for us). But whatever noble names we may give to these motives, they have grown from just those roots that we believed to be infused by evil poisons. There is no difference of kind between good and evil actions, but at most one of degree. Good actions are sublimated evil ones; evil actions are polluted and arrested good ones. Man acts as he can, that [is], as he must; his craving for self-gratification (together with the fear of losing it) demands satisfaction in all circumstances—be it in deeds of vanity, revenge, pleasure, convenience, malice, or cunning, be it in deeds of sacrifice, compassion, and dedication to knowledge. The degrees of discrimination decide in which direction one is drawn by this craving. Every society, every individual is continually aware of a scale of values according to which he determines his actions and judges those of others. But the standard of values changes constantly; many actions are called evil but are simply stupid because the degree of intelligence which decided for them was very low. Indeed, in a sense all our actions are at present still stupid; for the highest degree of human intelligence that can now be reached will certainly be yet surpassed. In retrospect then, all our actions and judgments will appear as narrow minded and precipitous as the actions and judgments of backward savages now appear to us. Gaining insight into this can be deeply painful, but there is a consolation—the pains are birth pangs. When a butterfly breaks through its chrysalis, it rends and tears it and then the unknown light, the realm of freedom, blinds and confuses it. Those men (and how few they are!) who are *susceptible* to such sorrow are the subjects of the first experiment to determine if mankind *can be transformed from a moral into a wise mankind.* The sun of a new gospel casts its first ray upon the highest peaks of the souls of those individuals, then the morning mists gather in a thick cloud and the brightest light mixes with nebulous gloom. Everything is necessity—thus speaks the new wisdom and this very wisdom is necessity. Everything is innocence, and wisdom is the way to insight into this innocence. Are pleasure, egoism, [and] vanity *necessary* for the creation of moral phenomena and their highest manifestations, namely, the affinity for truth and justice which is to be found in knowledge? Were error and delirium the only means through which mankind could raise itself gradually to this degree of self-enlightenment and self-redemption, who would dare to depreciate such means? Who would really be sad if he perceived the ends to which these means contribute? Everything in the sphere of morality has developed, is changeable, is fluctuating; everything flows like a river—that is true, but *everything within one* streams toward *one* goal. Even if the inherited practice of erroneous valuation, loving and hating, continues to reign, it will grow weaker under the influence of increasing wisdom. A new practice, that of understanding—of not loving and not hating—of a wide perspective is gradually taking root in us. In millennia, the new practice will perhaps be sufficiently strong to give humanity the strength to produce wise, innocent (enlightened innocence) men just as regularly as it now produces biased, guilt-stricken men: that means *not the opposite of the man of the future, but necessary preludes to them.*

XVII

Beyond the Neighbor. What? Can it be that the essence of true morality lies in our perceiving the most direct and immediate consequences of our actions for others, and that we make decisions accordingly? This is only a narrow-minded and petty bourgeois morality, even though it may be a morality. But it seems to me that it would be superior and more liberal to *look beyond* these immediate consequences for our neighbor and to encourage more distant purposes, even *at the risk of making others suffer,* as, for example, by encouraging the pursuit of knowledge in spite of the insight that our free thinking will, for the time being, plunge others into doubt, grief, and even worse afflictions. May we not at least treat our neighbor as we treat ourselves? And if we do not think in such a narrow and petty bourgeois fashion about our immediate welfare and sufferings, why must we do so about his? Granted that sacrifice made sense for us, what is to forbid us to sacrifice our neighbor along with ourselves, just as States and Sovereigns have hitherto sacrificed one citizen to the others, "for the sake of the general interest," as they say?

We too, however, have in mind the general interest, perhaps an even more general one than theirs: So why should not a few individuals of this generation be sacrificed for the benefit of generations to come? Can't affliction, unrest, despair, blunders and anxiety of the sacrificial victims be deemed essential if we view such victims as performing a function analogous to that of a new plough which is to break up the ground and render it fertile for all? Finally, we communicate at the same time to our neighbor the inclination to self-sacrifice by which he can *feel himself a martyr:* We persuade him to carry out the task for which we use him. Are we then devoid of all pity? If, however, we want to achieve a victory over ourselves *beyond our pity,* is this not a higher and freer attitude and state of mind than that in which we feel merely safe after having ascertained whether an action *benefits or harms* our neighbor? On the contrary, such an attitude toward sacrifice—including the sacrifice of ourselves *as well as of our neighbors*—would strengthen and elevate the general sense of human *power,* even supposing that we attain nothing more than this. But this alone would be a positive increase of *happiness.* Then, if even this . . . but not a word more! A glance suffices, you have understood me.

XVIII

The Cause of "Altruism." On the whole, men have spoken of love with so much emphasis and adoration simply *because they have had so little of it* and were never allowed to appease their appetite for this food: Thus it became their ambrosia. If a poet were to show the presence of *universal love of man* in his vision of a Utopia, he would certainly have to describe an agonizing and ridiculous state of affairs, the like of which was never seen on earth: Everyone would be gushed over, pestered and sighed for, not as at present by one lover, but by thousands, indeed by everybody, by dint of an irresistible drive, which would then be as much reviled and cursed as selfishness has been by men of past ages. The poets of such a Utopia, if only they had the time to write, would dream of nothing but the blissful, loveless past, of the divine selfishness, of the anonymity, neglect, and unpopularity that were once possible on earth; they would even dream of being hated and despised and of all the possible meannesses of the dear, animal world in which *we* live.

XIX

The Golden Maxim. Man has been bound by many chains to make him behave as an animal. And indeed he has become more temperate, more spiritual, more joyous, more reflective and considerate than any other animal. But now he still suffers from having borne his chains so long, from having lacked pure air and free movement for so long. I shall repeat it again and again that these chains are weighty and significant illusions derived from moral, religious, and metaphysical conceptions. Only after this "chain sickness" has been overcome do we reach the first great goal, the separation of man from the animal. At present we are still engaged in the work of removing the chains and in doing so we need to take the greatest precautions. *Freedom of spirit may be granted only to the ennobled man;* only he experiences an *alleviation of his lot* and his wounds alone are healed. He is the first who may say that he lives for the sake of *joyousness* and for no ulterior goal. His motto, "Let peace and the enjoyment of present things be with me," would be dangerous if uttered by anyone else. In thinking of this motto for individuals, he recalls an ancient saying, great and moving, which was addressed *to all,* and that has remained standing above all mankind as a motto and a beacon by which everyone who adorns his banner too early shall perish—the saying whereby Christianity perished. *The time has not yet come,* it seems, when *all* men can have the experience of those shepherds who saw the illumined heavens and heard the words: "Peace on earth and good will to men." This is still the time of the individual.

XX

The Morality of the Mature Individual. Until now altruism has been considered to be the essential characteristic of moral action; it has been shown that in the beginning it was on behalf of a good in which we share that all altruistic actions were praised and rewarded. Will not significant transformations of these views impend, now that we perceive ever more clearly that an action's usefulness for the community is greatest the more it is done from considerations of personal advantage? Actions most advantageous to the individual correspond most closely to today's concept of morality (a morality of the greatest general good). To develop our whole *person* and in all that we do to keep our *highest good* in view advances us more than those feelings of pity and actions done for the benefit of others. We all still suffer because we pay all too little attention to the personal in us; let us admit that it is badly developed. Our attention has been forcibly diverted from what is personal that has been offered as a sacrifice to the State, to science, or to the helpless, as if the personal were something bad which must be sacrificed. We are still willing to work for our fellow men, but only so far as we find our own greatest advantage in this work, no more and no less. It is only a question of what we understand to be to *our advantage;* the immature, undeveloped, crude individual will naturally understand "his advantage" in the crudest way.

XXI

Forward. Let us proceed upon the path of wisdom with firm, confident steps! Whatever you may be, be your own source of experience! Cast off the dissatisfaction with your own nature, forgive yourself your own ego, for in any case, you have in yourself a ladder with a hundred rungs upon which you can mount to knowledge. The age into which you regretfully feel yourself cast holds you to be blessed because of this good fortune; it calls out to you that you will still have experiences of which men of a later age perhaps must be deprived. Do not disdain having been religious; appreciate fully that you still had a genuine access to art. Can you not, with the help of these experiences, follow immense stretches of former humanity with a more sympathetic understanding? Is not *that* ground which sometimes displeases you so greatly, that ground of clouded thought, precisely the one upon which have grown many of the most glorious fruits of older civilizations? One must have loved religion and art as one loved his mother and his nurse, otherwise he cannot become wise. But one must become able to look beyond them, to grow beyond them; if one remains under their magic spell, one does not understand them. Likewise, you must be steeped in history and be familiar with that cautious toying with scales: "On the one hand—on the other hand." Wander back along the footsteps made by mankind in its sorrowful and long journey through the wilderness of the past, then you will be instructed most thoroughly which courses future mankind can never, and never should, traverse again. And while you wish with all your strength to foresee what riddles the future will pose, your own life will acquire the value of a tool and a means for knowledge. You can achieve a synthesis of all you have experienced in your ultimate goal—a synthesis of dead ends, mistakes, delusions, follies, your loves, and your hopes. This goal is to become yourself a necessary link in the Great Chain of Cultural Being and from the necessity you embody to infer the necessity that operates in the course of general culture. When your sight has become strong enough to fathom the dark depths of your nature and your knowledge, perhaps then you will be able to discern reflected therein the distant constellations of future cultures. Do you believe that such a life with such a goal is too taxing, too empty of all pleasantness? Then you have not learned that knowledge is sweeter than honey and that the clouds of melancholia will have to serve you as a spring from which you draw the purest water for your refreshment. When old age approaches, you will realize how much you have obeyed the voice of nature, that nature which governs the world through joy. The same life that reaches its peak in old age also reaches its peak in wisdom, in that mild sunshine of a continuous spiritual joyousness. Nature intended that you should meet both old age and wisdom, upon one ridge of life. Then it is time, and no reason for rancour that the shades of death approach. Your last glance—toward the light; your last sound—a paean to wisdom.

Francis Herbert Bradley (1846 – 1924)

Retired for most of his life by a chronic physical disability and unencumbered by teaching responsibilties, Bradley, during his more than half-century tenure as Fellow of Merton College, Oxford, succeeded to an unusual degree in devoting himself to philosophy. A warm admirer of Hegel, Bradley, however, was no mere slavish follower. And he deplored a similar though less extensive discipleship that grew about himself. His wit, brilliant style, and originality of mind combined to mark him as the dominant figure in British Idealism. In addition to *Ethical Studies* (1876), Bradley's most important writings are *Appearance and Reality* (1893), *The Principles of Logic* (1893), *Essays on Truth and Reality* (1914), and, finally, *Collected Essays* (1935).

MY STATION AND ITS DUTIES [1]

We have traversed by this time, however cursorily, a considerable field, and so far it might appear without any issue or at best with a merely negative result. Certainly in our anticipatory remarks (Essay II), we thought we found some answer to the question, What is the end? But that answer was too abstract to stand by itself. And, if we may be said to know thus much, that the end is self-realization, yet at present we do not seem to have learned anything about the self to be realized. And the detail of Essays II and III appears at most to have given us some knowledge of that which self-realization is not.

We have learned that the self to be realized is not the self as this or that feeling, or as any series of the particular feelings of our own or others' streams or trains of conscious-

ness. It is, in short, not the self to be pleased. The greatest sum of units of pleasure we found to be the idea of a mere collection, whereas, if we wanted morality, it was something like a universal that we wanted. Happiness, as the effort to construct that universal by the addition of particulars, gave us a futile and bastard product which carried its self-destruction within it, in the continual assertion of its own universality, together with its unceasing actual particularity and finitude; so that happiness was, if we chose, nowhere not realized; or again, if we chose, not anywhere realizable. And passing then to the opposite pole, to the universal as the negative of the particulars, to the supposed pure will or duty for duty's sake, we found that too was an unreal conception. It was a mere form which, to be will, must give itself a content, and which could give itself a content only at the cost of a self-contradiction. We saw, further, that any such content was in addition arbitrarily postu-

[1] Essay v, *Ethical Studies*, London, 1876.

450

lated and that, even then, the form was either never realized, because real in no particular content, or always and everywhere realized, because equally reconcilable with any content. And so, as before with happiness, we perceived that morality could have no existence if it meant anything more than the continual asseveration of an empty formula. And, if we had chosen, we might have gone on to exhibit the falsity of asceticism, to see that the self cannot be realized as its own mere negation, since morality is practice, is will to do something, is self-affirmation; and that a will to deny one's will is not self-realization, but rather is, strictly speaking, a psychical impossibility, a self-contradictory illusion. And the possibility, again, of taking as the self to be realized the self which I happen to have, my natural being, and of making life the end of life in the sense that each should live his life as he happens to find it in his own nature, has been precluded beforehand by the result derived from the consideration of the moral consciousness, viz., that morality implies a superior, a higher self, or at all events a universal something which is above this or that self and so above mine. And, to complete the account of our negations, we saw further, with respect to duty for duty's sake, that even were it possible (as it is not) to create a content from the formula and to elaborate in this manner a system of duties, yet even then the practice required by the theory would be impossible, and so too morality, since in practice particular duties must collide and the collision of duties, if we hold to duty for duty's sake, is the destruction of all duty save the unrealized form of duty in general.

But let us view this result, which seems so unsatisfactory, from the positive side; let us see after all with what we are left. We have self-realization left as the end, the self so far being defined as neither a collection of particular feelings nor an abstract universal. The self is to be realized as something not simply one or the other; it is to be realized further as will, will not being merely the natural will, or the will as it happens to exist and finds itself here or there, but the will as the *good* will, i. e., the will that realizes an end which is above this or that man, superior to them, and capable of confronting them in the shape of a law or an ought. This superior something further, which is a possible law or ought to the individual man, does not depend for its existence on his choice or opinion. Either there is no morality, so says the moral consciousness, or moral duties exist independently of their position by this or that person — my duty may be mine and no other man's, but I do not make it mine. If it is duty, it would be the duty of any person in my case and condition, whether they thought so or not — in a word, duty is 'objective,' in the sense of not being contingent on the opinion or choice of this or that subject.

What we have left then (to resume it) is this — the end is the realization of the good will which is superior to ourselves; and again the end is self-realization. Bringing these together we see the end is the realization of ourselves as the will which is above ourselves. And this will (if morality exists) we saw must be 'objective,' because not dependent on 'subjective' liking; and 'universal,' because not identifiable with any particular, but standing above all actual and possible particulars. Further, though universal it is not abstract since it belongs to its essence that it should be realized, and it has no real existence except in and through its particulars. The good will (for morality) is meaningless, if, whatever else it be, it be not the will of living human beings. It is a concrete universal because it not only is above but is within and throughout its details, and is so far only as they are. It is the life which can live only in and by them, as they are dead unless within it; it is the whole soul which lives so far as the body lives, which makes the body a living body and which without the body is as unreal an abstraction as the body without it. It is an organism and a moral organism; and it is conscious self-realization because only by the will of its self-conscious members can the moral organism give itself reality. It is the self-realization of the whole body because it is one and the same will which lives and acts in the life and action of each. It is the self-realization of each member because each member cannot find the function which makes him himself, apart from the whole to which he belongs; to be himself he must go beyond himself, to live his life he must live a life which is not *merely* his own, but which, none the less, but on the contrary all the more, is intensely and emphatically his own individuality. Here, and here first, are the contradictions which have beset us solved — here is a universal which can confront our wandering desires with a fixed and stern imperative, but which yet is no unreal form of the mind but a living soul that penetrates and stands fast in the detail of actual existence. It is real, and real for me. It is in its affirmation that I affirm myself, for I am but as a 'heart-beat in its system.' And I am real in it, for, when I give myself to it, it gives me the fruition of my own personal activity, the accomplished ideal of my life which is happiness. In the realized idea which, superior to me and yet here and now in and by me, affirms itself in a continuous process, we have found the end, we have found self-realization, duty, and

happiness in one — yes, we have found ourselves when we have found our station and its duties, our function as an organ in the social organism.

'Mere rhetoric,' we shall be told, 'a bad metaphysical dream, a stale old story once more warmed up, which cannot hold its own against the logic of facts. That the state was prior to the individual, that the whole was sometimes more than the sum of the parts, was an illusion which preyed on the thinkers of Greece. But that illusion has been traced to its source and dispelled and is in plain words exploded. The family, society, the state, and generally every community of men consists of individuals, and there is nothing in them real except the individuals. Individuals have made them, and make them, by placing themselves and by standing in certain relations. The individuals are real by themselves and it is because of them that the relations are real. They make them, they are real *in* them, not because of them, and they would be just as real *out* of them. The whole is the mere sum of the parts, and the parts are as real away from the whole as they are within the whole. Do you really suppose that the individual would perish if every form of community were destroyed? Do you think that anything real answers to the phrases of universal and organism? Everything is in the organism what it is out, and the universal is a name, the existing fact answering to which is particular persons in such and such relations. To put the matter shortly, the community is the sum of its parts, is made by the addition of parts, and the parts are as real before the addition as after; the relations they stand in do not make them what they are, but are accidental, not essential, to their being; and, as to the whole, if it is not a name for the individuals that compose it, it is a name of nothing actual. These are not metaphysical dreams. They are facts and verifiable facts.'

Are they facts? Facts should explain facts; and the view called 'individualism' (because the one reality that it believes in is the 'individual,' in the sense of this, that, and the other particular) should hence be the right explanation. What are the facts here to be explained? They are human communities, the family, society, and the state. Individualism has explained them long ago. They are 'collections' held together by force, illusion, or contract. It has told the story of their origin and to its own satisfaction cleared the matter up. Is the explanation satisfactory and verifiable? That would be a bold assertion when historical science has rejected and entirely discredited the individualistic origin of society, and when, if we turn to practice, we find everywhere the state asserting itself as a power which has, and, if need be, asserts the right to make use of and expend the property and person of the individual without regard to his wishes, and which, moreover, may destroy his life in punishment, and put forth other powers such as no theory of contract will explain except by the most palpable fictions, while at the same time no ordinary person calls their morality in question. Both history and practical politics refuse to verify the 'facts' of the individualist; and we should find still less to confirm his theory if we examined the family.

If, then, apart from metaphysic one looks at the history and present practice of society, these would not appear to establish the 'fact' that the individual is the one reality and communities mere collections. 'For all that,' we shall be told, 'it is the truth.' True that is, I suppose, not as fact but as metaphysic; and this is what one finds too often with those who deride meta-

physic and talk most of facts. Their minds, so far as such a thing may be, are not seldom mere 'collective unities' of metaphysical dogmas. They decry any real metaphysic because they dimly feel that their own will not stand criticism; and they appeal to facts because while their metaphysic stands they feel they need not be afraid of them. When their view is pushed as to plain realities, such as the nature of gregarious animals, the probable origin of mankind from them, the institutions of early society, actual existing communities with the common type impressed on all their members, their organic structure and the assertion of the whole body as of paramount importance in comparison with any of the members, then they must fall back on their metaphysic. And the point we wish here to emphasize is this, that their metaphysic is mere dogmatism. It is assumed, not proved. It has a right to no refutation, for assertion can demand no more than counter-assertion; and what is affirmed on the one side we on the other side can simply deny, and we intend to do so here.

A discussion that would go to the bottom of the question, What is an individual? is certainly wanted. It would certainly be desirable, showing first what an individual is, to show then that 'individualism' has not apprehended that, but taken an abstraction for reality. But, if I could do that (which I could not do), this would not be the place; nor perhaps should I have to say very much that has not been said before, and has not been attended to.

But we are not going to enter on a metaphysical question to which we are not equal; we meet the metaphysical assertion of the 'individualist' with a mere denial and, turning to facts, we will try to show that they lead us in another direction. To the assertion.

then, that selves are 'individual' in the sense of exclusive of other selves, we oppose the (equally justified) assertion that this is a mere fancy. We say that, out of theory, no such individual men exist; and we will try to show from fact that, in fact, what we call an individual man is what he is because of and by virtue of community, and that communities are thus not mere names but something real, and can be regarded (if we mean to keep to facts) only as the one in the many.

And to confine the subject and to keep to what is familiar, we will not call to our aid the life of animals, nor early societies, nor the course of history, but we will take men as they are now; we will take ourselves and endeavor to keep wholly to the teaching of experience.

Let us take a man, an Englishman as he is now, and try to point out that apart from what he has in common with others, apart from his sameness with others, he is not an Englishman— nor a man at all; that if you take him as something by himself, he is not what he is. Of course we do not mean to say that he cannot go out of England without disappearing, nor, even if all the rest of the nation perished that he would not survive. What we mean to say is that he is what he is because he is a born and educated social being, and a member of an individual social organism; that if you make abstraction of all this, which is the same in him and in others, what you have left is not an Englishman, nor a man, but some I know not what residuum, which never has existed by itself and does not so exist. If we suppose the world of relations, in which he was born and bred, never to have been, then we suppose the very essence of him not to be; if we take that away, we have taken him away; and hence he now is not an individual, in the sense of owing nothing to the sphere of relations in which he finds himself, but does contain those relations within himself as belonging to his very being; he is what he is, in brief, so far as he is what others also are.

But we shall be cut short here with an objection. 'It is impossible,' we shall be told, 'that two men should have the same thing in common. You are confusing sameness and likeness.' I say in answer that I am not, and that the too probable objector I am imagining too probably knows the meaning of neither one word nor the other. But this is a matter we do not intend to stay over, because it is a metaphysical question we cannot discuss, and which, moreover, we cannot be called on to discuss. We cannot be called on to discuss it because we have to do again here with sheer assertion, which either is ignorant of or ignores the critical investigation of the subject, and which, therefore, has no right to demand an answer. We allude to it merely because it has become a sort of catchword with 'advanced thinkers.' All that it comes to is this: first identity and diversity are assumed to exclude one another, and therefore, since diversity is a fact, it follows that there is no identity. Hence a difficulty; because it has been seen long ago and forces itself upon everyone, that denial of all identity brings you into sharp collision with ordinary fact and leads to total skepticism; [2] so, to avoid this, while we yet maintain the previous dogma, 'resemblance' is brought in — a conception which (I suppose I need not add) is not analyzed or properly

[2] Even from Mr. Mill (in controversy) we can quote, "If every general conception, instead of being 'the One in the Many,' were considered to be as many different conceptions as there are things to which it is applicable, there would be no such thing as general language."—*Logic*, 6th ed., I, 201.

defined, and so does all the better. Against these assertions I shall put some others, viz., that identity and diversity, sameness and difference, imply one another, and depend for their meaning on one another; that mere diversity is nonsense, just as mere identity is also nonsense; that resemblance or likeness, strictly speaking, falls not in the objects, but in the person contemplating (likening, *vergleichend*); that 'is A really like B?' does not mean 'does it seem like?' It may mean 'would it seem like to everybody?' but it generally means 'is there an "objective identity"?' Is there a point or points the same in both, whether anyone sees it or not?' We do not talk of cases of 'mistaken likeness'; we do not hang one man because he is 'exactly like' another, or at least we do not wish to do so. We are the same as we were, not merely more or less like. We have the same faith, hope, and purpose, and the same feelings as another man has now, as ourselves had at another time — not understanding thereby the numerical indistinguishedness of particular states and moments, but calling the feelings one and the same feeling because *what* is felt is the same, and not merely like. In short, so far is it from being true that 'sameness' is really 'likeness,' that it is utterly false that two things are really and objectively 'like,' unless that means 'more or less the same.' So much by way of counter-assertion; and now let us turn to our facts.

The 'individual' man, the man into whose essence his community with others does not enter, who does not include relation to others in his very being, is, we say, a fiction, and in the light of facts we have to examine him. Let us take him in the shape of an English child as soon as he is born; for I suppose we ought not to go further back. Let us take him as soon as he is separated from his mother and occupies a space clear and exclusive of all other human beings. At this time, education and custom will, I imagine, be allowed to have not as yet operated on him or lessened his 'individuality.' But is he now a mere 'individual,' in the sense of not implying in his being identity with others? We cannot say that if we hold to the teaching of modern physiology. Physiology would tell us, in one language or another, that even now the child's mind is no passive 'tabula rasa'; he has an inner, a yet undeveloped nature, which must largely determine his future individuality. What is this inner nature? Is it particular to himself? Certainly not all of it, will have to be the answer. The child is not fallen from heaven. He is born of certain parents who come of certain families, and he has in him the qualities of his parents, and, as breeders would say, of the strains from both sides. Much of it we can see and more we believe to be latent and, giving certain (possible or impossible) conditions, ready to come to light. On the descent of mental qualities modern investigation and popular experience, as expressed in uneducated vulgar opinion, altogether, I believe, support one another, and we need not linger here. But if the intellectual and active qualities do descend from ancestors, is it not, I would ask, quite clear that a man may have in him the same that his father and mother had, the same that his brothers and sisters have? And if anyone objects to the word 'same,' I would put this to him. If, concerning two dogs allied in blood, I were to ask a man, 'Is that of the same strain or stock as this?' and were answered, 'No, not the same, but similar,' should I not think one of these things, that the man either meant to deceive me, or was a 'thinker,' or a fool?

But the child is not merely the member of a family; he is born into other spheres, and (passing over the subordinate wholes which nevertheless do in many cases qualify him) he is born a member of the English nation. It is, I believe, a matter of fact that at birth the child of one race is not the same as the child of another; that in the children of the one race there is a certain identity, a developed or undeveloped national type which may be hard to recognize, or which at present may even be unrecognizable, but which nevertheless in some form will appear. If that be the fact, then again we must say that one English child is in some points, though perhaps it does not as yet show itself, the same as another. His being is so far common to him with others; he is not a mere 'individual.'

We see the child has been born at a certain time of parents of a certain race, and that means also of a certain degree of culture. It is the opinion of those best qualified to speak on the subject that civilization is to some not inconsiderable extent hereditary; that aptitudes are developed, and are latent in the child at birth; and that it is a very different thing, even apart from education, to be born of civilized and of uncivilized ancestors. These 'civilized tendencies,' if we may use the phrase, are part of the essence of the child. He would only partly (if at all) be himself without them; he owes them to his ancestors, and his ancestors owe them to society. The ancestors were made what they were by the society they lived in. If in answer it be replied, 'Yes, but individual ancestors were prior to their society,' then that, to say the least of it, is a hazardous and unproved assertion, since man, so far as history can trace him back, is social; and if Mr. Darwin's conjecture as to the development of man from a social

animal be received, we must say that man has never been anything but social, and society never was made by individual men. Nor, if the (baseless) assertion of the priority of individual men were allowed, would that destroy our case, for certainly our more immediate ancestors were social; and, whether society was manufactured previously by individuals or not, yet in their case it certainly was not so. They at all events have been so qualified by the common possessions of social mankind that, as members in the organism, they have become relative to the whole. If we suppose then that the results of the social life of the race are present in a latent and potential form in the child, can we deny that they are common property? Can we assert that they are not an element of sameness in all? Can we say that the individual is this individual because he is exclusive, when, if we deduct from him what he includes, he loses characteristics which make him himself, and when again he does include what the others include, and therefore does (how can we escape the consequence?) include in some sense the others also, just as they include him? By himself, then, what are we to call him? I confess I do not know unless we name him a theoretical attempt to isolate what cannot be isolated, and that, I suppose, has, out of our heads, no existence. But what he is really, and not in mere theory, can be described only as the specification or particularization of that which is common, which is the same amid diversity, and without which the 'individual' would be so other than he is that we could not call him the same.

Thus the child is at birth; and he is born not into a desert, but into a living world, a whole which has a true individuality of its own, and into a system and order which it is difficult to look at as anything else than an organism, and which, even in England, we are now beginning to call by that name. And I fear that the 'individuality' (the particularness) which the child brought into the light with him now stands but a poor chance, and that there is no help for him until he is old enough to become a 'philosopher.' We have seen that already he has in him inherited habits, or what will of themselves appear as such; but, in addition to this, he is not for one moment left alone, but continually tampered with; and the habituation which is applied from the outside is the more insidious that it answers to this inborn disposition. Who can resist it? Nay, who but a 'thinker' could wish to have resisted it? And yet the tender care that receives and guides him is impressing on him habits, habits, alas, not particular to himself, and the 'icy chains' of universal custom are hardening themselves round his cradled life. As the poet tells us, he has not yet thought of himself; his earliest notions come mixed to him of things and persons, not distinct from one another, nor divided from the feeling of his own existence. The need that he cannot understand moves him to foolish, but not futile, cries for what only another can give him; and the breast of his mother, and the soft warmth and touches and tones of his nurse, are made one with the feeling of his own pleasure and pain; nor is he yet a moralist to beware of such illusion and to see in them mere means to an end without them in his separate self. For he does not even think of his separate self; he grows with his world, his mind fills and orders itself; and when he can separate himself from that world, and know himself apart from it, then by that time his self, the object of his self-consciousness, is penetrated, infected, characterized by the existence of others. Its content implies in every fiber relations of community. He learns, or already perhaps has learned, to speak, and here he appropriates the common heritage of his race; the tongue that he makes his own is his country's language, it is (or it should be) the same that others speak, and it carries into his mind the ideas and sentiments of the race (over this I need not stay), and stamps them in indelibly. He grows up in an atmosphere of example and general custom, his life widens out from one little world to other and higher worlds, and he apprehends through successive stations the whole in which he lives, and in which he has lived. Is he now to try and develop his 'individuality,' his self which is not the same as other selves? Where is it? What is it? Where can he find it? The soul within him is saturated, is filled, is qualified by, it has assimilated, has got its substance, has built itself up from, it *is* one and the same life with the universal life, and if he turns against this he turns against himself; if he thrusts it from him, he tears his own vitals; if he attacks it, he sets his weapon against his own heart. He has found his life in the life of the whole, he lives that in himself, 'he is a pulsebeat of the whole system, and himself the whole system.'

'The child, in his character of the form of the possibility of a moral individual, is something subjective or negative; his growing to manhood is the ceasing to be of this form, and his education is the discipline or the compulsion thereof. The positive side and the essence is that he is suckled at the breast of the universal Ethos, lives in its absolute intuition, as in that of a foreign being first, then comprehends it more and more, and so passes over into the universal mind.' The writer proceeds to draw the weighty conclusion that virtue 'is not a troubling oneself about a peculiar and isolated morality of one's own, that the striving for a positive morality of one's own is futile, and in its very nature impossible of attainment; that in respect of morality the saying of the wisest men of antiquity is the only one which is true, that to be moral is to live in accordance with the moral tradition of one's country; and in respect of education the one true answer is that which a Pythagorean gave to him who asked what was the best education for his son, If you make him the citizen of a people with good institutions.' [3]

But this is to anticipate. So far, I think, without aid from metaphysics, we have seen that the 'individual' apart from the community is an abstraction. It is not anything real and hence not anything that we can realize, however much we may wish to do so. We have seen that I am myself by sharing with others, by including in my essence relations to them, the relations of the social state. If I wish to realize my true being I must therefore realize something beyond my being as a mere this or that, for my true being has in it a life which is not the life of any mere particular, and so must be called a universal life.

What is it then that I am to realize? We have said it in 'my station and its duties.' To know what a man is (as we have seen) you must not take him in isolation. He is one of a people, he was born in a family, he lives in a certain society, in a certain state. What he has to do depends on what his place is, what his function is, and that all comes from his station in the organism. Are there then such organisms in which he lives, and if so, what is their nature? Here we come to questions which must be answered in full by any complete system of Ethics, but which we cannot enter on. We

must content ourselves by pointing out that there are such facts as the family, then in a middle position a man's own profession and society, and, over all, the larger community of the state. Leaving out of sight the question of a society wider than the state, we must say that a man's life with its moral duties is in the main filled up by his station in that system of wholes which the state is, and that this, partly by its laws and institutions and still more by its spirit, gives him the life which he does live and ought to live. That objective institutions exist is of course an obvious fact; and it is a fact which every day is becoming plainer that these institutions are organic, and further, that they are moral. The assertion that communities have been manufactured by the addition of exclusive units is, as we have seen, a mere fable; and if, within the state, we take that which seems wholly to depend on individual caprice, e. g., marriage,[4] yet even here we find that a man does give up his self so far as it excludes others; he does bring himself under a unity which is superior to the particular person and the impulses that belong to his single existence, and which makes him fully as much as he makes it. In short, man is a social being; he is real only because he is social, and can realize himself only because it is as social that he realizes himself. The mere individual is a delusion of theory; and the attempt to realize it in practice is the starvation and mutilation of human nature, with total sterility or the production of monstrosities.

Let us now in detail compare the advantages of our present view with

[3] Hegel, *Philosophische Abhandlungen*, I, 389.

[4] Marriage is a contract, a contract to pass out of the sphere of contract; and this is possible only because the contracting parties are already beyond and above the sphere of mere contract.

the defects of 'duty for duty's sake.' The objections we found fatal to that view may be stated as follows: (1) The universal was abstract. There was no content which belonged to it and was one with it; and the consequence was that either nothing could be willed, or what was willed was willed not because of the universal, but capriciously. (2) The universal was 'subjective.' It certainly gave itself out as 'objective,' in the sense of being independent of this or that person, but still it was not real in the world. It did not come to us as what *was*, it came as what (merely) was to be, an inner notion in moral persons, which had not power to carry itself out and transform the world. And self-realization, if it means will, does mean that we put ourselves forth and see ourselves actual in outer existence. Hence, by identifying ourselves with that which has not this existence, which is not master of the outer world, we cannot secure our self-realization; since, when we have identified ourselves with the end, the end may still remain a mere inner end which does not accomplish itself, and so does not satisfy us. (3) The universal left a part of ourselves outside it. However much we tried to be good, however determined we were to make our will one with the good will, yet we never succeeded. There was always something left in us which was in contradiction with the good. And this we saw was even necessary because morality meant and implied this contradiction, unless we accepted that form of conscientiousness which consists in the simple identification of one's conscience with one's own self (unless, *i. e.*, the consciousness of the relation of my private self to myself as the good self be degraded into my self-consciousness of my mere private self as the good self); and this cannot be if we are in earnest with morality. There thus remains a perpetual contradiction in myself, no less than in the world, between the 'is to be' and the 'is,' a contradiction that cannot be got rid of without getting rid of morality; for, as we saw, it is inherent in morality. The man cannot realize himself in himself as moral because the conforming of his sensuous nature to the universal would be the entire suppression of it, and hence not only of himself but also of the morality which is constituted by the relation of himself to the universal law. The man then cannot find self-realization in the morality of pure duty because (1) he cannot look on his subjective self as the realized moral law; (2) he cannot look on the objective world as the realization of the moral law; (3) he cannot realize the moral law at all because it is defined as that which has no particular content, and therefore no reality; or, if he gives it a content, then it is not the law he realizes, since the content is got not from the law but from elsewhere. In short, duty for duty's sake is an unsolved contradiction, the standing 'is to be,' which, therefore, because it is to be, is *not;* and in which, therefore, since it is *not,* he cannot find himself realized nor satisfy himself.

These are serious defects. Let us see how they are mended by 'my station and its duties.' In that (1) the universal is concrete, (2) it is objective, (3) it leaves nothing of us outside it.

(1) It is concrete, and yet not given by caprice. Let us take the latter first. It is not given by caprice for, although within certain limits I may choose my station according to my own liking, yet I and everyone else must have some station with duties pertaining to it, and those duties do not depend on our opinion or liking. Certain circumstances, a certain position, call for a certain course. How I in particular

know what my right course is, is a question we shall recur to hereafter — but at present we may take it as an obvious fact that in my station my particular duties are prescribed to me, and I have them whether I wish to or not. And secondly, it is concrete. The universal to be realized is no abstraction, but an organic whole; a system where many spheres are subordinated to one sphere, and particular actions to spheres. This system is real in the detail of its functions, not out of them, and lives in its vital processes, not away from them. The organs are always at work for the whole, the whole is at work in the organs. And I am one of the organs. The universal then which I am to realize is the system which penetrates and subordinates to itself the particulars of all lives, and here and now in my life has this and that function in this and that case, in exercising which through my will it realizes itself as a whole, and me in it.

(2) It is 'objective'; and this means that it does not stand over against the outer world as mere 'subject' confronted by mere 'object.' In that sense of the words it is neither merely 'objective' nor merely 'subjective'; but it is that real identity of subject and object, which, as we have seen, is the only thing that satisfies our desires. The inner side does exist, but it is no more than the inside; it is one factor in the whole and must not be separated from the other factor; and the mistake which is made by the morality which confines itself to the individual man is just this attempt at the separation of what cannot be separated. The inner side certainly is a fact, and it can be distinguished from the rest of the whole; but it really is one element of the whole, depends on the whole for its being, and cannot be divided from it. Let us explain. The moral world, as we said, is a whole, and has

two sides. There is an outer side, systems and institutions, from the family to the nation; this we may call the body of the moral world. And there must also be a soul, or else the body goes to pieces; everyone knows that institutions without the spirit of them are dead. In the moral organism this spirit is in the will of the organs as the will of the whole which, in and by the organs, carries out the organism and makes it alive, and which also (and this is the point to which attention is requested) is and must be felt or known in each organ as his own inward and personal will. It is quite clear that a nation is not strong without public spirit, and is not public spirited unless the members of it are public spirited, i. e., feel the good of the public as a personal matter, or have it at their hearts. The point here is that you cannot have the moral world unless it is willed; that to be willed it must be willed by persons; and that these persons not only have the moral world as the content of their wills, but also must in some way be aware of themselves as willing this content. This being inwardly aware of oneself as willing the good will falls in the inside of the moral whole; we may call it the soul; and it is the sphere of personal morality, or morality in the narrower sense of the consciousness of the relation of my private self to the inwardly presented universal will, my being aware of and willing myself as one with that or contrary to that, as dutiful or bad. We must never let this out of our sight, that, where the moral world exists, you have and you must have these two sides; neither will stand apart from the other; moral institutions are carcasses without personal morality, and personal morality apart from moral institutions is an unreality, a soul without a body.

Now this inward, this 'subjective,' this personal side, this knowing in him self by the subject of the relation in which the will of him as this or that man stands to the will of the whole within him, or (as was rightly seen by 'duty for duty's sake') this consciousness in the one subject of himself as two selves, is, as we said, necessary for all morality. But the form in which it is present may vary·very much, and, beginning with the stage of mere feeling, goes on to that of explicit reflection. The reader who considers the matter will perceive that (whether in the life of mankind or of this or that man) we do not begin with a consciousness of good and evil, right and wrong, as such, or in the strict sense.[5] The child is taught to will a content which is universal and good, and he learns to identify his will with it so that he feels pleasure when he feels himself in accord with it, uneasiness or pain when his will is contrary thereto and he feels it is contrary. This is the beginning of personal morality, and from this we may pass to consider the end. That, so far as form went, was sufficiently exhibited in Essay IV. It consists in the explicit consciousness in myself of two elements which, even though they exist in disunion, are felt to be really one; these are myself as the will of this or that self, and again the universal will as the will for good; and this latter I feel to be my true self, and desire my other self to be subordinated to and so identified with it; in which case I feel the satisfaction of an inward realization. That so far as form goes is correct. But the important point on which 'duty for duty's sake' utterly failed us was as to the content of the universal will. We have seen that for action this must have a content, and now we see where the content comes from. The universal side in personal morality is, in short, the reflection of

[5] On this point see more in Essay VII.

the objective moral world into ourselves (or into itself). The outer universal which I have been taught to will as my will, and which I have grown to find myself in, is now presented by me inwardly to myself as the universal which is my true being, and which by my will I must realize, if need be, against my will as this or that man. So this inner universal has the same content as the outer universal, for it *is* the outer universal in another sphere; it is the inside *of* the outside. *There* was the whole system as an objective will, including my station, and realizing itself here and now in my function. *Here* is the same system presented as a will in me, standing above my will, which wills a certain act to be done by me as a will which is one with the universal will. This universal will is not a blank, but is filled by the consideration of my station in the whole with reference to habitual and special acts. The ideal self appealed to by the moral man is an ideally presented will, in his position and circumstances, which rightly particularizes the general laws which answer to the general functions and system of spheres of the moral organism. That is the content, and therefore, as we saw it, it is concrete and filled. And therefore also (which is equally important) it is not merely 'subjective.'

If, on the inner side of the moral whole, the universal factor were (as in would-be morality it is) filled with a content which is not the detail of the objective will particularizing itself in such and such functions, then there would be no true identity of subject and object, no need why that which is moral should be that which is real, and we should never escape from a practical postulate, which, as we saw, is a practical standing contradiction. But if, as we have seen, the universal on the inside is the universal on the outside reflected in us, or (since we cannot separate it and ourselves) into itself in us; if the objective will of the moral organism is real only in the will of its organs, and if, in willing morally, we will ourselves as that will, and that will wills itself in us—then we must hold that this universal on the inner side is the will of the whole, which is self-conscious in us, and wills itself in us against the actual or possible opposition of the false private self. This being so, when we will morally, the will of the objective world wills itself in us, and carries both us and itself out into the world of the moral will, which is its own realm. We see thus that when morals are looked at as a whole, the will of the inside, so far as it is moral, *is* the will of the outside, and the two are one and cannot be torn apart without *ipso facto* destroying the unity in which morality consists. To be moral I must will my station and its duties; that is, I will to particularize the moral system truly in a given case; and the other side to this act is that the moral system wills to particularize itself in a given station and functions, *i. e.*, in my actions and by my will. In other words, my moral self is not simply mine; it is not an inner which belongs simply to me; and further, it is not a mere inner at all, but it is the soul which animates the body and lives in it, and would not be the soul if it had not a body and *its* body. The objective organism, the systematized moral world, is the reality of the moral will; my duties on the inside answer to due functions on the outside. There is no need here for a pre-established or a postulated harmony, for the moral whole is the identity of both sides; my private choice, so far as I am moral, is the mere form of bestowing myself on and identifying myself with the will of the moral organism, which realizes in its process both itself and myself. Hence

we see that what I have to do I have not to force on a recalcitrant world; I have to fill my place—the place that waits for me to fill it; to make my private self the means, my life the sphere and the function of the soul of the whole, which thus, personal in me, externalizes both itself and me into a solid reality, which is both mine and its.

(3) What we come to now is the third superiority of 'my station and its duties.' The universal which is the end, and which we have seen is concrete and does realize itself, does also more. It gets rid of the contradiction between duty and the 'empirical' self; it does not in its realization leave me forever outside and unrealized.

In 'duty for duty's sake' we were always unsatisfied, no nearer our goal at the end than at the beginning. There we had the fixed antithesis of the sensuous self on one side, and a nonsensuous moral ideal on the other — a standing contradiction which brought with it a perpetual self-deceit, or the depressing perpetual confession that I am not what I ought to be in my inner heart, and that I never can be so. Duty, we thus saw, was an infinite process, an unending 'not-yet'; a continual 'not' with an everlasting 'to be,' or an abiding 'to be' with a ceaseless 'not.'

From this last peevish enemy we are again delivered by 'my station and its duties.' There I realize myself morally, so that not only what ought to be in the world is, but I am what I ought to be, and find so my contentment and satisfaction. If this were not the case, when we consider that the ordinary moral man is self-contented and happy, we should be forced to accuse him of immorality, and we do not do this; we say he most likely might be better, but we do not say that he is bad, or need consider himself so. Why is this? It is because 'my station and its duties' teaches us to identify others and ourselves with the station we fill; to consider that as good, and by virtue of that to consider others and ourselves good too. It teaches us that a man who does his work in the world is good, notwithstanding his faults, if his faults do not prevent him from fulfilling his station. It tells us that the heart is an idle abstraction; we are not to think of it, nor must we look at our insides, but at our work and our life, and say to ourselves, Am I fulfilling my appointed function or not? Fulfill it we can, if we will. What we have to do is not so much better than the world that we cannot do it; the world is there waiting for it; my duties are my rights. On the one hand, I am not likely to be much better than the world asks me to be; on the other hand, if I can take my place in the world I ought not to be discontented. Here we must not be misunderstood; we do not say that the false self, the habits and desires opposed to the good will, are extinguished. Though negated, they never are all of them entirely suppressed, and cannot be. Hence we must not say that any man really does fill his station to the full height of his capacity; nor must we say of any man that he cannot perform his function better than he does, for we all can do so, and should try to do so. We do not wish to deny what are plain moral facts, nor in any way to slur them over.

How then does the contradiction disappear? It disappears by my identifying myself with the good will that I realize in the world, by my refusing to identify myself with the bad will of my private self. So far as I am one with the good will, living as a member in the moral organism, I am to consider myself real and I am not to consider the false self real. That cannot be attributed to me in my character of member in the organism. Even in me

the false existence of it has been partly suppressed by that organism; and, so far as the organism is concerned, it is wholly suppressed because contradicted in its results, and allowed no reality. Hence, not existing for the organism, it does not exist for me as a member thereof; and only as a member thereof do I hold myself to be real. And yet this is not justification by faith, for we not only trust, but see, that despite our faults the moral world stands fast, and we in and by it. It is like faith, however, in this, that not merely by thinking ourselves, but by willing ourselves as such, can we look on ourselves as organs in a good whole, and so ourselves good. And further, the knowledge that as members of the system we are real, and not otherwise, encourages us more and more to identify ourselves with that system; to make ourselves better, and so more real, since we see that the good is real, and that nothing else is.

Or, to repeat it, in education my self by habituation has been growing into one with the good self around me, and by my free acceptance of my lot hereafter I consciously make myself one with the good, so that, though bad habits cling to and even arise in me, yet I cannot but be aware of myself as the reality of the good will. That is my essential side; my imperfections are not, and practically they do not matter. The good will in the world realizes itself by and in imperfect instruments, and in spite of them. The work is done, and so long as I will my part of the work and do it (as I do), I feel that, if I perform the function, I *am* the organ, and that my faults, if they do not matter to my station, do not matter to me. My heart I am not to think of, except to tell by my work whether it is in my work, and one with the moral whole; and if that is so, I have the consciousness of absolute reality in the good because of and by myself, and in myself because of and through the good; and with that I am satisfied, and have no right to be dissatisfied.

The individual's consciousness of himself is inseparable from the knowing himself as an organ of the whole; and the residuum falls more and more into the background, so that he thinks of it, if at all, not as himself, but as an idle appendage. For his nature now is not distinct from his 'artificial self.' He is related to the living moral system not as to a foreign body; his relation to it is 'too inward even for faith,' since faith implies a certain separation. It is no other-world that he cannot see but must trust to: he feels himself in it, and it in him; in a word, the self-consciousness of himself *is* the self-consciousness of the whole in him, and his will is the will which sees in him its accomplishment by him; it is the free will which knows itself as the free will, and as this beholds its realization and is more than content.

The non-theoretical person, if he be not immoral, is at peace with reality; and the man who in any degree has made this point of view his own becomes more and more reconciled to the world and to life, and the theories of 'advanced thinkers' come to him more and more as the thinnest and most miserable abstractions. He sees evils which cannot discourage him, since they point to the strength of the life which can endure such parasites and flourish in spite of them. If the popularizing of superficial views inclines him to bitterness, he comforts himself when he sees that they live in the head, and but little, if at all, in the heart and life; that still at the push the doctrinaire and the quacksalver go to the wall, and that even

that too is as it ought to be. He sees the true account of the state (which holds it to be neither mere force nor convention, but the moral organism, the real identity of might and right) unknown or 'refuted,' laughed at and despised, but he sees that state every day in its practice refute every other doctrine, and do with the moral approval of all what the explicit theory of scarcely one will morally justify. He sees instincts are better and stronger than so-called 'principles.' He sees in the hour of need what are called 'rights' laughed at, 'freedom,' the liberty to do what one pleases, tramped on, the claims of the individual trodden under foot, and theories burst like cobwebs. And he sees, as of old, the heart of a nation rise high and beat in the breast of each one of her citizens till her safety and her honor are dearer to each than life, till to those who live her shame and sorrow, if such is allotted, outweigh their loss, and death seems a little thing to those who go for her to their common and nameless grave. And he knows that what is stronger than death is hate or love, hate here for love's sake, and that love does not fear death because already it is the death into life of what our philosophers tell us is the only life and reality.

Yes, the state is not put together, but it lives; it is not a heap nor a machine; it is no mere extravagance when a poet talks of a nation's soul. It is the objective mind which is subjective and self-conscious in its citizens —it feels and knows itself in the heart of each. It speaks the word of command and gives the field of accomplishment, and in the activity of obedience it has and bestows individual life and satisfaction and happiness.

First in the community is the individual realized. He is here the embodiment of beauty, goodness, and truth—of truth because he corresponds to his universal conception, of beauty because he realizes it in a single form to the senses or imagination, of goodness because his will expresses and is the will of the universal.

'The realm of morality is nothing but the absolute spiritual unity of the essence of individuals, which exists in the independent reality of them. . . . The moral substance, looked at abstractedly from the mere side of its universality, is the law, and, as this, is only thought; but nonetheless is it, from another point of view, immediate real self-consciousness or custom: and conversely the individual exists as this single unit, inasmuch as it is conscious in its individuality of the universal consciousness as its own being, inasmuch as its action and existence are the universal Ethos. . . . They (the individuals) are aware in themselves that they possess this individual independent being because of the sacrifice of their individuality, because the universal substance is their soul and essence: and, on the other side, this universal is their individual action, the work that they as individuals have produced.

'The merely individual action and business of the separate person is concerned with the needs he is subject to as a natural being, as an individuality which exists. That even these his commonest functions do not come to nothing, but possess reality, is effected solely by the universal maintaining medium, by the power of the whole people. But it is not simply the form of persistence which the universal substance confers on his action; it gives also the content— what he does *is* the universal skill and custom of all. This content, just so far as it completely individualizes itself, is in its reality interlaced with the action of all. The work of the individual for his needs is a satisfaction of the needs of others as much as of his own; and he attains the satisfaction of his own only through the work of the others. The individual in his individual work thus accomplishes a universal work—he does so here *unconsciously;* but he also further accomplishes it as his *conscious* object: the whole as the whole is his work for which he sacrifices himself, and from which by that very sacrifice he gets again his self restored. Here there is nothing taken which is not given, nothing wherein the independent individual, by and in the resolution of his atomic existence, by and in the negation of his self, fails to give himself the positive significance of a being which exists by and for itself. The unity—on the one side of the being for another, or the making oneself into an outward thing, and on the other side of the being for oneself—this universal substance speaks its universal language in the usages and laws of his people: and yet this unchanging essence is itself nought else than the expression of the single individuality, which seems at first sight its mere opposite; the laws pronounce nothing but what everyone *is* and does. The individual recognizes the substance not only as his universal outward existence, but he recognizes also himself in it, particularized in his own individuality and in that of each of his fellow citizens. And so in the universal mind each one has nothing but self-certainty, the assurance of finding in existing reality nothing but himself. In all I contemplate independent beings, that are such, and are for themselves, only in the very same way that I am for myself; in them I see existing free unity of self with others, and existing by virtue of me and by virtue of the others alike.

Them as myself, myself as them.[6]

'In a free people, therefore, reason is realized in truth; it is present living mind, and in this not only does the individual find his destination, *i. e.*, his universal and singular essence, promulgated and ready to his hand as an outward existence, but he himself is this essence, and has also reached and fulfilled his destination. Hence the wisest men of antiquity have given judgment that wisdom and virtue consist in living agreeably to the Ethos of one's people.'—(Hegel, ii, 256-58.)

Once let us take the point of view which regards the community as the real moral organism, which in its members knows and wills itself and sees the individual to be real just so far as the universal self is in his self, as he in it, and we get the solution of most, if not all, of our previous difficulties. There is here no need to ask and by some scientific process find out what is moral, for morality exists all

[6] Let me illustrate from our great poet:

So they loved, as love in twain
Had the essence but in one;
Two distincts, division none:
Number there in love was slain.

Hearts remote yet not asunder;
Distance, and no space was seen—
So between them love did shine . . .
Either was the other's mine.

Property was thus appalled,
That the self was not the same;
Single nature's double name
Neither two nor one was called.

Reason, in itself confounded,
Saw division grow together:
To themselves yet either neither
Simple were so well compounded,

That it cried, How true a twain
Seemeth this concordant one!
Love hath reason, reason none,
If what parts can so remain.

—(*The Phoenix and the Turtle.*)

Surely philosophy does not reach its end till the 'reason of reason' is adequate to the 'reason of love.'

round us, and faces us, if need be, with a categorical imperative, while it surrounds us on the other side with an atmosphere of love.

The belief in this real moral organism is the one solution of ethical problems. It breaks down the antithesis of despotism and individualism; it denies them, while it preserves the truth of both. The truth of individualism is saved, because unless we have intense life and self-consciousness in the members of the state, the whole state is ossified. The truth of despotism is saved, because unless the member realizes the whole by and in himself, he fails to reach his own individuality. Considered in the main, the best communities are those which have the best men for their members, and the best men are the members of the best communities. Circle as this is, it is not a vicious circle. The two problems of the best man and best state are two sides, two distinguishable aspects of the one problem, how to realize in human nature the perfect unity of homogeneity and specification; and when we see that each of these without the other is unreal, then we see that (speaking in general) the welfare of the state and the welfare of its individuals are questions which it is mistaken and ruinous to separate. Personal morality and political and social institutions cannot exist apart, and (in general) the better the one the better the other. The community is moral because it realizes personal morality; personal morality is moral because and in so far as it realizes the moral whole.

It is here we find an answer to the complaint of our day on the dwindling of human nature. The higher the organism (we are told), the more are its functions specified, and hence narrowed. The man becomes a machine, or the piece of a machine; and, though the world grows, 'the individual withers.' On this we may first remark that, if what is meant is that the more centralized the system, the more narrow and monotonous is the life of the member, that is a very questionable assertion. If it be meant that the individual's life can be narrowed to 'file-packing,' or the like, without detriment to the intensity of the life of the whole, that is even more questionable. If again it be meant that in many cases we have a one-sided specification, which, despite the immediate stimulus of particular function implies ultimate loss of life to the body, that, I think, probably is so, but it is doubtful if we are compelled to think it always must be so. But the root of the whole complaint is a false view of things, which we have briefly noticed above.[7] The moral organism is not a mere animal organism. In the latter (it is no novel remark) the member is not aware of itself as such, while in the former it knows itself, and therefore knows the whole in itself. The narrow external function of the man is not the whole man. He has a life which we cannot see with our eyes; and there is no duty so mean that it is not the realization of this, and knowable as such. What counts is not the visible outer work so much as the spirit in which it is done. The breadth of my life is not measured by the multitude of my pursuits, nor the space I take up amongst other men, but by the fullness of the whole life which I know as mine. It is true that less now depends on each of us, as this or that man; it is not true that our individuality is therefore lessened, that therefore we have less in us.

Let us now consider our point of view in relation to certain antagonistic

7 [In the essay "Why Should I Be Moral," p. 73 of *Ethical Studies,* London, 1876.]

ideas; and first against the common error that there is something 'right in itself' for me to do, in the sense that either there must be some absolute rule of morality the same for all persons without distinction of times and places, or else that all morality is 'relative,' and hence no morality. Let us begin by remarking that there is no such fixed code or rule of right. It is abundantly clear that the morality of one time is not that of another time, that the men considered good in one age might in another age not be thought good, that what would be right for us here might be mean and base in another country, and what would be wrong for us here might there be our bounden duty. This is clear fact which is denied only in the interest of a foregone conclusion. The motive to deny it is the belief that it is fatal to morality. If what is right here is wrong there, then all morality (such is the notion) becomes chance and convention, and so ceases. But 'my station and its duties' holds that *unless* morals varied, there could be no morality; that a morality which was *not* relative would be futile, and I should have to ask for something 'more relative than this.'

Let us explain. We hold that man is φύσει πολιτικός, that apart from the community he is Θεὸς ἢ Θηρίον, no man at all. We hold again that the true nature of man, the oneness of homogeneity and specification, is being wrought out in history; in short, we believe in evolution. The process of evolution is the humanizing of the bestial foundation of man's nature by carrying out in it the true idea of man—in other words, by realizing man as an infinite whole. This realization is possible only by the individual's living as member in a higher life, and this higher life is slowly developed in a series of stages. Starting from and on the basis of animal nature, humanity has worked itself out by gradual advances of specification and systematization, and any other progress would, in the world we know, have been impossible. The notion that full-fledged moral ideas fell down from heaven is contrary to all the facts with which we are acquainted. If they had done so, it would have been for their own sake; for by us they certainly could not have been perceived, much less applied. At any given period to know more than he did, man must have been more than he was; for a human being is nothing if he is not the son of his time, and he must realize himself as that, or he will not do it at all.

Morality is 'relative,' but is nonetheless real. At every stage there is the solid fact of a world so far moralized. There is an objective morality in the accomplished will of the past and present, a higher self worked out by the infinite pain, the sweat and blood of generations, and now given to me by free grace and in love and faith as a sacred trust. It comes to me as the truth of my own nature, and the power and the law, which is stronger and higher than any caprice or opinion of my own.

'Evolution,' in this sense of the word, gives us over neither to chance nor alien necessity, for it is that self-realization which is the progressive conquest of both. But, on another understanding of the term, we cannot help asking, Is this still the case, and is 'my station' a tenable point of view?

Wholly tenable, in the form in which we have stated it, it is not. For if, in saying Morality has developed, all we mean is that something has happened different from earlier events, that human society has changed, and that the alterations, so far as we know them, are more or less of a certain sort; if 'progress' signifies that an advance has been set going and is kept up by chance in an unknown direc-

tion; that the higher is, in short, what *is* and what before was not, and that what will be, of whatever sort it is, will still be a step in progress; if, in short, the movement of history toward a goal is mere illusion, and the stages of that movement are nothing but the successes of what from time to time somehow happens to be best suited to the chance of circumstances—then it is clear in the first place that, teleology being banished, such words as evolution [8] and progress have lost their own

[8] With respect to 'evolution' I may remark in passing that, though this word may of course be used to stand for anything whatever, yet for all that it has a meaning of its own, which those who care to use words, not merely with *a* meaning, but also with *their* meaning, would do well to consider. To try to exhibit all that is contained in it would be a serious matter, but we may call attention to a part. And first, 'evolution,' 'development,' 'progress,' all imply something identical throughout, a subject of the evolution, which is one and the same. If what is there at the beginning is not there at the end, and the same as what was there at the beginning, then evolution is a word with no meaning. Something must evolve itself, and that something, which is the end, must also be the beginning. It must be what moves itself to the end, and must be the end which is the 'because' of the motion. Evolution must evolve itself to itself, progress itself go forward to a goal which is itself, development bring out nothing but what was in, and bring it out, not from external compulsion, but *because* it is in.

And further, unless what is at the end is different from that which was at the beginning, there is no evolution. That which develops, or evolves itself, both is and is not. It *is*, or it could not be *it* which develops, and which at the end has developed. It *is not*, or else it could not become. It becomes what it is; and, if this is nonsense, then evolution is nonsense.

Evolution is a contradiction; and, when

meaning, and that to speak of humanity realizing itself in history, and of myself finding in that movement the truth of myself worked out, would be simply to delude oneself with hollow phrases.

Thus far we must say that on such a view of 'development' the doctrine of 'my station' is grievously curtailed. But is it destroyed? Not wholly; though sorely mutilated, it still keeps its ground. We have rejected teleology but have not yet embraced individualism. We still believe that the universal self is more than a collection or an idea, that it is reality, and that apart from it the 'individuals' are the fictions of a theory. We have still the fact of the one self particularized in its many members; and the right and duty of gaining self-realization through the real universal is still as certain as is the impossibility of gaining it otherwise. And so 'my station' is after all a position, not indeed satisfactory, but not yet untenable.

But if the larger doctrine be the truth, if evolution is more than a tortured phrase, and progress to a goal no mere idea but an actual fact, then history is the working out of the true human nature through various incomplete stages toward completion, and 'my station' is the one satisfactory view of morals. Here (as we have seen) all morality is and must be 'relative' because the essence of realization is evolution through stages, and hence

---

the contradiction ceases, the evolution ceases. The process is a contradiction, and only *because* it is a contradiction can it be a process. So long as progress lasts, contradiction lasts; so long as anything becomes, it is not. To be realized is to cease to progress. To be at the end (in one sense) is to lose the end (in another), and that because (in both senses) all then comes to the end. For the process is a contradiction, and the solution of the contradiction is in every sense the *end* of the process.

existence in some one stage which is not final; here, on the other hand, all morality is 'absolute' because in every stage the essence of man *is* realized, however imperfectly; and yet again the distinction of right in itself against relative morality is not banished, because, from the point of view of a higher stage, we can see that lower stages failed to realize the truth completely enough, and also, mixed and one with their realization, did present features contrary to the true nature of man as we now see it. Yet herein the morality of every stage is justified for that stage; and the demand for a code of right in itself, apart from any stage, is seen to be the asking for an impossibility.

The next point we come to is the question, How do I get to know in particular what is right and wrong? and here again we find a strangely erroneous preconception. It is thought that moral philosophy has to accomplish this task for us, and the conclusion lies near at hand that any system which will not do this is worthless. Well, we first remark, and with some confidence, that there cannot be a moral philosophy which will tell us what in particular we are to do, and also that it is not the business of philosophy to do so. All philosophy has to do is 'to understand what is,' and moral philosophy has to understand morals which exist, not to make them or give directions for making them. Such a notion is simply ludicrous. Philosophy in general has not to anticipate the discoveries of the particular sciences nor the evolution of history; the philosophy of religion has not to make a new religion or teach an old one, but simply to understand the religious consciousness; and aesthetic has not to produce works of fine art, but to theorize the beautiful which it finds; political philosophy has not to play tricks with the state, but to understand it; and ethics has not to make the world moral, but to reduce to theory the morality current in the world. If we want it to do anything more, so much the worse for us; for it cannot possibly construct new morality, and, even if it could to any extent codify what exists (a point on which I do not enter), yet it surely is clear that in cases of collision of duties it would not help you to know what to do. Who would go to a learned theologian, as such, in a practical religious difficulty; to a system of aesthetic for suggestions on the handling of an artistic theme; to a physiologist, as such, for a diagnosis and prescription; to a political philosopher in practical politics; or to a psychologist in an intrigue of any kind? All these persons no doubt *might* be the best to go to, but that would not be because they were the best theorists, but because they were more. In short, the view which thinks moral philosophy is to supply us with particular moral prescriptions confuses science with art, and confuses, besides, reflective with intuitive judgment. That which tells us what in particular is right and wrong is not reflection but intuition. 9

We know what is right in a particular case by what we may call an immediate judgment, or an intuitive subsumption. These phrases are perhaps not very luminous, and the mat-

9 I must ask the reader here not to think of 'Intuitionalism,' or of 'Organs of the Absolute,' or of anything else of the sort. 'Intuitive' is used here as the opposite of 'reflective' or 'discursive'; 'intuition' as the opposite of 'reasoning' or 'explicit inferring.' If the reader dislike the word, he may substitute 'perception' or 'sense,' if he will; but then he must remember that neither are to exclude the intellectual, the understanding and its implicit judgments and inferences.

ter of the 'inituitive understanding' in general is doubtless difficult, and the special character of moral judgments not easy to define; and I do not say that I am in a position to explain these subjects at all, nor, I think, could anyone do so, except at considerable length. But the point that I do wish to establish here is, I think, not at all obscure. The reader has first to recognize that moral judgments are not discursive; next, that nevertheless they do start from and rest on a certain basis; and then if he puts the two together, he will see that they involve what he may call the 'intuitive understanding,' or any other name, so long as he keeps in sight the two elements and holds them together.

On the head that moral judgments are not discursive, no one, I think, will wish me to stay long. If the reader attends to the facts he will not want anything else; and if he does not, I confess I cannot prove my point. In practical morality, no doubt, we *may* reflect on our principles, but I think it is not too much to say that we *never* do so, except where we have come upon a difficulty of particular application. If anyone thinks that a man's *ordinary* judgment, 'this is right or wrong,' comes from the having a rule *before* the mind and bringing the particular case under it, he may be right, and I cannot try to show that he is wrong. I can only leave it to the reader to judge for himself. We say we 'see' and we 'feel' in these cases, not we 'conclude.' We prize the advice of persons who can give us no reasons for what they say. There is a general belief that the having a reason for all your actions is pedantic and absurd. There is a general belief that to try to have reasons for all that you do is sometimes very dangerous. Not only the woman but the man who deliberates may be lost. First thoughts are often the best,[10] and if once you begin to argue with the devil you are in a perilous state. And I think I may add (though I do it in fear) that women are remarkable for the fineness of their moral perceptions [11] and the quickness of their judgments, and yet are or (let me save myself by saying) 'may be' not remarkable for corresponding discursive ability.

Taking for granted then that our ordinary way of judging in morals is not by reflection and explicit reasoning, we have now to point to the other side of the fact, viz., that these judgments are not mere isolated impressions, but stand in an intimate and vital relation to a certain system, which is their basis. Here again we must ask the reader to pause, if in doubt, and consider the facts for himself. Different men, who have lived in different times and countries, judge a fresh case in morals differently. Why is this? There is probably no 'why' before the mind of either when he judges; but *we* perhaps can say, 'I know why A said so and B so,' because we find some general rule or principle different in each, and in each the basis of the judgment. Different people in the same society may judge points differently, and we sometimes know why. It is because A is struck by one aspect of the case, B by another; and one principle is (not *before,* but) *in* A's mind when he judges, and another in B's. Each has subsumed, but under a different head; the one perhaps jus-

tice, the other gratitude. Every man has the morality he has made his own in his mind, and he 'sees' or 'feels' or 'judges' accordingly, though he does not reason explicitly from data to a conclusion.

I think this will be clear to the reader; and so we must say that on their perceptive or intellectual side (and that, the reader must not forget, is the one side that we are considering) our moral judgments are intuitive subsumptions.

To the question, How am I to know what is right? the answer must be, By the αἴσθησις of the φρόνιμος; and the φρόνιμος is the man who has identified his will with the moral spirit of the community, and judges accordingly. If an immoral course be suggested to him, he 'feels' or 'sees' at once that the act is not in harmony with a good will, and he does not do this by saying, 'this is a breach of rule A, *therefore,* etc.,' but the first thing he is aware of is that he 'does not like it'; and what he has done, without being aware of it, is (at least in most cases) to seize the quality of the act, that quality being a general quality. Actions of a particular kind he does not like, and he has instinctively referred the particular act to that kind. What is right is perceived in the same way; courses suggest themselves, and one is approved of, because intuitively judged to be of a certain kind, which kind represents a principle of the good will.

If a man is to know what is right, he should have imbibed by precept, and still more by example, the spirit of his community, its general and special beliefs as to right and wrong, and, with this whole embodied in his mind should particularize it in any new case, not by a reflective deduction, but by an intuitive subsumption, which does not know that it is a subsump-

---

[10] It is right to remark that second thoughts are often the offspring of wrong desire, but not always so. They may arise from collisions, and in these cases we see how little is to be done by theoretical deduction.

[11] Not, perhaps, on *all* matters. Nor, again, will it do to say that *everywhere* women are pre-eminently intuitive, and men discursive. But in *practical* matters there seems not much doubt that it is so.

tion; [12] by a carrying out of the self

[12] Every act has, of course, many sides, many relations, many 'points of view from which it may be regarded,' and so many qualities. There are always several principles under which you can bring it, and hence there is not the smallest difficulty in exhibiting it as the realization of either right or wrong. No act in the world is without *some* side capable of being subsumed under a good rule, *e. g.*, theft is economy, care for one's relations, protest against bad institutions, really doing oneself but justice, etc.; and, if all else fails, it probably saves us from something worse, and therefore is good. Cowardice is prudence and a duty, courage rashness and a vice, and so on. The casuist must have little ingenuity, if there is anything he fails to justify or condemn according to his order. And the vice of casuistry is that, attempting to decide the particulars of morality by the deductions of the reflective understanding, it at once degenerates into finding a good reason for what you mean to do. You have principles of all sorts, and the case has all sorts of sides; *which* side is the essential side, and which principle is *the* principle *here*, rests in the end on your mere private choice, and that is determined by heaven knows what. No *reasoning* will tell you which the moral point of view *here* is. Hence the necessary immorality and the ruinous effects of practical casuistry. (Casuistry used not as a guide to conduct, but as a means to the theoretical investigation of moral principles, the casuistry used to discover the principle *from* the fact, and not to deduce the fact from the principle—is, of course, quite another thing.) Our moralists do not like casuistry; but if the current notion that moral philosophy has to tell you what to do is well founded, then casuistry, so far as I can see, at once follows, or should follow.

But the ordinary moral judgment is not discursive. It does not look to the right and left, and considering the case from all its sides, consciously subsume under one principle. When the case is presented, it fixes on one quality in the act, referring that unconsciously to one principle in which it feels the whole of itself, and

into a new case, wherein what is before the mind is the case and not the self to be carried out, and where it is indeed the whole that feels and sees, but all that is seen is seen in the form of *this* case, *this* point, *this* instance. Precept is good, but example is better; for by a series of particulars (as such forgotten) we get the general spirit, we identify ourselves both on the side of will and judgment with the basis, which basis (be it remembered) has not got to be explicit.[13]

There are a number of questions which invite consideration [14] here, but

_____

sees that whole in a single side of the act. So far as right and wrong are concerned it can perceive nothing but *this* quality of *this* case, and anything else it refuses to try to perceive. Practical morality means single-mindedness, the having one idea; it means what in other spheres would be the greatest narrowness. Point out to a man of simple morals that the case has other sides than the one he instinctively fixes on and he suspects you wish to corrupt him. And so you probably would if you went on. Apart from bad example, the readiest way to debauch the morality of any one is, on the side of principle, to confuse them by forcing them to see in all moral and immoral acts other sides and points of view, which alter the character of each; and, on the side of principle, to warp their instinctive apprehension through personal affection for yourself or some other individual.

[13] It is worth while in this connection to refer to the custom some persons have (and find useful) of calling before the mind, when in doubt, a known person of high character and quick judgment, and thinking what they would have done. This no doubt both delivers the mind from private considerations and also is to act in the spirit of the other person (so far as we know it), *i. e.*, from the general basis of his acts (certainly *not* the mere memory of his particular acts, or such memory plus inference).

[14] One of these would be as to how progress in morality is made.

we can not stop. We wished to point out briefly the character of our common moral judgments. This (on the intellectual side) is the way in which they are ordinarily made; and, in the main, there is not much practical difficulty. What is moral *in any particular given case* is seldom doubtful. Society pronounces beforehand; or, after some one course has been taken, it can say whether it was right or not; though society can not generalize much, and, if asked to reflect, is helpless and becomes incoherent. But I do not say there are no cases where the morally minded man has to doubt; most certainly such do arise, though not so many as some people think, far fewer than some would be glad to think. A very large number arise from reflection, which wants to act from an explicit principle, and so begins to abstract and divide, and, thus becoming one-sided, makes the relative absolute. Apart from this, however, collisions must take place; and here there is no guide whatever but the intuitive judgment of oneself or others.[15]

This intuition must not be confounded with what is sometimes miscalled 'conscience.' It is not mere individual opinion or caprice. It presupposes the morality of the community as its basis, and is subject to the approval thereof. Here, if anywhere, the idea of universal and impersonal morality is realized. For the final arbiters are the $\phi\rho\acute{o}\nu\iota\mu\omicron\iota$, persons with a will to do right, and not full of reflections and theories. If they fail you, you must judge for yourself, but practically they seldom do fail you. Their private peculiarities neutralize each other, and the result is an

intuition which does not belong merely to this or that man or collection of men. 'Conscience' is the antipodes of this. It wants you to have no law but yourself, and to be better than the world, you would be better than most likely you are, and that to wish to be better than the world is to be already on the threshold of immorality.

This perhaps 'is a hard saying,' but it is least hard to those who know life best; it is intolerable to those mainly who, from inexperience or preconceived theories, cannot see the world as it is. Explained it may be by saying that enthusiasm for good dies away—the ideal fades:

Dem Herrlichsten, was auch der Geist empfangen,
Drängt immer fremd und fremder Stoff sich an;

but better perhaps if we say that those who have seen most of the world (not one side of it)—old people of no one-sided profession nor of immoral life—know most also how much good there is in it. They are tolerant of new theories and youthful opinions that everything would be better upside down because they know that this also is as it should be, and that the world gets good even from these. They are intolerant only of those who are old enough, and should be wise enough, to know better than that they know better than the world; for in such people they cannot help seeing the self-conceit which is pardonable only in youth.

Let us be clear. What is that wish to be better, and to make the world better, which is on the threshold of immorality? What is the 'world' in this sense? It is the morality already existing ready to hand in laws, institutions, social usages, moral opinions and feelings. This is the element in which the young are brought up.

---

[15] I may remark on this (after Erdmann, and I suppose Plato) that collisions of duties are avoided mostly by each man keeping to his own immediate duties, and not trying to see from the point of view of other stations than his own.

It has given moral content to themselves and it is the only source of such content. It is not wrong, it is a duty, to take the best that there is, and to live up to the best. It is not wrong, it is a duty, standing on the basis of the existing, and in harmony with its general spirit, to try and make not only oneself but also the world better, or rather, and in preference, one's own world better. But it is another thing, starting from oneself, from ideals in one's head, to set oneself and them against the moral world. The moral world with its social institutions, etc., is a fact; it is real; our 'ideals' are not real. 'But we will make them real.' We should consider what we are, and what the world is. We should learn to see the great moral fact in the world, and to reflect on the likelihood of our private 'ideal' being anything more than an abstraction, which, because an abstraction, is all the better fitted for our heads, and all the worse fitted for actual existence.

We should consider whether the encouraging oneself in having opinions of one's own, in the sense of thinking differently from the world on moral subjects, be not, in any person other than a heaven-born prophet, sheer self-conceit. And though the disease may spend itself in the harmless and even entertaining sillinesses by which we are advised to assert our social 'individuality,' yet still the having theories of one's own in the face of the world is not far from having practice in the same direction; and if the latter is (as it often must be) immorality, the former has certainly but stopped at the threshold.

But the moral organism is strong against both. The person anxious to throw off the yoke of custom and develop his 'individuality' in startling directions, passes as a rule into the common Philistine, and learns that Philistinism is after all a good thing.

And the licentious young man, anxious for pleasure at any price, who, without troubling himself about 'principles,' does put into practice the principles of the former person, finds after all that the self within him can be satisfied only with that from whence it came. And some fine morning the dream is gone, the enchanted bower is a hideous phantasm, and the despised and common reality has become the ideal.

We have thus seen the community to be the real moral idea, to be stronger than the theories and the practice of its members against it, and to give us self-realization. And this is indeed limitation; it bids us say farewell to visions of superhuman morality, to ideal societies, and to practical 'ideals' generally. But perhaps the unlimited is not the perfect nor the true ideal. And, leaving 'ideals' out of sight, it is quite clear that if anybody wants to realize himself as a perfect man without trying to be a perfect member of his country and all his smaller communities, he makes what all sane persons would admit to be a great mistake. There is no more fatal enemy than theories which are not also facts; and when people inveigh against the vulgar antithesis of the two, they themselves should accept their own doctrine, and give up the harboring of theories of what should be and is not. Until they do that, the vulgar are in the right; for a theory of that which (only) is to be, is a theory of that which in fact is not, and that I suppose is only a theory.

There is nothing better than my station and its duties, nor anything higher or more truly beautiful. It holds and will hold its own against the worship of the 'individual,' whatever form that may take. It is strong against frantic theories and vehement passions, and in the end it triumphs over the fact and can smile at the literature, even of sentimentalism, however fulsome in its impulsive setting out, or sour in its disappointed end. It laughs at its frenzied apotheosis of the yet unsatisfied passion it calls love; and at that embitterment too which has lost its illusions, and yet cannot let them go—with its kindness for the genius too clever in general to do anything in particular, and its adoration of stargazing virgins with souls above their spheres, whose wish to be something in the world takes the form of wanting to do something with it, and who in the end do badly what they might have done in the beginning well; and, worse than all, its cynical contempt for what deserves only pity, sacrifice of a life for work to the best of one's lights, a sacrifice despised not simply because it has failed, but because it is stupid, and uninteresting, and altogether unsentimental.

And all these books (ah! how many) it puts into the one scale, and with them the writers of them; and into the other scale it puts three such lines as these:

"One place performs like any other place
The proper service every place on earth
Was framed to furnish man with"——
κόκκυ, μεθεῖτε· καὶ πολύ γε κατωτέρω
χωρεῖ τὸ τοῦδε,

Have we still to ask,
καὶ τί ποτ' ἐστὶ ταἴτιον;[16]

The theory which we have just exhibited (more or less in our own way), and over which perhaps we have heated ourselves a little, seems to us a great advance on anything we have had before, and indeed in the main to be satisfactory. It satisfies us be-

[16] Arist. *Frogs*, 1384. *Dionysos*—Cuckoo! Let go the scales; Aeschylos' side goes down, oh, much much the lowest. *Euripides*—Why, what ever is the reason?

cause in it our wills attain their realization; the content of the will is a whole, is systematic; and it is the same whole on both sides. On the outside and inside alike we have the same universal will in union with the particular personality; and in the identity of inside and outside in one single process we have reached the point where the 'is to be,' with all its contradictions, disappears, or remains but as a moment in a higher 'is.'

Nonetheless, however, must we consider this satisfaction neither ultimate, nor all-inclusive, nor anything but precarious. If put forth as that beyond which we do not need to go, as the end in itself, it is open to very serious objections, some of which we must now develop.

The point upon which 'my station and its duties' prided itself most, was that it had got rid of the opposition of 'ought' and 'is' in both its forms; viz., the opposition of the outer world to the 'ought' in me, and the opposition of my particular self to the 'ought' in general. We shall have to see it has not succeeded in doing either, or at least not completely.

(1) Within the sphere of my station and its duties the opposition is not vanquished; for:

(a) It is impossible to maintain the doctrine of what may be called 'justification by sight.' The self cannot be so seen to be identified with the moral whole that the bad self disappears. (i) In the moral man the consciousness of that unity cannot be present always, but only when he is fully engaged in satisfactory work. Then, I think, it is present; but when he is not so engaged, and the bad self shows itself, he can scarcely be self-contented, or, if he is so, scarcely because he *sees* that the bad self is unreal. He can only forget his faults when he is too busy to think of them; and he can hardly be so always. And he can not always *see* that his faults do not matter to the moral order of things—when it comes to that he can only trust. Further, (ii) the more or less immoral man who, because of past offenses, is now *unable* to perform his due function, or to perform it duly, cannot always in his work gain once more the self-content he has lost because that very work tells him of what should have been, and now is not and will not be, and the habits he has formed perhaps drag him still into the faults that made them. We cannot, without taking a low point of view, ask that this man's life, morally considered, should be more than a struggle; and it would be the most untrue Pharisaism or indifferentism to call him immoral because he struggles, and so far as he struggles. Here justification by sight is out of the question.

(b) Again, the moral man need not find himself realized in the world. (i) It is necessary to remark that the community in which he is a member may be in a confused or rotten condition, so that in it right and might do not always go together. And (ii) the very best community can only insure that correspondence in the gross; it cannot do so in every single detail. (iii) There are afflictions for which no moral organism has balm or physician, though it has alleviation; and these can mar the life of any man. (iv) The member may have to sacrifice himself for the community. In none of these cases can he *see* his realization; and here again the contradiction breaks out, and we must wrap ourselves in a virtue which is our own and not the world's, or seek a higher doctrine by which, through faith and through faith alone, self-suppression issues in a higher self-realization.

(2) Within the sphere of my station and its duties we see the contradiction is but partially solved, and the second objection is also very serious. You cannot confine a man to his station and its duties. Whether in another sense that formula would be all-embracing is a further question, but in the sense in which we took it, function in a 'visible' community, it certainly is not so. And we must remark here in passing that, if we accept (as I think we must) the fact that the essence of a man involves identity with others, the question what the final reality of that identity is, is still left unanswered. We should still have to ask what is the higher whole in which the individual is a function, and in which the relative wholes subsist, and to inquire whether that community is, or can be, a visible community at all.

Passing by this, however, let us develop our objection. A man cannot take his morality simply from the moral world he is in, for many reasons. (a) That moral world, being in a state of historical development, is not and cannot be self-consistent; and the man must thus stand before and above inconsistencies and reflect on them. This must lead to the knowledge that the world is not altogether as it should be, and to a process of trying to make it better. With this cooperates (b) what may be called cosmopolitan morality. Men nowadays know to some extent what is thought right and wrong in other communities now, and what has been thought at other times; and this leads to a notion of goodness not of any particular time and country. For numbers of persons no doubt this is unnecessary; but it is necessary for others, and they have the moral ideal (with the psychological origin of which we are not concerned) of a good man who is not good as member of this or that community, but who realizes himself in whatever community he finds himself. This, however, must mean also that he is not perfectly realized in any particular station.

(3) We have seen that the moral man can to a certain extent distinguish his moral essence from his particular function; and now a third objection at once follows, that the content of the ideal self does not fall wholly within any community, is in short *not* merely the ideal of a perfect social being. The making myself better does not always directly involve relation to others. The production of truth and beauty (together with what is called 'culture') may be recognized as a duty; and it will be very hard to reduce it in all cases to a duty of any station that I can see. If we like to say that these duties to myself are duties to humanity, that perhaps is true; but we must remember that humanity is not a visible community. If you mean by it only past, present, and future human beings, then you cannot show that in all cases my culture is of use (directly or indirectly) to anyone but myself. Unless you are prepared to restrict science and fine art to what is useful, i. e., to common arts and 'accomplishments,' you cannot hope to 'verify' such an assertion. You are in the region of belief, not knowledge; and this equally whether your belief is true or false. We must say then that, in aiming at truth and beauty, we are trying to realize ourself not as a member of any visible community.

And, finally, against this ideal self the particular person remains and must remain imperfect. The ideal self is not fully realized in us, in any way that we can see. We are aware of a ceaseless process, it is well if we can add progress, in which the false private self is constantly subdued but never disappears. And it never can disappear—we are never realized. The contradiction remains; and not to feel it demands something lower or something higher than a moral point of view.

Starting from these objections, our next Essay must try to make more clear what is involved in them, and to raise in a sharper form the difficulties as to the nature of morality. And our Concluding Remarks will again take up the same thread, after we have in some measure investigated in Essay VII the difficult problems of the bad self and selfishness.

NOTE

RIGHTS AND DUTIES

To handle this subject properly, more space would be wanted than I have at command. But I will make some remarks shortly and in outline.

A great to-do has been made about the ambiguity of the word 'right'; as I think, needlessly. Right is the rule, and what is conformable to the rule, whether that rule be physical or mental; e. g., a right line, a 'right English bull-dog' (Swift), a right conclusion, a right action.

Right is, generally, the expression of the universal. It is the emphasis of the universal side in the relation of particular and universal. It implies particulars, and therefore possibility of discrepancy between them and the universal. Hence right means law; which law may be carried out or merely stated. 'Is it right to do this?' means 'is the universal realized in this?' 'Have I a right?' means 'am I in this the expression of law?'

In the moral sphere, with which alone we are concerned, right means always the relation of the universal to the particular will. The emphasis is on the universal. Possibility of discrepancy with a conscious subject makes law here *command*.

Command is the simple proposal

of an action (or abstinence) to me by another will, as the content of that will. Or, from the side of the commander, it is the willing by me of some state of another will, such willing being presented by me as a fact to that will. Threat is not of the essence of command; command need not imply the holding forth or the anticipation of consequences.

To *have* rights is not merely to be the object with respect to which commands (positive or prohibitory) are addressed to others. If that were so, inanimate matter would have rights; *e. g.*, the very dirt in the road would 'have a right' to be taken up or let lie—and this is barbarous. To have rights is to be (or to be presumed to be) capable of realizing the universal command consciously as such.[17] This answers the question, Has a beast rights? He is the object of duties, not the subject of rights. Right is the universal in its relation to a will capable of recognizing it as such, whether it remain mere command or is also carried out in act.

Wherever in the moral world you have law you have also right and rights. These may be real or ideal. The first are the will of the state or society, the second the will of the

---

[17] 'I have rights against others,' or 'I have a right to this or that from others,' means, (1) it is right, it is the expression of the universal that they should do this or that in reference to me: I am the object of their duty. But this by itself does not give me 'rights.' To 'have a right' to anything from another, I must (2) be a subject which knows the universal as such, both (a) in its *immediate* relation to my will, in its expression through my acts; and (b) also here in its expression through the acts of others, which acts may concern me. When my will is the universal, and the universal as my will, calls for these acts, then I 'have a right' to them in the proper sense, but not otherwise.

ideal-social or nonsocial ideal. (*Vide* Essay VI.)

It is in order to secure the existence of right in the acts of particular wills that compulsion is used. But compulsion is not necessary to the general and abstract definition of right, and it cannot be immediately deduced from it.

What is duty? It is simply the other side of right. It is the same relation, viewed from the other pole or moment. It is the relation of the particular to the universal, with the emphasis on the particular. It is *my* will in its affirmative relation to the objective will. Right is the universal, existing for thought alone or also carried out. Duty is my will, either merely thought of as realizing this universal, or actually also doing so. 'This is my duty' means 'in this I identify, or am thought of as identifying, myself with right.'

Duty, like right, implies possible discordance of particular and universal. Like right, too, it implies more than this. It implies the consciousness (or presumed capacity for consciousness) of the relation of my will to the universal as the right. Hence a beast has no duties in the proper sense. If he has, then he has also rights.

Right is the universal will implying particular will. It is the objective side implying a subjective side, *i. e.*, duty. Duty is the particular will implying a universal will. It is the subjective side implying an objective side, *i. e.*, right. But the two sides are inseparable. No right without duty; no duty without right and rights. (To this we shall return.)

Right and duty are sides of a single whole. This whole is the good. Rights and duties imply the identity, and nonidentity, of the particular and universal wills. Right may remain a mere command, duty a mere 'ought to be,' the nonagreement of the particular and universal. They are both abstractions. They are both, if fixed and isolated one from the other, self-contradictions. Each by itself is a mere 'is to be,' each a willed idea, which, so long as apart from the other, remains a *mere, i. e., a not*-willed, idea. Each is a single side of one and the same relation, fixed apart from the other side. In the good the sides come together, and in the whole first cease to be abstractions and gain real existence. The right is carried out in duty. The duty realizes itself in the right.

But in the good rights and duties as such disappear. There is no more mere right or mere duty, no more particular and universal as such, no external relation of the two. They are now sides and elements in one whole; and, if they appear, it is only as, within the movement and life of the whole, here one element and there another has its relative emphasis. But outside the whole their reality fades into 'mere idea,' into legend and fable.

Rights and duties do not exist outside the moral world; and that world does not exist where there is not a sphere of inner morality, however immediate, the consciousness, however vague, of the relation of the private will to the universal, whether that universal be presented as outer (in the shape of tribal custom or of some individual) or again as inner. Where there is no morality there is no right; where there is no right there are no rights. Just so, where there are no rights there is no right, and where no right there no morality. Inner morality without an objective right and wrong is a self-delusion. Right and rights outside morality are a mere fiction.

It is here that every partial theory of morals and politics is wrecked and seen to be worthless. False theories of right either (1) fail to get to any objective universal except by some fond invention (of contract), which besides being an invention, presupposes what it is to create. (A contract outside the sphere of right and morality is nonsense.) Or (2) they take an objective universal (as positive law, will of the monarch, or what seems most convenient to the majority); and here they fail because their right is mere force, and is not moral, not right at all; and hence they cannot show that I am *in* the right to obey it, or in the wrong to disobey it, but merely that, if I do not obey it, it may (or may not) be inconvenient for me. So again in morals they either (1) posit a universal, such as the will of the Deity or of other human beings; and this fails because in it I do not affirm *my* self; or else (2) there is nothing anywhere objective and universal at all; and here I affirm nothing *but* myself. In either case there is no duty and no morality.

'But rights and duties,' we shall be told, 'collide.' They collide only as rights do with rights or duties with duties. Rights and duties of one sphere collide with those of another sphere, and again within each sphere they collide in different persons, and again in one and the same person. But that right as such can collide with duty as such is impossible. There is no right which is not a duty, no duty which is not a right. In either case right would cease to be right, and duty duty.

This will be denied. It will be said, (1) there are duties without rights; (2) rights without duties. As to the first (1) we say, If we have not a right to do anything, it is not right for us. If it is not right for us, then it is not our duty. It is quite true that *moral* duty may not be *legal* right, nor *legal* duty *moral* right, but this is not to the point.

As to the second (2), it seems harder to see that where I have no duties I have no rights. In the spheres of the state, of society, of ideal morality, I have a right to do this and not that, that and not the other. But can it be said that all these things that I have a right to do are my duties? Is not that nonsense?

No doubt there is much truth in this. It is almost as bad to have nothing *but* duties as it is to have no duties at all. For free individual self-development we must have both elements. Where the universal is all there is ossification; where the particular is all there is dissolution; in neither case life.

Is it true then that there are rights where there are no duties? No. In a sense, rights are wider than duties: but what does this mean? Does it mean there are rights outside the moral sphere? Certainly not. We shall see (Essay VI) that there is no limit to the moral sphere; and if there were a limit, then outside that rights would cease to be rights. "More rights than duties" then must be true, if at all, *within* the moral sphere. Does it hold there that there are more rights than duties? It is not a very hard puzzle. To make it easier let us double it, and say 'there are more duties than rights.' A man, for instance, has a certain indivisible sum to spend in charity. He has a duty to A, B, and C, but not a right to more than one because it is wrong if he gives more than his indivisible limited sum. Hence there are more duties than rights. All that it comes to is that, when you look on duties as possible, they are wider than what, when actually done, is right and actual duty. Just so possible rights are wider than what is actually duty and actually right.

The reason why this is noticed on the side of rights, and not on the side of duty, is very simple. We saw above that in right the emphasis is on the universal side. Now every act is

a determined this or that act, and what makes it a this or that act is the particularization. What I have a right to do thus depends on what my duty is; for duty, we saw, emphasized the particular side. Now, where there are no indifferents and no choice between them, rights are never wider than duties. It is where indifferents come in (cf. Essay VI), that possibility is wider than actuality. And because right emphasizes the side common to all the indifferents, *i. e.*, the undetermined side, it is therefore wider than duty, which emphasizes the particular side, and hence is narrower.

Thus, where the choice of my particular will comes in, that has rights and must be respected. But it has rights only because the sphere of its exercise, and therefore what it does therein, is duty. And it must be respected by others only so far as it thus expresses the universal will. If it has not right on its side, it has no rights whatever.

There is indeed a sphere where rights seem in collision with right. Wherever you have law you have this, since it comes from the nature of law. Thus I am *justified* in returning evil for evil; I have a right to do it, even where it is not right but wrong to do it. The same thing is found in the spheres of state law, social law, and mere moral law alike. This does not show that in these cases there is *no* moral universal; it shows that we are keeping to nothing *but* the universal. We have here the distinction of justice and equity. A merely just [18] act may

[18] What is justice? I have no space to develop or illustrate, but will set down what seems to be the fact. The just does not = right; injustice does not = wrong. Justice does not = giving to each deserts: 'nothing but justice' may be less or more than my deserts. Justice is not *mere* conforming to law; injustice is not *mere* acting against law; *e. g.*, murder is not

(we all know) be most unjust. The universal as law must be the same for all: it cannot be specified to meet every particular case. Hence, in keeping to this unspecified universal, I have 'right' on my side; but again, failing to specify it in my case, I do what is not right for me to do. I fail in duty, do not do, and am not, right.

The sphere of mere private right in the state cannot exist out of the moral whole. It is, for the sake of the development of the whole, created and kept up in the whole, but merely at the pleasure of the whole. Just so in morals there is a sphere of private liking, the sphere of indifferents, but this exists only because it ought to exist, only because duty is realized in its existence, though not by its particulars as particulars, *i. e.*, as this one against that one. The sphere of private right has rights only so long as it is right and is duty. It exists merely on sufferance; and the moment the right of the whole demands its suppression it has no rights. Public right everywhere overrides it in practice, if not in theory. This is the justification of such things as forcible expropriation, conscription, etc. The only proper way of regarding them is to say, In developing my property, etc.,

called 'unjust.' Justice and injustice mean this, but they imply something more.

Injustice is, while you explicity or implicity profess to go on a rule, the not going merely on the rule, but the making exceptions in favor of persons. Justice is the really going by nothing but one's ostensible rule in assigning advantage and disadvantage to persons.

What the rule is, is another matter. The rule may be the morally right. This is ideal justice. All lower sorts of law furnish each its own lower justice and injustice.

as this or that man, I am doing my duty to the state, for the state lives in its individuals: and I do my duty again in another way of giving up to the use of state my property and person, for the individual lives in the state. What other view will justify the facts of political life?

To repeat then: Right is the assertion of the universal will in relation to the particular will. Duty is the assertion of the particular will in the affirmation of the universal. Good is the identity, not the mere relation, of both. Right may be real, may actually exist; or be only ideal, merely thought of. So may duty. Rights and duties are elements in the good; they must go together. The universal cannot be affirmed except in the particular, the particular only affirms itself in the universal; but they should be suppressed in the good as anything more than elements, which reciprocally supplement each other, and should be regarded as two sides to one whole. It is not moral to stand on one's rights with the right; *i. e.*, right should not be *mere* right: nor moral to make a duty of all one's duties; *i. e.*, duty should not be *mere* duty.

We maintain the following theses. (1) It is false that you can have rights without duties. (2) It is false that you can have duties without rights. (3) It is false that right is merely negative.[19] (4) It is false that duty depends on possible compulsion, and a mere mistake that command always implies a threat; and (5) It is absolutely false that rights or duties can exist outside the moral world.

[19] Schopenhauer has developed this view with great clearness. He goes so far as to make wrong the original positive conception, right the mere negation of it.

Henry Sidgwick (1838—1900)

Although the influences of Mill, Kant, and Butler are evident in his thinking, Sidgwick is no mere eclectic. From Mill he inherited a utilitarianism that first attracted him because it seemed to provide the solution to the problem of justifying common-sense moral rules, but which, subsequently, left him dissatisfied with Mill's treatment of the relation between psychological and ethical hedonism. The need for justifying the subordination or sacrifice of interest in one's own happiness for the sake of the general happiness led him to accept an intuitionism, the key to which he gained from a reading of Kant. It was Butler's treatment of the relation between self-love and benevolence that provided the final impetus to his own view. In his *The Methods of Ethics*, Sidgwick's reliance upon common sense is evident. In almost conscious imitation of Aristotle's procedure, Sidgwick examines in painstaking detail and with admirable clarity the reasoned judgment of common sense. The outcome of this program is an intuitional utilitarianism that has had a lasting effect upon both contemporary intuitionism and utilitarianism.

THE METHODS OF ETHICS

ETHICAL JUDGMENTS [1]

§ 1. In the first chapter I spoke of actions that we judge to be right and what ought to be done as being "reasonable," or "rational," and similarly of ultimate ends as "prescribed by Reason": and I contrasted the motive to action supplied by the recognition of such reasonableness with "non-rational" desires and inclinations. This manner of speaking is employed by writers of different schools, and seems in accordance with the common view and language on the

[1] *The Methods of Ethics*, Bk. I, Chap. III, 5th Edition, London, 1893.

subject. For we commonly think that wrong conduct is essentially irrational, and can be shown to be so by argument; and though we do not conceive that it is by reason alone that men are influenced to act rightly, we still hold that appeals to the reason are an essential part of all moral persuasion, and that part which concerns the moralist or moral philosopher as distinct from the preacher or moral rhetorician. On the other hand it is widely maintained that, as Hume says, "Reason, meaning the judgment of truth and falsehood, can never of itself be any motive to the Will"—the motive to action being in all cases some feeling of the class that I have characterized as Non-rational Desires. It seems desirable to examine with some care the grounds of this contention before we proceed any further.

Let us begin by defining the issue raised, as clearly as possible. Every one, I suppose, has had experience of what is meant by the conflict of non-rational or irrational desires with reason: most of us (e.g.) occasionally feel bodily appetite prompting us to indulgences which we judge to be imprudent, and anger prompting us to acts which we disapprove as unjust or unkind. It is when this conflict occurs that the desires are said to be irrational, as impelling us to volitions opposed to our deliberate judgments: sometimes we yield to such seductive impulses, and sometimes not: and it is perhaps when we do *not* yield, that the impulsive force of such irrational desires is most definitely felt, as we have to exert in resisting them a voluntary effort somewhat analogous to that involved in any muscular exertion. Often, again, —since we are not always thinking either of our duty or of our interest, —desires of this kind take effect in voluntary actions without our having judged such actions to be either right or wrong, either prudent or imprudent; as (e.g.) when an ordinary healthy man eats his dinner. In such cases it seems most appropriate to call the desires "non-rational" rather than "irrational." Neither term is intended to imply that the desires spoken of—or at least the more important of them—are not normally accompanied by intellectual processes. It is true that some impulses to action seem to take effect, as we say "blindly" or "instinctively," without any definite consciousness either of the end at which the action is aimed, or of the means by which the end is to be attained: but this, I conceive, is only the case with impulses that do not occupy consciousness for an appreciable time, and ordinarily do not require any but very familiar and habitual actions for the attainment of their proximate ends. In all other cases—that is, in the case of the actions with which we are chiefly concerned in ethical discussion—the result aimed at, and some part at least of the means by which it is to be realised, are more or less distinctly represented in consciousness, previous to the volition that initiates the movements tending to its realisation. Hence the resultant forces of what I call "non-rational" desires, and the volitions to which they prompt, are continually modified by intellectual processes in two distinct ways; first by new perceptions or representations of means conducive to the desired ends, and secondly by new presentations or representations of facts actually existing or in prospect—especially more or less probable consequences of contemplated actions —which rouse new impulses of desire and aversion.

The question, then, is whether the account just given of the influence of the intellect on desire and volition is not exhaustive; and whether the experience which is commonly described as a "conflict of desire with reason" is not more properly conceived as merely a conflict among desires and aversions; the sole function of reason being to bring before the mind ideas of actual or possible facts, which modify in the manner above described the resultant force of our various impulses.

I hold that this is not the case; that the ordinary moral or prudential judgments which, in the case of all or most minds, have some—though too often not a predominant—influence on volition, cannot legitimately be interpreted as judgments respecting the present or future existence of human feelings or any facts of the sensible world; the fundamental notion represented by the word "ought" or "right,"[2] which such judgments contain expressly or by implication, being essentially different from all notions representing facts of physical or psychical experience. The question is one on which appeal must ultimately be made to the reflection of individuals on their practical judgments and reasonings: and in making this appeal it seems most convenient to begin by showing the inadequacy of all attempts to explain the practical judgments or propositions in which this fundamental notion is introduced, without recognising its unique character as above negatively defined. There is an element of truth in such explanations, in so far as they bring into view feelings which undoubtedly accompany moral or prudential judgments, and which ordinarily have more or less effect in determining the will to actions judged to be right; but so far as they profess to be interpretations of what such judgments mean, they appear to me to fail altogether.

In considering this question it will, I think, conduce to clearness to take separately the two species of judgments which I have distinguished as "moral" and "prudential" respectively; since though it is widely held that the ultimate obligation of all rules of duty must be rested on the self-interest of the individual to whom they are addressed—so that all valid moral rules have ultimately a prudential basis—it seems clear that in ordinary thought cognitions or judgments of duty present themselves as *primâ facie* distinct from cognitions or judgments as to what conduces to self-interest.

To begin then with the former, i.e., with moral judgments in the narrower sense: it is maintained by some that the judgments or propositions which

[2] The difference between the significations of the two words is discussed later.

we commonly call moral really affirm no more than the existence of a specific emotion in the mind of the person who utters them: that when I say 'Truth ought to be spoken' or 'Truthspeaking is right,' I mean no more than that the idea of truthspeaking excites in my mind a feeling of approbation or satisfaction. And probably some degree of such emotion, commonly distinguished as 'moral sentiment,' always or ordinarily accompanies moral judgments. But it is absurd to say that a mere statement of my approbation of truthspeaking is properly given in the proposition 'Truth ought to be spoken'; otherwise the fact of another man's disapprobation might equally be expressed by saying 'Truth ought not to be spoken'; and thus we should have two coexistent facts stated in two mutually contradictory propositions. This is so obvious, that we must suppose that those who hold the view which I am combating do not really intend to deny it: but rather to maintain that this subjective fact of my approbation is all that there is any *ground* for stating, or perhaps that it is all that any reasonable person is prepared on reflection to affirm. And no doubt there is a large class of statements, in form objective, which yet we are not commonly prepared to maintain as more than subjective if their validity is questioned. If I say that 'the air is sweet,' or 'the food disagreeable,' it would not be exactly true to say that I mean no more than that I like the one or dislike the other: but if my statement is challenged, I shall probably content myself with affirming the existence of such feelings in my own mind. But there appears to me to be a fundamental difference between this case and that of moral feelings. The peculiar emotion of moral approbation is, in my experience, inseparably bound up with the conviction, implicit or explicit, that the conduct approved is 'really' right—i.e. that it cannot, without error, be disapproved by any other mind. If I give up this conviction because others do not share it, or for any other reason, I may no doubt still retain a sentiment prompting to the conduct in question, or—what is perhaps more common—a sentiment of repugnance to the opposite conduct: but this sentiment will no longer have the special quality of 'moral sentiment' strictly so called. This difference between the two is often overlooked in ethical discussion: but any experience of a change in moral opinion produced by argument may afford an illustration of it. Suppose (e.g.) that any one habitually influenced by the sentiment of Veracity is convinced that under certain peculiar circumstances in which he finds himself, speaking truth is not right but wrong. He will probably still feel a repugnance against violating the rule of truth speaking: but it will be a feeling quite different in kind and degree from that which prompted him to veracity as a department of virtuous action. We might perhaps call the one a 'moral' and the other a 'quasi-moral' sentiment.

The argument just given holds equally against the view that approbation or disapprobation is not the mere liking or aversion of an individual for certain kinds of conduct, but this complicated by a sympathetic representation of similar likings or aversions felt by other human beings. No doubt such sympathy is a normal concomitant of moral emotion, and when the former is absent there is much greater difficulty in maintaining the latter: this, however, is partly because our moral beliefs commonly agree with those of other members of our society, and on this agreement depends to an important extent our confidence in the truth of these beliefs.[3] But if, as in the case just supposed, we are really led by argument to a new moral belief, opposed not only to our own habitual sentiment but also to that of the society in which we live, we have a crucial experiment proving the existence in us of moral sentiments as I have defined them, colliding with the represented sympathies of our fellow-men no less than with our own mere likings and aversions. And even if we imagine the sympathies opposed to our convictions extended until they include those of the whole human race, against whom we imagine ourselves to stand as *Athanasius contra mundum;* still, so long as our conviction of duty is firm, the emotion which we call moral stands out in imagination quite distinct from the complex sympathy opposed to it, however much we extend, complicate and intensify the latter.

§ 2. So far, then, from being prepared to admit that the proposition 'X ought to be done' *merely* expresses the existence of a certain sentiment in myself or others, I find it strictly impossible so to regard my own moral judgments without eliminating from the concomitant sentiment the peculiar quality signified by the term 'moral.' There is, however, another view in which moral judgments are considered to relate to the likings and aversions that men in general feel for certain kinds of conduct; not as sympathetically represented in the emotion of the person judging, and thus constituting the moral element in it, but as causes of pain to the person of whom 'ought' or 'duty' is predicated. On this view, when we say that a man 'ought' to do anything, or that it is his 'duty' to do it, we mean that he is bound under penalties to do it; the particular penalty considered being the pain that will accrue to him di-

3 See Book iii. chap. xi. par. 1.

rectly or indirectly from the dislike of his fellow-creatures.

It cannot be denied that this interpretation has some plausibility. For in using, as we commonly do, the term 'moral obligation' or 'boundness' as equivalent to that contained in the verb 'ought,' we imply an analogy between this notion and that of legal obligation; and in the case of positive law the connexion of 'obligation' and 'punishment' seems indissoluble: a law cannot be properly said to be actually established in a society if it is habitually violated with impunity. But a more careful reflection on the relation of Law to Morality, as ordinarily conceived, seems to show that it really affords no argument for the interpretation of 'ought' that I am now discussing. For the ideal distinction taken in common thought between legal and merely moral rules seems to lie in just this connexion of the former with punishment: we think that there are some things which a man ought to be compelled to do, or forbear, and others which he ought to do or forbear without compulsion, and that the former alone fall properly within the sphere of law. And it is otherwise evident that what we mean when we say that a man is "morally though not legally bound" to do a thing is not merely that he "will be punished by public opinion if he does not"; for we often join these two statements, clearly distinguishing their import: and further (since public opinion is known to be eminently fallible) there are many things which we judge men 'ought' to do, while perfectly aware that they will incur no serious social penalties for omitting them. In such cases, indeed, it would be commonly said that social disapprobation 'ought' to follow on immoral conduct; and in this very assertion it is clear that the term 'ought' cannot mean that social penalties are to be feared by those who

do not disapprove. Again, all or most men in whom the moral consciousness is strongly developed find themselves from time to time in conflict with the commonly received morality of the society to which they belong: and thus —as was before said—have a crucial experience proving that duty does not mean *to them* what other men will disapprove of them for not doing.

At the same time I admit, as indeed I have already suggested in par. 3 of chap. i., that we not unfrequently pass judgments resembling moral judgments in form, and not distinguished from them in ordinary thought, in cases where the obligation affirmed is found, on reflection, to depend on the existence of current opinions and sentiments as such. The members of modern civilised societies are under the sway of a code of Public Opinion, enforced by social penalties, which no reflective person obeying it identifies with the moral code, or regards as unconditionally binding: indeed the code is manifestly fluctuating and variable, different at the same time in different classes, professions, social circles, of the same political community. Such a code always supports to a considerable extent the commonly received code of morality; and most reflective persons think it generally reasonable to conform to the dictates of public opinion—to the code of Honour, we may say, in graver matters, or the rules of Politeness or Good Breeding in lighter matters—wherever these dictates do not positively conflict with morality; such conformity being maintained either on grounds of private interest, or because it is thought conducive to general happiness or well-being to keep as much as possible in harmony with one's fellow-men. Hence in the ordinary thought of unreflective persons the duties imposed by social opinion are often undistinguished from moral duties: and indeed this indistinctness is almost inherent in the common meaning of many terms. For instance, if we say that a man has been 'dishonoured' by a cowardly act, it is not quite clear whether we mean that he has incurred contempt, or that he has deserved it, or both: as becomes evident when we take a case in which the Code of Honour comes into conflict with Morality. If (e.g.) a man were to incur social ostracism anywhere for refusing a duel on religious grounds, some would say that he was 'dishonoured,' though he had acted rightly, others that there could be no real dishonour in a virtuous act. A similar ambiguity seems to lurk in the common notion of 'improper' or 'incorrect' behaviour. Still in all such cases the ambiguity becomes evident on reflection: and when discovered, merely serves to illustrate further the distinction between moral 'rightness' or 'goodness' of conduct, strictly so called, and mere conformity to the standard of current opinion.

There is, however, another way of interpreting 'ought' as connoting penalties, which is somewhat less easy to meet by a crucial psychological experiment. The moral imperative may be taken to be a law of God, to the breach of which Divine penalties are annexed; and these, no doubt, in a Christian society, are commonly conceived to be adequate and universally applicable. Still, it can hardly be said that this belief is shared by all the persons whose conduct is influenced by independent moral convictions, occasionally unsupported either by the law or the public opinion of their community. And even in the case of many of those who believe fully in the moral government of the world, the judgment "I ought to do this" cannot be identified with the judgment "God will punish me if I do not"; since the conviction that the former proposition is true is distinctly recognised as an important part of the grounds for believing the latter. Again, when Christians speak—as they commonly do—of the 'justice' (or other moral attributes) of God, as exhibited in punishing sinners and rewarding the righteous, they obviously imply not merely that God *will* thus punish and reward, but that it is 'right'[4] for Him to do so: which, of course, cannot be taken to mean that He is 'bound under penalties.'

Again, it is sometimes held not only that the affirmation that anything is "right" or "what ought to be" is always made with tacit—if not express—reference to some ulterior end; [5] but also that "rightness," being essentially an attribute of means not of ends, really signifies that the object to which it is applied is thought to be the only fit means, or the means best fitted, to the realization of some end. And I admit that this interpretation of the term, as used in common thought and discourse, would be admissible, if it were not found to be ever applied to ultimate ends or to the adoption of ends as ultimate. But it would be surely paradoxical to deny that we commonly think of certain ultimate ends—or the conscious adoption of certain ends—as "right," and obviously when the word is so used, the interpretation just suggested is inadmissible.[6]

[4] 'Ought' is here inapplicable, for a reason presently explained.

[5] Though I do not agree with this view, I shall presently try to shew that the adoption of it does not really get rid of the fundamental notion that we are now examining; it merely limits the application of "right" and "wrong" to consistency and inconsistency in volitions. See the last paragraph of this chapter.

[6] As, for instance, when Bentham explains (*Principles of Morals and Legislation*, Chap. I sec. i. note) that his fundamental principle "states the greatest happiness of all those whose interest is in question as being the right and proper end of human action," we cannot under-

§ 3. It seems then that the notion of 'ought' or 'moral obligation' as used in our common moral judgments, does not merely import (1) that there exists in the mind of the person judging a specific emotion (whether complicated or not by sympathetic representation of similar emotions in other minds); nor (2) that certain rules of conduct are supported by penalties which will follow on their violation (whether such penalties result from the general liking or aversion felt for the conduct prescribed or forbidden, or from some other source). What then, it may be asked, does it import? What definition can we give of 'ought,' 'right,' and other terms expressing the same fundamental notion? To this I should answer that the notion which these terms have in common is too elementary to admit of any formal definition; but if what the questioner wants is a complete account of the relation of what ought to be to what is, I should add that it does not belong to Ethics to furnish this, but to some more comprehensive study: at any rate this task is not undertaken in the present treatise which only attempts to methodize our practical judgments and reasonings, in which this fundamental notion must, I conceive, be taken as ultimate and unanalyzable.

In speaking of this fundamental notion as "unanalyzable," I do not mean that it belongs to the "original constitution of the mind"; i.e. that its presence in consciousness is not the result of a process of development.

stand him really to *mean* by the word "right" "conducive to the general happiness, though his language in other passages of the same chapter (secs. ix and x.) would seem to imply this; for the proposition that it is conducive to general happiness to take general happiness as an end of action, though not exactly a tautology, can hardly serve as the fundamental principle of a moral system.

I do not doubt that the whole fabric of human thought—including the conceptions that present themselves as most simple and elementary—has been developed, through a gradual process of psychical change, out of some lower life in which thought, properly speaking, had no place. But it is not therefore to be inferred, as regards this or any other notion, that it has not really the simplicity which it appears to have when we now reflect upon it. It is sometimes assumed that if we can show how thoughts have grown up—if we can point to the psychical antecedents of which they are the natural consequents—we may conclude that the thoughts in question are really compounds containing their antecedents as latent elements. But I know no justification for this transference of the conceptions of chemistry to psychology; [7] I know no reason for considering psychical antecedents as really constitutive of their psychical consequents, in spite of the apparent dissimilarity between the two. In default of such reasons, a psychologist must accept as elementary what introspection carefully performed declares to be so; and, using this criterion, I find the notion we have been examining elementary and un-

[7] In Chemistry we regard the antecedents (elements) as still existing in and constituting the consequent (compound) because the latter is exactly similar to the former in weight, and because we can generally cause this compound to disappear and obtain the elements in its place. But we find nothing at all like this in the growth of mental phenomena: the psychical consequent is in no respect exactly similar to its antecedents, nor can it be resolved into them. I should explain that I am not here arguing the question whether the *validity* of moral judgments is affected by a discovery of their psychical antecedents. This question I reserve for subsequent discussion. See Book iii. chap. i. sec. 4.

analyzable. As it now exists in our thought, it cannot be resolved into any more simple notions: it can only be made clearer by determining as precisely as possible its relation to other notions with which it is connected in ordinary thought, especially to those with which it is liable to be confounded.

Thus we have to note and distinguish two different implications with which the word "ought" is used; in the narrowest ethical sense what we judge 'ought to be' done, is always thought capable of being brought about by the volition of any individual to whom the judgment applies. I cannot conceive that I 'ought' to do anything which at the same time I judge that I cannot do. In a wider sense, however,—which cannot conveniently be discarded—I sometimes judge that I 'ought' to know what a wiser man would know, or feel as a better man would feel, in my place, though I may know that I could not directly produce in myself such knowledge or feeling by any effort of will. In this case the word merely implies an ideal or pattern which I 'ought'—in the stricter sense—to seek to imitate as far as possible. And this wider sense seems to be that in which the word is normally used in the precepts of Art generally, and in political judgments: when I judge that the laws and constitution of my country 'ought to be' other than they are, I do not of course imply that my own or any other individual's single volition can directly bring about the change.[8] In either

case, however, I imply that what ought to be is a possible object of knowledge: i.e. that what I judge ought to be must, unless I am in error, be similarly judged by all rational beings who judge truly of the matter.

In referring such judgments to the 'Reason,' I do not mean here to prejudge the question whether valid moral judgments are normally attained by a process of reasoning from universal principles or axioms, or by direct intuition of the particular duties of individuals. It is not uncommonly held that the moral faculty deals primarily with individual cases as they arise, applying directly to each case the general notion of duty, and deciding intuitively what ought to be done by this person in these particular circumstances. And I admit that on this view the apprehension of moral truth is more analogous to Sense-perception than to Rational Intuition (as commonly understood):[9] and hence the term Moral Sense might seem more appropriate. But the term Sense suggests a capacity for feelings which may vary from A to B without either being in error, rather than a faculty of cognition:[10] and, as it appears to me fundamentally important to avoid this suggestion, I have therefore thought it better to use the term Reason with the explanation above

---

[8] I do not even imply that any combination of individuals could completely realize the state of political relations which I conceive 'ought to' exist. My conception would be futile if it had no relation to practice: but it may merely delineate a pattern to which no more than an approximation is practically possible.

[9] We do not commonly say that particular physical facts are apprehended by the Reason: we consider this faculty to be conversant in its discursive operation with the relation of judgments or propositions: and the intuitive reason (which is here rather in question) we restrict to the apprehension of universal truths, such as the axioms of Logic and Mathematics.

[10] By cognition I always mean what some would rather call "apparent cognition"—that is, I do not mean to affirm the *validity* of the cognition, but only its existence as a psychical fact, and its claim to be valid.

given, to denote the faculty or moral cognition.[11]

Further, when I speak of the cognition or judgment that 'X ought to be done'—in the stricter ethical sense of the term ought [12]—as a 'dictate' or 'precept' of reason to the persons to whom it relates, I imply that in rational beings as such this cognition gives an impulse or motive to action: though in human beings, of course, this is only one motive among others which are liable to conflict with it, and is not always—perhaps not usually —a predominant motive. In fact, this possible conflict of motives seems to be connoted by the term 'dictate' or 'imperative,' which describes the relation of Reason to mere inclinations or non-rational impulses by comparing it to the relation between the will of a superior and the wills of his subordinates. This conflict seems also to be implied in the term 'ought,' 'duty,' 'moral obligation,' as used in ordinary moral discourse: and hence these terms cannot be applied to the actions of rational beings to whom we cannot attribute impulses conflicting with reason. We may, however, say of such beings that their actions are 'reasonable,' or (in an absolute sense) 'right.'

§ 4. I am aware that some persons will be disposed to answer all the preceding argument by a simple denial that they can find in their consciousness any such unconditional or categorical imperative as I have been trying to exhibit. If this is really the final result of self-examination in any case, there is no more to be said. I,

at least, do not know how to impart the notion of moral obligation to any one who is entirely devoid of it. I think, however, that many of those who give this denial only mean to deny that they have any consciousness of moral obligation to actions without reference to their consequences; and would not really deny that they recognise some universal end or ends— whether it be the general happiness, or well-being otherwise understood— as that at which it is ultimately reasonable to aim, subordinating to its attainment the gratification of any personal desires that may conflict with this aim. But in this view, as I have before said, the unconditional imperative plainly comes in as regards the end, which is—explicitly or implicitly —recognised as an end at which all men 'ought' to aim; and it can hardly be denied that the recognition of an end as ultimately reasonable involves the recognition of an obligation to do such acts as most conduce to the end. The obligation is not indeed "unconditional," but it does not depend on the existence of any non-rational desires or aversions. And nothing that has been said in the preceding section is intended as an argument in favour of Intuitionism, as against Utilitarianism or any other method that treats moral rules as relative to General Good or Well-being. For instance, nothing that I have said is inconsistent with the view that Truthspeaking is only valuable as a means to the preservation of society—only if it be admitted at it *is* valuable on this ground I should say that it is implied that the preservation of society—or some further end to which this preservation, again, is a means—must be valuable *per se*, and therefore something at which a rational being, as such, ought to aim. If it be granted that we need not look beyond the preservation of society, the primary 'dictate of reason' in this case

[11] A further justification for this extended use of the term Reason will be suggested in a subsequent chapter of this Book (chap. viii. sec. 3).

[12] This is the sense in which the term will always be used in the present treatise, except where the context makes it quite clear that only the wider meaning—that of the political 'ought'—is applicable.

would be 'that society *ought* to be preserved': but reason would also dictate that truth ought to be spoken, so far as truthspeaking is recognised as the indispensable or fittest means to this end: and the notion "ought" as used in either dictate is that which I have been trying to make clear.

So again, even those who hold that moral rules are only obligatory because it is the individual's interest to conform to them—thus regarding them as a particular species of prudential rules —do not thereby get rid of the 'dictate of reason,' so far as they recognise private interest or happiness as an end at which it is ultimately reasonable to aim. The conflict of Practical Reason with irrational desire remains an indubitable fact of our conscious experience, even if practical reason is interpreted to mean merely self-regarding Prudence. It is, indeed, maintained by Kant and others that it cannot properly be said to be a man's duty to promote his own happiness; since "what every one inevitably wills cannot be brought under the notion of duty." But even granting [13] it to be in some sense true that a man's volition is always directed to the attainment of his own happiness, it does not follow that a man always does what he believes will be conducive to his own *greatest* happiness or his 'good on the whole.' As Butler urges, it is a matter of common experience that men indulge appetite or passion even when, in their own view, the indulgence is as clearly opposed to what they conceive to be their interest as it is to what they conceive to be their duty. Thus the notion 'ought'—as expressing the relation of rational judgment to non-rational impulses—will find a place in the practical rules of any egoistic system, no less than in the rules of ordinary morality, understood as prescribing duty without reference to the agent's interest.

Even, finally, if we discard the belief, that any end of action is unconditionally or "categorically" prescribed by reason, the notion 'ought' as above explained is not thereby eliminated from our practical reasonings: it still remains in the "hypothetical imperative" which prescribes the fittest means to any end that we may have determined to aim at. When (e.g.) a physician says, "If you wish to be healthy you ought to rise early," this is not the same thing as saying "early rising is an indispensable condition of the attainment of health." This latter proposition expresses the relation of physiological facts on which the former is founded; but it is not merely this relation of facts that the word 'ought' imports; it also implies the unreasonableness of adopting an end and refusing to adopt the means indispensable to its attainment. It may perhaps be argued that this is not only unreasonable but impossible: since adoption of an end means the preponderance of a desire for it, and if aversion to the indispensable means causes them not to be adopted although recognised as indispensable, the desire for the end is *not* preponderant and it ceases to be adopted. But this view is due, in my opinion, to a defective psychological analysis. According to my observation of consciousness, the adoption of an end as paramount—either absolutely or within certain limits—is quite a distinct psychical phenomenon from desire: it is to be classed with volitions, though it is, of course, specifically different from a volition initiating a particular immediate action. As a species intermediate between the two, we may place resolutions to act in a certain way at some future time: we continually make such resolutions, and

[13] As will be seen from the next chapter, I do not grant this.

sometimes when the time comes for carrying them out, we do in fact act otherwise under the influence of passion or mere habit, without consciously cancelling our previous resolve: in this case the act is, I conceive, clearly irrational as inconsistent with a resolution that still persists in thought. Similarly the adoption of an end logically implies a resolution to take whatever means we may see to be indispensable to its attainment: and if, when the time comes, we do not take them while yet we do not consciously retract our adoption to the end, it must surely be admitted that we 'ought' in consistency to act otherwise than we do. That Reason dictates the avoidance of a contradiction will be allowed even by those who deny that it dictates anything else: and such a contradiction as I have described, between a general resolution and a particular volition, is surely a matter of common experience.

PHILOSOPHICAL INTUITIONISM [14]

§ 1. Is there . . . no possibility of attaining, by a . . . discriminating examination of our common moral thought, to real ethical axioms—intuitive propositions of real clearness and certainty?

This question leads us to the examination of that third phase of the intuitive method, which was called Philosophical Intuitionism.[15] For we conceive it as the aim of a philosopher, as such, to do somewhat more than define and formulate the common moral opinions of mankind. His function is to tell men what they ought to think, rather than what they do think: he is expected to transcend Common Sense in his premises, and is allowed a certain divergence from Common

[14] Chap. XIII, Book III, 5th Edition, London, 1893.
[15] Cf. *ante,* Book I. ch. viii. § 4.

Sense in his conclusions. It is true that the limits of this deviation are firmly, though indefinitely, fixed: the truth of a philosopher's premises will always be tested by the acceptability of his conclusions: if in any important point he be found in flagrant conflict with common opinion, his method is likely to be declared invalid. Still, though he is expected to establish and concatenate at least the main part of the commonly accepted moral rules, he is not necessarily bound to take them as the basis on which his own system is constructed. Rather, we should expect that the history of Moral Philosophy—so far at least as those whom we may call orthodox thinkers are concerned—would be a history of attempts to enunciate, in full breadth and clearness, those primary intuitions of Reason, by the scientific application of which the common moral thought of mankind may be at once systematized and corrected.

And this is to some extent the case. But Moral Philosophy, or philosophy as applied to Morality, has had other tasks to occupy it, even more profoundly difficult than that of penetrating to the fundamental principles of Duty. In modern times especially, it has admitted the necessity of demonstrating the harmony of Duty with Interest; that is, with the Happiness or Welfare of the agent on whom the duty in each case is imposed. It has also undertaken to determine the relation of Right or Good generally to the world of actual existence: a task which could hardly be satisfactorily accomplished without an adequate explanation of the existence of Evil. It has further been distracted by questions which, in my view, are of psychological rather than ethical importance, as to the 'innateness' of our notions of Duty, and the origin of the faculty that furnishes them. With their attention concentrated on these difficult subjects, each of which has been mixed up in various ways with the discussion of fundamental moral intuitions, philosophers have too easily been led to satisfy themselves with ethical formulae which implicitly accept the morality of Common Sense *en bloc*, ignoring its defects; and merely express a certain view of the relation of this morality to the individual mind or to the universe of actual existence. Perhaps also they have been hampered by the fear (not, as we have seen, unfounded) of losing the support given by 'general assent' if they set before themselves and their readers too rigid a standard of scientific precision. Still, in spite of all these drawbacks, we find that philosophers have provided us with a considerable number of comprehensive moral propositions, put forward as certain and self-evident, and such as at first sight may seem well adapted to serve as the first principles of scientific morality.

§ 2. But here a word of caution seems required, which has been somewhat anticipated in earlier chapters, but on which it is particularly needful to lay stress at this point of our discussion: against a certain class of sham-axioms, which are very apt to offer themselves to the mind that is earnestly seeking for a philosophical synthesis of practical rules, and to delude the unwary with a tempting aspect of clear self-evidence. These are principles which appear certain and self-evident because they are substantially tautological: because, when examined, they are found to affirm no more than that it is right to do that which is, in a certain department of life, under certain circumstances and conditions—right to be done. One important lesson which the history of moral philosophy teaches is that, in this region, even powerful intellects are liable to acquiesce in tautologies of this kind; sometimes expanded into

circular reasonings, sometimes hidden in the recesses of an obscure notion, often lying so near the surface that, when once they have been exposed, it is hard to understand how they could ever have presented themselves as important.

Let us turn, for illustration's sake, to the time-honoured Cardinal Virtues. If we are told that the dictates of Wisdom and Temperance may be summed up in clear and certain principles, and that these are respectively,

(1) It is right to act rationally,
(2) It is right that the Lower parts of our nature should be governed by the Higher,

we do not at first feel that we are not obtaining valuable information. But when we find (cf. *ante*, ch. xi. § 2) that "acting rationally" is merely another phrase for "doing what we see to be right," and, again, that the "higher part" of our nature to which the rest are to submit is explained to be Reason, so that "acting temperately" is only "acting rationally" under the condition of special non-rational impulses needing to be resisted, the tautology of our "principles" is obvious. Similarly when we are asked to accept as the principle of Justice "that we ought to give every man his own," the definition seems plausible—until it appears that we cannot define "his own" except as equivalent to "that which it is right he should have."

The definitions quoted may be found in modern writers: but it seems worthy of remark that throughout the ethical speculation of Greece,[16] such

---

[16] I am fully sensible of the peculiar interest and value of the ethical thought of ancient Greece. Indeed through a large part of the present work the influence of Plato and Aristotle on my treatment of this subject has been greater than that of any modern writer. But I am here only considering the value of the

universal affirmations as are presented to us concerning Virtue or Good conduct seem almost always to be propositions which can only be defended from the charge of tautology, if they are understood as definitions of the problem to be solved, and not as attempts at its solution. For example, Plato and Aristotle appear to offer as constructive moralists the scientific knowledge on ethical matters of which Socrates proclaimed the absence; knowledge, that is, of the Good and Bad in human life. And they seem to be agreed that such Good as can be realized in the concrete life of men and communities is chiefly Virtue,—or (as Aristotle more precisely puts it) the *exercise* of Virtue: so that the practical part of ethical science must consist mainly in the knowledge of Virtue. If, however, we ask how we are to ascertain the kind of conduct which is properly to be called Virtuous, it does not seem that Plato can tell us more of each virtue in turn than that It consists in (1) the knowledge of what is Good in certain circumstances and relations, and (2) such a harmony of the different elements of man's appetitive nature, that their resultant impulse may be always in accordance with this knowledge. But it is just this knowledge (or at least its principles and method) that we are expecting him to give us: and to explain to us instead the different exigencies under which we need it, in no way satisfies our expectation. Nor, again, does Aristotle bring us much nearer such knowledge by telling us that the Good in conduct is to be found somewhere between different kinds of Bad. This at best only indicates the *whereabouts* of Virtue: it does not give us a method for finding it.

---

general principles for determining what ought to be done, which the ancient systems profess to supply.

On the Stoic system,[17] as constructed by Zeno and Chrysippus, it is perhaps unfair to pronounce decisively, from the accounts given of it by adversaries like Plutarch, and such semi-intelligent expositors as Cicero, Diogenes Laertius, and Stobaeus. But, as far as we can judge of it, we must pronounce the exposition of its general principles a complicated enchainment of circular reasonings, by which the inquirer is continually deluded with an apparent approach to practical conclusions, and continually led back to the point from which he set out.

The most characteristic formula of Stoicism seems to have been that declaring 'Life according to Nature' to be the ultimate end of action. The spring of the motion that sustained this life was in the vegetable creation a mere unfelt impulse: in animals it was impulse accompanied with sensation: in man it was the direction of Reason, which in him was naturally supreme over all merely blind irrational impulses. What then does Reason direct? 'To live according to Nature' is one answer: and thus we get the circular exposition of ethical doctrine in its simplest form. Sometimes, however, we are told that it is 'Life according to Virtue:' which leads us into the circle already noticed in the Platonic-Aristotelian philosophy; as Virtue, by the Stoics also, is only defined as knowledge of Good and Bad in different circumstances and relations. Indeed, this latter circle is given by the Stoics more neatly and perfectly: for with Plato and Aristotle Virtue was not the *sole*, but only the

[17] The following remarks apply less to *later* Stoicism—especially the Roman Stoicism which we know at first hand in the writings of Seneca and Marcus Aurelius; in which the relation of the individual man to Humanity generally is more prominent than it is in the earlier form of the system.

chief content of the notion Good, in its application to human life: but in the view of Stoicism the two notions are absolutely coincident. The result, then, is that Virtue is knowledge of what is good and ought to be sought or chosen, and of what is bad and ought to be shunned or rejected: while at the same time there is nothing good or properly choice-worthy, nothing bad or truly formidable, except Virtue and Vice respectively. But if Virtue is thus declared to be a science that has no object except itself, the notion is inevitably emptied of all practical content. In order, therefore, to avoid this result and to reconcile their system with common sense, the Stoics explained that there were other things in human life which were in a manner preferable, though not strictly good, including in this class the primary objects of men's normal impulses. On what principle then are we to select these objects when our impulses are conflicting or ambiguous? If we can get an answer to this question, we shall at length have come to something practical. But here again the Stoic could find no other general answer except either that we were to choose what was Reasonable, or that we were to act in accordance with Nature: each of which answers obviously brings us back into the original circle at a different point.[18]

In Butler's use of the Stoic formula,

this circular reasoning seems to be avoided: but it is so only so long as the intrinsic reasonableness of right conduct is ignored or suppressed. Butler assumes with his opponents that it is reasonable to live according to Nature, and argues that Conscience or the faculty that imposes moral rules is naturally supreme in man. It is therefore reasonable to obey Conscience. But are the rules that Conscience lays down merely known to us as the dictates of arbitrary authority, and not as in themselves reasonable? This would give a surely dangerous absoluteness of authority to the possibly unenlightened conscience of any individual: and Butler is much too cautious to do this: in fact, in more than one passage of the Analogy [19] he expressly adopts the doctrine of Clarke, that the true rules of morality are essentially reasonable. But if Conscience is, after all, Reason applied to Practice, then Butler's argument seems to bend itself into the old circle: it is reasonable to live according to Nature, and it is natural to live according to Reason.

In the next chapter I shall have to call attention to another logical circle into which we are liable to slide, if we refer to the Good or Perfection, whether of the agent or of others, in giving an account of any special virtue; if we allow ourselves, in explaining Good or Perfection, to use the general notion of virtue (which is commonly regarded as an important

[18] It should be observed that in determining the particulars of external duty the Stoics to some extent used the notion 'nature' in a different way: they tried to derive guidance from the complex adaptation of means to ends exhibited in the organic world. But since in their view the whole course of the Universe was both perfect and completely predetermined, it was impossible for them to obtain from any observation of actual existence a clear and consistent principle for preferring and rejecting alternatives of conduct: and in fact their most characteristic practical precepts shew a curi-

ous conflict between the tendency to accept what was customary as 'natural,' and the tendency to reject what seemed arbitrary as unreasonable.

[19] Cf. *Analogy*, Pt. II, ch. i. and ch. viii. doctrine of Clarke, that the true rules of morality are essentially reasonable. But if Conscience is, after all, Reason applied to Practice, then Butler's argument seems to bend itself into the old circle: 'it is reasonable to live according to Nature, and it is natural to live according to Reason.'

element of either). Meanwhile I have already given, perhaps, more than sufficient illustration of one of the most important dangers that beset the student of Ethics. In the laudable attempt to escape from the doubtfulness, disputableness, and apparent arbitrariness of current moral opinions, he is liable to take refuge in principles that are incontrovertible but tautological and insignificant.

§ 3. Can we then, beween this Scylla and Charybdis of ethical inquiry, avoiding on the one hand doctrines that merely bring us back to common opinion with all its imperfections, and on the other hand doctrines that lead us round in a circle, find any way of obtaining self-evident moral principles of real significance? It would be disheartening to have to regard as altogether illusory the strong instinct of Common Sense that points to the existence of such principles, and the deliberate convictions of the long line of moralists who have enunciated them. At the same time, the more we extend our knowledge of man and his environment, the more we realize the vast variety of human natures and circumstances that have existed in different ages and countries, the less disposed we are to believe that there is any definite code of absolute rules, applicable to all human beings without exception. And we shall find, I think, that the truth lies between these two conclusions. There are certain absolute practical principles, the truth of which, when they are explicitly stated, is manifest; but they are of too abstract a nature, and too universal in their scope, to enable us to ascertain by immediate application of them what we ought to do in any particular case; particular duties have still to be determined by some other method.

One such principle was given in ch. i. § 3 of this Book; where I pointed out that whatever action any of us

judges to be right for himself, he implicitly judges to be right for all similar persons in similar circumstances. Or, as we may otherwise put it, 'if a kind of conduct that is right (or wrong) for me is not right (or wrong) for some one else, it must be on the ground of some difference between the two cases, other than the fact that I and he are different persons.' A corresponding proposition may be stated with equal truth in respect of what ought to be done *to*—not *by*— different individuals. These principles have been most widely recognized, not in their most abstract and universal form, but in their special application to the situation of two (or more) individuals similarly related to each other: as so applied, they appear in what is popularly known as the Golden Rule, 'Do to others as you would have them do to you.' This formula is obviously unprecise in statement; for one might wish for another's co-operation in sin, and be willing to reciprocate it. Nor is it even true to say that we ought to do to others only what we think it right for them to do to us; for no one will deny that there may be differences in the circumstances—and even in the natures—of two individuals, A and B, which would make it wrong for A to treat B in the way in which it is right for B to treat A. In short the self-evident principle strictly stated must take some such negative form as this; 'it cannot be right for A to treat B in a manner in which it would be wrong for B to treat A, merely on the ground that they are two different individuals, and without there being any difference between the natures or circumstances of the two which can be stated as a reasonable ground for difference of treatment.' Such a principle manifestly does not give complete guidance —indeed its effect, strictly speaking, is merely to throw a definite *onus probandi* on the man who applies to another a treatment of which he would complain if applied to himself; but Common Sense has amply recognized the practical importance of the maxim: and its truth, so far as it goes, appears to me self-evident.

A somewhat different application of the same fundamental principle that individuals in similar conditions should be treated similarly finds its sphere in the ordinary administration of Law, or (as we say) of 'Justice.' Accordingly in § 2 of ch. v. of this Book I drew attention to 'impartiality in the application of general rules,' as an important element in the common notion of Justice; indeed, there ultimately appeared to be no other element which could be intuitively known with perfect clearness and certainty. Here again it must be plain that this precept of impartiality is insufficient for the complete determination of just conduct, as it does not help us to decide what kind of rules should be thus impartially applied; though all admit the importance of excluding from government, and human conduct generally, all conscious partiality and 'respect of persons.'

The principle just discussed, which seems to be more or less clearly implied in the common notion of 'fairness' or 'equity,' is obtained by considering the similarity of the individuals that make up a Logical Whole or Genus. There are others, no less important, which emerge in the consideration of the similar parts of a Mathematical or Quantitative Whole. Such a Whole is presented in the common notion of the Good—or, as is sometimes said, 'good on the whole'—of any individual human being. The proposition 'that one ought to aim at one's own good' is sometimes given as the maxim of Rational Self-love or Prudence: but as so stated it does not clearly avoid tautology; since we may define 'good' as 'what

one ought to aim at.' If, however, we say 'one's good on the whole,' the addition suggests a principle which, when explicitly stated, is, at any rate, not tautological. I have already referred to this principle [20] as that 'of impartial concern for all parts of our conscious life':—we might express it concisely by saying 'that Hereafter as such is to be regarded neither less nor more than Now.' It is not, of course, meant that the good of the present may not reasonably be preferred to that of the future on account of its greater certainty: or again, that a week ten years hence may not be more important to us than a week now, through an increase in our means or capacities of happiness. All that the principle affirms is that the mere difference of priority and posteriority in time is not a reasonable ground for having more regard to the consciousness of one moment than to that of another. The form in which it practically presents itself to most men is 'that a smaller present good is not to be preferred to a greater future good' (allowing for difference of certainty): since Prudence is generally exercised in restraining a present desire (the object or satisfaction of which we commonly regard as *pro tanto* 'a good'), on account of the remoter consequences of gratifying it. The commonest view of the principle would no doubt be that the present *pleasure* or *happiness* is reasonably to be foregone with the view of obtaining greater pleasure or happiness hereafter: but the principle need not be restricted to a hedonistic application; it is equally applicable to any other interpretation of "one's own good,' in which good is conceived as a mathematical whole, of which the integrant parts are realized in different parts or moments of a lifetime. And therefore it is perhaps better to distinguish it here from the principle

[20] Cf. Bk. II, ch. ii, § 1.

'that Pleasure is the sole Ultimate Good,' which does not seem to have any logical connexion with it.

So far we have only been considering the 'Good on the Whole' of a single individual: but just as this notion is constructed by comparison and integration of the different 'goods' that succeed one another in the series of our conscious states, so we have formed the notion of Universal Good by comparison and integration of the goods of all individual human—or sentient—existences. And here again, just as in the former case, by considering the relation of the integrant parts to the whole and to each other, I obtain the self-evident principle that the good of any one individual is of no more importance, from the point of view (if I may say so) of the Universe, than the good of any other; unless, that is, there are special grounds for believing that more good is likely to be realized in the one case than in the other. And it is evident to me that as a rational being I am bound to aim at good generally,—so far as it is attainable by my efforts— not merely at a particular part of it.

From these two rational intuitions we may deduce, as a necessary inference, the maxim of Benevolence in an abstract form: viz. that each one is morally bound to regard the good of any other individual as much as his own, except in so far as he judges it to be less, when impartially viewed, or less certainly knowable or attainable by him. I before observed that the duty of Benevolence as recognized by common sense seems to fall somewhat short of this. But I think it may be fairly urged in explanation of this that *practically* each man, even with a view to universal Good, ought chiefly to concern himself with promoting the good of a limited number of human beings, and that generally in proportion to the closeness of their connexion with him. I think that a 'plain man,' in a modern civilised society, if his conscience were fairly brought to consider the hypothetical question, whether it would be morally right for him to seek his own happiness on any occasion if it involved a certain sacrifice of the greater happiness of some other human being,—without any counterbalancing gain to any one else—would answer unhesitatingly in the negative.

I have tried to shew how in the principles of Justice, Prudence, and Rational Benevolence as commonly recognized there is at least a self-evident element, immediately cognizable by abstract intuition; depending in each case on the relation which individuals and their particular ends bear as parts to their wholes, and to other parts of these wholes. I regard the apprehension, with more or less distinctness, of these abstract truths, as the permanent basis of the common conviction that the fundamental precepts of morality are essentially reasonable. No doubt these principles are often placed side by side with other precepts to which custom and general consent have given a merely illusory air of self-evidence: but the distinction between the two kinds of maxims appears to me to become manifest by merely reflecting upon them. I know by direct reflection that the propositions, 'I ought to speak the truth,' 'I ought to keep my promises'— however true they may be—are not self-evident to me; they present themselves as propositions requiring rational justification of some kind. On the other hand, the propositions, 'I ought not to prefer a present lesser good to a future greater good,' and 'I ought not to prefer my own lesser good to the greater good of another,' [21] do

21 To avoid misapprehension I should state that in these propositions the con-

present themselves as self-evident; as much (e. g.) as the mathematical axiom that 'if equals be added to equals the wholes are equal.'

It is on account of the fundamental and manifest importance, in my view, of the distinction above drawn between (1) the moral maxims which reflection shews not to possess ultimate validity, and (2) the moral maxims which are or involve genuine ethical axioms, that I refrained at the outset of this investigation from entering at length into the psychogonical question as to the origin of apparent moral intuitions. For no psychogonical theory has ever been put forward professing to discredit the propositions that I regard as really axiomatic, by shewing that the causes which produced them were such as had a tendency to make them false: while as regards the former class of maxims, a psychogonical proof that they are untrustworthy when taken as absolutely and without qualification true is, in my view, superfluous: since direct reflection shews me that they have no claim to be so taken. On the other hand, so far as psychogonical theory represents moral rules as, speaking broadly and generally, means to the ends of individuals and social good or well-being, it obviously tends to give a general support to the conclusions to which the preceding discussion has brought us by a different method: since it leads us to regard other moral rules as subordinate to the principles of Prudence and Benevolence.[22]

§ 4. I should, however, rely less confidently on the conclusions set forth in the preceding section, if they did not appear to me to be in substantial agreement—in spite of superficial differences—with the doctrines of those moralists who have been most in earnest in seeking among commonly received moral rules for genuine intuitions of the Practical Reason. I have already pointed out [23] that in the history of English Ethics the earlier intuitional school shew, in this respect, a turn of thought on the whole more philosophical than that which the reaction against Hume rendered prevalent. Among the writers of this school there is no one who shews more earnestness in the effort to penetrate to really self-evident principles than Clarke.[24] Accordingly, I find that Clarke lays down, in respect of our behaviour towards our fellowmen, two fundamental "rules of

---

siderate of the different degrees of *certainty* of Present and Future Good, Own and Others' Good respectively, is supposed to have been fully taken into account *before* the future or alien Good is judged to be greater.

[22] It may however be thought that in exhibiting this aspect of the morality of Common Sense, psychogonical theory leads us to define in a particular way the general notion of 'good' or 'well-being,' regarded as a result which morality has a demonstrable natural tendency to produce. This point will be considered subsequently (Ch. xiv. § 1 of this Book: and Book iv. ch. iv.).

[23] Cf. *ante*, Book I. ch. viii.

[24] In drawing attention to Clarke's system, I ought perhaps to remark that his anxiety to exhibit the parallelism between ethical and mathematical truth (on which Locke before him had insisted) renders his general terminology inappropriate and occasionally leads him into downright extravagances. *E.g.* it is patently absurd to say that "a man who wilfully acts contrary to Justice wills things to be what they are not and cannot be": nor are "Relations and Proportions" or "fitnesses and unfitnesses of things" very suitable designations for the matter of moral intuition. But for the present purpose there is no reason to dwell on these defects.

righteousness": [25] the first of which he terms Equity, and the second Love or Benevolence. The Rule of Equity he states thus: "Whatever I judge reasonable or unreasonable that another should do for me: that by the same judgment I declare reasonable or unreasonable that I should *in the like case* do for him" [26]—which is, of course, the 'Golden Rule' precisely stated. The obligation to "Universal Love or Benevolence" he exhibits as follows:—

"If there be a natural and necessary difference between Good and Evil: and that which is Good is fit and reasonable, and that which is Evil is unreasonable, to be done: and that which is the Greatest Good is always the most fit and reasonable to be chosen: then . . . every rational creature ought in its sphere and station, according to its respective powers and faculties, to do all the Good it can to its fellow-creatures: to which end, universal Love and Benevolence is plainly the most certain, direct and effectual means." [27]

Here the mere statement that a rational agent is bound to aim at universal good is open to the charge of tautology, since Clarke defines 'Good' as 'that which is fit and reasonable to be done.' But Clarke obviously holds that each individual 'rational crea-

ture' is capable of receiving good in a greater or less degree, such good being an integrant part of universal good. This indeed is implied in the common notion, which he uses, of 'doing Good to one's fellow-creatures,' or, as he otherwise expresses it, 'promoting their welfare and happiness.' And thus his principle is implicitly what was stated above, that the good or welfare of any one individual must as such be an object of rational aim to any other reasonable individual no less than his own similar good or welfare.

(It should be observed however that the proposition that Universal Benevolence is the right means to the attainment of universal good, is not quite self-evident; since the end may not always be best attained by directly aiming at it. Thus Rational Benevolence, like Rational Self-Love, may be self-limiting; may direct its own partial suppression in favor of other impulses.)

Among later moralists, Kant is especially noted for his rigour in separating the purely rational element of the moral code: and his ethical view also appears to me to coincide to a considerable extent, if not completely, with that set forth in the preceding section. I have already noticed that his fundamental principle of duty is the 'formal' rule of "acting on a maxim that one can will to law universal;" which, duly restricted, [28] is an immediate practical corollary from the principle that I first noticed in the preceding section. And we find that when he comes to consider the ends at which virtuous action is aimed, the only really ultimate end which he lays down is the object of Rational Benevolence

[25] Clarke's statement of the "Rule of Righteousness with respect to ourselves" I pass over, because it is, as he states it, a derivative and subordinate rule. It is that we should preserve our being, be temperate, industrious, &c., *with a view to the performance of Duty:* which of course supposes Duty (*i. e.* the ultimate and absolute rules of Duty) already determined. I may observe that the reasonableness of Prudence or Self-love is only recognized by Clarke indirectly; in a passage which I quoted before.

[26] *Boyle Lectures* (1705), &c. pp. 86, 87.

[27] *l. c.* p. 92.

[28] I think that Kant, in applying this axiom, does not take due account of certain restrictive considerations. Cf. ch. vii. § 3 of this Book, and also Book iv. ch. v. § 3.

as commonly conceived — the happiness of other men.[29] He regards it as evident *à priori* that each man as a rational agent is bound to aim at the happiness of other men: indeed, in his view, it can only be stated as a *duty* for me to seek my own happiness so far as I consider it as a part of the happiness of mankind in general. I disagree with the negative side of this statement, as I hold with Butler that "one's own happiness is a manifest obligation" independently of one's relation to other men; but, regarded on its positive side, Kant's conclusion appears to agree to a great extent with the view of the duty of Rational Benevolence that I have given:—though I am not altogether able to assent to the arguments by which Kant arrives at his conclusion.[30]

§ 5. I must now point out—if it has not long been apparent to the reader—that the self-evident principles laid down in § 3 do not specially belong to Intuitionism in the restricted sense which, for clear distinction of methods, I gave to this term at the outset of our investigation. The axiom of Prudence, as I have given it, is a self-evident principle, implied in Rational Egoism as commonly accepted.[31] Again, the axiom of Justice or

Equity as above stated—'that similar cases ought to be treated similarly'—belongs in all its applications to Utilitarianism as much as to any system commonly called Intuitional: while the axiom of Rational Benevolence is, in my view, required as a rational basis for the Utilitarian system.

Accordingly, I find that I arrive, in my search for really clear and certain ethical intuitions, at the fundamental principle of Utilitarianism. I must, however, admit that the thinkers who in recent times have taught this latter system, have not, for the most part, expressly tried to exhibit the truth of their first principle by means of any such procedure as that above given. Still when I examine the "proof" of the "principle of Utility" presented by the most persuasive and probably the most influential among English expositors of Utilitarianism,—J. S. Mill—I find the need of some such procedure to complete the argument very plain and palpable.

Mill begins by explaining [32] that though "questions of ultimate ends are not amenable" to "proof in the ordinary and popular meaning of the term," there is a "large meaning of the word proof" in which they are amenable to it. "The subject," he says, is "within the cognizance of the rational faculty . . . Considerations may be presented capable of determining the intellect to" accept "the Utilitarian formula." He subsequently makes clear that by "acceptance of the Utilitarian formula" he means the acceptance, not of the agent's own greatest happiness, but of "the greatest amount of happiness altogether" as the ultimate "end of human action" and "standard of morality:" to promote which is, in the Utilitarian view, the

[29] Kant no doubt gives the agent's own Perfection as another absolute end; but when we come to examine his notion of perfection, we find that it is not really determinate without the statement of other ends of reason, for the accomplishment of which we are to perfect ourselves. See *Tugendlehre, Einleitung*, § v. (A). "The perfection that belongs to men generally . . . can be nothing else than the cultivation of one's power, and also of one's will, to satisfy the requirements of duty in general."

[30] See note at the end of the chapter.

[31] On the relation of Rational Egoism to Rational Benevolence—which I regard as the profoundest problem of Ethics—

my final view is given in the last chapter of this treatise.

[32] *Utilitarianism*, chap. i.; *l. c.* chap. ii.

supreme "directive rule of human conduct." Then when he comes to give the "proof"—in the larger sense before explained—of this rule or formula, he offers the following argument. "The sole evidence it is possible to produce that anything is desirable, is that people do actually desire it. . . . No reason can be given why the general happiness is desirable, except that each person, so far as he believes it to be attainable, desires his own happiness. This, however, being a fact, we have not only all the proof which the case admits of, but all which it is possible to require, that happiness is a good: that each person's happiness is a good to that person, and the general happiness, therefore, a good to the aggregate of persons."[33] He then goes on to argue that pleasure, and pleasure alone, is what all men actually do desire.

Now, as we have seen, it is as a "standard of right and wrong," or "directive rule of conduct," that the utilitarian principle is put forward by Mill: hence, in giving as a statement of this principle that "the general happiness is *desirable*," he must be understood to mean (and his whole treatise shews that he does mean) that it is what each individual *ought* to desire, or at least—in the stricter sense of 'ought'—to aim at realizing in action.[34] But this proposition is not established by Mill's reasoning, even if we grant that what is actually desired may be legitimately inferred to be in this sense

[33] *l. c.* chap. iv. pp. 52, 53.
[34] It has been suggested that I have overlooked a confusion in Mill's mind between two possible meanings of the term 'desirable,' (1) what can be desired and (2) what ought to be desired. I intended to shew by the two first sentences of this paragraph that I was aware of this confusion, but thought it unnecessary for my present purpose to discuss it.

desirable. For an aggregate of actual desires, each directed towards a different part of the general happiness, does not constitute an actual desire for the general happiness, existing in any individual; and Mill would certainly not contend that a desire which does not exist in any individual can possibly exist in an aggregate of individuals. There being therefore no actual desire —so far as this reasoning goes—for the general happiness, the proposition that the general happiness is desirable cannot be in this way established: so that there is a gap in the expressed argument, which can, I think, only be filled by some such proposition as that which I have above tried to exhibit as the intuition of Rational Benevolence.

Utilitarianism is thus presented as the final form into which Intuitionism tends to pass, when the demand for really self-evident first principles is rigorously pressed. In order, however, to make this transition logically complete, we require to interpret 'Universal Good' as 'Universal Happiness.' And this interpretation cannot, in my view, be justified by arguing, as Mill does, from the psychological fact that Happiness is the sole object of men's actual desires, to the ethical conclusion that it alone is desirable or good: because in Book I, ch. iv, of this treatise I have attempted to shew that Happiness or Pleasure is not the only object that each for himself actually desires. The identification of Ultimate Good with Happiness is properly to be reached, I think, by a more indirect mode of reasoning; which I will endeavour to explain in the next Chapter.

NOTE.—The great influence at present exercised by Kant's teaching makes it worth while to state briefly the arguments by which he attempts to establish the duty of promoting the happiness of others, and the reasons why I am unable to regard these arguments as cogent. In some passages he attempts to exhibit this duty as an immediate deduction from his fundamental formula—"act from a maxim that thou canst will to be universal law" —when considered in combination with the desire for the kind of services of others which (as he assumes) the exigencies of life must arouse in every man. The maxim, he says, "that each should be left to take care of himself without either aid or interference," is one that we might indeed *conceive* existing as a universal law: but it would be impossible for us to *will* it to be such. "A will that resolved this would be inconsistent with itself, for many cases may arise in which the individual thus willing needs the benevolence and sympathy of others" (*Grundlegung*, p. 50 [Rosenkrantz]). Similarly elsewhere (*Metaph Anfangsgr. d. Tugendlehre,* Einleit. 8 and 30) he explains at more length that the Self-love which necessarily exists in every one involves the desire of being loved by others and receiving aid from them in case of need. We thus necessarily constitute ourselves an end for others, and claim that they shall contribute to our happiness: and so, according to Kant's fundamental principle, we must recognize the duty of making *their* happiness *our* end.

Now I cannot regard this reasoning as strictly cogent. In the first place, that every man in need wishes for the aid of others is an empirical proposition which Kant cannot know *à priori*. We can certainly conceive a man in whom the spirit of independence and the distaste for incurring obligations would be so strong that he would choose to endure any privations rather than receive aid from others. But even granting that every one, in the actual moment of distress, must necessarily wish for the assistance of others; still a strong man, after balancing the chances of life, may easily think that he and such as he have more to gain, on the whole, by the general adoption of the egoistic maxim; benevolence being likely to bring them more trouble than profit.

In other passages, however, Kant reaches the same conclusion by an apparently different line of argument. He lays down that, as all action of rational beings is done for some end, there must be some absolute end, corresponding to the absolute rule before given that imposes on our maxims the form of universal law. This absolute end, prescribed by Reason necessarily and *à priori* for all rational beings as such, can be nothing but Reason itself, or the Universe of Rationals; for what the rule inculcates is, in fact, that we should act as rational units in a universe of rational beings (and therefore on principles conceived and embraced as universally applicable). Or again, we may reach the same result negatively. For all particular ends at which men aim are constituted such by the existence of impulses directed towards some particular objects. Now we cannot tell *à priori* that any one of these special impulses forms part of the constitution of all men: and therefore we cannot state it as an absolute dictate of Reason that we should aim at any such special object. If, then, we thus exclude all particular empirical ends, there remains only the principle that "all Rational beings as such are ends to each:" or, as Kant sometimes put it, that "humanity exists as an end in itself."

Now, says Kant, so long as I confine myself to mere non-interference with others, I do not positively make Humanity my end; my aims remain selfish, though restricted by this condition of non-interference with others. My action, therefore, is not truly virtuous; for Virtue is exhibited and consists in the effort to realize the end of Reason in opposition to mere selfish impulses. Therefore "the ends of the subject, which is itself an end, must of necessity be my ends, if the representation of Humanity as an end in itself is to have its full weight with me" (*Grundlegung*, p. 59), and my action is to be truly rational and virtuous.

Here, again, I cannot accept the form of Kant's argument. The conception of "humanity as an end in itself" is perplexing: because by an End we commonly mean something to be realized, whereas "humanity" is, as Kant says, "a self-subsistent end:" moreover, there seems to be a sort of paralogism in the deduction of the principle of Benevolence by means of this conception. For the humanity which Kant maintains to be an end in itself is Man (or the aggregate of men) *in so far as rational.* But the subjective ends of other men, which Benevolence directs us to take as our own ends, would seem, according to Kant's own view, to depend upon and correspond to their non-rational impulses—their empirical desires and aversions. It is hard to see why, if man *as a rational being* is an absolute end to other rational beings, they must therefore adopt his subjective aims as determined by his non-rational impulses.

ULTIMATE GOOD [35]

§ 1. At the outset of this treatise [36] I noticed that there are two forms in which the object of ethical inquiry is considered; it is sometimes regarded as a Rule or Rules of Conduct, 'the Right,' sometimes as an end or ends, 'the Good.' I pointed out that in the moral consciousness of modern Europe the two notions are *primâ facie* distinct; since while it is commonly thought that the obligation to obey moral rules is absolute, it is not commonly held that the whole Good of man lies in such obedience; this view, we may say, is—vaguely and respectfully but unmistakably—repudiated as a Stoical paradox. The ultimate Good or Wellbeing of man is rather regarded as an ulterior result, the connexion of which with his Right Conduct is indeed held to be certain, but is frequently conceived as supernatural, and so beyond the range of independent ethical speculation. But now, if the conclusions of the preceding chapters are to be trusted, it would seem that the practical determination of Right Conduct depends on the determination of Ultimate Good. For we have seen (a) that most of the commonly

[35] Chap. XIV, Bk. III. 5th Edition, London, 1893.
[36] See Book I. ch. i. § 2.

received maxims of Duty—even of those which at first sight appear absolute and independent—are found when closely examined to contain an implicit subordination to the more general principles of Prudence and Benevolence: and (b) that no principles except these, and the formal principle of Justice or Equity can be admitted as at once intuitively clear and certain; while, again, these principles themselves, so far as they are self-evident, may be stated as precepts to seek (1) one's own good on the whole, repressing all seductive impulses prompting to undue preference of particular goods, and (2) others' good no less than one's own, repressing any undue preference for one individual over another. Thus we are brought round again to the old question with which ethical speculation in Europe began, "What is the Ultimate Good for man?"—though not in the egoistic form in which the old question was raised. When, however, we examine the controversies to which this question originally led, we see that the investigation which has brought us round to it has tended definitely to exclude one of the answers which early moral reflection was disposed to give to it. For to say that "General Good" consists solely in general Virtue —if we mean by Virtue conformity to such prescriptions and prohibitions as make up the main part of the morality of Common Sense—would obviously involve us in a logical circle; since we have seen that the exact determination of these prescriptions and prohibitions must depend on the definition of this General Good.

Nor, I conceive, can this argument be evaded by adopting the view of what I have called "Æsthetic Intuitionism" and regarding Virtues as excellences of conduct clearly discernible by trained insight, although their nature does not admit of being stated in definite formulæ. For our notions of special virtues do not really become more independent by becoming more indefinite: they still contain, though perhaps more latently, the same reference to "Good" or "Wellbeing" as an ultimate standard. This appears clearly when we consider any virtue in relation to the cognate vice—or at least *non-virtue*—into which it tends to pass over when pushed to an extreme, or exhibited under inappropriate conditions. For example, Common Sense may seem to regard Liberality, Frugality, Courage, Placability, as intrinsically desirable: but when we consider their relation respectively to Profusion, Meanness, Foolhardiness, Weakness, we find that Common Sense draws the line in each case not by immediate intuition, but by reference either to some definite maxim of duty, or to the general notion of "Good" or Wellbeing: and similarly when we ask at what point Candour, Generosity, Humility cease to be virtues by becoming "excessive." Other qualities commonly admired, such as Energy, Zeal, Self-control, Thoughtfulness, are obviously regarded as virtues only when they are directed to good ends. In short, the only so-called Virtues which can be thought to be essentially and always such, and incapable of excess, are such qualities as Wisdom, Universal Benevolence, and (in a sense) Justice; of which the notions manifestly involve this notion of Good, supposed already determinate. Wisdom is insight into Good and the means to Good; Benevolence is exhibited in the purposive actions called "doing Good": Justice (when regarded as essentially and always a Virtue) lies in distributing Good (or evil) impartially according to right rules. If then we are asked what is this Good which it is excellent to know, to bestow on others, to distribute impartially, it would be obviously absurd

to reply that it is just this knowledge, these beneficent purposes, this impartial distribution.

Nor, again, can I perceive that this difficulty is in any way met by regarding Virtue as a quality of "character" rather than of "conduct," and expressing the moral law in the form, "Be this," instead of the form, "Do this." [37] From a practical point of view, indeed, I fully recognise the importance of urging that men should aim at an ideal of character, and consider action in its effects on character. But I cannot infer from this that character and its elements—faculties, habits, or dispositions of any kind—are the constituents of Ultimate Good. It seems to me that the opposite is implied in the very conception of a faculty or disposition; it can only be defined as a tendency to act or feel in a certain way under certain conditions; and such a tendency appears to me clearly not valuable in itself but for the acts and feelings in which it takes effect, or for the ulterior consequences of these,—which consequences, again, cannot be regarded as Ultimate Good, so long as they are merely conceived as modifications of faculties, dispositions, etc. When, therefore, I say that effects on character are important, it is a summary way of saying that by the laws of our mental constitution the present act or feeling is a cause tending to modify importantly our acts and feelings in the indefinite future: the comparatively permanent result supposed to be produced in the mind or soul, being a tendency that will show itself in an indefinite number of particular acts and feelings, may easily be more important, in relation to the ultimate end, than a single act or the transient feeling of a single moment: but its comparative permanence appears to

[37] Cf. Leslie Stephen's *Science of Ethics*, chap. iv., § 16.

me no ground for regarding it as itself a constituent of ultimate good.

§ 2. So far, however, I have been speaking only of particular virtues, as exhibited in conduct judged to be objectively right: and it may be argued that this is too external a view of the Virtue that claims to constitute Ultimate Good. It may be said that the difficulty that I have been urging vanishes if we penetrate beyond the particular virtues to the root and essence of virtue in general,—the determination of the will to do whatever is judged to be right and to aim at realising whatever is judged to be best;—since this subjective rightness or goodness of will, being independent of knowledge of what is objectively right or good, is independent of that presupposition of Good as already known and determined, which we have seen to be implied in the common conceptions of virtue as manifested in outward acts. I admit that if subjective rightness or goodness of Will is affirmed to be the Ultimate Good, the affirmation does not exactly involve the logical difficulty that I have been urging. None the less is it fundamentally opposed to Common Sense; since the very notion of subjective rightness or goodness of will implies an objective standard, which it directs us to seek, but does not profess to supply. It would be a palpable and violent paradox to set before the right-seeking mind no end except this right-seeking itself, and to affirm this to be the sole Ultimate Good, denying that any effects of right volition can be in themselves good, except the subjective rightness of future volitions, whether of self or of others. It is true that no rule can be recognised, by any reasonable individual, as more authoritative than the rule of doing what he judges to be right; for, in deliberating with a view to my own immediate action, I cannot distinguish between doing what is objectively right, and realising my own subjective conception of rightness. But we are continually forced to make the distinction as regards the actions of others and to judge that conduct may be objectively wrong though subjectively right: and we continually judge conduct to be objectively wrong because it tends to cause pain and loss of happiness to others,—apart from any effect on the subjective rightness of their volitions. It is as so judging that we commonly recognise the mischief and danger of fanaticism:—meaning by a fanatic a man who resolutely and unswervingly carries out his own conception of rightness, when it is a plainly mistaken conception.

The same result may be reached even without supposing so palpable a divorce between subjective and objective rightness of volition as is implied in the notion of fanaticism. As I have already pointed out,[38] though the "dictates of Reason" are always to be obeyed, it does not follow that "the dictation of Reason"—the predominance of consciously moral over non-moral motives—is to be promoted without limits; and indeed Common Sense appears to hold that some things are likely to be better done, if they are done from other motives than conscious obedience to practical Reason or Conscience. It thus becomes a practical question how far the dictation of Reason, the predominance of moral choice and moral effort in human life, is a result to be aimed at; and the admission of this question implies that conscious rightness of volition is not the sole ultimate good. On the whole, then, we may conclude that neither (1) subjective rightness or goodness of volition, as distinct from objective, nor (2) virtuous char-

[38] Chap. xi., § 3; see also chap. xii., § 3.

acter, except as manifested or realised in virtuous conduct, can be regarded as constituting Ultimate Good: while, again, we are precluded from identifying Ultimate Good with virtuous conduct, because our conceptions of virtuous conduct, under the different heads or aspects denoted by the names of the particular virtues, have been found to presuppose the prior determination of the notion of Good—that Good which virtuous conduct is conceived as producing or promoting or rightly distributing.

And what has been said of Virtue, seems to me still more manifestly true of the other talents, gifts, and graces which make up the common notion of human excellence or Perfection. However immediately the excellent quality of such gifts and skills may be recognised and admired, reflection shows that they are only valuable on account of the good or desirable conscious life in which they are or will be actualised, or which will be somehow promoted by their exercise.

§ 3. Shall we then say that Ultimate Good is Good or Desirable conscious or sentient Life—of which Virtuous action is one element, but not the sole constituent? This seems in harmony with Common Sense; and the fact that particular virtues and talents and gifts are largely valued as means to ulterior good does not necessarily prevent us from regarding their exercise as also an element of Ultimate Good: just as the fact that physical action, nutrition, and repose, duly proportioned and combined, are means to the maintenance of our animal life, does not prevent us from regarding them as indispensable elements of such life. Still it seems difficult to conceive any kind of activity or process as both means and end, from precisely the same point of view and in respect of precisely the same quality: and in both the cases above mentioned it

is, I think, easy to distinguish the aspect in which the activities or processes in question are to be regarded as means from that in which they are to be regarded as in themselves good or desirable. Let us examine this first in the case of the physical processes. It is in their purely physical aspect, as complex processes of corporeal change, that they are means to the maintenance of life: but so long as we confine our attention to their corporeal aspect,—regarding them merely as complex movements of certain particles of organised matter, —it seems impossible to attribute to these movements, considered in themselves, either goodness or badness. I cannot conceive it to be an ultimate end of rational action to secure that these complex movements should be of one kind rather than another, or that they should be continued for a longer rather than a shorter period. In short, if a certain quality of human Life is that which is ultimately desirable, it must belong to human Life regarded on its psychical side, or, briefly, Consciousness.

But again: it is not all life regarded on its psychical side which we can judge to be ultimately desirable: since psychical life as known to us includes pain as well as pleasure, and so far as it is painful it is not desirable. I cannot therefore accept a view of the wellbeing or welfare of human beings—as of other living things—which is suggested by current zoölogical conceptions and apparently maintained with more or less definiteness by influential writers; according to which, when we attribute goodness or badness to the manner of existence of any living organism, we should be understood to attribute to it a tendency either (1) to self-preservation, or (2) to the preservation of the community or race to which it belongs—so that what "Wellbeing" adds to mere "being" is just promise of future being. It appears to me that this doctrine needs only to be distinctly contemplated in order to be rejected. If all life were as little desirable as some portions of it have been, in my own experience and in that (I believe) of all or most men, I should judge all tendency to the preservation of it to be unmitigatedly bad. Actually, no doubt as we generally hold that human life, even as now lived, has on the average, a balance of happiness, we regard what is preservative of life as generally good and what is destructive of life as bad: and I quite admit that a most fundamentally important part of the function of morality consists in maintaining such habits and sentiments as are necessary to the continued existence, in full numbers, of a society of human beings under their actual conditions of life. But this is not because the mere existence of human organisms, even if prolonged to eternity, appears to me in any way desirable; it is only assumed to be so because it is supposed to be accompanied by Consciousness on the whole desirable; it is therefore this Desirable Consciousness which we must regard as ultimate Good.

In the same way, so far as we judge virtuous activity to be a part of Ultimate Good, it is, I conceive, because the consciousness attending it is judged to be in itself desirable for the virtuous agent: though at the same time this consideration does not adequately represent the importance of Virtue to human wellbeing, since we have to consider its value as a means as well as its value as an end. We may make the distinction clearer by considering whether Virtuous life would remain on the whole good for the virtuous agent, if we suppose it combined with extreme pain. The affirmative answer to this question was strongly supported in Greek philo-

sophical discussion: but it is a paradox from which a modern thinker would recoil: he would hardly venture to assert that the portion of life spent by a martyr in tortures was in itself desirable,—though it might be his duty to suffer the pain with a view to the good of others, and even his interest to suffer it with a view to his own ultimate happiness.

§ 4. If then Ultimate Good can only be conceived as Desirable Consciousness,—including the Consciousness of Virtue as a part but only as a part, —are we to identify this notion with Happiness or Pleasure, and say with the Utilitarians that General Good is General Happiness? Many would at this point of the discussion regard this conclusion as inevitable: to say that all other things called good are only mean: to the end of making conscious life better or more desirable, seems to them the same as saying that they are means to the end of happiness. But very important distinctions remain to be considered. According to the view taken in a previous chapter,[39] in affirming Ultimate Good to be Happiness or Pleasure, we imply (1) that nothing is desirable except desirable feelings, and (2) that the desirability of each feeling is only directly cognisable by the sentient individual at the time of feeling it, and that therefore this particular judgment of the sentient individual must be taken as final [40] on the question how far each element of feeling has the quality of Ultimate Good. Now no one, I conceive, would estimate in any other way

[39] Book ii., chap. ii.

[40] Final, that is, so far as the quality of the present feeling is concerned. I have pointed out that so far as any estimate of the desirability or pleasantness of a feeling involves comparison with feelings only represented in idea, it is liable to be erroneous through imperfections in the representation.

the desirability of feeling considered merely as feeling: but it may be urged that our conscious experience includes besides Feelings, Cognitions and Volitions, and that the desirability of these must be taken into account, and is not to be estimated by the standard above stated. I think, however, that when we reflect on a cognition as a transient fact of an individual's psychical experience,—distinguishing it on the one hand from the feeling that normally accompanies it, and on the other hand from that relation of the knowing mind to the object known which is implied in the term "true" or "valid cognition," [41]—it is seen to be an element of consciousness quite neutral in respect of desirability: and the same may be said of Volitions, when we abstract from their concomitant feelings, and their relation to an objective norm or ideal, as well as from all their consequences. It is no doubt true that in ordinary thought certain states of consciousness—such as Cognition of Truth, Contemplation of Beauty, Volition to realise Freedom or Virtue—are sometimes judged to be preferable on other grounds than their pleasantness: but the general explanation of this seems to be (as was suggested in Book ii., chap. ii., § 2) that what in such cases we really prefer is not the present consciousness itself, but either effects on future consciousness more or less distinctly foreseen, or else something in the objective relations of the conscious being, not strictly included in his present consciousness.

The second of these alternatives may perhaps be made clearer by some illustrations. A man may prefer the mental state of apprehending truth to

the state of half-reliance on generally accredited fictions,[42] while recognising that the former state may be more painful than the latter, and independently of any effect which he expects either state to have upon his subsequent consciousness. Here, on my view, the real object of preference is not the consciousness of knowing truth, considered merely as consciousness,—the element of pleasure or satisfaction in this being more than outweighed by the concomitant pain,— but the relation between the mind and something else, which, as the very notion of "truth" implies, is whatever it is independently of our cognition of it, and which I therefore call objective. This may become more clear if we imagine ourselves learning afterwards that what we took for truth is not really such: for in this case we should certainly feel that our preference had been mistaken; whereas if our choice had really been between two elements of transient consciousness, its reasonableness could not be affected by any subsequent discovery.

Similarly, a man may prefer freedom and penury to a life of luxurious servitude, not because the pleasant consciousness of being free outweighs in prospect all the comforts and securities that the other life would afford, but because he has a predominant aversion to that relation between his will and the will of another which we call slavery: or, again, a philosopher may choose what he conceives as "inner freedom"—the consistent self-determination of the will— rather than the gratifications of appetite; though recognising that the latter are more desirable, considered merely as transient feelings. In either case, he will be led to regard his preference as mistaken, if he be after-

[41] The term "cognition" without qualification more often implies what is signified by "true" or "valid": but for the present purpose it is necessary to eliminate this implication.

[42] Cf. W. E. H. Lecky's *History of European Morals*, pp. 52 *seqq.*

wards persuaded that his conception of Freedom or self-determination was illusory; that we are all slaves of circumstances, destiny, etc.

So again, the preference of conformity to Virtue, or contemplation of Beauty, to a state of consciousness recognised as more pleasant seems to depend on a belief that one's conception of Virtue or Beauty correspond to an ideal to some extent objective and valid for all minds. Apart from any consideration of future consequences, we should generally agree that a man who sacrificed happiness to an erroneous conception of Virtue or Beauty made a mistaken choice.

Still, it may be said that this is merely a question of definition: that we may take "conscious life" in a wide sense, so as to include the objective relations of the conscious being implied in our notions of Virtue, Truth, Beauty, Freedom, and that from this point of view we may regard cognition of Truth, contemplation of Beauty, Free or Virtuous action, as in some measure preferable alternatives to Pleasure or Happiness—even though we admit that Happiness must be included as a part of Ultimate Good. In this case the principle of Rational Benevolence, which was stated in the last chapter as an indubitable intuition of the practical Reason, would not direct us to the pursuit of universal happiness alone, but of these "ideal goods" as well, as ends ultimately desirable for mankind generally.

§ 5. I think, however, that this view ought not to commend itself to the sober judgment of reflective persons. In order to show this, I must ask the reader to use the same twofold procedure that I before requested him to employ in considering the absolute and independent validity of common moral precepts. I appeal firstly to his intuitive judgment after due consideration of the question when fairly placed

before it and secondly to a comprehensive comparison of the ordinary judgments of mankind. As regards the first argument, to me at least it seems clear after reflection that these objective relations of the conscious subject, when distinguished from the consciousness accompanying and resulting from them, are not ultimately and intrinsically desirable; any more than material or other objects are, when considered apart from any relation to conscious existence. Admitting that we have actual experience of such preferences as have just been described, of which the ultimate object is something that is not merely consciousness: it still seems to me that when (to use Butler's phrase) we "sit down in a cool hour," we can only justify to ourselves the importance that we attach to any of these objects by considering its conduciveness, in one way or another, to the happiness of sentient beings.

The second argument, that refers to the common sense of mankind, obviously cannot be made completely cogent; since, as above stated, several cultivated persons do habitually judge that knowledge, art, etc.—not to speak of Virtue—are ends independently of the pleasure derived from them. But we may urge not only that all these elements of "ideal good" are productive of pleasure in various ways; but also that they seem to obtain the commendation of Common Sense, roughly speaking, in proportion to the degree of this productiveness. This seems obviously true of Beauty; and will hardly be denied in respect of any kind of social ideal. it is paradoxical to maintain that any degree of Freedom, or any form of social order, would still be commonly regarded as desirable even if we were certain that it had no tendency to promote the general happiness. The case of Knowledge is rather more complex; but certainly Common Sense is most impressed with the value of knowledge, when its "fruitfulness" has been demonstrated. It is, however, aware that experience has frequently shown how knowledge, long fruitless, may become unexpectedly fruitful, and how light may be shed on one part of the field of knowledge from another apparently remote: and even if any particular branch of scientific pursuit could be shown to be devoid of even this indirect utility, it would still deserve some respect on utilitarian grounds, both as furnishing to the inquirer the refined and innocent pleasures of curiosity, and because the intellectual disposition which it exhibits and sustains is likely on the whole to produce fruitful knowledge. Still in cases approximating to this last, Common Sense is somewhat disposed to complain of the misdirection of valuable effort; so that the meed of honour commonly paid to Science seems to be graduated, though perhaps unconsciously, by a tolerably exact utilitarian scale. Certainly the moment the legitimacy of any branch of scientific inquiry is seriously disputed, as in the recent case of vivisection, the controversy on both sides is generally conducted on an avowedly utilitiarian basis.

The case of Virtue requires special consideration: since the encouragement in each other of virtuous impulses and dispositions is a main aim of men's ordinary moral discourse; so that even to raise the question whether this encouragement can go too far has a paradoxical air. Still, our experience includes rare and exceptional cases in which the concentration of effort on the cultivation of virtue has seemed to have effects adverse to general happiness, through being intensified to the point of moral fanaticism, and so involving a neglect of other conditions of happiness. If, then,

we admit as actual or possible such "infelicific" effects of the cultivation of Virtue, I think we shall also generally admit that, in the case supposed, conduciveness to general happiness should be the criterion for deciding how far the cultivation of Virtue should be carried.

At the same time it must be allowed that we find in Common Sense an aversion to admit Happiness (when explained to mean a sum of pleasures) to be the sole ultimate end and standard of right conduct. But this, I think, can be fully accounted for by the following considerations.

I. The term Pleasure is not commonly used so as to include clearly *all* kinds of consciousness which we desire to retain or reproduce: in ordinary usage it suggests too prominently the coarser and commoner kinds of such feelings; and it is difficult even for those who are trying to use it scientifically to free their minds altogether from the associations of ordinary usage, and to mean by Pleasure only Desirable Consciousness or Feeling of whatever kind. Again, our knowledge of human life continually suggests to us instances of pleasures which will inevitably involve as concomitant or consequent either a greater amount of pain, or a loss of more important pleasures: and we naturally shrink from including even hypothetically in our conception of ultimate good these —in Bentham's phrase—"impure" pleasures; especially since we have, in many cases, moral or æsthetic instincts warning us against such pleasures.

II. We have seen [43] that many important pleasures can only be felt on condition of our experiencing desires for other things than pleasure. Thus the very acceptance of Pleasure as the ultimate end of conduct involves the

[43] Book i., chap. iv.; cf. Book ii., chap. iii.

practical rule that it is not always to be made the conscious end. Hence, even if we are considering merely the good of one human being taken alone, excluding from our view all effects of his conduct on others, still the reluctance of Common Sense to regard pleasure as the sole thing ultimately desirable may be justified by the consideration that human beings tend to be less happy if they are exclusively occupied with the desire of personal happiness. *E.g.* (as was before shown) we shall miss the valuable pleasures which attend the exercise of the benevolent affections if we do not experience genuinely disinterested impulses to procure happiness for others (which are, in fact, implied in the notion of "benevolent affections").

III. But again, I hold, as was expounded in the preceding chapter, that disinterested benevolence is not only thus generally in harmony with rational Self-love, but also in another sense and independently rational: that is, Reason shows me that if my happiness is desirable and a good, the equal happiness of any other person must be equally desirable. Now, when Happiness is spoken of as the sole ultimate good of man, the idea most commonly suggested is that each individual is to seek his own happiness at the expense (if necessary) or, at any rate, to the neglect of that of others: and this offends both our sympathetic and our rational regard for others' happiness. It is, in fact, rather the end of Egoistic than of Universalistic Hedonism, to which Common Sense feels an aversion. And certainly one's individual happiness is, in many respects, an unsatisfactory mark for one's supreme aim, apart from any direct collision into which the exclusive pursuit of it may bring us with rational or sympathetic Benevolence. It does not possess the characteristics which, as Aristotle says, we "divine" to belong

to Ultimate Good: being (so far, at least, as it can be empirically foreseen) so narrow and limited, of such necessarily brief duration, and so shifting and insecure while it lasts. But Universal Happiness, desirable consciousness or feeling for the innumerable multitude of sentient beings, present and to come, seems an End that satisfies our imagination by its vastness, and sustains our resolution by its comparative security.

It may, however, be said that if we require the individual to sacrifice his own happiness to the greater happiness of others on the ground that it is reasonable to do so, we really assign to the individual a different ultimate end from that which we lay down as the ultimate Good of the universe of sentient beings: since we direct him to take, as ultimate, Happiness for the Universe, but Conformity to Reason for himself. I admit the substantial truth of this statement, though I should avoid the language as tending to obscure the distinction before explained between "obeying the dictates" and "prompting the dictation" of reason. But granting the alleged difference, I do not see that it constitutes an argument against the view here maintained, since the individual is essentially and fundamentally different from the larger whole—the universe of sentient beings—of which he is conscious of being a part; just because he has a known relation to similar parts of the same whole, while the whole itself has no such relation. I accordingly see no inconsistency in holding that while it *would* be reasonable for the aggregate of sentient beings, if it could act collectively, to aim at its own happiness only as an ultimate end,—and would be reasonable for any individual to do the same, if he were the only sentient being in the universe,—it may yet be *actually* reasonable for an individual to sacrifice his own Good or happiness for the greater happiness of others.[44]

At the same time I admit that, in the earlier age of ethical thought which Greek philosophy represents, men sometimes judged an act to be "good" *for the agent,* even while recognising that its consequences would be on the whole painful to him,—as (*e. g.*) a heroic exchange of a life full of happiness for a painful death at the call of duty. I attribute this partly to a confusion of thought between what it is reasonable for an individual to desire, when he considers his own existence alone, and what he must recognise as reasonably to be desired, when he takes the point of view of a larger whole: partly, again, to a faith deeply rooted in the moral consciousness of mankind, that there cannot be really and ultimately any conflict between the two kinds of reasonableness.[45] But when "Reasonable Self-love" has been clearly distinguished from Conscience, as it is by Butler and his followers, we find it is naturally understood to mean desire for one's own Happiness: so that in fact the interpretation of "one's own good," which was almost peculiar in ancient thought to the Cyrenaic and Epicurean heresies, is adopted by some of the most orthodox of modern moralists. Indeed it often does not

[44] I ought at the same time to say that I hold it no less reasonable for an individual to take his own happiness as his ultimate end. This "Dualism of the Practical Reason" will be further discussed in the concluding chapter of the treatise.

[45] We may illustrate this double explanation by a reference to some of Plato's Dialogues, such as the *Gorgias,* where the ethical argument has a singularly mixed effect on the mind. Partly, it seems to us more or less dexterous sophistry, playing on a confusion of thought latent in the common notion of good: partly, a noble and stirring expression of a profound moral faith.

seem to have occurred to these latter that this notion can have any other interpretation.[46] If, then, when any one hypothetically concentrates his attention on himself, Good is naturally and almost inevitably conceived to be Pleasure, we may reasonably conclude that the Good of any number of similar beings, whatever their mutual relations may be, cannot be essentially different in quality.

IV. But lastly, from the universal point of view no less than from that of the individual, it seems true that Happiness is likely to be better attained if the extent to which we set ourselves consciously to aim at it be carefully restricted. And this not only because action is likely to be more effective if our effort is temporarily concentrated on the realisation of more limited ends —though this is no doubt an important reason:—but also because the fullest development of happy life for each individual seems to require that he should have other external objects of interest besides the happiness of other conscious beings. And thus we may conclude that the pursuit of the ideal objects before mentioned, Virtue, Truth, Freedom, Beauty, etc., *for their own sakes,* is indirectly and secondarily, though not primarily and absolutely, rational; on account not only of the happiness that will result from their attainment, but also of that which springs from their disinterested pursuit. While yet if we ask for a final criterion of the comparative value of the different objects of men's enthusiastic pursuit, and of the limits within which each may legitimately engross the attention of mankind, we shall none the less conceive it to depend upon the degree in which they respectively conduce to Happiness.

If, however, this view be rejected,

[46] Cf. D. Stewart's *Philosophy of the Active and Moral Powers,* Book ii., chap. i.

it remains to consider whether we can frame any other coherent account of Ultimate Good. If we are not to systematise human activities by taking Universal Happiness as their common end, on what other principles are we to systematise them? It should be observed that these principles must not only enable us to compare among themselves the values of the different non-Hedonistic ends which we have been considering, but must also provide a common standard for comparing these values with that of Happiness; unless we are prepared to adopt the paradoxical position of rejecting happiness as absolutely valueless. For we have a practical need of determining not only whether we should pursue Truth rather than Beauty, or Freedom or some ideal constitution of society rather than either, or perhaps desert all of these for the life of worship and religious contemplation; but also how far we should follow any of these lines of endeavour, when we foresee among its consequences the pains of human or other sentient beings, or even the loss of pleasures that might otherwise have been enjoyed by them.[47]

I have failed to find—and am unable

to construct—any systematic answer to this question that appears to me deserving of serious consideration: and hence I am finally led to the conclusion (which at the close of the last chapter seemed to be premature) that the Intuitional method rigorously applied yields as its final result the doctrine of pure Universalistic Hedonism,[48]—which it is convenient to denote by the single word, Utilitarianism.

---

[47] The controversy on vivisection, to which I referred just now, affords a good illustration of the need that I am pointing out. I do not observe that anyone in this controversy has ventured on the paradox that the pain of sentient beings is not *per se* to be avoided.

[48] I have before noticed (Book ii., chap. iii.) the metaphysical objection taken by certain writers to the view that Happiness is Ultimate Good; on the ground that Happiness (=sum of pleasures) can only be realized in successive parts, whereas a "Chief Good" must be "something of which some being can be conceived in possession"—something, that is, which he can have all at once. On considering this objection it seemed to me that, in so far as it is even plausible, its plausibility depends on the exact form of the notion "a Chief Good" (or "Summum Bonum"), which is perhaps inappropriate as applied to Happiness. I have therefore in this chapter used the notion of "Ultimate Good": as I can see no shadow of reason for affirming that that which is Good or Desirable *per se,* and not as a means to some further end, must *necessarily* be capable of being possessed all at once. I can understand that a man may aspire after a Good of this latter kind: but so long as Time is a necessary form of human existence, it can hardly be surprising that human good should be subject to the condition of being realised in successive parts.

G. E. Moore (1873–)

One of the most influential of contemporary ethical intuitionists, G. E. Moore has long been associated with Cambridge University, to which he came as a student in 1892 and which he left upon retirement from active teaching duties in 1939. A student of Sidgwick, he admired his teacher for his concern for clarity and belief in common sense. In both respects, however, Moore's writings, whether in ethics or in other branches of philosophy, are unexcelled. Moore's views have undergone change in many respects during the long career of his reflections, but he has never abandoned the basic ethical intuitionism that he inherited from Sidgwick. Among the most important of his writings are *Principia Ethica,* 1903; *Ethics,* 1912; *Philosophical Studies,* 1922; and his essay "A Reply to My Critics" in the collected volume of essays *The Philosophy of G. E. Moore,* 1942, edited by P. A. Schilpp.

GOODNESS AS A UNIQUE INDEFINABLE QUALITY [1]

5. (The) question, how 'good' is to be defined, is the most fundamental question in all Ethics. That which is meant by 'good' is, in fact, except its converse 'bad,' the *only* simple object of thought which is peculiar to Ethics. Its definition is, therefore, the most essential point in the definition of Ethics; and moreover a mistake with regard to it entails a far larger number of erroneous ethical judgments than any other. Unless this first question be fully understood, and its true answer clearly recognised, the rest of Ethics is as good as useless from the

[1] Reprinted with the permission of Cambridge University Press, from *Principia Ethica,* 1903, Chapter I, pp. 5-21.

point of view of systematic knowledge. . . .

6. What, then, is good? How is good to be defined? Now, it may be thought that this is a verbal question. A definition does indeed often mean the expressing of one word's meaning in other words. But this is not the sort of definition I am asking for. Such a definition can never be of ultimate importance in any study except lexicography. If I wanted that kind of definition I should have to consider in the first place how people generally used the word 'good'; but my business is not with its proper usage, as established by custom. I should, indeed, be foolish, if I tried to use it for something which it did not usually denote: if, for instance, I were to announce that, whenever I used the word 'good,' I must be

understood to be thinking of that object which is usually denoted by the word 'table.' I shall, therefore, use the word in the sense in which I think it is ordinarily used; but at the same time I am not anxious to discuss whether I am right in thinking that it is so used. My business is solely with that object or idea, which I hold, rightly or wrongly, that the word is generally used to stand for. What I want to discover is the nature of that object or idea, and about this I am extremely anxious to arrive at an agreement.

But, if we understand the question in this sense, my answer to it may seem a very disappointing one. If I am asked 'What is good?' my answer is that good is good, and that is the end of the matter. Or if I am asked 'How is good to be defined?' my answer is that it cannot be defined, and that is all I have to say about it. But disappointing as these answers may appear, they are of the very last importance. To readers who are familiar with philosophic terminology, I can express their importance by saying that they amount to this: That propositions about the good are all of them synthetic and never analytic; and that is plainly no trivial matter. And the same thing may be expressed more popularly, by saying that, if I am right, then nobody can foist upon us such an axiom as that 'Pleasure is the only good' or that 'The good is the desired' on the pretence that this is 'the very meaning of the word.'

7. Let us, then, consider this position. My point is that 'good' is a simple notion, just as 'yellow' is a simple notion; that, just as you cannot, by any manner of means, explain to any one who does not already know it, what yellow is, so you cannot explain what good is. Definitions of the kind that I was asking for, definitions which describe the real nature of the object

or notion denoted by a word, and which do not merely tell us what the word is used to mean, are only possible when the object or notion in question is something complex. You can give a definition of a horse, because a horse has many different properties and qualities, all of which you can enumerate. But when you have enumerated them all, when you have reduced a horse to his simplest terms, then you can no longer define those terms. They are simply something which you think of or perceive, and to any one who cannot think of or perceive them, you can never, by any definition, make their nature known. It may perhaps be objected to this that we are able to describe to others, objects which they have never seen or thought of. We can, for instance, make a man understand what a chimaera is, although he has never heard of one or seen one. You can tell him that it is an animal with a lioness's head and body, with a goat's head growing from the middle of its back, and with a snake in place of a tail. But here the object which you are describing is a complex object; it is entirely composed of parts, with which we are all perfectly familiar—a snake, a goat, a lioness; and we know, too, the manner in which those parts are to be put together, because we know what is meant by the middle of a lioness's back, and where her tail is wont to grow. And so it is with all objects, not previously known, which we are able to define: they are all complex; all composed of parts which may themselves, in the first instance, be capable of similar definition, but which must in the end be reducible to simplest parts, which can no longer be defined. But yellow and good, we say, are not complex: they are notions of that simple kind, out of which definitions are composed and with which the power of further defining ceases.

8. When we say, as Webster says, 'The definition of horse is "A hoofed quadruped of the genus Equus,"' we may, in fact, mean three different things. (1) We may mean merely: 'When I say "horse," you are to understand that I am talking about a hoofed quadruped of the genus Equus.' This might be called the arbitrary verbal definition: and I do not mean that good is indefinable in that sense. (2) We may mean, as Webster ought to mean: 'When most English people say "horse," they mean a hoofed quadruped of the genus Equus.' This may be called the verbal definition proper, and I do not say that good is indefinable in this sense either; for it is certainly possible to discover how people use a word: otherwise, we could never have known that 'good' may be translated by 'gut' in German and by 'bon' in French. But (3) we may, when we define horse, mean something much more important. We may mean that a certain object, which we all of us know, is composed in a certain manner: that it has four legs, a head, a heart, a liver, etc., etc., all of them arranged in definite relations to one another. It is in this sense that I deny good to be definable. I say that it is not composed of any parts, which we can substitute for it in our minds when we are thinking of it. We might think just as clearly and correctly about a horse, if we thought of all its parts and their arrangement instead of thinking of the whole: we could, I say, think how a horse differed from a donkey just as well, just as truly, in this way, as now we do, only not so easily; but there is nothing whatsoever which we could so substitute for good; and that is what I mean, when I say that good is indefinable.

9. But I am afraid I have still not removed the chief difficulty which may prevent acceptance of the proposition that good is indefinable. I do not mean to say that *the* good, that which is good, is thus indefinable; if I did think so, I should not be writing on Ethics, for my main object is to help towards discovering that definition. It is just because I think there will be less risk of error in our search for a definition of 'the good,' that I am now insisting that *good* is indefinable. I must try to explain the difference between these two. I suppose it may be granted that 'good' is an adjective. Well 'the good,' 'that which is good,' must therefore be the substantive to which the adjective 'good' will apply: it must be the whole of that to which the adjective will apply, and the adjective must *always* truly apply to it. But if it is that to which the adjective will apply, it must be something different from that adjective itself; and the whole of that something different, whatever it is, will be our definition of *the* good. Now it may be that this something will have other adjectives, beside 'good,' that will apply to it. It may be full of pleasure, for example; it may be intelligent: and if these two adjectives are really part of its definition, then it will certainly be true, that pleasure and intelligence are good. And many people appear to think that, if we say 'Pleasure and intelligence are good,' or if we say 'Only pleasure and intelligence are good,' we are defining 'good.' Well, I cannot deny that propositions of this nature may sometimes be called definitions; I do not know well enough how the word is generally used to decide upon this point. I only wish it to be understood that that is not what I mean when I say there is no possible definition of good, and that I shall not mean this if I use the word again. I do most fully believe that some true proposition of the form 'Intelligence is good and intelligence alone is good' can be found; if none could be found, our definition of *the* good would be

impossible. As it is, I believe *the* good to be definable; and yet I still say that good itself is indefinable.

10. 'Good,' then, if we mean by it that quality which we assert to belong to a thing, when we say that the thing is good, is incapable of any definition, in the most important sense of that word. The most important sense of 'definition' is that in which a definition states what are the parts which invariably compose a certain whole; and in this sense 'good' has no definition because it is simple and has no parts. It is one of these innumerable objects of thought which are themselves incapable of definition, because they are the ultimate terms by reference to which whatever *is* capable of definition must be defined. That there must be an indefinite number of such terms is obvious, on reflection; since we cannot define anything except by an analysis, which, when carried as far as it will go, refers us to something, which is simply different from anything else, and which by that ultimate difference explains the peculiarity of the whole which we are defining: for every whole contains some parts which are common to other wholes also. There is, therefore, no intrinsic difficulty in the contention that 'good' denotes a simple and indefinable quality. There are many other instances of such qualities.

Consider yellow, for example. We may try to define it, by describing its physical equivalent; we may state what kind of light-vibrations must stimulate the normal eye, in order that we may perceive it. But a moment's reflection is sufficient to shew that those light-vibrations are not themselves what we mean by yellow. *They* are not what we perceive. Indeed we should never have been able to discover their existence, unless we had first been struck by the patent difference of quality between the different

colours. The most we can be entitled to say of those vibrations is that they are what corresponds in space to the yellow which we actually perceive.

Yet a mistake of this simple kind has commonly been made about 'good.' It may be true that all things which are good are *also* something else, just as it is true that all things which are yellow produce a certain kind of vibration in the light. And it is a fact, that Ethics aims at discovering what are those other properties belonging to all things which are good. But far too many philosophers have thought that when they named those other properties they were actually defining good; that these properties, in fact, were simply not 'other,' but absolutely and entirely the same with goodness. This view I propose to call the 'naturalistic fallacy' and of it I shall now endeavour to dispose.

11. Let us consider what it is such philosophers say. And first it is to be noticed that they do not agree among themselves. They not only say that they are right as to what good is, but they endeavour to prove that other people who say that it is something else, are wrong. One, for instance, will affirm that good is pleasure, another, perhaps, that good is that which is desired; and each of these will argue eagerly to prove that the other is wrong. But how is that possible? One of them says that good is nothing but the object of desire, and at the same time tries to prove that it is not pleasure. But from his first assertion, that good just means the object of desire, one of two things must follow as regards his proof:

(1) He may be trying to prove that the object of desire is not pleasure. But, if this be all, where is his Ethics? The position he is maintaining is merely a psychological one. Desire is something which occurs in our minds, and pleasure is something else which

so occurs; and our would-be ethical philosopher is merely holding that the latter is not the object of the former. But what has that to do with the question in dispute? His opponent held the ethical proposition that pleasure was the good, and although he should prove a million times over the psychological proposition that pleasure is not the object of desire, he is no nearer proving his opponent to be wrong. The position is like this. One man says a triangle is a circle: another replies 'A triangle is a straight line, and I will prove to you that I am right: *for*' (this is the only argument) 'a straight line is not a circle.' 'That is quite true,' the other may reply; 'but nevertheless a triangle is a circle, and you have said nothing whatever to prove the contrary. What is proved is that one of us is wrong, for we agree that a triangle cannot be both a straight line and a circle: but which is wrong, there can be no earthly means of proving, since you define triangle as straight line and I define it as circle.'—Well, that is one alternative which any naturalistic Ethics has to face; if good is *defined* as something else, it is then impossible either to prove that any other definition is wrong or even to deny such definition.

(2) The other alternative will scarcely be more welcome. It is that the discussion is after all a verbal one. When A says 'Good means pleasant' and B says 'Good means desired,' they may merely wish to assert that most people have used the word for what is pleasant and for what is desired respectively. And this is quite an interesting subject for discussion: only it is not a whit more an ethical discussion than the last was. Nor do I think that any exponent of naturalistic Ethics would be willing to allow that this was all he meant. They are all so anxious to persuade us that what they call the good is what we really

ought to do. 'Do, pray, act so, because the word "good" is generally used to denote actions of this nature': such, on this view, would be the substance of their teaching. And in so far as they tell us how we ought to act, their teaching is truly ethical, as they mean it to be. But how perfectly absurd is the reason they would give for it! 'You are to do this, because most people use a certain word to denote conduct such as this.' 'You are not to say the thing which is not, because most people call it lying.' That is an argument just as good!—My dear sirs, what we want to know from you as ethical teachers, is not how people use a word; it is not even, what kind of actions they approve, which the use of this word 'good' may certainly imply: what we want to know is simply what *is* good. We may indeed agree that what most people do think good, is actually so; we shall at all events be glad to know their opinions about what *is* good, we do mean what we say; we do not care whether they call that thing which they mean 'horse' or 'table' or 'chair,' 'gut' or 'bon' or 'ἀγαθός'; we want to know what it is that they so call. When they say 'Pleasure is good,' we cannot believe that they merely mean 'Pleasure is pleasure' and nothing more than that.

12. Suppose a man says 'I am pleased'; and suppose that is not a lie or a mistake but the truth. Well, if it is true, what does that mean? It means that his mind, a certain definite mind, distinguished by certain definite marks from all others, has at this moment a certain definite feeling called pleasure. 'Pleased' *means* nothing but having pleasure, and though we may be more pleased or less pleased, and even, we may admit for the present, have one or another kind of pleasure; yet in so far as it is pleasure we have, whether there be more or less of it, and whether it be of one kind or

another, what we have is one definite thing, absolutely indefinable, some one thing that is the same in all the various degrees and in all the various kinds of it that there may be. We may be able to say how it is related to other things: that, for example, it is in the mind, that it causes desire, that we are conscious of it, etc., etc. We can, I say, describe its relations to other things, but define it we can *not*. And if anybody tried to define pleasure for us as being any other natural object; if anybody were to say, for instance, that pleasure *means* the sensation of red, and were to proceed to deduce from that that pleasure is a colour, we should be entitled to laugh at him and to distrust his future statements about pleasure. Well, that would be the same fallacy which I have called the naturalistic fallacy. That 'pleased' does not mean 'having the sensation of red,' or anything else whatever, does not prevent us from understanding what it does mean. It is enough for us to know that 'pleased' does mean 'having the sensation of pleasure,' and though pleasure is absolutely indefinable, though pleasure is pleasure and nothing else whatever, yet we feel no difficulty in saying that we are pleased. The reason is, of course, that when I say 'I am pleased,' I do *not* mean that 'I' am the same thing as 'having pleasure.' And similarly no difficulty need be found in my saying that 'pleasure is good' and yet not meaning that 'pleasure' is the same thing as 'good,' that pleasure *means* good, and that good *means* pleasure. If I were to imagine that when I said 'I am pleased,' I meant that I was exactly the same thing as 'pleased,' I should not indeed call that a naturalistic fallacy, although it would be the same fallacy as I have called naturalistic with reference to Ethics. The reason of this is obvious enough. When a man confuses two natural objects with one another, defining the one by the other, if for instance, he confuses himself, who is one natural object, with 'pleased' or with 'pleasure' which are others, then there is no reason to call the fallacy naturalistic. But if he confuses 'good,' which is not in the same sense a natural object, with any natural object whatever, then there is a reason for calling that a naturalistic fallacy; its being made with regard to 'good' marks it as something quite specific, and this specific mistake deserves a name because it is so common. As for the reasons why good is not to be considered a natural object, they may be reserved for discussion in another place. But, for the present, it is sufficient to notice this: Even if it were a natural object, that would not alter the nature of the fallacy nor diminish its importance one whit. All that I have said about it would remain quite equally true: only the name which I have called it would not be so appropriate as I think it is. And I do not care about the name: what I do care about is the fallacy. It does not matter what we call it, provided we recognise it when we meet with it. It is to be met with in almost every book on Ethics; and yet it is not recognised: and that is why it is necessary to multiply illustrations of it, and convenient to give it a name. It is a very simple fallacy indeed. When we say that an orange is yellow, we do not think our statement binds us to hold that 'orange' means nothing else than 'yellow,' or that nothing can be yellow but an orange. Supposing the orange is also sweet! Does that bind us to say that 'sweet' is exactly the same thing as 'yellow,' that 'sweet' must be defined as 'yellow'? And supposing it be recognised that 'yellow' just means 'yellow' and nothing else whatever, does that make it any more difficult to hold that oranges are yellow? Most

certainly it does not: on the contrary, it would be absolutely meaningless to say that oranges were yellow, unless yellow did in the end mean just 'yellow' and nothing else whatever—unless it was absolutely indefinable. We should not get any very clear notion about things, which are yellow—we should not get very far with our science, if we were bound to hold that everything which was yellow, *meant* exactly the same thing as yellow. We should find we had to hold that an orange was exactly the same thing as a stool, a piece of paper, a lemon, anything you like. We could prove any number of absurdities; but should we be the nearer to the truth? Why, then, should it be different with 'good'? Why, if good is good and indefinable, should I be held to deny that pleasure is good? Is there any difficulty in holding both to be true at once? On the contrary, there is no meaning in saying that pleasure is good, unless good is something different from pleasure. It is absolutely useless, so far as Ethics is concerned, to prove, as Mr. Spencer tries to do, that increase of pleasure coincides with increase of life, unless good *means* something different from either life or pleasure. He might just as well try to prove that an orange is yellow by shewing that it always is wrapped up in paper.

13. In fact, if it is not the case that 'good' denotes something simple and indefinable, only two alternatives are possible: either it is a complex, a given whole, about the correct analysis of which there may be disagreement; or else it means nothing at all, and there is no such subject as Ethics. In general, however, ethical philosophers have attempted to define good, without recognising what such an attempt must mean. They actually use arguments which involve one or both of the absurdities considered in § 11.

We are, therefore, justified in concluding that the attempt to define good is chiefly due to want of clearness as to the possible nature of definition. There are, in fact, only two serious alternatives to be considered, in order to establish the conclusion that 'good' does denote a simple and indefinable notion. It might possibly denote a complex, as 'horse' does; or it might have no meaning at all. Neither of these possibilities has, however, been clearly conceived and seriously maintained, as such, by those who presume to define good; and both may be dismissed by a simple appeal to facts.

(1) The hypothesis that disagreement about the meaning of good is disagreement with regard to the correct analysis of a given whole, may be most plainly seen to be incorrect by consideration of the fact that, whatever definition be offered, it may be always asked, with significance, of the complex so defined, whether it is itself good. To take, for instance, one of the more plausible, because one of the more complicated, of such proposed definitions, it may easily be thought, at first sight, that to be good may mean to be that which we desire to desire. Thus if we apply this definition to a particular instance and say 'When we think that A is good, we are thinking that A is one of the things which we desire to desire,' our proposition may seem quite plausible. But, if we carry the investigation further, and ask ourselves 'Is it good to desire to desire A?" it is apparent, on a little reflection, that this question is itself as intelligible, as the original question 'Is A good?'—that we are, in fact, now asking for exactly the same information about the desire to desire A, for which we formerly asked with regard to A itself. But it is also apparent that the meaning of this second question cannot be correctly analysed into 'Is the desire to desire A one of

the things which we desire to desire?': we have not before our minds anything so complicated as the question 'Do we desire to desire to desire to desire A?' Moreover any one can easily convince himself by inspection that the predicate of this proposition—'good'—is positively different from the notion of 'desiring to desire' which enters into its subject: 'That we should desire to desire A is good' is *not* merely equivalent to 'That A should be good is good.' It may indeed be true that what we desire to desire is always also good; perhaps, even the converse may be true: but it is very doubtful whether this is the case, and the mere fact that we understand very well what is meant by doubting it, shews clearly that we have two different notions before our minds.

(2) And the same consideration is sufficient to dismiss the hypothesis that 'good' has no meaning whatsoever. It is very natural to make the mistake of supposing that what is universally true is of such a nature that its negation would be self-contradictory: the importance which has been assigned to analytic propositions in the history of philosophy shews how easy such a mistake is. And thus it is very easy to conclude that what seems to be a universal ethical principle is in fact an identical proposition; that, if, for example, whatever is called 'good' seems to be pleasant, the proposition 'Pleasure is the good' does not assert a connection between two different notions, but involves only one, that of pleasure, which is easily recognised as a distinct entity. But whoever will attentively consider with himself what is actually before his mind when he asks the question 'Is pleasure (or whatever it may be) after all good?' can easily satisfy himself that he is not merely wondering whether pleasure is pleasant. And if he will try this experiment with each

suggested definition in succession, he may become expert enough to recognise that in every case he has before his mind a unique object, with regard to the connection of which with any other object, a distinct question may be asked. Every one does in fact understand the question 'Is this good?' When he thinks of it, his state of mind is different from what it would be, were he asked 'Is this pleasant, or desired, or approved?' It has a distinct meaning for him, even though he may not recognise in what respect it is distinct. Whenever he thinks of 'intrinsic value,' or 'intrinsic worth,' or says that a thing 'ought to exist,' he has before his mind the unique object—the unique property of things—which I mean by 'good.' Everybody is constantly aware of this notion, although he may never become aware at all that it is different from other notions of which he is also aware. But, for correct ethical reasoning, it is extremely important that he should become aware of this fact; and, as soon as the nature of the problem is clearly understood, there should be little difficulty in advancing so far in analysis.

14. 'Good,' then, is indefinable; and yet, so far as I know, there is only one ethical writer, Prof. Henry Sidgwick, who has clearly recognised and stated this fact. We shall see, indeed, how far many of the most reputed ethical systems fall short of drawing the conclusions which follow from such a recognition. At present I will only quote one instance, which will serve to illustrate the meaning and importance of this principle that 'good' is indefinable, or, as Prof. Sidgwick says, an 'unanalysable notion.' It is an instance to which Prof. Sidgwick himself refers in a note on the passage, in which he argues that 'ought' is unanalysable.[2]

[2] *Methods of Ethics,* Bk. I, Chapter III, §§ 2–3.

'Bentham,' says Sidgwick, 'explains that his fundamental principle "states the greatest happiness of all those whose interest is in question as being the right and proper end of human action"'; and yet 'his language in other passages of the same chapter would seem to imply' that he *means* by the word "right" "conducive to the general happiness." Prof. Sidgwick sees that, if you take these two statements together, you get the absurd result that 'greatest happiness is the end of human action, which is conducive to the general happiness'; and so absurd does it seem to him to call this result, as Bentham calls it, 'the fundamental principle of a moral system,' that he suggests that Bentham cannot have meant it. Yet Prof. Sidgwick himself states elsewhere [3] that Psychological Hedonism is 'not seldom confounded with Egoistic Hedonism'; and that confusion, as we shall see, rests chiefly on that same fallacy, the naturalistic fallacy, which is implied in Bentham's statements. Prof. Sidgwick admits therefore that this fallacy is sometimes committed, absurd as it is; and I am inclined to think that Bentham may really have been one of those who committed it. Mill . . . certainly did commit it. In any case, whether Bentham committed it or not, his doctrine, as above quoted, will serve as a very good illustration of this fallacy, and of the importance of the contrary proposition that good is indefinable.

Let us consider this doctrine. Bentham seems to imply, so Prof. Sidgwick says, that the word 'right' *means* 'conducive to general happiness.' Now this, by itself, need not necessarily involve the naturalistic fallacy. For the word 'right' is very commonly appropriated to actions which lead to the

[3] *Methods of Ethics,* Bk. I, Chap. IV, § 1.

attainment of what is good; which are regarded as *means* to the ideal and not as ends-in-themselves. This use of 'right,' as denoting what is good as a means, whether or not it be also good as an end, is indeed the use to which I shall confine the word. Had Bentham been using 'right' in this sense, it might be perfectly consistent for him to *define* right as 'conducive to the general happiness,' *provided only* (and notice this proviso) he had already proved, or laid down as an axiom, that general happiness was *the* good, or (what is equivalent to this) that general happiness alone was good. For in that case he would have already defined *the* good as general happiness (a position perfectly consistent, as we have seen, with the contention that 'good' is indefinable), and, since right was to be defined as 'conducive to *the* good,' it would actually *mean* 'conducive to general happiness.' But this method of escape from the charge of having committed the naturalistic fallacy has been closed by Bentham himself. For his fundamental principle is, we see, that the greatest happiness of all concerned is the *right* and proper *end* of human action. He applies the word 'right,' therefore, to the end as such, not only to the means which are conducive to it; and, that being so, right can no longer be defined as 'conducive to the general happiness,' without involving the fallacy in question. For now it is obvious that the definition of right as conducive to general happiness can be used by him in support of the fundamental principle that general happiness is the right end; instead of being itself derived from that principle. If right, by definition, means conducive to general happiness, then it is obvious that general happiness is the right end. It is not necessary now first to prove or assert that general happiness is the right end, before right is defined as conducive to general happiness—a perfectly valid procedure; but on the contrary the definition of right as conducive to general happiness proves general happiness to be the right end—a perfectly invalid procedure, since in this case the statement that 'general happiness is the right end of human action' is not an ethical principle at all, but either, as we have seen, a proposition about the meaning of words, or else a proposition about the *nature* of general happiness, not about its rightness or goodness.

Now, I do not wish the importance I assign to this fallacy to be misunderstood. The discovery of it does not at all refute Bentham's contention that greatest happiness is the proper end of human action, if that be understood as an ethical proposition, as he undoubtedly intended it. That principle may be true all the same; we shall consider whether it is so in succeeding chapters. Bentham might have maintained it, as Professor Sidgwick does, even if the fallacy had been pointed out to him. What I am maintaining is that the *reasons* which he actually gives for his ethical proposition are fallacious ones, so far as they consist in a definition of right. What I suggest is that he did not perceive them to be fallacious; that, if he had done so, he would have been led to seek for other reasons in support of his Utilitarianism; and that, had he sought for other reasons, he *might* have found none which he thought to be sufficient. In that case he would have changed his whole system —a most important consequence. It is undoubtedly also possible that he would have thought other reasons to be sufficient, and in that case his ethical system, in its main results, would still have stood. But, even in this latter case, his use of the fallacy would be a serious objection to him as an ethical philosopher. For it is the

business of Ethics, I must insist, not only to obtain true results, but also to find valid reasons for them. The direct object of Ethics is knowledge and not practice; and any one who uses the naturalistic fallacy has certainly not fulfilled this first object, however correct his practical principles may be.

My objections to Naturalism are then, in the first place, that it offers no reason at all, far less any valid reason, for any ethical principle whatever; and in this it already fails to satisfy the requirements of Ethics, as a scientific study. But in the second place I contend that, though it gives a reason for no ethical principle, it is a *cause* of the acceptance of false principles—it deludes the mind into accepting ethical principles, which are false; and in this it is contrary to every aim of Ethics. It is easy to see that if we start with a definition of right conduct as conduct conducive to general happiness; then, knowing that right conduct is universally conduct conducive to the good, we very easily arrive at the result that the good is general happiness. If, on the other hand, we once recognise that we must start our Ethics without a definition, we shall be much more apt to look about us, before we adopt any ethical principle whatever; and the more we look about us, the less likely are we to adopt a false one. It may be replied to this: Yes, but we shall look about us just as much, before we settle on our definition, and are therefore just as likely to be right. But I will try to shew that this is not the case. If we start with the conviction that a definition of good can be found, we start with the conviction that good *can mean* nothing else than some one property of things; and our only business will then be to discover what that property is. But if we recognise that, so far as the meaning of good goes, anything whatever may be good, we start with a much more open mind. Moreover, apart from the fact that, when we think we have a definition, we cannot logically defend our ethical principles in any way whatever, we shall also be much less apt to defend them well, even if illogically. For we shall start with the conviction that good must mean so and so, and shall therefore be inclined either to misunderstand our opponent's arguments or to cut them short with the reply, 'This is not an open question: the very meaning of the word decides it; no one can think otherwise except through confusion.'

H. A. Prichard (1871 – 1947)

The extent of Prichard's influence upon contemporary ethical intuitionism is not to be measured by the amount of his writings. In addition to the volume *Kant's Theory of Knowledge,* Prichard's only writings published during his lifetime are several short essays that appeared in various journals. Nevertheless, as teacher for many years at the University of Oxford and as writer of several incisive and challenging essays, he has had a decisive influence in shaping the character of one type of ethical intuitionism, the main insistence of which has been the irreducibility of the rightness of an act to the goodness of it, the agent, the consequences or anything else. In addition to the essay reprinted here, the most important of Prichard's writings have been *Duty and Interest,* his inaugural lecture (1928) as White's Professor at Oxford, and a number of essays, some of which had not been published previously, in the posthumous volume *Moral Obligation.*

DOES MORAL PHILOSOPHY REST ON A MISTAKE? [1]

Probably to most students of Moral Philosophy there comes a time when they feel a vague sense of dissatisfaction with the whole subject. And the sense of dissatisfaction tends to grow rather than to diminish. It is not so much that the positions, and still more the arguments, of particular thinkers seem unconvincing, though this is true. It is rather that the aim of the subject becomes increasingly obscure. "What," it is asked, "are we really going to learn by Moral Philosophy?" "What are books on Moral Philosophy really trying to show, and when their aim is clear, why are they so unconvincing and artificial?" And again: "Why is it so difficult to substitute anything better?" Personally, I have been led by growing dissatisfaction of this kind to wonder whether the reason may not be that the subject, at any rate as usually understood, consists in the attempt to answer an improper question. And in this article, I shall venture to contend that the existence of the whole subject, as usually understood, rests on a mistake, and on a mistake parallel to that on which rests, as I think, the subject usually called the Theory of Knowledge.

If we reflect on our own mental history or on the history of the subject, we feel no doubt about the nature of the demand which originates the subject. Any one who, stimulated by education, has come to feel the force of the various obligations in life,

[1] This essay, which appeared first in *Mind,* N. S., Vol. 21, 1912, and, subsequently, in a posthumously published book of essays by Prichard entitled *Moral Obligation,* Oxford, 1949, is reprinted here with the kind permission of the Editor of *Mind,* Professor G. Ryle.

at some time or other comes to feel the irksomeness of carrying them out, and to recognise the sacrifice of interest involved; and, if thoughtful, he inevitably puts to himself the question: "Is there really a reason why I should act in the ways in which hitherto I have thought I ought to act? May I not have been all the time under an illusion in so thinking? Should not I really be justified in simply trying to have a good time?" Yet, like Glaucon, feeling that somehow he ought after all to act in these ways, he asks for a *proof* that this feeling is justified. In other words, he asks "*Why* should I do these things?" and his and other people's moral philosophising is an attempt to supply the answer, *i. e.* to supply by a process of reflexion a proof of the truth of what he and they have prior to reflexion believed immediately or without proof. This frame of mind seems to present a close parallel to the frame of mind which originates the Theory of Knowledge. Just as the recognition that the doing of our duty often vitally interferes with the satisfaction of our inclinations leads us to wonder whether we really ought to do what we usually call our duty, so the recognition that we and others are liable to mistakes in knowledge generally leads us, as it did Descartes, to wonder whether hitherto we may not have been always mistaken. And just as we try to find a proof, based on the general consideration of action and of human life, that we ought to act in the ways usually called moral, so we, like Descartes, propose by a process of reflexion on our thinking to find a test of knowledge, *i. e.* a principle by applying which we can show that a certain condition of mind was really knowledge, a condition which *ex hypothesi* existed independently of the process of reflexion.

Now, how has the moral question been answered? So far as I can see, the answers all fall, and fall from the necessities of the case, into one of two species. *Either* they state that we ought to do so and so, because, as we see when we fully apprehend the facts, doing so will be for our good, *i. e.* really, as I would rather say, for our advantage, or, better still, for our happiness; *or* they state that we ought to do so and so, because something realised either in or by the action is good. In other words, the reason 'why' is stated in terms either of the agent's happiness or of the goodness of something involved in the action.

To see the prevalence of the former species of answer, we have only to consider the history of Moral Philosophy. To take obvious instances, Plato, Butler, Hutcheson, Paley, Mill, each in his own way seeks at bottom to convince the individual that he ought to act in so-called moral ways by showing that to do so will really be for his happiness. Plato is perhaps the most significant instance, because of all philosophers he is the one to whom we are least willing to ascribe a mistake on such matters, and a mistake on his part would be evidence of the deep-rootedness of the tendency to make it. To show that Plato really justifies morality by its profitableness, it is only necessary to point out (1) that the very formulation of the thesis to be met, viz., that justice is ἀλλότριον ἀγαθόν, implies that any refutation must consist in showing that justice is οἰκεῖον ἀγαθόν, *i. e.* really, as the context shows, one's own advantage, and (2) that the term λυσιτελεῖν supplies the keynote not only to the problem but also to its solution.

The tendency to justify acting on moral rules in this way is natural. For if, as often happens, we put to ourselves the question "Why should we do so and so?" we are satisfied by being convinced either that the doing so will lead to something which we want (*e. g.* that taking certain medicine will heal our disease), or that the doing so itself, as we see when we appreciate its nature, is something that we want or should like, *e. g.* playing golf. The formulation of the question implies a state of unwillingness or indifference towards the action, and we are brought into a condition of willingness by the answer. And this process seems to be precisely what we desire when we ask, *e. g.*, "Why should we keep our engagements to our own loss?" for it is just the fact that the keeping our engagements runs counter to the satisfaction of our desires which produced the question.

The answer is, of course, not an answer, for it fails to convince us that we ought to keep our engagements; even if successful on its own lines, it only makes us *want* to keep them. And Kant was really only pointing out this fact when he distinguished hypothetical and categorical imperatives, even though he obscured the nature of the fact by wrongly describing his so-called 'hypothetical imperatives' as imperatives. But if this answer be no answer, what other can be offered? Only, it seems, an answer which bases the obligation to do something on the *goodness* either of something to which the act leads or of the act itself. Suppose, when wondering whether we really ought to act in the ways usually called moral, we are told as a means of resolving our doubt that those acts are right which produce happiness. We at once ask "Whose happiness?" If we are told "Our own happiness," then, though we shall lose our hesitation to act in these ways, we shall not recover our sense that we ought to do so. But how can this result be avoided? Apparently, only by being told one of two things; *either* that any one's happiness is a thing good in

itself, and that *therefore* we ought to do whatever will produce it, *or* that the working for happiness is itself good, and that the intrinsic goodness of such an action is the reason why we ought to do it. The advantage of this appeal to the goodness of something consists in the fact that it avoids reference to desire, and, instead, refers to something impersonal and objective. In this way it seems possible to avoid the resolution of obligation into inclination. But just for this reason it is of the essence of the answer, that, to be effective, it must neither include nor involve the view that the apprehension of the goodness of anything necessarily arouses the desire for it. Otherwise the answer resolves itself into a form of the former answer by substituting desire or inclination for the sense of obligation, and in this way it loses what seems its special advantage.

Now it seems to me that both forms of this answer break down, though each for a different reason.

Consider the first form. It is what may be called Utilitarianism in the generic sense in which what is good is not limited to pleasure. It takes its stand upon the distinction between something which is not itself an action but which can be produced by an action and the action which will produce it, and contends that if something which is not an action is good, then we *ought* to undertake the action which will, directly or indirectly, originate it.[2]

But this argument, if it is to restore the sense of obligation to act, must presuppose an intermediate link, *viz.*, the further thesis that what is good ought to be.[3] The necessity of this

[2] *Cf.* Dr. Rashdall's *Theory of Good and Evil*, vol. i., p. 138.

[3] Dr. Rashdall, if I understand him rightly, supplies this link (*cf. Theory of Good and Evil*, vol. i., pp. 135–136).

link is obvious. An 'ought,' if it is to be derived at all, can only be derived from another 'ought.' Moreover this link tacitly presupposes another, *viz.*, that the apprehension that something good which is not an action ought to be involves just the feeling of imperativeness or obligation which is to be aroused by the thought of the action which will originate it. Otherwise the argument will not lead us to feel the obligation to produce it by the action. And, surely, both this link and its implication are false.[4] The word 'ought' refers to actions and to actions alone. The proper language is never "So and so ought to be," but "I ought to do so and so." Even if we are sometimes moved to say that the world or something in it is not what it ought to be, what we really mean is that God or some human being has not made something what he ought to have made it. And it is merely stating another side of this fact to urge that we can only feel the imperativeness upon us of something which is in our power; for it is actions and actions alone which, directly at least, are in our power.

Perhaps, however, the best way to see the failure of this view is to see its failure to correspond to our actual moral convictions. Suppose we ask ourselves whether our sense that we ought to pay our debts or to tell the truth arises from our recognition that in doing so we should be originating something good, *e. g.*, material comfort in A or true belief in B, *i. e.*, suppose we ask ourselves whether it is this aspect of the action which leads to our recognition that we ought to do it. We, at once, and without hesitation

answer 'No.' Again, if we take as our illustration our sense that we ought to act justly as between two parties, we have, if possible, even less hesitation in giving a similar answer; for the balance of resulting good may be, and often is, not on the side of justice.

At best it can only be maintained that there is this element of truth in the Utilitarian view that unless we recognised that something which an act will originate is good, we should not recognise that we ought to do the action. Unless we thought knowledge a good thing, it may be urged, we should not think that we ought to tell the truth; unless we thought pain a bad thing, we should not think the infliction of it, without special reason, wrong. But this is not to imply that the badness of error is the reason why it is wrong to lie, or the badness of pain the reason why we ought not to inflict it without special cause.[5]

It is, I think, just because this form of the view is so plainly at variance with our moral consciousness that we become driven to adopt the other form of the view, *viz.*, that the act is good in itself and that its intrinsic goodness is the reason why it ought to be done. It is this form which has always made the most serious appeal; for the goodness of the act itself seems more closely related to the obligation to do it than that of its mere consequences or results, and therefore, if obligation is to be based on the goodness of something, it would seem that this goodness should be that of the act itself. Moreover, the view gains plausibility from the fact that moral actions are most

---

[4] When we speak of anything, *e.g.*, of some emotion or of some quality of a human being, as good, we never dream in our ordinary consciousness of going on to say that therefore it ought to be.

[5] It may be noted that if the badness of pain were the reason why we ought not to inflict pain on another, it would equally be a reason why we ought not to inflict pain on ourselves; yet, though we should allow the wanton infliction of pain on ourselves to be foolish, we should not think of describing it as wrong.

conspicuously those to which the term 'intrinsically good' is applicable.

Nevertheless this view, though perhaps less superficial, is equally untenable. For it leads to precisely the dilemma which faces every one who tries to solve the problem raised by Kant's theory of the good will. To see this, we need only consider the nature of the acts to which we apply the term 'intrinsically good.'

There is, of course, no doubt that we approve and even admire certain actions, and also that we should describe them as good, and as good in themselves. But it is, I think, equally unquestionable that our approval and our use of the term 'good' is always in respect of the motive and refers to actions which have been actually done and of which we think we know the motive. Further, the actions of which we approve and which we should describe as intrinsically good are of two and only two kinds. They are either actions in which the agent did what he did because he thought he ought to do it, or actions of which the motive was a desire prompted by some good emotion, such as gratitude, affection, family feeling, or public spirit, the most prominent of such desires in books on Moral Philosophy being that ascribed to what is vaguely called benevolence. For the sake of simplicity I omit the case of actions done partly from some such desire and partly from a sense of duty; for even if all good actions are done from a combination of these motives, the argument will not be affected. The dilemma is this. If the motive in respect of which we think an action good is the sense of obligation, then so far from the sense that we ought to do it being derived from our apprehension of its goodness, our apprehension of its goodness will presuppose the sense that we ought to do it. In other words, in this case the recog-

nition that the act is good will plainly *presuppose* the recognition that the act is right, whereas the view under consideration is that the recognition of the goodness of the act *gives rise* to the recognition of its rightness. On the other hand, if the motive in respect of which we think an action good is some intrinsically good desire, such as the desire to help a friend, the recognition of the goodness of the act will equally fail to give rise to the sense of obligation to do it. For we cannot feel that we ought to do that the doing of which is *ex hypothesi* prompted solely by the desire to do it.[6]

The fallacy underlying the view is that while to base the rightness of an act upon its intrinsic goodness implies that the goodness in question is that of the motive, in reality the rightness or wrongness of an act has nothing to do with any question of motives at all. For, as any instance will show, the rightness of an action concerns an action not in the fuller sense of the term in which we include the motive in the action, but in the narrower and commoner sense in which we distinguish an action from its motive and mean by an action merely the conscious origination of something, an origination which on different occasions or in different people may be prompted by different motives. The question "Ought I to pay my bills?" really means simply "Ought I to bring about my tradesmen's possession of what by my previous acts I explicitly or implicitly promised them?" There is, and can be, no question of whether I ought to pay my debts from a particular motive. No doubt we know that if we pay our bills we shall pay them with a motive, but in considering whether we ought to pay them we

[6] It is, I think, on this latter horn of the dilemma that Martineau's view falls; cf. *Types of Ethical Theory,* part ii, book i.

inevitably think of the act in abstraction from the motive. Even if we know what our motive would be if we did the act, we should not be any nearer an answer to the question.

Moreover, if we eventually pay our bills from fear of the county court, we shall still have done *what* we ought, even though we shall not have done it *as* we ought. The attempt to bring in the motive involves a mistake similar to that involved in supposing that we can will to will. To feel that I ought to pay my bills is to be *moved towards paying them*. But what I can be moved towards must always be an action and not an action in which I am moved in a particular way, *i. e.* an action from a particular motive; otherwise I should be moved towards being moved, which is impossible. Yet the view under consideration involves this impossibility; for it really resolves the sense that I ought to do so and so, into the sense that I ought to be moved to do it in a particular way.[7]

So far my contentions have been mainly negative, but they form, I think, a useful, if not a necessary, introduction to what I take to be the truth. This I will now endeavour to state, first formulating what, as I think, is the real nature of our apprehension or appreciation of moral obligations, and then applying the result to elucidate the question of the existence of Moral Philosophy.

The sense of obligation to do, or of the rightness of, an action of a particular kind is absolutely underivative or immediate. The rightness of an action consists in its being the origination of something of a certain kind A in a situation of a certain kind, a situa-

[7] It is of course not denied here that an action done from a particular motive may be good; it is only denied that the *rightness* of an action depends on its being done with a particular motive.

tion consisting in a certain relation B of the agent to others or to his own nature. To appreciate its rightness two preliminaries may be necessary. We may have to follow out the consequences of the proposed action more fully than we have hitherto done, in order to realise that in the action we should originate A. Thus we may not appreciate the wrongness of telling a certain story until we realise that we should thereby be hurting the feelings of one of our audience. Again, we may have to take into account the relation B involved in the situation, which we had hitherto failed to notice. For instance, we may not appreciate the obligation to give X a present, until we remember that he has done us an act of kindness. But, given that by a process which is, of course, merely a process of general and not of moral thinking we come to recognise that the proposed act is one by which we shall originate A in a relation B, then we appreciate the obligation immediately or directly, the appreciation being an activity of *moral* thinking. We recognise, for instance, that this performance of a service to X, who has done us a service, just in virtue of its being the performance of a service to one who has rendered a service to the would-be agent, ought to be done by us. This apprehension is immediate, in precisely the sense in which a mathematical apprehension is immediate, *e.g.*, the apprehension that this three-sided figure, in virtue of its being three-sided, must have three angles. Both apprehensions are immediate in the sense that in both insight into the nature of the subject directly leads us to recognise its possession of the predicate, and it is only stating this fact from the other side to say that in both cases the fact apprehended is self-evident.

The plausibility of the view that obligations are not self-evident but need proof lies in the fact that an act which is referred to as an obligation may be incompletely stated, what I have called the preliminaries to appreciating the obligation being incomplete. If, *e. g.*, we refer to the act of repaying X by a present merely as giving X a present, it appears, and indeed is, necessary to give a reason. In other words, wherever a moral act is regarded in this incomplete way the question, *"Why* should I do it?" is perfectly legitimate. This fact suggests, but suggests wrongly, that even if the nature of the act is completely stated, it is still necessary to give a reason, or, in other words, to supply a proof.

The relations involved in obligations of various kinds, are, of course, very different. The relation in certain cases is a relation to others due to a past act of theirs or ours. The obligation to repay a benefit involves a relation due to a past act of the benefactor. The obligation to pay a bill involves a relation due to a past act of ours in which we have either said or implied that we would make a certain return, for something which we have asked for and received. On the other hand the obligation to speak the truth implies no such definite act; it involves a relation consisting in the fact that others are trusting us to speak the truth, a relation the apprehension of which gives rise to the sense that communication of the truth is something owing by us to them. Again the obligation not to hurt the feelings of another, involves no special relation of us to that other, *i. e.*, no relation other than that involved in our both being men and men in one and the same world. Moreover, it seems that the relation involved in an obligation need not be a relation to another at all. Thus we should admit that there is an obligation to overcome our natural timidity or greediness, and that this involves no relations to others. Still there is a relation involved, *viz.*, a relation to our own disposition. It is simply because we can and because others cannot directly modify our disposition that it is our business to improve it, and that it is not theirs, or, at least, not theirs to the same extent.

The negative side of all this is, of course, that we do not come to appreciate an obligation by an *argument,* *i. e.* by a proces of nonmoral thinking, and that, in particular, we do not do so by an argument of which a premise is the ethical but not moral activity of appreciating the goodness either of the act or of a consequence of the act; *i. e.* that our sense of the rightness of an act is not a conclusion from our appreciation of the goodness either of it or of anything else.

It will probably be urged that on this view our various obligations form, like Aristotle's categories, an unrelated chaos in which it is impossible to acquiesce. For, according to it, the obligation to repay a benefit, or to pay a debt, or to keep a promise, presupposes a previous act of another; whereas the obligation to speak the truth or not to harm another does not; and, again, the obligation to remove our timidity involves no relations to others at all. Yet, at any rate, an effective *argumentum ad hominem* is at hand in the fact that the various qualities which we recognise as good are equally unrelated; *e. g.* courage, humility, and interest in knowledge. If, as is plainly the case, ἀγαθά (goods) differ ᾗ ἀγαθά (*qua* goods), why should not obligations equally differ *qua* their obligatoriness? Moreover if this were not so, there could in the end be only one obligation, which is palpably contrary to fact.[8]

[8] Two other objections may be anticipated: (1) that obligations cannot be self-evident, since many actions regarded

Certain observations will help to make the view clearer.

In the first place, it may seem that the view, being—as it is—avowedly put forward in opposition to the view that what is right is derived from what is good, must itself involve the opposite of this, viz., the Kantian position that what is good is based upon what is right, i. e., that an act, if it be good, is good because it is right. But this is not so. For, on the view put forward, the rightness of a right action lies solely in the origination in which the act consists, whereas the intrinsic goodness of an action lies solely in its motive; and this implies that a morally good action is morally good not simply because it is a right action but because it is a right action done because it is right, i. e., from a sense of obligation. And this implication, it may be re-

as obligations by some are not so regarded by others; and (2) that if obligations are self-evident, the problem of how we ought to act in the presence of conflicting obligations is insoluble.

To the first I should reply:—

(a)   That the appreciation of an obligation is, of course, only possible for a developed moral being, and that different degrees of development are possible.

(b)   That the failure to recognise some particular obligation is usually due to the fact that, owing to a lack of thoughtfulness, what I have called the preliminaries to this recognition are incomplete.

(c)   That the view put forward is consistent with the admission that, owing to a lack of thoughtfulness, even the best men are blind to many of their obligations, and that in the end our obligations are seen to be co-extensive with almost the whole of our life.

To the second objection I should reply that obligation admits of degrees, and that where obligations conflict, the decision of what we ought to do turns not on the question "Which of the alternative courses of action will originate the greater good?" but on the question "Which is the greater obligation?"

marked incidentally, seems plainly true.

In the second place the view involves that when, or rather so far as, we act from a sense of obligation, we have no purpose or end. By a 'purpose' or 'end' we really mean something the existence of which we desire, and desire of the existence of which leads us to act. Usually our purpose is something which the act will originate, as when we turn round in order to look at a picture. But it may be the action itself, i. e., the origination of something, as when we hit a golf ball into a hole or kill some one out of revenge.[9] Now if by a purpose we mean something the existence of which we desire and desire for which leads us to act, then plainly so far as we act from a sense of obligation, we have no purpose, consisting either in the action itself or in anything which it will produce. This is so obvious that it scarcely seems worth pointing out. But I do so for two reasons. (1) If we fail to scrutinise the meaning of the terms 'end' and 'purpose,' we are apt to assume uncritically that all deliberate action, i. e., action proper, must have a purpose; we then become puzzled both when we look for the purpose of an action done from a sense of obligation, and also when we try to apply to such an action the distinction of means and end, the truth all the time being that since there is no end, there is no means either. (2) The attempt to base the sense of obligation on the recognition of the goodness of something is really an attempt to find a purpose in a moral

[9] It is no objection to urge that an action cannot be its own purpose, since the purpose of something cannot be the thing itself. For, speaking strictly, the purpose is not the *action's* purpose but *our* purpose, and there is no contradiction in holding that our purpose in acting may be the action.

action in the shape of something good which, as good, we want. And the expectation that the goodness of something underlies an obligation disappears as soon as we cease to look for a purpose.

The thesis, however, that, so far as we act from a sense of obligation, we have no purpose must not be misunderstood. It must not be taken either to mean or to imply that so far as we so act we have no *motive*. No doubt in ordinary speech the words 'motive' and 'purpose' are usually treated as correlatives, 'motive' standing for the desire which induces us to act, and 'purpose' standing for the object of this desire. But this is only because, when we are looking for the motive of some action, say some crime, we are usually presupposing that the act in question is prompted by a desire and not by the sense of obligation. At bottom, however, we mean by a motive what moves us to act; a sense of obligation does sometimes move us to act; and in our ordinary consciousness we should not hesitate to allow that the action we were considering might have had as its motive a sense of obligation. Desire and the sense of obligation are co-ordinate forms or species of motive.

In the third place, if the view put forward be right, we must sharply distinguish morality and virtue as independent, though related, species of goodness, neither being an aspect of something of which the other is an aspect, nor again a form or species of the other, nor again something deducible from the other; and we must at the same time allow that it is possible to do the same act either virtuously or morally or in both ways at once. And surely this is true. An act, to be virtuous, must, as Aristotle saw, be done willingly or with pleasure; as such it is just not done from a sense of obligation but from some desire which

is intrinsically good, as arising from some intrinsically good emotion. Thus in an act of generosity the motive is the desire to help another arising from sympathy with that other; in an act which is courageous and no more, *i. e.* in an act which is not at the same time an act of public spirit or family affection or the like, we prevent ourselves from being dominated by a feeling of terror, desiring to do so from a sense of shame at being terrified. The goodness of such an act is different from the goodness of an act to which we apply the term moral in the strict and narrow sense, *viz.* an act done from a sense of obligation. Its goodness lies in the intrinsic goodness of the emotion and the consequent desire under which we act, the goodness of this motive being different from the goodness of the moral motive proper, *viz.*, the sense of duty or obligation. Nevertheless, at any rate in certain cases, an act can be done either virtuously or morally or in both ways at once. It is possible to repay a benefit either from desire to repay it or from the feeling that we ought to do so or from both motives combined. A doctor may tend his patients either from a desire arising out of interest in his patients or in the exercise of skill or from a sense of duty, or from a desire and a sense of duty combined. Further, although we recognise that in each case the act possesses an intrinsic goodness, we regard that action as the best in which both motives are combined; in other words, we regard as the really best man the man in whom virtue and morality are united.

It may be objected that the distinction between the two kinds of motive is untenable on the ground that the *desire* to repay a benefit, for example, is only the manifestation of that which manifests itself as the *sense of obligation* to repay whenever we think of something in the action which is other than the repayment and which we should not like, such as the loss or pain involved. Yet the distinction can, I think, easily be shown to be tenable. For, in the analogous case of revenge, the desire to return the injury and the sense that we ought not to do so, leading, as they do, in opposite directions, are plainly distinct; and the obviousness of the distinction here seems to remove any difficulty in admitting the existence of a parallel distinction between the desire to return a benefit and the sense that we ought to return it.[10]

Further the view implies that an obligation can no more be based on or derived from a virtue than a virtue can be derived from an obligation, in which latter case a virtue would consist in carrying out an obligation. And the implication is surely true and important. Take the case of courage. It is untrue to urge that, since courage is a virtue, we ought to act courageously. It is and must be untrue, because, as we see in the end, to feel an obligation to act courageously would involve a contradiction. For, as I have urged before, we can only feel an obligation to *act*; we cannot feel an obligation to *act from a certain desire*,

[10] This sharp distinction of virtue and morality as co-ordinate and independent forms of goodness will explain a fact which otherwise it is difficult to account for. If we turn from books on Moral Philosophy to any vivid account of human life and action such as we find in Shakespeare, nothing strikes us more than the comparative remoteness of the discussions of Moral Philosophy from the facts of actual life. Is not this largely because, while Moral Philosophy has, quite rightly, concentrated its attention on the fact of obligation, in the case of many of those whom we admire most and whose lives are of the greatest interest, the sense of obligation, though it may be an important, is not a dominating factor in their lives?

in this case the desire to conquer one's feelings to terror arising from the sense of shame which they arouse. Moreover, if the sense of obligation to act in a particular way leads to an action, the action will be an action done from a sense of obligation, and therefore not, if the above analysis of virtue be right, an act of courage.

The mistake of supposing that there can be an obligation to act courageously seems to arise from two causes. In the first place, there is often an obligation to do that which involves the conquering or controlling our fear in the doing of it, e. g., the obligation to walk along the side of a precipice to fetch a doctor for a member of our family. Here the acting on the obligation is externally, though only externally, the same as an act of courage proper. In the second place there is an obligation to acquire courage, i. e., to do such things as will enable us afterwards to act courageously, and this may be mistaken for an obligation to act courageously. The same considerations can, of course, be applied, *mutatis mutandis*, to the other virtues.

The fact, if it be a fact, that virtue is no basis for morality will explain what otherwise it is difficult to account for, viz., the extreme sense of dissatisfaction produced by a close reading of Aristotle's *Ethics*. Why is the *Ethics* so disappointing? Not, I think, because it really answers two radically different questions as if they were one: (1) "What is the happy life?" (2) "What is the virtuous life?" It is, rather, because Aristotle does not do what we as Moral Philosophers want him to do, viz., to convince us that we really ought to do what in our non-reflective consciousness we have hitherto believed we ought to do, or, if not, to tell us what, if any, are the other things which we really ought to do, and to prove to us that he is right. Now, if what I have just been contending is true, a systematic account of the virtuous character cannot possibly satisfy this demand. At best it can only make clear to us the details of one of our obligations, viz., the obligation to make ourselves better men; but the achievement of this does not help us to discover what we ought to do in life as a whole and why; to think that it did would be to think that our only business in life was self-improvement. Hence it is not surprising that Aristotle's account of the good man strikes us as almost wholly of academic value, with little relation to our real demand, which is formulated in Plato's words: οὐ γὰρ περὶ τοῦ ἐπιτυχόντος ὁ λόγος ἀλλά περὶ τοῦ ὅντινα τρόπον χρὴ ζῆν.

I am not, of course, *criticising* Aristotle for failing to satisfy this demand, except so far as here and there he leads us to think that he intends to satisfy it. For my main contention is that the demand cannot be satisfied and cannot be satisfied because it is illegitimate. Thus we are brought to the question: "Is there really such a thing as Moral Philosophy, and, if there is, in what sense?"

We should first consider the parallel case — as it appears to be — of the Theory of Knowledge. As I urged before, at some time or other in the history of all of us, if we are thoughtful, the frequency of our own and of others' mistakes is bound to lead to the reflexion that possibly we and others have *always* been mistaken in consequence of some radical defect of our faculties. In consequence certain things which previously we should have said without hesitation that we *knew*, as e. g., that $4 \times 7 = 28$, become subject to doubt; we become able only to say that we thought we knew these things. We inevitably go on to look for some general procedure by which we can ascertain that a given condition of mind is really one of knowl-

edge. And this involves the search for a criterion of knowledge, i. e. for a principle by applying which we can settle that a given state of mind is really knowledge. The search for this criterion and the application of it, when found, is what is called the Theory of Knowledge. The search implies that instead of its being the fact that the knowledge that A is B is obtained directly by consideration of the nature of A and B, the knowledge that A is B, in the full or complete sense, can only be obtained by first knowing that A is B, and then knowing that we knew it, by applying a criterion, such as Descartes' principle that what we clearly and distinctly conceive is true.

Now it is easy to show that the doubt whether A is B based on this speculative or general ground, could, if genuine, never be set at rest. For if, in order really to know that A is B, we must first know that we knew it, then really to know that we knew it, we must first know that we knew that we knew it. But—what is more important—it is also easy to show that this doubt is not a genuine doubt but rests on a confusion the exposure of which removes the doubt. For when we *say* we doubt whether our previous condition was one of knowledge, what we *mean,* if we mean anything at all, is that we doubt whether our previous *belief* was *true,* a belief which we should express as the *thinking* that A is B. For in order to doubt whether our previous condition was one of knowledge, we have to think of it not as knowledge but as only belief, and our only question can be "Was this belief true?" But as soon as we see that we are thinking of our previous condition as only one of belief, we see that what we are now doubting is not what we first *said* we were doubting, viz., whether a previous condition of knowledge was really knowledge. Hence, to remove the doubt, it is only necessary to appreciate the real nature of our consciousness in apprehending, e. g., that $7 \times 4 = 28$, and thereby see that it was no mere condition of believing but a condition of knowing, and then to notice that in our subsequent doubt what we are really doubting is not whether this consciousness was really knowledge, but whether a consciousness of another kind, viz., a belief that $7 \times 4 = 28$, was true. We thereby see that though a doubt based on speculative grounds is possible, it is not a doubt concerning what we believed the doubt concerned, and that a doubt concerning this latter is impossible.

Two results follow. In the first place, if, as is usually the case, we mean by the 'Theory of Knowledge' the knowledge which supplies the answer to the question "Is what we have hitherto thought knowledge really knowledge?" there is and can be no such thing, and the supposition that there can is simply due to a confusion. There can be no answer to an illegitimate question, except that the question is illegitimate. Nevertheless the question is one which we continue to put until we realise the inevitable immediacy of knowledge. And it is positive knowledge that knowledge is immediate and neither can be, nor needs to be, improved or vindicated by the further knowledge that it was knowledge. This positive knowledge sets at rest the inevitable doubt, and, so far as by the 'Theory of Knowledge' is meant this knowledge, then even though this knowledge be the knowledge that there is no Theory of Knowledge in the former sense, to that extent the Theory of Knowledge exists.

In the second place, suppose we come genuinely to doubt whether, e. g., $7 \times 4 = 28$ owing to a genuine doubt whether we were right in believing yesterday that $7 \times 4 = 28$, a doubt which can in fact only arise if we have lost our hold of, i. e., no longer remember, the real nature of our consciousness of yesterday, and so think of it as consisting in believing. Plainly, the only remedy is to do the sum again. Or, to put the matter generally, if we do come to doubt whether it is true that A is B, as we once thought, the remedy lies not in any process of reflection but in such a reconsideration of the nature of A and B as leads to the knowledge that A is B.

With these considerations in mind, consider the parallel which, as it seems to me, is presented—though with certain differences—by Moral Philosophy. The sense that we ought to do certain things arises in our unreflective consciousness, being an activity of moral thinking occasioned by the various situations in which we find ourselves. At this stage our attitude to these obligations is one of unquestioning confidence. But inevitably the appreciation of the degree to which the execution of these obligations is contrary to our interest raises the doubt whether after all these obligations are really obligatory, i. e., whether our sense that we ought not to do certain things is not illusion. We then want to have it *proved* to us that we ought to do so, i. e., to be convinced of this by a process which, as an argument, is different in kind from our original and unreflective appreciation of it. This demand is, as I have argued, illegitimate.

Hence in the first place, if, as is almost universally the case, by Moral Philosophy is meant the knowledge which would satisfy this demand, there is no such knowledge, and all attempts to attain it are doomed to failure because they rest on a mistake, the mistake of supposing the possibility of proving what can only be apprehended directly by an act of moral thinking. Nevertheless the demand, though illegitimate, is inevitable until we have carried the process of reflexion far enough to realise the self-evidence of our obligations, *i. e.*, the immediacy of our apprehension of them. This realisation of their self-evidence is positive knowledge, and so far, and so far only, as the term Moral Philosophy is confined to this knowledge and to the knowledge of the parallel immediacy of the apprehension of the goodness of the various virtues and of good dispositions generally, is there such a thing as Moral Philosophy. But since this knowledge may allay doubts which often affect the whole conduct of life, it is, though not extensive, important and even vitally important.

In the second place, suppose we come genuinely to doubt whether we ought, for example, to pay our debts owing to a genuine doubt whether our previous conviction that we ought to do so is true, a doubt which can, in fact, only arise if we fail to remember the real nature of what we now call our past conviction. The only remedy lies in actually getting into a situation which occasions the obligation, or—if our imagination be strong enough—in imagining ourselves in that situation, and then letting our moral capacities of thinking do their work. Or, to put the matter generally, if we do doubt whether there is really an obligation to originate A in a situation B, the remedy lies not in any process of general thinking, but in getting face to face with a particular instance of the situation B, and then directly appreciating the obligation to originate A in that situation.

Index